Equivalence and Substituted Compliance in Financial Markets Law

Equivalence and Substituted Compliance in Financial Markets Law

JONAS SCHÜRGER

OXFORD
UNIVERSITY PRESS

OXFORD
UNIVERSITY PRESS

Great Clarendon Street, Oxford, OX2 6DP,
United Kingdom

Oxford University Press is a department of the University of Oxford.
It furthers the University's objective of excellence in research, scholarship,
and education by publishing worldwide. Oxford is a registered trade mark of
Oxford University Press in the UK and in certain other countries

First Edition published in 2023

Published in the United States of America by Oxford University Press
198 Madison Avenue, New York, NY 10016, United States of America

British Library Cataloguing in Publication Data
Data available

Library of Congress Control Number:2023932450

ISBN 978–0–19–887674–8

DOI: 10.1093/oso/9780198876748.001.0001

Printed and bound by
CPI Group (UK) Ltd, Croydon, CR0 4YY

To my family

Acknowledgements

This book was written during my time at the universities of Bonn and Vienna and was accepted by the Faculty of Law and Political Sciences of the Rheinische Friedrich-Wilhelms-Universität Bonn in the summer semester of 2022. The cut-off date for information to be considered in the manuscript was 1 March 2023.

The book has benefited greatly from the valuable discussions, interaction, and support of many people, some of whom I would like to mention specifically:

First and foremost, I am deeply indebted to my supervisor, Prof Dr Matthias Lehmann. He has always encouraged and supported my academic endeavours. Prof Lehmann provided me with the opportunity to work on numerous exciting projects and, at the same time, gave me enough space to conduct the research for this work. The three years I spent at his chairs in Bonn and Vienna were very enriching and rewarding, both academically and personally.

Likewise, I would like to thank my second academic teacher, Prof Dr Matthias Herdegen, who provided the second review for this thesis. In the nearly five years in which I had the privilege of working at his chair, I gained a lot of insights into EU constitutional and administrative law as well as world trade law, from which this thesis has immensely benefited.

The time in Bonn and Vienna would not have been the same without my colleagues' and friends' constant exchange, support, and many off-campus adventures. Therefore, I would like to express my special thanks to all of you, in particular Felix, Verena, Emeric, Karolina, Paul, Robert, Vanessa, and Vicky from Vienna as well as Carl, Isabel, Jule, Konstantin, Magnus, Martha, Matthias, Max, Nicole, and Thomas from Bonn, who have also greatly shaped the long journey through college. Particularly noteworthy are my two best friends: Max and Ruben. You have made every day of school, university, and in our shared flat unique. I very much hope that we will remain close friends and share many more memories.

Furthermore, a big thank you is owed to my wife, Annabel. She has supported me continuously and with much love over the last eight years. Annabel improved the thesis with many valuable hints and provided the necessary balance when the work threatened to overwhelm. I deeply wish that we will continue to tackle and overcome all future challenges together.

Finally, I owe the greatest thanks to my family, especially my parents, Carsten and Ulrike, and my siblings, Lukas and Niklas. Only your constant support and unwavering trust in me have made it possible to complete this book. It is therefore dedicated to you.

Jonas Schürger
Bonn, March 2023

Contents

Detailed Contents

Table of Cases

I. INTERNATIONAL COURT OF JUSTICE

II. DISPUTE SETTLEMENT IN THE WORLD TRADE ORGANIZATION

1. Appellate Body

2. Panel

III. COURT OF JUSTICE OF THE EUROPEAN UNION AND ADVOCATES GENERAL

1. European Court of Justice

2. General Court

3. Advocates General

IV. NATIONAL COURTS

1. Switzerland

2. United States of America

3. Germany

Table of Legislation

I. EUROPEAN UNION LAW

1. European Primary Law

2. European Secondary Law

a) Regulations and Directives

b) Delegated Legislation

c) (Implementing) Decisions

II. LAW OF THE WORLD TRADE ORGANIZATION

III. LAW OF SWITZERLAND

1. Federal Acts

2. Ordinances by the Swiss Federal Council

3. Ordinances by FINMA, FAOA, and the National Bank

4. Self-Regulation of Swiss Trading Venues

IV. LAW OF THE UNITED STATES

1. Federal Law

2. Rules by Federal Agencies and State law

V. OTHER COUNTRIES AND INTERNATIONAL AGREEMENTS

1. Law of Germany

2. Law of France

3. Law of the United Kingdom

4. Ireland

5. Law of Australia

6. Law of Singapore

7. International Agreements

Table of Policy Documents

I. EUROPEAN UNION

1. European Parliament

2. European Commission

3. European Central Bank

4. European Supervisory Authorities

a) European Banking Authority

c) EIOPA and CEIOPS

II. SWITZERLAND

1. Legislative Materials

2. FINMA, FAOA, and Swiss National Bank

finma.ch/en/~/media/finma/dokumente/dokumentencenter/myfinma/4dokumentation/finma-aufsichtsmitteilungen/20210203-finma-aufsichtsmitteilung-01-2021.pdf?la=en (accessed 12 November 2022) 211n.397
Swiss National Bank, 'Turnover in foreign exchange and derivatives markets in Switzerland—BIS Triennial Survey' (April 2022) https://data.snb.ch/en/topics/texts/doc/ddum_2022 (accessed 28 February 2023) 182n.193
FINMA, 'Guidelines on submitting applications for recognition of foreign trading venues under Article 41 FMIA' (22 October 2020) https://finma.ch/en/~/media/finma/dokumente/dokumentencenter/myfinma/1bewilligung/wl-boersen-ausl-d.pdf?la=en (accessed 12 November 2022) 193n.272
FINMA, 'Recognised credit rating agencies' (8 November 2022) https://www.finma.ch/en/~/media/finma/dokumente/finmapublic/bewilligungstraeger/ratingagenturen.pdf?sc_lang=en&hash=3EF6A5637E13BC76972B2B9670C3C0F3 (accessed 28 February 2023) 167n.75

3. Miscellaneous

Federal Department of Finance, 'Richtlinien für Finanzmarktregulierung' (September 2005) https://www.finews.ch/images/download/richtlinien.pdf (accessed 12 November 2022) 200n.327, 201n.329, 210n.392, 210n.394
Expertengruppe Finanzmarktaufsicht, 'Finanzmarktregulierung und -Aufsicht in der Schweiz' (Zufferey-Bericht) (November 2010) http://docplayer.org/108102443-Integrierte-finanzmarktaufsicht-gesetzgeberische-folgearbeiten-zum-schlussbericht-der-expertengruppe-finanzmarktaufsicht-bericht-zufferey.html (accessed 12 November 2022) 180n.183, 211n.395
Expertengruppe zur Weiterentwicklung der Finanzmarktstrategie, 'Schlussbericht' (Brunetti Bericht) (2014) https://www.newsd.admin.ch/newsd/message/attachments/37585.pdf (accessed 12 November 2022) 210n.392
Federal Council, 'Derzeit kein Bedarf für Benchmark-Regulierung' Press Release (4 March 2016) https://www.admin.ch/gov/de/start/dokumentation/medienmitteilungen.msg-id-60870.html (accessed 12 November 2022) 171n.109, 201n.331
Federal Council, 'Financial Market Policy for a Competitive Swiss Financial Centre' Report (November 2016) https://www.sif.admin.ch/dam/sif/en/dokumente/Publicationen/Bericht_Finanzmarktpolitik.pdf.download.pdf/Financial%20market%20policy%20for%20a%20competitive%20Swiss%20financial%20centre%20.pdf (accessed 12 November 2022). 201nn.328–29, 210n.392
SIX Swiss Exchange, 'Swiss Indices Endorsed Under the EU Benchmarks Regulation' Press Release (5 February 2020) https://www.six-group.com/en/newsroom/media-releases/2020/20200205-swiss-indices-endorsed.html (accessed 12 November 2022) . . . 171n.110
Federal Council, 'Leading worldwide, rooted in Switzerland' (4 December 2020) https://www.sif.admin.ch/dam/sif/en/bilder/politik-finanzplatz-schweiz/politik-finanzplatz-schweiz-bericht.pdf.download.pdf/politik-finanzplatz-schweiz-bericht.pdf (accessed 12 November 2022) 209n.383
State Secretariat for Economic Affairs, 'Services Trade Cockpit 2020 Rev. 1' (January 2021) https://www.seco.admin.ch/dam/seco/en/dokumente/Aussenwirtschaft/Wirtschaftsbeziehungen/Handel%20mit%20Dienstleistungen/services_trade_cockpit.pdf.download.pdf/Services%20Trade%20Cockpit%202020.pdf (accessed 12 November 2022) . . . 209n.386

III. UNITED STATES OF AMERICA

1. SEC

2. CFTC

3. PCAOB

4. Miscellaneous

IV. UNITED KINGDOM

V. AUSTRALIA

VI. OTHER INTERNATIONAL ORGANIZATIONS, FORA, AND THE LIKE

List of Abbreviations

I. Legal Journals

AcP	Archiv für die civilistische Praxis
AG	Die Aktiengesellschaft
AJIL	American Journal of International Law
AJP/PJA	Aktuelle Juristische Praxis/Pratique Juridique Actuelle
Am Bus LJ	American Business Law Journal
Ann Rev Bank & Fin L	Annual Review of Banking & Financial Law
AöR	Archiv des öffentlichen Rechts
BC L Rev	Boston College Law Review
BJ Intl Ban & Fin L	Butterworths Journal of International Banking and Financial Law
BKR	Zeitschrift für Bank- und Kapitalmarktrecht
Brit Y B Intl L	British Yearbook of International Law
Brook J Corp Fin & Com L	Brooklyn Journal of Corporate, Financial and Commercial Law
Brook J Intl L	Brooklyn Journal of International Law
Brook L Rev	Brooklyn Law Review
BU Intl LJ	Boston University International Law Journal
BU L Rev	Boston University Law Review
Bus L Intl	Business Law International
Bus L Rev	Business Law Review
Bus Law	Business Lawyer
Cal L Rev	California Law Review
Cambridge LJ	Cambridge Law Journal
Cambridge YB Eur Legal Stud	Cambridge Yearbook of European Legal Studies
Cardozo J Intl & Comp L	Cardozo Journal of International and Comparative Law
Case W Res J Intl L	Case Western Reserve Journal of International Law
Case W Res L Rev	Case Western Reserve Law Review
Chic J Intl L	Chicago Journal of International Law
CMLJ	Capital Markets Law Journal
CMLR	Common Market Law Review
Colum Bus L Rev	Columbia Business Law Review
Colum J Eur L	Columbia Journal of European Law
Colum J Transnatl L	Columbia Journal of Transnational Law
Colum L Rev	Columbia Law Review
Cornell Intl LJ	Cornell International Law Journal

Cornell L Rev	Cornell Law Review
DQ	Dovenschmidt Quarterly
DVBl	Das Deutsche Verwaltungsblatt
EBLR	European Business Law Review
EBOR	European Business Organization Law Review
ECFR	European Company and Financial Law Review
ECL	European Company Law
ECLIC	EU and Comparative Law Issues and Challenges Series
Econ J	The Economic Journal
EF	Expert-Focus
EJIL	The European Journal of International Law
EJTR	eJournal of Tax Research
Ethics & Intl Aff	Ethics & International Affairs
EuR	Europarecht
Eur J Legal Stud	European Journal of Legal Studies
Eur J Risk Reg	European Journal of Risk Regulation
Eur JL Reform	European Journal of Law Reform
Eur L Rev	European Law Review
Eur LJ	European Law Journal
Eur Rev Priv L	European Review of Private International Law
EUREDIA	Revue Européenne de droit bancaire & financier
EuZW	Europäischer Zeitschrift für Wirtschaftsrecht
EWS	Europäisches Wirtschafts- und Steuerrecht
Fed Res Bull	Federal Reserve Bulletin
Fin Reg Intl	Financial Regulation International
Fordham Intl LJ	Fordham International Law Journal
Fordham L Rev	Fordham Law Review
Foreign Aff	Foreign Affairs
Geo J Intl L	Georgetown Journal of International Law
Geo JL & Pub Pol'y	Georgetown Journal of Law & Public Policy
Geo Wash J Intl L & Econ	George Washington Journal of International Law and Economics
George LJ	The Georgetown Law Journal
German LJ	German Law Journal
GesKR	Gesellschafts- und Kapitalmarktrecht
Harv Bus L Rev	Harvard Business Law Review
Harv Intl LJ	Harvard International Law Journal
Hastings Bus LJ	Hastings Business Law Journal
Hong Kong LJ	Hong Kong Law Journal
Hous J Intl L	Houston Journal of International Law
ICCLR	International Company and Commercial Law Review
Ind J Global Legal Stud	Indiana Journal of Global Legal Studies
Intl & Comp LQ	International and Comparative Law Quarterly
Intl Fin L Rev	International Financial Law Review

Intl Lawyer	International Lawyer
Intl Organization	International Organization
Intl Tax J	International Tax Journal
Iowa L Rev	Iowa L Review
IPrax	Praxis des Internationalen Privat- und Verfahrensrechts
J Acct Res	Journal of Accounting Research
J Bank Reg	Journal of Banking Regulation
J Bus & Sec L	Journal of Business & Securities Law
J Comp Econ	Journal of Comparative Economics
J Corp L	Journal of Corporation Law
J Eur Integr	Journal of European Integration
J Eur Public Policy	Journal of European Public Policy
J Financ Intermediation	Journal of Financial Intermediation
J Intl Bus & L	Journal of International Business and Law
J Invest Compliance	Journal of Investment Compliance
J Legal Stud	Journal of Legal Studies
J Fin	The Journal of Finance
J of Intl Bus Research	Journal of International Business Research
J of Risk and Ins	The Journal of Risk and Insurance
J of Sec Oper & Cust	Journal of Securities Operations & Custody
J WTO & China	Journal of WTO and China
JFR	Journal of Financial Regulation
JIBLR	Journal of International Banking Law and Regulation
JIEL	Journal of International Economic Law
JuS	Juristische Schulung
JWT	Journal of World Trade
JZ	Juristenzeitung
KritV	Kritische Vierteljahresschrift für Gesetzgebung und Rechtswissenschaft
Law & Pol'y Intl Bus	Law and Policy in International Business
Legal Issues of Econ Integ	Legal Issues of Economic Integration
Lex ET Scientia Intl J	Lex ET Scientia International Journal
Macquarie J Bus L	Macquarie Journal of Business Law
Md J Intl L	Maryland Journal of International Law
Melb J Intl L	Melbourne Journal of International Law
Mich L Rev	Michigan Law Review
Minn J Intl L	Minnesota Journal of International Law
Minn LR	Minnesota Law Review
MLR	The Modern Law Review
NC J Intl L & Com Reg	North Carolina Journal of International Law and Commercial Regulation
Nev LJ	Nevada Law Journal
NJW	Neue Juristische Wochenschrift

NW J Intl L & Bus	Northwestern Journal of International Law & Business
NYLS L Rev	New York Law School Law Review
NYU J Intl L & Pol	New York University Journal of International Law and Politics
NYU J Legis & Pub Pol'y	New York University Journal of Legislation and Public Policy
NYU JL & Bus	New York University Journal of Law and Business
NZG	Neue Zeitschrift für Gesellschaftsrecht
OBLB	Oxford Business Law Blog
Ohio State LJ	Ohio State Law Journal
OJLS	Oxford Journal of Legal Studies
Okla L Rev	Oklahoma Law Review
Oxf Dev Stud	Oxford Development Studies
Oxf Rev Econ Policy	Oxford Review of Economic Policy
RabelsZ	Rabels Zeitschrift für ausländisches und internationales Privatrecht
RB	Revue Banque/Banque & Droit
RdF	Recht der Finanzinstrumente
Rec des Cours	Recueil des cours - Académie de Droit International de La Haye
recht	Zeitschrift für juristische Weiterbildung und Praxis
Rev Intl Polit Econ	Review of International Political Economy
Rich Econ Rev	Richmond Economic Review
Rich J Global L & Bus	Richmond Journal of Global Law and Business
RISF/JFS	Revue Internationale des Services Financiers/ International Journal for Financial Services
RIW	Recht der Internationalen Wirtschaft
RRDE	Revista Romana de Drept European
RSDA	Revue Suisse de Droit des Affaires et du Marché Financier
RSF	The Russell Sage Foundation Journal of the Social Sciences
RW	Zeitschrift für rechtswissenschaftliche Forschung
S Cal L Rev	Southern California Law Review
SJZ	Schweizer Juristen-Zeitung
St John's L Rev	St. John's Law Review
Stan JL Bus & Fin	Stanford Journal of Law, Business & Finance
Suffolk Transnatl L Rev	Suffolk Transnational Law Review
Syracuse J Intl L & Com	Syracuse Journal of International Law and Commerce
SZW	Schweizerische Zeitschrift für Wirtschafts- und Finanzmarktrecht
Tex J Bus L	Texas Journal of Business Law
Tex L Rev	Texas Law Review
Theoretical Inq L	Theoretical Inquiries in Law

U Cin L Rev	University of Cincinnati Law Review
U Colo L Rev	University of Colorado Law Review
U Ill L Rev	University of Illinois Law Review
U Pa J Bus L	University of Pennsylvania Journal of Business Law
U Pa J Intl L	University of Pennsylvania Journal of International Law
U Pa L Rev	University of Pennsylvania Law Review
UC Irvine J Intl Transnatl & Comp L	UC Irvine Journal of International, Transnational, and Comparative Law
Wash U J L & Pol'y	Washington University Journal of Law & Policy
Wash U L Q	Washington University Law Quarterly
West Eur Pol	West European Politics
WM	Wertpapier-Mitteilungen – Zeitschrift für Wirtschafts- und Bankrecht
World Trade Rev	World Trade Review
Yale J on Reg	Yale Journal on Regulation
Yale LJ	Yale Law Journal
YBEL	Yearbook of European Law
YPIL	Yearbook of Private International Law
ZBB/JBB	Zeitschrift für Bankrecht und Bankwirtschaft/ Journal of Banking Law and Banking
ZEuS	Zeitschrift für Europarechtliche Studien
ZGR	Zeitschrift für Unternehmens- und Gesellschaftsrecht
ZIP	Zeitschrift für Wirtschaftsrecht
ZSR	Zeitschrift für Schweizerisches Recht
ZVglRWiss	Zeitschrift für Vergleichende Rechtswissenschaft

II. Legislation

AIFMD	Alternative Investment Fund Managers Directive
AVO	Supervisory Ordinance (Aufsichtsverordnung)
Banking Act	Swiss Federal Act on Banks and Savings Banks (Bankengesetz)
Banking Ordinance	Ordinance on Banks and Savings Banks (Bankenverordnung)
BEHG	Swiss Stock Exchange Act (Börsengesetz)
BEHV	Swiss Stock Exchange Ordinance (Börsenverordnung)
BMR	Benchmark Regulation
CEA	Commodity Exchange Act
CFR	Charter of the Fundamental Rights of the European Union
CRA Regulation	Credit Rating Agency Regulation
CRD V	Capital Requirements Directive V

CRR II	Capital Requirements Regulation II
CSDR	Central Securities Depositories Regulation
EinSiG	German Deposit Guarantee Act (Einlagensicherungsgesetz)
EMIR	European Market Infrastructure Regulation
FIDLEG	Financial Services Act (Finanzdienstleistungsgesetz)
FIDLEV	Financial Services Ordinance (Finanzdienstleistungsverordnung)
FinfraG	Financial Market Infrastructure Act (Finanzmarktinfrastrukturgesetz)
FinfraV	Financial Market Infrastructure Ordinance (Finanzmarktinfrastrukturverordnung)
FINIG	Financial Institutions Act (Finanzinstitutsgesetz)
FINIV	Financial Institutions Ordinance (Finanzinstitutsverordnung)
FINMAG	Financial Market Supervision Act (Finanzmarktaufsichtsgesetz)
Foreign Banks Ordinance-FINMA	Auslandbankenverordnung-FINMA (ABV-FINMA)
GATS	General Agreement on Trade in Services
GATT	General Agreement on Tariffs and Trade
GDPR	General Data Protection Regulation
GWG	Anti-Money Laundering Act (Geldwäschereigesetz)
HGB	German Commercial Code (Handelsgesetzbuch)
IAA	Investment Advisers Act of 1940
ICA	Investment Company Act of 1940
IDD	Insurance Distribution Directive
KAG	Collective Investment Schemes Act (Kollektivanlagengesetz)
KAGB	Capital Investment Code (Kapitalanlagegesetzbuch)
KKV	Collective Investment Schemes Ordinance (Kollektivanlagenverordnung)
KKV-FINMA	FINMA Collective Investment Schemes Ordinance (Kollektivanlagenverordnung-FINMA)
KWG	German Banking Act (Kreditwesengesetz)
Law of Obligations	Obligationenrecht
MAR	Market Abuse Regulation
MiFID II	Markets in Financial Instruments Directive II
MiFIR	Markets in Financial Instruments Regulation
PfG	Pfandbriefgesetz
PRIIP Regulation	Packaged Retail and Insurance-Based Investment Products Regulation
PSD II	Payment Services Directive II
RAG	Auditor Oversight Act (Revisionsaufsichtsgesetz)
RAV	Auditor Oversight Ordinance (Revisionsaufsichtsverordnung)

SAD	Statutory Audit Directive
SFT Regulation	Securities Financing Transactions Regulation
SPS-Agreement	Agreement on the Application of Sanitary and Phytosanitary Measures
SSM Regulation	Single Supervisory Mechanism Regulation
SSR	Short Selling Regulation
TBT-Agreement	Agreement on Technical Barriers to Trade
TEU	Treaty on European Union
TFEU	Treaty on the Functioning of the European Union
UCITS Directive	Undertakings for Collective Investment in Transferable Securities Directive
VAG	Insurance Supervision Law (Versicherungsaufsichtsgesetz)
WpHG	German Securities Trading Act (Wertpapierhandelsgesetz)
WPO	German Auditors' Code (Wirtschaftsprüferordnung)
ZAG	German Payment Services Supervision Act (Zahlungsdiensteaufsichtsgesetz)

III. Other Abbreviations

AIF	Alternative Investment Funds
BaFin	Federal Financial Supervisory Authority (Bundesanstalt für Finanzdienstleistungsaufsicht)
BCBS	Basel Committee on Banking Supervision
CCP	Central Counterparty
CEIOPS	Committee of European Insurance and Occupational Pensions Supervisors
CESR	Committee of European Securities Regulators
CFTC	Commodity Futures Trading Commission
CJEU	Court of Justice of the European Union
CRA	Credit Rating Agency
CPSS-IOSCO	Committee on Payment and Settlement Systems-IOSCO
CSD	Central securities depository
DG	Directorate-General
EBA	European Banking Authority
EC	European Communities
ECB	European Central Bank
ECJ	European Court of Justice
EEA	European Economic Area
EEC	European Economic Community
EIOPA	European Insurance and Occupational Pensions Authority

ESAs	European supervisory authorities
ESG	Environmental Social Governance
ESMA	European Securities and Markets Authority
EU	European Union
FAOA	Federal Audit Oversight Authority (Revisionsaufsichtsbehörde)
FATF	Financial Action Task Force on Money Laundering
FSB	Financial Stability Board
FINMA	Financial Market Supervisory Authority (Eidgenössische Finanzmarktaufsicht)
FinTech	Financial technology
GAAP	Generally Accepted Accounting Principles
GAAS	Generally Accepted Auditing Standards
GC	General Court
GFC	Global financial crisis
IAASB	International Auditing and Assurance Standards Board
IAIS	International Association of Insurance Supervisors
IAS	International Accounting Standards
IASB	International Accounting Standards Board
ICJ	International Court of Justice
IFRS	International Financial Reporting Standards
IMF	International Monetary Fund
IOSCO	International Organization of Securities Commissions
IOSCO Principles for PRAs	IOSCO Principles for Price Reporting Agencies
LIBOR	London Interbank Offered Rate
MFN treatment	Most-Favoured-Nation Treatment
MoU	Memorandum of Understanding
MTF	Multilateral trading facility
NCA	National competent authority
OECD	Organisation for Economic Co-operation and Development
OTC	Over-the-counter
OTF	Organised trading facility
PCAOB	Public Company Accounting Oversight Board
PFMI	Principles for Financial Market Infrastructures
SEC	United States Securities and Exchange Commission
SFTs	Securities Financing Transactions
Swiss GAAP FER	Swiss General Accepted Accounting Principles (Fachempfehlungen zur Rechnungslegung)
UK	United Kingdom
US	United States
WTO	World Trade Organization

The world must learn to work together, or finally it will not work at all.[1]

—Dwight D Eisenhower

[1] Dwight D Eisenhower (34th President of the United States), 'Address at the Ground-breaking Ceremonies for the Eisenhower Library' in Abilene, Kansas (13 October 1959), © The American Presidency Project.

1

Access to EU Financial Markets: Equivalence as a New Approach

A) Introduction: Fragmentary legislation without a uniform concept

I. Globalized financial markets without 'globalized law'

The globalization of financial markets has been progressing for more than half a century. This development is characterized by an ever-stronger interconnectedness of national markets, as the global financial crisis (GFC) of 2007 impressively demonstrated. Financial crises no longer stop at national borders but have a direct impact on the global financial system. This phenomenon is aptly described by the term *systemic risk*.[1] This interdependence of national markets has recently been surpassed by the emergence of 'real' global financial market players—namely services that operate on the basis of financial technology (FinTechs)—such as new payment solutions or cryptocurrencies. Although a precise definition of FinTech is hardly feasible, FinTech services have specific characteristics in common: ubiquity, disintermediation, and concentration.[2] Their business model is built on economies of scale and only works in a global, non-fragmented market. FinTechs can address clients all over the world (ubiquity) and operate from a single point, which is why they do not need branches or subsidiaries in each and every country (concentration). Even 'more global' are FinTechs that work on the basis of distributed ledger technologies, for instance, blockchain technology. Cryptocurrencies, such as Bitcoin or LIBRA, can hardly be allocated to a state anymore because of the decentralization of this technology.[3] Thus, due to a lack of connection to a single state, these players and phenomena can be described as truly global.

This ongoing globalization of financial markets creates challenges for supervision that have been dealt with to only a certain extent.[4] Many questions have not yet been

[1] Steven L Schwarcz, 'Systemic Risk' (2008) 97 George LJ 193; Hal S Scott, *The Global Financial Crisis* (New York Foundation Press 2009) 11ff; Douglas W Arner and others (eds), *Systemic Risk in the Financial Sector: Ten Years after the Great Crash* (CIGI 2019).

[2] Matthias Lehmann, 'Global Rules for a Global Market Place? The Regulation and Supervision of FinTech Providers' (2020) 38 BU Intl LJ 118, 123ff; generally on the characterization of FinTech see Jelena Madir, 'Introduction: What is FinTech?' in Jelena Madir (ed), *FinTech: Law and Regulation* (Edward Elgar Publishing 2019) 1ff; on the evolution of FinTech see Douglas W Arner, Janos Barberis, and Ross P Buckley, 'The Evolution of FinTech: A New Post-Crisis Paradigm' (2016) 47 Geo J Intl L 1271.

[3] On the phenomenon of decentralized finance and related problems for regulation see Dirk A Zetzsche, Douglas W Arner, and Ross P Buckley, 'Decentralized Finance' (2020) 6 JFR 172.

[4] See eg Ross P Buckley and Douglas W Arner, 'Redesigning the Architecture of the Global Financial System' (2010) 11 Melb J Intl L 1; Ross P Buckley, Emilios Avgouleas, and Douglas W Arner (eds),

Equivalence and Substituted Compliance in Financial Markets Law. Jonas Schürger,
Oxford University Press. © Jonas Schürger 2023. DOI: 10.1093/oso/9780198876748.003.0001

sufficiently answered. How can a global market be supervised without 'globalized law'? How can supervision work without a global regulator and without harmonized law—two features that are not realistically going to evolve in the near future? Who is responsible for the supervision of global players such as FinTechs in the first place?

Looking at this continuing development, the fragmented international approach to the regulation of financial markets seems surprising and irritating.[5] Although there have been increasing efforts since the financial crisis to provide at least a uniform basis for regulation through soft law by international fora and organizations such as the G20, the Financial Stability Board (FSB), the Bank for International Settlements and the Basel Committee on Banking Supervision (BCBS),[6] financial markets law as a whole is far from being harmonized.[7] It is even more surprising that this lack of harmonization is not limited to uniform standards for the supervision of financial service providers, i.e. to substantive law. Even the preliminary question of cross-border market access is far from being harmonized and no uniform concept has yet emerged.[8] There is no common understanding regarding the requirements that a financial service provider must fulfil to offer services outside its home state. In fact, states use very different models to regulate market access.

Since there is no globally accepted way of accessing a market, broadly speaking, countries can theoretically choose from three different approaches, whereas in practice these are often combined and mixed.[9] A very liberal approach is the country-of-origin principle or principle of home state supervision.[10] Under this principle, at least in its strict reading, states allow foreign products or service providers to enter their market without demanding prior authorization and without subjecting them to regulation or supervision, simply because they trust in the home state's regulation and supervision. However, this approach is rarely encountered in practice, and when used, it is limited to specific sectors. This is because states following this approach give up their regulatory power without requiring minimum standards from the foreign law. Without such minimum standards, there is the danger of a *laissez-faire* attitude in the foreign country when it comes to supervision. Furthermore, there is the risk of regulatory

Reconceptualising Global Finance and Its Regulation (CUP 2016); concerning the regulation of FinTech see Lehmann (n 2).

[5] Sharing this finding see Hannah L Buxbaum, 'Transnational Legal Ordering and Regulatory Conflict' (2016) 1 UC Irvine J Intl Transnatl & Comp L 91, 94: 'The gap between the global scale of the markets and the domestic scale of regulation poses significant challenges to the transnational economic order'.

[6] Other important fora and organizations include IOSCO, IAIS, IASB or FATF. These more informal organizations are complemented by the World Bank Group and the IMF that are linked to the United Nations. See extensively Peter Nobel, *Schweizerisches Finanzmarktrecht* (4th edn, Stämpfli 2019) § 3.

[7] Cally Jordan, *International Capital Markets: Law and Institutions* (OUP 2014) 291.

[8] Mirjam Eggen and Rupert Schaefer, 'Regulierung grenzüberschreitender Tätigkeiten im Finanzmarktrecht' (2013) 8 GesKR 368, 371.

[9] On different regulatory approaches in the field of securities regulation see Hal S Scott, 'International finance' in Andrew T Guzman and Alan O Sykes (eds), *Research Handbook in International Economic Law* (Edward Elgar Publishing 2007) 370ff; see also the comparative analysis by IOSCO, 'Task Force on Cross-Border Regulation' Final Report (September 2015) https://www.iosco.org/library/pubdocs/pdf/IOSCOPD507.pdf (accessed 12 November 2022).

[10] Wulf-Henning Roth, 'Mutual Recognition' in Panos Koutrakos and Jukka Snell (eds), *The Law of the EU's Internal Market* (Edward Elgar Publishing 2017) 433f; Matthias Lehmann in Jan von Hein (ed), *MüKo/BGB*, vol 13 (8th edn, CH Beck 2021) pt 12, paras 123ff.

arbitrage.[11] If a certain number of states unconditionally accept foreign supervision, market participants will relocate their seats to countries with weak financial regulation. Even worse, competition between countries to attract financial institutions could result in a downward spiral (race to the bottom) of supervisory standards and enforcement. An example of the country-of-origin principle is the concept of passporting for financial services inside the EU, more precisely inside the European Economic Area (EEA).[12] Due to the passports, European firms established and licensed in a Member State may provide services inside the entire EEA without further approval and without the need to relocate. However, most of the regulatory requirements are harmonized in the EEA, and the partly centralized supervision is at least coordinated. That way, many of the above-described risks are minimized.

Another way of dealing with cross-border services is to demand prior registration. As a consequence, a product or service provider can only access the market if the authorities of the host state have granted authorization.[13] Thereafter, the national supervisory law of the host state applies and supervision is exercised by its competent authorities. This concept is also referred to as the principle of host state supervision. On closer inspection, a further distinction can be made as to whether the host state imposes the same requirements on foreign financial service providers as on domestic ones (national treatment), modifies these requirements (modified national treatment) or subjects them to a completely different regulation that applies solely to foreign firms. Regardless of this differentiation, the application of national law to foreign products or financial service providers is to be classified as an extraterritorial application of the law.[14] From a public international law perspective, a state can apply its laws extraterritorially if there is a genuine connection.[15] This link can, inter alia, be seen in the law of the place of performance (*lex loci solutionis*).[16] Another link would be the nationality of the customers/investors of that state (principle of nationality).[17] Furthermore, a genuine link is constituted by the effects doctrine.[18] Often, activities

[11] Victor Fleischer, 'Regulatory Arbitrage' (2010) 89 Tex L Rev 227; Wolf-Georg Ringe, *Regulatory Competition in Global Financial Markets* (Annals of Corporate Governance 2016) 175.

[12] Lehmann (n 10) para 124.

[13] See eg MiFID II, art 5(1); CRD V, art 8(1); EMIR, art 14(1); CRA Regulation, art 14(1); UCITS Directive, art 5(1).

[14] See on extraterritorial application of law Michael Akehurst, 'Jurisdiction in International Law' (1972–1973) 46 Brit Y B Intl L 145, 179ff; Werner Meng, *Extraterritoriale Jurisdiktion im öffentlichen Wirtschaftsrecht* (Springer 1994); specifically on extraterritoriality in financial markets law see John C Coffee Jr, 'Extraterritorial Financial Regulation: Why E.T. Can't Come Home' (2014) 99 Cornell L Rev 1259; Matthias Lehmann, 'Legal Fragmentation, Extraterritoriality and Uncertainty in Global Financial Regulation' (2017) 37 OJLS 406; see on the different types of extraterritoriality Chris Brummer, 'Territoriality as a Regulatory Technique: Notes from the Financial Crisis' (2010) 79 U Cin L Rev 499, 504ff.

[15] Landmark decisions include *SS Lotus, France v Turkey*, Judgment [1927] PCIJ (ser A) No 10; *Nottebohm Case, Liechtenstein v Guatemala* (second phase), Judgment [1955] ICJ Reports 1955, 4; *Barcelona Traction, Light and Power Co. Case, Belgium v Spain*, Judgment [1970] ICJ Reports 1970, 6; see also American Law Institute, Restatement (Fourth) of the Foreign Relations Law of the US § 402 (2018); Cedric Ryngaert, *Jurisdiction in International Law* (2nd edn, OUP 2015) 43 and 84ff; on 'triggers' used by the EU to expand the territorial application of its law see Joanne Scott, 'The New EU "Extraterritoriality"' (2014) 51 CMLR 1343, 1347ff.

[16] Walter A Stoffel, 'Place of Performance-Jurisdiction and Plaintiff's Interests in Contemporary Societies' (2002) 4 Eur JL Reform 185.

[17] James Crawford, *Brownlie's Principles of Public International Law* (9th edn, OUP 2019) 444ff; Malcolm N Shaw, *International Law* (9th edn, CUP 2021) 567ff.

[18] Crawford (n 17) 447ff; Shaw (n 17) 592ff.

taking place exclusively on foreign markets will impact domestic markets because they are interconnected as described above.[19] Consequently, the extraterritorial application is justified from a public international law perspective. This finding, however, does not mean that an extraterritorial application of the law is always the best choice. Even though it is widespread in practice, it comes along with significant disadvantages. If a host state applies its laws extraterritorially to foreign companies and the latter are already subject to the regulation of their home state, companies must comply with several legal systems in different countries. This compliance causes high opportunity costs for the company. Moreover, conflicts between the two legal systems may arise, making it impossible for market players to operate in multiple jurisdictions. The same is true for supervision. In the case of extraterritorial application of laws, this supervision is carried out by multiple national authorities from different jurisdictions, which increases the global costs of supervision. On the other hand, supervision could be more stringent as indicated by the proverb 'two heads are better than one'. However, this requires close coordination between the supervisory authorities, including an intense exchange of data.[20] If this coordination does not function well, there is the danger of blind spots in the supervision. There is also moral hazard in relying on other supervisors, and without effective information sharing, risks spreading across borders may not be detected in time. Again, there is a risk of supervisory conflicts. Those conflicts will keep service providers away from foreign jurisdictions. All in all, it can be summarized that 'too much' extraterritorial application creates fragmented markets. These are less efficient and force financial firms to withdraw from foreign markets, which reduces the supply for investors, results in welfare losses, and generally jeopardizes the benefits of globalization.

One last and even more restrictive way of dealing with cross-border services is to additionally demand the presence of the service provider in the host state.[21] The law could either require the establishment of a branch or a subsidiary. That way, supervision is simplified for the authorities as they will have a contact person in their jurisdiction and may be more effective in enforcing oversight measures. This approach could be described as 'forced territoriality' and is even stricter than the simple form of extraterritoriality. At the starting point, it faces the same issues described above. On top of that, it is even more costly for market participants because they have to bear not only the licensing costs but also the costs of setting up and maintaining a branch or subsidiary. This is particularly burdensome if one thinks of either multinational players or FinTechs whose business model is based on the idea of operating from a single point in the world (centralization).

[19] One example of the effects doctrine can be found in art 4(1)(a)(v) of the EMIR, which extends the clearing obligation to contracts between two third country entities if the contract has a 'direct, substantial and foreseeable effect within the Union'. Similarly, in the US see US Commodity Exchange Act, s 2(i) (7 USC § 2(i)).

[20] Eddy Wymeersch, 'The Future of Financial Regulation and Supervision in Europe' 42 CMLR (2005) 987, 994ff; Fabian Walla, 'Capital Markets Supervision' in Rüdiger Veil (ed), *European Capital Markets Law* (3rd edn, Hart Publishing 2022) § 11 paras 43ff.

[21] Examples include MiFID II, art 39(1), which leaves Member States the choice of whether to impose a duty on financial service providers addressing retail investors to establish a branch. See also Solvency II, art 162(2)(b); Swiss VAG, art 15(1)(b).

The fact that there is no uniform global response to the question of what requirements should be imposed when granting market access to foreign financial service providers is worrying against the backdrop of globalized markets. Even more problematic, however, is that there is no uniform policy within the EU when it comes to dealing with financial service providers from third countries. This area of law is partly harmonized and partly left to the Member States.[22] Furthermore, the ways of market access for third country financial service providers also depend on the type of market participant in question.[23] The prerequisites vary, for example, between credit institutions, investment firms and even between undertakings for collective investment in transferable securities (UCITS) and alternative investment funds (AIFs). Various options of market access compete, such as the establishment of a branch or a subsidiary or the mere offering of cross-border services.[24] These many differentiations make the current system extremely complex and confusing. It is not built on a single philosophy but on many competing ways to regulate cross-border services. It is therefore referred to as a hopelessly fragmented legal framework.[25] Moreover, access to European markets is concomitant with extraterritorial application of law and, in part, forced territoriality. Both are incompatible with a global approach to regulation and supervision.

Since 2003, a new mechanism has been added to this diffuse mix of market access options: equivalence. Equivalence is now embedded in sixteen European legal acts, including key acts such as the Markets in Financial Instruments Regulation (MiFIR), the European Market Infrastructure Regulation (EMIR), and the Alternative Investment Fund Managers Directive (AIFMD). When granting equivalence, it is first examined whether the supervisory law of a foreign state is equivalent to EU law and enforced in an equivalent way. If this—and other conditions—are fulfilled, the EU adopts an equivalence decision. As a result of this decision, financial service providers from third countries can access the European market without having to obtain approval from European or Member State authorities and without having to comply with European supervisory law.[26] The concept of withdrawing regulatory and supervisory powers over foreign service providers and products, if they are already regulated in a comparable way by their home country, is not limited to the EU. It is advocated at the G20 level and has been implemented by multiple countries, such as Switzerland and Australia.[27]

[22] See eg MiFID II, art 39(1), which leaves the obligation to establish a branch up to the Member States. However, where a Member State has introduced such an obligation, the requirements for the third country firm are exhaustively regulated in MiFID II, art 39(2) and full harmonization therefore exists. See for other examples Hans Kuhn, 'Handel mit Dienstleistungen' in Herbert Kronke, Werner Melis, and Hans Kuhn (eds), *Handbuch Internationales Wirtschaftsrecht* (2nd edn, Otto Schmidt 2017) pt C paras 301ff.

[23] Kuhn (n 22) pt C para 299.

[24] Eddy Wymeersch, 'Third-Country Equivalence and Access to the EU Financial Markets Including in Case of Brexit' (2018) 4 JFR 209, 212ff; Matthias Lehmann and Dirk A Zetzsche, 'How Does It Feel to Be a Third Country? The Consequences of Brexit for Financial Market Law' in Oonagh E Fitzgerald and Eva Lein (eds), *Complexity's Embrace* (Queen's UP 2018) 120ff.

[25] Kuhn (n 22) pt C para 299: 'heillos zersplitterter Rechtsrahmen'.

[26] Not all equivalence decisions grant some form of market access. See ch 2 C).

[27] Concerning the G20 see G20 St Petersburg Summit, 'G20 Leaders' Declaration' (6 September 2013) para 71 http://www.g20.utoronto.ca/2013/2013-0906-declaration.html (accessed 12 November 2022); for national implementations of deference see the FSB's comparative analysis: FSB, 'Jurisdictions' ability to defer to each other's OTC derivatives market regulatory regimes' Report to G20 Finance Ministers and Central Bank Governors (18 September 2014) https://www.fsb.org/wp-content/uploads/r_140918.pdf (accessed 12 November 2022); on the Swiss approach see ch 3; on the Australian approach see ASIC,

In the US, it is treated under the name of substituted compliance.[28] The generic term used in this book for equivalence and substituted compliance is deference.[29]

The main difference between deference and all other options of market access presented is that it neither leads to an extraterritorial application of law nor to a 'forced territoriality', but on the contrary entails a withdrawal of (supra-)national regulatory power. This difference offers a unique chance to build a new global supervisory system without fragmented markets. If this cooperative approach is applied in a consistent manner and constantly developed, deference could become a decisive component of a new globalized financial market architecture. In fact, it is argued in this book that deference is the only realistic way to overcome fragmented markets.

II. Course of the investigation

This book is divided into five chapters. The first chapter introduces the European concept of equivalence by setting out the historical context and examining the scope of equivalence provisions as well as the process of how equivalence is granted. The second chapter provides a more in-depth discussion of equivalence and analyses its main requirements and legal consequences. The third and fourth chapters leave the European framework and present and critically assess the Swiss and US systems of market access for foreign service providers, in particular their approach to deference. The fifth and final chapter ventures an outlook on future developments of deference in general and equivalence in the EU in particular and proposes reform proposals.

1. An introduction to history, scope of application, and process of equivalence in the EU

In the first part of this chapter, the different options for financial service providers to access the European financial market are presented.[30] It will be shown that European law does not offer a uniform approach but provides different ways to access the internal market. Nevertheless, each way is connected to decisive disadvantages. In particular, European rules are often applied extraterritorially, and third country financial service providers are forced to move to the EU ('forced territoriality') so that they can be supervised more effectively. This leads to a legal fragmentation of markets and thus to high opportunity costs, legal conflicts, and a distortion of competition.

'Principles for cross-border financial regulation' Regulatory Guide 54 (June 2012) 25ff https://asic.gov.au/media/1238990/rg54-published-29-june-2012.pdf (accessed 12 November 2022); Greg Tanzer, 'Substituted Compliance: An Australian Regulator's Perspective' (2007) 48 Harv Intl LJ Online 21; Jennifer G Hill, 'Regulatory Cooperation in Securities Market Regulation: Perspectives from Australia' (2020) 17 ECFR 11, 26ff.

[28] Ethiopis Tafara and Robert J Peterson, 'A Blueprint for Cross-Border Access to U.S. Investors: A New International Framework' (2007) 48 Harv Intl LJ 31; Howell E Jackson, 'Substituted Compliance' (2015) 1 JFR 169; see extensively on the US approach ch 4.

[29] Deference is also used as a generic term in Lehmann (n 14) 429ff; characterizing equivalence as a deference model see Niamh Moloney, 'Reflections on the EU Third Country Regime for Capital Markets in the Shadow of Brexit' (2020) 17 ECFR 35, 39.

[30] See ch 1 B).

The new approach of equivalence is one solution to this problem. The first chapter discusses its historical roots, the areas of financial law covered by it, and the procedure for obtaining equivalence. The idea of equivalence does not originate from financial markets law.[31] Equivalence in the form of mutual recognition has contributed to the creation of the EU single market.[32] The concept of equivalence has also been embedded in various legal acts of world trade law since 1980. A similar concept is provided for in EU data protection law, in the form of an adequacy decision, which will be compared to equivalence. Since the beginning of this millennium, equivalence has been incorporated into EU financial markets law on a large scale.[33] Many of the key legislative acts in this area contain an equivalence mechanism. Nevertheless, some important areas, such as market access for credit institutions and direct insurers, are not covered for reasons presented later.[34] The process of how equivalence is obtained varies depending on the regime applicable. Sometimes there is just one equivalence decision; other times, an additional registration is required, or even a second decision must be adopted by the Member States' national competent authorities (NCAs). These differences in the procedure are analysed at the end of the first chapter.[35]

2. A closer look at key requirements, decision-making, and legal consequences of equivalence in the EU

The second chapter argues that equivalence provisions in the various directives and regulations are all based on a uniform concept. Although the prerequisites, the process and legal consequences are not completely homogeneous, the essential preconditions and outcomes are identical or at least based on the same regulatory philosophy. The granting of market access via equivalence is often subject to various requirements.[36] However, a condition *sine qua non* is the equivalence decision by the European Commission. If equivalence—as advocated in this study—is based on a uniform concept, this has far-reaching implications for the interpretation of individual equivalence provisions.

Subsequently, the equivalence decision as the core prerequisite of each equivalence mechanism is being examined.[37] The crucial question that arises here is what is to be understood by 'equivalence'.[38] What does the term mean? How can it be determined in theory as well as in practice whether two legal systems are equivalent? Is the same or just a comparable level of supervision needed? These and similar questions will be addressed in two steps: first, by an interpretation of the legal concept and, secondly, by an analysis of the current practice of the Commission and the European supervisory authorities (ESAs). The analysis is complemented by a proposal for a methodology on how to determine equivalence. A consistent methodology underlying equivalence

[31] Tzung-bor Wei, 'The Equivalence Approach to Securities Regulation' (2007) 27 NW J Intl L & Bus 255, 263; see on the history ch 1 C)I.

[32] Roth (n 10) 435ff; Vassilis Hatzopoulos, 'Forms of mutual recognition in the field of services' in Ioannis Lianos and Okeoghene Odudu (eds), *Regulating Trade in Services in the EU and the WTO* (CUP 2012) 59ff.

[33] See for an overview of all EU regimes ch 1 C)II.

[34] See ch 1 C)II.6 below.

[35] See ch 1 C)III.

[36] See ch 2 A)I.

[37] See ch 2 B).

[38] See ch 2 B)I.

decisions would increase predictability and transparency, the absence of which is one of the main shortcomings of the current system of equivalence.

After having analysed what is meant by equivalence, the focus shifts to the key player of equivalence assessments and the question of discretion in the administrative decision-making.[39] The Commission is responsible for issuing equivalence decisions, which poses a problem because it includes political considerations in its decision-making and behaves more like a political actor than an administrative authority. It will be argued that equivalence provisions as well as world trade law and EU primary law require a strict legal interpretation of equivalence and therefore do not permit any political considerations on the part of the Commission. Such a strict legal interpretation ('juridification') of equivalence has the benefit of resulting in a more coherent and transparent system of cross-border regulation and greater efficiency of equivalence in practice, which could play a decisive role, for example, in the context of Brexit. If the equivalence decision is understood as a legal one, many other constitutional and administrative law principles apply to the decision-making process.

One issue all equivalence provisions have in common is that of changing legal environments. Equivalence is a permanent state unless the decision is being withdrawn. For this reason, continuous observation of equivalence is necessary. The process and quality of this monitoring and review, possible grounds for and administrative as well as constitutional limits to withdrawal decisions are analysed.[40] All of this promotes a juridification, which is advocated throughout this book.

Discretion in administrative decision-making and the question of judicial review of these decisions are two sides of the same coin. Whether and to what extent equivalence decisions of the Commission can be reviewed by courts, in particular the Court of Justice of the European Union (CJEU), is a crucial question. So far, the literature lacks an in-depth assessment of the applicable type of action, the right to bring an action (*locus standi*) and potential grounds for annulment, which is why this book addresses these issues.[41]

Finally, the legal consequences of equivalence are described.[42] Equivalence provisions are formulated very differently and do not achieve the same outcomes. The results range from a mere waiver of individual requirements through partial market access up to full market access for third country products or market participants. Although the consequences may look very different at first sight, they are based on the same regulatory philosophy.

3. A more liberal approach to market access in Switzerland

The third chapter of this book goes a step further and leaves the legal framework of the EU. Deference is not a particular European phenomenon. Instead, it is advocated at the G20 level, and various countries have implemented deference.[43] Among these jurisdictions, this chapter will concentrate on Switzerland because of its unique role

[39] See ch 2 B)II.
[40] See ch 2 B)III.
[41] See ch 2 B)IV.
[42] See ch 2 C).
[43] See n 27 (ch 1).

for the European financial sector, which does not only derive from its location in the heart of Europe.

Compared to the EU and the US, Switzerland pursues a more liberal approach with extensive market access for foreign service providers. In the case of merely cross-border services, Switzerland often refrains from making market access for foreign companies subject to registration. This considerably facilitates market access for foreign entities. Once they have entered the market, foreign firms must nevertheless comply with the stringent rules of Swiss supervisory law. These rules are primarily based on international standards, which play a paramount role for the Swiss legislator, and in particular on European law, which Switzerland autonomously replicates, primarily to achieve the equivalence status in the EU. This liberal approach has only been slightly restricted by the recent comprehensive reform of Swiss financial law. Interestingly, not only the concept of equivalence but also that of 'appropriateness' exists in Switzerland, which is a more liberal version of equivalence, as it is a form of recognition based on international standards. The Swiss regulatory approach can be explained in particular against the background of Switzerland's economic situation. It is characterized by the great importance of its financial industry for the economy as a whole and by the state of being surrounded by a large internal market.

4. Substituted compliance in the US: Different terminology, but same concept?

The US has also established deference mechanisms under the name of substituted compliance, which allow for a withdrawal of domestic law following a qualitative analysis of a foreign legal system. The current state of deference in the US, however, lags behind the developments in the EU and Switzerland. For a long time, the US predominantly followed the principle of national treatment by subjecting foreign service providers to the same regulation as domestic ones in order to create a level playing field. It was only when pressure increased significantly due to the declining dominance of the US capital market compared to other markets, the EU's advancement of the concept of equivalence and the increasing desire of US investors to invest abroad that the US retreated, at least partially, from the principle of national treatment.

However, this development, which traced back to a proposal by two United States Securities and Exchange Commission (SEC) officials, came to an abrupt end with the GFC before it could be widely implemented. After the financial crisis, the idea of substituted compliance experienced a comeback in the area of derivatives regulation. The extent to which substituted compliance has found its way into the US system, how the regimes have changed before and after the financial crisis, and what similarities and differences exist to the European and Swiss approaches are analysed in this chapter.

5. A look into the crystal ball

The fifth chapter leaves the current regime and attempts to give an outlook on the future global financial market architecture. The first section addresses the highly controversial topic of the conception of a new global financial market architecture.[44] Is there a need for a harmonized and thus globally uniform supervisory law, or is competition

[44] See ch 5 A).

between different national legal systems the better way for the future? This book aims at striking a balance between these extreme positions by combining the advantages of both. Deference in the form of appropriateness, equivalence and substituted compliance leads to far-reaching convergence of different supervisory regimes without, however, completely eliminating competition. In this way, the idea of trial and error is maintained and systemic risks arising from uniformly applied, ineffective regulation are largely avoided. Therefore, the concept of deference should be further enhanced, strengthened, and expanded. If that is achieved, deference will be a key component of any future global financial market architecture that is also capable of managing new phenomena such as the regulation of FinTech.

The second section of the last chapter is devoted to the future of equivalence in the EU.[45] European equivalence mechanisms should be further refined and improved to overcome the challenges identified in the first two chapters. For this development *de lege ferenda*, insights can be drawn from the experiences of deference regimes in Switzerland and the US.

III. Approach of this book

Equivalence is deeply rooted in financial markets law. In total, there are 40 provisions in European supervisory law containing an equivalence regime.[46] Due to the sheer number of—in part very diverging—regimes, it is not a realistic approach to go into the details of every single provision. This would not be possible for reasons of space alone. What is more, the variety of provisions and their details would blur the vision of the bigger picture. For these reasons, an overview of the scope and functioning of equivalence mechanisms is given at the beginning.[47] All other parts treat equivalence as a uniform principle and examine the upcoming questions from a holistic perspective.

The overarching aim is to draw a bigger picture by pointing out differences and similarities between the regimes and highlighting the general philosophy behind the concept of equivalence. Administrative and constitutional limits are identified, consequences for a new global financial market architecture are discussed, and the European approach is compared to that of Switzerland and the US. There will be illustrative examples showing the specifics of selected equivalence provisions.

For readers who want to find out what the legal situation in a particular equivalence regime of the EU is like, tables will be provided at the end of the second chapter. These tables address most of the questions raised during this analysis and include all provisions containing equivalence regimes.[48]

[45] See ch 5 B).

[46] This number varies depending on the definition of an equivalence mechanism. See for the definition used in this book ch 1 C); see for a full list of all provisions included ch 2 D).

[47] See ch 1 C)II.

[48] See 'Tables on equivalence provisions—Article-by-Article overview', ch 2 D).

B) Access to EU financial markets

When the question of access to the EU market for third country firms is raised, it is already presupposed that there is a single European market and a single access to it. Contrary to this presumption, there could be 27 different markets with diverging access conditions. If this were the case, would it not be more appropriate to analyse the law governing access to these markets instead of focusing on the European level?

Indeed, there is no European agency deciding on market access for service providers in large parts of financial market law. For instance, investment firms, central counterparties, direct insurances and reinsurances or management companies of UCITS are not authorized by a European agency, but by NCAs.[49] Two main exceptions are the authorization of credit institutions, which is carried out by both the European Central Bank (ECB) and NCAs, and the registration of credit rating agencies by the European Securities and Markets Authority (ESMA).[50] The fact that the Member States are primarily responsible for the authorization applies to European financial service providers as well as to those from third countries. So why does this research not address the national legislation, but instead focuses on the European legal framework? There are several reasons for this. First, the fact that NCAs must authorize financial service providers is prescribed in EU law.[51] Secondly, many of the requirements that need to be fulfilled by market participants to obtain a national licence are determined by EU law. Many EU texts even provide for full harmonization. That means that all requirements are set by EU law and national legislators cannot impose further conditions. Thirdly, the focus of this book is on equivalence. Equivalence provisions are to be found primarily in EU law and the decision on equivalence is also taken by the Commission at the European level. That means that equivalence mechanisms are truly European instruments. Because of the above-mentioned arguments, it is worth looking at the European level. In fact, this is the only way to understand fully how access to financial markets for service providers works.

I. How does access to EU financial markets work?

An important distinction has to be made before the different ways in which service providers access European markets can be identified. The regime applicable to market access depends on whether the service provider is from the EEA[52] or from a third country. A third country in this context refers to a country that is not part of the EEA.

[49] MiFID II, art 5(1); EMIR, art 14(1); Solvency II, art 14(1) and (2) and UCITS Directive, art 6(1).

[50] In relation to credit institutions see SSM Regulation, arts 4(1)(a) and 14(1) and (2); with regard to credit rating agencies see CRA Regulation, arts 14(1) and 15(1).

[51] See the examples listed in n 13 (ch 1).

[52] Members of the Agreement on the EEA include the European Union, all Member States of the EU and in addition Norway, Lichtenstein, and Iceland. The United Kingdom is now neither a member of the EU nor of the EEA.

1. Access inside the European Economic Area: Passporting

At the outset, almost every financial service provider must obtain a licence before it is allowed to offer services.[53] Such a licence could theoretically be granted by an EU institution for the entire internal market, but this is rarely the case.[54] There is not even a single licence in the area of banking where the ECB is involved in the process of authorization.[55] Consequently, authorization is almost exclusively granted at national level.

As a consequence, a financial service provider would have to go through 27 different authorization proceedings in order to be able to satisfy the entire European market. This would take much time, cause excessive costs, lead to a multiplication of applicable regulatory and supervisory regimes, and would altogether contravene the idea of freedom of services. In fact, the entire concept of a single market would be endangered. To avoid these consequences, the EU introduced the concept of passports.[56] On the basis of passports, a service provider needs to obtain only one licence from the NCA of its home state (so-called country-of-origin principle or principle of home state regulation).[57] This licence suffices for the entire single market, including the EEA, meaning that no further authorization process is required.[58]

This approach is built on the idea of mutual recognition. The concept of mutual recognition is closely connected to the free movement of goods and the *Cassis-de-Dijon* judgment of the European Court of Justice (ECJ) and will be discussed extensively below.[59]

To sum it up, market access through passports is a major step towards a single market for financial services and products. Nonetheless, there is no perfect competition within the EU because diverging legal situations in the Member States lead to competitive differences.[60]

2. Access for third country financial service providers

The access for third country financial service providers is very different from that of EEA firms. Third country firms can enter the internal market in multiple ways. Each of

[53] See examples listed in n 13 (ch 1).

[54] One important exception is the registration of credit rating agencies directly by ESMA pursuant to CRA Regulation, arts 14(1), 15(1), and 16(3). Rüdiger Veil, 'Rating Agencies' in Rüdiger Veil (ed), *European Capital Markets Law* (3rd edn, Hart Publishing 2022) § 27 para 55.

[55] See SSM Regulation, arts 4(1)(a) and 14(1) and (2); Heinrich Nemeczek and Sebastian Pitz, 'Cross-Border Business of UK Credit Institutions and Investment Firms with German Clients in light of Brexit, MiFIR and MiFID II' (2018) 29 EBLR 425, 428.

[56] See eg MiFID II, arts 6(3), 34(1), and 35(1); CRD V, arts 33 and 34(1); CRA Reg, art 14(2); AIFMD, art 33(1); UCITS Directive, arts 5(1) and 6(1); Solvency II, art 15(1); see Roth (n 10) 446ff; generally on the concept of passporting see Andrew Godwin, Ian Ramsay, and Edwin Sayes, 'Assessing Financial Regulatory Coordination and Integration with Reference to OTC Derivatives Regulation' (2017) 12 CMLJ 38, 56ff.

[57] Lehmann and Zetzsche (n 24) 109.

[58] Before services can be offered in another Member State, the provider must usually notify the NCA of its home state of its intention to do so. See eg MiFID II, art 34(2); CRD V, art 35; AIFMD, arts 32(2) and 33(2).

[59] Case C-120/78 *Cassis-de-Dijon* ECLI:EU:C:1979:42; Roth (n 10) 435f; see ch 1 C)I.1.

[60] See eg the unfinished projects of a banking and capital markets union. Diego Valiante, 'CMU and the Deepening of Financial Integration' in Danny Busch, Emilios Avgouleas, and Guido Ferrarini (eds), *Capital Markets Union in Europe* (OUP 2018) paras 2.01ff; speech delivered by Benoît Cœuré, 'Completing the single market in capital' ICMA Capital Market Lecture Series (19 May 2014) https://www.ecb.europa.eu/press/key/date/2014/html/sp140519_1.en.html (accessed 12 November 2022).

them is fraught with major problems, as will be demonstrated in the following. First, service providers can obtain a national licence by the NCA of the host state, including for the mere offering of cross-border services (a)). Moreover, they can opt for the creation of a subsidiary inside the EEA, which will then be regarded as an EU company (b)). Finally, firms can confine themselves to passive marketing, so-called reverse solicitation (c)).

a) Principle of host state regulation

Market participants from third countries must obtain a licence from the NCA of the state they want to provide services in.[61] This licence is limited to the territory of the Member State concerned, which means that market access is granted on a bilateral basis. There is no passporting for financial service providers from third countries[62] and no system of mutual recognition applies. Consequently, third country firms need to go through 27 approval proceedings. This approach leads to the problems described above: waste of time, excessive costs, legal conflicts, multiplication of applicable supervision, and consequently potential conflicts between supervisory authorities.

The last two, in particular, pose a problem when thinking about a new global financial market architecture. An investment firm from the United States, for example, that wants to offer investment services in the US and the EU would need to follow 28 different legal regimes. On top of that, the firm might be forced to set up a branch in the respective country in which it offers its services.[63] If the US investment firm expands into other countries, for instance in Asia, additional legal regimes apply, and new branches may have to be established. This goes along with high opportunity costs and legal conflicts that could, in the end, prevent an investment firm from becoming active in some parts of the world. The same holds true for supervision. The investment firm would be supervised by multiple competent authorities, each applying different laws. This may lead to misunderstandings, coordination issues, and most likely blind spots in the supervision due to issues in the delineation of competences. These shortcomings will become even more evident as financial markets in less developed parts of the world evolve. Market access on the basis of national licences, i.e. through the principle of host state regulation, is therefore not only very unattractive for third country firms but also unsuitable for a global financial market. It leads to fragmented markets.[64]

b) Establishment of a subsidiary

Another way to enter the European financial market is by establishing a legally independent subsidiary within the EEA. Due to its legal independence, this subsidiary is regarded as a European entity from the perspective of European law.[65] This entails a

[61] In relation to investment firms see eg Rolf Sethe, 'Das Drittstaatenregime von MiFIR und MiFID II' (2014) 86 SZW 615, 617–19.

[62] Lehmann and Zetzsche (n 24) 109, 122.

[63] See eg Solvency II, arts 162ff; Dirk A Zetzsche, 'Drittstaaten im Europäischen Bank- und Finanzdienstleistungsrecht' in Gregor Bachmann and Burkhard Breig (eds), *Finanzmarktregulierung zwischen Innovation und Kontinuität in Deutschland, Europa und Russland* (Mohr Siebeck 2014) 100–101.

[64] See Kenneth A Armstrong, 'Mutual Recognition' in Catherine Barnard and Joanne Scott (eds), *The Law of the Single European Market* (Hart Publishing 2002) 229.

[65] André Prüm, 'Brexit: Options for Banks from the UK to Access the EU Market' (2017) 28 EuZW 988, 990ff.

number of advantages, including the applicability of the rules on passports. Hence, the subsidiary only needs to obtain one licence, which all other members of the EEA will then recognize. Consequently, the subsidiary will not have to comply with numerous different supervisory regimes, but just with the one of its home Member State. It will also be supervised solely by the competent authority of its home state. In addition, the subsidiary can invoke the freedom to provide services (Articles 56ff TFEU) and the freedom of establishment (Articles 49ff TFEU) *ex origine* since it is regarded as a European company.

Nevertheless, this approach has several drawbacks. If there is a strong interconnectedness with the parent company, enforcement of supervisory measures by NCAs can be hampered. This issue is addressed by some EU legal acts that enable the competent authorities to refuse authorization in cases where effective supervision is endangered.[66] Furthermore, systemic risks could unnoticedly spread through the institutional channel, as different competent authorities supervise the parent company and the subsidiary. Hence, close cooperation between supervisory authorities is needed. Additionally, it is cost-intensive for the financial service provider to set up a full-fledged subsidiary with sufficiently qualified personnel. This could tempt especially smaller institutions to establish letter-box companies that outsource most of the work to the parent company. This poses a threat to sound supervision by NCAs. As a result, supervisory authorities will try to limit the process of outsourcing to counter the danger of supervising 'empty shells'.[67] This leads to a 'forced territoriality', which is connected to a loss of efficiency caused by the need for dual organization. Besides, smaller service providers without the means to set up a fully equipped branch will not have the opportunity to enter new markets. As a result, competition is distorted to the advantage of big companies, which will increase the too-big-to-fail dilemma. Another negative consequence of forced territoriality is the disruption of the business model of FinTech services. As pointed out in the introductory part, these global players rely on economies of scale. The benefits of economies of scale erode if the same service is subject to myriad laws and supervisory authorities. On top of that, the important characteristic of FinTechs of operating from a single point on earth—concentration—is incompatible with the idea of forced territoriality and the duty to set up subsidiaries in every jurisdiction.

To sum up, accessing the financial market through establishing a legally independent subsidiary has some advantages. Nevertheless, it is not the most economically efficient way of providing financial services. It leads to high opportunity costs, distorts competition and hampers the rise of FinTech, which is not favourable from an economic point of view.[68]

[66] See eg MiFID II, art 10(1); CRD V, art 14(3); AIFMD, art 8(3)(b); see Lehmann and Zetzsche (n 24) 120f.

[67] See extensive prohibitions eg in AIFMD, art 20(3); see Zetzsche (n 63) 89f; in the context of Brexit see ESMA, 'Opinion: General Principles to support supervisory convergence in the context of the United Kingdom withdrawing from the European Union' ESMA42-110-433 (31 May 2017); Gunnar Schuster, 'A tightened European framework for banks following Brexit' (2019) 31 ZBB/JBB 297.

[68] See on the challenges for FinTechs Lehmann (n 2) 140–41.

c) Reverse solicitation

One way to provide services in the EEA without having to obtain a licence and without being subjected to supervision by an EU authority is the concept of reverse solicitation. The concept is part of the freedom of services of EU citizens guaranteed in Articles 56, 57 TFEU[69] and is also foreseen in European secondary legislation.[70] Reverse solicitation is the right of an EU citizen to receive services passively across borders from any (EU or third country) firm.[71] Therefore, if the EU citizen approaches the third country firm on his initiative, the firm will neither need a licence nor will it be supervised by an authority in the EEA.[72] In fact, European financial markets law will not apply in the first place. Only the supervisory law of the home state of the service provider might apply. This clear separation of applicable legal orders will prevent conflicts of law and conflicting supervisory acts.

Nonetheless, two decisive disadvantages associated with reverse solicitation remain for financial service providers. First, they have very limited market access rights because a supplier cannot provide its services without the initiative of an EU citizen. In the wake of Brexit, the scope of application has even been reduced,[73] and EU institutions are generally more alert in relation to topics such as empty shells, outsourcing, dual-hatting, or similar techniques preventing effective supervision by EU authorities.[74] Secondly, there is no clear demarcation between passive and active freedom of services. This is especially problematic in view of the drastic sanctions provided for in some Member States for operating without a licence.[75]

II. Access through equivalence: A new approach

A relatively new approach is market access through equivalence. An equivalence mechanism regulating market access for third country firms or financial products was first introduced in the 2003 Prospectus Directive.[76] In its pure form, equivalence is very different from the other forms of market access that have just been described because market access is also granted for the active provision of services (as opposed to reverse solicitation) and, at the same time, the foreign company is not subjected to European or Member State supervisory law.[77] Insofar, it is different from the principle

[69] Joined Cases C-286/82 and 26/83 *Luisi and Carbone v Ministero dello Tesoro* ECLI:EU:C:1984:35, para 10.

[70] See eg AIFMD, recital 70; MiFIR, art 46(5) subpara 3; MiFID II, art 42.

[71] Lehmann and Zetzsche (n 24) 124.

[72] Nemeczek and Pitz (n 55) 458ff; in the context of MiFID II and MiFIR see ESMA, 'Questions and Answers: On MiFID II and MiFIR investor protection and intermediaries topics' ESMA35-43-349 (3 October 2018) 109ff.

[73] See MiFIR, art 46(5) subpara 3 second and third sentence.

[74] See eg ECB, 'Supervisory Expectations on Booking Models' (2018) https://www.bankingsupervision.europa.eu/banking/relocating/shared/pdf/ssm.supervisoryexpectationsbookingmodels_201808.en.pdf (accessed 12 November 2022).

[75] See eg German Banking Act (KWG), § 54(1) no 2; see in France the Code monétaire et financier, art L353-1 no 1.

[76] Prospectus Directive, art 20 (no longer in force).

[77] These characteristics do not apply to all equivalence mechanisms to the same extent. The details of the various mechanisms will be set out in more detail in the course of this book.

of host state regulation and the establishment of a subsidiary. No authorization is needed, no ongoing prudential supervision by authorities inside the EEA takes place, and no EU supervisory law needs to be followed. Equivalence strictly follows the country-of-origin principle. Hence, there is neither an extraterritorial application of law nor forced territoriality. These consequences are very similar to those of the principle of mutual recognition, which governs European passports.

C) Equivalence in the EU: History, scope of application, and process

Before an in-depth analysis of equivalence can be undertaken, the meaning of this concept needs to be elaborated. There is no legal definition of equivalence. In fact, a closer look at the numerous regimes reveals that their scope, prerequisites, and legal consequences vary considerably. It is, therefore, best to approach equivalence through its central idea. The guiding principle is the withdrawal of regulatory power with regard to third country market participants in order to avoid legal conflicts and market fragmentation whenever an extraterritorial application of the law is unnecessary because the regulation and supervision in the third country are as effective (in other words 'equivalent') as that in the EU and its Member States.[78] Unnecessary in that context means that the objectives of the specific law of the EU—often investor protection, safeguarding the functioning of markets, and systemic stability—are met by the foreign regulatory and supervisory system on an equal footing. As a result of equivalence, market access is granted, or the financial service provider is at least exempted from certain regulatory requirements. In this sense, the equivalence decision of the European Commission is the door opener for third country service providers into the EU.[79]

It follows from this definition that this book does not address provisions demanding equivalence in an intra-EU context.[80] It does also not encompass national rules of Member States concerning equivalence, neither purely national-based equivalence regimes nor national legislation transposing European Directives where the equivalence decision is adopted at the national level.[81] Hence, this book focuses on equivalence mechanisms where the equivalence decision is taken at the European level.[82] For a list

[78] Moloney (n 29) 39.

[79] Wymeersch (n 24) 210.

[80] See eg UCITS Directive, art 32(5) subpara 3 in the version of 31 May 2013.

[81] See for purely national regimes under German law KWG, § 2(5); KWG, § 53c(1) no 2; German Securities Trading Act (WpHG), § 91; see for a national equivalence mechanism transposing a European directive in the context of deposit guarantee schemes § 59 of the German Deposit Guarantee Act (EinSiG) transposing art 15 of the Directive 2014/49/EU of 16 April 2014 (Deposit Guarantee Schemes Directive).

[82] Olivier Girard identifies three different types of equivalence provisions: 1. national equivalence clauses, 2. decentralized equivalence clauses, and 3. centralized equivalence clauses. Only the latter consists of mechanisms in which the Commission is responsible for the decision-making. Following this terminology, this book focuses only on 'centralised equivalence decisions'. See Olivier Girard, 'Les méthodes de suppression des frontières au plan mondial dans le domaine bancaire et financier' (2007–2008) 3 EUREDIA 349, 361–64.

of all 40 equivalence provisions included in this book, see the 'Tables on equivalence provisions' in Chapter 2 D).

In the following section, the history of equivalence is examined, inter alia, on the basis of similar legal concepts. Subsequently, a detailed overview of all areas of financial markets law containing equivalence provisions is provided. Finally, equivalence mechanisms are categorized according to the process that governs them. The key requirements, in particular the equivalence decision, as well as the legal consequences will be analysed in Chapter 2.

I. Where does equivalence come from? History and related concepts

Equivalence as such is not a concept limited to capital markets law or even to law in general. The idea of equivalence is part of Albert Einstein's general theory of relativity and is also used in financial mathematics to compare and value cash flows. In law, there are equivalence principles in insurance, tax, antitrust and environmental law, as well as in the case law of the CJEU on the enforcement of EU law in Member States.[83] However, all these principles have little or nothing in common with the concept presented here.

Equivalence can be compared to the general principle of recognition. The difference is that equivalence, unlike recognition, requires that the third country legal system is equivalent to that of the EU, a status that is determined by a Commission equivalence decision. Equivalence can therefore be understood as a subcategory of recognition.[84] In cases where equivalence demands reciprocal treatment by the third country, it is a subcategory of mutual recognition.[85]

As equivalence in capital markets law is a rather new concept established just a little less than two decades ago, it makes sense to look at the superordinate concept of (mutual) recognition. Granting effect to foreign legal rules or acts through recognition has a long history in public international law as well as private international law.[86] Examples include the recognition of states in international law, the recognition of the legal status of foreign marriages, or the recognition of foreign judgments. Although these mechanisms are all labelled with the catchphrase 'recognition', it is obvious that the rules governing them differ tremendously. Even within one area of law, recognition

[83] Wei (n 31) 263.

[84] See in detail Eilís V Ferran, 'Financial Supervision' in Daniel Mügge (ed), *Europe and the Governance of Global Finance* (OUP 2014) 23; Joel P Trachtman, 'Embedding Mutual Recognition at the WTO' (2007) 14 J Eur Public Policy 780, 782ff and in particular 784; see for the discussion regarding the terminology Hatzopoulos (n 32) 68–70; a different view is expressed by Tilman Imm, *Der finanz- und kapitalmarktrechtliche Gleichwertigkeitsmechanismus* (Mohr Siebeck 2020) 143; see in more detail ch 2 B) I.1.a)ee).

[85] Ferran (n 84) 23; see also the accurate characterization by Francesco Pennesi, 'Equivalence in the Area of Financial Services' (2021) 58 CMLR 39, 48.

[86] Hersch Lauterpacht, 'Recognition of States in International Law' (1944) 53 Yale LJ 385; Stefan Talmon, *Recognition in International Law* (Martinus Nijhoff 2000); Pierre Mayer, 'Les méthodes de la reconnaissance en droit international privé' in *Le droit international privé: esprit et méthodes, Mélanges en l'honneur de Paul Lagarde* (Dalloz 2005); Paul Lagarde, *La reconnaissance des actes publics dans les règlements européens de droit international privé* (Pedone 2013).

has different meanings.[87] Nevertheless, individual manifestations of the idea of recognition have changed the way one can think about equivalence in financial markets law and consequently influence its interpretation. Those manifestations can be found in EU law in the form of mutual recognition, in world trade law, as well as data protection law.

1. Mutual recognition and the creation of a single capital market in the EU: A model for third country regimes?

The creation of a single capital market in the EU is a process that has been ongoing for decades and is not yet completed in some areas, which is why it cannot be described in detail here.[88] A milestone in this development, however, is the principle of mutual recognition. As equivalence is a subcategory of mutual recognition, the question arises whether the experiences gained from the creation of an internal capital market in the EU can be transferred to the shaping of third country regimes.

The principle of mutual recognition is embedded in the primary law and specified in the secondary law of the EU.[89] The *Cassis-de-Dijon* case of the ECJ largely influences its interpretation and it was a key factor in the evolvement of the single market.[90] In its 1985 White Paper, the Commission had already identified the dilemma that positive integration in the form of harmonization at the European level alone is not sufficient to create a single market.[91] Relying solely on harmonization leads to overregulation, takes a long time to implement and hampers innovation.[92] Especially in a highly detailed and technical area such as financial markets law, complete harmonization also reaches its factual limits. For these reasons, negative integration in the form of mutual recognition is needed alongside harmonization efforts to create a single market.[93]

Shortly after the 'new strategy' was proclaimed in the 1985 White Paper, the EU reacted by adopting the Mutual Recognition Directive, which amended the Listing Particulars Directive.[94] Furthermore, the EU adopted the predecessor of the current

[87] See for differences even within private international law Dagmar Coester-Waltjen, 'Das Anerkennungsprinzip im Dornröschenschlaf?' in Heinz-Peter Mansel and others (eds), *Festschrift für Erik Jayme*, vol 1 (Sellier 2004) 122; Katja Funken, *Das Anerkennungsprinzip im internationalen Privatrecht* (Mohr Siebeck 2009) 23ff; Dominique Bureau and Horatia Muir Watt (eds), *Droit international privé*, vol 1 (4th edn, Thémis 2017) § 238–39.

[88] See the Segré Report (Report of a group of experts appointed by the EEC Commission), 'The Development of a European Capital Market' (November 1966) http://aei.pitt.edu/31823/1/Dev_Eur_Cap_Mkt_1966.pdf (accessed 12 November 2022); on the development see Jennifer Payne and Elizabeth Howell, 'The Creation of a European Capital Market' in Panos Koutrakos and Jukka Snell (eds), *The Law of the EU's Internal Market* (Edward Elgar Publishing 2017) 241; see extensively Daniel Mügge, 'Reordering the Marketplace: Competition Politics in European Finance' (2006) 44 J Common Mkt Stud 991.

[89] See TFEU, arts 53(1), 81 and 82. Matteo Ortino, 'The Role and Functioning of Mutual Recognition in the European Market of Financial Services' (2007) 56 Intl & Comp LQ 309; Payne and Howell (n 88) 241–62.

[90] Case C-120/78 *Cassis-de-Dijon* (n 59); Roth (n 10) 427.

[91] Commission, 'Completing the Internal Market' White Paper COM (85) 310, paras 13 and 61–64; with regard to financial services see paras 101–107.

[92] Commission (n 91) para 64.

[93] Daniel-Erasmus Khan and Dominik Eisenhut in Rudolf Geiger, Daniel-Erasmus Khan, and Markus Kotzur (eds), *European Union Treaties* (CH Beck 2015) art 114 paras 9–11; Thomas von Danwitz in Manfred A Dauses and Markus Ludwigs, *Handbuch des EU-Wirtschaftsrechts* (CH Beck as of February 2021) B. II. para 93.

[94] Manning G Warren III, 'Regulatory Harmony in the European Communities: The Common Market Prospectus' (1990) 16 Brook J Intl L 19, 29–31.

UCITS Directive (Council Directive 85/611/EEC—UCITS I), which introduced a passport for UCITS, the first passport in capital markets law.[95] The passport system is founded on the idea of mutual recognition and host state regulation and continues to form the backbone of cross-border financial services in the EU to this day. In retrospect, the approach of minimum harmonization combined with negative integration has taken the objective of a single capital market to the next level.

The factual limits of a complete harmonization of supervisory law become even clearer at the global level, not to mention that it would not be beneficial either.[96] Therefore, overcoming fragmented markets will also depend on negative integration. But can the concept of mutual recognition simply be transferred to EU third country regimes?

There are two central differences between (mutual) recognition in EU law and equivalence as provided for in third country regimes. First, mutual recognition does not require that the other legal system is equivalent. The terminology is not used consistently in the literature as some use the terms (mutual) recognition and equivalence as synonyms.[97] But there is a clear difference between recognition and equivalence. The ECJ ruled that no equivalence is needed for the duty of recognition.[98] From this perspective, mutual recognition is less demanding than equivalence.[99] At the European level, mutual recognition without demanding minimum standards from other legal systems was only feasible because Union law already prescribed a minimum level of harmonization. Such binding minimum requirements, however, do not exist at the global level. There is no regulator at the global level and minimum harmonization takes place only in the form of soft law. States therefore have the choice whether they want to implement the proposals made. Due to this lack of globally binding minimum standards, negative integration can only be achieved in the form of equivalence and not through recognition.

Secondly, mutual recognition in EU law is designed as a duty for Member States. The CJEU and national courts can enforce it. In contrast, granting market access through equivalence is, in principle, a voluntary decision by the respective state. This highlights that a considerable amount of goodwill on the part of states is needed to promote the shared goal of a common market.

Ultimately, the process of creating the single market within the EU cannot be blindly transferred to third country regimes. However, the successful path taken by the EU to reduce market access and trade barriers proves that negative integration is an essential tool to achieve the goal of a common market. This success story is also often discussed as a model for the US system of treating foreign financial service providers.[100]

[95] Council Directive 85/611/EEC of 20 December 1985, art 4(1) (UCITS I); see Payne and Howell (n 88) 243.

[96] Christian Tietje and Matthias Lehmann, 'The Role and Prospects of International Law in Financial Regulation and Supervision' (2010) 13 JIEL 663, 679–81.

[97] See on the terminology used Christine Janssens, *The Principle of Mutual Recognition in EU Law* (OUP 2013) 31–41; Hatzopoulos (n 32) 68–70; Ortino (n 89) 313–17.

[98] Case C-288/89 *Collectieve Antennevoorziening Gouda* ECLI:EU:C:1991:323, para 12.

[99] Ferran (n 84) 23.

[100] See the discussion in Pierre-Hugues Verdier, 'Mutual Recognition in International Finance' (2011) 52 Harv Intl LJ 56, 71ff, who rejects a transfer to the US because of the peculiarities of the EU, especially the strong supranational bodies. See also Eric J Pan, 'A European Solution to the Regulation of Cross-Border

Interestingly, it is not so much the third country regimes of the EU that are used as a comparison, but rather the creation of the internal market is taken as a historical blueprint.[101] This historical comparison thus demonstrates that harmonization at the global level alone will not suffice to reach the aim of a common global market, but that deference—respectively equivalence in the EU—is needed as an additional pillar to achieve it.

2. Recognition in world trade law

Recognition as a means of trade liberalization has played an important role in world trade law since 1980.[102] The Agreement on the Application of Sanitary and Phytosanitary Measures (SPS), the Agreement on Technical Barriers to Trade (TBT) as well as the General Agreement on Trade in Services (GATS) include provisions on recognition. However, only the latter deals directly with financial services. Since the EU is a member of the World Trade Organization (WTO), it is bound by these agreements and its secondary law has to be interpreted in accordance with them.[103] Apart from that, the legislative bodies of the EU had the world trade regimes in mind when drafting equivalence provisions in capital markets law.[104] This can be demonstrated by the fact that Recital 7 of EMIR refers to the recognition under the GATS.[105]

Pursuant to the equivalence regime in Article 4 SPS Agreement, Members must recognize foreign sanitary or phytosanitary measures if the exporting Member proves the equivalence of its measures to the importing Member. The standards do not need to be identical. Article 2.7 TBT Agreement is not as far-reaching as the SPS Agreement but still demands 'positive consideration' of accepting equivalent standards by other Members if 'these regulations adequately fulfil the objectives of their own regulations'. Again, a word-by-word transfer is not required, but rather the outcomes are compared against the background of the goals of the regulation. This outcome-based approach, as opposed to a line-by-line analysis, can be transferred to the interpretation of equivalence in capital markets law.[106] Furthermore, both the SPS Agreement and TBT

Markets' (2007) 2 Brook J Corp Fin & Com L 133; Susan Wolburgh Jenah, 'Commentary on a Blueprint for Cross-Border Access to U.S. Investors' (2007) 48 Harv Intl LJ 69, 76.

[101] Jenah (n 100).

[102] See Tokyo Round Codes on Technical Barriers to Trade, entry into force on 1 January1980, art 5.2; Humberto Zúñiga Schroder, *Harmonization, Equivalence and Mutual Recognition of Standards in WTO Law* (Wolters Kluwer 2011) 99; for a good overview see Trachtman (n 84) 787ff; drawing the connection between equivalence in the GATT and equivalence in financial markets law see Dirk A Zetzsche and Robin Veidt, 'The AIFMD's Third-Country Rules and the Equivalence Concept' in Dirk A Zetzsche (ed), *The Alternative Investment Fund Managers Directive* (3rd edn, Wolters Kluwer 2020) 829.

[103] TFEU, art 216(2); Case C-61/94 *Commission v Germany (International Dairy Arrangement)* ECLI:EU:C:1996:313, para 52; Joined Cases C-300/98 and 392/98 *Parfums Christian Dior* ECLI:EU:C:2000:688, para 47; in more detail see Mitsuo Matsushita and others, *The World Trade Organization* (3rd edn, OUP 2015) 37ff.

[104] Wei (n 31) 263.

[105] Furthermore, the G20 summits, which promoted the principle of deference and consequently the global spread of equivalence, repeatedly refer to world trade law. See G20 Pittsburgh Summit, 'G20 Leaders' Statement' (24–25 September 2009) paras 48f http://www.g20.utoronto.ca/2009/2009communique0925.html (accessed 12 November 2022); G20 St Petersburg Summit, 'G20 Leaders' Declaration' (n 27) paras 41ff.

[106] In more detail see ch 2 B)I.1.a)aa).

Agreement are based on the principle of proportionality.[107] The idea of proportionality has recently gained importance in the context of equivalence in capital markets law. The new reform of EMIR (EMIR 2.2) follows a risk-sensitive and proportionate approach.[108] Recent statements of the Commission also stress both concepts.[109] These examples show that comparable questions arise in the context of recognition regimes and that experiences and insights gained from world trade law can, in principle, be transferred to capital markets law.

The GATS applies to almost all kinds of services pursuant to the definitions in Article I. Its scope of application also covers financial services, which are further specified in two Annexes.[110] Article VII GATS provides for the recognition of professional experience or qualifications in two ways, either by agreement or by autonomous decisions of a member. This recognition is less far-reaching than that provided for in the SPS and TBT-Agreements. It leaves the recognition of foreign standards to the discretion of the Members. It does also not address the concept of equivalence. Interestingly, the GATS Annex on Financial Services contains a separate provision on recognition. In case of an autonomous recognition, Members must provide other Members with an 'adequate opportunity' to prove that their prudential measures provide for 'equivalent regulation, oversight and implementation of such regulation' pursuant to para 3(b) sentence 2 of the Annex. If a member proves that it provides for an equivalent regulation, it must be recognized as well. This provision is intended to prevent discrimination.[111] It has major implications for the interpretation of the scope of discretion in the Commission's equivalence decision in capital markets law, as will be demonstrated later.[112]

3. Recognition in data protection law: Adequacy decision

A concept similar to equivalence is the adequacy decision in Article 45(3) GDPR. Pursuant to that provision, personal data can be transferred from within the EU to third countries in case the Commission has adopted an adequacy decision.[113] As with the equivalence mechanism, the Commission's decision is the door opener,

[107] Schroder (n 102) 103–107, 126–28; Mads Andenas and Stefan Zleptnig, 'Proportionality and Balancing in WTO Law: A Comparative Perspective' in Kern Alexander and Mads Andenas (eds), *The World Trade Organization and Trade in Services* (Martinus Nijhoff 2008) 160ff.

[108] Commission, 'Equivalence in the area of financial services' Communication COM (2019) 349 final, 6; ESMA, 'Final Report: Final technical advice on criteria for tiering under Article 25(2a) of EMIR 2.2' ESMA70-151-2682 (11 November 2019) paras 34–42.

[109] Commission (n 108) 5–8.

[110] See Annex on Financial Services and Second Annex on Financial Services to the GATS.

[111] Armin von Bogdandy and Joseph Windsor in Rüdiger Wolfrum, Peter-Tobias Stoll, and Clemens Feinäugle (eds), *WTO—Trade in Services* (Martinus Nijhoff 2008) Annex on Financial Services para 27; for a concurring, but more restrained view see Wolfgang Weiß, *WTO Law and Domestic Regulation* (CH Beck 2020) 346 para 128.

[112] See ch 2 B)II.2.b)cc)(2).

[113] Besides the adequacy decision, there is also the possibility to transfer personal data to third countries in case of appropriate safeguards pursuant to art 46 of the GDPR. The European Commission may decide that so-called standard contractual clauses (SCCs) provide such sufficient data protection safeguards for the data transfer to third countries. In the absence of an adequacy decision or of appropriate safeguards, the data transfer can still take place in any of the situations listed in art 49 of the GDPR ('Derogations for specific situations'). Alexander Golland, 'Datenschutzrechtliche Anforderungen an internationale Datentransfers' (2020) 73 NJW 2593.

although data leaves the EU this time, and nothing enters it instead. In its decision, the Commission must assess whether the third country ensures an adequate level of data protection. This analysis must include, among other factors, whether one or more independent supervisory authorities are in place and effectively functioning and whether the country has entered into international agreements or multilateral systems ensuring the protection of personal data.[114] Accordingly, some equivalence provisions in capital markets law require effective supervision in the third country and conformity with international standards. Another similarity is the ongoing supervision by the Commission and the right to withdraw or amend its decision, which is explicitly stated in Article 45(4) and (5) GDPR.

In light of these common features, it is particularly interesting that the ECJ has ruled in the *Schrems I*[115] and *Schrems II*[116] cases on the validity of the Commission's adequacy decision regarding the data transfer to the United States. In *Schrems I*, the ECJ held that the Commission's decision on the adequacy of the protection provided by the safe harbour privacy principles and related frequently asked questions issued by the US Department of Commerce was invalid.[117] Before that decision, the prevailing view was that 'adequate' does not require an equivalent regime but would excuse some weaknesses in the third country's system.[118] Contrary to that, the Court found that 'adequate' does not demand an identical level of protection, but at least an 'essentially equivalent' one protecting the fundamental rights and freedoms of EU citizens.[119] Furthermore, this equivalence needs to be proven not just on paper but 'in practice'.[120] By this interpretation, the Court approximated the adequacy decision of the GDPR to the equivalence decision of financial markets law. This close connection is also demonstrated by the fact that some of the equivalence provisions in financial markets law relating to data transfer use the term adequacy.[121]

The invalidated Safe-Harbour Agreement was subsequently replaced by the EU-US Privacy Shield, negotiated between the EU and the US and implemented in the EU by the Commission.[122] In *Schrems II*, the ECJ declared that the EU-US Privacy Shield was invalid as well because US surveillance programmes based on section 702 of the Foreign Intelligence Surveillance Act of 1978 and Executive Order 12333 did not guarantee an adequate level of data protection for EU citizens.[123] The ECJ thereby underlined its interpretation from the *Schrems I* ruling that the level of data protection in the third country must be 'essentially equivalent'. Although this interpretation cannot be

[114] GDPR, art 45(2)(b) and (c).

[115] Case C-362/14 *Schrems I* ECLI:EU:C:2015:650; more precisely, the judgment did not refer to art 45 of the GDPR, but to the previous provision, namely art 25 of Directive 95/46/EC of 24 October 1995 (Data Protection Directive).

[116] Case C-311/18 *Schrems II* ECLI:EU:C:2020:559.

[117] Case C-362/14 *Schrems I* (n 115) para 98; Safe Harbour Privacy Principles as set out in Commission Decision 2000/520/EC of 26 July 2000.

[118] Peter Schantz in Spiros Simitis, Gerrit Hornung, and Indra Spiecker (eds), *Datenschutzrecht: DSVGVO mit BDSG* (Nomos 2019) DSGVO, art 45 para 6.

[119] Case C-362/14 *Schrems I* (n 115) paras 71–74; see also Opinion 1/15 *EU–Canada PNR Agreement* ECLI:EU:C:2017:592, para 134.

[120] Case C-362/14 *Schrems I* (n 115) para 74.

[121] See eg SAD, art 47(1)(c).

[122] See Commission Implementing Decision (EU) 2016/1250 of 12 July 2016.

[123] Case C-311/18 *Schrems II* (n 116) paras 168ff; Golland (n 113).

transferred to equivalence provisions in financial markets law without modifications, since the protection of fundamental rights is more central in data protection law and thus influences the interpretation more than in financial markets law, the judgments nevertheless demonstrate that the ECJ is willing and able to subject equivalence decisions relating to third countries to close legal scrutiny. Also, the mere fact that a third country is the subject of the decision does not render the decision a matter of foreign policy, but it remains an administrative decision. These findings are essential for the interpretation and judicial scrutiny of equivalence decisions in capital markets law.

4. The early regulation of cross-border banking

In 1975, the Committee on Banking Regulations and Supervisory Practices, today called the Basel Committee on Banking Supervision, published a report on the supervision of banks' foreign establishments.[124] The issue came on the agenda after, among others, the Bankhaus Herstatt in West Germany caused distortions on the international markets.[125] In its report, the Committee called for a better demarcation of responsibilities between home and host state authorities and more cooperation between them to avoid supervisory gaps. This report triggered a series of other reports that further refined the challenge of the proper allocation of responsibilities between home and host state authorities.[126]

These reports are interesting from the perspective of deference. Although they discuss a topic that lies at the heart of deference, the terms deference, recognition, equivalence or substituted compliance hardly appear. This is attributable to the fact that many of the proposals have their origin in some kind of crisis. In most cases, a risk materialized through a (supposed) supervisory gap, which caused a tightening of cross-border regulation and supervision.[127]

This crisis-driven regulation explains, on the one hand, why the liberal approach of deference did not play an important role. The development also illustrates why deference—as will be shown later—is completely underdeveloped in the banking sector.[128] Moreover, this evolution reveals where some of the roots of today's fragmentation lie, namely in the desire to close regulatory and supervisory gaps through more regulation and supervision. This has led to double and multiple regulation and supervision and ultimately to increasingly fragmented markets, a phenomenon that is being fought against today. As will be shown later, deference is one essential instrument to counter this problem of overregulation and fragmentation.

[124] BCBS, 'Report to the Governors on the supervision of banks' foreign establishments' BS/75/44e (28 September 1975); Kern Alexander, Rahul Dhumale, and John Eatwell, *Global Governance of Financial Systems* (OUP 2005) 47ff.

[125] Charles Goodhart, *The Basel Committee on Banking Supervision* (CUP 2011) 31ff.

[126] In particular, BCBS, 'Principles for the Supervision of Banks' Foreign Establishments: Basel Revised Concordat' (28 May 1983); BCBS, 'The Supervision of Cross-Border Banking' (4 October 1996); on the development see Christos Gortsos, *Fundamentals of Public International Financial Law* (Nomos 2012) 238–48.

[127] See among others the Banco Ambrosiano crisis of June 1982, the 1982 MAB crisis (Mexico, Argentina, and Brazil), and the BCCI scandal of 1991; Charles Goodhart, *The Basel Committee on Banking Supervision* (CUP 2011)104ff; Richard Dale, *The Regulation of International Banking* (Woodhead-Faulkner 1984) 156–67.

[128] See ch 1 C)II.3.b).

5. Development of equivalence in financial markets law

The development of equivalence mechanisms in financial markets law can be roughly divided into three phases: first, preliminary stages in the 1970s to 1990s; secondly, the emergence of equivalence provisions before the GFC of 2007; and, thirdly, the broad expansion and centralization of equivalence following the crisis. Today we may be at the beginning of a new fourth phase, the 'post-Brexit era'.

a) Emergence of third country regimes: Negotiation-based mechanisms

The focus of the EU legislator in the late 20th century was not on third countries but rather on creating a single market within the Union through harmonization and mutual recognition.[129] In a world that was not as globalized as it is today, third country regimes did not have the same significance.[130] Nevertheless, even then, many directives contained third country provisions.[131] Unlike today, these provisions were often not based on unilateral decisions but allowed for the negotiation of mutual agreements by the Community.[132] However, some directives introduced in the 1990s enabled Member States to take unilateral decisions and provided for more comprehensive third country regimes.[133] The idea of equivalence was already reflected in the fact that many provisions required an 'adequate protection' of investors.[134] That is why these regimes can be considered as predecessors of modern equivalence provisions.

b) More sophisticated mechanisms based on unilateral decisions

At the beginning of the new millennium, the Commission's strategy slowly shifted towards more comprehensive equivalence mechanisms based on unilateral decisions, as the previous negotiating system was unsuccessful.[135] The Commission further transferred its experience from the internal market that 'convergence alone is not the solution' to third country regimes.[136] The bottom line was that identical approaches on an international basis are neither realistic nor necessary, but that common regulatory objectives and 'broadly equivalent approaches' are sufficient to recognize foreign

[129] Commission (n 91) 310; Hal S Scott, *International Finance: Law and Regulation* (Sweet & Maxwell 2004) 99ff.

[130] This does not mean, however, that globalization was not already taking place. See for the securities market David E Ayling, *The Internationalisation of Stockmarkets* (Gower 1986).

[131] See eg First Council Directive 73/239/EEC of 24 July 1973, art 29 (First Non-Life Insurance Directive); First Council Directive 77/780/EEC of 12 December 1977, art 9(3) (First Banking Directive); First Council Directive 79/267/EEC of 5 March 1979, art 32 (First Life Insurance Directive); Council Directive 87/345/EEC, art 25a (Mutual Recognition Directive); Council Directive 89/298/EEC of 17 April 1989, art 24 (Public Offering Prospectus Directive); Directive 2001/34/EC, art 41 (Consolidated and Admissions and Reporting Directive).

[132] For a late example of such a provision: see—in addition to the examples given in n 131—Directive 2005/68/EC of 16 November 2005, art 50 (Reinsurance Directive).

[133] Council Directive 93/6/EEC of 15 March 1993, art 2(4) (Capital Adequacy Directive); Council Directive 93/22/EEC of 10 May 1993, art 2(2)(g)(iii) and art 7 (Investment Services Directive).

[134] First Non-Life Insurance Directive, art 29; First Life Insurance Directive, art 32.

[135] This was put in a nutshell by Alexander Schaub: '[m]y sense and that of my Commissioner has been that if we spend our time in discussions about terms such as 'reciprocity', 'national treatment' and 'mutual recognition', we will not get anywhere. We have to make a fresh start.' See Alexander Schaub (DG Internal Market), 'Testimony before the Committee on Financial Services U.S. House of Representatives' (13 May 2004) 5 https://www.iasplus.com/en/binary/resource/051304as.pdf (accessed 12 November 2022).

[136] ibid 8–9.

regulation and supervision.[137] The idea of equivalence emerged mainly in the context of mutual recognition vis-à-vis the US.[138]

This shift was most notably reflected in the amendment of three areas.[139] The first legal act was the Financial Conglomerates Directive, which extended supervision to parent undertakings established in third countries if any entity in the conglomerate provided services inside the EU.[140] The Directive was a response to the finding that stand-alone supervision in a globalized world with financial conglomerates was not effective anymore.[141] However, the Directive granted the opportunity to exempt third country holdings from being supervised if they were subject to equivalent supervision by the competent authority of their home country.[142] The national authority (the coordinator) was responsible for this determination of equivalence. The second legal act providing for an equivalence mechanism was the Prospectus Directive of 2003.[143] It was the first Directive under which the Commission was competent to decide on equivalence unilaterally.[144] The last area was that of accounting standards and auditing, notably the introduction of the Transparency Directive in 2004 and the related Commission Regulation of 2007 on the determination of equivalence of accounting standards as well as the Statutory Audit Directive of 2006.

c) *The financial crisis and the global breakthrough*

The third phase of development is marked by the response to the GFC, which leveraged the breakthrough of equivalence.[145] The crisis demonstrated that the financial system as a whole is put at risk if regulation and supervision are not equally robust in all states because risks no longer stop at national borders. States concluded from this, on the one hand, that minimum standards must be coordinated and defined globally. This observation led to increasing efforts, especially at the urging of the G20, to adopt soft law at the global level.[146] On the other hand, states extended the territorial reach of their regulation to parties and transactions that were not domiciled in their markets but affected them. This increasing extraterritoriality led to significant market fragmentation as legal and regulatory conflicts became more likely and market access barriers rose. States attempted to counter this problem by implementing deference regimes, under which states would withdraw regulatory and supervisory

[137] ibid; see also Wei (n 31) 258ff.

[138] See eg Commission, 'A stronger EU–US Partnership and a more open market for the 21st century' Communication COM (2005) 196 final, 9f; see also the US–EU regulatory dialogue which is discussed in Kern Alexander and others, 'Transatlantic Financial Services Regulatory Dialogue' (2006) 7 EBOR 647.

[139] Another area was the Markets in Financial Instruments Directive 2004/39 (MiFID I), which only included minor equivalence mechanisms. See MiFID I, arts 19(6) and 24(4).

[140] Directive 2002/87/EC of 16 December 2002, art 5(3) (Financial Conglomerates Directive).

[141] Wei (n 31) 272; Scott (n 9) 384f.

[142] Financial Conglomerates Directive, art 18(1).

[143] Directive 2003/71/EC of 4 November 2003, art 20(3) (Prospectus Directive). This example is a good illustration of the transition from rules based on the conclusion of agreements to unilateral decisions. The preceding provision from 2001 was still based on the conclusion of agreements. See Consolidated and Admissions and Reporting Directive, art 41.

[144] Lehmann and Zetzsche (n 24) 111.

[145] Imm (n 84) 92ff; Lucia Quaglia, 'The Politics of "Third Country Equivalence" in Post-Crisis Financial Services Regulation in the European Union' (2015) 38 West Eur Pol 167, 168.

[146] Especially the G20 Pittsburgh Summit (n 105); John Armour and others, *Principles of Financial Regulation* (OUP 2016) 616–43.

powers vis-à-vis states having comparable or equivalent regulatory and supervisory standards. This concept was promoted at the level of the G20, whose leaders at the St Petersburg conference declared: 'We agree that jurisdictions and regulators should be able to defer to each other when it is justified by the quality of their respective regulatory and enforcement regimes, based on similar outcomes, in a non-discriminatory way, paying due respect to home country regulation regimes.'[147]

The three phenomena of increasing extraterritoriality, advancing convergence of supervisory law and the rise of deference were thus closely interrelated. Increasing extraterritoriality made the need for deference mechanisms particularly pressing. Convergence of national supervisory law was a prerequisite for deference, as otherwise comparability would not have been achieved and deference more generally would therefore not have been possible. Deference was therefore a reaction to increasing extraterritoriality and global convergence a precondition for it.

As a result of this international breakthrough, most legal acts passed in the EU after the crisis contained equivalence mechanisms.[148] An important example directly influenced by the FSB is the derivatives area.[149] The EU adopted six different equivalence regimes in EMIR alone. These have either the function to grant market access or at least facilitate cross-border derivatives transactions. They are all based on unilateral decisions and are detailed and sophisticated, which are typical features of more recent regimes adopted after the GFC. The rapid spread of equivalence in the EU can therefore not be explained without the crisis.

This development was not restricted to the EU. Especially in the field of derivatives regulation, many jurisdictions adopted instruments based on deference. In Switzerland and in the US, where the concept is referred to as substituted compliance, deference has been widely implemented in the derivatives sector.[150] Other countries like Canada, Australia, Japan, South Africa, Singapore, or Russia have followed the advice of the G20 and included deference, at least in the field of OTC derivatives.[151]

d) *The post-Brexit era*

Currently, we may be at the beginning of a new era—the post-Brexit era.[152] As equivalence was not originally designed for a country so close—not just geographically—and interconnected to the European continent, the European legislator faces new uncertainties and problems discussed under the heading of 'high-impact countries'.[153] The

[147] G20 St Petersburg Summit, 'G20 Leaders' Declaration' (n 27) para 71. The Chairman of the FSB later described it in the following way: 'Deferring to each other's market regulatory regimes where they achieve equivalent outcomes'; FSB, 'Chair's Letter to G20 Ministers and Governors on financial reforms' (23 February 2014) https://www.fsb.org/wp-content/uploads/r_140222.pdf (accessed 12 November 2022).

[148] See explicitly referring to the G20 summit in Pittsburgh EMIR, recital 7.

[149] Lehmann and Zetzsche (n 24) 111; on the FSB see Eva Hüpkes, 'Globale Finanzstabilität—Wer setzt die Standards?' (2015) 87 SZW 570.

[150] See generally on the concept in the US Jackson (n 28).

[151] In 2014, the FSB reported that all but five jurisdictions (Argentina, Brazil, China, India, and Indonesia) have some capability to defer in the field of OTC Derivatives. FSB (n 27).

[152] See similar analysis in Moloney (n 29) 48ff.

[153] Economic Governance Support Unit (DG for Internal Policies), 'Third country equivalence in EU banking and financial regulation' In Depth Analysis, PE 614.495 (August 2019) https://www.europarl.europa.eu/RegData/etudes/IDAN/2018/614495/IPOL_IDA(2018)614495_EN.pdf (accessed 12 November 2022).

current uncertainty is reflected in the absence of equivalence in recent legislative acts, which can, however, be integrated after a review.[154]

Yet, there is much evidence to suggest that the Parliament and Commission will not renounce equivalence.[155] The intention to keep relying on equivalence in the future becomes particularly evident when looking at the current draft of the regulation for an EU Green Bond Standard.[156] This draft regulation contains a comprehensive equivalence regime for third country external reviewers.[157] In addition, the negotiated EU–UK Trade and Cooperation Agreement does not contain any significant substantive provisions with regard to financial services.[158] This silence reveals that both the EU and the UK believe that market access rights should continue to be granted unilaterally through equivalence decisions. This assumption is confirmed by the Joint Declaration on Financial Services, which calls for 'transparency and appropriate dialogue' regarding equivalence decisions.

Instead of abolishing equivalence, the EU will be stricter in its application, especially with regard to the assessment of equivalence. The legislator emphasizes that passporting is distinct from equivalence, reminding that equivalence can be withdrawn as demonstrated in the case of Swiss stock exchanges and underlining that equivalence is not a tool to liberalize trade.[159] Moreover, new criteria such as the systemic importance of investment firms or central counterparties (CCPs) found their way into equivalence provisions, further limiting market access for high-impact countries.[160]

It remains to be seen how the situation develops, but it is clear that the EU will not abandon equivalence. Instead, it will adapt it to the new circumstances. This

[154] Regulation (EU) 2017/2402 of 12 December 2017, art 46(e) (Securitisation Regulation); Commission, 'Proposal for a Regulation of the European Parliament and of the Council on markets in crypto-assets, and amending Directive (EU) 2019/1937' COM (2020) 593 final, art 122(2)(k); Regulation (EU) 2020/1503 of 7 October 2020, art 45(2)(q) (Crowdfunding Regulation); Jim Brunsden, 'Brussels Signals Tough Stance on UK Bank Bonuses after Brexit' *Financial Times* (19 December 2017) https://www.ft.com/content/98c9a2b4-e4a0-11e7-97e2-916d4fbac0da (accessed 12 November 2022).

[155] This hypothesis is supported by the fact that recent reforms of MiFIR and EMIR did not waive equivalence, but rather advanced the concept. The same holds true for the new Prospectus Regulation. What is more, the Commission pointed out in 2019 that '[e]quivalence is one of the key instruments at the EU's disposal in furthering that goal in the external dimension of the internal market.'. See Commission (n 108) 3; for a consenting view see Moloney (n 29) 49.

[156] Commission, 'Proposal for a Regulation of the European Parliament and of the Council on European green bonds' COM (2021) 391 final.

[157] ibid arts 31, 32, and 59; Nikolai Badenhoop, 'Green Bonds: An assessment of the proposed EU Green Bond Standard and its potential to prevent greenwashing' IPOL Study PE 703.359 (31 March 2022) 80–81 https://www.europarl.europa.eu/RegData/etudes/STUD/2022/703359/IPOL_STU(2022)703359_EN.pdf (accessed 12 November 2022).

[158] Trade and Cooperation Agreement between the European Union and the European Atomic Energy Community, of the one part, and the United Kingdom of Great Britain and Northern Ireland, of the other part [2021] OJ L149/10-2539; Emil Nästegård, 'Equivalence Decisions in the EU and UK Financial Services Sectors Post-Brexit' (2022) 33 EBLR 463, 464f; Adam Bennett and David Vines, 'The EU–UK Trade and Cooperation Agreement' (2022) 38 Oxf Rev Econ Policy 68, 74f.

[159] European Parliament, 'Resolution of 11 September 2018 on relationships between the EU and third countries concerning financial services regulation and supervision' (2018) OJ C433/19, lit B and nos 15, 16, 19, and 22; Commission, 'EU Equivalence decisions in financial services policy: An Assessment' (Staff Working Document) SWD (2017) 102 final, 5 and 9; Commission (n 108) 9–11.

[160] Regulation (EU) 2019/2099 of 23 October 2019, art 63 (Investment Firm Regulation).

adaptation is currently taking the form of a more restrictive approach, particularly regarding high-impact countries, and a (detrimental) politicization of the process.

II. Where can equivalence be found? An overview

As outlined above, the first equivalence mechanisms as defined in this book were established in the early 2000s.[161] Since then, the scope of application has been constantly widened. To the present day, there are a total of 40 equivalence provisions, which makes it difficult to keep an overview. What adds to the difficulty is that these regimes are often interconnected and overlapping. For instance, an equivalence decision on accounting standards of a third country influences the information to be published under the Prospectus Regulation as well as the Transparency Directive. Another example is the five different equivalence mechanisms dealing with the equivalence of third country markets.[162] For a clear overview, it is best to sort the provisions according to subject areas. The following areas can be identified: disclosure obligations (1.), gatekeepers and benchmarks (2.), financial intermediaries (3.), trading venues and financial market infrastructure (4.) and exemptions for central banks and public bodies of third countries (5.). After this overview, some central ideas of the legislator are identified, which partly explain the creation of this fragmented picture (6.).

1. Disclosure obligations under capital markets law

The first area of capital markets law covered by equivalence was that of disclosure. Disclosure obligations can be divided into three stages depending on the phase of market participation of the company.[163] Within these stages, an additional differentiation can be made between the obligation to publish information on the one hand and the specific content that the information to be published must have on the other.

a) First stage: Obligation to draw up a prospectus

At the first stage, disclosure requirements arise on the primary market when a company makes a public offering.[164] Such an obligation was first imposed on issuers by the Admission Directive in 1979.[165] It was applied to EU issuers and non-EU issuers offering securities to the public in the Union, as prospectus law has always been a 'product driven' regulation, applicable irrespective of the issuer.[166] Much later,

[161] See ch 1 C)I.5.b).

[162] SSR, art 17(2); EMIR, art 2a(2); MiFID II, art 25(4); MiFIR, arts 28(4) and 38(3).

[163] Hanno Merkt, *Unternehmenspublizität* (Mohr Siebeck 2001) 141; Hendrik Brinckmann, 'Disclosure System: Foundations' in Rüdiger Veil (ed), *European Capital Markets Law* (3rd edn, Hart Publishing 2022) § 16 para 37.

[164] Prospectus Regulation, art 3(1); more generally see Kitty Lieverse, 'The Obligation to Publish a Prospectus and Exemptions' in Danny Busch, Guido Ferrarini, and Jan P Franx (eds), *Prospectus Regulation and Prospectus Liability* (OUP 2020) paras 7.01ff.

[165] Council Directive 79/279/EEC of 5 March 1979 (Admission Directive); see for a historical summary Niamh Moloney, *EU Securities and Financial Markets Regulation* (3rd edn, OUP 2014) 71ff; Warren (n 94).

[166] Pierre Schammo, *EU Prospectus Law* (CUP 2011) 142.

the Prospectus Directive of 2003 introduced the system of passporting[167] as well as equivalence provisions for third country issuers.

The Prospectus Directive of 2003 included two different forms of equivalence.[168] The first concerned the exemption from the obligation to publish a prospectus for securities offered to employees by their employer, provided that the company has its head office or registered office in the Union.[169] This exemption was expanded to employers based in a third country if the Commission had adopted an equivalence decision. This equivalence mechanism is no longer included in the new Prospectus Regulation. The exemption now applies to third country employers, irrespective of an equivalence decision.[170] Therefore, the Prospectus Regulation has provided for liberalization in this respect.

The second and only remaining equivalence provision was provided for in Article 20 Prospectus Directive and can now be found in Article 29 Prospectus Regulation.[171] If an equivalence decision has been adopted and the NCA approves a prospectus drawn up in accordance with the laws of that third country, a third country issuer may offer securities to the public in the Union without having to prepare a prospectus in accordance with the Prospectus Regulation. This means that issuers from third countries are exempted from drawing up a prospectus in accordance with EU law. Instead, the third country prospectus is recognized as a substitute in the entire Union (passporting).[172] If the third country system has shortcomings, the prospectus can still be approved if it contains additional information that makes up for the deficit (so-called equivalence 'wrap').[173] This constitutes a far-reaching liberalization and considerably enhances market access for third country issuers. However, this liberalization has not yet materialized in practice since the Commission has been very reluctant to adopt equivalence decisions and because, even after such a decision has been taken, the national authorities still have discretion in relation to the approval of the third country prospectus.[174] Thus equivalence currently exists only in theory, which explains why it

[167] Konstantinos Sergakis, *The Law of Capital Markets in the EU: Disclosure and Enforcement* (Palgrave Macmillan 2018) 58ff.

[168] Schammo (n 166) 142–43 names three different equivalence mechanisms because he includes the equivalence of accounting standards. Strictly speaking, this equivalence is not contained in the Prospectus Directive even though it influences the prospectus to be published.

[169] Prospectus Directive, art 4(1)(e); see extensively Schammo (n 166) 160ff.

[170] Prospectus Regulation, art 1(4)(i); see also Prospectus Regulation, recital 17 fourth and fifth sentence; Peter Young (Norton Rose Fulbright), 'Market Access after Brexit: Prospectus Equivalence' (May 2017) https://www.nortonrosefulbright.com/de-de/wissen/publications/79f084b3/market-access-after-brexit-prospectus-equivalence (accessed 12 November 2022).

[171] n Sergakis (n 167) 83f; on the equivalence mechanism of art 20 of the Prospectus Directive see Christoph Sandberger, 'Die EU-Prospektrichtlinie: "Europäischer Pass für Emittenten"' (2004) 12 EWS 298, 303; Moloney (n 165) 122ff.

[172] Sandberger (n 171) 303.

[173] See the opinion of ESMA, 'Framework for the assessment of third country prospectuses under Article 20 of the Prospectus Directive' ESMA/2013/317 (20 March 2013).

[174] The Commission has realized that the current regime is not appropriate. In a draft dated 7 December 2022, the Commission proposes to amend the equivalence regime to make it 'workable'. According to this draft, prospectuses recognized in third countries that the Commission considers equivalent will no longer have to be approved by NCAs. Instead, the prospectuses only have to be filed with the NCAs. See Commission, 'Proposal for a Regulation of the European Parliament and of the Council amending Regulations (EU) 2017/1129, (EU) No 596/2014 and (EU) No 600/2014 to make public capital markets in the Union more attractive for companies and to facilitate access to capital for small and medium-sized enterprises' COM (2022) 762 final, art 1(22).

is often overlooked.[175] In relation to key information documents required under the PRIIP Regulation, such an equivalence regime does not exist.[176]

If a third country issuer has to draw up a prospectus under the Prospectus Regulation because no equivalence decision has been adopted, the question arises as to the content of the prospectus. A prospectus needs to contain certain minimum information, which is further specified in Annex 1 of the Commission's Delegated Regulation (EU) 2019/980.[177] According to this Delegated Regulation, the financial information provided for in the prospectus must be prepared in accordance with International Financial Reporting Standards (IFRS) as outlined in Regulation (EC) No 1606/2002.[178] Consequently, third country firms cannot apply their home country's accounting standards when drawing up a prospectus. This changes if the Commission finds that the General Accepted Accounting Principles (GAAP) of a third country are equivalent to EU IFRS.[179] After the adoption of an equivalence decision, the third country issuer may use the GAAP of its home country to draw up a prospectus under the Prospectus Regulation. All in all, equivalence is largely in place at the first stage of disclosure requirements.

b) Second stage: Disclosure on the secondary market

At the second stage, activities on the secondary market are accompanied by periodic and event-driven disclosure obligations. These obligations are numerous, which is why the following analysis will focus on those duties covered by equivalence.[180]

aa) Periodic disclosure Periodic disclosure obligations are mainly regulated in the Transparency Directive.[181] The Directive sets out a catalogue of periodic disclosure requirements in its Chapter II, which principally apply equally to both EU issuers as well as non-EU issuers.[182] This information to be published includes an annual financial report, a half-yearly financial report, and a report on payments to governments.[183] It also covers disclosure obligations concerning corporate governance issues.[184] Third country companies may be exempted from these requirements pursuant to the

[175] The entire book *Prospectus Regulation and Prospectus Liability* does not contain a single reference to art 29 of the Prospectus Regulation, although it contains a chapter on Brexit where equivalence may be the decisive tool. See Simon Gleeson, 'The Prospectus Regime and Brexit' in Danny Busch, Guido Ferrarini, and Jan P Franx (eds), *Prospectus Regulation and Prospectus Liability* (OUP 2020) paras 17.01ff.

[176] Lieverse (n 164) paras 7.01ff.

[177] Prospectus Regulation, art 13 and Commission Delegated Regulation (EU) 2019/980 of 14 March 2019, art 2.

[178] See Commission Delegated Regulation (EU) 2019/980 of 14 March 2019, s 18.1.3.

[179] Commission Regulation (EC) No 1569/2007 of 21 December 2007, arts 2 and 3; generally on third country GAAP in this context see Schammo (n 166) 150ff.

[180] For a full overview of disclosure obligations see Thomas C Jutzi, *Unternehmenspublizität* (Stämpfli 2017); Rüdiger Veil (ed), *European Capital Markets Law* (3rd edn, Hart Publishing 2022) §§ 16–22.

[181] Rüdiger Veil, 'The Reform of the Transparency Regime in European Capital Markets Laws' (2013) 10 ECFR 18.

[182] Wolf-Georg Ringe in Matthias Lehmann and Christoph Kumpan (eds), *European Financial Services Law* (Nomos 2019) TD, art 23 para 4; Rüdiger Veil, 'Disclosure of Major Holdings' in Rüdiger Veil (ed), *European Capital Markets Law* (3rd edn, Hart Publishing 2022) § 20 para 15.

[183] Transparency Directive, arts 4–6.

[184] See ibid arts 16–18; Rüdiger Veil, 'Corporate Governance and Shareholder Rights' in Rüdiger Veil (ed), *European Capital Markets Law* (3rd edn, Hart Publishing 2022) § 22.

equivalence mechanism in Article 23 Transparency Directive by the NCA of its home Member State.[185] Where the authorities of the Member States have not granted a full exemption, the third country company may at least use the GAAP of its home country if the third country's GAAP have been recognized as equivalent to EU IFRS by the Commission.[186]

Another periodic disclosure obligation is provided for in the Takeover Directive.[187] Companies whose securities are at least partially traded on a regulated market must publish detailed information in their annual report, particularly on their capital structure. This obligation is not covered by the equivalence provision of Article 23 Transparency Directive. Instead, the rules on the equivalence of third country GAAP apply, which may lead to an exemption.[188]

Additional reporting obligations apply to large undertakings and all public-interest entities active in the extractive industry or the logging of primary forests.[189] A so-called country-by-country report must be prepared and made public on an annual basis under the Accounting Directive.[190] However, undertakings preparing and publishing a report in accordance with equivalent third country reporting requirements can be exempted from this obligation.[191]

Moreover, the Accounting Directive requires public-interest entities, whose securities are admitted to trading on a regulated market in the EU, to publish corporate governance statements in their management reports.[192] The equivalence mechanism of the Accounting Directive does not apply to corporate governance disclosures. This is not a major concern in light of the fact that the extraterritorial effect of the duty is limited to cases of dual listings, as the obligation applies only to securities admitted to trading in a Member State.

bb) Event-driven disclosure Event-driven disclosure obligations can be found in various regulations and directives throughout capital markets law. A distinction can be made between disclosure obligations concerning major holdings, inside information and directors' dealing.

The disclosure of major holdings is regulated in Section I of Chapter III of the Transparency Directive and is composed of two steps. First, the shareholder who

[185] n Sergakis (n 167) 84. Art 2(i) of the Transparency Directive determines the 'home Member State' of an issuer. In Germany, the BaFin is responsible for evaluating equivalence pursuant to § 118(4) of the WpHG. Once the Commission has adopted an equivalence decision, the BaFin may not deviate from that assessment. Anna Heidelbach and Günter Doleczik in Eberhard Schwark and Daniel Zimmer (eds), *Kapitalmarktrechts-Kommentar* (5th edn, CH Beck 2020) § 118 WpHG para 19.

[186] Transparency Directive, art 23(4) subpara 3; Commission Regulation (EC) No 1569/2007 of 21 December 2007, arts 2 and 3; Eilís V Ferran, *Building an EU Securities Market* (CUP 2004) 161f. Such an equivalence decision may have further consequences. See eg German Commercial Code (HGB), § 292(1) no 1(d), which refers to this equivalence decision as part of a national equivalence mechanism which provides for an exemption of consolidated financial statements from third countries. This national provision transposes art 23(8) of the Accounting Directive.

[187] Directive 2004/25/EC of 21 April 2004, art 10 (Takeover Directive).

[188] Commission Regulation (EC) No 1569/2007 of 21 December 2007, arts 2 and 3.

[189] Jutzi (n 180) para 444.

[190] Accounting Directive, arts 42 and 44.

[191] ibid arts 46(1) and 47.

[192] ibid art 20; Veil (n 184) § 22 paras 5ff; Jutzi (n 180) paras 546ff.

acquires or disposes of shares must notify the issuer and the supervisory authority thereof.[193] Secondly, the issuer must then make public the information received.[194] Issuers whose registered office is situated in a third country can, however, be exempted from this obligation pursuant to Article 23 Transparency Directive provided that their rules on the disclosure of major holdings are equivalent to those of the EU. The same equivalence exemption applies to the duties under Articles 14 and 15 Transparency Directive.

Moreover, issuers of financial instruments must disclose inside information under the Market Abuse Regulation (MAR).[195] The scope of this obligation is limited to issuers who have requested or approved the admission of their financial instruments to a trading venue in a Member State.[196] The volume of trade on these markets is irrelevant for the applicability.[197] This way, transactions that appear to be non-EU trades at first glance may turn out to be regulated by the MAR, and the disclosure of inside information may be required.[198] The MAR therefore has a significant extraterritorial dimension and third country issuers may easily be affected by it.[199] This extraterritorial effect is only slightly reduced by the equivalence provision concerning public bodies and central banks of third countries contained in the MAR.[200]

Notifications of major holdings under the Transparency Directive may also trigger disclosure obligations under the MAR.[201] In such cases, the question arises whether an equivalence decision under the Transparency Directive will equally affect the disclosure obligations of the MAR. The fact that the aim and purpose of the laws are comparable speaks for such an influence. Both laws aim to improve investor protection by providing investors with all relevant information to dispose of or acquire financial instruments.[202] Nevertheless, their purposes are not identical. The MAR focuses much more on equal treatment of investors and their confidence in the system.[203] Furthermore, the differences concerning the timing and type of publication argue against an influence.[204] That is why an equivalence decision under the Transparency Directive is without prejudice to disclosure obligations under the MAR.[205] The MAR

[193] Transparency Directive, arts 9, 10, and 19(3).
[194] ibid art 12(6).
[195] MAR, art 17.
[196] See ibid art 17(1) subpara 3 and recital 49 fifth sentence. The obligation also applies to emission allowance market participants, so-called EAMPs (MAR, art 17(2)).
[197] For a different approach, see SSR, art 16, which provides for an exemption if the principal trading venue is in a third country.
[198] See for a good example Leonard Ng, 'Market Abuse Update' (2016) OBLB https://www.law.ox.ac.uk/business-law-blog/blog/2016/06/market-abuse-update (accessed 12 November 2022).
[199] This represents a major change compared to Directive 2003/6/EC of 28 January 2003 (Market Abuse Directive). See MAR, recital 8.
[200] MAR, art 6(5) and (6); ch 1 C)II.5.
[201] Ringe (n 182) MAR, art 17 para 26.
[202] See Transparency Directive, recital 18; MAR, recital 7.
[203] Rüdiger Veil, 'Disclosure of Inside Information' in Rüdiger Veil (ed), *European Capital Markets Law* (3rd edn, Hart 2022) § 19 para 16.
[204] Heribert Hirte in Heribert Hirte and Thomas M J Möllers (eds), *Kölner Kommentar zum WpHG* (2nd edn, Carl Heymanns 2014) § 21 para 56.
[205] See also Case C-628/13 *Lafonta v AMF* ECLI:EU:C:2015:162; Veil (n 182) § 20 para 20; Lars Klöhn in Lars Klöhn (ed), *Marktmissbrauchsverordnung* (CH Beck 2018) art 17 para 44; Lars Klöhn, 'Lafonta/AFM: Die neue cause célèbre des europäischen Insiderrechts?' (2014) 35 ZIP 945, 952.

further requires persons discharging managerial responsibilities and persons closely connected with them to notify issuers and the competent authority of specific transactions.[206] Again, the scope of issuers addressed is limited and is in line with the definition of Article 17(1) subparagraph 3 MAR. Therefore, a far-reaching equivalence provision is not included.[207]

c) Third stage: Market exits

The third stage concerns market exits, including delistings. There are no specific mandatory disclosure obligations for market exits at the European level.[208] Consequently, no equivalence mechanism can be found here.

2. Gatekeepers and benchmarks

Gatekeepers can be characterized as independent market actors who provide verification or certification services to investors or the market in general.[209] Among others, credit rating agencies (a)) and auditors (b)) can be considered as gatekeepers. Related to this is the regulation (of administrators) of benchmarks as they must have a high degree of credibility, allowing markets to use them as a basis for financial instruments and contracts (c)).

a) Credit rating agencies

The Credit Rating Agencies Regulation is a product of the GFC, the emergence of which, in the opinion of many, has also been a consequence of insufficient regulation of rating agencies, especially the big players situated in the US.[210] In order to improve the regulation and supervision of those third country rating agencies, ratings demanded from financial service providers may be used for regulatory purposes only if the rating agency is established in the Union—forced territoriality—and registered in accordance with the CRA Regulation.[211]

This restrictive approach does not, however, reflect the heavy reliance on US rating agencies, which is why Articles 4(3) and 5 CRA Regulation mitigate the strict territorial approach.[212] Under stringent conditions, the former allows the endorsement of credit ratings issued in a third country by rating agencies belonging to the same group and established in the Union.[213] Inter alia, the analysis leading to the rating in the

[206] MAR, art 19.

[207] ibid art 19(4); Stephan Semrau in Lars Klöhn (ed), *Marktmissbrauchsverordnung* (CH Beck 2018) art 19 para 15.

[208] Brinckmann (n 163) § 16 para 37. This does not mean that there are no disclosure duties at the national level. See with regard to German law Benjamin M Schmitz, *Die Entwicklung des Anlegerschutzes beim regulären Delisting in Deutschland* (Peter Lang 2019).

[209] Moloney (n 165) 634; Jennifer Payne, 'The Role of Gatekeepers' in Niamh Moloney, Eilís V Ferran, and Jennifer Payne (eds), *The Oxford Handbook of Financial Regulation* (OUP 2015) 254–79.

[210] John C Coffee Jr, 'Ratings Reform: The Good, the Bad, and the Ugly' (2011) 1 Harv Bus L Rev 231, 236ff; Commission, 'Proposal for a Regulation of the European Parliament and of the Council on Credit Rating Agencies' COM (2008) 704 final, 2; Olivia Schmid, 'Rebuilding the Fallen House of Cards: A New Approach to Regulating Credit Rating Agencies' (2012) 2012 Colum Bus L Rev 994, 1000ff.

[211] CRA Regulation, art 4(1); Veil (n 54) § 27 para 55; concerning the registration procedure see Tim Wittenberg, 'Regulatory Evolution of the EU Credit Rating Agency Framework' (2015) 16 EBOR 669, 697.

[212] Moloney (n 165) 678.

[213] Francesco Pennesi, *Equivalence in Financial Services* (Palgrave Macmillan 2022) 117–18.

third country must be subject to requirements at least as stringent as those under EU law. ESMA has changed its administrative practice in this respect and no longer considers that this condition is fulfilled once an equivalence decision has been issued in relation to the third country concerned.[214] This interpretation renders the 'at least as stringent as-criterion' more restrictive than the equivalence requirement of the CRA Regulation. Although *de lege lata* ESMA's interpretation is correct, it is reasonable *de lege ferenda* to abandon the 'as strict as-criterion' once an equivalence decision has been taken because the differences between the assessments are of such marginal nature that they do not justify a separate assessment.

The latter is a certification regime based on an equivalence decision by the Commission.[215] Remarkably, this regime only applies to ratings of entities established or financial instruments issued in third countries. Consequently, equivalence does not exist with regard to ratings for entities established or financial instruments issued in the EU, for instance, sovereign bonds of Member States.[216] Certification is further limited to third country entities and financial instruments without systemic importance.[217] This restriction is in line with recent developments, which can also be observed in relation to third country regimes for CCPs and investment firms. All in all, the equivalence mechanism is rather restrictive and mainly designed for smaller rating agencies that are not supported by a globally operating group necessary for endorsement.[218]

b) Statutory auditors

The Directive on Statutory Audits (SAD) lays down rules for the audit and assurance of annual and consolidated accounts as well as sustainability reporting.[219] Statutory auditors and audit firms must be approved by the NCA of its home Member State, entered in a public register and effectively supervised.[220] This approval must be recognized by other Member States (passporting).[221] Auditors from third countries are governed by Chapter XI of the SAD.

Third country auditors may be approved by the NCA if they prove to have equivalent qualifications and knowledge as required under the SAD.[222] This is a purely national equivalence mechanism, limited to the granting of authorization. Third-country

[214] ESMA, 'Final Report: Update of the guidelines on the application of the endorsement regime under Article 4(3) of the Credit Rating Agencies Regulation' ESMA33-9-205 (17 November 2017) paras 10ff; Christoph Kumpan and Ronny Grütze in Matthias Lehmann and Christoph Kumpan (eds), *European Financial Services Law* (Nomos 2019) CRA Regulation, art 4 para 6; see extensively on the role of ESMA in the CRA Regulation Gudula Deipenbrock, 'Direct Supervisory Powers of the European Securities and Markets Authority (ESMA) in the Realm of Credit Rating Agencies' (2018) 29 EBLR 169.

[215] n Sergakis (n 167) 273; Fabian Amtenbrink and Klaus Heine, 'Regulating Credit Rating Agencies in the European Union: Lessons from Behavioural Finance' (2013) 2013 DQ 2, 10; Kristina St Charles, 'Regulatory Imperialism: The Worldwide Export of European Regulatory Principles on Credit Rating Agencies' (2010) 19 Minn J Intl L 399, 421f.

[216] Moloney (n 165) 679.

[217] CRA Regulation, art 5(1)(d) and Commission Delegated Regulation (EU) No 449/2012 of 21 March 2012, art 28.

[218] Moloney (n 165) 679.

[219] SAD, art 1.

[220] ibid arts 3(1), 15–20, and 32–36a.

[221] ibid art 3a.

[222] ibid art 44(1) and arts 4 and 6–13; see for the German transposition: Auditors' Code (WPO), § 28(3).

auditors will still need to be registered, comply with other obligations under the SAD and will be supervised by the NCA.

Third country auditors issuing an audit report on an undertaking incorporated outside the Union whose securities are admitted to trading on a regulated market in a Member State must be registered and supervised by the NCA.[223] This provision gives the Directive an extraterritorial scope of application to ensure that a possibly poor audit quality in third countries does not undermine the high quality of EU audits.[224] If third country auditors are not registered with the NCA, their audits will have no legal effect in the Union.[225] To prevent unnecessary regulatory overlap, Member States may exempt third country auditors from this registration (or at least some of its requirements) and supervision pursuant to Article 46(1) SAD if equivalence to the quality assurance system, the systems of investigations and sanctions as well as the principles of public oversight is ensured.[226] The Commission is empowered to decide upon that equivalence.[227] Remarkably, the equivalence mechanism does not apply to the auditing of undertakings incorporated in the Union.

In the absence of a derogation under Article 46 SAD, the third country audit entity needs to be registered with an NCA in accordance with the requirements laid down in Article 45 SAD. A registration requires, among other things, that the auditing entity applies international auditing standards as defined in the SAD to its audits of annual or consolidated financial statements. However, the auditing entity may also apply other auditing standards if they are equivalent to these international standards. Where such an equivalence decision has been adopted, the auditing entity may apply its home auditing standards.[228]

To enhance cooperation with third country authorities, the SAD provides for another equivalence mechanism concerning the transfer of audit working papers to the supervisory authorities of third countries.[229] Such a transfer is subject to strict conditions, including that the competent authorities of the third country concerned meet requirements determined by the Commission to be 'adequate'.[230] Moreover, working arrangements based on the principle of reciprocity must exist between the authorities.[231]

c) Benchmarks and their administrators

The regulation of benchmarks and their administrators in the Benchmark Regulation (BMR) is a recent phenomenon and a direct consequence of scandals such as the manipulation of benchmarks like the London Interbank Offered Rate (LIBOR).[232]

[223] SAD, art 45(1) and (3).

[224] See Commission, 'Proposal for a Directive of the European Parliament and of the Council on statutory audit of annual accounts and consolidated accounts and amending Council Directive 78/660/EEC and 83/349/EEC' COM (2004) 177 final, p. 9.

[225] SAD, art 45(4).

[226] See Commission (n 224) 9.

[227] SAD, art 46(2); on the mechanism in general see Wymeersch (n 24) 240f.

[228] SAD, art 45(6) and (5)(c).

[229] ibid art 47.

[230] ibid art 47(1)(c) and (3).

[231] ibid art 47(1)(d).

[232] BMR, recital 1; Wymeersch (n 24) 273; see extensively on the different manipulations Kristina L Gütte, *Regulierung finanzieller Referenzwerte* (Mohr Siebeck 2020) 27ff.

The European regulation is inspired by the International Organization of Securities Commissions (IOSCO) Principles for Financial Benchmarks of July 2013.[233] At the outset, a supervised entity may use a benchmark in the EU only if the benchmark is provided by a regulated and supervised EU benchmark administrator registered with ESMA.[234] The administrator is the person who has control over the provision of a benchmark.[235] In addition, under the third country regime of Articles 30, 32 and 33, benchmarks and managers from third countries may also be used and operated in the EU.[236]

The structure of the BMR third country regime is very similar to that of the CRA Regulation.[237] First, benchmarks provided by a third country administrator can be used inside the Union if both the administrator as well as the benchmark are registered with ESMA.[238] A prerequisite for this registration is an equivalence decision by the Commission, which demands that the administrator of the benchmark in the third country is subject to binding requirements that are equivalent to those of the BMR and the IOSCO principles and that these requirements are effectively enforced on an ongoing basis.[239] Interestingly, the Commission can either adopt an equivalence decision referring to all third country administrators (paragraph 2) or just to specific administrators (paragraph 3). Further prerequisites for the registration are the authorization or registration as well as supervision of the administrator in the third country, its consent regarding the usage in the Union and the existence of cooperation agreements.[240] Under certain conditions set out in Article 32 BMR, ESMA is authorized to withdraw the registration.[241]

Secondly, if no equivalence decision has been adopted, an administrator may get recognized by ESMA.[242] In that scenario, the benchmark may be used by all entities in the Union (passport). However, the benchmark administrator will largely have to comply with the requirements of the BMR and appoint a representative in the Union who is jointly responsible for the oversight function and, in that respect, is accountable to the NCA.[243] Such recognition also generally requires the existence of cooperation agreements between ESMA and the competent authority in the third country.[244]

[233] See, inter alia, BMR, recitals 44–46; Beat Brändli, Basil Guggenheim, and Matthias Jüttner, 'Financial Benchmarks: Bedeutung, Problematik und regulatorische Ansätze' (2016) 88 SZW 162, 166.

[234] BMR, arts 29(1) first alternative, 36(1)(a), and 34.

[235] ibid art 3(1) no (6).

[236] Alexander Sajnovits, 'Die Auswirkungen des Brexit auf die Verwendung des LIBOR und anderer UK-Benchmarks' (2018) 27 WM 1247, 1248f; Eilís V Ferran, 'The UK as a Third Country Actor in EU Financial Services Regulation' (2017) 3 JFR 40, 50ff.

[237] An overview of the third country regime of the BMR is provided for in Stephen Farrell and Mark Cankett, 'EU Benchmark Regulation: Our translation, your transition and the timeframe' (2018) 10 J of Sec Oper & Cust 279, 281f.

[238] BMR, arts 30(1) and 36(1)(b); Sajnovits (n 236) 1248.

[239] The Commission has the power to specify these requirements in delegated acts. It also has the right to make the equivalence decision subject to the fulfilment of extra conditions aimed at ensuring equivalence. See Regulation (EU) 2019/2175 of 18 December 2019, art 5(9)(a)–(d).

[240] BMR, art 30(1)(b)–(d). ESMA also needs to take into consideration when concluding a cooperation agreement, whether the third country is on the list of jurisdictions having strategic deficiencies in their national anti-money laundering and countering the financing of terrorism regimes. See BMR, art 30(4) subpara 1 second sentence.

[241] Gütte (n 232) 371.

[242] BMR, arts 32 and 36(1)(c); for the so-called 'prior recognition' regime see Wymeersch (n 24) 274.

[243] BMR, art 32(2) and (3).

[244] BMR, art 32(5) subpara 3 second sentence.

Thirdly, benchmarks—just like credit ratings—can be endorsed by EU benchmark administrators under strict conditions, including that the provision of the third country benchmark on a mandatory or on a voluntary basis meets requirements 'at least as stringent as' the requirements provided for under the BMR.[245] This determination should be made with reference to the equivalence criterion and the IOSCO principles, which again underlines the importance of the concept of equivalence and the alignment of the BMR with international standards.[246]

Finally, there is a transitional provision regarding benchmarks referred to or to which a reference is added prior to 31 December 2023.[247] This exemption does not apply to benchmarks provided by administrators who relocated from the Union to a third country during the transitional period.

Against the background of the economic relevance of benchmarks, it is important to prevent potential abuses due to monopolistic positions of individual benchmarks, which can arise due to networking effects.[248] That is why the question of access rights to benchmarks arises, more specifically to their price and data feeds, as well as licences for their usage, for example, when benchmarks are used as an underlying in a derivative contract. To prevent such abuses, access to benchmarks shall be granted on a non-discriminatory and speedy basis as provided for in Article 37 MiFIR. Since EU benchmarks may also be underlying a cross-border or purely foreign financial contract or instrument, trading venues and CCPs established in third countries may have a substantial interest in having the same access rights to price and data feeds and licences. These rights are granted to them if the Commission adopts a decision determining that the legal and supervisory framework of the respective third country is equivalent to that of the EU.[249] Equivalence is fulfilled if trading venues in the third country are subject to authorization as well as ongoing effective supervision and enforcement, and reciprocal treatment is ensured with regard to access rights of foreign trading venues and CCPs.[250] Foreign trading venues and CCPs in this sense are those located outside the third country, such as EU trading venues and CCPs.

3. Financial intermediaries

A financial intermediary can be described as an entity that intermediates between providers and users of financial capital.[251] Examples of financial intermediaries within the meaning of this definition include investment firms, credit institutions, insurances,

[245] BMR, arts 33 and 36(1)(c); Sajnovits (n 236) 1249.

[246] Jakobus Feldkamp, 'Alle ein bisschen LIBOR? Die neue Referenzwertordnung und ihre Folgen' (2016) 6 RdF 180, 186.

[247] BMR, art 51(5).

[248] Matthias Lehmann in Matthias Lehmann and Christoph Kumpan (eds), *European Financial Services Law* (Nomos 2019) MiFIR, arts 35–37 para 1.

[249] MiFIR, art 38(2) and (3).

[250] Lehmann (n 248) MiFIR, art 38 para 2.

[251] There are various ways of defining financial intermediaries. The definition used here is taken from Stuart I Greenbaum, Anjan V Thakor, and Arnoud WA Boot, *Contemporary Financial Intermediation* (4th edn, Elsevier 2021) 24.

and investment funds. Although considerable similarities can be identified, each of them is regulated in a separate legal act.[252]

a) Investment firms and MiFID II/MiFIR

In relation to intra-EU services, the Markets in Financial Instruments Directive II (MiFID II) foresees a passport regime whereby services, irrespective of the clients addressed, can be provided either on a purely cross-border basis or through a branch established in a Member State.[253] The regulation of market access for third country investment firms is more complex. MiFID II and the Markets in Financial Instruments Regulation (MiFIR) contain different rules depending on the client being addressed and depending on whether the service is provided through a branch or on a purely cross-border basis.[254] As always, services based on the exclusive initiative of EU customers (reverse solicitation) are excluded from the regulation described in the following, which is explicitly stated in Article 42 MiFID II.

Investment firms from third countries may provide services to *wholesale clients* throughout the entire EEA without the establishment of a branch and without having to obey the requirements of MiFID II, MiFIR and the Capital Requirements Directive V (CRD V) if they are registered with ESMA.[255] Wholesale clients are to be understood in this context as eligible counterparties and per se professional clients.[256] The registration with ESMA requires an equivalence decision by the Commission, authorization and effective supervision of the firm in its home country, a cooperation agreement between the authorities involved as well as the ability of the firm to report the data required under paragraph 6a.[257] Therefore, the equivalence decision by the Commission and the subsequent registration with ESMA partly open the market for cross-border services by investment firms from third countries. Such registered third country firms may also operate as systematic internalizers.[258]

In response to Brexit, MiFIR was reformed by the EU.[259] The equivalence decision now requires not only equivalent third country rules, effective supervision and enforcement, as well as reciprocity, but the assessment also depends on whether the services provided by the firms are likely to be of systemic importance.[260] In this scenario, the assessment must be more detailed and granular, and the Commission is entitled to attach specific operational conditions to its equivalence decision. Moreover,

[252] Critical with regard to this separated regulation are Veerle Colaert and Danny Busch, 'Summary and Conclusions' in Veerle Colaert, Danny Busch, and Thomas Incalza (eds), *European Financial Regulation: Levelling the Cross-Sectoral Playing Field* (Hart Publishing 2019) 455ff.

[253] See MiFID II, arts 6(3), 34(1), and 35(1).

[254] Sethe (n 61) 630; Jan Ceyssens and Andreas Tarde, 'Äquivalenz im Finanzdienstleistungsrecht der Europäischen Union' (2019) 31 EuZW 805, 808ff.

[255] MiFIR, arts 46(1) and (2); more convincing is Sethe (n 61) 626. The scope of the derogation from EU law can be deduced from the matters reviewed in the equivalence decision. Therefore, the scope of art 47(1)(a) of MiFIR is decisive. For a dissenting view see Eggen and Schaefer (n 8) 378, who only recognize an exemption from the code of conduct rules.

[256] See for the definitions MiFID II, art 4(1) no (9)–(11).

[257] MiFIR, art 46(2)(a)–(d).

[258] ESMA, 'Questions and Answers: On MiFID II and MiFIR market structures topics' ESMA70-872942901-38 (29 May 2020) 31 (Answer 30).

[259] Investment Firm Regulation, art 63; Ceyssens and Tarde (n 254) 809f; Moloney (n 29) 55ff.

[260] Investment Firm Regulation, art 47(1) subpara 2.

investment firms that carry out proprietary trading or the underwriting of financial instruments and/or placing of financial instruments on a firm commitment basis and whose assets equal or exceed the threshold of €30 billion (so-called Class 1a investment firms) will henceforth be considered credit institutions within the meaning of the Capital Requirements Regulation II (CRR II) and thus be subject to the stricter third country regime for banks.[261]

The equivalence mechanism of MiFIR is limited in two important ways. First, it only applies to wholesale clients. The requirements for addressing retail clients are dealt with in Chapter IV of MiFID II, which does not include an equivalence mechanism.[262] When regulating investment services for retail clients, Member States are free to decide whether they want to oblige third country firms to establish a branch in their Member State.[263] If they opt for a branching obligation, MiFID II provides a set of detailed rules governing the establishment of that branch.[264] If Member States do not impose a branching obligation, they are free to determine the conditions for market access. Even where a branch is required, the provision of services by that branch is restricted to clients in the respective Member State and the system of passporting does not apply.

Secondly, the equivalence mechanism of MiFIR is restricted to the provision of cross-border services and does not grant investment firms the right to establish branches in the EU. The prerequisites for the establishment of a branch in the Union are instead exclusively set out in MiFID II. However, where a third country investment firm has set up a branch in a Member State pursuant to Article 39 MiFID II and where the respective third country firm is registered with ESMA following an equivalence decision, a branch obtains what is called a 'European passport light'.[265] As a result, wholesale clients in all Member States can be approached not only by the third country investment firm but also through its branch.

All in all, the third country regime of MiFID II and MiFIR can be described as a balanced system that properly weighs up the various interests at stake, such as the opening of markets on the one hand and the need for strong protection of retail investors on the other. The equivalence mechanism of MiFIR can be characterized as being modern and elaborated.

[261] See ibid art 62(3)(a) and (b) amending the definition of a credit institution in art 4(1) no (1) of the CRR II; on Class 1a investment firms see Gunnar Schuster and Heinrich Nemeczek, 'IFR, IFD und WpIG—Neuer Rechtsrahmen für Wertpapierfirmen (Teil 1)' (2021) 33 ZBB/JBB 35, 38ff; Andreas Schwennicke, 'Die künftige Beaufsichtigung der Wertpapierfirmen in Deutschland' (2021) 21 BKR 150, 153.

[262] See extensively on this part Thierry R Ammann, *Der europäische Marktzugang für Schweizer Banken* (Dike 2020) ch 9.

[263] MiFID II, art 39(1); Sethe (n 61) 628; Jochen Eichhorn and Ulf Klebeck, 'Drittstaatenregulierung der MiFID II und MiFIR' (2014) 4 RdF 189, 190ff; for a critical view see Detmar Loff, 'Die Nutzung des vereinfachten Marktzugangs für Schweizer Banken' (2014) 9 GesKR 376, 386.

[264] MiFID II, art 39(2).

[265] MiFIR, art 47(3) subpara 1; Christian Hoops, 'Die Drittstaatenregelung von MiFIR/MiFID und ihre Umsetzung im geplanten Finanzmarktnovellierungsgesetz' (2016) 28 ZBB/JBB 47, 50f; Sethe (n 61) 626; Nemeczek and Pitz (n 55) 452ff.

b) Credit institutions and CRD V/CRR II

Credit institutions are regulated in the EU by CRD V and CRR II and are to be understood as institutions that engage in the deposit-taking business or take other repayable funds from the public and grant credits for their own account.[266] As a result of the recent reform by the Investment Firm Regulation, Class 1a investment firms are now also defined as CRR credit institutions.[267]

aa) Market access for third country credit institutions Third country credit institutions may access the European market in different ways. They can establish a subsidiary in one of the Member States, which will subsequently benefit from the advantages of the passport since it will be regarded as an independent legal entity.[268] This subsidiary must be authorized and will have to comply with CRD V and CRR II obligations. A third country credit institution can also establish a branch within a Member State according to the national law of that state. Again, approval by the Member State's competent authority is required, and compliance with banking regulation must be ensured.[269] However, a branch can only operate within the Member State in which it has been authorized. Passporting does not apply to branches of third country credit institutions.[270] The last way to access the European financial market is through the concept of reverse solicitation.[271] What is missing is access to the financial market via a European equivalence mechanism.[272] This is a significant gap considering the importance of banks in the financial system.

bb) Existing equivalence mechanisms in CRR II In the area of capital requirements for credit risks, multiple equivalence provisions exist. However, some of these provisions only address EU institutions, which is a specificity of these mechanisms. The link with third countries exists solely in the form of exposures of EU institutions towards third country institutions. The CRR II uses a risk-weighted assets approach to identify credit risks and calculate capital requirements on that basis. The higher the risk, the higher the capital adequacy ratio and the higher the institution's capital requirements in general. Pursuant to Article 107(1) CRR II, credit institutions must calculate their risk-weighted exposure amounts. For this calculation, institutions may treat exposures to third country investment firms, credit institutions, clearinghouses,

[266] See CRR II, art 4(1) no (1).

[267] See note 261 (ch 1).

[268] CRD V, arts 33 and 35. Authorization will be granted in accordance with the procedure laid down in the SSM Regulation. See Matthias Haentjens and Pierre de Gioia-Carabellese, *European Banking and Financial Law* (2nd edn, Routledge 2020) 125.

[269] Mathias Hanten and Osman Sacarcelik, 'Pandora's Box: EU Market Access for UK-Based Banks and Investment Firms After Brexit' (2018) 15 ECL 126, 129f.

[270] See CRD V, recital 23; Henning Berger and Nikolai Badenhoop, 'Financial Services and Brexit: Navigating Towards Future Market Access' (2018) 19 EBOR 679, 685.

[271] See ch 1 B)I.2.c); Lehmann and Zetzsche (n 24) 124f.

[272] John Armour, 'Brexit and Financial Services: Bargaining in the Shadow of Equivalence' in John Armour and Horst Eidenmüller (eds), *Negotiating Brexit* (CH Beck 2017) 30. Equivalence regimes do exist at national level, but they can only grant market access to the respective Member State and not to the Internal Market of the EU. See eg KWG, § 53c(1)(2) and § 53; Hanten and Sacarcelik (n 269) 130.

and exchanges in the same way as exposures to institutions based in the Union if an equivalence decision has been adopted.[273]

Articles 114, 115 and 116 CRR II regulate the calculation of risk-weighted exposures to central governments and central banks, regional governments, and local authorities, as well as to public sector entities. Again, these public bodies from third countries can be treated like European ones if equivalence is fulfilled.

In addition, the CRR contains two further equivalence mechanisms. The first deals with exposures to large financial sector entities. When calculating risk-weighted exposures, institutions can either use the Standardized Approach of Chapter 2 or, if permitted, the Internal Ratings Based Approach provided for in Chapter 3.[274] Under the Internal Ratings Based Approach, exposures to large financial sector entities are calculated pursuant to Article 153(2) CRR II.[275] For this purpose, large financial sector entities are defined in Article 142(1) no (4) CRR II. According to this definition, the entity needs to be subject to prudential regulation in the Union or a third country with equivalent supervisory and regulatory requirements. Hence, privileges for calculating capital requirements are available when an equivalence decision has been issued. The second mechanism concerns Part 4 of CRR II on large exposures. Following an equivalence decision by the Commission under Article 391(2) CRR II, third country undertakings can be considered as 'institutions' for the purposes of the large exposure regulation, which entails significant advantages. In the absence of such an equivalence decision, third country undertakings will be classified as unregulated financial sector entities within the meaning of Article 142(1) no 5 CRR II.

cc) A wide gap: Payment services and settlement finality The absence of an equivalence mechanism is not limited to market access for credit institutions. With regard to payment services, the Payment Services Directive (PSD II) does not contain an equivalence mechanism either.[276] This deficiency can harbour significant risks, which were, for example, imminent in the wake of Brexit. To avoid disadvantages for the functioning or the stability of payment systems, the German legislator, for instance, introduced a provision that enables the Federal Financial Supervisory Authority (BaFin) to allow British payment service providers to continue to provide payment services to Germany in the event of a hard Brexit.[277]

The same risks existed in the context of Brexit in relation to the transfer of financial instruments and the settlement of payments. In case of a hard Brexit, the UK Continuous Linked Settlement payment system would have no longer been recognized under the Settlement Finality Directive.[278] This Directive does not contain an

[273] CRR II, art 107(3).
[274] ibid art 107(1).
[275] See Ronny Hahn, in Reinfrid Fischer and Hermann Schulte-Mattler (eds), *KWG, CRR-VO* (6th edn, CH Beck 2023) CRR, art 153.
[276] Ferran (n 236) 43; Arun Srivastava and Nina Moffatt, 'EU Equivalence Regime' in Jonathan Herbst and Simon Lovegrove (eds), *Brexit and Financial Regulation* (OUP 2020) para 4.22.
[277] See German Payment Services Supervision Act (ZAG), § 39(8), which was introduced by the Brexit-Steuerbegleitgesetz. Matthias Lehmann and Jonas Schürger, 'Brexit-Steuerbegleitgesetz und Brexit-Übergangsgesetz: Sicherheit trotz Unsicherheit?' (2019) 19 BKR 365, 368.
[278] Directive 98/26/EC of 19 May 1998.

equivalence mechanism that allows for such a recognition.[279] However, according to Recital 7 Settlement Finality Directive, Member States may extend the Directive's provisions to their domestic institutions directly participating in third country systems. Based on this recital, some Member States adopted national equivalence mechanisms to avert the risks that could have arisen from a hard Brexit.[280]

As a result, it can be stated that the regulation of credit institutions, payment services, and settlements remains one of the blind spots when it comes to equivalence in European financial law.[281]

c) Insurances and Solvency II and the IDD

Insurance is a global business, which is why the issue of cross-border regulation is of particular importance.[282] In the following, a distinction is made between issues of market access for insurance undertakings, questions of supervision and solvency requirements of insurance groups, as well as matters relating to insurance distribution.

aa) Market access for third country (re)insurance undertakings At the outset, Solvency II sets high barriers to the cross-border provision of insurance services. Third country insurers offering services to EEA customers must obtain prior authorization, establish a branch in the Union and meet various other requirements.[283] As a result of this restrictive approach, there is a great risk of legal and supervisory conflicts, which makes equivalence a key concern.[284]

When analysing market access conditions, a distinction must be made between direct insurers and reinsurers. Market access for direct insurers works in a similar way to that of credit institutions. Direct insurers must obtain prior authorization before taking-up business.[285] Again, insurers may establish a subsidiary or branch in the EEA or operate on the principle of reverse solicitation.[286] If they establish an independent subsidiary, its authorization is valid for the entire EEA.[287] With respect to market access for direct insurers, there is no equivalence provision in Solvency II.

[279] Ferran (n 236) 43.

[280] See eg ch 7 Withdrawal of the United Kingdom from the European Union (Consequential Provisions) Act, 2019 (Private Act No 8 of 2019) of Ireland, particularly s 63(2)(b) of that bill. See also Loi n° 2019-486 du 22 mai 2019 relative à la croissance et la transformation des entreprises, art 84 no 2° (PACTE Law) in France; see now Code monétaire et financier, art 330-1.

[281] Armour (n 272) 30.

[282] See Aerdt Houben and Mark Teunissen, 'The Systemicness of Insurance Companies' in Patrick M Liedtke and Jan Monkiewicz (eds), *The Future of Insurance Regulation and Supervision* (Palgrave Macmillan 2011) 246ff.

[283] Solvency II, art 162; Rolf H Weber and Rainer Baisch, *Versicherungsaufsichtsrecht* (2nd edn, Stämpfli 2017) § 2 paras 67f.

[284] See on equivalence in insurance law Bradley L Kading and Leila Madeiros, 'Insurance Regulation: Mutual Recognition, Equivalence and International Standards' in Patrick M Liedtke and Jan Monkiewicz (eds), *The Future of Insurance Regulation and Supervision* (Palgrave Macmillan 2011) 389ff; Hermann Geiger, 'Transnational supervisory recognition' in Julian Burling and Kevin Lazarus (eds), *Research Handbook on International Insurance Law and Regulation* (Edward Elgar Publishing 2011) 308ff.

[285] Solvency II, arts 14(1) and 162.

[286] Julian Burling, 'The Potential Effect of Brexit on Insurance Regulation in the UK' in Pierpaolo Marano and Michele Siri (eds), *Insurance Regulation in the European Union* (Palgrave Macmillan 2017) 87–93.

[287] Solvency II, art 15(1); n Burling (n 286) 82.

For third country reinsurers, Solvency II foresees a special regime. In principle, the regulation of third country reinsurance undertakings is left to the Member States. However, the regulatory freedom of Member States is limited in two ways. First, Member States may not treat third country reinsurers more favourably than reinsurers established in the EEA.[288] Secondly, Article 172 Solvency II contains an equivalence mechanism for third country reinsurance undertakings. On the basis of the criteria laid down in a Commission's delegated act,[289] the Commission may adopt equivalence decisions stating that the solvency regime of a third country regarding reinsurers is equivalent to that of Solvency II.[290] As a consequence of such a decision, reinsurance contracts concluded with undertakings having their head office in that third country must be treated like contracts concluded with EEA-reinsurers. Therefore, no prior authorization is needed, and no additional requirements can be demanded by the Member States, which limits their regulatory freedom.[291] This equivalence mechanism is inspired by the Discussion Paper on the Mutual Recognition of Reinsurance Supervision from October 2007 of the IAIS.[292] Additionally, the EU may conclude agreements with third countries on the basis of equivalence in accordance with Article 175 Solvency II.

bb) Group supervision and group solvency calculation In light of the growing cross-border nature of the insurance business, the EU moved away from purely solo supervision of insurance undertakings and adopted the Insurance Groups Directive, which was later integrated into Solvency II.[293] Group supervision generally applies at the level of the ultimate parent undertaking having its head office in the EU and is carried out by a single supervisor, called the group supervisor.[294] Where the group is headquartered in a third country, the group supervisor must apply the Solvency II requirements *mutatis mutandis*.[295] However, if the group is already subject to equivalent supervision by a third country supervisory authority, Member States shall rely on this group supervision and cooperate closely with the third country authority.[296]

Solvency II also entails special solvency capital requirements for group insurers.[297] EEA-group insurers must consider the capital position of any related undertaking—especially subsidiaries of the group—for their group solvency calculation.[298] Third

[288] Solvency II, art 174.

[289] Commission Delegated Regulation (EU) 2015/35 of 10 October 2014, art 378.

[290] Solvency II, art 172(2) and (1).

[291] Kern Alexander, 'The UK's Third-Country Status Following Brexit' in Kern Alexander and others (eds), *Brexit and Financial Services: Law and Policy* (Hart Publishing 2018) 142; concerning the predecessor in the Reinsurance Directive see Geiger (n 284) 313.

[292] n Kading and Madeiros (n 284) 394ff.

[293] Angelo Borselli, 'Insurance Group Supervision in the European Union' in Pierpaolo Marano and Michele Siri (eds), *Insurance Regulation in the European Union* (Palgrave Macmillan 2017) 202ff.

[294] Solvency II, arts 215 and 247.

[295] ibid arts 262(1) and 260(4).

[296] ibid arts 261 and 260; n Burling (n 286) 89f.

[297] Meinrad Dreher, *Treatises on Solvency II* (Springer 2015) 106–107; on solvency requirements in general see Rob Curtis, 'Solvency as a Focal Point of Prudential Regulation' in Patrick M Liedtke and Jan Monkiewicz (eds), *The Future of Insurance Regulation and Supervision* (Palgrave Macmillan 2011) 87ff.

[298] Solvency II, arts 225 and 226; for the definition of a 'related undertaking', see Solvency II, art 212(1)(b).

country subsidiaries of that group shall use the Solvency II standards when calculating their capital requirements for the group's calculation.[299] This means that subsidiaries from third countries will have to perform two calculations: one in accordance with the rules of its home country; and one under Solvency II. This burden of double calculation is eliminated if the alternative method for the calculation pursuant to Article 233 Solvency II is used, and an equivalence decision has been adopted either by the Commission or the competent group supervisor.[300]

cc) Insurance distribution Finally, it is necessary to take a brief look at the insurance distribution activities regulated under the new Insurance Distribution Directive (IDD), which has replaced the Insurance Mediation Directive. The IDD obliges Member States to require registration of insurance intermediaries, which is then, however, subject to the passporting regime.[301] The IDD does not apply to third country firms and therefore has a limited territorial scope.[302] Member States' regulatory freedom is only limited to the extent that they may not treat insurance mediation services provided by third country firms more favourably than those provided by EU companies operating under the passport regime.[303] Due to the lack of an elaborated third country regime at the European level, the IDD does not provide for an equivalence mechanism.

d) Investment funds and UCITS Directive/AIFMD

Two Directives govern investment funds in the EU: the UCITS Directive and the AIFM Directive. UCITS must be organized as open-ended investment funds, may only invest in certain investment instruments, in particular transferable securities and money market instruments admitted to or traded on regulated markets, and need to comply with the principle of risk-spreading.[304] AIFs are all investment funds that do not qualify as UCITS.[305]

What makes it difficult to present the cross-border context of investment funds is the fact that there are several elements that may constitute a link to a third country. First, the fund itself can be established in a Member State or in a third country. Secondly, the legal person managing the fund can have its registered office either in a Member State or a third country. Thirdly, there must be a depositary for each fund that can also be located in a third country. Fourthly, the fund may be invested in instruments that are traded in third countries. Finally, the fund can be marketed within or outside the Union.

[299] ibid art 227(1).

[300] The Commission may decide about equivalence pursuant to art 227(3) and (4) of Solvency II. If the Commission has not taken a decision, the group supervisor is responsible for a decision on equivalence in accordance with art 227(2) of Solvency II.

[301] Concerning the registration see IDD, art 3; concerning passporting see IDD, arts 4 and 6.

[302] ibid art 1(6).

[303] ibid art 1(6) subpara 2.

[304] See UCITS Directive, art 1 and Chapter VII ('Obligations Concerning the Investment Policies of UCITS').

[305] See the formulation by the German legislator in Capital Investment Code (KAGB), § 1(3). The AIFMD defines AIFs in its art 4(1)(a). Gerald Spindler and Sara Tancredi, 'Die Richtlinie über Alternative Investmentfonds (AIFM-Richtlinie)—Teil I' (2011) 67 WM 1393, 1396.

aa) UCITS Directive UCITS are undertakings established within a Member State of the EU.[306] They must be authorized by the NCA of their home Member State.[307] This authorization is valid for all Member States (passporting).[308] Therefore, undertakings originating from a third country are not subject to the UCITS Directive but are regulated under the more complex and restrictive regime of the AIFMD.[309]

Managers of UCITS also need prior approval, and here too, the rules of passporting apply.[310] The rules for third country managers in the UCITS Directive are very limited and refer mainly to Article 15(1) MiFID I, which has no corresponding provision in MiFID II.[311] That is why the responsibility for regulation under the UCITS Directive lies primarily with the Member States.[312] An equivalence provision at the European level is not included. The legislator has refrained from updating the UCITS Directive by including a reference to the equivalence mechanism of MiFIR, which would have harmonized and liberalized the third country regime. UCITS must therefore be managed and administrated in the EU.[313] The only exception is the delegation of specific functions to third country undertakings, which is restricted in that cooperation between the supervisory authorities must be ensured and the creation of letter-box entities must be avoided.[314]

The UCITS Directive further requires that a depositary is appointed for each fund.[315] These depositaries need to have their registered office or be established in the UCITS home Member State, which means they can neither be established in another Member State (no passporting) nor in a third country.[316] Again, these EU-depositaries can delegate functions to third country undertakings. This delegation is subject to strict conditions, is limited to safekeeping functions and does not include control functions.[317]

The assets in which UCITS may invest are generally not limited to EU assets.[318] Nonetheless, there are some limitations to this rule. For example, UCITS may only invest in units of collective undertakings established in a third country if this undertaking is, inter alia, subject to supervision considered equivalent by the competent authority at the level of the Member State.[319] Consequently, the UCITS Directive does

306 UCITS Directive, art 1(1)e.
307 ibid art 5(1).
308 ibid art 5(1).
309 Wymeersch (n 24) 247.
310 UCITS Directive, art 6(1).
311 The reference to art 15 of the MiFID I is included in art 9(1) of the UCITS Directive. According to art 94 and Annex IV of the MiFID II, this provision does not have a corresponding provision. See Thomas C Jutzi and Christoph Feuz, 'MiFID II, AIFMD und UCITSD: Auswirkungen des EU-Vermögensverwaltungsrechts auf das grenzüberschreitende Geschäft Schweizer Finanzintermediäre' (2016) Jusletter Next 1, para 29.
312 Detmar Loff and Jasper Lembke, 'Zugang von Drittstaaten-Finanzmarktakteuren in die EU' (2016) 6 RdF 101, 102; Dirk A Zetzsche and Dominik Nast in Matthias Lehmann and Christoph Kumpan (eds), *European Financial Services Law* (Nomos 2019) UCITS Directive, art 9 para 1.
313 UCITS Directive, art 7(1)(d).
314 ibid art 13(1)(d); see ibid recital 16; Wymeersch (n 24) 246f.
315 UCITS Directive, art 22(1).
316 ibid art 23(1).
317 ibid art 22a(1) and (2); Zetzsche and Nast (n 312) UCITSD, art 22a para 3.
318 Wymeersch (n 24) 247.
319 UCITS Directive, art 50(1)(e). This is a purely national equivalence regime. See Dörte Poelzig and Max Bärnreuther, 'Die finanzmarktrechtlichen Konsequenzen des Brexit' in Malte Kramme, Christian

not include any equivalence provision at the European level, is rather strict when it comes to foreign influences and mostly requires an establishment within the Union.

bb) AIFMD As explained above, investment funds originating from third countries are not covered by the UCITS Directive but fall within the scope of the AIFMD, which is consequently of greater importance in a cross-border context.[320] With the AIFMD, the European legislator has largely abandoned, at least in theory,[321] the approach that questions of third country regulation are left to the discretion of Member States.[322] Instead, competences have been shifted almost entirely to the EU level.

The territorial scope of the AIFMD is defined in Article 2(1) in a very far-reaching manner. The directive applies to EU alternative investment funds managers (AIFMs) managing AIFs irrespective of where these funds are domiciled, to non-EU AIFMs managing EU AIFs and to non-EU AIFMs managing non-EU AIFs marketed in the Union.[323] Again, a distinction must be made between the different elements that may create the cross-border dimension.[324]

(1) Non-EU AIF

In relation to EU AIFs, Member States must ensure that EU AIFMs are allowed to market units or shares of any EU AIF in the home Member State of the manager (Article 31(1) AIFMD). To allow cross-border marketing within the EU, Article 32(1) AIFMD requires Member States to allow marketing in Member States other than the home Member State and thereby establishes a product passport.[325]

Unlike the UCITS Directive, the AIFMD explicitly foresees the possibility of non-EU funds.[326] A non-EU AIF is a fund established and registered outside the Union and having its registered/head office in a third country.[327] With regard to these non-EU AIFs, it has to be differentiated between two scenarios: they can either be managed by an EU AIFM or by a non-EU AIFM.

In the first case, a further distinction must be made depending on whether the AIF is marketed in the Union or not. Suppose the non-EU AIF is managed by an EU AIFM and is *not* marketed in a Member State. In that case, Article 34 AIFMD applies, which exempts the manager from the duties regarding the depositary and the

Baldus, and Martin Schmidt-Kessel (eds), *Brexit: Privat- und wirtschaftsrechtliche Folgen* (2nd edn, Nomos 2020) § 15 para 20.

320 See especially concerning the case of Brexit Ferran (n 236) 52.

321 Only in theory, as most of the third country provisions included in the AIFMD have not yet come into force. See further below.

322 Lukas Lezzi, *Regulierung und Aufsicht über kollektive Kapitalanlagen für alternative Anlagen* (Schulthess 2012) para 603.

323 ibid paras 622ff.

324 A good overview is provided by the table in Mirzha J De Manuel Aramendía, 'Third Country Rules for Alternative Investments: Passport flexibility comes at a price' ECMI Commentary No. 27/16 (December 2010) 5 https://www.ceps.eu/wp-content/uploads/2010/12/ECMI%20Commentary%20No%2027.pdf (accessed 12 November 2022); Gerald Spindler and Sara Tancredi, 'Die Richtlinie über Alternative Investmentfonds (AIFM-Richtlinie)—Teil II' (2011) 67 WM 1441, 1447ff; see extensively Zetzsche and Veidt (n 102) ch 33.

325 Christian Schmies in Matthias Lehmann and Christoph Kumpan (eds), *European Financial Services Law* (Nomos 2019) AIFMD, art 32 para 1.

326 AIFMD, art 4(1)(aa).

327 ibid art 4(1)(k); Ferran (n 236) 53.

annual report but demands appropriate cooperation agreements to be concluded between the competent third country authority and the competent authority of the home Member State of the manager.[328] If the non-EU AIF *is* marketed to professional investors in the Union, Article 35 AIFMD grants the opportunity of a product passport for the marketing of that non-EU AIF in the Union subject to strict conditions including an appropriate cooperation agreement, the third country not being listed as a Non-Cooperative Country and Territory by the Financial Action Task Force on Money Laundering (FATF) and compliance with Article 26 of the OECD Model Tax Convention on Income and on Capital.[329] These requirements are recurring elements of third country regimes of the AIFMD.[330] This product passport will, however, only be valid after it has been activated by the Commission pursuant to Article 67(6) AIFMD, which has not yet been achieved.[331] Without prejudice to the product passport, Member States may also allow the marketing to professional investors of non-EU AIFs under the national private placement regime and the conditions set out in Article 36 AIFMD.[332]

In the second case, two regimes apply cumulatively.[333] First, the non-EU AIFM marketing the non-EU AIF to professional investors in a Member State must be authorized in accordance with Article 37 AIFMD.[334] Secondly, a product passport for the non-EU AIF is granted if the requirements of Article 40 AIFMD are met, which are very similar to the ones described above in relation to Article 35(2) AIFMD. But, again, both mechanisms have yet to be activated in accordance with Article 67(6) AIFMD.

(2) Non-EU AIFM

The supervision of funds is primarily based on the supervision of its managers, who must be authorized in their home state in order to manage funds.[335] This approval is valid for the entire EU[336] and, because of the management company passport, enables

[328] Lezzi (n 322) paras 800ff.

[329] AIFMD, art 35(2); Lezzi (n 322) paras 803ff.

[330] For this reason, they are also referred to as the 'Four-Pillar System'. See Zetzsche and Veidt (n 102) 818ff.

[331] The course of this procedure is described in detail in Jutzi and Feuz (n 311) paras 46ff. So far, ESMA has issued positive advice for some jurisdictions (ESMA, 'Advice to the European Parliament, the Council and the Commission on the application of the AIFMD passport to non-EU AIFMs and AIFs' ESMA/2015/1236 (30 July 2015)). However, the Commission was not satisfied and asked for more countries to be assessed (Commission, 'Letter by the Commission to ESMA' (17 December 2015) https://www.esma.europa.eu/sites/default/files/library/eu_commission_letter_aifmd_passport.pdf (accessed 12 November 2022)). Following this letter, ESMA published a second advice containing further jurisdictions (ESMA, 'Advice to the European Parliament, the Council and the Commission on the application of the AIFMD passport to non-EU AIFMs and AIFs' ESMA/2016/1140 (12 September 2016)). The legislator then introduced art 69a of the AIFMD which demands from the Commission to submit a report to the European Parliament and to the Council before the adoption of the delegated act (Directive (EU) 2019/1160 of 20 June 2019). One of the last comments was published by the Commission in July 2020 (Commission, 'Report from the Commission to the European Parliament and the Council: assessing the application and the scope of Directive 2011/61/EU of the European Parliament and of the Council on Alternative Investment Fund Manager' COM (2020) 232 final).

[332] The marketing without a passport is of particular importance in practice, as the passport has not yet been activated pursuant to art 67(6) of the AIFMD. Zetzsche and Veidt (n 102) 806ff.

[333] Schmies (n 325) AIFMD, art 40 para 1.

[334] See extensively in the next section.

[335] AIFMD, arts 6ff and 31; Loff and Lembke (n 312) 103.

[336] AIFMD, art 8(1) subpara 2.

EU AIFMs to market the units or shares of EU AIFs in any Member State either directly or by establishing a branch (Article 33(1) AIFMD).[337] Again, the question arises whether such a management company passport exists for non-EU AIFMs.

This is the case because non-EU AIFMs can obtain authorization pursuant to Article 37(1) AIFMD if they intend to manage or market EU AIFs in the Union.[338] This provision has to be read in conjunction with Article 39 AIFMD for the marketing of EU AIFs, in conjunction with Article 40 AIFMD for the marketing of non-EU AIFs and in conjunction with Article 41 AIFMD for the marketing of EU AIFs established in a Member State other than the Member State of reference of the non-EU AIFM.[339] The competent Member State of reference for the authorization under Article 37 AIFMD is to be determined in accordance with the complex procedure in paragraph 4.[340] A non-EU AIFM must comply with the AIFMD, with the exception of Chapter VI, in order to prevent systemic risk from arising in the EU. In addition, the authorization is subject to further recurrent requirements of the AIFMD, such as the conclusion of cooperation agreements or the appointment of a legal representative in the Member State of reference by the non-EU AIFM.[341] However, in the event of incompatibility of the AIFMD with the national law by which the non-EU AIFM is governed, a possibility exists to suspend certain duties of the AIFMD. This exemption requires that the foreign law provides for an 'equivalent rule having the same regulatory purpose and offering the same level of protection to the investors' and that the non-EU AIFM complies with this rule.[342] Apart from that, there is no equivalence mechanism for managers in the AIFMD. Non-EU managers of AIFs consequently always require prior authorization by a competent authority in the Union and must in principle comply with all obligations of the AIFMD, irrespective of an already applicable regulation imposed on the manager in its home state. The idea of equivalence is, therefore, only weakly developed. A delegation of managing functions to non-EU third parties is possible but limited to prevent the creation of letter-box entities.[343]

Against the background that the Commission has not yet activated the third country regime of the AIFMD and passports are thus not available, Member States may allow the marketing of AIFs to professional investors on its territory by non-EU AIFMs according to the national private placement regime.[344] Such authorization by

[337] Schmies (n 325) AIFMD, art 33 para 1.

[338] Again, the applicability of the third country manager passport according to art 37 of the AIFMD must first be prescribed in the form of a delegated act pursuant to art 67(6) of the AIFMD, which has not happened yet.

[339] From a systematic point of view, art 37 of the AIFMD establishes the manager passport for the non-EU AIFM and arts 39 and 40 the corresponding product passport. Therefore, art 37 is the corresponding provision to art 33 for non-EU AIFM. Arts 39 and 40 are the corresponding provisions to arts 32 and 35 for the marketing of EU AIF respectively non-EU AIF by EU AIFM. See also Zetzsche and Veidt (n 102) 817.

[340] Lezzi (n 322) paras 819ff.

[341] In particular AIFMD, art 37(3), (7), and (8); Schmies (n 325) AIFMD, art 37 para 8.

[342] AIFMD, art 37(2)(b) and (c).

[343] ibid art 20 and Commission Delegated Regulation (EU) No 231/2013 of 19 December 2012; Ulf Klebeck and Jürg Frick in Frank Dornseifer and others (eds), *AIFM-Richtlinie* (CH Beck 2013) art 37 paras 154ff.

[344] AIFMD, art 42; on the national private placement regime in general see Zetzsche and Veidt (n 102) 806ff; on the German implementation see Christian Schmies, 'Germany' in Lodewijk van Setten and Danny Busch (eds), *Alternative Investment Funds in Europe* (OUP 2014) para 4.112.

Member States is subject to certain minimum requirements, including compliance with some of the duties of the AIFMD, appropriate cooperation agreements being in place and that the third country is not listed as a Non-Cooperative Country and Territory by the FATF.[345]

(3) Depositary

Like the UCITS Directive, the AIFMD generally requires from the manager to assure that one depositary is appointed for each AIF it manages.[346] This depositary must be established in the home Member State of the AIF for EU-AIFs.[347] In the case of non-EU AIFs, the AIFM has the right to choose the location of the depositary between the third country where the AIF is domiciled and the home Member State (in the case of an EU AIFM) respectively the reference Member State (in the case of a non-EU AIFM).[348] However, the depositary can only be located in the third country subject to strict conditions.[349] The regulation and supervision in the third country must, inter alia, have 'the same effect as Union law'.[350] The wording suggests that this requires more than an 'equivalent effect' as foreseen in Article 47(1)(a) MiFIR, although it remains unclear whether this terminological difference is intended. Only the Commission is competent to adopt such equivalence decisions.[351] The other requirements of the mechanism are controlled at the national level, which means that the national authorities are responsible for the approval of non-EU depositaries.

cc) **Overly protectionist approach of EU fund regulation** As a result, it can be stated that equivalence has not yet conquered the area of funds regulation.[352] This is partly attributable to the fact that a substantial amount of decision-making is still done at the national level and has not yet been harmonized. The UCITS Directive barely contains any third country provisions. The AIFMD has a sophisticated third country regime, but the Commission has not yet activated it. Consequently, equivalence regimes have developed rather at the national level.[353]

This hesitation on the European level seems surprising in light of the fact that the UCITS Directive was one of the pioneers of the passport.[354] This restraint also fails

345 Schmies (n 325) AIFMD, art 42 paras 3ff.

346 AIFMD, art 21(1).

347 ibid art 21(5)(a).

348 ibid art 21(5)(b). This choice is remarkable because it results in a quasi-depositary passport giving third country AIFs competitive advantages over EU AIFs. See Sebastiaan N Hooghiemstra, 'Depositary Regulation' in Dirk A Zetzsche (ed), *The Alternative Investment Fund Managers Directive* (3rd edn, Wolters Kluwer 2020) 450 and 453.

349 AIFMD, art 21(6); Schmies (n 325) AIFMD, art 21 para 7.

350 AIFMD, art 21(6)(b); see the detailed criteria at Level 2 in Commission Delegated Regulation (EU) No 231/2013 of 19 December 2012, art 84 and in ESMA, 'Final report: ESMA's technical advice to the European Commission on possible implementing measures of the Alternative Investment Fund Managers Directive' ESMA/2011/379 (16 November 2011) 144ff.

351 AIFMD, art 21(6) subpara 3; Caroline Specht in Frank Dornseifer and others (eds), *AIFM-Richtlinie* (CH Beck 2013) art 21 para 67. This follows from the fact that subpara 2 does not refer to lit b) and that the decision by the Commission under subpara 3 is of a binding nature ('shall').

352 See Wymeersch (n 24) 254.

353 See for an assessment of the situation for funds in Germany after Brexit Harald Glander and Yaprak Ağırman, 'Auswirkungen des Brexit auf die deutsche Fondsindustrie und den Marktzugang von UK-Finanzdienstleistern' (2019) 9 RdF 4.

354 UCITS I, art 4(1) subpara 2; Payne and Howell (n 88) 242–43.

to take into account the economic reality. The vast majority of alternative funds have a link to a third country and are not purely European.[355] With regard to the UCITS Directive, one explanation for the cautious approach is the high need for investor protection in the area of funds.[356]

The argument of investor protection is not equally convincing in the case of the AIFMD, as AIFs can generally only be marketed to professional clients. The AIFMD was also created in response to the GFC and therefore focuses much more on systemic risks than on investor protection.[357] In view of the wide (extraterritorial) scope of application of the AIFMD, the lack of an operational third country regime is particularly problematic for AIFs. Since non-EU AIFMs still need to be authorized and comply with the directive under the third country regime of Article 37 AIFMD, it is also not apparent why systemic risks are associated with the authorization.

More likely than a legal justification for not activating the regime is a political motivation. Because of Brexit, the EU is reluctant to open its market to third countries further and prefers to use equivalence as a bargaining chip.[358] However, as will be explained later, such political considerations are economically harmful and legally highly questionable.[359] It is thus time finally to put the third country regime into force.[360]

4. Trading venues and financial market infrastructures

There are different types of trading venues in European capital markets law. These are regulated markets, multilateral trading facilities and organized trading facilities as opposed to OTC trading that does not take place on organized venues. These trading venues are defined and comprehensively regulated in MiFID II and MiFIR. Closely related to the regulation of trading venues is that of market infrastructures, which includes clearing and settlement services through central counterparties, recording data about financial transactions by trade repositories, and depositing securities by central securities depositories.[361]

[355] David Clarkson, Stefan Jaecklin, and Kamil Kaczmarski (Oliver Wyman), 'Domiciles of Alternative Investment Funds' (2014) https://www.oliverwyman.com/content/dam/oliver-wyman/global/en/2014/dec/Oliver_Wyman_Domiciles_of_Alternative_Investment_Funds.pdf (accessed 12 November 2022); Ulf Klebeck and Catia Meyer, 'Drittstaatenregulierung der AIFM-Richtlinie' (2012) 2 RdF 95, 95–96.

[356] Jonathan Fisher and Jane Bewsey, *The Law of Investor Protection* (Sweet & Maxwell 1997) 377ff. The goal of investor protection is mentioned 10 times in the recitals of the UCITS Directive alone.

[357] AIFMD, recitals 2 and 3; Lezzi (n 322) para 945.

[358] Zetzsche and Veidt (n 102) 838; anticipating this risk of non-activation already in 2010 see Aramendía (n 324) 3.

[359] See ch 2 B)II.2.b).

[360] ESMA has already assessed 18 countries, which makes the Commission's objection cited above in n 331 (ch 1) that ESMA has not made sufficient progress in its evaluations of countries invalid. See ESMA, 'Advice to the European Parliament, the Council and the Commission on the application of the AIFMD passport to non-EU AIFMs and AIFs' ESMA/2016/1140 (n 331) and ESMA, 'Advice to the European Parliament, the Council and the Commission on the application of the AIFMD passport to non-EU AIFMs and AIFs' ESMA/2015/1236 (n 331); for a summary of the results see Zetzsche and Veidt (n 102) 836f.

[361] In Swiss financial markets law, the term 'market infrastructure' also includes trading venues (*Handelsplätze*, FinfraG, art 26(a)), which supports the argument of a close connection between the two. See FinfraG, art 2(a).

a) Trading venues

The classification of trading venues is at the heart of MiFID II. Trading venue is the generic term for regulated markets, multilateral trading facilities (MTFs) and organized trading facilities (OTFs).[362] Systematic internalizers are not qualified as trading venues because they do not operate a multilateral but a bilateral system. However, systematic internalizers are subject to a "tailored 'venue-like' regulation".[363] In this context, the question arises on how to deal with third country markets on the one hand and third country participants accessing EU markets on the other hand.

aa) Operation of EU trading venues A regulated market is operated or managed by a market operator who needs to be authorized by the competent authority of the respective Member State.[364] MTFs and OTFs can either be operated by market operators or investment firms. An operation in the form of an investment firm is possible because the operation of an MTF/OTF is qualified as an investment service. The same applies with regard to the dealing on own account, which is why the activity as a systematic internalizer is also qualified as an investment service.

MiFID II and MiFIR do not contain a third country regime for foreign operators of EU regulated markets. The regulation of such market access is not harmonized but remains within the competence of Member States.[365] The situation is different for the operation of MTFs and OTFs, as the third country regime in Articles 46ff MiFIR concerning investment firms applies because the operation of MTFs and OTFs is qualified as an investment service. Hence, third country investment firms registered with ESMA may operate an MTF or OTF domiciled in the EU.

bb) Specific obligations relating to trading venues There are numerous provisions referring to trading venues and linking various requirements and legal consequences to the existence of a specific trading venue. For example, EU law sometimes prescribes that specific trades must be carried out on EU trading venues. In a globalized world and in view of the extraterritorial scope of many European legal acts, third country trading venues must be classified into this scheme. In the above example, the question must therefore be answered as to whether the trading obligation can also be fulfilled on an equivalent third country trading venue. As there is no general equivalence mechanism governing trading venues, each obligation has its own equivalence mechanism.[366]

One example of a classification of a foreign trading venue is the definition of OTC derivatives in Article 2(7) EMIR. To meet the definition, the derivative contract must be executed outside of a regulated market and outside of a third country market equivalent to a regulated market. The Commission adopts implementing acts

362 MiFID II, art 4(1) no (24); Peter K Andersen, *EU Trading Venues* (Djøf Forlag 2018) 21–26.
363 Moloney (n 165) 462.
364 See MiFID II, art 4(1) no (18) and (21).
365 Danny Busch and Marije Louisse, 'MiFID II/MiFIR's Regime for Third-country Firms' in Danny Busch and Guido Ferrarini (eds), *Regulation of the EU Financial Markets: MiFID II and MiFIR* (OUP 2017) para 10.14.
366 This approach is subsequently identified as being 'obligation-based' and, because of the many disadvantages it entails, a reform is proposed in ch 5 B)I.

determining whether a third country market is regulated and supervised in an equivalent way to the requirements of Title III of MiFID II concerning regulated markets.[367] If that is not the case, a contract executed on the third country market is to be regarded as an OTC derivative.

Another equivalence provision concerning trading venues is included in the execution-only regime of MiFID II.[368] Articles 24 and 25 MiFID II set out the core of the conduct-of-business rules for investment firms when providing services to their clients.[369] An integral part of these rules is the appropriateness assessment, whereby the investment firm must determine whether the proposed product is suitable for the individual client by collecting information about them (know-your-customer principle).[370] However, there is an exemption from this obligation in the case of investment services consisting only in the execution or reception and transmission of client orders (execution-only regime).[371] In order for the exception to apply, four conditions must be met cumulatively. One of these requirements is that the service relates to a specific financial instrument, which includes shares traded on a third country market deemed equivalent to a regulated market as defined in MiFID II.[372] Consequently, the execution-only exception can also apply if the shares are traded on an equivalent third country market. The scope of this equivalence mechanism is, however, not limited to the execution-only regime. Article 23 MiFIR imposes a trading obligation on investment firms when trading in shares to ensure substantial trading takes place on organized markets or using systematic internalizers.[373] The trading obligation can also be fulfilled by trading on a venue located in a third country and recognized under MiFID II. Therefore, by allowing the trading of shares in third countries, market fragmentation is reduced.

A further trading obligation exists in the area of derivatives for financial and non-financial counterparties.[374] This obligation is a direct consequence of the GFC, and the subsequent reform initiated by the G20 Pittsburgh Summit.[375] These counterparties are not only European parties but may also encompass counterparties from third countries.[376] Hence, the trading obligation is applied extraterritorially. In addition to this extraterritorial application of the law, other legal systems may include a trading obligation that they likewise apply extraterritorially.[377] This creates the danger that

[367] EMIR, art 2a(1) and (2).

[368] MiFID II, art 25(4)(a).

[369] Martin Brenncke in Matthias Lehmann and Christoph Kumpan (eds), *European Financial Services Law* (Nomos 2019) MiFID II, art 25 para 1; Rüdiger Veil, 'Investment Services' in Rüdiger Veil (ed), *European Capital Markets Law* (3rd edn, Hart Publishing 2022) § 30; Matthias Lehmann, *Grundriss des Bank- und Kapitalmarktrechts* (CF Müller 2016) 107–11; Haentjens and de Gioia-Carabellese (n 268) 96–8.

[370] MiFID II, art 25(3).

[371] ibid art 25(4).

[372] ibid art 4(1) no (21).

[373] See MiFIR, recital 11; Christoph Kumpan and Finn Schmidt in Matthias Lehmann and Christoph Kumpan (eds), *European Financial Services Law* (Nomos 2019) MiFIR, art 23 para 1; on this equivalence mechanism from a Swiss perspective see Marco Toni and Lea Hungerbühler, 'Neue Handelspflicht für Aktien in der EU' (2017) 12 GesKR 205.

[374] MiFIR, art 28(1) and arts 32 and 34.

[375] G20 Pittsburgh Summit (n 105) para 13 third bullet point.

[376] MiFIR, art 28(2); Rezah Stegeman and Aron Berket, 'Derivatives' in Danny Busch and Guido Ferrarini (eds), *Regulation of the EU Financial Markets: MiFID II and MiFIR* (OUP 2017) para 15.14.

[377] See in Switzerland eg FinfraG, art 112.

transactions have to be executed twice (duplicative trading).[378] To mitigate this risk, the trading obligation can also be fulfilled by trading on a third country trading venue recognized as equivalent.[379] Even more far-reaching than the recognition of a third country trading venue is the recognition that a third country legal system is equivalent in the field of derivatives. If the Commission has adopted such an equivalence decision, a counterparty entering into a transaction subject to MiFIR is exempt from complying with the trading obligation (Article 28 MiFIR) as well as the clearing obligation for derivatives traded on regulated markets (Article 29 MiFIR).[380] This mechanism helps to avoid duplicative regulation as well as the emergence of legal conflicts.

Another example of the classification of third country trading venues into the European system exists in the area of market making. Market makers can be described as persons who are continuously available as counterparties to other market participants and enable them to realize transactions immediately.[381] They are mainly regulated in MiFIR and MiFID II. However, market makers enjoy some privileges in other legal acts. The Short Selling Regulation (SSR), for instance, contains strict notification and disclosure requirements as well as restrictions on uncovered short sales.[382] Market makers are exempted from these obligations because they contribute to the efficiency of and provide liquidity for capital markets.[383] What is considered a market making activity is defined in Article 2(1)(k) SSR. The activity needs to take place on a trading venue, or a third country market deemed equivalent by the Commission.[384] Therefore, market making activities on third country markets may also be exempted from the obligations under the SSR.

Further examples include the special relationship between CCPs and trading venues, more specifically, the mutual access rights of the two, which will be discussed in the next section. The question of access rights of third country trading venues and CCPS to benchmarks, set out in Article 38(2) and (3) MiFIR, has already been discussed in the section on benchmarks.[385]

MiFID II and MiFIR as the applicable public law apply only to EU regulated markets.[386] That is why they do not regulate third country trading venues granting direct market access to EU trading participants. This does, however, not lead to a gap in protection, as national legal orders often provide for a licensing requirement for third country markets in this respect.[387]

[378] Lehmann (n 248) MiFIR, art 28 para 25.
[379] MiFIR, art 28(1)(d) and (4).
[380] MiFIR, art 33(2); see concerning the clearing obligation also the next section.
[381] The definition in MiFID II, art 4(7) is very similar to the definition used above.
[382] See SSR, art 17(1) and arts 5–7 and 12–14.
[383] Klaus Ulrich Schmolke in Matthias Lehmann and Christoph Kumpan (eds), *European Financial Services Law* (Nomos 2019) SSR, art 17 para 1; SSR, recital 26.
[384] SSR, arts 2(1)(k) and 17(2).
[385] See ch 1 C)II.2.c).
[386] That is because MiFIR/MiFID II apply only, according to art 44(4) of the MiFID II, if the regulated market is registered in a Member State. This means *e contrario* that regulated markets registered in third countries do not fall under the remit of MiFIR/MiFID II. With a focus on German law see Lehmann (n 10) paras 263ff.
[387] See in Germany, for example, § 102 of the WpHG which interestingly exempts third country markets from the licensing obligation if the Commission adopted equivalence decisions relating to third country markets or investment firms in similar contexts. See in the French legal system Règlement Général de L'autorité des Marchés Financiers, art 513-3.

The different equivalence mechanisms described above all aim to integrate third country trading venues into the EU system and are all very alike. However, due to the obligation-based approach of the EU, there are five different mechanisms to determine equivalence, five different decisions by the Commission have to be made, and five different systems of monitoring and review of these decisions are in place.[388] This situation adversely affects the coherence of the legal acts, the consistency of the decision-making and it wastes much-needed resources, which is why the last chapter proposes the introduction of a sectoral approach.[389]

b) Central counterparties

Central counterparties (CCPs) are entities performing two primary functions as intermediaries in a transaction: clearing and settlement. As CCPs are the counterparty in many transactions, they reallocate counterparty risks and often pool these risks, which is why they are strictly regulated.[390] CCPs exist in both the securities and the derivatives market, with regulation focusing on the latter due to the experiences from the GFC.[391]

One reason for the key role of CCPs in the financial system is the clearing obligation for derivatives. This obligation is twofold: it is provided for in EMIR and MiFIR.[392] Under EMIR, CCPs must clear all OTC derivatives pertaining to a specific class that have been declared subject to that obligation.[393] Under MiFIR, operators of regulated markets must ensure that all transactions in derivatives traded on their markets are cleared by a CCP.[394] Against the background that various countries have implemented extraterritorial clearing obligations for cross-border derivative transactions, the chances of duplicative or conflicting rules are high. This leads to a fragmentation of the derivatives market, which in turn weakens CCPs as the positive network effects are reduced and they become less efficient. To avoid duplicative or even conflicting rules, both EMIR and MiFIR provide for the possibility to be exempted from the clearing obligation if the Commission adopts an equivalence decision regarding a third country and at least one party to the contract is established in that third country.[395]

When a derivative transaction must be cleared, this clearing obligation may be fulfilled by an authorized CCP established in the Union or a third country CCP recognized by ESMA. Legal persons providing clearing services as a CCP in the EU have to be authorized by the NCA and observe organizational and prudential requirements and the conduct of business rules.[396] This authorization is effective for the entire

[388] MiFID II, art 25(4); MiFIR, arts 28(1) and 38(1); EMIR, art (2a); SSR, art 17(2).
[389] See extensively in ch 5 B)I.
[390] Paolo Saguato and Guido Ferrarini, 'Clearing House and Systemic Risk' in Douglas W Arner and others (eds), *Systemic Risk in the Financial Sector: Ten Years after the Great Crash* (CIGI 2019) 101ff; Evariest Callens, *Regulation of Central Counterparties (CCPs) in Light of Systemic Risk* (Intersentia 2022).
[391] Jon Gregory, *Central Counterparties* (Wiley 2014) 41ff; Maximilian Brambring, *Zentrales Clearing von OTC-Derivaten unter EMIR* (Mohr Siebeck 2017) 123ff.
[392] Regarding the interplay of the two obligations see Lehmann (n 248) MiFIR, art 29 para 5; Stegeman and Berket (n 376) paras 15.32–15.34.
[393] EMIR, arts 4(1) and 5(2).
[394] MiFIR, art 29.
[395] EMIR, art 13(3) and (2); MIFIR, art 33(3) and (2).
[396] EMIR, art 14(1); see EMIR Title IV for the requirements for CCPs.

Union.[397] CCPs established in a third country may only provide clearing services in the Union if they are recognized by ESMA pursuant to Article 25(1) and (2) EMIR. This recognition is based on an equivalence decision by the Commission.[398] It further requires that the CCP is authorized and subject to effective supervision and enforcement in the third country, that a cooperation agreement has been established between the competent authorities and that the third country does not have strategic deficiencies in its national anti-money laundering and counter financing of terrorism regime. Since the latest reform of EMIR 2.2, the CCP must also be a Tier 1 CCP and not a Tier 2 CCP.[399] The latter are CCPs that ESMA has identified as being systemically important or likely to become systemically important for the financial stability of the Union or a Member State.[400] ESMA can only recognize Tier 2 CCPs under additional conditions, and, in the case of particularly systemically relevant CCPs, recognition can even be completely denied.[401] Hence, the requirements of the equivalence mechanisms have been tightened significantly.

Since CCPs thus play an important role under the current regulatory framework, the question of access rights to CCPs and of CCPs to trading venues arises. In general, CCPs and trading venues must grant access in a non-discriminatory and transparent manner.[402] Third country trading venues may, however, only request access to CCPs established in the Union if the Commission adopts a decision determining that these trading venues comply with equivalent requirements.[403] For the third country trading venue to be permitted to make use of the access rights, an additional equivalence decision by the Commission pursuant to Article 38(3) MiFIR has to be adopted. Similar rules apply to the access of third country CCPs to trading venues established in the Union. Again, two equivalence decisions are required. First, third country CCPs must be recognized by ESMA in accordance with Article 25 EMIR and, secondly, an equivalence decision by the Commission is required pursuant to Article 38(3) MiFIR.[404] The issue of access rights of third country CCPs to EU benchmarks has been outlined above.[405]

c) Central securities depositories

Central securities depositories (CSDs) may perform notary services, central maintenance or settlement services and are regulated under the CSD Regulation (CSDR). CSDs must be authorized by the NCA of the Member State in which they are established.[406] This authorization is valid for the entire EEA (passporting).[407] At the outset,

[397] ibid art 14(2).

[398] EMIR, art 25(2)(a) and (6); see extensively n Pennesi (n 213) 178–80; Callens (n 390) 437–518.

[399] See the newly introduced EMIR, art 25(2)(e); Pennesi (n 213n) 185–98; Matthias Lehmann, 'Derivateclearing post-Brexit' (2021) 33 ZBB/JBB 177, 184ff; Sebastian Steuer, 'EMIR 2.2 und die Aufsicht über systemrelevante Drittstaaten-CCPs' (2021) 21 BKR 272, 274f.

[400] EMIR, art 25(2a); Pablo Iglesias-Rodriguez, 'Supervisory Cooperation in the Single Market for Financial Services: United in Diversity' (2018) 41 Fordham Intl LJ 589, 658–61.

[401] EMIR, art 25(2b) and (2c); referring to these CCPs as 'Tier 2 plus CCPs' see Lehmann (n 399) 186.

[402] EMIR, arts 7(1) and 8(1); MiFIR, arts 35(1) and 36(1).

[403] MiFIR, arts 38(1) first sentence and 28(4).

[404] See Lehmann (n 248) MiFIR, art 38 para 3.

[405] See ch 1 C)II.2.c).

[406] CSDR, arts 10 and 16(1).

[407] ibid art 23(1).

third country CSDs may provide services within the Union without being regulated.[408] However, if CSDs provide core services (notary services, central maintenance services or settlement services) or want to set up a branch in a Member State, they must be authorized by the NCA and are subject to the CSDR.[409] Alternatively, a CSD may apply for recognition to ESMA pursuant to Article 25(4) CSDR. Among other conditions, an equivalence decision by the Commission is needed for the recognition by ESMA.[410] As a consequence of the recognition, CSDs may provide services within the territory of the Union without being subject to the obligations of the CSDR and without being supervised by a national authority.[411]

d) Trade repositories

To enhance transparency in the derivatives market, Article 9 EMIR provides for a reporting obligation for counterparties and CCPs for exchange-traded derivatives as well as OTC derivatives.[412] The reporting shall be submitted either to a trade repository registered with ESMA and established in the Union or to a third country trade repository recognized by ESMA. A recognition by ESMA requires, inter alia, an equivalence decision by the Commission.[413] A full exemption from the reporting obligation is provided for by the equivalence mechanism of Article 13(2) and (3) EMIR, where an equivalence decision has been adopted and one of the parties is established in that third country. To further improve the quality and transparency of the reported data, the updated EMIR 2.2 grants supervisory authorities from third countries the right to have direct access to information in trade repositories established in the Union on the basis of equivalence and reciprocity.[414]

An additional reporting obligation can be found in the SFT Regulation for counterparties to so-called securities financing transactions (SFTs).[415] Again, the reporting shall be submitted either to a trade repository registered with ESMA and established in the Union or to a third country trade repository recognized by ESMA, conditional upon a prior equivalence decision by the Commission.[416] This mechanism is modelled on the general one in EMIR and is worded almost identically. The fact that the legislator introduced an additional mechanism for SFTs is a consequence of the obligation-based approach, which is one of the main reasons for the lack of clarity of equivalence, as will be discussed extensively later.[417] A further equivalence regime is provided for in Article 21 SFT Regulation, which again replicates the general regime of EMIR. The provision does not grant market access to third country trade repositories. However, it

[408] ibid art 25(1).
[409] ibid art 25(2).
[410] ibid art 25(9); Wymeersch (n 24) 270f.
[411] CSDR, art 25(11).
[412] Paolo Lucantoni in Matthias Lehmann and Christoph Kumpan (eds), *European Financial Services Law* (Nomos 2019) EMIR, art 9 para 1. The regime outlined in the following will be fundamentally changed according to the Commission's current proposals of 7 December 2022. At the time of publication of this book, it was not yet foreseeable how the proposals would develop. They were therefore left aside.
[413] EMIR, arts 77(1) and 75(1).
[414] ibid art 76a, as amended by Regulation (EU) 2019/834 of 20 November 2019.
[415] SFT Regulation, art 4(1); for the definition of SFTs, see SFT Regulation, art 1(11).
[416] SFT Regulation, art 19(3)–(5) and (1).
[417] See ch 5 B)I.

exempts counterparties from the reporting obligation if the Commission has adopted an implementing act establishing equivalence of the third country legal framework with the reporting obligation of the SFT Regulation and one of the parties is established in that third country.

5. Exemptions for central banks and public bodies of third countries

A number of legal acts exempt the European System of Central Banks and other public bodies from its application. One example of that is provided for in MiFIR, which excludes the application of certain provisions for specific transactions where the counterparty is a member of the European System of Central Banks.[418] These provisions include pre- and post-trade transparency requirements for trading venues as well as certain disclosure obligations for investment firms, particularly systematic internalizers.[419] These types of exemptions are expanded in some instances to third country central banks and public bodies. The MiFIR exemption just described can, for instance, be extended to the Bank for International Settlement and central banks of third countries in case the Commission issues an equivalence decision.[420] Another example is the restriction of the application of EMIR to central banks and public bodies from third countries following an equivalence decision by the Commission.[421] The same applies to the reporting obligation and the requirements concerning the reuse of financial instruments received under a collateral agreement for securities financing transactions, which do not apply if the Commission adopts a delegated act.[422] A further example in which third country central banks and public bodies can be exempted from obligations can be found in Article 6 MAR. This provision empowers the Commission to exempt public bodies and central banks of third countries from the application of the MAR, but only for reasons of monetary and public debt management activities (paragraph 5) and for measures concerning the fight against climate change (paragraph 6).

One reason for the privileged treatment certainly is the motive to avoid interference with the monetary policy executed by these organs.[423] This is reflected in the fact that many exceptions demand that the activities pursue specific purposes, such as monetary policy.[424] Moreover, public institutions often have statutory obligations in place limiting their scope of action, for example, mechanisms to ensure non-discriminatory treatment of price-sensitive information regarding the MAR.[425] Hence, an additional regulation is not necessary.

418 MiFIR, art 1(6).

419 The provisions contained in the exemption are MiFIR, arts 8, 10, 18, and 21.

420 MiFIR, art 1(9); see also Commission Delegated Regulation (EU) 2017/1799 of 12 June 2017; CEPS, 'Study on exemptions for third-country central banks and other entities under the Market Abuse Regulation and the Markets in Financial Instruments Regulation' MARKT/2014/069/G3/ST/OP (2015) https://www.ecmi.eu/sites/default/files/study_on_exemptions_for_third-country_central_banks_and_other_entities_under_mar_and_mifir.pdf (accessed 12 November 2022).

421 EMIR, art 1(6) and (4).

422 SFT Regulation, art 2(4) and (2) regarding the obligations of SFT Regulation, arts 4 and 15.

423 Lucantoni (n 412) EMIR, art 3 para 14.

424 See eg MiFIR, art 1(6); MAR, art 6(1).

425 See MAR, recitals 21 and 22; Carsten Gerner-Beuerle in Matthias Lehmann and Christoph Kumpan (eds), *European Financial Services Law* (Nomos 2019) MAR, art 6 para 1.

6. Legislative system behind the fragmented picture

A closer look at where equivalence provisions can be found reveals a very fragmented picture.[426] At first sight, there seems to be no system as to whether equivalence provisions have been included in legal acts or not. That is why the equivalence approach has been described as being 'piece-meal'.[427] Because almost all relevant legal acts have been amended since equivalence first became law, a lack of time does not explain why equivalence has not yet been included.[428] *Sharon Bowles*, who was chair of the ECON Committee and chaired some of the trilogue negotiations, summarized the situation regarding consistency in the legislation as follows:

> To be honest, I think that this [creating consistency] is the job of the Commission, and they have fallen down on it again, because they are in the negotiation. It has happened a lot, especially on third countries. Third-country regimes always seem to get pushed right to the end. There is a big danger that you get what is, if you like, some rubbish compromise out of it.[429]

The Commission tried to justify these significant differences by referring to the uniqueness of each regulatory area and a need for a tailor-made approach.[430] Even though this justification is not fully convincing, some legislative concepts can be recognized behind the fragmented legislation.

a) Focus on professional investors and protection of retail investors

One guiding principle seems to be the restriction of equivalence to professional parties in the broader sense. Retail clients with typically fewer assets, less experience and less knowledge are considered more vulnerable by the legislator, which is why they are not equally affected by equivalence.

Proof of this thesis is the regulation of third country investment firms, which, following an equivalence decision by the Commission and a registration with ESMA, are only allowed to provide services to professional clients. This guiding principle also explains why foreign prospectuses are recognized under the Prospectus Regulation but foreign key information documents under the PRIIP Regulation are not. Based on this finding, the conclusion can be drawn that the more the interests of retail investors are affected, the more limited is the scope of equivalence. The UCITS Directive, for instance, guaranteeing a high level of investor protection, does not contain an equivalence provision. The AIFMD, on the other hand, which deals with higher-risk investment funds, provides for an equivalence mechanism. This hypothesis also explains

[426] Ceyssens and Tarde (n 254) 812; for a very critical view see Ferran (n 236) 50ff.

[427] Niamh Moloney, 'Brexit, the EU and Its Investment Banker: Rethinking "Equivalence" for the EU Capital Market' (2017) LSE Working Paper Series 5/2017, 46 http://eprints.lse.ac.uk/73429/1/WPS2017-05_Moloney.pdf (accessed 12 November 2022).

[428] However, time is an argument for different wordings and styles of writing, as will be shown in ch 2 A) III.1.

[429] See House of Lords, 'Review of the EU Financial Regulatory Framework' Inquiry (22 July 2014) Question 15 http://data.parliament.uk/writtenevidence/committeeevidence.svc/evidencedocument/eu-sub-a-economic-and-financial-affairs-committee/review-of-the-eu-financial-regulatory-framework/oral/11723.html (accessed 12 November 2022).

[430] Commission (n 108) 4ff.

why equivalence provisions are missing in important areas such as banking (deposit-taking), lending, payment services, mortgage lending and direct insurance, which all greatly affect retail investors.

b) Market access solely to ensure functioning of EU markets

Another motive of the legislator is to safeguard the functioning of the financial system in the Union while at the same time not opening markets more than necessary. The attempt to achieve this balance could be well observed in the context of Brexit with regard to the equivalence for CCPs in EMIR. Many CCPs are located in London and their clearing capacity is needed for the European derivatives market. Complete exclusion of British CCPs could therefore have endangered Europe as a financial centre, at least temporarily,[431] which is why the EU still allows CCPs from the UK to enter the European market via equivalence. However, the EU does not want to give all CCPs access to the European market via equivalence, as this would make the EU dependent on the UK and deprive it of control over such an important market infrastructure. That is why the EU limits market access primarily to Tier 1 CCPs (not systemically important).[432] The Commission has also put a time limit on its equivalence decision for UK CCPs.[433] In this way, the EU ensures the proper functioning of its markets while at the same time providing incentives for CCPs from third countries to re-establish themselves in the Union.

Further evidence of this hypothesis is provided by the equivalence provisions concerning statutory auditors in the SAD. On the one hand, after an equivalence decision has been adopted, statutory auditors do not need to be registered in the Union to audit undertakings established in a third country. Without such an arrangement, duplicative regulation and supervision would occur, which would keep companies out of the European market. On the other hand, auditors are not allowed to audit undertakings established in the Union. A similar regulation exists for credit rating agencies. Under the equivalence mechanism of the CRA Regulation, ratings are eligible for regulatory purposes for third country entities or financial instruments but not for undertakings established or financial instruments issued in the Union. Again, a restriction to entities and financial instruments without systemic importance can be observed.

This restrictive approach is underlined by the Commission's current plan announced on 7 December 2022 to deepen the Capital Markets Union. The Commission proposes to amend the recognition of third country CCPs. According to the draft, the Commission has the power to adopt an equivalence decision even if the regulation and supervision in a third country is not equivalent, as long as such a decision is 'in the interests of the Union' and is 'considering the potential risks for the Union financial stability'.[434]

[431] Thierry Philipponnat, 'The Landscape for Post-Brexit European Financial Services' in John Armour and Horst Eidenmüller (eds), *Negotiating Brexit* (CH Beck 2017) 19–20; Lehmann and Schürger (n 277) 368.

[432] EMIR, art 25(2)(e). Market access barriers for Tier 2 CCPs are much higher and some particularly systemically relevant CCPs are a priori excluded from market access via equivalence.

[433] Commission Implementing Decision (EU) 2020/1308 of 21 September 2020, art 2. This equivalence decision was extended but again temporarily restricted to encourage UK based CCPs to relocate to the EU. See Commission Implementing Decision (EU) 2022/174 of 8 February 2022, art 2.

[434] Commission, 'Proposal for a Regulation of the European Parliament and of the Council amending Regulations (EU) No 648/2012, (EU) No 575/2013 and (EU) 2017/1131 as regards measures to mitigate

To put it in a nutshell, the Commission nowadays tries to restrict market access as far as possible without damaging the European market. This overly protective approach seems surprising in view of the rather liberal founding idea of equivalence, as expressed by Frits Bolkestein and Alexander Schaub, and can only be explained in light of the GFC and Brexit.[435] This approach creates the risk that market access for third country financial service providers will be unduly hindered and that third country market participants will even stay out of the European market altogether, thereby depriving European markets of the necessary liquidity and excessively limiting the supply to the detriment of investors in the Union. From a global perspective, the policy leads to a far-reaching fragmentation of markets, thereby hampering the building of a global financial market.

c) Avoiding dependencies and attracting foreign players

A third central theme is the avoidance of dependencies on foreign supervision and the corresponding aim of encouraging financial market players to settle in Europe. This reduction of dependencies is one of the central lessons from the GFC. The objective of regulatory sovereignty has recently been fortified by Brexit and the fact that it has led to the emergence of a new third country market directly next to the EU. A typical example of that goal is the many equivalence regimes limiting (or at least setting higher barriers regarding) market access for systemically important players, particularly ratings in the CRA Regulation, CCPs in EMIR, and investment firms in MiFIR. The location policy pursued by the EU in this way is also being communicated more and more openly, as can be seen from the example of CCP regulation.[436]

III. How does equivalence work? Investigating the process

This section will take a closer look at the process of how equivalence in the different legal acts is obtained. In most cases, the procedure for obtaining equivalence is not identical with the adoption of just an equivalence decision.[437] Usually, the equivalence decision is only one among several prerequisites for equivalence. Some regimes even require two equivalence decisions.[438] The final stage of equivalence is to be understood in this context as the stage at which the legal consequences, which will be described in Chapter 2 C), take effect.

excessive exposures to third-country central counterparties and improve the efficiency of Union clearing markets' COM (2022) 697 final.

[435] See ch 1 C)I.5.c) and d); see the speeches by Frits Bolkestein (EU Commission), 'EU-US regulatory co-operation on financial markets: A matter of necessity' SPEECH/03/96 (24 February 2003) and Alexander Schaub (DG Internal Market), 'Testimony before the Committee on Financial Services U.S. House of Representatives' (n 135).

[436] See ECB, 'Eurosystem Oversight Policy Framework' (July 2016) 12ff https://www.ecb.europa.eu/pub/pdf/other/eurosystemoversightpolicyframework201607.en.pdf (accessed 12 November 2022); this policy is also indicated in recitals 6–8, as well as 19 and 20 of Commission Implementing Decision (EU) 2022/174 of 8 February 2022, which justifies the time limit included in the equivalence decision in relation to UK CCPs.

[437] This section will not deal with the process of issuing an equivalence decision. See ch 2 A)I.1.

[438] See eg for the access of third country CCPs to trading venues established in the Union art 38(1) second sentence of MiFIR, which requires equivalence decisions pursuant to art 25 of EMIR and art 38(3) of MiFIR.

There are basically three different ways of how equivalence is obtained in EU legislation. It can be differentiated between mechanisms where the equivalence decision is sufficient to bring about the legal consequences (1.). Other EU acts require some kind of additional registration—usually with one of the ESAs—from the third country firm after the decision has been adopted (2.). The third type consists of two different discretionary measures, an equivalence decision at the first level and a decision by a national authority at the second level (3.).

1. One-step process

The shortest and easiest way for financial service providers to reap the benefits of equivalence is a one-step process. In regimes consisting of one-step processes, the legal consequences of equivalence will automatically take effect after the equivalence decision has been adopted. There will be no other authority or agency deciding on this matter. This may be the only situation where the procedure and requirements of equivalence are identical to those of the equivalence decision, as the decision may be the only prerequisite for equivalence. This is the case, for example, with the equivalence regime in relation to the country-by-country reporting under the Accounting Directive. But there may also be additional prerequisites for equivalence, such as reciprocity in MiFIR regarding the admission of third country trading venues for the trading obligation.[439] However, these other prerequisites do not include (discretionary) acts by the administration. Typical examples of this one-step process are equivalence mechanisms in relation to third country central banks and other public bodies, which are exempted from specific regulation.[440] Other examples include the provisions in the Transparency Directive, the AIFMD, and all equivalence mechanisms in the CRR II. These one-step processes are either conducted exclusively at the European or national level, while this book deals only with the former category of mechanisms.[441]

On the one hand, such one-step processes achieve full harmonization of the Member States' relations with third countries, thereby creating a single foreign policy with regard to market access for financial actors. They prevent a downward spiral, which can result from the fact that Member States, in the fight over third country service providers, impose ever lower requirements on them. Such a race to the bottom could possibly endanger the financial stability in the Union. Furthermore, one-step processes simplify the legal situation for third country firms that no longer have to look into different national legal systems to find out the obligations imposed on them for market access. On the other hand, these processes interfere more deeply with the national sovereignty of Member States than two-step processes. In other words, there is no right or wrong solution even though from an economic point of view, one-step

[439] MiFIR, art 28(1)(d).

[440] EMIR, art 1(6); SFT Regulation, art 2(4); MiFIR, art 1(9); MAR, art 6(5) and (6).

[441] One exception is AIFMD, art 37(2) regulating non-EU AIFM intending to manage EU AIFs and/or market AIFs managed by them in the Union. This equivalence mechanism is provided for in a European directive, but the decision is adopted at the national level. The mechanism is included because of its importance and because ESMA plays an important role in the decision-making (see AIFMD, art 37(9)).

processes are preferable. Rather, the choice of the process is the result of a political weighing.[442]

2. Two-step process involving ESAs

Similar to the procedure just presented is the two-step process involving ESAs. At the outset, there is again just one discretionary act, i.e. the equivalence decision. In addition, however, there is a 'registration procedure' in which the individual market participant must register with one of the ESAs following the equivalence decision. The legal effects of equivalence only take effect after this registration. The terminology used by the legislator to describe this 'registration procedure' varies between the terms registration (e.g. Article 46(2) MiFIR), recognition (e.g. Article 25(2) EMIR) and certification (e.g. Article 5(2) CRA Regulation).[443]

The equivalence mechanism for investment firms under MiFIR is the epitome of this process. According to Article 46(1) MiFIR, third country firms may only provide investment services to eligible counterparties and per se professional clients if they are registered with ESMA. The registration with ESMA requires, among other things, an equivalence decision by the Commission.[444] Therefore, an equivalence decision does not trigger the legal consequences but registration with ESMA. Other legislation containing such a registration includes the CRA Regulation, EMIR for CCPs and trade repositories, the CSDR for central securities depositories, the SFT Regulation regarding trade repositories, and the BMR for administrators of benchmarks.

Registration in the current legal acts is always with ESMA, which is why it could be described as a 'gatekeeper'.[445] In principle, registration is a formal step because ESMA does not have any room for manoeuvre.[446] The registration, therefore, does not serve the purpose of keeping out third country market participants. It rather creates more transparency on the European market. The list of all third country market participants who are allowed to access the market without having to be supervised facilitates their identification by supervisory authorities. Moreover, the list includes the specific services the undertaking is permitted to provide. Since the competent supervisory authority of the third country is also included in the register, it is easier to coordinate with that agency. Besides, as the register must be publicly accessible, investors can check whether their investment service provider is allowed to provide such services and by whom it is supervised.

One exception to this rule is ESMA's decision on the registration of third country CCPs under EMIR, which appears to be a discretionary act.[447] Pursuant to Article 25(2) EMIR, ESMA 'may' recognize a CCP established in a third country. The original draft of the provision by the Commission was still based on a binding decision,[448] but was

[442] Concerning the distribution of competences in equivalence mechanisms relating to disclosure see Schammo (n 166) 148ff.

[443] In the following, all types of registration are meant unless explicitly stated otherwise.

[444] MiFIR, art 46(2)(a).

[445] Moloney (n 29) 44; Niamh Moloney, *The Age of ESMA* (Hart Publishing 2018) 338.

[446] In relation to the registration under MiFIR see Ammann (n 262) paras 187ff.

[447] A second exception is CSDR, art 25(4). Overall, the same considerations as those under EMIR apply to this exemption.

[448] See 'shall' in Commission, 'Proposal for a Regulation of the European Parliament and of the Council on OTC derivatives, central counterparties and trade repositories' COM (2010) 484 final, art 23(2).

later amended by the European Parliament without further justification.[449] It is unclear in what way ESMA should have discretionary powers. In view of the *Meroni* doctrine by the ECJ and the fact that the Commission has already exercised discretion regarding the equivalence decision, there are many indications that ESMA's discretion is very limited.[450] Otherwise, conflicts would also arise with the Commission. Both ESMA and the Commission need to review whether the CCP is 'subject to effective supervision and enforcement'.[451] Potential conflicts can only be mitigated if ESMA's assessment is restricted to an entity-based review and does not encompass the general level of supervision and enforcement already analysed in the equivalence decision.[452]

3. Two-step process involving NCAs

The course of the two-step process differs from the first two in that it does not solely take place at the European level. Instead, most of these mechanisms are designed as purely national procedures. If a set of requirements, including equivalence of the third country legal framework in a given sector, is fulfilled, the NCA of a Member State may grant market access or at least exempt third country firms from certain obligations. Thus, these mechanisms appear as one-step processes operative at the national level.

To ensure uniform application, the Commission may, however, decide on the prerequisite of equivalence. In this way, these regimes are transformed into a two-step process. In a first step, the Commission adopts an equivalence decision. This equivalence decision is a prerequisite for further proceedings at the second level by the NCA. The legal consequences of equivalence take effect only after the NCA has adopted a decision in a second step. One example of a two-step process is the acceptance of a prospectus drawn up in accordance with the laws of a third country.[453] First, the Commission may adopt an equivalence decision stating that the requirements imposed by the third country on the issuer are equivalent to the requirements under the Prospectus Regulation.[454] Second, the NCA of the home Member State of a third country issuer may approve that prospectus for an offer of securities to the public or admission to trading on a regulated market in Europe.[455] Other examples include third country statutory auditors under the SAD, the provisions on group solvency for related third country insurers as well as the supervision of insurers with a parent undertaking outside the Union under Solvency II.

Therefore, different from the one-step process described at the beginning, this process takes place at both the European (level 1) as well as the national level (level 2). As a

[449] European Parliament, 'Amendments by the European Parliament to the Commission proposal' A7-0223/34 (2012) https://www.europarl.europa.eu/doceo/document/A-7-2011-0223-AM-034-034_EN.pdf?redirect (accessed 12 November 2022).

[450] Case C-9/56 *Meroni v High Authority* ECLI:EU:C:1958:7; on the *Meroni* doctrine see in more detail ch 5 B)II.1.a).

[451] See EMIR, art 25(2)(b) and art 25(6)(b); on that conflict see IRSG, 'The EU's Third Country Regimes and Alternatives to Passporting' (23 January 2017) p. 64–65 https://www.irsg.co.uk/assets/IRSG-Full-report-The-EUs-third-country-regimes-and-alternatives-to-passporting.pdf (accessed 12 November 2022).

[452] Nevertheless, critical of this new mechanism in EMIR 2.2 see ch 5 B)II.3.b).

[453] Prospectus Regulation, art 29. This regulation is currently being revised and there are plans to convert it into a one-step process. See Commission (n 174) art 1(22).

[454] ibid art 29(3) subpara 2.

[455] ibid art 29(1); see ibid art 2(m)(iii) for the definition of a 'home Member State' concerning an issuer established in a third country.

result, the two-step process is more vulnerable to supervisory and political influences and consequently less likely to promote a consistent European solution regarding the treatment of third country actors.[456] Hence, this approach is more cumbersome and less attractive for third country market participants. Since most of the relevant legal factors have already been considered in the Commission's discretionary act at the first level, the question arises as to which additional factors should be assessed by NCAs as part of their discretion at the second level.[457] In many cases, only political considerations remain, which should, however, not be included in the decision-making process at all.[458] All these factors render the process less liberal. Yet, the two-step process preserves national sovereignty, which is why the choice of process is ultimately a political one.

456 Schammo (n 166) 181f.
457 This question is also raised in Schammo (n 166) 168.
458 See for a detailed discussion on why political considerations should not be included ch 2 B)II.2.b).

2
Equivalence in the EU: Key Requirements, Equivalence Decision, and Legal Consequences

A) Is equivalence a uniform concept or just a catchphrase? Similarities and differences between the 40 mechanisms

As outlined above, neither a legal definition of equivalence nor a common understanding of the term exists.[1] This unclear situation is hardly surprising in light of the 40 existing mechanisms with different prerequisites, processes, and legal consequences. The current state of equivalence is also strongly criticized by various scholars for this reason.[2] It is described as 'piece-meal, inconsistent and subject to a range of different procedures and conditions depending on the measure in question'.[3] Others observe that '[t]he resulting complexity is considerable and has been widely regretted'.[4]

The following analysis attempts to present and evaluate the main similarities and differences between the requirements of the various mechanisms (I.). Afterwards, some peculiarities of selected equivalence provisions are outlined, whereby the necessity of such tailor-made requirements is challenged since they are linked to considerable disadvantages (II.).

[1] See ch 1 C); Vassilis Hatzopoulos, 'Forms of Mutual Recognition in the Field of Services' in Ioannis Lianos and Okeoghene Odudu (eds), *Regulating Trade in Services in the EU and the WTO* (CUP 2012) 68–70; Eilís V Ferran, 'Financial Supervision' in Daniel Mügge (ed), *Europe and the Governance of Global Finance* (OUP 2014) 23. The closest it gets to a definition is Commission Regulation (EC) No 1569/2007 of 21 December 2007, art 2.

[2] Aleksandra Visekruna, 'The Access to the EU Financial Market for the Companies from Non-Member States' (2018) 2 ECLIC 656, 664; Eilís V Ferran, 'The UK as a Third Country Actor in EU Financial Services Regulation' (2017) 3 JFR 40, 56; Karel Lannoo, 'EU Financial Market Access After Brexit' (2016) 51 Intereconomics 255, 258: 'highly complex puzzle'. Even the European Parliament recognizes the need for a reform: 'underlines the need to evolve towards a consistent and coherent system of sensible recognition'. See European Parliament, 'Report on Stocktaking and Challenges of the EU Financial Services Regulation' A8-0360/2015 (2015) para 40 https://www.europarl.europa.eu/doceo/document/A-8-2015-0360_EN.pdf (accessed 12 November 2022).

[3] Niamh Moloney, 'Brexit, the EU and Its Investment Banker: Rethinking "Equivalence" for the EU Capital Market' (2017) LSE Working Paper Series 5/2017, 46 http://eprints.lse.ac.uk/73429/1/WPS2017-05_Moloney.pdf (accessed 12 November 2022).

[4] Eddy Wymeersch, 'Third-Country Equivalence and Access to the EU Financial Markets Including in Case of Brexit' (2018) 4 JFR 209, 221. For a warning of further complication in the course of the reforms see Nathan de Arriba-Sellier, 'The Brexit Reform of European Financial Supervision: Lost in Transition?' (2019) 30 EBLR 695, 718f.

Equivalence and Substituted Compliance in Financial Markets Law. Jonas Schürger,
Oxford University Press. © Jonas Schürger 2023. DOI: 10.1093/oso/9780198876748.003.0002

I. Key requirements

In the analysis of the requirements, a distinction can be made between the three steps described above.[5] Some requirements may exist at the level of the equivalence decision; others only become relevant at the time of registration. However, the allocation of the requirements does not appear to be based on substantive considerations and will therefore be left aside in the following.[6] In the scenario of a two-step process, Member States may also demand additional requirements at the second level unless the respective EU legal act demands full harmonization. In view that full harmonization nowadays is the rule rather than the exception, the leeway of national legislators is very limited, which is why the national level is excluded from this analysis.[7] The prerequisites presented in the following are arranged according to the frequency of their occurrence in equivalence mechanisms.

1. Equivalence decision

The constitutive element of all regimes is the equivalence decision. Depending on the level responsible for the decision-making, a differentiation can be made between national or European mechanisms, whereas this book deals exclusively with the latter.[8] But even if the EU is in principle competent for the decision on equivalence, some mechanisms allow national competent authorities (NCAs) to take an equivalence decision if no decision has yet been adopted at the European level. However, from the moment the EU adopts an equivalence decision, Member States are no longer allowed to deviate from that decision unless otherwise provided.[9] This 'blocking effect' of the European decision is explicitly laid down in some regimes.[10] In other cases, it follows from the rationale of equivalence decisions at the European level, which is 'to ensure uniform conditions', as is explicitly stated in some provisions.[11] Yet, the blocking

[5] See ch 1 C)III.

[6] Almost all requirements can be found at both decision-making levels. A notable exception is that of cooperation agreements, which is never part of the equivalence decision, but only exists at the second level. This is because ESAs and NCAs, which are competent for the second level, are also responsible for the conclusion of such agreements.

[7] There are many factors contributing to the limited room for action of Member States, including that directives have largely been replaced by regulations, that the *Lamfalussy* process allows the EU to regulate in greater detail, including on technical issues, that supervision has shifted more to the European level and that the objective of a 'single rulebook' is more actively pursued. See Rüdiger Veil, 'Europäische Kapitalmarktunion' (2014) 43 ZGR 544; Rüdiger Veil, 'Legislative Powers for Regulating and Harmonising Capital Markets' in Rüdiger Veil (ed), *European Capital Markets Law* (3rd edn, Hart Publishing 2022) § 3 para 17.

[8] See art 5 of the CRA Regulation for a purely European regime and art 50(1)(e) of the UCITS Directive concerning the investment policy for a purely national one. There are also hybrid mechanisms, such as art 18 of the Financial Conglomerates Directive, in which guidance is provided at the European level, but the final decision is adopted at the national level. See Olivier Girard, 'Les méthodes de suppression des frontières au plan mondial dans le domaine bancaire et financier' (2007–2008) 3 EUREDIA 349, 361–64.

[9] See eg SAD, art 46(2), which contains the general rule as well as an exception to this rule.

[10] See Solvency II, arts 227(2) subpara 1 and 260(1) subpara 2; only in certain instances see SAD, art 46(2).

[11] See Transparency Directive, art 23(4) subpara 1; SAD, arts 45(6) subpara 1 and 46(2) subpara 1; see also TFEU, art 291(2), which is the enabling provision for the equivalence decisions; for a consenting view see Pierre Schammo, *EU Prospectus Law* (CUP 2011) 152; see the detailed analysis in ibid 176ff; see also the case law of the ECJ in Case C-22/70 *AETR* ECLI:EU:C:1971:32, paras 17–18 and Case C-476/98 *Commission v Germany* ECLI:EU:C:2002:631, paras 109–110.

effect will only apply when the EU adopts a formal decision. If the Commission rejects equivalence informally and outside of the official decision-making process, Member States remain responsible.[12]

Each time the EU has the sole decision-making power, it is the Commission's duty to act. In the case of hybrid mechanisms characterized by the involvement of the European as well as the national level in the equivalence decision, other EU institutions also play a role. One example is Article 37 of the Alternative Investment Fund Managers Directive (AIFMD), which requires the European Securities and Markets Authority (ESMA) to issue advice to NCAs, which are then in charge of the final decision.[13]

a) Procedure of the decision-making

The Commission adopts equivalence decisions in the form of implementing acts, mostly based on Article 291(2) of the Treaty on the Functioning of the European Union (TFEU).[14] Unfortunately, the relevant equivalence provisions do not specify many details regarding the procedure, which is why the reader is left in the dark. This is one reason why the procedure is often criticized as being opaque.[15] To shed light on this process, general principles of administrative and constitutional law need to be taken into account.[16]

The initiation of an administrative proceeding, which may lead to the adoption of an equivalence decision, is left to the discretion of the Commission. Only in a few cases, an explicit right for Member States or third country authorities to request such a procedure is foreseen.[17] Whether service providers from third countries have a right to a decision will be discussed extensively later.[18]

Many equivalence provisions refer to the examination procedure of the 2011 Comitology Regulation, in which a committee composed of representatives of the Member States delivers an opinion to the Commission.[19] This allows national interests to be taken into account in the decision, but at the same time, entails the risk of

[12] Otherwise, legal certainty would be unduly impaired because it would be unclear when Member States would lose their competence. This result can also be inferred from Case C-22/70 *AETR* (n 11) paras 17–18. Whether the Commission can formally adopt negative equivalence decisions depends on the wording of the respective legal act. If the Commission has the competence to do so, this decision has a blocking effect on the Member States. This follows from the telos, which is to ensure a uniform stance in the EU.

[13] AIFMD, art 37(2) and (9); see Ulf Klebeck and Jürg Frick in Frank Dornseifer and others (eds), *AIFM-Richtlinie* (CH Beck 2013) art 37 paras 221–26. Similar guidance procedures, not dealt with in this book, include art 116 of the CRD V regarding confidentiality regimes and art 127 of the CRD V regarding consolidated supervision.

[14] See Niamh Moloney, 'Capital Markets Union, Third Countries, and Equivalence' in Danny Busch, Emilios Avgouleas, and Guido Ferrarini (eds), *Capital Markets Union in Europe* (OUP 2018) para 6.18; see in general Paul P Craig, 'Delegated Acts, Implementing Acts and the New Comitology Regulation' (2011) 36 Eur L Rev 671.

[15] Moloney (n 14) para 6.19; Visekruna (n 2) 664; in the context of the US system see Tzung-bor Wei, 'The Equivalence Approach to Securities Regulation' (2007) 27 NW J Intl L & Bus 255, 292f.

[16] See ch 2 B)II.4.

[17] MiFID II, art 25(4)(a) subparas 2 and 3; EMIR, art 76a(2).

[18] ch 2 B)II.5.

[19] See eg MiFIR, arts 47(1) and 51(2); Robert Schütze (ed), *European Constitutional Law* (3rd edn, OUP 2021) 322ff.

politicization at the national level.[20] In some equivalence mechanisms, the European Securities Committee is also involved in the decision-making.[21] Where proceedings are opened, there is, in principle, no time limit for the Commission. Nonetheless, the European Court of Justice (ECJ) has always demanded a decision to be taken within a 'reasonable time'.[22] This case law is now laid down in Article 41(1) of the Charter of the Fundamental Rights of the European Union (CFR) and will be further analysed below.[23]

b) Constitutive effect of equivalence decisions

The design that a decision on equivalence is necessary to trigger the legal consequences is by no means mandatory. An alternative approach would be equivalence *ipso iure*, meaning that if a third country legal system is equivalent to that of the EU, no decision establishing this would be required. Rather the consequences would take effect by operation of law (*ex lege*). Such a design would be very liberal and market-oriented, as political interferences would be eliminated. Nevertheless, there are good reasons why the legislator opted for a model in which an equivalence decision is a prerequisite. The determination of whether a legal system of a third country is equivalent to that of the EU is very complex and technical.[24] If there is no decision, but legal consequences come into effect *ipso iure*, great legal uncertainty arises. This is particularly true for later changes in either the legal system of the EU or that of the third country, which may result in a loss of equivalence. Owing to the lack of legal certainty, financial service providers will also not trust in the market entrance via equivalence. Instead, they will opt for another way to access EU markets, such as establishing a subsidiary. This distrust is reasonable because of the high sanctions imposed for providing services without a licence, including criminal charges.[25]

Nonetheless, major concerns remain with regard to the equivalence decision. No uniform methodology for determining equivalence has yet emerged and the decision is a gateway for political considerations damaging the concept of equivalence. This tendency could be observed during the process of negotiating Brexit as well as during the negotiations of the Institutional Framework Agreement between the EU and Switzerland. These and other problems of equivalence decisions will be addressed in more detail in Chapter 2 B) below.

[20] Regarding the withdrawal of an equivalence decision see Dirk A Zetzsche in Matthias Lehmann and Christoph Kumpan (eds), *European Financial Services Law* (Nomos 2019) MiFIR, art 47 para 14.

[21] See eg AIFMD, art 59(1); MiFID II, art 89a(1); CRA Regulation, art 38(1), all referring to Commission Decision 2001/528/EC of 6 June 2001.

[22] Joined Cases C-238/99 P, 244/99 P, 245/99 P, 247/99 P, 250/99 P–252/99 P and 254/99 P *Limburgse Vinyl Maatschappij and Others v Commission* ECLI:EU:C:2002:582, para 179; Case C-113/04 P *Technische Unie v Commission* ECLI:EU:C:2006:593, para 40; Thomas von Danwitz, *Europäisches Verwaltungsrecht* (Springer 2008) 359–60.

[23] ch 2 B)II.4.c)aa).

[24] The technical nature of the decision already follows from the fact that the Commission normally requests technical advice from ESMA prior to adopting a decision. See extensively ch 2 B)I.

[25] See eg German Banking Act (KWG), § 54(1) no 2 or Code monétaire et financier, art L353-1 no 1.

c) Margin of appreciation

Since the legislator opted for a system that requires a decision on equivalence, the follow-up question needs to be addressed: does the competent authority have discretionary powers or is it a rule-bound process with full legal review and no room for manoeuvre for the authorities?[26] Here, the legislator was clearly in favour of leaving competent authorities room to act. Almost all equivalence provisions state that the Commission 'may' adopt implementing decisions. Even if a Member State requests an evaluation of a specific third country legal system, the Commission is often not bound by this request. This concept is expressed, for instance, in Recital 41 subparagraph 3 of the Markets in Financial Instruments Regulation (MiFIR).[27] The only exceptions to this rule are Article 21(6) subparagraph 3 AIFMD and Article 23(4) subparagraphs 1 and 3 Transparency Directive.

However, this finding does not prejudge the way in which discretion has to be exercised. The scope of action of authorities must be limited to ensure effective legal protection as guaranteed by Article 19(1) of the Treaty on the European Union (TEU) and Article 47 CFR.[28] These boundaries are of paramount importance, inter alia in the process of Brexit, and will be dealt with below.[29]

d) Involvement of European supervisory authorities

The European Banking Authority (EBA), ESMA, and the European Insurance and Occupational Pensions Authority (EIOPA), collectively the European supervisory authorities (ESAs), are involved in equivalence mechanisms at various points.[30] The ESAs are often responsible for the negotiation of cooperation agreements, they assess the systemic importance of service providers from third countries, in some mechanisms, they are competent for the registration, recognition or certification of those service providers, and they are part of the reviewing and monitoring process in the aftermath of an equivalence decision.[31] Most importantly in this context, however, is the fact that they are also involved in the equivalence decision.[32]

The role of ESAs in the equivalence assessment is often not expressly defined in the relevant provisions.[33] This is different for EIOPA in the insurance sector. All three

[26] See Wymeersch (n 4) 223–27. The terms margin of appreciation, room for manoeuvre, discretion, and decision-making leeway are used interchangeably in this book.

[27] 'The Commission should initiate ...'. The recital does not state that the Commission 'shall' initiate a proceeding, as would be the case if the assessment were mandatory.

[28] This concept was developed in: Case C-294/83 *Les Verts v Parliament* ECLI:EU:C:1986:166, para 23.

[29] ch 2 B)II.

[30] See extensively on the role of agencies in third country equivalence assessments Pieter Van Cleynenbreugel, 'Accountability Challenges for EU Agencies in the Context of Third Country Equivalence Assessments' in Herwig CH Hofmann, Ellen Vos, and Merijn Chamon (eds), *The External Dimension of EU Agencies and Bodies* (Edward Elgar Publishing 2019) 145ff.

[31] See ESAs Regulations, art 33. These are Regulation (EU) No 1093/2010 of 24 November 2010 (EBA Regulation), Regulation (EU) No 1094/2010 of 24 November 2010 (EIOPA Regulation), and Regulation (EU) No 1095/2010 of 24 November 2010 (ESMA Regulation), together referred to in this book as the ESAs Regulations.

[32] Arun Srivastava and Nina Moffatt, 'EU Equivalence Regime' in Jonathan Herbst and Simon Lovegrove (eds), *Brexit and Financial Regulation* (OUP 2020) para 4.28; Niamh Moloney, 'Reflections on the EU Third Country Regime for Capital Markets in the Shadow of Brexit' (2020) 17 ECFR 35, 42–48.

[33] See for an exception to this rule Transparency Directive, art 23(8); see also extensively on ESMA's role in equivalence decisions Niamh Moloney, *The Age of ESMA* (Hart Publishing 2018) 332ff.

equivalence provisions in Solvency II directly refer to the assistance of EIOPA in the process of determining equivalence.[34] For reasons of transparency, EIOPA also publishes a list of all third countries assessed as equivalent by the Commission.[35] However, this does not mean that ESAs do not contribute to other equivalence assessments. Based on Article 33(2) ESAs Regulations, the Commission may always request advice from them.[36]

This advice plays a key role in practice, as ESAs carry out thorough assessments.[37] Yet, the technical advice provided by ESAs is not binding on the Commission and thus has very little *legal* effect.[38] Since the Commission would act contradictorily if it first requests advice and afterwards completely disregards it, it must at least take into account the advice provided when adopting an equivalence decision. This limited binding effect creates the risk of tensions between the Commission and ESAs.[39] It also adds to the opacity of the process because it is unclear on what basis the Commission deviates from the authorities' advice. There is also no timetable for such decision-making processes.

These disadvantages have given rise to calls for greater involvement of ESAs.[40] An increased influence of technocratic authorities may also depoliticize the question. As Niamh Moloney put it:

> Yet ironically, this fear of politicization likely under-appreciates the merits of leaving decisions to technocrats, which is precisely what the democratically opaque structure of the Commission, and a fortiori the delegation of the initial assessment to the European Supervisory Authorities (ESAs), is intended to achieve.[41]

The best way to achieve a depoliticization is to transform equivalence decisions into implementing technical standards, respectively decisions in the meaning of Article 15 ESAs Regulations. This proposal will be extensively discussed in Chapter 5.[42]

[34] Solvency II, arts 172(2) subpara 1, 227(4) subpara 1, and 260(3) subpara 1.

[35] ibid arts 172(2) subpara 3, 227(4) subpara 3, and 260(3) subpara 3.

[36] See n 31 (ch 2); see ESMA and EIOPA Regulation, art 16a(4); EBA Regulation, art 34(1).

[37] Niamh Moloney, *EU Securities and Financial Markets Regulation* (3rd edn, OUP 2014) 920; see eg in-depth analyses: ESMA, 'Final report: Technical advice on CRA regulatory equivalence—US, Canada and Australia' ESMA/2012/259 (18 April 2012) and ESMA, 'Final report: Technical advice on third country regulatory equivalence under EMIR—US' ESMA/2013/1157 (1 September 2013).

[38] See the wording of ESMA Regulation, arts 16a and 33(2); see also ESMA, 'Final report—US' (n 37) 31; Niamh Moloney states that the advice is 'crucial but informal' (Moloney (n 33) 116). This follows also from the *Meroni* case law of the ECJ. See Case C-9/56 *Meroni v High Authority* ECLI:EU:C:1958:7.

[39] Moloney (n 37) 921.

[40] EBA, 'Opinion of the European Banking Authority on cooperation with third countries—Article 161(7) CRD' EBA/Op/2015/19 (10 December 2015); European Parliament, 'Resolution of 11 September 2018 on relationships between the EU and third countries concerning financial services regulation and supervision' (2018) OJ C433/19, nos 17–20 and 23; Ferran (n 2) 58.

[41] Niamh Moloney (House of Commons Economy Committee), 'The Impact of the EU Exit on Financial Services' (11 October 2016); see also Niamh Moloney, 'The European Union in International Financial Governance' (2017) 3 RSF 138.

[42] See ch 5 B)II.1.

2. Home country authorization and supervision of service providers
The requirement of an equivalent third country legal system would be superfluous if that system existed only as 'law in the books' but not as 'law in practice'. In other words: compliance with the requirements of the third country law must be ensured.[43] To achieve this, the financial service provider or product must first be authorized by its competent home country authority. In addition, it must be subject to effective supervision and enforcement to ensure 'full compliance with the requirements applicable in that third country', as formulated in MiFIR as a representative example of other mechanisms.[44]

Such a requirement is part of 26 of the 40 equivalence provisions examined. It is not included in the exemptions for third country central banks and public bodies as they are not supervised.[45] For the same reason, the requirement is missing in mechanisms concerning data exchange with third country authorities.[46] Authorization and supervision are finally not required in equivalence regimes dealing with third country accounting standards.[47] As a result, it can be stated that the requirement is included whenever it is reasonable to do so.

The concept of trust in the supervision of foreign authorities is one of the key features of equivalence, considering that it is the only way of market access that is not linked to (additional) EU supervision. The withdrawal of supervisory competences must be seen against the background of the principle of deference at the global level, which aims precisely at avoiding double supervision and supervisory conflicts.[48] It is thus a feature that is gaining particular importance in a globalized world and without which equivalence cannot function. In this context, the new developments in MiFIR and the European Market Infrastructure Regulation (EMIR) 2.2, which provide for partial application of European supervisory law and the possibility of onsite inspections on foreign territory,[49] are particularly worrying, as they gradually abandon the principle of trust and return to the idea of home country supervision. This development deprives equivalence of its core idea and will be discussed at length in Chapter 5 of this book.[50] Nonetheless, a withdrawal of supervisory competences is only feasible if supervisory authorities cooperate well, which leads to the next requirement included in most equivalence provisions.

[43] Matthias Lehmann, 'Legal Fragmentation, Extraterritoriality and Uncertainty in Global Financial Regulation' (2017) 37 OJLS 406, 430f.

[44] MiFIR, art 46(2)(b); see EMIR, art 25(6)(b) as an example where the requirement is also part of the equivalence decision.

[45] See EMIR, art 1(6); SFT Regulation, art 2(4); MiFIR, art 1(9); MAR, art 6(5) and (6); CRR II, arts 114(7), 115(4), and 116(5).

[46] See SAD, art 47.

[47] See SAD, art 45(5)(c); Transparency Directive, art 23(4) and (1); similarly, see Accounting Directive, art 46(1), which deals with third country reporting requirements in relation to country-by-country reports.

[48] See eg FSB, 'Jurisdictions' ability to defer to each other's OTC derivatives market regulatory regimes' Report to G20 Finance Ministers and Central Bank Governors (18 September 2014) 6 https://www.fsb.org/wp-content/uploads/r_140918.pdf (accessed 12 November 2022).

[49] Matthias Lehmann, 'La coopération avec les États tiers en matière bancaire et financière: La confiance n'exclut pas le contrôle' (2020) RB 35, 41; Moloney (n 32) 55ff.

[50] See ch 5 B)II.3.

3. Cooperation agreements

Supervisory cooperation plays a paramount role in a globalized world. This is not just true in an intra-EU context but also for the cooperation of NCAs and of ESAs with third country supervisory authorities.[51] The global financial crisis (GFC) has impressively demonstrated the consequences of failure to detect systemic risks and the lack of proper cooperation between supervisory authorities around the world.[52]

In the case of equivalence, close cooperation has several advantages. First and foremost, it promotes the mutual understanding of each other's supervisory legal system and practice. Without knowledge, insights and trust in the work of other authorities, the withdrawal of supervisory power by way of equivalence would not be feasible. Once equivalence has been established, close collaboration is needed to identify systemic risks. To maintain an equivalent level of investor protection, legislative proposals and their consequences need to be discussed and evaluated early on. As soon as the level of protection decreases in one country, equivalence needs to be withdrawn, which can only be prevented by timely discussions. Moreover, if information is exchanged on a broad basis, the supervision of individual units of multinational companies becomes much more effective.[53] To put it in a nutshell, regulatory dialogues and fora are key to working equivalence mechanisms.[54]

This conclusion is reflected in the fact that almost all equivalence mechanisms granting market access for service providers or financial products explicitly require the prior conclusion of cooperation agreements.[55] Even where it is not explicitly demanded, some provisions hint at the possibility of cooperation arrangements.[56] Moreover, a voluntary conclusion of agreements is always possible even if the respective legislation does not touch upon this issue. From the standpoint of consistency and legal certainty, extending the obligation of cooperation agreements to all equivalence mechanisms leading to market access would still be preferable.

The collaboration of supervisors may take different forms. Often a so-called Memorandum of Understanding (MoU) is concluded, which is a rather informal agreement, although it may have binding effects to some degree.[57] The content of such MoUs is not predetermined and authorities have a wide room for manoeuvre, yet some equivalence mechanisms dictate a certain minimum content. This minimum content may include provisions regarding the exchange of information, investigative

[51] See Lehmann (n 49); on the intra-EU context see Pablo Iglesias-Rodriguez, 'Supervisory Cooperation in the Single Market for Financial Services: United in Diversity' (2018) 41 Fordham Intl LJ 589; see for the lessons learned from the GFC regarding supervisory cooperation ESMA Regulation, recital 44.

[52] Lehmann (n 49) 35–37; David Zaring, 'International Institutional Performance in Crisis' (2010) 10 Chic J Intl L 475.

[53] Lehmann (n 49) 39.

[54] Commission, 'Equivalence in the area of financial services' (Communication) COM (2019) 349 final, 10.

[55] In total, 12 equivalence mechanisms contain an obligation to conclude cooperation agreements.

[56] See eg SAD, art 46(3)(b).

[57] Eric J Pan, 'Challenge of International Cooperation and Institutional Design in Financial Supervision: Beyond Transgovernmental Networks' (2010) 11 Chic J Intl L 243, 248 and 258–62; see as an example of limited binding effects SEC–ESMA, 'Memorandum of Understanding concerning Consultation, Cooperation and the Exchange of Information related to the Supervision of Cross-Border regulated Entities' (2012) art 2 paras 9–11 https://www.sec.gov/about/offices/oia/oia_bilateral/esma-mou.pdf (accessed 12 November 2022).

powers such as onsite inspections, notification obligations or specific procedures of third country authorities.[58] One example of a successful cooperation is the US–EU Financial Markets Regulatory Dialogue, which led, inter alia, to the convergence of US Generally Accepted Accounting Principles (GAAP) and International Financial Reporting Standards (IFRS) and consequently an equivalence and substituted compliance determination on the part of the EU and US.[59] Another area in which the EU has been very active is the more than 1,000 bilateral MoUs concluded with the support of centrally negotiated MoUs by ESMA.[60] Depending on the specific regime, either NCAs or ESAs are responsible for the conclusion of supervisory agreements. Even where ESAs are not responsible, they may develop contacts and enter into administrative arrangements with third country agencies, although these arrangements will not create legal obligations.[61]

One weakness of cooperation agreements is their non-binding nature.[62] Since both sides depend on the other party's goodwill, the effectiveness of such agreements is fragile. However, equivalence mechanisms set strong incentives for both sides to keep cooperating. First, service providers from third countries will lose their access rights through equivalence if the cooperation does not work anymore.[63] In order to avoid harming their service providers, third country supervisory authorities are therefore interested in maintaining the collaboration.[64] Secondly, interdependencies increase in cases where equivalence requires reciprocity and both sides supervise the service providers of the other country. That is why the dependency is mutual with strong incentives to collaborate (*do ut des*).

4. Reciprocity

Reciprocity is an ancient principle of law dating back as far as Hammurabi's Code (around 1754 BC). Back then, it reflected the concept of 'an eye for an eye, a tooth for a tooth' and described the relationship between a criminal offence and a punishment. *Thomas Hobbes* used the idea of reciprocity in his Second Law of Nature to explain why a man grants freedom to others.[65] In the prisoner's dilemma in game theory, it is described by the tit-for-tat strategy.[66] In short, reciprocity means returning like behaviour and explains the mutuality of actions. In the case of equivalence, this means that

[58] See eg EMIR, art 25(7); MiFIR, art 47(2); CRA Regulation, art 5(7).

[59] On the part of the EU see Commission Decision 2008/961/EC of 12 December 2008, art 1(c) (no longer in force); on the reaction of the US and the SEC's substituted compliance determination see ch 4 B)I.1.a); on the regulatory dialogue see Kern Alexander and others, 'Transatlantic Financial Services Regulatory Dialogue' (2006) 7 EBOR 647.

[60] ESMA, 'Annual Report 2012' 46 https://www.esma.europa.eu/sites/default/files/library/2015/11/esma_annual_report_2012_final_2.pdf (accessed 12 November 2022); Moloney (n 37) 992–93.

[61] See ESAs Regulations, art 33(1); more generally on the global dimension see Edoardo Chiti, 'An Important Part of the EU's Institutional Machinery: Features, Problems and Perspectives of European Agencies' (2009) 46 CMLR 1395, 1413–16.

[62] See extensively Lehmann (n 49) 37–38.

[63] See explicitly EMIR, art 25(7) subpara 2; implicitly the mechanism in MiFIR, arts 46(2)(c) and 47(2); Lehmann (n 49) 40.

[64] ibid 38–39.

[65] Thomas Hobbes, *Leviathan* (Liberal Arts Press 1958) 110 (original from 1651); regarding international law in general see Francesco Parisi and Nita Ghei, 'The Role of Reciprocity in International Law' (2003) 36 Cornell Intl LJ 93.

[66] Robert Axelrod, *The Evolution of Cooperation* (Basic Books 1984) 20–21.

the EU allows market access on the basis of equivalence only if the third country grants market access to European financial service providers on an equal footing. Only eight of the 40 equivalence mechanisms demand an element of reciprocity, making it the exception rather than the rule.[67] Reciprocity is mostly demanded in situations where equivalence concerns the question of market access. The reciprocity requirement does not usually apply where equivalence merely results in an exemption from specific obligations under EU law.

A closer look reveals that there are different degrees of the required level of reciprocity. In the strictest sense, 'concrete' reciprocity is demanded, which is only fulfilled if market access has *actually* been granted to European service providers in the specific sector in question. The predecessors of today's equivalence provisions were formulated in this sense, as they allowed the conclusion of an agreement only if reciprocity was part of that agreement.[68] Less restrictive is an 'abstract' reciprocity, which examines whether the legal system of the third country generally allows European service providers access to its markets. Most of the present equivalence provisions are modelled on such an abstract reciprocity.[69] Nevertheless, the provisions demand an 'effective equivalent system' for recognizing EU service providers, thus introducing a qualitative element to the assessment of market access opportunities under the third country legal system. This does not mean that the third country must have an equivalence mechanism mirroring the European one, but the third country mechanism needs to be as effective as its European counterpart.[70]

The call for reciprocal treatment is often criticized as being incompatible with the Most-Favoured-Nation (MFN) principle in Article II of the General Agreement on Trade in Services (GATS).[71] The MFN principle requires Members to 'accord immediately and unconditionally ... treatment no less favourable than that it accords to like services and service suppliers of any other country'. The reciprocity requirement could be seen as an additional precondition to equal treatment and thus a violation of Article II GATS. However, the EU applies the criterion of reciprocity equally to all Members and therefore does not treat any Member less favourably. This result is also underlined by the telos of the MFN principle, which is designed to prevent discrimination. If a Member demands reciprocal treatment from all Members, there is no discrimination against any particular one.[72] Moreover, such a restriction of the MFN

[67] Wymeersch (n 4) 228.

[68] See eg First Banking Directive, art 9(3); First Non-Life Insurance Directive, art 29; Mutual Recognition Directive, art 25a; see ch 1 C)I.5.a).

[69] See CSDR, art 25(9); EMIR, art 25(6)(c); MiFIR, arts 28(1)(d), 38(3) subpara 2(b), and 47(1)(c).

[70] See for different systems that were still accepted by the Commission as effectively equivalent Commission Implementing Decision (EU) 2015/2040 of 13 November 2015, recitals 26–28 and Commission Implementing Decision (EU) 2014/753 of 30 October 2014, recitals 19–22; see also Thierry R Ammann, *Der europäische Marktzugang für Schweizer Banken* (Dike 2020) paras 248ff.

[71] Juliane Kokott, 'Liberalisierung der Finanzdienstleistungen im Rahmen der WTO—Auswirkungen auf Deutschland, Österreich und die Schweiz' (2000) 8 RIW 402, 405; see on the criticism particularly in Switzerland Benjamin Leisinger in Rolf Sethe and others (eds), *SK zum FinfraG* (Schulthess 2017) art 40 para 26; on the special situation of Switzerland see ch 3 B)IV.2.a)aa). The compatibility is also seen critically in the UK. See House of Lords, 'MiFID II: Getting it Right for the City and EU Financial Services Industry' European Union Committee—Second Report (2012) para 56 https://publications.parliament.uk/pa/ld201213/ldselect/ldeucom/28/2802.htm (accessed 12 November 2022).

[72] Regarding the telos see George A Papaconstantinou, 'The GATS and Financial Regulation: Time to Clear-House?' (2020) 19 World Trade Rev 379, 393.

principle would be justified in the area of financial services on the basis of the prudential carve-out because reciprocity prevents the externalization of risks.[73] Only if both states concerned allow foreign financial service providers on their markets, an equal distribution of risks is ensured and thus there is an incentive for supervisory authorities to monitor closely the actions of their domestic service providers on foreign markets.

5. Conformity with international standards

Seven equivalence regimes demand that the third country concerned complies with international standards.[74] This is a rather recent development, as the requirement has been introduced primarily over the last few years. Expert groups such as international organizations, groups of states, or private organizations from the industry develop international standards.[75] International standards lay down minimum requirements in the form of recommendations, guidelines, or principles and are not legally binding on states or market participants.[76] The standards are enforced by states voluntarily incorporating them into their national laws, thereby changing the legal nature from soft law to hard law.[77] International standards have had a major influence on regulatory reforms since the GFC.[78]

The criterion of conformity with international standards in equivalence is not always drafted as a mandatory requirement, but where it is part of an equivalence decision, it is formulated as a factor that needs to be considered in the decision-making.[79] The concrete international standard referred to depends on the respective equivalence provision. Four equivalence mechanisms demand that the third country does not have deficiencies in its national anti-money laundering and counter financing of terrorism regime as stipulated under the recommendations of the Financial Action Task Force on Money Laundering (FATF) and related Union law.[80] Two provisions refer

[73] The further relationship between world trade law and equivalence will be discussed in detail in ch 2 B) II.2.b)cc). The argument regarding the externalization of risks is also presented in more detail in ch 5 A) II.1.d).

[74] See MiFIR, art 47(1a) subpara 3; EMIR, art 25(2)(d); AIFMD, art 21(6) subpara 1(c) and (d); BMR, art 33(1) subpara 2 (representing two equivalence mechanisms); CSDR, art 25(9) subpara 2; Prospectus Regulation, art 30(1); see for an introduction to different international standards Michael Raffan, 'International Standards' in Jonathan Herbst and Simon Lovegrove (eds), *Brexit and Financial Regulation* (OUP 2020) 31ff.

[75] On the notion of 'international standards' in general see Peter Nobel, *Schweizerisches Finanzmarktrecht* (4th edn, Stämpfli 2019) § 3 paras 99ff; Reto Schiltknecht, 'Internationale Standards in den Vorlagen zur neuen Finanzmarktarchitektur' (2015) 87 SZW 598, 598f; see for examples of expert groups in n 6 (ch 1). These expert groups are often dominated by economically powerful countries, which is one of many reasons for the justified accusation that international standards have a democratic deficit. See Vera Schreiber, *Internationale Standards—Neues Recht für die Weltmärkte* (Haupt 2005) 170.

[76] On the legal nature see Juliane Kokott, 'Soft Law Standards under Public International Law' in Peter Nobel (ed), *International Standards and the Law* (Bern 2005) 15ff.

[77] Moreover, they can also be 'enforced' by market pressure when companies are discriminated against on the basis of non-compliance with international standards. Peter Nobel, 'Was heisst "Internationale Standards"?' (2015) 87 SZW 556, 560.

[78] Stefan A Wandel, 'Global Financial Standards and Regulatory Reforms' (2015) 87 SZW 562.

[79] See MiFIR, art 47(1a) subpara 3; BMR, art 33(1) subpara 2; CSDR, art 25(9) subpara 2.

[80] The four regimes include MiFIR, art 47(1a) subpara 3; EMIR, art 25(2)(d); Prospectus Regulation, art 30(1); AIFMD, art 21(6) subpara 1(c). The first two refer to the Union Directive in question: Directive (EU) 2015/849 of 20 May 2015 (Anti-Money Laundering Directive).

to standards regarding tax matters and tax evasion. Another three relate to different principles of the International Organization of Securities Commissions (IOSCO), namely the IOSCO principles for financial benchmarks, the IOSCO principles for price reporting agencies and the Committee on Payment and Settlement Systems (CPSS)-IOSCO principles for financial market infrastructures.[81] Surprisingly, the new Prospectus Regulation does not demand the third country prospectus to comply with the IOSCO principles, even though the former Prospectus Directive contained such an obligation.[82] The Commission's draft for the new Prospectus Regulation had not included such a reference without giving further reasons.[83] This is unfortunate given the positive impact of taking international standards into account.[84]

6. Systemic importance

A rather new criterion, which has only been included in three equivalence provisions, is the standard of systemic importance. It was first introduced in the Credit Rating Agency (CRA) Regulation of 2009, which gives entities established or financial instruments issued in a third country the opportunity to use ratings for regulatory purposes from rating agencies established outside the Union. According to Article 5(1)(d) CRA Regulation, these ratings can, however, not be used if the agency and its rating activities are of systemic importance to the financial stability or integrity of the financial markets of one or more Member States.[85] Rating agencies with such systemic importance must either endorse their ratings or establish a legal person within the Union and subsequently obtain a licence.[86] By excluding systemically important agencies, the CRA Regulation promotes smaller rating agencies and leaves larger agencies to the process of endorsement.[87] This is in line with the overall aim of the CRA Regulation to enhance competition in the field of credit ratings.[88] Moreover, the dependence on foreign supervision is reduced, which is a lesson learned from the GFC in which agencies failed to rate residential mortgage-backed securities and collateralized debt obligations adequately.[89]

The other two regulations containing the element of 'systemic importance' are MiFIR and EMIR, which were both recently amended.[90] However, the set-up of the

[81] See BMR, art 33(1) subpara 2; CSDR, art 25(9) subpara 2; generally on IOSCO see Antonio Marcacci, 'IOSCO: The World Standard Setter for Globalized Financial Markets' (2012) 12 Rich J Global L & Bus 23.

[82] See Prospectus Regulation, art 29(1) in comparison to Prospectus Directive, art 20(1)(a).

[83] Commission, 'Proposal for a Regulation of the European Parliament and of the Council on the prospectus to be published when securities are offered to the public or admitted to trading' COM (2015) 583 final, art 27.

[84] On the merits of including international standards as a baseline for deference assessments see ch 5 A) II.1.c).

[85] See for the assessment of the systemic importance Commission Delegated Regulation (EU) No 449/2012 of 21 March 2012, art 28 and Annex XII.

[86] ESMA, 'Consultation paper: Guidelines and recommendations on the scope of the CRA Regulation' ESMA/2012/841 (20 December 2012) para 24.

[87] Moloney (n 37) 679.

[88] See also the compulsory rotation system of the CRA Regulation; Tim Wittenberg, 'Regulatory Evolution of the EU Credit Rating Agency Framework' (2015) 16 EBOR 669, 686–88.

[89] Harry McVea, 'Credit Rating Agencies, the Subprime Mortgage Debacle and Global Governance: The EU Strikes Back' (2010) 59 Intl & Comp LQ 701.

[90] See for MiFIR, Investment Firm Regulation, art 63; see for EMIR, Regulation (EU) 2019/2099 of 23 October 2019; see Jan Ceyssens and Andreas Tarde, 'Äquivalenz im Finanzdienstleistungsrecht der Europäischen Union' (2019) 31 EuZW 805, 809f and 811f.

element varies considerably between MiFIR, EMIR, and the CRA Regulation. Unlike in the CRA Regulation and EMIR, where the assessment of systemic importance is part of the certification/registration process by ESMA (step 2), the systemic relevance of investment firms is linked to the equivalence decision under MiFIR (step 1). It is consequently in the hands of the Commission. Furthermore, the degree of systemic importance required differs. The rating agency needs to be of systemic importance, whereas it is sufficient that an investment firm is 'likely to be' of systemic importance or, even more far-reaching in the case of EMIR, a central counterparty (CCP) is systemically important or likely to become so in the future (so-called Tier 2 CCP). Besides, the point of reference in MiFIR and EMIR is not the market of a Member State like in the CRA Regulation but that of the Union. What is more, the legal consequences of the three regulations do not match. A rating agency of systemic importance cannot get certified, whereas a Tier 2 CCP may get recognized if it fulfils additional requirements.[91] Where a third country investment firm under MiFIR is (or is likely to be) of systemic importance, the Commission may still adopt an equivalence decision but only 'after a detailed and granular assessment'.[92] The Commission may also attach additional operational requirements to the equivalence decision, similar to the regulation in EMIR.[93]

Since systemic stability is a key goal of capital markets regulation, it is plausible to include the criterion of systemic importance in the assessment. Otherwise, systemic risks could spread to the EU without authorities noticing it and thus being able to intervene. However, the use of the element of systemic importance is a vivid example of inconsistencies within equivalence provisions.[94] One reason for these inconsistencies could be the time in which the provisions were drafted. The criterion of systemic importance under the CRA Regulation is a decade older than the recently amended mechanisms in EMIR and MiFIR. Another explanation would be the need for a tailor-made approach in each regulation or simply bad communication within the Directorate-General (DG) of the Commission. Whatever the justification is, such an uncoordinated approach has major drawbacks. It produces complicated and hardly manageable equivalence provisions, creates legal ambiguity and consequently weakens the efficiency of equivalence.

II. Special features of selected equivalence regimes

Although most equivalence provisions consist of the key requirements described above, many mechanisms contain further prerequisites. These prerequisites are

[91] EMIR, art 25(2b). This possibility of recognition finds its limit with CCPs that are considered too important for the systemic stability of the EU. See EMIR, art 25(2c).

[92] MiFIR, art 47(1) subpara 2.

[93] ibid art 47(1a) subpara 2; Francesco Pennesi, *Equivalence in Financial Services* (Palgrave Macmillan 2022) 138.

[94] Calling the reforms in EMIR and MiFIR a 'piece-meal' approach see Francesco Pennesi, 'The EU equivalence regime in financial services: an effective instrument to preserve financial stability after Brexit?' (2020) ECMI Policy Brief No 27, 14 http://www.eurocapitalmarkets.org/sites/default/files/the_eu_equivalence_regime_in_financial_services_ecmi_policy_brief.pdf (accessed 12 November 2022).

difficult to categorize because they are tailored to the specific service provider or financial product concerned and therefore have little in common. Nonetheless, some recurring elements can be identified. Many provisions require equivalent guarantees of professional secrecy in the exchange of information or compliance of data transfers with European data protection law.[95] Others demand a legally binding and enforceable provision in the third country legal system obliging service providers to transfer relevant information to EU authorities.[96]

The equivalence mechanism with the most 'special' obligations is the one dealing with market access for third country investment firms. Investment firms wanting to register with ESMA need to make sure to have arrangements and procedures in place, which enable them to inform ESMA about their services extensively.[97] ESMA can even demand more information if necessary. The investment firm must additionally keep all information relating to orders and transactions in the Union at the disposal of ESMA for five years.[98] Besides the extensive information duties to ESMA, investment firms must make their customers aware—prior to providing services—of certain facts, for instance, that they are not supervised in the Union.[99] Another curious and rather unclear provision is Article 46(6) MiFIR, which obliges the third country investment firm to offer the client that any dispute arising in relation to the services or activities may be settled before a court or arbitral tribunal in a Member State. The scope of application as well as the legal consequences of a violation are largely unclear.[100]

These tailor-made requirements have the downside of further complicating already highly intricate regimes. This worsens comprehensibility for practitioners and creates inconsistencies. For this reason, it will be advocated in Chapter 5 to consolidate most requirements, thereby promoting the comprehensibility of equivalence and paving the way for a sectoral approach presented in that chapter.[101]

III. Conclusion

1. Equivalence as a uniform concept

A closer look at equivalence mechanisms reveals that the requirements in the single provisions are not yet harmonized and inconsistencies remain. Nevertheless, they are all designed in a similar way. All provisions demand that the third country legal system is equivalent to that of the EU. Thus, equivalence is the defining element of

[95] See MiFIR, art 33(2)(b); SFT Regulation, arts 19(1) subpara 1(c) and 21(1)(b); EMIR, arts 13(2)(b), 75(1) subpara 1(c), and 76a(2)(c); see regarding data protection law SAD, art 47(1)(e).

[96] SFT Regulation, arts 19(1) subpara 1(d) and 21(1)(d); EMIR, arts 77(2) subpara 1(b) and 75(2); EMIR, art 76a(2)(d).

[97] MiFIR, art 46(2)(d) and (6a) subpara 1.

[98] ibid art 46(6a) subpara 3 and (6b) subpara 1.

[99] ibid art 46(5); see Dirk A Zetzsche and Matthias Lehmann, 'Das Vereinigte Königreich als Drittstaat?—Die Auswirkungen des Brexit auf das Finanzmarktrecht' (2017) 62 AG 651, 656; Rolf H Weber and Rolf Sethe, 'Äquivalenz als Regelungskriterium im Finanzmarktrecht' (2014) 110 SJZ 569, 575.

[100] Matthias Lehmann and Dirk A Zetzsche, 'How Does It Feel to Be a Third Country? The Consequences of Brexit for Financial Market Law' in Oonagh E Fitzgerald and Eva Lein (eds), *Complexity's Embrace* (Queen's UP 2018) 116–18.

[101] See ch 5 B)III.2.b); see for the proposal of a sectoral approach: ch 5 B)I.

all provisions and, at the same time, the most important and controversial barrier to access the European market. Furthermore, all provisions demand effective home country control of service providers or products to ensure compliance with the third country legal order, where such a requirement is appropriate.

The other four recurrent requirements, namely the conclusion of cooperation agreements, reciprocity, conformity with international standards and the criterion of systemic importance, are only included in some equivalence regimes. This is partly due to the fact that it does not always make sense to demand them. For example, if no international standard exists in a specific area, it is impossible to demand compliance. Other times, insisting on them would be too cumbersome given the small effects of some equivalence mechanisms, for example, if equivalence provisions only exempt third country service providers from individual obligations. Moreover, equivalence provisions were introduced and amended at different times. Events changed the political landscape and thus the priorities of the legislator. The circumstances shortly after the GFC varied tremendously from the situation after the referendum on Brexit.[102] That is why, for example, the equivalence regime for credit rating agencies, which was drafted in response to the financial crisis, differs from the recently reformed mechanism in EMIR dealing with market access for CCPs, which was designed with Brexit in mind. Hence, equivalence mechanisms designed at different points in time have their distinctive character.

As a rule of thumb, however, more recent regimes cover most of the requirements, as can be seen from equivalence provisions concerning investment firms in MiFIR or CCPs in EMIR. This development should be welcomed, as most of the requirements have positive effects.[103] Inter alia, cooperation agreements increase trust in the work of other supervisory authorities and thereby stabilize the status of equivalence, reciprocity creates a level playing field and consequently eliminates competitive disadvantages, and international standards are a way of harmonizing global standards in general and thus reduce the fragmentation of markets. It is, therefore, in principle advisable to include all requirements in equivalence mechanisms. This would, at the same time, reduce inconsistencies between the regimes. To further eliminate inconsistencies stemming from the fact that provisions were drafted at different points in time, it would be best to reduce the number of mechanisms by adopting a sectoral instead of an obligation-based approach. This reform will be advocated in Chapter 5.[104]

The remaining requirements, which are only part of specific equivalence provisions, must be eliminated to create a consistent and comprehensible equivalence system.[105] Such an elimination can take different forms. Unnecessary preconditions can be deleted, some can be formulated in a more abstract manner, others may be included in the equivalence decision, and still others can be moved to legislation at Level 2.

To sum up, current equivalence provisions are not identical and there are manifest inconsistencies. Nevertheless, there is an underlying system behind the individual

[102] Moloney (n 32) 48–50.
[103] See extensively: ch 5 A)II.1.c) and d).
[104] ch 5 B)I.
[105] See ch 5 B)III.2.b).

provisions, which is why equivalence can be described as a uniform concept: an equivalence *principle* or equivalence *concept*.[106]

2. Consequences for the interpretation of single equivalence provisions

What can be deduced from the finding that all equivalence provisions are part of a uniform concept? When interpreting provisions of EU law, four methods of interpretation must be observed.[107] A literal interpretation, a systematic or contextual interpretation, a historical or genetic interpretation and a teleological interpretation. A systematic interpretation demands that an interpretation is not limited to the specific provision in question. Instead, as the ECJ put it, 'every provision of Community law must be placed in its context and interpreted in the light of the provisions of Community law as a whole'.[108] The legislator is assumed to be a rational actor who created a consistent and complete system.[109] This contextual view is not restricted to individual legislation but also takes place across legal acts.[110] As a result, one equivalence provision cannot be interpreted in isolation. On the contrary, all other 39 equivalence mechanisms must be considered.

A teleological interpretation underlines the necessity for such a contextual view.[111] The guiding principle of equivalence is the withdrawal of regulatory and supervisory competences in relation to third country service providers to avoid legal conflicts and market fragmentation whenever an extraterritorial application of the law is unnecessary because the regulation and supervision in the third country meet the objectives of the EU legislation in question equally effectively (i.e. it is 'equivalent').[112] Therefore, if all equivalence provisions are based on the same rationale, they must be interpreted consistently and with due regard to that rationale.

More specifically, with regard to the upcoming questions, it follows from this conclusion that the term equivalence, even though it has different reference points in the individual regimes, basically has the same meaning in all 40 mechanisms. Furthermore, the administrative and constitutional limits that govern the entire process of obtaining equivalence, particularly the Commission's discretion, are the same. The identical limits apply to the withdrawal of equivalence. Likewise, the possibilities of judicial review and the level of judicial scrutiny are similar.

[106] Veronika E-M Köpfer, *Anwendung und Auswirkungen des europäischen Kapitalmarktrechts auf Akteure aus Drittstaaten* (2015) https://www.e-helvetica.nb.admin.ch/api/download/urn%3Anbn%3Ach%3Abel-523480%3Adis4410.pdf/dis4410.pdf (accessed 12 November 2022); for a critical view see Tilman Imm, *Der finanz- und kapitalmarktrechtliche Gleichwertigkeitsmechanismus* (Mohr Siebeck 2020) 89.

[107] These four elements trace back to Friedrich C von Savigny, *System des heutigen Römischen Rechts*, vol 1 (Veit 1840) 213f; Karl Riesenhuber, 'Die Auslegung' in Karl Riesenhuber (ed), *Europäische Methodenlehre* (4th edn, De Gruyter 2021) 285ff; Giulio Itzcovich, 'The Interpretation of Community Law by the European Court of Justice' (2009) 10 German LJ 537.

[108] Case C-283/81 *CILFIT v Ministero della Sanità* ECLI:EU:C:1982:335, para 20.

[109] Koen Lenaerts and Jose A Gutierrez-Fons, 'To Say What the Law of the EU Is: Methods of Interpretation and the European Court of Justice' (2014) 20 Colum J Eur L 3, 17.

[110] Riesenhuber (n 107) 298f.

[111] See regarding the teleological interpretation eg Case C-465/04 *Honyvem Informazioni Commerciali* ECLI:EU:C:2006:199, paras 17ff and 26; Lenaerts and Gutierrez-Fons (n 109) 31–37; Miguel Poiares Maduro, 'Interpreting European Law: Judicial Adjudication in a Context of Constitutional Pluralism' (2008) 1 Eur J Leg Stud 137.

[112] See on this guiding idea ch 1 C).

B) Equivalence decision as the crucial point

The decision on equivalence by the Commission is the central prerequisite of all regimes.[113] At the same time, the decision is surrounded by much uncertainty.[114] The meaning of the legal term 'equivalent' is unclear, and the process of how equivalence is determined is opaque. The Commission has hardly disclosed its practice, and the practice of ESAs, which has barely been discussed in the academic literature, is not always consistent.[115] What is missing is a common methodology to assess equivalence.

Additional uncertainty arises due to the discretionary nature of equivalence decisions. What factors does the Commission take into account in its decision-making? Is it a technical or a policy decision? Furthermore, the process of decision-making has not yet been examined in detail, both in practice and in academic literature, which is why many questions remain unanswered. Is there a time limit for decisions? Do service providers from third countries have a right to a decision, a right to be heard or a right to a reasoned decision?

This ambiguity is even enhanced by the fact that the Commission can withdraw equivalence decisions at any time. Hence, market access rights are always in a floating state with the permanent risk of a withdrawal resulting in a loss of access rights. The position of service providers is further exacerbated insofar as the Commission has taken the view that it can withdraw equivalence also for political reasons.

All this uncertainty could at least be reduced by judicial control and consistent case law. However, there has not yet been a single case dealing with equivalence questions in financial markets law. Even in the literature, problems of judicial review in the context of equivalence decisions have barely been touched upon.

In the following, the meaning of equivalence and the process for its determination are evaluated (I.). Next, the administrative decision-making leeway and its limits as well as other administrative and constitutional boundaries to the decision are analysed (II.). Finally, the withdrawal of equivalence and limits to it (III.) as well as ways of judicial protection (IV.) are outlined. All this leads to a juridification that helps to overcome the shortcomings of equivalence (V.).

I. Pivotal question: What is meant by equivalence and how can it be determined?

The following analysis is subdivided into two parts. The first part deals with the definition of equivalence. The analysis begins with a legal interpretation of the term and is

[113] Moloney (n 32) 38; see extensively, also on the controversial aspects of it Srivastava and Moffatt (n 32) 81–83.

[114] Imm (n 106) 113; Michael Hahn, 'The Day After: Access to the Single Market in Times of Brexit, Equivalence and Extraterritoriality' (2018) 21 ZEuS 409, 414: 'far from an exact science'.

[115] A short discussion can be found in Moloney (n 32) 44–48; for a very critical view with regard to the practice of ESMA in the area of the AIFMD see Dirk A Zetzsche and Robin Veidt, 'The AIFMD's Third-Country Rules and the Equivalence Concept' in Dirk A Zetzsche (ed), *The Alternative Investment Fund Managers Directive* (3rd edn, Wolters Kluwer 2020) 837f.

followed by the Commission's and ESAs' understanding of what equivalence means. In the second part, a closer look is taken at how equivalence is assessed. The practice of the Commission and ESAs will be analysed and critically reviewed. Finally, a proposal is made on the methodology for this assessment.

1. Meaning of equivalence

a) Interpretation of the legal term 'equivalence'

aa) Functional equivalence of regulatory outcomes from a holistic perspective The wording of the equivalence requirement in the different provisions is very alike. At the centre of the requirement is the term 'equivalence' or 'equivalent'.[116] These terms are used in most languages.[117] One exception to this rule is the German version, which uses the term *gleichwertig* instead of *äquivalent*. Since these terms are synonyms, there is no difference in the content.[118] The Latin etymology of the word is *aequivalentem*, which is made up of two parts, *aequus* and *valere*.[119] This emphasizes equivalence's literal meaning, which can be paraphrased with equal in value, effect, or significance.[120] This already shows that equivalence provisions do not demand that the third country legal system is identical to that of the EU.[121] It is not necessary to copy EU legislation.[122] Third countries can even have a totally different approach.[123] What matters is not the approach, tool, or regulatory technique used by the third country, but that the regulatory aims of the EU legislator are fulfilled on an equal footing by the third country legal system. Consequently, the outcomes that abstract rules produce on financial markets and market participants in relation to the goals of investor protection, the functioning of financial markets, as well as financial stability should be at the centre of the assessment. Other legal consequences are irrelevant in that context. In other words, the third country legal system must fulfil the same function as EU law by producing the same regulatory outcomes. Hence, equivalence means a functional equivalence of regulatory outcomes (so-called outcome-based approach). This approach was already reflected in one of the first equivalence mechanisms in the

[116] In the context of data protection, the term 'adequacy' is used instead of 'equivalent'. See SAD, art 47(1)(c) and (3). In the cases of exemptions for central banks and public bodies of third countries, the term equivalence is not used but paraphrased. Often a 'comparative analysis' is required. See EMIR, art 1(6) subpara 3; MAR, art 6(5) subpara 3; SFT Regulation, art 2(4) subpara 3.

[117] In French: *équivalence/équivalent*; in Spanish: *equivalencia/equivalente*; in Italian: *equivalenza/equivalente*.

[118] Wolfang Müller, *Duden: Sinn- und sachverwandte Wörter und Wendungen*, vol 8 (Duden 1972) 58; Clara-Erika Dietl and Egon Lorenz (eds), *Dictionary of Legal, Commercial and Political Terms*, pt 1 (6th edn, CH Beck 2000) 284.

[119] See https://www.etymonline.com/word/equivalent (accessed 12 November 2022).

[120] Bryan A Garner (ed), *Black's Law Dictionary* (11th edn, West 2021) 682; see Peter H Collin, Sigrid Janssen, and Anke Kornmüller (eds), *PONS: Fachwörterbuch Recht* (Ernst Klett 1990) 112: 'to have the same value as'.

[121] Pennesi (n 94) 4.

[122] Strongly emphasizing this aspect see Lehmann (n 43) 430.

[123] See eg CESR, 'Technical Advice to the European Commission on the Equivalence between the US Regulatory and Supervisory Framework and the EU Regulatory Regime for Credit Rating Agencies' CESR/10-332 (21 May 2010) 40–55 and 161. Here, CESR identified a 'fundamental difference in terms of the philosophy' of the US regulation resulting in major differences. However, they still assessed the US as 'broadly equivalent'.

Financial Conglomerates Directive, Recital 13 of which called for 'equivalent and appropriate supplementary supervisory arrangements which achieve objectives and results similar to those pursued by the provisions of this Directive'. Some equivalence provisions hint to that interpretation when they demand that third country requirements should be 'in effect equivalent to the requirements' of the EU.[124] Article 37(2)(b) AIFMD, which demands 'an equivalent rule having the same regulatory purpose and offering the same level of protection to the investors of the relevant AIF', even expressly confirms this interpretation.

A teleological interpretation further underlines this reading. The rationale of equivalence is the withdrawal of regulatory and supervisory powers vis-à-vis market participants from third countries if an extraterritorial application of the law is disproportionate because the regulation and supervision in the third country meet the objectives as effectively (i.e. 'equivalently') as that of the EU legislation in question.[125] If the same outcomes are achieved, there is no point wasting resources and increasing market fragmentation through double regulation and supervision. A withdrawal of legislative and supervisory power is reasonable.[126] Thus, the telos supports an interpretation that demands functional equivalence of regulatory outcomes.

It also follows from this central idea that equivalence must be assessed from a holistic perspective, i.e. a helicopter view.[127] It is irrelevant whether individual EU provisions have counterparts within the legislation of the third country in question, as long as the third country legal system *as a whole* achieves the same level of protection.[128] Otherwise, there is an inevitable risk of carrying out a line-by-line analysis and transferring the European approach to the third country system, which is not what equivalence demands.

At the same time, this guiding principle defines the lower end of equivalence. The goals of EU legislation need to be met on an equal footing to allow deference to the foreign regulation. Otherwise, EU investors would not be equally well protected, financial markets would not function as effectively, or market stability would be at risk. Furthermore, competition would be distorted to the detriment of EU service providers, who would face stricter regulation than their third country competitors. As a result, it is not sufficient if third country provisions meet the goals of EU legislation only to a comparable but lower degree.[129]

However, the third country regime may be stricter than EU legislation. Stricter in this context means that the objectives of the EU act in question are exceeded. Eilís V Ferran describes this situation as 'super-equivalent'.[130] Against the background that

[124] CSDR, art 25(9) subpara 1; see also MiFIR, art 47(1)(a): 'which have equivalent effect'; AIFMD, art 21(6)(b): 'which have the same effect as Union law'; Regulation (EU) No 462/2013 of 21 May 2013, recital 48: 'It is important to recall in this respect that a third-country regulatory regime does not have to have identical rules as those provided for in this Regulation. As already provided for in Regulation (EC) No 1060/2009, in order to be considered equivalent to or as stringent as the Union regulatory regime, it should be sufficient that the third-country regulatory regime achieve the same objectives and effects in practice.'

[125] See also Moloney (n 32) 39.

[126] Köpfer (n 106) 325.

[127] Matthias Lehmann speaks in this context of a 'cosmopolitan perspective'. See Lehmann (n 43) 430.

[128] CESR (n 123) para 38 lit a) and para 40; Moloney (n 14) para 6.49.

[129] The interpretation of the ECJ with regard to adequacy decisions in data protection law already goes in this direction. See Case C-362/14 *Schrems I* ECLI:EU:C:2015:650, paras 71–74; see ch 1 C)I.3.

[130] Ferran (n 2) 62.

some equivalence mechanisms require a third country regulation to be 'at least equivalent', it could be concluded from an *argumentum e contrario* that other mechanisms do not recognize more stringent regimes as equivalent.[131] However, if the objectives of EU law are even surpassed (and not just fulfilled equally), the denial of market access would be even more disproportionate (*argumentum a maiore ad minus*). Consequently, equivalence requires that third country provisions achieve the same result in terms of meeting the objectives of the legislation in question (lower limit), but equivalence has no upper limit and is therefore amenable to more effective regulation that achieves the objectives of the European legislator to a greater extent.

bb) Cost equivalence Some scholars advocate an approach that requires cost equivalence in addition to functional equivalence.[132] Cost equivalence demands that the costs imposed on the service providers by the third country are comparable to those incurred under the EU legal system. Otherwise, competition would be affected to the detriment of EU service providers.[133] However, most equivalence decisions do not mention costs as a factor. There is no evidence supporting the idea that all equivalence mechanisms are based on the idea that competitive disadvantages of EU service providers must be prevented, which would turn equivalence into a protectionist tool.[134] Such an approach would also be inconsistent with the GATS, as the EU would discriminate against foreign service providers based on a non-prudential element.[135] Also, equivalence does not have a punitive function. The opposite is true: if a third country succeeds in establishing an equivalent system, which at the same time entails lower costs for service providers, it has come up with a more efficient solution and the EU should amend its legislation instead of punishing the third country. Such an adjustment would also be an expression of a functioning regulatory competition. Consequently, equivalence assessments do not include the notion of cost equivalence.

cc) Reference points It must be differentiated between two reference points. On the one hand, it is necessary to identify the reference point within the EU legal system against which the equivalence of the third country must be assessed. On the other hand, the point of reference within the third country legal system, which can be used to determine equivalence, must be located.

The reference point for equivalence within the EU legal system depends on the specific equivalence mechanism in question and cannot be defined universally. However, even the legislative technique varies between the different provisions. Some provisions demand equivalence in relation to all requirements of the respective legal act,[136] while most refer only to specific chapters or provisions of either the legislation in question or

[131] See eg CRR II, arts 107(4), 114(7), and 115(4); EMIR, art 75(1)(c); raising this question and dismissing the idea of super-equivalence see Ferran (n 2) 62; for a consenting view see Imm (n 106) 146.

[132] Dirk A Zetzsche, 'Competitiveness of Financial Centers in Light of Financial and Tax Law Equivalence Requirements' in Ross P Buckley, Emilios Avgouleas, and Douglas W Arner (eds), *Reconceptualising Global Finance and Its Regulation* (CUP 2016) 395; Zetzsche and Veidt (n 115) 830.

[133] Zetzsche and Veidt (n 115) 830.

[134] Imm (n 106) 145.

[135] See GATS, Annex on Financial Services, para 2(a); in more detail see ch 2 B)II.2.b)cc)(2).

[136] See eg BMR, art 30(2)(a); Prospectus Regulation, art 29(1)(a); SFT Regulation, art 19(1)(a); CRA Regulation, art 5(6) subpara 1.

sometimes other regulations or directives.[137] Almost half of the provisions delegate the task of a further specification to the Commission, which thus indirectly determines the reference points for equivalence in delegated acts at Level 2.[138] One very extensive and comprehensive example of such a Level 2 act is Commission Directive 2007/14/EC laying down detailed rules for the implementation of the equivalence mechanism in the Transparency Directive.[139] This Directive defines the minimum content that a legal system of a third country must contain to be considered equivalent. Another example from the insurance sector is Commission Delegated Regulation (EU) 2015/35.[140] From the point of view of legal certainty, specifications at Level 2 are preferable as the requirements to be fulfilled by the third country are much clearer in this scenario.

But what parts of the third country 'legal system' can be used to establish equivalence? Again, the terminology used in equivalence provisions is inconsistent. Some refer to 'third country laws', others to the 'legal and supervisory arrangements of a third country', and again others simply refer to 'supervision and enforcement' in that third country.[141] The interpretation must be guided by the rationale of equivalence. In the end, the same outcomes must be produced by the third country legal system to guarantee investor protection, efficient financial markets, and market stability. How these results are achieved is irrelevant from the standpoint of equivalence. It can be the legislation specifically dealing with the service provider or product at issue, more general legislation or even persistent administrative practice. Reference can be made to ex-ante or ex-post regulation, and public as well as private enforcement tools may be considered to establish equivalence. This bird's eye view on the legal system of third countries is a direct consequence of the 'holistic perspective' advocated above.[142] In order to guarantee that these requirements are fulfilled, the reference is limited to legally binding rules, an idea that is also explicitly laid down in some equivalence provisions.[143] Consequently, the entire legal order as well as the supervisory practice must be used as a reference point.

dd) Granularity, risk-sensitivity, and proportionality The granularity and risk-sensitivity of an assessment as well as the principle of proportionality are three elements that are closely linked to one another.[144] They all gained in importance as a result

[137] See eg EMIR, art 13(2)(a); and Accounting Directive, art 46(1); see MiFIR, arts 28(4) subpara 1 and 47(1)(a) as examples where reference is made to other legal acts.

[138] See eg Prospectus Regulation, art 29(3) subpara 2; Solvency II, arts 227(3) and 260(2); EMIR, art 25(6a).

[139] Commission Directive 2007/14/EC of 8 March 2007; see also Commission Regulation (EC) No 1569/2007 of 21 December 2007 concerning the Transparency and Prospectus Directive.

[140] Commission Delegated Regulation (EU) 2015/35 of 10 October 2014, arts 378–80.

[141] Prospectus Regulation, art 29(1); EMIR, art 25(6)(a); MiFIR, art 46(2)(b).

[142] See eg CESR, 'Final concept paper on equivalence of certain third country GAAP and on description of certain third countries' mechanism of enforcement of financial information' CESR/04~509C (February 2005) 5; ESMA, 'Supplement to the Final report: Technical advice on third country regulatory equivalence under EMIR—Japan' ESMA/2014/123 (27 January 2014) 8.

[143] See eg MiFIR, art 47(1); BMR, art 30(2)(b); Commission, 'EU Equivalence decisions in financial services policy: An Assessment' (Staff Working Document) SWD (2017) 102 final, 7; ESMA, 'Final report—US' (n 37) 5; see extensively in relation to the equivalence mechanism under MiFIR Ammann (n 70) paras 222ff.

[144] See Moloney (n 3) 15.

of the MiFIR and EMIR 2.2 reforms.[145] Article 47(1) subparagraph 2 MiFIR states that where activities of third country firms are likely to be of systemic importance for the Union, the Commission may only adopt an equivalence decision 'after a detailed and granular assessment'. The underlying idea behind this additional prerequisite is that equivalence assessments can be more or less granular. The analysis of ESAs and the Commission may immerse deeply into the functioning of the third country legal framework in question or remain on the surface of it. The granularity of the assessment is supposed to depend on the risks associated with an equivalence decision. Where greater risks to the financial stability of EU markets exist, for example, as a consequence of the size of the third country market, the analysis needs to be more detailed and granular. This follows from the fact that financial stability, particularly since the GFC, has been one of the primary objectives of the European legislator.[146] The legislator also emphasized the risk-sensitivity of equivalence in the new reforms of MiFIR and EMIR, both of which introduced the criterion of systemic importance.[147] Hence, the granularity of an assessment depends on the risks associated with the equivalence decision.

Risk-sensitivity determines not only the granularity of the assessment but also the outcome in the form of a different balancing of similarities and differences. This influence of risks on the result of the assessment is treated under the principle of proportionality.[148] If, for example, two third countries have a completely identical legal system, one may be considered equivalent, while the other will not be regarded as equivalent, depending on the risks associated with market access by service providers from these countries.[149] In the case of market access for service providers from lower impact jurisdictions, differences do not create the same risks for EU financial markets compared to market access for service providers from higher impact jurisdictions.[150] Such differentiation is legitimate as it is rooted in the legislator's objective to ensure a stable financial system. The stability of financial markets is also a prudential criterion within the meaning of the GATS. Even though the principle of proportionality is not explicitly laid down in most equivalence provisions, it still applies because it is a general principle of EU law embedded in Article 5(4) TEU.[151]

ee) Is equivalence an example of substitution or recognition? Finally, the question can be raised whether equivalence is a case of an already known principle/institution. Two possibilities can be considered here. First, equivalence as a case of substitution, a

[145] Moloney (n 32) 54–61.

[146] Philipp Hartmann and Olivier de Bandt, 'Systemic Risk in Banking after the Great Financial Crisis' in Allen N Berger, Philip Molyneux, and John OS Wilson (eds), *The Oxford Handbook of Banking* (3rd edn, OUP 2019) 847ff.

[147] See Commission (n 54) 6. However, systemic relevance in EMIR is a criterion that is only taken into account at the second level, namely in the process of recognition by ESMA. See in more detail ch 5 B)II.3.b).

[148] See eg Commission (n 54) 5–8; Commission (n 143) 8–11.

[149] A case in point was the Commission's recognition of CCPs from Singapore and the US. The US had to meet more stringent conditions because its CCPs posed greater risks to the EU. See with further references Francesco Pennesi, 'Equivalence in the Area of Financial Services' (2021) 58 CMLR 39, 52f.

[150] Commission (n 54) 7.

[151] Settled case law, see eg Joined Cases C-41/79, 121/79 and 796/79 *Testa v Bundesanstalt für Arbeit* ECLI:EU:C:1980:163, para 21; Marcus Klamert in Manuel Kellerbauer, Marcus Klamert, and Jonathan Tomkin (eds), *Commentary on the EU Treaties and the Charter of Fundamental Rights* (OUP 2019) art 5 paras 5 and 37.

principle of private international law, and second, as a case of recognition as found in international economic law.

(1) Equivalence as a form of substitution

What substitution precisely means is part of a broader debate.[152] For present purposes, substitution can be defined as an operation where a legal relationship or act established under a foreign legal system may produce all or some of the effects provided for under the substantive law applicable by virtue of the choice-of-law rules.[153] A substitution is feasible if the rule of the applicable substantive law can be interpreted as being open to such an operation, meaning that it is not a priori limited to a domestic legal relationship or act (1.) and if the foreign legal relationship or act is equivalent to the legal relationship or act as required under the applicable substantive law (2.).[154] It has been argued that equivalence is precisely that: provisions that are expressly open to accept foreign legal institutions if they are equivalent to the regulation in the EU.[155]

Indeed, substitution and equivalence have much in common. They are founded on the idea that it is disproportionate to insist on domestic legal relationships, acts or requirements if these obligations are fulfilled in an equivalent manner by a foreign legal system. Also, the result is similar as the foreign legal act is in a way recognized within the domestic system. Nevertheless, equivalence is not just a case of substitution. The concept of substitution presupposes that domestic law is applicable. The legal consequence of equivalence, however, is that the EU supervisory law is a priori not applied to third country firms or products. These firms are only subject to their equivalent home country law and only supervised by their home country authorities. Hence, the domestic law, i.e. the European supervisory law, is not applicable and equivalence is therefore not just the recognition of a single act but the withdrawal of regulatory and supervisory powers in general.[156] Moreover, substitution is an instrument of private international law, whereas equivalence in capital markets law deals with supervisory law, which qualifies as public law. The instruments of private international law cannot be blindly transferred to public international law.[157] Furthermore, there is no big takeaway from such a categorization.[158] In private international law, equivalence

[152] For a very detailed account see Imm (n 106) 7–45; Jan D Lüttringhaus, 'Substitution' in Jürgen Basedow and others (eds), *Encyclopedia of Private International Law*, vol 2 (Edward Elgar Publishing 2017) 1675–76; Gerd J van Venrooy, *Internationalprivatrechtliche Substitution* (Hartung-Gorre 1999) 35–39; the concept of substitution was first mentioned in Hans Lewald, 'Règles générales des conflits de lois' (1939) 69 Rec des Cours 5, 130ff.

[153] The definition of the Institut de Droit International is similar to the one used here: 'La substitution permet à un rapport de droit ou un acte établi sous l'empire d'une loi donnée de produire tout ou partie des effets attachés à un rapport de droit ou un acte similaires connus de la loi d'un autre État.' Première Commission Résolution, 27 octobre 2007, art 1, published in Erik Jayme and Andreas Bucher, 'Première Commission/First Commission Résolution' (2008) 28 IPrax 297.

[154] Jan von Hein, 'Einleitung zum Internationalan Privatrecht' in Jan von Hein (ed), *MüKo/BGB*, vol 12, pt 1 (8th edn, CH Beck 2020) paras 255ff; Christian von Bar and Peter Mankowski, *Internationales Privatrecht*, vol 1 (2nd edn, CH Beck 2003) § 7 para 243.

[155] Imm (n 106) 138–44.

[156] See Lehmann (n 43) 429–31. Admittedly, the extent of deference depends on the equivalence mechanism in question and may sometimes be restricted to an exemption from single obligations of EU law.

[157] See on their relationship: von Bar and Mankowski (n 154) § 4 paras 53–54.

[158] The rejection of cost equivalence, which is justified with the general principles of substitution in the thesis of *Tilman Imm*, can also be challenged for other reasons. See ch 2 B)I.1.a)bb). Imm (n 106) 145.

is also understood as a 'functional equivalence'.[159] However, no methodology has yet emerged in the literature on how functional equivalence can be determined, which is why the benefit of such a categorization is limited.

(2) Equivalence as a form of recognition

Recognition, as found for instance in the GATS, means that 'one jurisdiction accepts that compliance with the rules of another jurisdiction is sufficient to authorize access to the first jurisdiction's markets'.[160] This definition accurately describes equivalence in financial markets law. It can be differentiated between unilateral and mutual recognition. Historically, mutual recognition was and still is in the centre of state practice. The mere fact that recognition usually applies regardless of the quality of the foreign regulation does not mean that equivalence is not a case of recognition.[161] Rather, equivalence is a subcategory of recognition because it entails an additional requirement in the form of an equivalence decision.[162] If equivalence demands reciprocity, it can also be understood as a subcategory of mutual recognition.[163]

b) Interpretation of the European Commission and ESAs

Already at a very early stage, the Commission promoted equivalence and defended its central idea. In a testimony in 2004, Alexander Schaub, Director-General of the DG Internal Market of the European Commission at the time, emphasized that, although convergence and 'aiming at the same basic goals' is extremely important, it is unrealistic fully to harmonize legal systems in every detail.[164] Consequently, identical approaches are not feasible. Instead, the focus should be on 'broadly equivalent approaches', which share 'the same goal', an approach he referred to as a 'rule of reason approach'.[165]

Today, equivalence is a much more developed concept. The Commission has published its first comprehensive analysis of the principle in 2017.[166] Although it is formulated a lot more restrictive than the initial remarks of Alexander Schaub,[167] the basic ideas remained the same: equivalence still is described as an outcome-based process

[159] In great detail see Sabine Hug, *Die Substitution im internationalen Privatrecht. Anhand von Beispielen aus dem internationalen Familienrecht* (Florentz 1983) 131–41.

[160] Andrew Lang, 'The "Default Option"? The WTO and Cross-Border Financial Services Trade after Brexit' in Kern Alexander and others (eds), *Brexit and Financial Services: Law and Policy* (Hart Publishing 2018) 204.

[161] A dissenting view is taken by Tilman Imm, who concludes from this difference that equivalence is not a case of recognition. See Imm (n 106) 143.

[162] For a consenting view see Eilís V Ferran, 'Regulatory Parity in Post-Brexit UK–EU Financial Regulation' in Kern Alexander and others (eds), *Brexit and Financial Services: Law and Policy* (Hart Publishing 2018) 5; Lehmann (n 43) 430; see above ch 1 C)I.

[163] Ferran (n 1); see ch 1 C)I.

[164] Alexander Schaub (DG Internal Market), 'Testimony before the Committee on Financial Services U.S. House of Representatives' (13 May 2004) 6 and 8 https://www.iasplus.com/en/binary/resource/051304as.pdf (accessed 12 November 2022).

[165] ibid 8.

[166] Commission (n 143).

[167] ibid 5: 'Equivalence is not a vehicle for liberalising international trade in financial services, but a key instrument to effectively manage cross-border activity of market players in a sound and secure prudential environment with third-country jurisdictions that adhere to, implement and enforce rigorously the same high standards of prudential rules as the EU.'

in which the same results as in the corresponding EU legislation and supervision must be achieved.[168] The provisions must be interpreted in light of the objectives pursued by them, such as investor protection or financial stability.[169] Proportionality and a risk-based approach are supposed to guide the equivalence assessment.[170]

The latest statement of the Commission from 2019 is in line with earlier assessments.[171] The goal of equivalence is described in a slightly more liberal way by also referring to the promotion of 'open, fair and efficient financial markets', although this objective is put into perspective in the same sentence by the constraint of 'rigorous prudential and conduct frameworks'.[172] Apart from that, the outcome-based approach is emphasized, which again highlights that the systems do not need to be identical. However, the results achieved by the third country system must correspond to the level of protection in the EU. Against the background of the latest reforms of EMIR and MiFIR in light of Brexit, the Commission's statement stresses that equivalence follows a risk-sensitive approach with varying degrees of granularity in the assessment and a strict application of the principle of proportionality, especially if high-impact third countries are involved.[173]

This interpretation of the Commission corresponds to the statements published by ESAs. Already in 2005, CESR, ESMA's predecessor, pointed out that equivalence does not require an identical approach of the third country in question. Rather, it is sufficient that the third country legal system allows investors to take similar decisions based on the information to be published.[174] In 2010, CESR explicitly stated in the context of credit rating agencies that equivalence means an outcome-based approach from a holistic perspective reaching the same level of consumer protection as the EU legislation, without demanding a line-by-line transfer of EU legislation to the third country legislation.[175] ESMA subsequently recalled this view on several occasions.[176] Also, CEIOPS, EIOPA's predecessor, concurred with this interpretation in its consultation paper on the methodology for equivalence assessments under Solvency II.[177] The same applies to EBA, which published a methodology demanding that third country rules achieve 'similar outcomes as the EU framework' in terms of the major legislative aims expressed by the EU legislator.[178] All in all, the Commission's and

[168] ibid 7.
[169] ibid.
[170] ibid 8.
[171] Commission (n 54).
[172] ibid 3.
[173] ibid 5–8.
[174] CESR (n 142) paras 1ff.
[175] CESR, 'Technical Advice to the European Commission on the Equivalence between the Japanese Regulatory and Supervisory Framework and the EU Regulatory Regime for Credit Rating Agencies' CESR/10-333 (9 June 2010) paras 31–35.
[176] See eg Steven Maijoor (Chair of ESMA), 'Dinner Address—FESE Convention' Speech ESMA71-319-120 (4 June 2019) 5 https://www.esma.europa.eu/sites/default/files/library/esma71-319-120_fese_dinner_address_dublin_june_2019_steven_maijoor.pdf (accessed 12 November 2022); ESMA (n 142) 4; ESMA, 'Final report—US' (n 37) 5.
[177] CEIOPS, 'Consultation Paper no 82: The methodology for equivalence assessments by CEIOPS under Solvency II' CEIOPS-CP-82/10 (27 September 2010) 5f.
[178] EBA, 'Questionnaire on the Assessment of the Equivalence with European regulatory and supervisory framework' (Questionnaire—Annex I) (2015) 1 www.eba.europa.eu/documents/10180/1094990/Annex+I+-+EBA+questionnaire+on+regulatory+equivalence_publication.pdf (accessed 12 November 2022).

ESAs' general understanding of the term 'equivalence' is in line with the interpretation of this book.[179]

2. Process of determination: Identifying a methodology

More complex than evaluating the abstract meaning of equivalence is the actual assessment of whether a third country legal system is equivalent. Unfortunately, the relevant directives and regulations are rather silent on this question. Much is therefore left to administrative practice, which makes a consistent and transparent practice even more important.

a) Practice of the European Commission

The practice of the Commission is difficult to determine and therefore remains opaque. There are many underlying causes for this situation. First, the Commission only adopts positive equivalence decisions. Whenever it assesses a third country legal system and finds it to be not equivalent, no official decision is taken, let alone published. Consequently, the reasons for the rejection remain in the dark. This is particularly unfortunate in cases in which the Commission deviates from the advice of ESAs, as the differences in the evaluation are not disclosed. Secondly, the decision-making is often influenced by political considerations and does not reflect a purely technical analysis.[180] Political factors are per se hard to anticipate and detect as they are not expressed openly. Thirdly, positive equivalence decisions are brief in their reasoning as to why a third country system is considered equivalent. Most recitals merely repeat the legislative text, the result of the technical advice by ESAs as well as objectives pursued by the legislation. As a result of this lack of transparency, third countries cannot respond adequately to the denial of equivalence and make targeted adjustments to their legal systems. Given the outstanding role of the Commission in equivalence mechanisms, this shortcoming is one of the main challenges for the concept of equivalence.

b) Practice of ESAs

aa) Practice of ESMA respectively CESR ESMA has long been involved in the equivalence assessment by issuing technical advice to the Commission.[181] Three areas, in particular, can be identified which provide deep insights into the methodology of ESMA's assessment.

CESR published the first statement on the methodology of equivalence in a concept paper on the equivalence of certain third country GAAP in 2005.[182] This methodology was confirmed multiple times.[183] In a first step, CESR recapitulated four general principles of IFRS, namely understandability, relevance, reliability and comparability,

[179] This does not apply to the question of whether the equivalence decision is a technical or a policy decision. See on that problem ch 2 B)II.2.

[180] See extensively on political influences ch 2 B)II.2.

[181] Moloney (n 33) 116–19.

[182] CESR (n 142); see for an extensive analysis of the practice of CESR Schammo (n 11) 152ff.

[183] See eg CESR, 'Technical advice on equivalence of certain third country GAAP and International Financial Reporting Standards' CESR/05~230 b (June 2005); CESR, 'Technical advice on a mechanism for determining the equivalence of the generally accepted accounting principles of third countries' CESR/07~289 (30 May 2007).

which were already listed in the Commission's mandate to CESR.[184] In a second step, CESR conducted a technical assessment, which was subdivided into two parts. In the first part of the technical assessment, CESR asked third country authorities whether and in what way the general principles identified in the first step and other principles of IFRS are met or pursued in their legal order.[185] The legal order in this sense included the third country GAAP as well as other mandatory guidance or regulation concerning these principles.[186] This consultation disclosed the differences between the legal systems. The second part of the technical assessment tried to evaluate the 'significance' of the differences found.[187] As the legal systems did not need to be identical, differences were not per se harmful to a positive equivalence evaluation. On the contrary, as long as investors were in a position to make investment decisions on the basis of understandable, relevant, reliable and comparable information, differences were irrelevant.[188] A hypothetical test could therefore be whether an investor would make similar investment decisions when looking either only at European standards or only at the third country GAAP.[189] This hypothetical test already reveals that a rule's protection level can hardly be determined in the abstract.[190] Laws function and unfold their effects only when they are applied to individual cases. However, cases and circumstances vary; for instance, different securities do not have the same characteristics and investors have different levels of experience, practice, knowledge, and preferences, making it hard—if not impossible—to define a precise level of protection of an abstract rule. It, therefore, makes sense to focus on commonly found cases as advocated by CESR.[191] Another crucial issue is the balancing of similarities and differences. Is the economic effect of a divergent regime, for example, severe enough to lead to a finding of non-equivalence? This decisive question has neither been specified in the methodology of CESR nor of ESMA.

Another area where CESR and later ESMA have fully disclosed their methodology for determining equivalence is the regulation of credit rating agencies. CESR commenced its technical advice on the US and Japan in 2010 with general considerations on the approach for assessing equivalence.[192] First, it drafted a questionnaire to be answered by the third country supervisor for self-assessment, as it is best placed to explain its legal system. Secondly, CESR identified conditions that are of major importance to the EU CRA Regulation, and which must be met by the third country to be assessed as equivalent. These conditions were rather broad and included that the rules of the third country are legally binding, that they are formulated in detail rather than in the abstract and that they are already in force. Thirdly, CESR detected similarities and differences between the legal systems based on the questionnaire and evaluated whether these differences impact the goals expressed by the EU legislator.

[184] CESR (n 142) paras 17ff.
[185] ibid paras 40ff.
[186] ibid para 42.
[187] ibid paras 46ff.
[188] ibid para 9.
[189] This is the proposal of a 'Market-based test' by Tzung Bor Wei, which will be discussed in more detail below. See ch 2 B)I.2.c)bb)(2).
[190] CESR (n 142) para 49.
[191] ibid para 50.
[192] CESR (n 123); CESR (n 175).

The fourth step consisted of aggregating these findings from a holistic perspective (also called 'global assessment').[193] The crucial question is whether the differences identified in the third step led to a finding of equivalence or non-equivalence of the third country legal system. Hence, this approach is very similar to the one used for assessing the equivalence of accounting standards, although the steps are not described identically.

A third area where ESMA provided detailed information in its technical advice concerns equivalence assessments under EMIR. As outlined above, EMIR contains several equivalence mechanisms covering inter alia CCPs and trade repositories. Although the technical advice differentiates between these regimes, the general approach is the same. Different from other areas, ESMA did not disclose a general methodology regarding the process of how equivalence is determined. The very detailed technical advice nevertheless reveals that its approach is akin to that in other areas.[194] It is an outcome-based approach from a holistic perspective. The basic aims of the EU legislator are identified, differences and similarities of the third country are disclosed and finally weighed up. The three representative examples, therefore, show that ESMA's approach to assessing equivalence is quite consistent and homogeneous.

bb) Practice of EIOPA respectively CEIOPS The procedure of equivalence assessments conducted by EIOPA is very similar to that of ESMA.[195] After having identified the main goals of the EU insurance legislation, CEIOPS also created a questionnaire for the authorities of the third country in question.[196] Intensive discussions follow this questionnaire, even including an onsite visit by EIOPA, to identify the main differences and similarities between the rules.[197] In the last step, EIOPA performs, just like ESMA, a balancing of these differences. Here, EIOPA uses five categories to further differentiate between the two extremes of equivalent and non-equivalent (observed, largely observed, partly observed, not observed, and not applicable).[198] This categorization makes the balancing process more comprehensible and transparent and is better than ESMA's approach in this respect. It nevertheless does not go far enough because clear criteria are still missing for the balancing. Remarkably, CEIOPS also published an indicative timeline for its assessment.[199] Since the final decision on equivalence is in the hands of the Commission, this will barely help the third country in question, however. Furthermore, EIOPA published guidelines on the methodology

[193] CESR (n 123) 18.

[194] ESMA, 'Final report—US' (n 37); ESMA, 'Final report: Technical advice on third country regulatory equivalence under EMIR—Australia' ESMA/2013/1159 (1 September 2013); Moloney (n 32) 47.

[195] See for an analysis of the approach of CEIOPS Bradley L Kading and Leila Madeiros, 'Insurance Regulation: Mutual Recognition, Equivalence and International Standards' in Patrick M Liedtke and Jan Monkiewicz (eds), *The Future of Insurance Regulation and Supervision* (Palgrave Macmillan 2011) 396ff.

[196] CEIOPS (n 177) 11ff; see for an example of such an assessment EIOPA, 'Advice to the European Commission: Equivalence assessment of the Bermudan supervisory system in relation to articles 172, 227 and 260 of the Solvency II Directive' EIOPA-BoS-11-029 (2011).

[197] CEIOPS (n 177) 8.

[198] ibid 9.

[199] ibid 10.

for equivalence assessments by NCAs under Solvency II to further harmonize assessments within the EU.[200]

cc) Practice of EBA EBA's approach is also comparable to that of ESMA and EIOPA. It identifies the main goals of the EU legislator, consults the third country supervisory authority in the form of a questionnaire and in the form of onsite inspections to identify similarities and differences between the legal systems, and weighs these differences in the last step. However, EBA recently changed its consultation by using two questionnaires instead of one.[201] In a first step, the third country authority needs to fill out a 'Pre-screening questionnaire' mainly consisting of questions that can be answered 'simply with a YES/NO'.[202] Subsequently, a more detailed questionnaire is sent out, containing various references to EU regulation and its goals.[203] These references aid the third country in understanding what its supervisory system is supposed to achieve. A special feature of EBA's second questionnaire is that it uses a 'five-grading scoring scale', differentiating between super equivalent, equivalent, largely equivalent, partially equivalent, and non-equivalent, to weigh differences within the subcategories of its assessment.[204] Thereby, EBA weighs the differences already when identifying similarities and differences. The grading scale is similar to the five groups used by EIOPA. As noted above, such a grading scale objectifies the final evaluation, as the extent of divergence between EU and third country rules has already been more finely categorized. In the last step, EBA aggregates these findings and transforms them into a two-grading scoring scale as used by the other ESAs: equivalent or non-equivalent.[205]

Another difference of EBA's practice is that it focuses solely on abstract rules and the supervisory framework and not on individual cases, claiming that such an approach would be too complicated.[206] Looking at concrete cases indeed complicates the assessment. However, to determine whether a third country legal system achieves the same regulatory outcomes, there is no way around looking at the effects produced in individual cases. Of course, this does not mean that ESAs have to analyse thousands of individual cases. However, they must at least look at how abstract rules are generally applied and enforced within a legal system and thus how they influence individuals in commonly found cases.

[200] EIOPA, 'Guidelines on the methodology for equivalence assessments by National Supervisory Authorities under Solvency II' EIOPA-BoS-14-182 (2014).

[201] In the past, EBA had just one questionnaire: see EBA (n 178).

[202] EBA, 'Regulatory and Supervisory Equivalence—Pre-screening questionnaire (STEP1)' (2019) https://eba.europa.eu/sites/default/documents/files/documents/10180/2613666/ec3d2202-a08e-42f6-9216-f5df332fa1a5/EBA%20methodology%20for%20the%20assessment%20of%20regulatory%20and%20supervisory%20equivalence%20of%20third%20countries%20-%201st%20step.pdf (accessed 12 November 2022).

[203] EBA, 'Questionnaire on the Assessment of the Equivalence with European regulatory and supervisory framework' (21 February 2022) https://www.eba.europa.eu/sites/default/documents/files/document_library/Publications/Other%20publications/2022/1027291/EBA%20Questionnaire%20Equivalence%202st%20step.pdf (accessed 12 March 2023).

[204] EBA, 'Opinion of the European Banking Authority on the Equivalence of Supervisory and Regulatory Requirements in relation to Turkey and New Zealand' EBA/Op/2015/21 (17 December 2015) 2.

[205] ibid.

[206] ibid.

dd) Do ESAs meet their expectations? As ESAs claim to follow both a self-imposed methodology and an understanding of the legal concept of equivalence which has been defined as an outcome-based approach from a holistic perspective focused on the main regulatory goals of the EU, it is necessary to verify these claims against some representative examples of technical advice issued.[207]

The technical advice issued by CESR on the equivalence of accounting standards of Canada, Japan, and the US is a perfect example of CESR strictly adhering to its methodology.[208] The assessment is displayed in a spreadsheet with the first column referring to IFRS, the second containing a description of the third country GAAP in question, the third column assessing the differences and the fourth column proposing a remedy. After having identified the differences, CESR examines the impact of these on investors' decisions.[209] In doing so, CESR takes into account the effect of such differences on financial markets, which constitutes an outcome-based approach. CESR stuck to that approach when it evaluated the equivalence of legal systems in relation to credit rating agencies. CESR and ESMA still refer to and consider the differences of the effects on investors.[210] Furthermore, CESR assessed the US system as 'broadly equivalent' on the grounds that the EU and the US shared the same overall objectives, even though the philosophy behind the regulation was very different.[211] With regard to the regulation of CCPs under EMIR, ESMA also claims to follow an outcome-based approach. Indeed, differences are still recognized as being broadly equivalent if the third country takes another approach.[212]

Under Solvency II, not many equivalence decisions have been adopted. The most extensive technical advice by EIOPA was adopted concerning the Bermudan supervisory system and its equivalence to Solvency II as required under Articles 172, 227, and 260.[213] This assessment is based on 12 principles identified by EIOPA as being at the centre of Solvency II. Each assessment starts with a short recapitulation of the goal of the EU regulation and is followed by an analysis of the Bermudan legal system. The result is based on the five groups introduced in the general methodology. Some of the assessments tend to miss the target of an outcome-based approach from a holistic perspective because they focus too much on technicalities demanded in EU legislation and thereby come close to a line-by-line assessment.[214] This risk is mitigated in the results, as a final balancing offers an opportunity to see the full picture and focus on the

[207] See concerning the third country regime of the AIFMD Zetzsche and Veidt (n 115) 837.

[208] CESR, 'Technical advice on equivalence of certain third country GAAP and International Financial Reporting Standards' (n 183).

[209] See eg Standard IFRS 2 or IAS Standards 18 and 19 (third column) in CESR, 'Technical advice on equivalence of certain third country GAAP and International Financial Reporting Standards' (n 183) 31 and 36.

[210] ESMA, 'Final Report: Technical advice on CRA regulatory equivalence—Argentina, Brazil, Mexico, Hong Kong and Singapore' ESMA/2013/626 (30 May 2013) 39.

[211] CESR (n 123) 40–55 and 161.

[212] See eg Australian CCPs do not need a remuneration committee. However, they are required to have compensation agreements in place to secure the soundness and effectiveness of risk management. ESMA regarded this different regulatory technique as broadly equivalent. See ESMA, 'Final report—Australia' (n 194) 26.

[213] EIOPA, 'Advice to the European Commission' (n 196).

[214] See eg the analysis of capital requirements, which goes into great detail on EU legislation. EIOPA, 'Advice to the European Commission' (n 196) 41ff.

general outcomes. By concluding that the Bermudan supervisory system meets the criteria for an equivalence assessment in relation to some insurers with few caveats, although some of the EU principles were only partly equivalent,[215] EIOPA returns to the path of an outcome-based approach from a holistic perspective. The approach taken in the technical advice relating to Bermuda is very similar to that in other cases.[216] All in all, EIOPA generally follows its methodology and interpretation of equivalence.

As outlined above, EBA created two questionnaires that must be answered by the third country to be assessed. Both questionnaires focus solely on technical aspects and do not include policy considerations, which is in line with EBA's general methodology. The second, more comprehensive questionnaire is divided into 16 thematic sections and focuses on the main goals of the EU legislator. As claimed by EBA, it does not go into technical particularities. All EBA opinions include a detailed analysis of the legal systems in their annex. This annex starts by giving a general overview of the third country financial system, including market participants, banking system, and Basel III implementation. Afterwards, the analysis is displayed in a spreadsheet in which the results of the specific sectors are rated according to the five-grading scoring scale mentioned above. In 2015, EBA assessed the regulatory systems of Turkey and New Zealand and found them to be equivalent.[217] Even though EBA identified some parts of the regulation as being only 'partially equivalent' and even 'not equivalent',[218] these conclusions did not result in a general finding of non-equivalence. This underlines the holistic perspective taken by EBA. It is therefore not harmful if parts of the assessment are rather technical, as this does not directly lead to the finding of non-equivalence. Unfortunately, EBA does not consider the effects different rules have on investors. Also, the actual enforcement is not part of the assessment, as EBA openly admits.[219] By putting aside these effects on the economy, EBA performs more of an 'abstract outcome-based' than a 'concrete outcome-based' assessment.

All in all, ESAs adhere to the approach outlined in their methodology.[220] At times, it seems that ESAs are moving towards a line-by-line analysis, but in the overall assessment, they mostly maintain a holistic approach. However, what is missing in the assessments of ESAs is more reference to real economic outcomes rather than abstract rules.

c) *Critical analysis and theoretical foundation*

As indicated at the beginning of this section, a consistent and transparent administrative practice in relation to the process of determining equivalence is a key component in creating legal certainty by enhancing the comprehensibility of equivalence mechanisms and the predictability of their results.[221] An examination of the Commission's

[215] See eg Principle 3 concerning the taking-up of business, ibid 26.

[216] See eg EIOPA, 'Advice to the European Commission: Equivalence assessment of the Japanese supervisory system in relation to article 172 of the Solvency II Directive' EIOPA-BoS-11-030 (2011).

[217] EBA (n 204) 3.

[218] ibid Annex 21 and 24. The same is true for other assessments: see eg EBA, 'Opinion of the European Banking Authority on the Equivalence of supervisory and regulatory requirements in relation to Serbia and South Korea' EBA/Op/2020-01 (23 January 2020).

[219] EBA (n 204) 2.

[220] For a consenting view see Moloney (n 32) 44–48.

[221] See also IOSCO, 'Good Practices on Processes for Deference' Report (June 2020) 11ff (Good Practice 1) https://www.iosco.org/library/pubdocs/pdf/IOSCOPD659.pdf (accessed 12 November 2022).

practice has shown that much remains in the dark, as the Commission only publishes positive equivalence decisions and only provides brief explanations. Positive equivalence decisions can be interpreted as consent not only to the result of equivalence but also to the methodology used by ESAs. However, such a conclusion is fraught with considerable uncertainty.

The administrative practice of ESAs is much more transparent, which is also why it is proposed in Chapter 5 that more responsibility should be shifted to them.[222] Many of the technical analyses contain a section on their methodology. As can be seen from the examples above, there is no common methodology but different ones for different equivalence mechanisms. Although these methodologies are very similar, some differences persist, which is unfortunate in view of the fact that equivalence is a uniform concept. Hence, it would be better to establish one common methodology applicable to all equivalence regimes (aa)). Moreover, when ESAs evaluate the differences between the legal systems and their effects on EU markets and investors, an underlying theoretical concept seems to be missing. Some evaluations, such as assessments by EBA, remain very abstract and do not look at individual outcomes. Other analyses tend to be rather subjective and detached from objective criteria, which again creates legal ambiguity. The following analysis attempts to map out a theoretical framework for the process of evaluating and weighing up differences between legal systems (bb)).

aa) Common methodology: Functional comparison A closer look at the approaches of ESAs analysed above reveals that they are all very close to the method of functional comparison. This method was coined by Konrad Zweigert and Hein Kötz in their book *An Introduction to Comparative Law*.[223] This method starts from the hypothesis that two things in law are only comparable if they fulfil the same function. A functional legal comparison requires that the preconditions of the domestic legal system are completely eradicated. Familiar concepts must be set aside. The questions posed to the third country legal system must be purely functional.[224] Applied to equivalence, this means that the central aims of the EU legislation in question must first be identified. What is the function of the EU legislation, and why did the legislator prescribe certain rules? Here, an orientation along the origin of the rules and the circumstances that led to their adoption as well as the recitals of the legislation may be helpful. Once these aims have been defined, the second step is to look at the third country legal system and locate rules that pursue the same objectives without transferring European concepts to the third country system. In practice, this is done by questionnaires and consultations of third country supervisory authorities. These authorities are best placed to explain their legal system. Positive side-effects of this procedure are that it reduces the workload on the side of the EU, it strengthens supervisory cooperation, and intensifies supervisory communication. When looking at foreign systems, Zweigert and Kötz underline that the 'comparatist must treat as a source of law whatever moulds or affects the living law

[222] See ch 5 B)II.1.

[223] Konrad Zweigert and Hein Kötz, *An Introduction to Comparative Law*, vol 1 (1st edn, North-Holland 1977) 23–41.

[224] ibid 27–31; Kirsten Scheiwe, 'Was ist ein funktionales Äquivalent in der Rechtsvergleichung?' (2000) 83 KritV 30.

in his chosen system'.[225] This is exactly the approach taken by ESAs in equivalence assessments. As long as the rules, be it statutory or customary law, case law or administrative practice, have a binding effect, they are relevant for the outcomes produced in real life and must thus be taken into account.[226]

Once the rules of the third country system having the same function or task as the European rules have been identified, in a third step, differences and similarities need to be detected, yet without critically evaluating them.[227] This is often done by ESAs in the form of a chart indicating in one column the rules of the EU legal system and in another column the third country rules that fulfil the same function. However, not much is gained by just listing differences and similarities.[228] Since the third country law does not have to be identical but only equivalent, differences alone are insufficient to establish a finding of (non-) equivalence.

That is why, in a fourth step, an evaluation or weighing up of these differences needs to take place. In the methodology of functional comparison, this step is described as a 'critical evaluation' of the identified differences and similarities.[229] This evaluation is very difficult because abstract rules, when considered in isolation, do not have a level of protection. Rather, the level of protection depends on the outcome of individual cases governed by these rules. What further complicates the process is that the evaluation must also include supervisory and judicial practice. It is not sufficient to look at the 'law in the books'; instead, the legal practice must be used as the basis of the evaluation. To objectify the evaluation with regard to the 'law in practice', it is essential to consider empirical research.[230] The entire evaluation is also linked to the risk of what is referred to as legal-cultural imperialism.[231] Cultural imperialism means the oversimplified assumption that the domestic legal system has a smarter and more efficient solution to a problem without questioning both ideas from a neutral perspective. This bias is based on the human reflex that something familiar must be better than an alien approach. To prevent such tendencies and objectify the evaluation, it is best to develop a theoretical framework for the balancing process, as proposed in the next section.

bb) Evaluating differences: Economic analysis As seen, the process of evaluating differences is a complex and opaque one.[232] Even though equivalence mechanisms are all based on a uniform concept, the balancing in each case has its particular challenges. The EU legislator puts different aims in the centre of legislative acts, the legal consequences of equivalence provisions differ, and each third country legal system

[225] Zweigert and Kötz (n 223) 27.
[226] See n 143 (ch 2).
[227] Zweigert and Kötz (n 223) 35.
[228] ibid 36; see also the criticism raised in Geoffrey Samuel, *An Introduction to Comparative Law Theory and Method* (Hart Publishing 2014) 65–95.
[229] Zweigert and Kötz (n 223) 40–41; Ralf Michaels, 'Functional Method' in Mathias Reimann and Reinhard Zimmermann (eds), *The Oxford Handbook of Comparative Law* (2nd edn, OUP 2019) 379–81.
[230] See eg Peter Cane and Herbert M Kritzer (eds), *The Oxford Handbook of Empirical Legal Research* (OUP 2010); Uwe Kischel, *Comparative Law* (OUP 2019) 112–30.
[231] Kischel (n 230) 48–50.
[232] With regard to the third country regime of the AIFMD and the assessments by ESMA, the missing transparency is explicitly criticized in Zetzsche and Veidt (n 115) 837: 'We note, however, that the methodology of the equivalence assessment is not transparent. In particular, the weighing up of individual provisions by ESMA is unclear and it is not clear on what exact information ESMA bases its decisions.'

has its own historical, cultural, and legal specificities. Because of these differences, it is impossible to formulate a step-by-step instruction on how to perform the evaluation. Such an instruction for practice, which can simply be applied to all cases, is not a realistic goal. Instead, three economic concepts will be introduced in the following, which may function as a future basis for evaluations. A normative approach to comparative law, built on the groundwork of economic theories, will objectify evaluations.[233] It prevents cultural imperialism and the hiding behind vague terms.[234] Hence, economic theories increase the foreseeability of results and legal certainty.

(1) Statistical comparison

Statistical comparison is a rather new method of comparing and evaluating rules in different legal systems.[235] It emerged in the area of business law and is still largely limited to this area.[236] The major difference between statistical comparison and other methods of comparative law is that statistical comparison does not describe and evaluate rules with words but translates these abstract rules into numbers.[237] So far, statistics have only been used in the field of sociology of law to describe the reality, i.e. in the case of capital markets law, the effects empirical data suggests rules have on investors and the economy.[238] The unique characteristic of the new approach is that the rule itself is transformed into a statistic.

A renowned study in capital markets law is that of La Porta, Lopez-de-Silanes, and Shleifer.[239] In this study, they compared the legal requirements as well as the enforcement in 49 countries with respect to initial public offerings.[240] Afterwards, they determined the power and size of the capital markets of the respective countries and tried to draw conclusions from the regulatory level of a country to the power and size of its capital market. They concluded, inter alia, that the strength of a capital market depends on the regulatory level of the country in question: the stronger the regulatory level, the stronger the capital market.[241] For the purposes of the equivalence assessment, only the first step is of relevance. To ascertain the regulatory level, the authors

[233] Florian Faust, 'Economic Analysis of Law' in Mathias Reimann and Reinhard Zimmermann (eds), *The Oxford Handbook of Comparative Law* (2nd edn, OUP 2019) 834–36.

[234] ibid 835.

[235] Simeon Djankov and others, 'The New Comparative Economics' (2003) 31 J Comp Econ 595; Mathias M Siems, 'Statistische Rechtsvergleichung' (2008) 72 RabelsZ 354; Claude Ménard and Bertrand du Marais, 'Can We Rank Legal Systems According to Their Economic Efficiency?' (2008) 26 Wash U J L & Pol'y 55; critical of this view is Kischel (n 230) 134–43.

[236] Kischel (n 230) 134.

[237] Siems (n 235) 355f.

[238] See in general Cane and Kritzer (n 230); Robert M Lawless, Jennifer K Robbennolt, and Thomas S Ulen (eds), *Empirical Methods in Law* (2nd edn, Wolters Kluwer 2016).

[239] Rafael La Porta, Florencio Lopez-de-Silanes, and Andrei Shleifer, 'What Works in Securities Laws?' (2006) 61 J Fin 1; critical of this view is Mathias M Siems, 'What Does Not Work in Comparing Securities Laws: A Critique on La Porta et al.'s Methodology' (2005) 16 ICCLR 300; Mathias M Siems, 'Numerical Comparative Law: Do We Need Statistical Evidence in Law in Order to Reduce Complexity' (2005) 13 Cardozo J Intl & Comp L 521, 531–33. A similar study is the 'Doing Business Report' of the World Bank Group; see for the 2020 report World Bank Group, 'Doing Business Report' (2020) https://openknowledge.worldbank.org/bitstream/handle/10986/32436/9781464814402.pdf (accessed 12 November 2022).

[240] La Porta, Lopez-de-Silanes, and Shleifer (n 239) 3–5.

[241] They also concluded that some legal requirements play a bigger role than others and that, as a general rule, common law countries have a better regulation than civil law countries. See ibid 27f.

assigned a value to a country for each obligation, such as the obligation to publish a prospectus. If the obligation was part of the country's legal system, the country scored a 1, if the duty did not exist, it got a 0, and if the obligation was somehow restricted, it was assigned a 0.5. Next, the figures were aggregated and an average was calculated to assign a number to each country in a particular area, which was supposed to describe the strength of its legal system. In the field of disclosure requirements, for example, Germany scored 0.42, Switzerland 0.67, France 0.75, the UK 0.83, and the US 1.0.[242] In the context of equivalence, the conclusion from this calculation would be that the US legal system concerning disclosure obligations is equivalent to all other systems mentioned. The Swiss system would, however, not be equivalent to that of France or the UK but equivalent to that of Germany.

This study has been criticized on many different grounds.[243] From the perspective of equivalence, three objections are of particular importance. First, simply translating abstract rules into numbers is at odds with an outcome-based approach. The goal of equivalence is to evaluate the effects abstract rules have on markets and investors to determine how far the aims of the legislator are fulfilled.[244] Statistical comparison looks only at abstract rules and not at the effects they create on the market. It might be objected that the second step of the study establishes a correlation between abstract rules and the size of markets. However, correlation is not the same as causality, which is mixed up here.[245] There are many other reasons for a correlation, such as cultural and political influences. Besides, the market size does not necessarily allow the conclusion that investors are protected and resources are allocated more efficiently on these markets. Secondly, assigning a number to single rules contradicts the idea of a holistic perspective. Not national ideas/concepts, but functionality must be at the centre of the evaluation, which is disregarded if only single rules are compared.[246] Thirdly, the reduction of abstract rules to three numbers (0; 0.5 and 1) oversimplifies reality.[247] Effects of rules and their efficiency are complex, have many sides and come in subtle shades rather than black and white. Hence, it is inappropriate to categorize detailed rules and reflect them in just three numbers. As a result, the approach of statistical comparison is not suitable to aid in evaluating equivalence. It may give a rough orientation if the numbers assigned were more nuanced (e.g. in steps of 0.1: 0.1–1.0), but it cannot be used as a definite yardstick.

(2) Market-based test

In 2007, Tzung-bor Wei had already suggested what he called a market-based test for equivalence:

> An alternative approach is to focus on economic effects rather than law per se. Here the appropriate questions are: How do regulations affect capital markets? Are these

[242] ibid 15f. One has to keep in mind that this study is from 2006. In those days, the harmonization in capital markets law, particularly within the EU, was not as advanced as it is today.
[243] Siems, 'What Does Not Work in Comparing Securities Laws (n 239); Kischel (n 230) 136–43.
[244] See extensively: ch 2 B)I.1.a)aa).
[245] Kischel (n 230) 140f.
[246] Siems, 'Numerical Comparative Law' (n 239) 531–33.
[247] ibid 529–31; Kischel (n 230) 136–39.

> effects similar or different? How do market participants react to the regulations? Under this view, two regulatory regimes that have different legal characteristics may nonetheless be 'equivalent' if they produce the same economic effects, ie if capital markets treat the regimes as interchangeable.[248]

One example where such a test has been undertaken is a study that compared accounting standards, namely IAS to US GAAP.[249] CESR has also applied the market-based test, paraphrasing it as follows:

> Rather CESR believes that, in the framework of the mandate given by the European Commission, third country GAAP can be declared as equivalent to IAS/IFRS when financial statements prepared under such third country GAAP enable investors to take similar decision in terms of whether to invest or divest, as if they were provided with financial statements prepared on the basis of IAS/IFRS.[250]

Later, this test was even included in the definition of equivalence by the Commission in Article 2 Commission Regulation (EC) No 1569/2007 of 21 December 2007, requiring that 'investors are likely to make the same decisions'. The advantage of such an approach is twofold. First, it focuses on what equivalence really is, an outcome-based approach from a holistic perspective that rather looks at economic effects than at abstract rules. Secondly, underlying the test is an economic concept that can either be verified or falsified and thus it objectifies the evaluation. Nonetheless, two objections remain. The first problem relates to the difficulty of determining economic outcomes in practice.[251] How can it be determined whether a rule leads to different results in a foreign jurisdiction? Even if there is a different outcome in a foreign jurisdiction, how can causality be established? Was it the different rule or rather another factor that led to a different result? This objection has some truth to it. Indeed, it is difficult to figure out such causal links, especially in areas where economic data is missing. However, practical difficulties do not challenge the concept itself. As already indicated, it is better to have a theoretical framework underlying the evaluation, even if it might not be a step-by-step introduction for all cases, than to argue detached from real effects and rational reasons. Hence, whenever it is feasible to conduct a market-based test, it should be carried out. The second challenge is more fundamental. Why is it necessary that the third country legal system produces the *same* economic outcome? This insinuates that the EU legislator created the 'best' solution in terms of the goals pursued in capital markets law. It leaves out the option that the third country came up with an approach that achieves an even higher level of investor protection and greater efficiency of capital markets.[252] That is why the fact that a third country legal system

[248] Wei (n 15) 262.

[249] Christian Leuz, 'IAS versus U.S. GAAP: Information-Asymmetry Based Evidence from Germany's New Market' (2003) 41 J Acct Res 445.

[250] CESR (n 142) para 1.

[251] Imm (n 106) 115f.

[252] See on this demarcation between undesirable regulatory arbitrage and beneficial regulatory competition Sean J Griffith, 'Substituted Compliance and Systemic Risk: How to Make a Global Market in Derivatives Regulation' (2014) 98 Minn LR 1291, 3126ff.

produces the same economic effects as the EU legislation is a sufficient test but not a necessary requirement to establish equivalence.

(3) Kaldor-Hicks improvement

Since the market-based test is a sufficient but not a necessary requirement, a method that goes beyond this test needs to be identified. Such a method could be a Kaldor-Hicks improvement. Nicholas Kaldor and John Hicks developed a theory to overcome deficiencies arising from the Pareto principle when comparing two conditions against the benchmark of efficiency.[253] According to Kaldor and Hicks, a reallocation of resources is more efficient and thus an improvement if those that are made better off could hypothetically compensate those that are made worse off and lead to a Pareto-improving outcome.[254] With the help of this formula, legislators can figure out whether rule A is more or less efficient than rule B. It is therefore often used in regulatory impact assessments, especially in capital markets law.[255] In the context of equivalence, the question arises as to whether this formula can be used by the Commission and ESAs to determine if a third country rule A is 'equivalent' to rule B of the European Union, where rule A and B may also mean a set of rules. This presupposes that efficiency is not only an instrument for the legislator but can also be used by the administration and courts to interpret laws. Some scholars are rather restrictive in this respect. However, even they acknowledge that efficiency may be a tool for interpreting rules if the legislator has based the law on the principle of efficiency.[256] Under this condition, an economic interpretation is always a teleological interpretation because the legislator sought to draft a regulation that is as efficient as possible.

Hence, the *Kaldor-Hicks* improvement can only be applied in an area of law solely based on the concept of efficiency.[257] Legislation in capital markets is often founded on three aims: functioning markets, investor protection and systemic stability.[258] The concept of functioning markets has three components, namely allocative, institutional and operational efficiency.[259] Investors will only invest money if they are protected and markets function properly, as only functioning markets will provide them with reasonable pricing as well as low transaction costs and will guarantee equal treatment. That is why functioning markets and investor protection are two sides of the same

[253] Nicholas Kaldor, 'Welfare Propositions of Economics and Interpersonal Comparisons of Utility' (1939) 49 Econ J 549. See Emanuel V Towfigh in Emanuel V Towfigh and Niels Petersen (eds), *Ökonomische Methoden im Recht* (2nd edn, Mohr Siebeck 2017) 42–43.

[254] John S Chipman, 'Compensation Principle' in *The New Palgrave Dictionary of Economics* (3rd edn, Macmillan 2018) 1912ff; Hans-Bernd Schäfer and Claus Ott, *Lehrbuch der ökonomischen Analyse des Zivilrechts* (6th edn, Springer 2020) 21f.

[255] Wolf-Georg Ringe, '"Alternativen: Keine"? Gesetzesfolgenabschätzung in der Finanzmarktregulierung' in Matthias Casper and others (eds), *Festschrift für Johannes Köndgen zum 70. Geburtstag* (RWS 2016) 65.

[256] Horst Eidenmüller, *Effizienz als Rechtsprinzip* (4th edn, Mohr Siebeck 2015) 454–59; less restrictive regarding civil law: Gerhard Wagner, 'Prävention und Verhaltenssteuerung durch Privatrecht—Anmaßung oder legitime Aufgabe' (2006) 206 AcP 352, 425–31.

[257] Daniel M Häusermann, 'Eine annahmenbasierte Rechtssetzungsmethode für das Handelsrecht' (2015) 6 RW 49, 51.

[258] See eg Transparency Directive, recital 1.

[259] Rüdiger Veil, 'Concepts and Aims of Capital Market Regulation' in Rüdiger Veil (ed), *European Capital Markets Law* (3rd edn, Hart Publishing 2022) § 2 paras 6ff.

coin.[260] Moreover, investors will only invest money if the financial system itself is stable. A stable system, however, requires sufficient liquidity, which is only provided if investors have confidence in the system. There can be no investor protection without functioning markets or systemic stability, and vice versa. Consequently, it can be argued that EU capital markets law is solely based on the idea of efficiency.[261]

These objectives of the EU legislator correspond to the formula of the Kaldor-Hicks improvement. Whenever a 'third country rule' constitutes a Kaldor-Hicks improvement compared to the 'EU rule', resources are reallocated to more efficient investments. Therefore, they lead to a better functioning market. At the same time, better-functioning markets increase investor protection, which in turn leads to more investments and thus to more stable markets. As a result, a 'third country rule', which is a Kaldor-Hicks improvement compared to the 'EU rule', surpasses the goals of the EU legislator and is therefore equivalent to the 'EU rule'. This also applies if the 'third country rule' is not a Kaldor-Hicks improvement, but if those that are made better off can hypothetically compensate those that are made worse off without making any profit. Consequently, the theory of Kaldor-Hicks improvement can generally be transferred to equivalence assessments.

Nevertheless, two concerns remain. First, it can be doubted that the legislator only focuses on efficiency in capital markets law. In recent years, new factors primarily based on ethical and moral convictions have influenced the legislation, such as environmental aspects, questions of health and safety regulations or compliance and human rights issues.[262] These factors are often dealt with under the buzzwords sustainable finance and ESG.[263] However, even these considerations can often be expressed in economic terms.[264] Environmental challenges, for example, cause natural disasters, famines, and scarcity of resources, all of which may lead to systemic risks that must be priced in. Without pricing them in, markets are not efficient, and investors bear greater risks than anticipated. Thus, even factors that at first sight do not appear to be economic in nature may have an economic dimension on closer examination. In exceptional cases, where such considerations cannot be traced back to the principle of

[260] Klaus J Hopt, *Der Kapitalanlegerschutz im Recht der Banken* (CH Beck 1975) 52, who described the relationship as two 'communicating vessels'.

[261] Thomas M Möllers, 'Efficiency as a Standard in Capital Market Law' (2009) 20 EBLR 243, 246–50; see also Richard A Posner, *Economic Analysis of Law* (9th edn, Wolters Kluwer 2014) ch 16.

[262] See eg the new Regulation (EU) 2020/852 of 18 June 2020 (Taxonomy Regulation); see Commission, 'Action Plan: Financing Sustainable Growth' (Communication) COM (2018) 97 final; High-Level Expert Group on Sustainable Finance, 'Final Report 2018: Financing a Sustainable European Economy' (2018) https://ec.europa.eu/info/sites/info/files/180131-sustainable-finance-final-report_en.pdf (accessed 12 November 2022).

[263] See Harald Glander and Daniel Lühmann, 'Auswirkungen der europäischen ESG-Regulierung auf Asset Manager' (2020) 10 RdF 12; Markus Lange, 'Sustainable Finance: Nachhaltigkeit durch Regulierung?' (2020) 20 BKR 216 (pt 1) and 261 (pt 2); Susan N Gary, 'Best Interests in the Long Term: Fiduciary Duties and ESG Integration' (2019) 90 U Colo L Rev 731; Dirk Schoenmaker and Willem Schramade, *Principles of Sustainable Finance* (OUP 2018); Bernard Paranque, Roland Perez, and William Sun (eds), *Finance Reconsidered: New Perspectives for a Responsible and Sustainable Finance* (Bingley Emerald 2016).

[264] See for an economic analysis of some of these topics ch 8, 9, 17, and 18 in A Mitchell Polinsky and Steven Shavell (eds), *Handbook of Law and Economics*, vols 1 and 2 (Elsevier 2007); Susmita Dasgupta, 'Environmental Regulation and Development: A Cross-country Empirical Analysis' (2001) 29 Oxf Dev Stud 173; Mary Dowell-Jones and David Kinley, 'Minding the Gap: Global Finance and Human Rights' (2011) 25 Ethics & Intl Aff 183.

efficiency, an exception from the proposed application of the Kaldor-Hicks improvement must be made.

Secondly, the proposed solution is connected to practical obstacles.[265] How is the Commission supposed to determine the effects of a rule, i.e. the reallocation of goods in the formula? What are the underlying hypotheses for such assumptions? As Mitchell Polinsky put it: 'Probably the most difficult problem in undertaking an economic analysis of a legal rule is putting dollar values on the relevant costs and benefits.'[266] Indeed, there are numerous problems when measuring the costs and benefits of rules. There will often be a lack of information, the causality between rules and effects on markets will be uncertain, and situations will be too complex to reduce them to simple causalities.[267] That is why, to perform the analysis in practice, the formula must be based on assumptions. When formulating these assumptions, the Commission must be granted room for manoeuvre. It must compare different assumptions and choose the one it finds most realistic. It is sufficient if the choice is made plausible.[268] This assumption-based approach reveals that equivalence is not a bright-line test, at least not in practice, where the underlying hypotheses are not definite. Instead, there is a range of 'correct' results for equivalence, depending on the underlying assumptions. Consequently, a Kaldor-Hicks improvement can only be calculated precisely in theory. In practice, it cannot be used as a mathematical formula since much depends on the assumptions used by the Commission. Rather, it can be utilized as a pattern for argumentation, where much depends on the justification by the Commission. Courts can only review whether the Commission's reasoning is in line with the theory of Kaldor-Hicks and whether the assessments are based on plausible assumptions. This leaves a margin of discretion to the Commission on the one hand, but on the other hand makes the assessment much more fact-oriented, predictable and less arbitrary.

(4) Conclusion

It has been demonstrated in this chapter that the evaluation of differences between the third country legal system and the EU legal system should be based on an economic analysis. An economic analysis brings light into the assessment, thereby increasing foreseeability and legal certainty, enabling the granting of legal protection, and eliminating the risk of cultural imperialism. The approach of a statistical comparison is not suitable as a basis for the evaluation because it focuses only on abstract rules and not regulatory outcomes and oversimplifies reality. It can, therefore, merely be used as a first orientation.

A market-based test for equivalence, as advocated by Tzung-bor Wei, is a good way of looking at equivalence outcomes, as the market reaction is at the centre of this theory. However, it is too restrictive because it does not cover the option that the third country legal system produces different but better regulatory outcomes. It is, therefore a sufficient, but not a necessary requirement. The preferred option is an assumption-based evaluation following the theory of a Kaldor-Hicks improvement. Whenever the

[265] Imm (n 106) 115.
[266] A Mitchell Polinsky, *An Introduction to Law and Economics* (5th edn, Wolters Kluwer 2019) 171.
[267] See extensively on the problems Häusermann (n 257) 62–76.
[268] ibid 78–83.

legal system of a third country represents a Kaldor-Hicks improvement on the basis of plausible assumptions made by the Commission, its legal system is equivalent to that of the EU.

II. Administrative decision-making leeway

As pointed out above, the equivalence decision is the crucial point in the entire procedure, which is why it is so important to assess what equivalence means and how it is determined. However, this can only be a starting point. It is of no use for financial service providers if the legal system of their home country is equivalent to that of the EU, but the Commission does not adopt an equivalence decision. The Commission has a decision-making leeway, which it has so far exploited extensively by operating as a political actor instead of a rule-bound administrative authority. This approach of the Commission has been identified as one of the main shortcomings of equivalence and has been widely criticized.[269]

In the following, some general concepts of European administrative law are outlined (1.) before an in-depth analysis of the nature of equivalence decisions as policy or technical decisions is undertaken (2.). The precise scope of the Commission's discretionary powers will then be examined (3.). Afterwards, further legal limits and individual rights that shape equivalence decisions are mapped out (4.). Finally, the question of whether there is a right to a decision for third countries or their financial service providers is addressed (5.). All this leads to a 'juridification' of equivalence.

1. General concepts of EU administrative law in the light of equivalence

a) Institutional role of the European Commission

The Commission is a genuinely supranational institution and shall, according to the Treaties, promote the general interest of the Union.[270] Its President is proposed by the European Council and elected by the European Parliament. The Commission as an institution is completely independent and responsible only to the Parliament.[271] It can be characterized as a Janus-faced institution due to the fact that it has extensive powers belonging to different branches. This is one reason why a clear separation of executive and legislative in European law is somewhat challenging.[272] The Commission is part of the legislative process and is considered 'the engine of integration' because it, in

[269] Jeremy Bacharach, 'L'équivalence: entre question technique et instrument de realpolitik' Centre de droit bancaire et financier (19 August 2019) https://www.cdbf.ch/1081/ (accessed 12 November 2022); Pierre-Henri Conac, 'The International Organisation of Securities Commissions (IOSCO), Europe, Brexit, and Rethinking Cross-border Regulation' (2020) 17 ECFR 72, 76–79; Wymeersch (n 4) 223–27; Elizabeth Howell, 'Post-"Brexit" Financial Governance' (2020) 83 MLR 128, 137f; on the political importance of market access in general see Eric Helleiner and Stefano Pagliari, 'The End of an Era in International Financial Regulation? A Post-Crisis Research Agenda' (2011) 65 Intl Organization 169.

[270] TEU, art 17(1); see Matthias Herdegen, *Europarecht* (24th edn, CH Beck 2023) § 7 paras 58ff.

[271] TEU, art 17(3) subpara 3 and (8).

[272] Eberhard Schmidt-Aßmann, 'Der Europäische Verwaltungsverbund und die Rolle des Verwaltungsrechts' in Eberhard Schmidt-Aßmann and Bettina Schöndorf-Haubold (eds), *Der Europäische Verwaltungsverbund* (Mohr Siebeck 2005) 12–14; see extensively Christoph Möllers, *Die Drei Gewalten* (Velbrück 2008) 175–77.

principle, has the sole power to initiate legislation.[273] As the 'guardian of the Treaties', the Commission also needs to ensure the implementation of the Treaties.[274] It can therefore initiate infringement proceedings and is a privileged applicant for actions for annulment and actions for failure to act. In addition, the Commission is also involved in the foreign policy of the EU[275] and is responsible for executing the budget.[276]

Of particular interest in the context of equivalence is the fact that the Commission is also tasked with delegated rulemaking and administrative duties. Delegated rulemaking takes place at Level 2 of the *Lamfalussy* process.[277] Since the Lisbon Treaties, there is a fundamental distinction between delegated acts pursuant to Article 290 TFEU and implementing acts pursuant to Article 291 TFEU. The former is described as non-legislative acts of general application which supplement or amend certain non-essential elements of the legislative act. Thus, delegated acts can be characterized as administrative law-making. The latter category of implementing acts is not defined in the Treaties. The key difference, however, is that delegated acts make minor changes to the basic act ('amend') or add new non-essential elements to it ('supplement') while implementing acts only help to give effect to the rules of the basic act.[278] This is why the Commission acts as a 'quasi-legislative' organ when adopting delegated acts.[279] The situation is completely different for implementing acts, where its 'power is purely executive', as found by the Commission itself.[280] Another difference is that the Commission is responsible for implementing acts only where uniform acts are needed, whereas it is always responsible for delegated acts when the legislative act contains a delegation.[281] Within the category of implementing acts, a further distinction can be made between implementing regulations, directives, and decisions. Implementing acts are governed by the Comitology Regulation of 2011, which lays down procedural rules granting rights to Member States to control the Commission in the adoption of these acts.[282]

In the context of equivalence, both delegated and implementing acts often play a role. Article 29(3) Prospectus Regulation illustrates this phenomenon. Pursuant to subparagraph 1, the Commission is empowered to adopt delegated acts establishing general criteria that should be considered in the equivalence decision. The Commission thereby adds new non-essential elements to the basic act and supplements it. The

[273] Walter Hallstein, *Der unvollendete Bundesstaat* (Econ 1969) 34.

[274] Rudolf Geiger in Rudolf Geiger, Daniel-Erasmus Khan, and Markus Kotzur (eds), *European Union Treaties* (CH Beck 2015) art 17 para 11.

[275] See eg TFEU, art 218(3); Matthias Herdegen, *Europarecht* (24th edn, CH Beck 2023) § 7 para 70.

[276] See TFEU, art 317.

[277] See Susanne Kalss, 'Kapitalmarktrecht' in Karl Riesenhuber (ed), *Europäische Methodenlehre* (4th edn, De Gruyter 2021) 601ff.

[278] Thomas Christiansen and Mathias Dobbels, 'Non-Legislative Rule Making after the Lisbon Treaty: Implementing the New System of Comitology and Delegated Acts' (2013) 19 Eur LJ 42, 44.

[279] Commission, 'Implementation of Article 290 of the Treaty on the Functioning of the European Union' (Communication) COM (2009) 673 final, 3; Joana Mendes, 'Delegated and Implementing Rule Making: Proceduralisation and Constitutional Design' (2013) 19 Eur LJ 22, 28.

[280] Mendes (n 279); Moloney (n 33) 117; Andreas Glaser, *Die Entwicklung des Europäischen Verwaltungsrechts aus der Perspektive der Handlungsformenlehre* (Mohr Siebeck 2013) 34ff.

[281] See the limitation in TFEU, art 291(2); Matthias Ruffert in Christian Calliess and Matthias Ruffert (eds), *EUV/AEUV* (6th edn, CH Beck 2022) AEUV, art 291 para 6.

[282] Regulation (EU) No 182/2011 of 16 February 2011 (Comitology Regulation).

second subparagraph allows the Commission to adopt implementing acts on the basis of the criteria developed above. This act takes the form of an implementing decision. In terms of the Comitology Regulation, it is adopted under the examination procedure (Article 5).[283]

To sum up, the Commission is involved at various stages of equivalence which is of great importance for the forthcoming analysis: it initiates legislative acts as a political actor at Level 1, it is competent for specifying these acts at Level 2 as a 'quasi-legislative' organ, and it, later on, adopts equivalence decisions as an administrative authority. At the same time, the Commission monitors Member States' compliance with these rules.

b) Margin of appreciation and judicial review

The bottom line of the previous analysis is that equivalence decisions are implementing decisions pursuant to Article 291(2) TFEU, in which the Commission acts as an administrative authority with purely executive powers. Yet, as was also found above, almost every equivalence decision has an element of discretion—an administrative decision-making leeway—which is subject to limited judicial review.[284] The leeway of the administration in European law is much greater than in German law.[285] Good examples of the clash of these concepts can be observed in the *Gauweiler* and *Weiss* decisions, where the ECJ, unlike the German Constitutional Court, highlighted the 'broad discretion' of the ECB.[286] The ECJ even established a presumption of legality for European Union measures.[287]

EU law does also not differentiate between margins of appreciation regarding preconditions and legal consequences, which is a fundamental difference to German administrative law (so-called *Beurteilungs- und Ermessensspielraum*).[288] Another difference is that the Court of Justice of the European Union (CJEU), just like courts in France, does not establish the facts ex officio.[289] It is the parties' duty to establish the facts of the matter. However, the CJEU is then in charge to control the facts for accuracy, validity and completeness. The CJEU also follows the *qualification juridique des faits* of French administrative law, according to which the appraisal of facts is to be strictly separated from the mere gathering of facts and where the former is subject only to very limited judicial review.[290] Moreover, the CJEU does not substitute its

[283] Ammann (n 70) para 204; on the procedure see Craig (n 14) 680f.

[284] See ch 2 A)I.1.c).

[285] Claus D Classen, 'Der EuGH und die Herausbildung eines europäischen Verwaltungsrechts' in Ralf P Schenke and Joachim Suerbaum (eds), *Verwaltungsgerichtsbarkeit in der Europäischen Union* (Nomos 2016) 15–21.

[286] Case C-62/14 *Gauweiler and Others* ECLI:EU:C:2015:400, para 68; Case C-493/17 *Weiss and Others* ECLI:EU:C:2018:1000, paras 73 and 91–92; for a dissenting view see German Constitutional Court, judgment of the Second Senate of 5 May 2020, 2 BvR 859/15 *Weiss* ECLI:DE:BVerfG:2020:rs20200505.2bvr085915, paras 140–53.

[287] Settled case law includes Case C-272/12 P *Commission v Ireland and Others* ECLI:EU:C:2013:812, para 54; Case C-475/01 *Commission v Greece* ECLI:EU:C:2004:585, para 18; Case C-137/92 P *Commission v BASF and Others* ECLI:EU:C:1994:247, para 48.

[288] See von Danwitz (n 22) 300.

[289] Classen (n 285) 21; with regard to French law see Jean Waline, *Droit administratif* (28th edn, Dalloz 2020) para 707.

[290] Waline (n 289) paras 680ff; von Danwitz (n 22) 299.

appraisal for that of the Commission. This is particularly apparent for complex economic matters in which the appraisal by the Commission is only checked for manifest errors, a misuse of power or whether the authority did clearly exceed the limits of its discretion.[291] It is settled case law that 'a decision may amount to a misuse of powers only if it appears, on the basis of objective, relevant, and consistent factors, to have been taken with the exclusive purpose, or at any rate the main purpose, of achieving an end other than that stated or evading a procedure specifically prescribed by the Treaty for dealing with the circumstances of the case'.[292]

The equivalence decision is a very complex, technical, and economic decision. It also involves prognostic elements, for instance, concerning the impact market access of third country firms will have on financial stability. Therefore, judicial review is limited. The CJEU will only check the Commission's appraisal for manifest errors, misuse of power and a clear overstepping of discretionary limits.[293]

2. Policy decision versus technical decision

As already mentioned, the impact and effectiveness of equivalence depend largely on how the Commission uses the room for manoeuvre granted to it.

On the one hand, the Commission could interpret the decision as a political one and an instrument of foreign policy. Political respectively policy considerations are understood in this book as all objectives unrelated to the regulation of financial markets, i.e. all objectives that are neither linked to the goal of investor protection nor to ensuring the functioning of financial markets nor to systemic stability. Since European financial markets are very important for third country service providers, simply because of their size encompassing 461 Million inhabitants, this creates considerable negotiation power on the side of the EU.[294] The granting of market access could be used as a bargaining chip for political goals such as the conclusion of favourable trade agreements.[295] Integrating political considerations into the decision-making will turn equivalence into a protectionist mechanism, at least in the long run.[296] If more states focus primarily on their national advantages, comparative cost advantages are diminished, ultimately resulting in considerable global welfare losses. Such a development is highly likely, as other countries are critical of an extraterritorial application

[291] Case C-29/77 *Roquette v France* ECLI:EU:C:1977:164, paras 19–20; Case C-42/84 *Remia v Commission* ECLI:EU:C:1985:327, para 34. This case law was slightly restricted in Case C-199/11 *Otis* ECLI:EU:C:2012:684, para 59; Herdegen (n 275) § 9 paras 44ff.

[292] Case C-331/88 *FEDESA and Others* ECLI:EU:C:1990:391, para 24; see also Case C-285/94 *Italy v Commission* ECLI:EU:C:1997:313, para 52; Case C-180/96 *United Kingdom v Commission* ECLI:EU:C:1998:192, para 64.

[293] The precise content of the scope of discretion will be evaluated in ch 2 B)II.3.

[294] John Armour, 'Brexit and Financial Services: Bargaining in the Shadow of Equivalence' in John Armour and Horst Eidenmüller (eds), *Negotiating Brexit* (CH Beck 2017) 21.

[295] Ammann (n 70) para 212; in relation to Switzerland see Bacharach (n 269); Jim Brunsden, Philip Stafford, and David Keohane, 'EU regulators seek solution to post-Brexit derivatives rule clash' *Financial Times* (16 November 2020): 'Officials in Brussels note that it is unlikely the bloc will announce any decisions on equivalence while talks over a broader trade deal continue, given the political sensitivities.' https://www.ft.com/content/ad60293f-cdb4-4566-8644-b970ecf98ad4 (accessed 12 November 2022).

[296] Discussing new protectionism in Europe post GFC see Stefano Pagliari, 'A Wall around Europe? The European Regulatory Response to the Global Financial Crisis and the Turn in Transatlantic Relations' (2012) 35 J Eur Integr 391; Andreas Dür, 'Fortress Europe or open door Europe? The external impact of the EU's single market in financial services' (2011) 18 J Eur Public Policy 619.

of law combined with unilateral recognition of foreign standards influenced by policy considerations. They will feel like 'rule-takers' forced to obey a European 'benchmark' and may react with retaliation.[297] With regard to economically weaker and therefore dependent states, this approach could even be described as a policy of New Imperialism.[298]

On the other hand, the Commission could use its margin of discretion purely for legal considerations. In this scenario, investor protection, the functioning of financial markets and financial stability would be the predominant factors to be taken into account. The assessment of whether a third country legal regime is equivalent to that of the EU would consequently be a purely technical decision. This is also how ESMA interprets its mandate when it provides technical advice to the Commission. It regards its analysis as an 'advice ... of a factual nature, not a policy one'.[299] Even with this reading of a purely technical decision, the Commission continues to have room for manoeuvre, for instance, in evaluating the extent to which third country laws protect European investors. Such an approach would be more market-oriented and increase transparency, as political considerations are hardly predictable and make decisions opaque.

Hereinafter, in a first step, the current practice of the Commission is examined. In a second step, the question of whether the Commission may take political considerations into account in its decision or whether it is a purely technical assessment is examined. The distant aim advocated in this book, which is further developed through reform proposals in Chapter 5,[300] is an unbundling of policy and technical decisions and thus a juridification.

a) *European Commission as a political actor*

As of July 2019, the Commission adopted over 280 equivalence decisions for more than 30 countries.[301] Hence, there are many practical examples to analyse the decision-making. The Commission claims to carry out mainly a technical assessment. It highlights the need to include the *technical expertise* of ESAs, establish *technical contacts* within the third country and continue with *technical work* in the aftermath of an equivalence decision.[302] In addition, the Commission endorses the advice of ESAs in many cases. There are also just a few decisions in which a political reasoning can be

[297] Lucia Quaglia, 'The Politics of 'Third Country Equivalence' in Post-Crisis Financial Services Regulation in the European Union' (2015) 38 West Eur Pol 167, 168; described as the 'political economy problem' in Chris Brummer, 'Territoriality as a Regulatory Technique: Notes from the Financial Crisis' (2010) 79 U Cin L Rev 499, 509ff. The term 'rule-taker' became a buzzword in the Brexit discussions. See eg Caroline Binham, 'Fear EU Deal Puts City of London at Risk of "Rule-taking"' *Financial Times* (23 January 2020) https://www.ft.com/content/d56ee33a-3d3d-11ea-b232-000f4477fbca (accessed 12 November 2022).

[298] See in relation to the US Kristina St Charles, 'Regulatory Imperialism: The Worldwide Export of European Regulatory Principles on Credit Rating Agencies' (2010) 19 Minn J Intl L 399; comparing equivalence to 'Realpolitik', see Bacharach (n 269); see regarding the term 'Realpolitik' Henry Kissinger, *World Order* (Penguin 2014) 302–308; see also Niamh Moloney, 'The Legacy Effects of the Financial Crisis on Regulatory Design in the EU' in Eilís V Ferran and others (eds), *The Regulatory Aftermath of the Global Financial Crisis* (CUP 2012) 111, 148, who characterizes the European system as 'regulatory imperialism'.

[299] See eg ESMA, 'Final report—US' (n 37) 6.

[300] See ch 5 B).

[301] Commission (n 54) 2.

[302] ibid 6–8 and 10; Commission (n 143) 8–10.

identified, which allows the conclusion that the Commission mostly argues on a technical level.

However, there are also statements by the Commission as well as practical cases that prove the opposite.[303] These cases are particularly serious because all future decisions are at risk of being influenced by political motives. It is like third countries and their service providers have the Sword of Damocles hanging over their heads. What is more, political reasons will only be used as a bargaining chip in cases that have a strong influence on markets, as the Commission's negotiating position will be particularly powerful here. The European Parliament also admits that equivalence decisions have a 'clear political dimension'.[304] The Commission does not put it as clear as the Parliament and rather speaks of 'factor[ing] in wider external policy priorities and concerns in particular with respect to the promotion of common values and shared regulatory objectives at international level'.[305] Nevertheless, it essentially means the same.

Three cases can be used to illustrate that political considerations have played a role in the decision-making. First, it took almost three and a half years to finalize the EU–US deal on equivalence concerning the recognition of CCPs, although ESMA's extensive technical advice was published within one year and came to an optimistic conclusion.[306] The delay of more than two years following the advice is often explained in the light of political differences that arose, inter alia, over the wide extraterritorial reach of the Dodd-Frank Act, to which EU regulators opposed.[307] A second case is the equivalence mechanism regarding non-EU AIFMs marketing AIFs in the EU. This mechanism is not in force, as it requires an implementing act from the Commission, which has not adopted such an act yet.[308] In 2015, ESMA had already issued advice to the Commission on several countries and concluded in relation to Jersey that 'there are no significant obstacles ... impeding the application of the AIFMD passport to Jersey'.[309] Jersey had EU-style legislation, entered into cooperation agreements with ESMA, had positive feedback from the latter, and still, the Commission did not adopt an implementing act because they demanded more countries to be assessed.[310] However, such a requirement, namely that many jurisdictions must first be examined before the Commission can activate the third country regime, is not foreseen in the AIFMD. Even after ESMA assessed further countries, the Commission did not activate the third country regime.[311] These actions by the Commission have been widely

303 See eg Commission (n 143) 9.
304 European Parliament (n 40) no 14.
305 Commission (n 143) 9.
306 ESMA, 'Final report—US' (n 37) 20–21.
307 See generally Edward F Greene and Ilona Potiha, 'Issues in the Extraterritorial Application of Dodd–Frank's Derivatives and Clearing Rules, the Impact on Global Markets and the Inevitability of Cross-border and US Domestic Coordination' (2013) 8 CMLJ 338; n Pennesi (n 93) 181–85.
308 AIFMD, art 67(6); see in general Stephen Sims, Patrick Brandt, and Greg Norman, 'AIFMD Passport: Europe Must Try Harder' (2016) 17 J Invest Compliance 10; Rodrigo Zepeda, 'To EU, or Not to EU: That Is the AIFMD Question' (2014) 29 JIBLR 82.
309 ESMA, 'Advice to the European Parliament, the Council and the Commission on the application of the AIFMD passport to non-EU AIFMs and AIFs' ESMA/2015/1236 (30 July 2015).
310 Commission, 'Letter by the Commission to ESMA' (17 December 2015) https://www.esma.europa.eu/sites/default/files/library/eu_commission_letter_aifmd_passport.pdf (accessed 12 November 2022).
311 In more detail see n 331 (ch 1) and n 360 (ch 1).

interpreted as being politically motivated.[312] The last and most unambiguous case occurred in 2019 when the Commission did not prolong equivalence for Swiss stock exchanges explicitly for political reasons.[313] This decision had a great response in the media and was widely interpreted as a warning shot for the United Kingdom in the course of Brexit.[314] This proves once again that the Commission uses equivalence as a bargaining chip.[315]

But why does the Commission sometimes opt for a political interpretation in view of the disadvantages outlined above? The Commission's approach can be explained against the background of the history of equivalence, wrong incentives and the Commission's institutional structure. The predecessors of equivalence were based on bilateral negotiations and not designed as unilateral decisions.[316] The Commission has remained in its role as a negotiator, even though the legal background has changed. This partly explains why the Commission still factors in non-technical parameters. Moreover, the Commission is appointed for five years only.[317] Its members have an incentive to focus on achieving short-term goals by using equivalence as a bargaining chip rather than aiming for long-term achievements to get re-elected. Furthermore, the Commission is involved at many stages and tends to mix these up. The Commission has different faces and is both a political institution as well as an administrative authority. It has a right to initiate legislation, is involved in the adoption of delegated acts specifying the criteria to be considered in the equivalence decision, and afterwards adopts implementing decisions based on these criteria. As the first two stages are policy decisions, the Commission is inclined to convey political considerations into the third decision.

b) Against a political interpretation and for a juridification of equivalence

Since there are several cases where the Commission has used political arguments to justify equivalence related decisions, the question arises whether this practice, which, as shown above, is neither economically nor politically wise, is at least

312 Ferran (n 2) 60; Eilís V Ferran, 'After the Crisis: The Regulation of Hedge Funds and Private Equity in the EU' (2011) 12 EBOR 379, 394–99.

313 Commission Implementing Decision (EU) 2018/2047 of 20 December 2018, recitals 30 and 32; see also Commission, 'Commission Proposes to Extend Equivalence for Swiss Share Trading Venues for Six Months' Press Release (17 December 2018) https://ec.europa.eu/commission/presscorner/detail/en/IP_18_6801 (accessed 12 November 2022). In this press release, the Commission linked the extension to the finalization of the Institutional Framework Agreement; see European Parliament (n 40) no 15; see also n Pennesi (n 93) 90–91; explicitly calling it a political decision see Nobel (n 75) § 2 para 70.

314 See eg Attracta Mooney, 'Will London Be Berned Like the Swiss?' *Financial Times* (6 July 2019) https://www.ft.com/content/fe903f9b-926d-36c8-b950-f2f56e014cff?ftcamp=engage%2Femail%2Fnewsletters%2Fsmart_brief%2Fsmartbriefnewsletterscontraf (accessed 12 November 2022); Mehreen Khan and Philip Stafford, 'EU-based Traders Caught in Swiss "Equivalence" Spat' *Financial Times* (30 June 2019) https://www.ft.com/content/41091f2c-9ad0-11e9-9c06-a4640c9feebb (accessed 12 November 2022).

315 See also Brunsden, Stafford, and Keohane (n 295); Emil Nästegård, 'Equivalence Decisions in the EU and UK Financial Services Sectors Post-Brexit' (2022) 33 EBLR 463, 472.

316 See ch 1 C)I.5.a).

317 TEU, art 17(3).

lawful.[318] To review the legality of a decision, different legal levels need to be taken into account.

aa) Interpretation of equivalence provisions Most equivalence provisions state that the Commission 'may' adopt an equivalence decision without further defining the content of the discretion. However, legal consequences cannot be interpreted independently, as European administrative law does not differentiate between the margin of appreciation concerning preconditions and legal consequences.[319] Hence, the wording of the preconditions of equivalence needs to be included in the interpretation. Since equivalence provisions are to be interpreted as a uniform concept, as shown above, arguments derived from one mechanism can be transferred to all other equivalence mechanisms unless otherwise stated. Some provisions scarcely specify the content of equivalence.[320] Others stipulate a point of reference for equivalence determinations by listing European rules to which equivalence must be fulfilled.[321] These points of reference are always supervisory requirements, but not political aspects. Again, other provisions leave the definition to the delegated legislation by the Commission, which is then in charge of specifying criteria that need to be considered.[322] Yet this delegated legislation is restricted. The definition of general equivalence criteria in the Prospectus Regulation must, for instance, be based on the requirements regarding the prospectus, the prospectus summary, the base prospectus, as well as the minimum information and format.[323] In the Transparency Directive, the general equivalence criteria must be 'regarding accounting standards' and do therefore not include policy considerations. Thus, equivalence provisions never explicitly allow policy considerations to enter the decision-making process. The reference to exclusively prudential aspects and the limited authorization for delegated legislation consequently supports a purely technical and legal interpretation.

Besides this literal and systematic interpretation, the historical development of equivalence provisions needs to be observed.[324] In the past, equivalence was based on bilateral negotiations rendering it a foreign policy issue rather than an administrative one. This has changed: equivalence is not a bargaining process anymore but a unilateral decision. This change must be accompanied by a corresponding change in

[318] Pennesi argues that: 'It is normal and legitimate for the European Commission to take on-board political considerations when assessing whether to provide equivalence status to third countries. After all, what kind of trade relationship the EU should have with other jurisdictions, including in the area of financial services, constitutes first and foremost a political question.' See n Pennesi (n 93) 232. See also Paolo Saguato, Guido Ferrarini, and Eric Pan, 'Financial Market Infrastructures: The International Approach and the Current Challenges' in Jens-Hinrich Binder and Paolo Saguato (eds) *Financial Market Infrastructures* (OUP 2022) para 4.42, stating: 'And an equivalence determination is the ultimate political decision.' This assumption will be challenged in the following pages.

[319] Joanna Dervisopoulos, 'Nichtigkeitsklage' in Hans-Werner Rengeling, Andreas Middeke, and Martin Gellermann (eds), *Handbuch des Rechtsschutzes in der Europäischen Union* (3rd edn, CH Beck 2014) § 7 para 117.

[320] See eg CRR II, arts 107(4) and 114(7) subpara 2.

[321] See eg MiFIR, art 47(1)(a); EMIR, art 25(6)(a).

[322] See eg Prospectus Regulation, art 29(3); Transparency Directive, art 23(4) subpara 4.

[323] Prospectus Regulation, art 29(3) subpara 1 and arts 6, 7, 8, and 13.

[324] See for the interpretation of European law in general Riesenhuber (n 107) 285ff.

the legal interpretation, moving away from a foreign policy and towards a technical decision.

bb) Interpretation in conformity with EU Treaties European secondary law must be interpreted in accordance with the EU Treaties.[325] This follows from the principle of coherence of EU law and the supremacy of primary law. Another justification is that the judiciary needs to respect the legislator's authority for reasons of institutional balance as much as possible.[326] Rather, this is done by interpreting secondary law in conformity with the Treaties than by declaring it null and void.

The argument regarding the EU Treaties has already been mapped out in the analysis of the institutional role of the Commission.[327] When adopting an equivalence decision in the form of an implementing decision based on Article 291 TFEU, the Commission acts as an administrative authority and thus as part of the executive.[328] To preserve the institutional balance of the Union, it is important to separate legislative and administrative decision-making. When the Commission is tasked with deciding matters as an administrative authority, it must not at the same time 'think like a legislator' by including policy considerations in the decision. If executive and legislative thinking were allowed to coexist in one decision, the institutional balance would be seriously threatened to the detriment of the judiciary, as the judiciary would not be able to effectively control the executive branch anymore. This is especially true in view of the fact that policy considerations a priori evade judicial review. Such a loss of power for the judiciary would also result in a lack of legal protection for financial service providers and infringe their constitutionally guaranteed rights under Article 47 CFR and Article 19 TEU. This is particularly problematic in an area such as banking and capital markets law, which is a subgroup of regulatory law and police law and in which the state-citizen relationship is characterized by superiority and subordination. Finally, such an approach would be incompatible with the dogma advocated by the CJEU of a Union 'based on the rule of law'.[329] Consequently, the EU Treaties require that equivalence decisions are based solely on supervisory concerns and not on policy considerations.

This analysis is further supported by the wording of Article 291(2) TFEU, which is the legal basis of equivalence decisions. The sole purpose of such implementing acts is to create uniform conditions in the Union, i.e. to reduce differences between the otherwise competent national levels. The Commission's stated objective of pursuing 'wider external policy priorities and concerns' and promoting 'common values and shared regulatory objectives' is not covered by the enabling statute. For this reason, a political interpretation is also not in line with the Treaties.

[325] Joined Cases C-201/85 and 202/85 *Klensch v Secrétaire d'État* ECLI:EU:C:1986:439, para 21; Case C-1/02 *Borgmann* ECLI:EU:C:2004:202, para 30; Case C-499/04 *Werhof* ECLI:EU:C:2006:168, para 32; Stefan Leible and Ronny Domröse, 'Die primärrechtskonforme Auslegung' in Karl Riesenhuber (ed), *Europäische Methodenlehre* (4th edn, De Gruyter 2021) 209ff.

[326] Clemens Höpfner, *Die systemkonforme Auslegung* (Mohr Siebeck 2008) 229f.

[327] See ch 2 B)II.1.a).

[328] With regard to the equivalence decision see Moloney (n 14) para 6.18; more generally see Michael Dougan, 'The Treaty of Lisbon 2007: Winning Minds, Not Hearts' (2008) 45 CMLR 617, 649.

[329] Case C-294/83 *Les Verts v Parliament* (n 28) para 23.

It could be objected that equivalence decisions are a matter of foreign policy, given that the decisions concern the assessment of third countries' legal systems and should therefore not be subject to the standards of administrative law. However, the decision merely implements European supervisory—i.e. administrative—law and the legal consequences take effect solely within the national and European administrative system. The mere fact that the subject matter of the decision is an international one does not render the decision a foreign policy decision. Moreover, strict judicial review is possible even in an area with a foreign dimension, as the *Schrems I and II* cases impressively demonstrated. Hence, equivalence decisions are of a purely administrative nature.

cc) Interpretation in conformity with world trade law Another level that must be included in the analysis is the law of the WTO. The EU has been a member of the WTO since 1995 and is bound by its agreements. It follows from Article 216(2) TFEU that world trade law is superior to European secondary law, and therefore directives and regulations must be interpreted in accordance with it.[330] Even the ECJ, which is very restrictive when applying world trade law,[331] has meanwhile acknowledged that fact.[332] In addition, the application of the law by EU institutions, i.e. in this context, the Commission's administrative practice with regard to equivalence decisions, must also be measured against the duties of world trade law.[333] However, this does not mean that world trade law grants individuals an enforceable legal position since the question of subjective rights is to be distinguished from the objective interpretation of a provision.[334]

(1) GATS: Scope of application and general obligations

In the context of financial services, the GATS and its Annex on Financial Services play an important role.[335] The GATS applies to all 'measures by Members affecting trade in services', whereby the supply of a service can take place in four different modes.[336] The scope of application of the Annex is also very broad, defining a financial service as 'any

[330] Matthias Herdegen, *Principles of International Economic Law* (2nd edn, OUP 2016) 315; Mitsuo Matsushita and others, *The World Trade Organization* (3rd edn, OUP 2015) 37ff.

[331] See eg Case C-377/02 *Van Parys* ECLI:EU:C:2005:121, paras 46–52; Herdegen (n 330) 313ff; see regarding the case law Jan Wouters and others (eds), *The Law of EU External Relations* (3rd edn, OUP 2021) 443–63.

[332] Case C-53/96 *Hermès International v FHT Marketing Choice* ECLI:EU:C:1998:292, para 28; Joined Cases C-300/98 and 392/98 *Parfums Christian Dior* ECLI:EU:C:2000:688, para 47; see Hans-Joachim Prieß and Georg M Berrisch, 'Die Geltung und Durchsetzung des WTO-Rechts im Gemeinschaftsrecht' in Hans-Joachim Prieß and Georg M Berrisch (eds), *WTO-Handbuch* (CH Beck 2003) 764.

[333] Papaconstantinou (n 72) 384.

[334] Friedrich Erlbacher in Manuel Kellerbauer, Marcus Klamert, and Jonathan Tomkin (eds), *Commentary on the EU Treaties and the Charter of Fundamental Rights* (OUP 2019) TFEU, art 216 para 12; Marc Bungenberg, 'Europäisches Verwaltungsrecht und WTO-Recht' in Jörg P Terhechte (ed), *Verwaltungsrecht der Europäischen Union* (Nomos 2011) § 11 paras 30–33 and 34–36.

[335] For extensive analysis with regard to equivalence see Lang (n 160) 202ff; more generally on the interrelation between the GATS and financial services see Kern Alexander, 'The GATS and Financial Services' in Kern Alexander and Mads Andenas (eds), *The World Trade Organization and Trade in Services* (Martinus Nijhoff 2008) 561ff.

[336] GATS, art I:1 and I:2; see for the wide interpretation Appellate Body Report, *European Communities—Regime for the Importation, Sale and Distribution of Bananas*, WT/DS27/AB/R (adopted 9 September 1997) para 220; Panel Report, *Mexico—Measures Affecting Telecommunications Services*, WT/DS204/R (adopted 2 April 2004) para 7.41; in relation to the modes of supply see Ammann (n 70) paras 57f.

service of a financial nature offered by a financial service supplier of a Member', which 'include[s] all insurance and insurance-related services, and all banking and other financial services (excluding insurance)'.[337]

The GATS sets forth several obligations. Amongst them are, as part of the general obligations, the Most-Favoured-Nation Treatment (Article II) and rules concerning Domestic Regulation (Article VI) as well as Recognition (Article VII). Moreover, the GATS contains specific commitments relating to Market Access (Article XVI) and National Treatment (Article XVII). These specific commitments are, however, only guaranteed to the extent to which the Members voluntarily signed up for them in the Schedules (so-called positive list approach), which is why a universal right to access foreign markets does not exist.[338] In the following, the compatibility of a political interpretation will only be examined in light of the Most-Favoured-Nation principle of the GATS.[339]

(2) Most-Favoured-Nation Treatment, prudential carve-out, and standard of 'adequate opportunity'

The principle of Most-Favoured-Nation Treatment (MFN) is a general principle of world trade law embedded in almost all its legal acts.[340] In the words of Article II GATS, it requires that 'each Member shall accord immediately and unconditionally to services and service suppliers of any other Member treatment no less favourable than that it accords to like services and service suppliers of any other country'. This rule aims at preventing unjustified discrimination between Members, an objective that is one of the cornerstones of the WTO.[341] It follows from that principle that, as soon as the Commission recognizes a third country as equivalent, it needs to adopt equivalence decisions in relation to all other third countries with an equivalent level of prudential regulation.

Such a far-reaching commitment could, however, discourage countries from recognizing other Members in the first place. This result would be at odds with the WTO's other goal of liberalizing trade. Consequently, the GATS contains two exceptions that are of relevance here: first, the prudential carve-out and, second, the reduced standard of 'adequate opportunity' concerning recognitions.

The prudential carve-out in paragraph 2(a) of the Annex on Financial Services was designed to allow Members to protect their investors adequately and ensure the functioning and stability of financial markets.[342] The provision is interpreted very broadly

[337] GATS, Annex on Financial Services, para 5(a); see Rolf Sethe and Matthias Lehmann, 'Internationales Bank- und Finanzdienstleistungsrecht' in Christian Tietje (ed), *Internationales Wirtschaftsrecht* (3rd edn, De Gruyter 2021) § 15 para 12; Matsushita and others (n 330) 560ff and 629.

[338] Matsushita and others (n 330) 593–603.

[339] See Lang (n 160) 202ff for an extensive analysis against the background of GATS, art VII. See with regard to the equivalence mechanism in EMIR concerning third country CCPs: Papaconstantinou (n 72).

[340] In relation to the GATS see Aaditya Mattoo, 'MFN and the GATS' in Thomas Cottier and Petros C Mavroidis (eds), *Regulatory Barriers and the Principle of Non Discrimination* (University of Michigan Press 2000) 51ff; Apostolos Gkoutzinis, 'International Trade in Banking Services and the Role of the WTO' (2005) 39 Intl Lawyer 877, 898f.

[341] Papaconstantinou (n 72) 393.

[342] See on the prudential carve-out Juan Marchetti, 'The GATS Prudential Carve-Out' in Panagiotis Delimatsis and Nils Herger (eds), *Financial Regulation at the Crossroads* (Kluwer Law International 2011) 279–95; Mamiko Yokoi-Arai, 'GATS' Prudential Carve Out in Financial Services and Its Relation with Prudential Regulation' (2008) 57 Intl & Comp LQ 613; Wei Wang, 'The Prudential Carve-Out' in Kern

and leaves a considerable margin of appreciation to Members. In the *Argentina–Financial Services* case, the panel found that three requirements must be fulfilled for the exception to apply.[343] The second of these conditions is that the measure was taken for prudential reasons, with the panel splitting this question into two parts. In the first part, the panel demands that the reasons for the measure are of a 'prudential' nature. The term 'prudential' must be read in conjunction with the indicative list and can be described as 'precautionary'.[344] This reading precludes the inclusion of purely political considerations that are not intended to protect investors or markets.[345]

Moreover, the prudential carve-out shall not be used to circumvent commitments or obligations under the agreement, as expressively stated in the second sentence of paragraph 2(a). The prudential carve-out is based on the principle of good faith and must be interpreted against the background of the introductory sentence—the chapeau—of Article XIV GATS and Article XX GATT from which it is deduced.[346] This chapeau demands that an exception cannot be applied as 'a means of arbitrary or unjustifiable discrimination between countries where the same conditions prevail'.[347] Consequently, political reasons are not of a prudential nature, and the prudential carve-out cannot justify the interference with the MFN principle.[348]

A justification of the interference with the MFN principle could, however, be achieved via the reduced standard of paragraph 3(b) second sentence of the Annex on Financial Services.[349] This provision deals with the possibility for Members to recognize prudential measures of other countries through bilateral agreements or unilateral decisions. Equivalence in European financial markets law is exactly this: a unilateral

Alexander and Mads Andenas (eds), *The World Trade Organization and Trade in Services* (Martinus Nijhoff 2008) 601ff.

[343] Panel Report, *Argentina—Financial Services*, WT/DS453/R (adopted 30 September 2015) paras 7.853–7.945; see also Appellate Body Report, *Argentina—Financial Services*, WT/DS453/AB/R (adopted 9 May 2016); on the case see Sethe and Lehmann (n 337) § 15 para 15; Rolf H Weber and Rika Koch, 'Relevance of WTO Law for Financial Services Lessons from "Argentina—Financial Services"' (2017) 89 SZW 163, 167ff; Panagiotis Delimatsis and Bernard Hoekman, 'National Tax Regulation, Voluntary International Standards, and the GATS: Argentina–Financial Services' (2018) 17 World Trade Rev 265; Andrew D Mitchell, Jennifer K Hawkins, and Neha Mishra, 'Dear Prudence: Allowances under International Trade and Investment Law for Prudential Regulation in the Financial Services Sector' (2016) 19 JIEL 787, 801ff.

[344] Panel Report, *Argentina—Financial Services* (n 343) paras 7.867 and 7.869; Armin von Bogdandy and Joseph Windsor in Rüdiger Wolfrum, Peter-Tobias Stoll, and Clemens Feinäugle (eds), *WTO—Trade in Services* (Martinus Nijhoff 2008) Annex on Financial Services, para 22.

[345] In the same direction see Pennesi (n 149) 45.

[346] Yokoi-Arai (n 342).

[347] Appellate Body Report, *United States—Standards for Reformulated and Conventional Gasoline*, WT/DS2/AB/R (adopted 20 May 1996); Appellate Body Report, *United States—Import Prohibition of Certain Shrimp and Shrimp Products*, WT/DS58/AB/R (adopted 6 November 1998); Appellate Body Report, *United States Measures Affecting the Cross-border Supply of Gambling and Betting Services*, WT/DS285/AB/R (adopted 20 April 2005); see Herdegen (n 330) 237f; Lorand Bartels, 'The Chapeau of the General Exceptions in the WTO GATT and GATS Agreements: A Reconstruction' (2015) 109 AJIL 95.

[348] Wolfgang Vahldiek, 'GATS und Bankenaufsichtsrecht' (2003) 3 BKR 971, 972.

[349] See Eric H Leroux, 'Trade in Financial Services under the World Trade Organization' (2002) 36 JWT 413, 431f; a very interesting analysis with regard to Mutual Recognition Agreements and MFN treatment is provided for in Kalypso Nicolaïdis, 'Non-Discriminatory Mutual Recognition' in Thomas Cottier and Petros C Mavroidis (eds), *Regulatory Barriers and the Principle of Non Discrimination* (University of Michigan Press 2000) 267ff.

recognition of foreign prudential measures.[350] Hence, the provision is applicable. If a Member grants an autonomous recognition, it shall 'afford adequate opportunity for any other Member to demonstrate that such circumstances exist'. This obligation is less demanding than the MFN principle because it does not require unconditional equal treatment but only an 'adequate opportunity'.[351]

This raises the question of what is to be understood by such 'adequate opportunity' and whether this standard excludes political justifications. The provision must be interpreted in the light of the general recognition clause in Article VII GATS.[352] This general rule demands that the recognition shall not be accorded 'in a manner which would constitute a means of discrimination ... or a disguised restriction on trade in services'.[353] It can therefore be inferred from the general provision that the basic idea of the standard is to avoid unjustified discriminatory treatment of other Members and disguised restrictions on trade.[354] Including political arguments in the recognition is both: a discrimination detached from prudential reasons and a disguised restriction on trade in services and is therefore prohibited.

The inclusion of political considerations would also turn the possibility for a state to demonstrate the equivalence of its supervisory law into an empty promise. If the recognition is not based on objective grounds, it will be impossible for states to demonstrate equivalence. Consequently, if the European Commission adopts an equivalence decision, the MFN principle and the prudential carve-out require that subsequent equivalence decisions in this area are taken only on the basis of prudential concerns and that political considerations are not part of the decision-making.

c) Conclusion

The above analysis has shown that the Commission must not use political considerations to justify equivalence decisions. Equivalence assessments are purely technical decisions, as can already be seen from the interpretation of the equivalence provisions. Moreover, political decision-making violates the EU Treaties and the MFN treatment of the GATS. Equivalence decisions based on political factors are thus unlawful.[355] It follows from this that the Commission's decision mentioned above not to extend equivalence for Swiss stock exchanges for political reasons was not lawful.[356]

[350] Lang (n 160) 204f; in the context of MiFIR see Kern Alexander, 'The UK's Third-Country Status Following Brexit' in Kern Alexander and others (eds), *Brexit and Financial Services: Law and Policy* (Hart Publishing 2018) 132; in the context of EMIR see Papaconstantinou (n 72) 398.

[351] Owing to this hierarchy of requirements, the prudential carve-out is seen here as an exception to MFN treatment. However, it would also be possible to understand the prudential carve-out as a separate and independent duty. This dogmatic question has no influence on the result found here. The prudential carve-out is also classified as an exception in: Weber and Sethe (n 99) 575.

[352] On the systematic relationship of the provisions see Papaconstantinou (n 72) 397.

[353] GATS, art VII:3.

[354] See the same result in von Bogdandy and Windsor (n 344) Annex on Financial Services, para 27.

[355] Also critical towards a political decision: Matthias Lehmann, 'CCP supervision after Brexit' (2023) 18 CMLR 5, 14–15; Wymeersch (n 4) 223–27.

[356] More specifically, Commission Implementing Decision (EU) 2018/2047 of 20 December 2018 is unlawful; see on the case ch 2 B)II.2.a).

3. Determination of the scope of discretion

As the Commission is not allowed to consider political aspects, the equivalence decision is merely a technical comparison of two legal systems. Within this technical analysis, a distinction must now be made between aspects subject to full judicial review and those that fall within the Commission's discretion and are therefore only subject to limited judicial review. The following classification is based on the method developed above for determining equivalence.[357]

In a first step, the central aims of EU regulatory law must be identified. This determination consists of a legal interpretation only and does not involve any forecasts or subjective assessments. Hence, it is subject to full judicial review.[358]

In a second step, binding rules in the third country system having the same objective as EU regulatory law must be identified. This is done through consultations with supervisory authorities of the third country in question. Therefore, this step consists only of identifying foreign legal acts (fact-finding) and interpreting them. The CJEU can review this finding for completeness, validity and accuracy, which is why there is almost full judicial review.

The third step consists of detecting similarities and differences between the EU and third country legal system in question, without yet weighing them up. This process is also more of a descriptive and not normative nature. As the process is not limited to the written law but also involves an analysis of the administrative practice and case law, the CJEU does not have the resources to review the Commission's findings for completeness. Nevertheless, it can check the information provided by the Commission for correctness—or at least plausibility—and accuracy. As a result, the decision is subject to strict judicial scrutiny up to this point.

This changes in the fourth step, in which the weighing of similarities and differences is carried out by the Commission to establish a finding of (non-)equivalence. This balancing comprises prognostic elements, requires special expertise and is economically complex.[359] For all these reasons, the decision is in the Commission's discretion and accordingly subject to limited judicial review.[360] For example, the Commission will have room for manoeuvre when evaluating the level of investor protection guaranteed by a third country rule. What effects will rule A of country B have in the EU? What level of protection does rule C of the EU guarantee for EU investors? Will rule A of country B protect investors in the same way as rule C of the EU? How is rule A enforced in country B? Is it just law in the books? Is the enforcement equivalent to that of NCAs or ESAs? Regarding these and similar questions, there is no full legal review by the courts.

[357] See ch 2 B)I.2.c).

[358] See for the full judicial review of purely 'legal questions': Case C-42/84 *Remia v Commission* (n 291) para 34; Case C-7/95 P *Deere v Commission* ECLI:EU:C:1998:256, para 34; Case C-194/99 P *Thyssen Stahl v Commission* ECLI:EU:C:2003:527, para 78; von Danwitz (n 22) 368.

[359] Concerning complex economic matters: Case C-42/84 *Remia v Commission* (n 291) para 34; Case C-7/95 P *Deere v Commission* (n 358) para 34; Case C-194/99 P *Thyssen Stahl v Commission* (n 358) para 78; with further references see von Danwitz (n 22) 363f.

[360] See on other potential grounds for granting discretion Barbara Widmer, *Verwaltungsermessen im Recht der Europäischen Union* (CH Beck 2014) paras 90ff.

Moreover, the Commission can determine the general level of equivalence required by demanding fewer discrepancies between the legal systems. An increase of the general level of equivalence can, for instance, be justified with potential threats for financial stability. This would set the bar higher for all third countries in an equal manner, without discriminating individual countries based on political reasoning. And even if there were a less favourable treatment of individual countries, this would be justified by objective reasons such as the impact on financial stability. Furthermore, there is no full legal review when it comes to predictions of the future. Such forecasts must only be consistent and based on a solid factual basis.

However, the finding of discretionary elements in the balancing (step four) does not mean that there is no judicial review. The CJEU will check the Commission's appraisal for manifest errors, misuse of power and a clear excess of discretionary boundaries.[361] If the CJEU endorses the economic methodology advocated above, it can also measure the Commission's reasoning against the yardstick of the theory of a Kaldor-Hicks improvement and review the assumptions used for this evaluation for plausibility. Especially against the background of an increasing shift of direct administrative competences to the European level, the CJEU must adequately fulfil its task of controlling administrative discretion. The call for more judicial review by Advocate General Jacobs in the *TU Munich* case of 1991 is, therefore, more valid today than ever before: 'The Court cannot shy away from technical questions and must in an appropriate case be prepared to resolve such questions ... '[362]

4. Further legal limits to equivalence decisions

The analysis has revealed that the equivalence decision is merely a technical comparison of two legal systems. Nonetheless, the Commission has a wide margin of appreciation in weighing the similarities and differences of the two legal regimes. Since the judicial review exercised by the CJEU is somewhat limited in this regard, it is compensated by general principles of EU constitutional and administrative law, in particular a strict formal review of procedural guarantees outlined in the following.[363]

a) Inquisitorial principle

A typical example of a principle that compensates for the limited judicial review is the inquisitorial principle.[364] It obliges the administration to examine and consider all relevant matters of law and facts, especially if the complainant brought it to the Commission's attention.[365] That way, judicial control of administrative reasoning is

[361] Case C-42/84 *Remia v Commission* (n 291) para 34; Case C-7/95 P *Deere v Commission* (n 358) para 34; Case C-194/99 P *Thyssen Stahl v Commission* (n 358) para 78; regarding the last criterion see Case C-390/95 P *Antillean Rice Mills and Others* ECLI:EU:C:1999:66, para 48; Case C-301/97 *Netherlands v Council* ECLI:EU:C:2001:621, para 74.

[362] Opinion of Advocate General Jacobs delivered on 11 July 1991 in Case C-269/90 *TU München v Hauptzollamt München-Mitte* ECLI:EU:C:1991:317, para 13.

[363] The ECJ explicitly establishes this connection in its case law. See Case C-269/90 *TU München v Hauptzollamt München-Mitte* ECLI:EU:C:1991:438, para 14; von Danwitz (n 22) 300.

[364] Case C-269/90 *TU München v Hauptzollamt München-Mitte* (n 363) para 14; von Danwitz (n 22) 518.

[365] Joined Cases C-142/84 and 156/84 *BAT and Reynolds v Commission* ECLI:EU:C:1987:490, para 20; Case C-269/90 *TU München v Hauptzollamt München-Mitte* (n 363) para 14; Case C-449/98 P *IECC v Commission* ECLI:EU:C:2001:275, para 45; see also TFEU, art 337.

greatly simplified and enhanced. In the case of equivalence, this principle gains particular importance considering the very technical nature of the decision. It allows third countries and their service providers to increase their chances to be recognized by providing the Commission with detailed facts regarding their home legal system. These facts must then be taken into account by the Commission in its decision, which in turn is subject to judicial review.

b) Protection of service providers by fundamental freedoms and rights

Service providers inside the Union are well protected by the fundamental freedoms of the internal market provided for in the TFEU as well as the fundamental rights of the CFR, which binds all institutions of the Union.[366] But to what extent does that protection apply to service providers from third countries? And how does it change the interpretation of equivalence decisions?

aa) Freedom of services and freedom of capital The fundamental freedom most relevant for financial services is the freedom to provide services.[367] It is, however, limited to nationals of Member States and does not apply to third country persons.[368] Service providers from third countries can only indirectly benefit from the passive freedom of services of EU citizens in the form of reverse solicitation.[369] Contrary to the freedom to provide services, the freedom of capital also applies to third country nationals.[370] In view of this difference and the fact that both freedoms will be relevant in many cases relating to financial services, a demarcation must therefore be made. In the *Fidium Finanz* case, the ECJ decided that it will only consider one freedom if it prevails over the other because one of them is entirely secondary in relation to the other.[371] In the context of equivalence, the freedom to provide services will often prevail, as it did in the *Fidium Finanz* case. Thus, the level of protection provided by the fundamental freedoms for service providers from third countries is rather low.[372]

bb) Freedom to conduct a business and right to property In the context of fundamental rights, the freedom to conduct a business (Article 16 CFR) and the right to property (Article 17 CFR) need to be examined. The freedom to conduct business is

366 Regarding the institutions bound by the CFR see Matthias Herdegen, 'Grundrechte der Europäischen Union' in Josef Isensee and Paul Kirchhof (eds), *Handbuch des Staatsrechts*, vol 10 (3rd edn, CF Müller 2012) § 211 para 27.

367 TFEU, arts 26 and 56–62.

368 Jonathan Tomkin in Manuel Kellerbauer, Marcus Klamert, and Jonathan Tomkin (eds), *Commentary on the EU Treaties and the Charter of Fundamental Rights* (OUP 2019) TFEU, art 56 paras 5ff.

369 See on reverse solicitation ch 1 B)I.2.c).

370 TFEU, arts 26 and 63–66; John A Usher, 'The Evolution of the Free Movement of Capital' (2008) 31 Fordham Intl LJ 1533, 1562–69.

371 Case C-452/04 *Fidium Finanz* ECLI:EU:C:2006:631, para 34; for a dissenting view see the Opinion of Advocate General Stix-Hackl delivered on 16 March 2006 in Case C-452/04 *Fidium Finanz* ECLI:EU:C:2006:182, para 70; see also Martha O'Brien, 'Case C-452/04, Fidium Finanz AG v. Bundesanstalt für Finanzdienstleistungsaufsicht, judgment of the Court of Justice (Grand Chamber) of 3 October 2006, [2006] ECR I-9521' (2007) 44 CMLR 1483.

372 In particular, fundamental freedoms do not guarantee a right of market access for firms from third countries. See Dörte Poelzig, 'Drittstaaten und Gleichwertigkeit' in Lars Klöhn and Sebastian Mock (eds), *Festschrift 25 Jahre WpHG* (De Gruyter 2020) 1141ff.

a corollary of the right to property,[373] yet at the same time one of the most controversial rights in the CFR.[374] Already at a very early stage, the ECJ pointed out in the *Nold* case that the freedom to engage in business is protected as a general principle of EU law.[375] The core of this freedom is the freedom to exercise economic and commercial activities such as financial services. At the outset, this freedom also applies to third country nationals since the wording of Article 16 CFR does not provide otherwise.[376] Nonetheless, this freedom is restricted in two important ways. First, the freedom is only recognized 'in accordance with Community law and national laws'. Therefore, it is not absolute but must be interpreted in accordance with its social function as laid down in the legal system.[377] As a result, EU institutions have a particularly wide margin of appreciation to regulate the market. Secondly, the freedom to conduct a business cannot be interpreted in a way that the restriction of the free movement of services, which is granted to Union citizens only, is circumvented by extending the freedom to third country nationals through the back door. Thus, the freedom to conduct business applies to third country nationals only after market access has been granted.[378] Article 16 CFR, therefore, neither protects the right to enter a market nor the right to stay on the market for third country nationals, which is why it has no impact on the interpretation of equivalence provisions.

The right to property does not protect the granting of market access either. However, once market access has been established, it may be regarded as protected property in the sense of Article 17 CFR. In that case, the withdrawal of equivalence by the Commission, which will either deprive the third country financial service provider ipso facto of its access rights (in one-step processes) or will lead to a loss of market access rights through the competent ESAs or national authorities (in two-step processes) must be in conformity with Article 17 CFR. For the protection of the right to property to apply, third country nationals must first be part of the personal scope of application of Article 17 CFR and, secondly, the substantive scope of protection must cover the legal position acquired by the equivalence decision. First, fundamental rights in the CFR always include third country nationals unless otherwise provided.[379]

[373] Case C-59/83 *Biovilac v EEC* ECLI:EU:C:1984:380, para 21; Michele Everson and Rui Correia Gonçalves in Steve Peers and others (eds), *The EU Charter of Fundamental Rights* (Hart Publishing 2014) paras 16.01–16.10.

[374] Everson and Gonçalves (n 373) para 16.11.

[375] Settled case law includes Case C-4/73 *Nold KG v Commission* ECLI:EU:C:1975:114, para 14; Case C-230/78 *Eridana* ECLI:EU:C:1979:216, para 21; more recently: Case C-544/10 *Deutsches Weintor* ECLI:EU:C:2012:526, para 44.

[376] Case C-84/95 *Bosphorus v Minister for Transport, Energy and Communications and Others* ECLI:EU:C:1996:312; Thorsten Sasse, 'Die Grundrechtsberechtigung juristischer Personen durch die unternehmerische Freiheit gemäß Art 16 der Europäischen Grundrechtecharta' (2012) 47 EuR 628, 636–43.

[377] Joined Cases C-184/02 and 223/02 *Spain and Finland v Parliament and Council* ECLI:EU:C:2004:497, paras 51–52; Case C-544/10 *Deutsches Weintor* (n 375) para 54; Case C-283/11 *Sky Österreich* ECLI:EU:C:2013:28, paras 45–46; Tobias Lock in Manuel Kellerbauer, Marcus Klamert, and Jonathan Tomkin (eds), *Commentary on the EU Treaties and the Charter of Fundamental Rights* (OUP 2019) CFR, art 16 para 6.

[378] Sasse (n 376) 641–43.

[379] Norbert Bernsdorff in Jürgen Meyer and Sven Hölscheidt (eds), *Charta der Grundrechte der Europäischen Union* (5th edn, Nomos 2019) CFR, art 16 para 19; Walter Frenz, *Handbuch Europarecht*, vol 4 (Springer 2009) para 310.

According to the wording of Article 17(1) CFR, 'every person' is entitled to the right to property; thus, it includes third country nationals.[380]

Secondly, the equivalence decision, more specifically the legal status reached by it, must be included in the material scope of application. One particularity of Article 17 CFR is that the legislator itself partly defines the substantive scope of application. Mere commercial interests or opportunities are not protected because they are part of an economic risk that cannot be guaranteed in a free market economy.[381] As mentioned in the introduction, equivalence decisions function like a door opener for third country services. Once it has been adopted, service providers from third countries may enter the EU financial markets. In this sense, equivalence decisions are like state approvals. Whether such state approvals are part of the protected property under Article 17 CFR is the subject of vigorous debate.[382] The CJEU follows a very restrictive approach when qualifying the consequences of market regulation as protected property. Benefits obtained from production quotas, reference quantities, and similar instruments are not protected under the case law of the CJEU.[383] There is much to be said for this approach. If a company were protected against a mere change in the legal and political framework, the legislator would be unduly restricted. Furthermore, the restriction to Union citizens as foreseen for the fundamental freedoms of services and establishment would again be circumvented. Finally, service providers have not contributed anything to the granting of market access, even though contribution is an important reason to protect property in the first place.[384] Hence, the status obtained through an equivalence decision is not protected as property under Article 17 CFR.

As a result, third country service providers are therefore neither protected under Article 16 nor Article 17 CFR. Since equivalence decisions often lead to concrete and burdensome consequences, legal protection is nevertheless necessary. This protection can, however, be guaranteed through the right to good administration and its individual manifestations described in the next section.

c) *Right to good administration: Article 41 CFR*

As mentioned above, many administrative principles were developed in the case law of the CJEU and not spelt out in legal acts. This changed with the proclamation of the CFR, which has 'the same legal value as the Treaties' pursuant to Article 6 TEU. In relation to equivalence decisions, the codification of the right to good administration in

[380] Case T-496/10 *Bank Mellat v Council of the European Union* ECLI:EU:T:2013:39, paras 36–46; Ferdinand Wollenschläger in Steve Peers and others (eds), *The EU Charter of Fundamental Rights* (Hart Publishing 2014) para 17(1).14.

[381] Joined Cases C-120/06 P and 121/06 P *FIAMM and Others v Council and Commission* ECLI:EU:C:2008:476, para 185; Case C-283/11 *Sky Österreich* (n 377) para 34.

[382] Jürgen Kühling in Matthias Pechstein, Carsten Nowak, and Ulrich Häde (eds), *Frankfurter Kommentar*, vol 1 (Mohr Siebeck 2017) GRC, art 17 paras 11–12 and 18; Hans D Jarass in Hans D Jarass (ed), *Charta der Grundrechte der EU* (4th edn, CH Beck 2021) art 17 paras 11–12.

[383] Case C-2/92 *Bostock* ECLI:EU:C:1994:116, para 19; Case C-210/03 *Swedish Match* ECLI:EU:C:2004:802, para 73; Case C-275/05 *Kibler* ECLI:EU:C:2006:682, para 27; Joined Cases T-466/93, 469/93, 473/93, 474/93 and 477/93 *O'Dwyer and Others v Council* ECLI:EU:T:1995:136, para 101.

[384] Thomas von Danwitz, 'Eigentumsschutz in Europa und im Wirtschaftsvölkerrecht' in Thomas von Danwitz, Otto Depenheuer, and Christoph Engel (eds), *Bericht zur Lage des Eigentums* (Springer 2002) 235f; Wollenschläger (n 380) para 17(1).22.

Article 41 CFR, which has previously been developed in the case law of the CJEU,[385] is of particular importance. It has many facets, such as the right to an impartial and fair decision or the right to be heard, and it creates a legal position for individual citizens against administrative authorities. Because Article 41 CFR is part of Title V, which has the heading 'Citizens' Rights', it may be assumed that it only applies to citizens of the Union.[386] This is indeed true for most provisions in this Title, which grant rights only to citizens or partly also to persons residing or having its registered office in the Union.[387] However, the right to good administration applies to '[e]very person' and thus includes third country nationals in its personal scope of application.[388] The right must be interpreted in light of the guarantees provided for the European administration in Article 298 TFEU.[389]

aa) Right to timely treatment: Time limits for decision-making The assessment of equivalence is a very time-consuming procedure, as illustrated by the two case examples above.[390] In the EU–US deal on equivalence concerning the recognition of CCPs, it took more than three years for the Commission to adopt an equivalence decision. This poses a problem for service providers of third countries and the credibility of the equivalence system as a whole. Hence, the question arises whether there are time limits for the decision-making.

Article 41(1) CFR states that '[e]very person has the right to have his or her affairs handled ... within a reasonable time' and thereby stipulates a right to timely treatment, which has long been recognized in the case law of the ECJ.[391] For service providers to invoke the right to a timely decision, the equivalence decision must be regarded as 'his or her affairs'. A narrow interpretation would demand that the individual is addressed by the decision and, therefore, a party to the administrative proceeding. However, the wording of neither the German (*ihre Angelegenheiten*) nor the French (*ses affaires*) nor the English version uses the word 'party'. This interpretation would also run contrary to the right to a decision, which can also exist for persons who are not the addressees of the respective measure. The right to a decision and to a timely decision must go hand in hand. Furthermore, such a narrow interpretation is not necessary to achieve the rationale of the limitation, namely to avoid an *actio popularis*.[392] In line with the case law of the CJEU, it is therefore sufficient to demand a legitimate interest in the

[385] Case C-255/90 P *Burban v Parliament* ECLI:EU:C:1992:153; Case T-167/94 *Nölle v Council and Commission* ECLI:EU:T:1995:169; Case T-231/97 *New Europe Consulting and Brown v Commission* ECLI:EU:T:1999:146; Paul P Craig in Steve Peers and others (eds), *The EU Charter of Fundamental Rights* (Hart Publishing 2014) para 41.7.

[386] Jill Wakefield, *The Right to Good Administration* (Wolters Kluwer 2007) 65–66.

[387] See eg CFR, arts 39(1), 40, and 42–46.

[388] Lock (n 377) CFR, art 41 para 3.

[389] Widmer (n 360) para 51.

[390] See ch 2 B)II.2.a).

[391] Joined Cases C-238/99 P, 244/99 P, 245/99 P, 247/99 P, 250/99 P–252/99 P and 254/99 P *Limburgse Vinyl Maatschappij and Others v Commission* (n 22) para 179; Case C-105/04 P *Nederlandse Federatieve Vereniging voor de Groothandel op Elektrotechnisch Gebied v Commission* ECLI:EU:C:2006:592, para 35; Case C-113/04 P *Technische Unie v Commission* (n 22) para 40.

[392] Klara Kanska, 'Towards Administrative Human Rights in the EU: Impact of the Charter of Fundamental Rights' (2004) 10 Eur LJ 296, 310.

decision.[393] Service providers whose market access rights depend on the equivalence decision have such an interest, which is why the decision is issued in their affairs.

It follows from this interpretation that third country firms have a right to a decision within a reasonable time. What is to be understood by a 'reasonable' time depends on the specific case.[394] The two months deadlines of Article 17(1) of the European Code of Good Administrative Behaviour and Article 265(2) TFEU can provide guidance and be used as a starting point.[395] In view of the high technicality and complexity as well as the discretionary elements of equivalence decisions, the deadlines should not be too tight. When determining a time limit, the particularities of the respective equivalence mechanism must also be taken into account. An equivalence decision in relation to the country-by-country reporting under the Accounting Directive is, for example, less complex than an equivalence decision regarding the regulation of investment firms under MiFIR, and a decision must therefore be adopted much faster. In addition, the cooperation of the third country in question needs to be considered.[396] If the country provides a detailed analysis to the Commission, the time limits may be shorter. For these reasons, it is not possible to define a deadline applicable to all cases. However, any artificial delaying of the decision is prohibited.

bb) Right to be heard The right to be heard is provided for in Article 41(2)(a) CFR. It is restricted to individual measures which adversely affect the natural or legal person concerned. Hence, the scope of application is restricted in two ways: first, it must be an individual measure[397] and, secondly, it must adversely affect a person. Equivalence decisions are regulatory acts and thus acts of general application.[398] Therefore, there is no right to be heard for service providers, which is unfortunate against the backdrop that the case law of the CJEU used to be more liberal before the proclamation of the CFR in this respect.[399]

cc) Right to access his or her files The right to access one's files in Article 41(2)(b) CFR must be regarded in conjunction with the general right to information and the right of access to documents in Article 42 CFR. The latter does not apply to third country firms, as it is restricted to citizens and natural or legal persons residing or having their registered office in the Union, whereas the other two apply to third

[393] Case T-167/94 *Nölle v Council and Commission* (n 385) para 76; Lock (n 377) CFR, art 41 para 6; with further references see Jörg P Terhechte in Matthias Pechstein, Carsten Nowak, and Ulrich Häde (eds), *Frankfurter Kommentar*, vol 1 (Mohr Siebeck 2017) GRC, art 41 para 11.

[394] Case T-81/95 *Interhotel v Commission* ECLI:EU:T:1997:117, para 65; Joined Cases T-213/95 and 18/96 *SCK and FNK v Commission* ECLI:EU:T:1997:157, para 57; Matthias Klatt in Hans von der Groeben, Jürgen Schwarze, and Armin Hatje (eds), *Europäisches Unionsrecht*, vol 1 (7th edn, Nomos 2015) GRC, art 41 para 12.

[395] Kanska (n 392) 313; critical of this view is Frenz (n 379) para 4553. The European Code of Good Administrative Behaviour is available at https://www.cvce.eu/content/publication/2003/3/10/1b633730-1555-4b88-ac05-b868ae5cc6ac/publishable_en.pdf (accessed 12 November 2022).

[396] Joined Cases T-213/95 and T-18/96 *SCK and FNK v Commission* (n 394) para 57.

[397] Case C-221/09 *AJD Tuna* ECLI:EU:C:2011:153, para 49; Jarass (n 382) art 41 para 20; Craig (n 385) paras 41.33–41.34.

[398] See extensively ch 2 B)IV.1.a)aa)(1). The situation is different with regard to the registration that is following the equivalence decision in a second step in some mechanisms.

[399] Case C-49/88 *Al-Jubail Fertilizer Company and Others v Council* ECLI:EU:C:1991:276, para 15.

country firms. A right to information and, more specifically, a right to one's file are essential to make effective legal protection feasible.[400] Without knowledge of the arguments and considerations of the opposing side, there can hardly be effective legal protection.

For the right to apply, the files must be 'his or hers'. Some scholars advocate a narrow interpretation and demand that the administrative measure addresses the person.[401] This interpretation is not in line with the principle of effective legal protection under Article 47 CFR. It is also not reflected in other language versions, which are formulated more openly. The German, French, and Spanish versions simply require that the files concern the person (*den sie betreffenden Akten*; *dossier qui la concerne*; *que le concierna*). Moreover, only a wider interpretation creates consistency between the right to a decision, the right to information, and the right to a reasoned decision. Thus, service providers need only be concerned by the file's content, which is the case when the equivalence decision is adopted in relation to their home country.[402]

Yet, it is somewhat difficult for the Commission to grant access to files for all service providers concerned.[403] In some cases, this may be thousands of parties. It is, therefore, necessary to limit the obligation to the extent that the Commission is capable of granting access to files without abandoning other tasks. Nevertheless, in light of the importance of the right for the prospects of actions, the standards for applying the exception must be fairly high.

dd) Right to a reasoned decision The right to a reasoned decision[404] in Article 41(2)(c) CFR is probably the most important right for service providers affected by equivalence decisions because only clear reasoning will enable them to assess the prospects of success of actions, and only clear reasoning will enable the court to exercise judicial review.[405] Therefore, it is a precondition for effective legal protection as guaranteed under Article 47 CFR. Moreover, it will shed light on the process of how equivalence is determined. It also demonstrates whether the Commission has fulfilled its duties under the inquisitorial principle.

The institution adopting the act 'must disclose in a clear and unequivocal fashion the reasoning' of the decision in a way that puts the parties affected in a position to assess the legality of the act.[406] The personal scope of application is not specified in paragraph 2 lit c), why is why recourse can be made to the general scope of application as outlined in paragraph 1 ('his or her affairs').[407] As advocated above, it is sufficient to have a legitimate interest, which is fulfilled in the case of third country service providers. This interpretation is underlined by the strong link between the duty to give a

400 Craig (n 385) paras 41.37–41.38.
401 Lock (n 377) CFR, art 41 para 9.
402 For a view in favour of a broad interpretation see Terhechte (n 393) GRC, art 41 para 18; Klatt (n 394) GRC, art 41 para 14.
403 On this problem see Craig (n 385) para 41.38.
404 See also TFEU, art 296(2) for a legal obligation to give a reasoned decision.
405 Joined Cases C-78/16 and 79/16 *Pesce and Others* ECLI:EU:C:2016:428, para 88; Craig (n 385) para 41.49.
406 Case C-367/95 P *Commission v Sytraval and Brink's France* ECLI:EU:C:1998:154, para 63; Case C-269/90 *TU München v Hauptzollamt München-Mitte* (n 363) para 26; Craig (n 385) para 41.51.
407 Klatt (n 394) GRC, art 41 para 15.

reasoned decision and the right to effective legal protection. Since service providers have the legal standing to bring an action, they must also have the right to a reasoned decision.[408]

The precise standards that the reasoning needs to fulfil vary depending on the circumstances of each case. Generally, the obligation does not 'require a specific statement of reasons for each of the technical choices made by the institution'.[409] However, it is not sufficient to simply reproduce the wording of the enabling provision.[410] Rather, the legal and factual basis of the decision must be presented. The concrete limits must be determined with regard to the wording and the context of the decision.[411] The reasoning must be more detailed for administrative than for legislative decisions,[412] it must be more in-depth if there is a wide margin of appreciation[413] or if there is a deviation from an administrative practice, and the burden of justification increases the more severe the implications of the decision.[414] Accordingly, equivalence decisions, as administrative decisions with a wide margin of appreciation and major implications for market access of service providers, must contain an in-depth justification. Since equivalence decisions are very technical decisions by nature, the requirements for the justification are again rather high.

d) Other constitutional principles

Surprisingly, the EU Treaties rarely contain specific constitutional principles limiting administrative actions. As there is no EU legislation dealing with questions of general administrative law either,[415] the CJEU was called to develop general principles of administrative law deriving from the Treaties. The CJEU performed this mission extensively to prevent a denial of justice, recurring particularly to the principle of the rule of law as well as a comparative study of the Member States' legal orders.[416] These principles, which have emerged from case law, and their influence on equivalence decisions, are analysed below.

aa) **Proportionality** The principle of proportionality is one of the most fundamental principles in EU law. It has been developed and formed in the case law of the ECJ and is now foreseen in Article 5(4) TEU.[417] The Commission itself highlights the importance

[408] See for the discussion of legal standing ch 2 B)IV.1.a).

[409] Joined Cases C-78/16 and 79/16 *Pesce and Others* (n 405) para 90; Case C-122/94 *Commission v Council* ECLI:EU:C:1996:68, para 29.

[410] Case C-269/90 *TU München v Hauptzollamt München-Mitte* (n 363) para 27.

[411] See references in n 409 (ch 2).

[412] Craig (n 385) paras 41.53–41.54.

[413] Case C-269/90 *TU München v Hauptzollamt München-Mitte* (n 363) para 14.

[414] Case C-41/00 P *Interporc v Commission* ECLI:EU:C:2003:125, para 55; Case C-185/85 *Usinor v Commission* ECLI:EU:C:1986:276, paras 20–23; Klatt (n 394) GRC, art 41 para 15.

[415] Widmer (n 360) para 30.

[416] For a landmark decision see Joined Cases C-7/56 and 3/57–7/57 *Algera and Others v Assemblée commune* ECLI:EU:C:1957:7, p. 55ff; von Danwitz (n 22) 344.

[417] Concerning the case law of the ECJ see Tor-Inge Harbo, 'The Function of the Proportionality Principle in EU Law' (2010) 16 Eur LJ 158, 171ff.

of a proportional approach in its equivalence assessment, which is why it makes sense to look at it from a constitutional perspective.[418]

The principle of proportionality demands that acts of EU institutions are suitable for pursuing a legitimate objective as set out in the legislation at issue and should not go beyond what is necessary to achieve the objective.[419] An act is 'necessary' if it is the least restrictive measure among different alternatives equally achieving the legitimate objective and if the measure is not manifestly disproportionate in terms of a cost-benefit balance.[420] With regard to equivalence decisions, two interests are at stake: on the one hand, the idea of open and unhindered competition by granting market access to third country service providers and, on the other hand, the maintenance of a high level of investor protection and the stability of the financial system as a whole. Hence, the rejection of an equivalence decision on political grounds, i.e. on the grounds that are not in line with the objective of investor protection and financial stability, must, in addition to the reasons already described above,[421] be regarded as an unsuitable measure and therefore as an infringement of the principle of proportionality.

If the Commission justifies the rejection of equivalence with potential risks for investor protection or financial stability, the proportionality test boils down to *stricto sensu* proportionality, which is the balancing element of the test.[422] This raises the question of whether even a minor shortfall of the third country legal system is sufficient to deny market access through equivalence completely. The CJEU has constantly reduced its judicial scrutiny when assessing measures of EU institutions.[423] It justified this reduction with different explanations, for instance, if the decision is adopted in an area involving discretionary elements,[424] in an area demanding complex technical assessments[425] or if the decision does not result in penalties or far-reaching restrictions of fundamental rights[426]. All these explanations apply here cumulatively, which is why the CJEU will scarcely control the necessity of a denial of equivalence. Furthermore, the CJEU is very restrained in its control of protectionist measures vis-à-vis third countries, as can be seen especially from the ruling on the *EU banana regime*.[427] As a result, the CJEU will only intervene in cases of a clear and manifest violation.

Nevertheless, from the perspective of third country service providers, it is a good signal that the Commission intends to pay particular attention to the proportionality

[418] Commission (n 54) 7f; Commission (n 143) 8 and 10–11.

[419] Settled case law includes Case C-59/11 *Association Kokopelli* ECLI:EU:C:2012:447, para 38; see with further references in Case C-493/17 *Weiss and Others* (n 286) para 72; Case C-62/14 *Gauweiler and Others* (n 286) para 67.

[420] Case C-331/88 *FEDESA and Others* (n 292) para 13; Wolf Sauter, 'Proportionality in EU Law: A Balancing Act' (2012–2013) 15 Cambridge YB Eur Leg Stud 439, 448.

[421] See ch 2 B)II.2.b).

[422] See on *stricto sensu* proportionality Paul P Craig, *EU Administrative Law* (3rd edn, OUP 2018) 653–55.

[423] Sauter (n 420) 449–52; see extensively Oliver Koch, *Der Grundsatz der Verhältnismäßigkeit in der Rechtsprechung des Gerichtshofs der Europäischen Gemeinschaften* (Duncker & Humblot 2003) 290–414.

[424] Case C-331/88 *FEDESA and Others* (n 292) para 13; Case C-265/87 *Schräder v Hauptzollamt Gronau* ECLI:EU:C:1989:303, paras 21–22; Gráinne De Búrca, 'The Principle of Proportionality and its Application in EC Law' (1993) 13 YBEL 105, 115–26.

[425] Case C-122/00 *Omega Air and Others* ECLI:EU:C:2002:161, paras 64–65; Joined Cases C-248/95 and 249/95 *SAM Schiffahrt and Stapf v Germany* ECLI:EU:C:1997:377, paras 23–25; Harbo (n 417) 177.

[426] Craig (n 422) 664–68.

[427] Case C-280/93 *Germany v Council* ECLI:EU:C:1994:367, paras 103ff; Koch (n 423) 361–65.

test.[428] When the Commission constantly applies a strict proportionality test, the principle may gain in importance through the backdoor, namely through the principle of equal treatment and the binding effects of administrative practice (see in more detail under cc)).

bb) Protection of legitimate expectations Already in the early stages of the EU, the ECJ developed the general principle of protection of legitimate expectations as a subcategory of the principle of legal certainty.[429] For the principle of the protection of legitimate expectations to apply, three requirements must be cumulatively fulfilled: 1. the institution must have given rise to justified expectations (objective element); 2. the person concerned must have trusted in these expectations (subjective element); and 3. a balancing of interests must show that the individual interest outweighs the Union interest.[430]

In the case of equivalence, service providers can only develop little trust in the equivalence decision because the Commission highlights its power to withdraw it at any time.[431] What is more, numerous mechanisms explicitly refer to the possibility of a withdrawal.[432] Furthermore, the ECJ found that in the 'sphere of the common organization of the market whose purpose involves constant adjustments to meet changes in the economic situation, economic operators cannot legitimately expect that they will not be subject to restrictions arising out of future rules of market or structural policy'.[433] Reliance on the persistence of the equivalence status is therefore little worthy of protection.

However, the limits outlined above in relation to the equivalence decision of the Commission also apply to the act of withdrawal. Both decisions are purely technical and not of a policy nature. It follows from this that, by adopting an equivalence decision, the Commission gives rise to justified hopes among service providers that the Commission will continue to regard a third country legal system as equivalent unless there is a change in the legal system of either the EU or the third country concerned leading to a finding of non-equivalence. Service providers can therefore rely on the assessment and need not fear a change in policy considerations. If the Commission withdraws equivalence for political reasons, this constitutes, inter alia, a breach of the principle of the protection of legitimate expectations.

cc) Equal treatment and binding effects of administrative practice In case the Commission has already adopted equivalence decisions, another general principle of

[428] Commission (n 54) 7f; Commission (n 143) 8 and 11.

[429] Case C-111/63 *Lemmerz-Werke GmbH v High Authority of the ECSC* ECLI:EU:C:1965:76, p. 691–93; Case C-112/77 *Töpfer v Commission* ECLI:EU:C:1978:94, paras 18–20; Case C-14/81 *Alpha Steel v Commission* ECLI:EU:C:1982:76, paras 28–31; Jörg P Terhechte, 'Europäisches Verwaltungsrecht und europäisches Verfassungsrecht' in Jörg P Terhechte (ed), *Verwaltungsrecht der Europäischen Union* (Nomos 2011) § 7 para 24.

[430] Terhechte (n 429) § 7 para 24; Jürgen Schwarze, *Europarecht* (Nomos 2012) 646–48.

[431] Commission (n 54) 9–11; eg MiFIR, art 47(4); EMIR, art 25p(1)(e).

[432] EMIR, art 13(4); EMIR, art 25p(1)(e); MiFIR, art 33(4) subpara 2; Solvency II, art 172(2) subpara 2.

[433] Case C-177/90 *Kühn v Landwirtschaftskammer Weser-Ems* ECLI:EU:C:1992:2, para 13; previously see Joined Cases C-424/85 and 425/85 *Frico v Voedselvoorzienings In- en Verkoopbureau* ECLI:EU:C:1987:296, para 33; Case C-120/86 *Mulder v Minister van Landbouw en Visserij* ECLI:EU:C:1988:213, para 23.

EU law applies, which has long been established in the case law of the ECJ: the principle of equal treatment.[434] The principle of equal treatment is stipulated in Article 20 CFR. It requires that similar situations should not be treated differently, and different situations should not be treated identically unless such differentiation is objectively justified.[435] From this principle and the principle of legitimate expectations, the ECJ has derived the idea that an institution is bound by its exercise of discretion in former cases and cannot depart from those rules unless there are objective reasons for a different treatment.[436] Thus, the Commission is bound by former equivalence decisions. If the Commission recognizes the supervisory system of a third country as equivalent, it must treat comparable cases of other countries in the same manner if there are no objective reasons for differentiation. Therefore, if country A is recognized as equivalent, the Commission must generally adopt an equivalence decision in relation to country B if its legal system is equivalent to that of the EU *or* country A.[437] An example of an objective ground for differentiation in this case will be if the market of country B poses greater risks for the financial stability in the EU due to its size. This does not only apply to the final decision on equivalence but also to preliminary questions. For instance, if the Commission found that rule A of country A concerning the content of a prospectus to be published guarantees an equivalent level of investor protection, it must come to the same conclusion for country B if it has the same or an equivalent rule to country A. Conversely, the Commission must come to a different decision if the third countries' legal systems are not similar. Accordingly, a growing administrative practice leads to an increasing degree of juridification due to a reduction of the administrative decision-making leeway. This enhances legal certainty and transparency in future decisions by the Commission.

5. Right to a decision

The Commission and many scholars reject the idea that there is an individual right of third countries or their service providers to an equivalence decision.[438] From a comparative law perspective, this concept would constitute a special path of the EU. The

[434] Joined Cases C-17/61 and 20/61 *Klöckner-Werke AG and Others v High Authority* ECLI:EU:C:1962:30, p. 344–46; Joined Cases C-117/76 and 16/77 *Ruckdeschel and Others v Hauptzollamt Hamburg-St Annen* ECLI:EU:C:1977:160, para 7; Joined Cases C-124/76 and 20/77 *Moulins Pont-à-Mousson v ONIC* ECLI:EU:C:1977:161, paras 14–17.

[435] Case C-217/91 *Spain v Commission* ECLI:EU:C:1993:293, para 37.

[436] Joined Cases C-189/02 P, 202/02 P, 205/02 P–208/02 P and 213/02 P *Dansk Rørindustri and Others v Commission* ECLI:EU:C:2005:408, para 211; see also von Danwitz (n 22) 353–56; Gilbert Gornig and Christiane Trüe, 'Die Rechtsprechung des EuGH und des EuG zum europäischen allgemeinen Verwaltungsrecht' (2000) 55 JZ 446, 889.

[437] The only exception to this is if the decision regarding country A was already unlawful. There is no right to the adoption of an unlawful decision. In Germany, this situation is referred to as *Keine Gleichheit im Unrecht*. See Svenja Lemke in Hans von der Groeben, Jürgen Schwarze, and Armin Hatje (eds), *Europäisches Unionsrecht*, vol 1 (7th edn, Nomos 2015) GRC, art 20 para 18.

[438] Commission (n 143) 8; Commission (n 54) 8; Srivastava and Moffatt (n 32) para 4.27; Andy Tarrant, Peter Holmes, and R Daniel Kelemen, 'Equivalence, Mutual Recognition in Financial Services and the UK Negotiating Position' (January 2019) University of Sussex Briefing Paper No 27, 3 https://blogs.sussex.ac.uk/uktpo/files/2019/01/BP27print.pdf (accessed 12 November 2022); Rolf Sethe, 'Das Drittstaatenregime von MiFIR und MiFID II' (2014) 86 SZW 615, 624; Evariest Callens, 'Third Country CCP Supervision as a Catalyst for More Centralized EU CCP Supervision?' (2023) EBI Working Paper Series No 134, 18–19 <<https://ssrn.com/abstract=4349597> (accessed 5 March 2023).

EU is the only legal system worldwide that uses deference but at the same time claims that there is no possibility to request such a decision.[439] The CFTC, for instance, grants such a right of request not only to foreign regulators and affected firms but also to foreign trade associations or similar groups acting on behalf of the firms.[440] For this reason alone, and in view of the fact that the EU has extended equivalence, particularly on the basis of the G20 proposals, this hypothesis must be subjected to a critical examination.

a) Basis of a right to a decision

Without a right to a decision, the approach of market access through equivalence appears to be rather protectionist and leaves (service providers from) third countries in a weak position. Neither the Commission nor scholars give proper reasoning for their view that there is no right to a decision. Sometimes reference is made to the Commission's discretion; other times the nature of a *political* decision is underlined.[441] These arguments are not convincing.

As has been extensively outlined above, the decision is purely technical and not a political one. Including political considerations is not in conformity with equivalence provisions and violates the EU Treaties as well as world trade law. While the Commission does indeed have discretionary powers when deciding on equivalence and judicial review is limited in this respect, this does not mean, however, that the Commission can do whatever it pleases. The *Schrems I* and *II* cases are only two examples where the ECJ has set clear limits to the Commission's room for manoeuvre in comparable situations.[442]

Another ground-breaking case in this regard is *Camar and Tico*.[443] Two Italian companies (*Camar* and *Tico*) wanted to import bananas from third countries because they could no longer supply the Italian market as their imports from Somalia nosedived after war broke out there. The import of bananas was subject to strict quotas under the common organization of the market in bananas scheme.[444] However, the Commission had the power to adopt special measures to overcome situations of a sensitive nature if it judged it necessary.[445] The two companies requested such measures multiple times. In this case, the General Court ruled that even though the Commission had 'broad discretion' in its decision with limited judicial review, the Commission unlawfully failed to take the necessary measures.[446] This judgment, which was upheld by the ECJ

[439] FSB (n 48) 6 https://www.fsb.org/wp-content/uploads/r_140918.pdf (accessed 12 November 2022). However, MiFID II, art 25(4)(a) subparas 2 and 3 and EMIR, art 76a(2) expressly provide for such a right. With these two equivalence mechanisms, the possibility of requesting a decision cannot be disputed.

[440] CFTC, 'Interpretive Guidance and Policy Statement Regarding Compliance With Certain Swap Regulations' 78 Fed Reg 45292, 45344 (26 July 2013) https://www.cftc.gov/sites/default/files/idc/groups/public/@lrfederalregister/documents/file/2013-17958a.pdf (accessed 12 November 2022).

[441] Commission (n 143) 8; Srivastava and Moffatt (n 32) para 4.31.

[442] See ch 1 C)I.3.

[443] Joined Cases T-79/96, 260/97 and 117/98 *Camar and Tiko v Commission and Council* ECLI:EU:T:2000:147.

[444] Council Regulation (EEC) No 404/93 of 13 February 1993 (Market in Bananas Regime).

[445] Council Regulation (EEC) No 404/93 of 13 February 1993, art 30.

[446] Joined Cases T-79/96, 260/97 and 117/98 *Camar and Tiko v Commission and Council* (n 443) paras 138, 145, 149, and 152.

in the parts relevant here,[447] underlines that broad discretion and a right to a decision are not mutually exclusive.[448]

Another line of argumentation against a right to a decision could be that equivalence decisions are issued in the form of regulatory acts which are of a general and not individual nature. Since service providers are not the addressees of such decisions, they should not have a right to request the adoption of such general acts. Being the addressee of a decision is, however, not a prerequisite for the right to a decision. The requested decision of the Commission in the *Camar and Tico* case was also a measure of general application.[449] Thus, the argument is not substantiated.

A right to a decision for third country *service providers* may derive either from primary or secondary law.[450] The European legal system is more open in recognizing individual rights than, for instance, German law, which requires that a provision intends to serve individual interests (*Schutznormtheorie*).[451] EU law is rather modelled on the French system, in which any legitimate interest (*intérêt pour agir*) suffices.[452] The ECJ often examines whether the decision affects the individual concerned.[453] However, academia and jurisprudence are far from developing a consistent system of when individual rights exist.[454] Based on the current state of the discussion, as seen, any legitimate interest is sufficient. Although the Commission stresses that equivalence is not an instrument to liberalize trade, market access or exemptions from certain obligations for third country service providers depend on the Commission's decision. Therefore, service providers have a substantial interest in such a decision, as their market access depends on it. Consequently, in principle, they have an individual right to an equivalence decision deriving from the provisions enabling the Commission to

[447] Case C-312/00 P *Commission v Camar and Tiko* ECLI:EU:C:2002:736.

[448] Joanna Dervisopoulos, 'Untätigkeitsklage' in Hans-Werner Rengeling, Andreas Middeke, and Martin Gellermann (eds), *Handbuch des Rechtsschutzes in der Europäischen Union* (3rd edn, CH Beck 2014) § 8 para 49; Matthias Pechstein in Matthias Pechstein, Carsten Nowak, and Ulrich Häde (eds), *Frankfurter Kommentar*, vol 4 (Mohr Siebeck 2017) AEUV, art 265 para 66.

[449] Joined Cases T-79/96, 260/97 and 117/98 *Camar and Tiko v Commission and Council* (n 443) para 82; see also Case T-496/11 *United Kingdom v ECB* ECLI:EU:T:2015:133, para 30, stating that: '[a]n action for annulment is available in the case of all measures adopted by the institutions, whatever their nature or form, which are intended to have legal effects'.

[450] Joined Cases C-10/68 and 18/68 *Eridania Zuccherifici and Others v Commission* ECLI:EU:C:1969:66, para 16; Koen Lenaerts, Ignace Maselis, and Kathleen Gutman, *EU Procedural Law* (OUP 2014) para 8.06. Whether such a right for individuals can also be derived from world trade law is disputed but has been rejected by the ECJ in settled case law. This case law, according to which provisions of world trade law are not directly applicable in Union law and individuals cannot rely on them, is to be opposed because it circumvents the EU's obligations under international law. See references in n 456 (ch 2).

[451] von Danwitz (n 22) 513–15; Mathias Hong, 'Subjektive Rechte und Schutznormtheorie im europäischen Verwaltungsrechtsraum' (2012) 67 JZ 381, 381f.

[452] See Dervisopoulos (n 319) § 7 para 56; André Legrand and Céline Wiener, *Le droit public* (La Documentation française 2017) 147.

[453] With regard to state liability in the area of deposit insurance: Case C-571/16 *Kantarev* ECLI:EU:C:2018:807, para 103.

[454] Martin Nettesheim, 'Subjektive Rechte im Unionsrecht' (2007) 132 AöR 333, 350. This is because the individual's right to bring an action does not depend on a subjective legal position. Even without such a position, an action may be admissible. Moreover, the ECJ examines the legality of the contested act irrespective of whether the infringement also violates the rights of the individual. For this reason, the question of when individual rights exist is rather of a theoretical nature. See ibid 351ff. This is different in the case of an action for failure to act, where an infringement of the Treaties is required, which in the present cases occurs only if there is a right to a decision.

adopt an equivalence decision. Once the Commission has adopted an equivalence decision, this interpretation is underlined by the general principle of equal treatment and the doctrine that administrative practice is binding on the institution concerned.[455]

A right to a decision for *third countries* may derive from world trade law. As discussed, paragraph 3(b) second sentence of the Annex on Financial Services of the GATS obliges the EU to give third countries that are members of the WTO an 'adequate opportunity' to demonstrate that their legal system is equivalent once an equivalence decision has been adopted in relation to another Member. It follows from this duty that the EU must allow countries to apply for equivalence if it has previously taken an equivalence decision vis-à-vis another state in the given field. This opportunity constitutes a right to a decision for third countries. However, it is highly unlikely that the ECJ will accept such a right arising directly from world trade law. In general, the ECJ takes a rather restrictive stance towards the recognition of subjective rights as well as the direct applicability of world trade law, as can be seen from multiple cases, including *International Fruit Company*, *EU banana regime*, and *Van Parys*.[456]

Ultimately, *service providers* from third countries generally have a right to a decision. Such a right will most likely not be recognized by the ECJ for *third countries*. This hesitant position towards world trade law by the ECJ is to be seen critically but has only minor practical consequences in the present context.[457]

b) Limits of a right to a decision

This right to a decision is limited in two important ways. First of all, it must not be disregarded that equivalence decisions are discretionary acts.[458] For reasons of separation of powers, the judiciary shall not interfere in the leeway of the administration.[459] Consequently, the right to a decision of service providers is limited in that they are not entitled to a positive equivalence decision unless the only possible lawful decision would be to determine equivalence,[460] which is unlikely to be the case due to the high complexity and technical nature of such decisions leading to a wide margin of discretion on the part of the Commission. Usually, service providers, therefore, only have a right to request a decision free of any assessment errors.[461]

Secondly, the limited resources of the Commission must be considered. The Commission is not capable of carrying out equivalence investigations of dozens of third countries on numerous equivalence mechanisms simultaneously. It has a right to prioritize. The order in which the Commission conducts its investigations is also

[455] See in more detail ch 2 B)II.4.d)cc).

[456] Joined Cases C-21/72–24/72 *International Fruit Company* ECLI:EU:C:1972:115, paras 19ff; Case C-280/93 *Germany v Council* (n 427) paras 103ff; Case C-377/02 *Van Parys* (n 331) paras 46ff; critical of this case law is Herdegen (n 330) 313ff.

[457] The question is of little practical relevance in this context because actions by third countries against equivalence acts before the CJEU are inadmissible, as will be explained later. Instead, the legal protection of third countries is limited to the dispute settlement system of world trade law. See ch 2 B)IV.

[458] Two exceptions include AIFMD, art 21(6) subpara 3 and Transparency Directive, art 23(4) subpara 2, where the limitation on the right to a decision does consequently not apply.

[459] Alexander Fritzsche, 'Discretion, Scope of Judicial Review and Institutional Balance in European Law' (2010) 47 CMLR 361, 381–92.

[460] Dervisopoulos (n 448) § 8 para 49.

[461] Markus Kotzur in Rudolf Geiger, Daniel-Erasmus Khan, and Markus Kotzur (eds), *European Union Treaties* (CH Beck 2015) art 265 para 11; Wakefield (n 386) 148–50.

subject to its discretion. Again, the Commission is not allowed to prioritize on political grounds. Prioritization must be based on criteria underlying financial market regulation in general, i.e. investor protection, functioning of financial markets and systemic stability.[462] Third countries and service providers can therefore request an equivalence analysis from the Commission, but they only have a right to a lawful consideration of their request.

c) *The special case of Brexit*

Since the United Kingdom has left the EU, it is now a third country. Nevertheless, the UK is not a third country like any other.[463] Its financial economy is important for and closely intertwined with that of the EU, which is why the EU refers to the UK in this context as a 'high-impact country'.[464] Moreover, the UK prescribed in its Withdrawal Act the retention of indirect EU and the incorporation of direct EU legislation into UK law after exit day.[465] Through the incorporation of Union law, the legal system of the UK is equivalent to that of the EU.[466] Because the British supervisory authorities were long part of the European supervisory system, there is also no evidence suggesting that the supervision is not equivalent.[467] The mere fact that the Commission wants to carry out a very thorough examination in the case of high-impact countries does not change the finding of equivalence in the case of identical legal regimes. Likewise, the mere expectation that the UK will change its regulation in the future is not a legitimate ground for refusing to issue an equivalence decision.[468] Should this fear materialize, the Commission can withdraw equivalence at any time.

Consequently, if the UK or its service providers request an equivalence decision by the Commission, they have a right to a lawful consideration of that request. The Commission must then process this request based on objective grounds established for prioritization. When it is the UK's turn according to these criteria, they have a right to a decision free of any errors of assessment. Provided that the two legal systems remain identical, this right to a decision free of any errors of assessment even turns into a right to a positive equivalence decision.

[462] A good example of a prioritization along such objective grounds can be found in: CEIOPS, 'Advice to the European Commission: Equivalence assessments to be undertaken in relation to Articles 172, 227 and 260 of the Solvency II Directive' CEIOPS-DOC-92-10 (31 August 2010) 3.

[463] Niccolò Lorenzotti, 'Third-country equivalence and its suitability in the context of Brexit' (2019) 22 Fin Reg Intl 1, 8f.

[464] Economic Governance Support Unit (DG for Internal Policies), 'Third country equivalence in EU banking and financial regulation' In Depth Analysis, PE 614.495 (August 2019) https://www.europarl.europa.eu/RegData/etudes/IDAN/2018/614495/IPOL_IDA(2018)614495_EN.pdf (accessed 12 November 2022); see indirectly Commission (n 54) 7.

[465] European Union (Withdrawal) Act 2018, §§ 2–3.

[466] Wymeersch (n 4) 226f.

[467] Moloney (n 3) 22. The UK has already negotiated an MoU with the EU which, among other things, establishes a Joint EU-UK Financial Regulatory Forum. The existence of such an MoU is a prerequisite required in many equivalence provisions. See Lucy McNulty, 'Here is the UK-EU Brexit deal for finance' *Financial Times* (1 April 2021) https://www.fnlondon.com/articles/here-is-the-uk-eu-brexit-deal-for-finance-20210401 (accessed 12 November 2022).

[468] An exception can only be made if a legislative initiative is already in the process of becoming law and this initiative would lead to non-equivalence. In this scenario, it would not make sense to issue an equivalence decision, which would then have to be immediately withdrawn.

However, these observations only apply as long as the UK autonomously adopts EU law. As soon as the UK deviates from EU law, it loses its right to a positive equivalence determination. Instead, it will only have a right to a decision free of any errors of assessment. Owing to the strong influence the UK economy has on the financial stability of the EU, the Commission may apply high standards when weighing the similarities and differences. Nevertheless, no identical legal systems can be demanded. The decision must continue to be based on an outcome-based approach. When the UK achieves an equivalent result with different rules, the Commission must adopt an equivalence decision.[469]

III. Withdrawal of equivalence decisions

In an ideal world, equivalence describes not the single moment of the equivalence decision but a continuous state. In that world, legal orders evolve parallel to each other and therefore remain equivalent. In reality, this will often not be the case. There is a risk of diverging legal situations between the EU and the respective third country after an equivalence decision has been adopted. A different legal environment may result in a situation where equivalence between the legal orders no longer exists. If the level of protection drops in the third country, it can be dangerous for investors and the soundness of financial markets when European law is no longer applied extraterritorially, and EU authorities no longer supervise third country market participants. The Commission identified and addressed this threat in its Staff Working Document of 2017 and its Communication of 2019.[470]

Because of this risk, many equivalence mechanisms include statutes enabling competent authorities to withdraw equivalence unilaterally.[471] But some regimes do not contain such a clause.[472] Here, the question arises whether the decision can still be withdrawn. Even though it is not foreseen *expressis verbis*, simply the fact that the state of equivalence is a prerequisite for the decision underlines that a decision can be revoked if this requirement is no longer met.[473] Also, from a teleological standpoint, the Commission must be able to take back its decisions if the legal regime changes in a way that jeopardizes consumers and financial markets. In addition, the concept of *actus*

[469] It seems likely that the UK will shift more to a principle-based regulatory approach, as this fits better to the common law tradition. This approach will automatically move away from the European one, which focuses on regulating in as much detail as possible. It is to be hoped that the EU will respect this different regulatory approach and will look only at the outcomes it produces for investor protection, the functioning of financial markets and financial stability. See on the development in the UK post-Brexit Christy Ann Petit and Thorsten Beck, 'Recent trends in UK financial sector regulation and possible implications for the EU, including its approach to equivalence' IPOL Study PE 740.067 (February 2023) https://www.europarl.europa.eu/RegData/etudes/STUD/2023/740067/IPOL_STU(2023)740067_EN.pdf (accessed 5 March 2023).

[470] Commission (n 143) 9; Commission (n 54) 9–11.

[471] See eg EMIR, art 13(4); EMIR, art 25p(1)(e); MiFIR, art 33(4) subpara 2; Solvency II, art 172(2) subpara 2.

[472] See eg Transparency Directive, art 23(4); CRR II, art 107(4); SSR, art 17(2).

[473] Wymeersch (n 4) 227.

contrarius, which the General Court describes as a 'general principle of law', argues in favour of a possibility to withdraw the decision.[474]

Again, a distinction must be drawn between the withdrawal of equivalence as a whole, the withdrawal of an equivalence decision, and deregistration where a register is involved in the process. If an equivalence regime is classified as a one-step process, only the equivalence decision can be revoked. If registration is a prerequisite for market access, there are two scenarios in which a third country firm may lose its rights derived from equivalence. The first scenario is the withdrawal of registration/recognition/certification, for instance, for CCPs under EMIR or investments firms under MiFIR by ESMA. This automatically leads to a loss of market access, as registration/recognition/certification is the key condition for triggering the legal consequences.[475] This logging off from the register is not the same as the withdrawal of an equivalence decision, even though the former may result in the latter.[476] The second scenario is a withdrawal of the equivalence decision by the Commission, which does not directly lead to a revocation of market access rights. However, in the absence of a decision on equivalence, the conditions under which ESMA may register a company are no longer fulfilled. ESMA will deregister the company, thereby depriving it of market access rights. When an equivalence mechanism consists of a two-step process, both decisions can therefore be withdrawn.

To assess whether a withdrawal of an equivalence decision is necessary, the Commission observes the legal system of the third country. In this context, the Commission differentiates between 'monitoring' and 'reviewing'.[477] Monitoring describes an ongoing technical comparison of two evolving legal systems and a dynamic market carried out by the Commission and ESAs.[478] An important prerequisite for the functioning of monitoring is the existence of cooperation agreements and regulatory dialogues and fora with third country regulators and supervisory agencies. Therefore, the Commission believes that monitoring contributes to understanding market and regulatory developments in third countries and should therefore not be regarded as a risk of possible withdrawals but as a means to prevent them due to ongoing cooperation.[479]

An equivalence review, however, may take place on an ad hoc or regular basis and 'involves a more structured and more strictly defined analysis'.[480] In this assessment, all criteria for equivalence and all requirements contained in the decision are checked, and the review may result in a withdrawal of the equivalence decision. Again, ESAs may be involved in the form of technical assessments, which is why they are a key part

[474] Case T-251/00 *Lagardère v Commission* ECLI:EU:T:2002:278, para 130; Herwig CH Hofmann, Gerard C Rowe, and Alexander H Türk, *Administrative Law and Policy of the European Union* (OUP 2011) 632; Alfred Bleckmann, 'Die actus-contrarius-Doktrin' (1988) 28 JuS 174.

[475] EMIR, art 25(5) and (1); MiFIR, arts 49 and 46(1).

[476] See eg MiFIR, arts 49(3) and 47(4); Zetzsche (n 20) MiFIR, art 49 para 4.

[477] Commission (n 54) 9–11.

[478] For a critical view with regard to the intensity of the control which comes close to an ongoing supervision see Moloney (n 32) 44. A look at ESMA's annual report shows that Moloney's criticism is at least partially justified, given that ESMA interprets its task very broadly in the report. ESMA, '2016 Annual Report and 2017 Work Programme' ESMA80-1467488426-27 (3 February 2017) 61ff.

[479] Commission (n 54) 10.

[480] Commission (n 143) 11–12.

of both monitoring and reviewing. Apart from a withdrawal, the Commission can also amend, e.g. restrict or extend, already adopted equivalence decisions (*argumentum a fortiori*).[481]

The revocation of equivalence decisions poses potential challenges for third country financial service providers. First, it remains unclear on what grounds equivalence decisions can be withdrawn. The Commission proposes to consider changes in the legal orders, relevant market developments, as well as 'wider external policy priorities and concerns in particular with respect to the promotion of common values and shared regulatory objectives . . . .'[482] An example of the latter reasoning was the expiration of equivalence regarding Swiss stock exchanges, which was justified by the lack of process in concluding a common Institutional Framework Agreement.[483] The exercise of discretion in the withdrawal decision must be guided by the standards of the initial decision. The Commission must therefore focus on the characteristics of the legal systems. At the same time, it can also consider market developments that may affect the required level of equivalence depending on the degree of the markets' interdependence. However, political considerations must not be taken into account by the Commission. The expiration of equivalence in relation to Swiss stock exchanges was therefore unlawful.

Secondly, it is potentially dangerous for service providers that the Member States may influence the withdrawal process.[484] This risk stems from the fact that many equivalence provisions refer to the Comitology Regulation laying down rules for the control by the Member States of the Commission's exercise of implementing powers. This influence is mainly done through a committee comprised of representatives of the Member States.[485] That way, political discords can affect market access, even though these considerations should not be part of the decision-making process.

Thirdly, the withdrawal of equivalence may take place at little or even no notice. The EMIR mechanism to avoid duplicative or conflicting rules for counterparties, for instance, provides for a 30-day period within which the Commission must decide on a withdrawal. These short deadlines create considerable legal uncertainty for financial service providers, which are unnecessary, at least if no imminent systemic risks for EU markets arise during a transitional period. The short deadlines also prevent third countries from adjusting their legal systems to the EU's to preserve their market access rights. Such an alignment would be a preferable outcome compared to a complete withdrawal of equivalence because it prevents the fragmentation of markets. It is therefore advisable to include grace/transition periods in future legislation.[486]

Fourthly, the process of withdrawal is rather opaque, making it difficult to anticipate such decisions, which in turn increases legal uncertainty.[487] This is at odds with

[481] ibid 12.

[482] ibid 9 and 12.

[483] Commission Implementing Decision (EU) 2018/2047 of 20 December 2018, recitals 30 and 32; See also Commission (n 313). The decision linked the extension to the finalization of the Institutional Framework Agreement. Explicitly: European Parliament (n 40) no 15f; explicitly calling it a political decision: Nobel (n 75) § 2 para 70.

[484] Zetzsche (n 20) MiFIR, art 47 para 14.

[485] See Comitology Regulation, art 3(2).

[486] This reform proposal is presented in more detail in ch 5 B)III.3.b).

[487] Admonishing the lack of transparency: European Parliament (n 40) nos 16 and 19.

the case law of the ECJ and European primary law, which require a due and fair as well as transparent process in administrative proceedings.[488] The Union is based on the rule of law as developed in the case law of the ECJ, inter alia, on Article 19 TEU.[489] Meanwhile, this settled case law has been reflected as a subjective right to good administration in Article 41 CFR. Both the equivalence decision and the withdrawal of it are administrative decisions by the Commission.[490] In the course of these decisions, the Commission must comply with the right of diligent and impartial examination, the right to have access to his or her files and the right to receive a reasoned explanation for the decision. By adhering to these principles of good administration, legal certainty can be increased for third countries and the process will be further 'juridified' as advocated throughout this book.

IV. Judicial review of equivalence decisions

As many contentious issues are surrounding the equivalence decision, such as the limits to the administrative decision-making leeway or the procedural rights of third country service providers, the possibilities of legal protection against it are of utmost importance. This is especially true against the background of the European self-conception as a 'Community based on the rule of law'.[491] Surprisingly, this question has hardly been discussed so far.[492] Some claim that equivalence decisions are subject to judicial review,[493] while others deny any possibility of judicial review without further justification.[494] The latter view will be challenged in the following.

Since an analysis of legal protection limited to equivalence decisions does not provide a complete picture, a potential decision at the second level by ESAs or NCAs is also included in the following. Legal protection against these equivalence acts can take place at three different levels: the national level, the EU level (1.) and the level of world trade law (2.). The national level will be left out in the following analysis, as legal protection differs depending on the respective Member State.[495]

[488] Case C-255/90 P *Burban v Parliament* (n 385); Michael Fehling, 'Europäisches Verwaltungsverfahren und Verwaltungsprozessrecht' in Jörg P Terhechte (ed), *Verwaltungsrecht der Europäischen Union* (Nomos 2011) § 12 paras 12–51; see in the context of equivalence: Wymeersch (n 4) 227.

[489] Case C-294/83 *Les Verts v Parliament* (n 28) para 23.

[490] Moloney (n 14) para 6.18.

[491] Case C-294/83 *Les Verts v Parliament* (n 28) para 23. This term was coined in the German translation (*Rechtsgemeinschaft*) by Walter Hallstein. See Walter Hallstein, *Die Europäische Gemeinschaft* (Econ 1973) 31–54; Wolfgang Blomeyer and Karl Albrecht Schachtschneider, *Die Europäische Union als Rechtsgemeinschaft* (Duncker & Humblot 1995).

[492] Two notable exceptions include the analysis of Howell (n 269) 138ff and of Imm (n 106) 120ff.

[493] See Wymeersch (n 4) 216f, stating, without further explanation, that such decisions are reviewable. Likewise, see Srivastava and Moffatt (n 32) para 4.34; Heikki Marjosola, 'Regulate Thy Neighbour' (2016) EUI Working Papers 2016/01, 12 http://hdl.handle.net/1814/39022 (accessed 12 November 2022).

[494] Jonathan Herbst and Rachel Kent, 'Q: Is Equivalence a Backdoor Route for UK Firms to Maintain Access to EU Markets' (2017) 36 Intl Fin L Rev 14, 15; Doris Döhmel in Heinz-Dieter Assmann, Uwe H Schneider, and Peter O Mülbert (eds), *Wertpapierhandelsrecht* (8th edn, Otto Schmidt 2023) VO (EU) Nr 600/2014, art 47 para 5; Franca Contratto, 'Sanktionen: Neue Gretchenfrage im Ringen um den Marktzugang in die EU?' (2018) 90 SZW 653, 659.

[495] See for legal remedies under German law Imm (n 106) 132ff.

1. Legal protection before the CJEU

The type of action brought before the CJEU and its chances of success depend on numerous factors. In particular, the concrete applicant, the specific situation they face, and the type of equivalence mechanism. That is why the following analysis distinguishes between the type of applicant (a), b) and c)) and, within these subheadings, where appropriate, between the type of equivalence mechanism.

a) Third countries and third country firms as applicants

The goal of a third country and its firms is to have their country recognized as equivalent by the EU. If an equivalence status does not yet exist because the Commission has not adopted an equivalence decision or the competent ESA has not granted registration/recognition/certification, the action for failure to act is the applicable type of action (Article 265 TFEU). In cases where equivalence was established, but the Commission withdrew the equivalence decision or the competent ESA revoked the registration/recognition/certification[496], the action for annulment is the appropriate legal remedy (Article 263 TFEU).

aa) One-step process In situations where the legal consequences automatically take effect following an equivalence decision (one-step process),[497] as is the case, for instance, in the Accounting Directive in relation to the obligation to perform a country-by-country reporting, the identification of the subject matter is relatively easy. The available legal remedy is either an action for failure to act where the Commission has not adopted an equivalence decision or an action for annulment where the Commission has withdrawn the equivalence decision. The General Court is responsible for these kinds of proceedings.[498] Two questions seem to be relevant when examining the prospects of success of actions: first, the applicant needs to have the capacity to bring an action—*locus standi* (admissibility). Secondly, there must be a ground for an annulment or a right to a decision (merits).

(1) *Locus standi* (admissibility)

With regard to the legal standing of the applicant (*locus standi*), both types of actions that are relevant here differentiate between privileged and non-privileged applicants.[499] Third countries and their financial service providers, if at all, fall into the latter category. This category includes 'any natural or legal person' and is therefore not limited to EU citizens or private companies. Hence, third countries[500] and

[496] When reference is made to the registration decision in the following, this encompasses the decision on recognition and certification. See note 443 (ch 1).

[497] See on one-step processes: ch 1 C)III.1.

[498] This follows from art 256(1) of the TFEU and the fact that the exceptions listed in art 51 of the Statute of the Court of Justice of the European Union only refer to certain actions initiated by Member States or institutions of the Union but not to other natural or legal persons. Matthias Pechstein, *EU-Prozessrecht* (4th edn, Mohr Siebeck 2011) para 351.

[499] The action for annulment further introduces the category of semi-privileged applicants which does not apply here.

[500] The CJEU has not yet explicitly stated that third countries are to be considered 'legal person[s]' in the sense of TFEU, arts 263(4) and 265(3). However, the CJEU has already hinted at that solution: Case C-70/04 *Swiss Confederation v Commission* ECLI:EU:C:2005:468 and Case T-319/05 *Switzerland v Commission* ECLI:EU:T:2010:367. It has also allowed an intervention of a third country: see Joined Cases C-91/82 and 200/82 *Chris International Foods v Commission* ECLI:EU:C:1983:45, p. 419; see the explanation in Lenaerts, Maselis, and Gutman (n 450) para 7.82, n 315.

their nationals[501] are included. In the case of an action for annulment initiated by non-privileged applicants, Article 263(4) TFEU applies, providing three options.[502] Whether these options also apply in the context of the action for failure to act, which has a different wording, is controversial and must be assessed separately for each option.

Pursuant to the first alternative, the action is admissible if the applicant is the addressee of the decision. This alternative also applies to the action for failure to act. An equivalence or withdrawal decision, as an implementing decision, does neither individually address the third country nor its service providers. Third countries are not parties but rather the subject of the decision. Service providers are just generally affected by the decision, which is not sufficient to qualify as an addressee.[503]

According to the second alternative, applicants also have the capacity to bring an action if they are directly and individually concerned. However, these criteria are highly controversial and are interpreted very narrowly by the ECJ.[504] In the *Plaumann* case, the ECJ decided that persons are individually concerned only if 'by reason of certain attributes which are peculiar to them or by reason of circumstances in which they are differentiated from all other persons and by virtue of these factors distinguishes them individually'.[505] In the case of an equivalence decision or its withdrawal, all financial service providers from the respective third country are affected in the same manner. Hence, none of them stands out and is *individually* concerned according to the *Plaumann* judgment.

The last alternative for applicants to institute proceedings is in the case of regulatory acts which are of direct concern to them and do not entail implementing measures. Thus, an individual concern is not required in these situations.[506] A regulatory act is defined by the CJEU as an act of general application (1st element), apart from legislative acts (2nd element).[507] Again, this classification is highly controversial because many voices disagree with the exclusion of legislative acts.[508] Since

[501] Case T-143/06 *MTZ Polyfilms v Council* ECLI:EU:T:2009:441; Case T-122/09 *Zhejiang Xinshiji Foods Co and Hubei Zinshiji Foods Co v Council* ECLI:EU:T:2011:46; Case T-262/10 *Microban International and Microban (Europe) v Commission* ECLI:EU:T:2011:623.

[502] Albertina Albors-Llorens, 'Judicial Protection before the Court of Justice of the European Union' in Catherine Barnard and Steve Peers (eds), *European Union Law* (3rd edn, OUP 2020) 295ff; see extensively on the relationship between art 263(4) of the TFEU and arts 290 and 291 of the TFEU with regard to judicial review Maria Bergström, 'Judicial Protection for Private Parties in European Commission Rulemaking' in Carl F Bergström and Dominique Ritleng (eds), *Rulemaking by the European Commission* (OUP 2016) 205ff.

[503] Imm (n 106) 121; see extensively Alexander H Türk, *The Concept of Legislation in European Community Law* (Wolters Kluwer 2006) 82–120.

[504] See Marilina Eliantonio and Nelly Stratieva, 'From Plaumann, through UPA and Jego-Quere, to the Lisbon Treaty: The Locus Standi of Private Applicants under Article 230(4) EC through a Political Lens' (2010) 2010 RRDE 43; Bernhard Kluttig, 'Die Klagebefugnis Privater gegen EU-Rechtsakte in der Rechtsprechung des Europäischen Gerichtshofes: Und die Hoffnung stirbt zuletzt ... ' (2004) 30 Beiträge zum Transnationalen Wirtschaftsrecht 5.

[505] Case C-25/62 *Plaumann v Commission* ECLI:EU:C:1963:17, p. 107.

[506] Lenaerts, Maselis, and Gutman (n 450) para 7.107.

[507] Case T-18/10 *Inuit Tapiriit Kanatami and Others v Parliament and Council* ECLI:EU:T:2011:419, paras 41–56; confirmed on appeal: Case C-583/11 P *Inuit Tapiriit Kanatami and Others v Parliament and Council* ECLI:EU:C:2013:625, para 60; Case T-262/10 *Microban International and Microban (Europe) v Commission* (n 501) paras 20–25.

[508] Niklas Görlitz and Philipp Kubicki, 'Rechtsakte "mit schwierigem Charakter"' (2011) 22 EuZW 248; Jürgen Schwarze and Philipp Voet van Vormizeele in Jürgen Schwarze and others (eds), *EU-Kommentar* (4th edn, Nomos 2019) art 263 paras 51–52.

neither equivalence nor withdrawal decisions—as implementing decisions within the meaning of Article 291(2) TFEU—qualify as legislative acts, this discussion is not of relevance for the present purposes.[509]

Nevertheless, the decision needs to be a matter of general and not individual application according to the first element of the definition. The ECJ qualifies an act as a matter of general application if it lays down generally applicable principles, applies to objectively defined situations and produces legal effects for categories of persons determined in an abstract manner.[510] On the one hand, it could be argued that it is an individual decision because the undertakings affected by the decision are at least identifiable at the moment of its adoption. Moreover, the legal consequences take effect *ipso iure* after the decision has been adopted, and therefore concrete consequences are produced by the decision in individual cases. In the case of the Accounting Directive, financial service providers are, for instance, exempted from the obligation to prepare a country-by-country report in accordance with the Directive.

On the other hand, the affected recipients are identified only in an abstract manner based on their establishment in the third country. Therefore, the decision deals with categories of persons and not individuals. According to the case law of the ECJ, it is not decisive that the measure ultimately affects only a limited group of persons but that this group of persons is determined according to abstract criteria.[511] This is the case for equivalence decisions, which in the abstract concern all third country firms or products. What is more, the legal consequences (e.g. market access and exemption from supervisory obligations) are not set out in the decision itself. They only take effect if other requirements are fulfilled cumulatively. The decision determines a state of equivalence which may then have concrete effects at a later level on the basis of these objectively defined situations.[512] This finding is further supported by looking at other set-ups of equivalence. In two-step processes, in which the national level must decide about the specific consequences, the equivalence decision only harmonizes different administrative practices and does not regulate individual cases. Even though implementing decisions are addressed to the Member States in these scenarios, they are still qualified as being of general application.[513] The set-up of equivalence does, however, not change the legal nature of the decision, which is why the decision is always of general application. As a result, equivalence and withdrawal decisions are regulatory acts in the sense of Article 263(4) third alternative TFEU.[514]

[509] Jürgen Bast, 'New Categories of Acts After the Lisbon Reform: Dynamics of Parliamentarization in EU Law' (2012) 49 CMLR 885; see for a definition of legislative acts Lenaerts, Maselis, and Gutman (n 450) para 7.108.

[510] Joined Cases C-36/58, 37/58, 38/58, 40/58 and 41/58 *Simet and Others v High Authority* ECLI:EU:C:1959:19, p. 166; see also Case T-262/10 *Microban International and Microban (Europe) v Commission* (n 501) para 23; Lenaerts, Maselis, and Gutman (n 450) para 7.108.

[511] Joined Cases C-622/16 P–624/16 P *Scuola Elementare Maria Montessori v Commission* ECLI:EU:C:2018:873, paras 34–39.

[512] The GC even qualified a decision by the Commission as a regulatory act that directly produced legal consequences. See Case T-262/10 *Microban International and Microban (Europe) v Commission* (n 501) paras 23–24.

[513] Case T-262/10 *Microban International and Microban (Europe) v Commission* (n 501) paras 23 and 29; Haakon Roer-Eide and Mariolina Eliantonio, 'The Meaning of Regulatory Act Explained: Are There Any Significant Improvements for the Standing of Non-Privileged Applicants in Annulment Actions' (2013) 14 German LJ 1851, 1859.

[514] Howell (n 269) 139; Imm (n 106) 121.

The third alternative further requires that the act is of direct concern. An act is of direct concern if it directly affects the situation of individuals and therefore produces legal consequences for them.[515] This is rather not the case for third countries, as the mechanisms do not foresee any specific results for the countries themselves. They are the object but not the subject of the decision.[516] This is different for individual firms, whose legal status is directly changed by the decision in one-step processes. Thus, they are directly concerned by the decision.

Finally, the regulatory act must not entail implementing measures. The decisions in such one-step processes directly take effect and do not need to be implemented. As a result, third country firms have legal standing to bring actions for annulment under the third alternative of Article 263(4). Actions brought by third countries are not admissible because they are not directly concerned by the equivalence/withdrawal decision.

Now the question arises whether the third alternative of Article 263(4) TFEU can be transferred to situations of an action for failure to act pursuant to Article 265(3) TFEU where an equivalence decision as a regulatory act has not yet been adopted. Neither does the provision expressly state such an option, nor has the CJEU decided on the question so far.[517] However, the action for annulment and the action for failure to act should be interpreted in parallel to prevent the existence of loopholes in legal protection.[518] What is more, the question of legal protection must not depend on whether an authority has acted or not and thus be left to its discretion.[519] Therefore, it is best to recognize an action for failure to adopt a regulatory act in Article 265 TFEU.[520]

To sum up, actions by third country firms against the failure to adopt an equivalence decision and actions for the annulment of the withdrawal of an equivalence decision are admissible. The third country itself cannot initiate proceedings, but it may join the case as an intervener since it has an economic 'interest in the result'.[521]

[515] This definition corresponds to the meaning of 'direct concern' in the second alternative: Case T-262/10 *Microban International and Microban (Europe) v Commission* (n 501) paras 26–32; Case T-18/10 *Inuit Tapiriit Kanatami and Others v Parliament and Council* (n 507) para 71; Lenaerts, Maselis, and Gutman (n 450) paras 7.90 and 7.109.

[516] For a dissenting view see Imm (n 106) 122ff, for whom the economic effect on those countries is sufficient.

[517] Lenaerts, Maselis, and Gutman (n 450) para 8.13.

[518] Under the old regime see Case C-15/70 *Chevalley v Commission* ECLI:EU:C:1970:95, paras 5–7; Alexander H Türk, *Judicial Review in EU Law* (Edward Elgar Publishing 2009) 194.

[519] Under the old regime: Case C-68/95 *T Port v Bundesanstalt für Landwirtschaft und Ernährung* ECLI:EU:C:1996:452, para 59; Wolfram Cremer in Christian Calliess and Matthias Ruffert (eds), *EUV/AEUV* (6th edn, CH Beck 2022) AEUV, art 265 para 8.

[520] Opinion of Advocate General Bobek delivered on 25 April 2017 in Joined Cases C-596/16 P and 597/15 P *Bionorica and Diapharm* ECLI:EU:C:2017:297, paras 111–17; for a consenting view see Pechstein (n 498) para 624; in this direction see Lenaerts, Maselis, and Gutman (n 450) para 8.13; for a dissenting view see Oliver Dörr in Eberhard Grabitz, Meinhard Hilf, and Martin Nettesheim (eds), *Das Recht der Europäischen Union* (76th edn, CH Beck 2022) art 265 para 19.

[521] Statute of the Court of Justice of the European Union, art 40(2); the ECJ qualified a third country as 'any other person', see Joined Cases C-91/82 and 200/82 *Chris International Foods v Commission* (n 500) p. 419; Charlotte Gaitanides in Hans von der Groeben, Jürgen Schwarze, and Armin Hatje (eds), *Europäisches Unionsrecht*, vol 4 (7th edn, Nomos 2015) AEUV, art 263 para 44.

(2) Merits

For the action to be well-founded, there must be a ground for annulment in relation to the withdrawal decision, or the failure to act must infringe the Treaties. As regards the action for annulment, Article 263(2) TFEU restricts judicial review to 'grounds of lack of competence, infringement of an essential procedural requirement, infringement of the Treaties or of any rule of law relating to their application, or misuse of powers'.[522] Against the background that the allocation of responsibilities in equivalence mechanisms is clear and the notion of a 'misuse of power' is interpreted very narrowly by the CJEU, these grounds are of little relevance in this context.[523]

When examining whether an essential procedural requirement has been infringed, the CJEU reviews the decision-making process for formal errors, inter alia, the failure to give reasons.[524] With regard to the 'infringement of the Treaties', among others, the line of reasoning can be controlled for unlawful considerations such as political ones, and the CJEU will review potential violations of fundamental rights like the right to equal treatment and the right to good administration. If the Commission sticks to technical considerations to justify equivalence decisions, the courts will not consider its expediency or replace the Commission's reasoning with their own due to the discretionary nature of the decisions.[525]

As regards the action for failure to act, Article 265(1) TFEU requires an infringement of the Treaties. Such a violation occurs if the Commission was under an obligation to act and did not act even though it was called upon to do so.[526] An obligation exists if the service provider has a right to a decision deriving either from primary or secondary law.[527] As advocated above, such a right, in principle, exists, although it will in practice often be limited to a right to a lawful consideration of an equivalence request and not to a decision due to the discretionary elements contained in many provisions.[528] Hence, the prospects of success for actions for failure to act will be rather low.[529] However, they are increasing as administrative practice increases because the Commission must apply its general practice in each case unless different treatment is justified on objective grounds.[530] This follows

[522] See Augustin Fuerea, 'The ECJ Case-Law on the Annulment Action: Grounds, Effects and Illegality Plea' (2017) 24 Lex ET Scientia Intl J 61.

[523] See ch 2 B)II.1.b) regarding the definition of a 'misuse of power' by the CJEUh .

[524] See on the formal errors which might be relevant here: ch 2 B)II.4. Concerning the right to a reasoned decision which often leads to the annulment of the decision: Bernhard Schima in Manuel Kellerbauer, Marcus Klamert, and Jonathan Tomkin (eds), *Commentary on the EU Treaties and the Charter of Fundamental Rights* (OUP 2019) art 263 para 61.

[525] Case C-84/94 *United Kingdom v Council* ECLI:EU:C:1996:431, para 23; Joana Mendes, 'Bounded Discretion in EU Law: A Limited Judicial Paradigm in a Changing EU' (2017) 80 MLR 443.

[526] Lenaerts, Maselis, and Gutman (n 450) para 8.03.

[527] Joined Cases C-10/68 and 18/68 *Eridania Zuccherifici and Others v Commission* (n 450) para 16; Lenaerts, Maselis, and Gutman (n 450) para 8.06.

[528] See ch 2 B)II.5. Two exceptions are AIFMD, art 21(6) subpara 3 and Transparency Directive, art 23(4) subpara 2.

[529] That does not mean, however, that there are no chances of success. See for a successful action for failure to act despite discretionary elements: Joined Cases T-79/96, 260/97 and 117/98 *Camar and Tiko v Commission and Council* (n 443) (approved by Case C-312/00 P *Commission v Camar and Tiko* (n 447)); Wakefield (n 386) 148–50.

[530] Case C-268/84 *Valsabbia v Commission* ECLI:EU:C:1987:19, paras 14f.

from the principle of equal treatment and the principle of protection of legitimate interests.[531]

bb) Two-step process involving ESAs In equivalence regimes where ESAs are involved at the second level,[532] the situation regarding legal protection changes. One example of such a two-step process is the granting of market access for third country investment firms. There is an equivalence decision at the first level and subsequently a registration with ESMA. Again, the action for failure to act applies where the Commission has not adopted an equivalence decision or where ESAs have neglected registration. Where the Commission adopted a withdrawal decision or where the competent ESA deregistered the service provider, the service providers may initiate an action for annulment. The General Court is again competent for these kinds of proceedings.[533] In the following, it must be distinguished between the granting of legal protection at the first and the second level.

(1) First level: Equivalence decision and withdrawal

With regard to the equivalence decision and its withdrawal (first level), it must be examined whether the prospects of success of actions are the same as in one-step processes. For an action to be admissible, the applicant needs to have legal standing. As discussed above, the decisions are to be classified as regulatory acts in the meaning of Article 263(4) third alternative TFEU.

Again, unlike service providers, third countries are not directly concerned by the decision, and their actions are thus inadmissible. Actions by third country service providers, however, are admissible if the decision does not entail implementing decisions. In contrast to one-step processes, the two-step process requires a second decision for legal consequences to take effect. In the case of MiFIR, this second decision is the registration of investment firms with ESMA. Contrary to the interpretation of Article 263(4) second alternative TFEU, where the ECJ has ruled that an action is inadmissible only if the implementing decision is a discretionary one,[534] the criterion of 'implementing decision' in the third alternative is to be understood as any decision irrespective of discretionary elements and therefore more formalistic.[535] This strict reading is justified by the objective of the new alternative to avoid situations in which the applicant would have to break the law to get access to courts.[536] Hence, equivalence mechanisms composed of a two-step process entail implementing decisions,

[531] See ch 2 B)II.4.d)cc); Case C-217/91 *Spain v Commission* (n 435) para 37; Joined Cases C-189/02 P, 202/02 P, 205/02 P–208/02 P and 213/02 P *Dansk Rørindustri and Others v Commission* (n 436) para 211; von Danwitz (n 22) 353–56; Jürgen Schwarze, 'Rechtsstaatliche Grundsätze für das Verwaltungshandeln in der Rechtsprechung des Gerichtshofs' in Ninon Colneric and others (eds), *Une Communauté de droit: Festschrift für Gil Carlos Rodriguez Iglesias* (BWV 2003) 151f.

[532] See on this kind of process: ch 1 C)III.2.

[533] See note 498 (ch 2).

[534] Case C-386/96 P *Dreyfus v Commission* ECLI:EU:C:1998:193, para 43.

[535] Case C-274/12 P *Telefónica v Commission* ECLI:EU:C:2013:852, paras 27–29; Alexander Thiele, *Europäisches Prozessrecht* (2nd edn, CH Beck 2014) 149–50; very critical of this judgment: Georg M Berrisch, 'Beihilferecht: Direktklagen gegen beihilferechtliche Entscheidung der Kommission nach Art 263 IV AEUV' (2014) 25 EuZW 228, 231f.

[536] Secretariat of the European Convention, 'Final Report of the discussion circle on the Court of Justice' (2003) CONV 636/03, CERCLE I 13, para 21; Opinion of Advocate General Kokott delivered on 21 March 2013 in Case C-274/12 P *Telefónica v Commission* ECLI:EU:C:2013:204, paras 40f.

which is why actions of service providers against equivalence or withdrawal decisions are inadmissible.[537]

With regard to the action for failure to act, the possibilities of legal protection against regulatory acts can again be transposed to Article 265(3) TFEU.[538] However, the question arises whether the additional precondition of Article 263(4) third alternative that the regulatory act 'does not entail implementing measures' has to be transferred to Article 265(3) TFEU as well. On the one hand, in light of the principle of effective legal protection, it appears appropriate to allow the applicant to proceed against various acts without restrictions. On the other hand, to ensure parallelism between the action for annulment and the action for failure to act, as advocated above,[539] it is more appropriate to transfer the restrictions of actions against regulatory acts as well. This interpretation is underlined by the purpose and history of the provision.[540]

Consequently, actions of third countries and their service providers against equivalence and withdrawal decisions, i.e. at the first level, are inadmissible in two-step processes involving ESAs. However, these decisions are incidentally reviewed in legal actions at the second level, as will be shown in the next section, which is why effective legal protection is ensured.

(2) Second level: Recognition, registration, or certification

Against the background that actions against measures at the first level are inadmissible, legal protection of service providers boils down to actions against decisions by ESAs (second level). A service provider's recognition, registration, or certification[541] is an implementing decision addressed to the specific service provider by the competent ESA. Consequently, service providers are addressees and have *locus standi* under Article 263(4) first alternative TFEU. The same applies to the decision to deregister a service provider. The court will also review the Commission's preceding equivalence related decisions ('basic act') in these proceedings, namely the equivalence decision or its withdrawal.[542] However, before a matter can be taken to court, an administrative appeal must, in principle, be conducted (Article 61 ESAs Regulations).[543] According to Article 60 ESAs Regulations, the Board of Appeal shall decide in these proceedings.

The prospects of success of the action depend primarily on the stage of the process at which the alleged infringement has occurred. If the violation took place at the level of the equivalence decision or its withdrawal (first level), the chances are identical to those outlined above in one step proceedings.[544] If the alleged infringement occurs at

537 Imm (n 106) 123.

538 See at the end of ch 2 B)IV.1.a)aa)(1).

539 Case C-15/70 *Chevalley v Commission* (n 518) para 6; Case C-68/95 *T Port v Bundesanstalt für Landwirtschaft und Ernährung* (n 519) para 59.

540 See n 536 (ch 2).

541 The specific measure depends on the equivalence mechanism in question. However, these are primarily terminological differences. See eg MiFIR, arts 46 and 48 (= registration); EMIR, art 25 (= recognition); CRA Regulation, art 5 (= certification).

542 See on this procedure Case C-274/12 P *Telefónica v Commission* (n 535) para 29.

543 Ammann (n 70) paras 309ff; Lennart Dahmen and Jochen Kindermann, 'Zwischen Passport und Niederlassungszwang' in Hanno Teuber and Ulrich Schröer (eds), *MiFID II/MiFIR: Umsetzung in der Bankpraxis* (Finanz Colloquium 2015) paras 609ff.

544 See ch 2 B)IV.1.a)aa)(2).

the second level, chances are significantly higher because ESAs have no discretion in the registration decision.[545]

cc) Two-step process involving NCAs Legal protection in two-step processes involving the national level works similarly to the one just described.[546] Direct legal protection against equivalence or withdrawal decisions by the Commission does not exist since service providers as well as third countries lack *locus standi*. As explained above, this is due to the broad interpretation of the term 'implementing measure', pursuant to which equivalence decisions in two-step processes must be implemented. Since the second decision will be adopted at the Member State level, legal protection will take place before national courts.[547] When decisions of NCAs are reviewed, national courts will incidentally control whether the Commission's measures at the first level, i.e. the equivalence decision or its withdrawal, were lawful and might initiate a preliminary ruling according to Article 267 TFEU.[548] In the course of this preliminary ruling, national courts can ask the ECJ whether the Commission has failed to adopt an equivalence decision or has unlawfully withdrawn it.[549] Whether this design of indirect control of Union measures by national courts is appropriate appears extremely doubtful. Direct control by the CJEU could be achieved if the term 'implementing measure' were to be interpreted more restrictively. This would greatly facilitate legal protection.

b) The Member States, the European Council and Parliament as applicants

The legal remedies available to the Member States, the European Council and the European Parliament differ significantly from those available to service providers, as they are privileged applicants in the sense of Articles 263(2) and 265(1) TFEU. Consequently, they have *locus standi* to bring an action without further requirements.[550] Therefore, the above-mentioned problems regarding the admissibility of an action do not occur.

The General Court has jurisdiction over actions brought by the Member States because the exception in Article 51(1)(a) Statute of the Court of Justice of the European Union, which would transfer the competence back to the ECJ, does not apply to non-legislative acts by the Commission. The situation is different for actions by institutions of the Union since lit (b) of this article explicitly mentions acts by the Commission.

[545] See ch 1 C)III.2.

[546] See on two-step processes involving NCAs: ch 1 C)III.3.

[547] This vertical division of jurisdiction within the EU follows the general rule that each jurisdiction within the EU reviews the decisions of its own institutions. On the allocation of jurisdiction in the Banking Union: Matthias Lehmann, 'Jurisdiction, Locus Standi and the Circulation of Judgments in the Banking Union' in Chiara Zilioli and Karl-Philipp Wojcik (eds), *Judicial Review in the European Banking Union* (Edward Elgar Publishing 2021) para 6.05.

[548] On this situation see Case C-294/83 *Les Verts v Parliament* (n 28) para 23; Case C-583/11 P *Inuit Tapiriit Kanatami and Others v Parliament and Council* (n 507) para 93; Case C-274/12 P *Telefónica v Commission* (n 535) para 29; Cremer (n 519) AEUV, art 263 para 73.

[549] Such a preliminary question is permissible if no direct legal protection can be obtained against the European legal act, as is the case here. See Case C-511/03 *Ten Kate Musselkanaal and Others* ECLI:EU:C:2005:625, para 29; Case C-50/00 P *Unión de Pequeños Agricultores v Council* ECLI:EU:C:2002:462, para 42; Lenaerts, Maselis, and Gutman (n 450) para 10.12.

[550] Kotzur (n 461) art 263 para 16 and art 265 para 8.

Therefore, the ECJ is responsible for actions brought by EU institutions. This distinction between Member States and EU institutions is at odds with the general idea that they are treated equally as privileged applicants and does not appear to be based on objective grounds.[551] Given that these differences have existed for a long time and were explicitly confirmed in this form by Regulation (EU, Euratom) 2019/629 of 17 April 2019, it cannot be assumed, however, that there was a drafting error.[552] Hence, the distinction must be accepted as a deliberate choice of the legislator.

As regards the merits of the claim, prospects of success are identical to that of third country service providers as applicants. In practice, the question may arise as to why players should start such a procedure in the first place. Just to mention some reasons: European institutions may find that the Commission is not applying the laws in the way envisaged and may want to intervene. Member States may have an interest in opening up their markets to third country service providers to extend the supply for their nationals. If, contrary to other Member States, they have already opened up their national markets to these operators, a proceeding could also be initiated to create a level playing field in the Union by forcing the other Member States to grant access to these players by way of equivalence. Conversely, European organs and Member States may also want to challenge an equivalence measure to prevent market access of third country service providers. Consequently, actions by privileged applicants are not completely unrealistic, although they may not be the rule.

c) EU service providers and investors as applicants

EU service providers may also seek to prevent access by service providers from third countries. In situations where the third country legal regime is not equivalent, but the Commission has adopted an equivalence decision, competition would be distorted to the detriment of European players. Furthermore, investor protection and financial stability are at stake if supervision is ineffective in the third country. This risk could be a motivation for European investors to take legal action against equivalence decisions.

In those scenarios, European service providers and investors may initiate an action for annulment of either the equivalence decision or, in two-step processes, the decision of the competent ESA. Where a national authority is competent for the second step, legal protection takes place at the national level.

It is, however, questionable whether European service providers and investors have legal standing to file such an action. As those service providers and investors are non-privileged applicants, they need to have *locus standi* pursuant to Article 263(4) TFEU. Because they are neither addressed by the equivalence nor the registration decision of ESAs, the first alternative does not apply. For both the second and third alternatives of Article 263(4) TFEU, investors and service providers would need to be directly concerned by the decision. With regard to European *investors*, neither the equivalence decision nor the decision by the competent ESA has direct consequences for them, as only the legal position of third country service providers is changed. The mere fact that their investments may be at risk because financial stability is jeopardized as a consequence of access by these service providers does not constitute a direct causal link

[551] Thiele (n 535) 31.

[552] Assuming a drafting error with regard to the previous version: ibid.

as required for a 'direct concern'.[553] Another interpretation would allow for an *actio popularis*, which is to be avoided.[554] Hence, actions by EU investors are inadmissible.

The situation is slightly different for European *service providers*, as the level playing field may be directly affected if service providers from third countries are exempted from obligations or allowed to access the market purely on the basis of their home country laws. If these laws are not equivalent, competition is distorted to the detriment of European competitors. In relation to equivalence decisions as regulatory acts, competitors must show that they are directly affected and that no implementing measures are necessary (third alternative). In relation to registration decisions by ESAs, which are not regulatory acts, competitors will even need to demonstrate that they are directly and *individually* concerned and implementing measures are not entailed (second alternative).[555]

To sum up, European investors cannot challenge equivalence related decisions before the CJEU. The admissibility of actions by European service providers depends on the specific circumstances, more specifically on whether they are directly and possibly individually affected as competitors.

2. Legal protection in the WTO's dispute settlement mechanism

With the adoption of the WTO Agreement in 1995, a new dispute resolution system was introduced.[556] The Dispute Settlement Understanding, as the relevant law, establishes the Dispute Settlement Body, which has the power to establish panels and adopt panel and appellate body reports. As the EU is itself a member of the WTO, its acts can be controlled by the Dispute Settlement Body.[557] Third countries that are members of the WTO may request the establishment of such a panel as complainants.[558] That way, equivalence related decisions by the Commission or ESAs may be reviewed for their compatibility with world trade law.[559] As outlined above, such decisions breach the GATS if they are based on political considerations. Likewise, other breaches of the third country's 'adequate opportunity' to demonstrate the equivalence of its legal system under paragraph 3(b) sentence 2 of the Annex to the GATS, such as artificially delaying a decision, will lead to a condemnation of the EU.

If the Dispute Settlement Body adopts a report of the panel or appellate body finding such a violation, these reports are binding on the parties to the disputes. Owing to the 'negative consensus' decision-making process, which was part of the reform, the dispute settlement is much stricter and more effective than before.[560] If the respondent

[553] ibid 134.

[554] Lenaerts, Maselis, and Gutman (n 450) para 7.88.

[555] On the case law concerning the admissibility of actions brought by competitors: Pechstein (n 498) paras 481ff.

[556] See for a historical classification: Robert Howse, 'The World Trade Organization 20 Years On: Global Governance by Judiciary' (2016) 27 EJIL 9; Peter van den Bossche, 'The making of the "World Trade Court"' in Rufus Yerxa and Bruce Wilson (eds), *Key Issues in WTO Dispute Settlement: The first ten years* (CUP 2005) 63.

[557] This applies both to an active act and to an omission. See World Trade Organization, *A Handbook on the WTO Dispute Settlement System* (2nd edn, CUP 2017) 41f.

[558] See on the membership of the EU: WTO Agreement, arts IX:1 and XII:2.

[559] Howell (n 269) 156ff; see extensively, also differentiating between formal and substantive claims, Lang (n 160) 208ff.

[560] See eg Dispute Settlement Understanding, arts 6.1, 16.4, 17.14, and 22.6; Matsushita and others (n 330) 92; World Trade Organization (n 557) 25.

does not comply with the Dispute Settlement Body's recommendations, there are two types of sanctions: compensation and retaliation.[561] In the case of compensation, the defeated Member must approach the other and agree through negotiation on a mutually acceptable compensation, for example, the payment of a lump sum. If no agreement on compensation is reached, the party may apply to the Dispute Settlement Body for authorization to take retaliatory measures. Retaliation is primarily focused on suspending concessions with respect to the same economic sector in which the violation has been found but can extend to other sectors ('cross-retaliation') or even other WTO agreements ('cross-agreement retaliation').[562] In principle, the dispute settlement is therefore not a toothless instrument, had it not been obstructed by the United States, which is currently preventing the filling of vacancies in the appellate body, leading the WTO in its biggest crisis to date.[563] Consequently, third countries not only have a right to a decision deriving from world trade law but also have a corresponding right to bring actions under world trade law.

V. Conclusion: Taming equivalence through juridification

The preceding analysis has shown that there are two main weaknesses of equivalence that are interrelated: politicization and opacity. The two are related because, on the one hand, politicization leads to a detachment from legally defined arguments and thus promotes uncertainty and creates opacity. On the other hand, the opacity of the process facilitates the inclusion of political arguments by hampering judicial and public control.

Politicization and opacity of equivalence are associated with many disadvantages. First, they prevent a meaningful public dialogue about the methods and whether the standards applied are too light or strict. Secondly, uncertainty deters market participants from accessing the EU market via equivalence, which in turn reinforces market fragmentation. Thirdly, opacity prevents third countries from aligning their legal systems with the EU's, not because they are unwilling to do so, but because the standards are unclear. This again reduces the export of the EU supervisory rules. Finally, the willingness of third countries to admit European financial service providers to their markets via deference decreases when they face political pressure or feel unfairly treated. The spread of deference depends largely on reciprocal treatment based on factual and prudential reasons.

The solution to overcome these weaknesses has been set out in detail above. It consists of establishing and disclosing a consistent methodology of determining

561 Extensively on enforcement: Matsushita and others (n 330) 111ff; World Trade Organization (n 557) 133ff.

562 Dispute Settlement Understanding, art 22(3); Matsushita and others (n 330) 96.

563 Yang Guohua, 'The Causes of the Crisis Confronting the WTO Appellate Body' (2019) 9 J WTO & China 102; Shi Jingxia and Bai Fangyan, 'A Practical Response to the WTO Appellate Body Crisis: Utilizing Arbitration to Resolve Trade Disputes' (2019) 9 J WTO & China 35; Pieter J Kuijper, 'From the Board: The US Attack on the WTO Appellate Body' (2018) 45 Legal Issues of Econ Integ 1; see on the criticism from the side of the US: Claude E Barfield, 'Free Trade, Sovereignty, Democracy, The Future of the WTO' (2001) 2 Chic J Intl L 403.

equivalence, setting clear legal limits to the Commission's discretion, and thereby enabling effective judicial review. This could be described as a juridification of equivalence, an idea that is further pursued in Chapter 5 in the form of reform proposals.

C) Legal consequences

A first look at the legal consequences of equivalence mechanisms reveals that they are formulated very differently and do not seem to have much in common. To get an overview of the numerous mechanisms, it is best to divide them into groups.[564] The categorization obviously depends primarily on the criteria used for the classification, and there is no 'right' or 'wrong' solution.[565] The following categorization is based on the regulatory technique used by the legislator. The results are determined strictly according to the wording and not to (indirect) economic consequences or the legislator's long-term objectives.

I. First category: Exemption from regulatory obligations

Equivalence regimes in the first category provide a (limited) exemption from or modification of regulatory obligations of EU law. They generally do not lead to market access rights.[566] It can be further distinguished within this category between two different regulatory techniques used to grant an exemption. Many provisions explicitly state that certain obligations do not apply to the third country players concerned or that they are exempt from these requirements. Other mechanisms use an irrebuttable presumption to achieve the same result ('shall be deemed to have fulfilled').[567] However, this distinction has no practical implications, which is why they belong to the same category.

The extent of these exemptions varies considerably. A far-reaching waiver exists, for example, in the MAR, where the entire regulation does not apply to public bodies and central banks of third countries designated by the Commission.[568] Less far-reaching are legal acts which only exempt from the requirements of individual parts of the law, such as the Accounting Directive, where third country undertakings are only exempted from Chapter 10 of the Accounting Directive and thus the duties relating to country-by-country reports.[569] Most equivalence provisions only exempt third country companies or products from certain enumerated obligations. A good

564 The following categorization leaves out two mechanisms which are very different from all other regimes. They relate to access and exchange of data (SAD, art 47(1) and EMIR, art 76a(1)).

565 See for another categorization: Susan Emmenegger and Andrea Bigler, 'Fortress Europe: Die Äquivalenzverfahren der EU im Bereich der Finanzdienstleistungen' (2019) 91 SZW 155, 158ff.

566 One exception is the equivalence mechanism in art 46(1) of the SAD, which allows Member States to exempt third country auditors from registration and oversight, thereby granting them market access.

567 See eg Accounting Directive, art 46(1); EMIR, art 13(3); SFT Regulation, art 21(2); MiFIR, art 33(3).

568 See MAR, art 6(5) and (6). Another example is EMIR, art 1(6).

569 Accounting Directive, art 46(1). Another example where an exemption is also granted from a specific chapter is art 37(2) of the AIFMD. However, this exemption is limited to a situation of a legal conflict between the European and the third country legal system.

example is the Transparency Directive mechanism which, among other things, exempts third country issuers from the obligation to produce an annual financial report in accordance with Article 4 Transparency Directive. Another example is Article 33(3) MiFIR, which exempts counterparties from the trading and clearing obligation.[570]

II. Second category: Equal treatment

The mechanisms belonging to the second category are characterized by a legal prescription of equal treatment of the third country with the EU. According to Article 28(1) MiFIR, the trading obligation of counterparties cannot only be fulfilled on regulated markets, MTFs and OTFs, but also on equivalent third country markets. Therefore, these markets are treated in the same way as European markets in the context of the trading obligation. With regard to trading venues, similar provisions exist, inter alia, in Article 25(4)(a)(i) MiFID II, Article 2(7) EMIR, and Article 2(1)(k) SSR.

A further example of this category can be found in relation to reinsurance undertakings. Article 172(3) Solvency II states that insurance contracts concluded with equivalent third country reinsurers 'shall be treated in the same manner as insurance contracts concluded with undertakings authorized in accordance with this Directive'. This equal treatment of insurance contracts gives third country reinsurance undertakings access to the European single market. These examples already show that the regulatory technique used does not necessarily prejudge the legal outcome. Equal treatment of third country trading venues aims at facilitating the fulfilment of a European obligation, whereas equal treatment of third country reinsurance undertakings leads to market access rights.

III. Third category: Partial market access

Equivalence provisions in the third and fourth categories are characterized by the fact that the provisions are worded in a way that directly points to granting market access. This market access is, however, restricted in some form in the third category. A prime example of this group is equivalence concerning investment firms in MiFIR. After the registration of a third country investment firm with ESMA, which presupposes a prior equivalence decision by the Commission, a 'firm may provide investment services ... to eligible counterparties and to professional clients ... established throughout the Union without the establishment of a branch' and without having to obey the requirements of MiFID II, MiFIR and CRD V.[571] The market access provided is limited, as it only suffices for services to eligible counterparties and per se professional clients and does not include services to retail clients.

Another example is the regulation of credit rating agencies under the CRA Regulation. In general, credit ratings can be used for regulatory purposes only if the

[570] Other examples include EMIR, art 13(3); SFT Regulation, art 2(4); MiFIR, art 1(9).

[571] MiFIR, art 46(1); Sethe (n 438) 626; Ferran (n 2) 48f; Scott Morrison, 'Third-country equivalence: a Brexit scenario for UK financial services' (2018) 29 ICCLR 1, 3ff.

rating agency is established in the EU and registered in accordance with the CRA Regulation.[572] As a consequence of equivalence, ratings related to entities established or financial instruments issued in third countries can also be used for regulatory purposes in the EU.[573] That way, ratings can, in a sense, 'enter' the European market because they can be used in case European supervisory law demands them. Nevertheless, this exception is limited to entities and instruments established or issued in third countries and does not include ratings relating to European entities or instruments. This is why the market access is limited.

These two illustrative mechanisms already show that a further distinction can be made between active and passive market access. Active market access is indicated by the phrase 'can provide services/activities' in the Union, while passive market access is described by the expression 'can be used' in the Union.[574] This differentiation is solely based on the nature of the regulated product or service and not on differences in content.

IV. Fourth category: Full market access

The fourth category again encompasses equivalence provisions whose wording is directed at market access. As opposed to category number three, there are no limitations regarding clients that can be addressed or products that are affected. Following an equivalence decision and a recognition by ESMA, trade repositories may, for instance, provide their services and activities to all entities established in the Union.[575]

It is striking that the rights granted in fourth category equivalence provisions are very similar to those of passporting.[576] In the case of passporting, a financial service provider from one Member State only needs an authorization from its home state to provide services in other Member States. The authority of the service providers' home state exclusively supervises them, and the other Member States cannot demand additional requirements.[577] The same is true for equivalence decisions in the fourth category. A third country service provider does not need authorization from a national authority of the host state anymore. It is not being supervised by authorities of the host state and does not need to obey the host state's supervisory law. This demonstrates that the legal consequences of equivalence in the fourth category and of passporting are almost identical. The differences between these regimes lie at the level of the prerequisites and not in the legal consequences.[578] Therefore, equivalence provisions leading to

[572] CRA Regulation, art 4(1).

[573] McVea (n 89) 723f.

[574] Emmenegger and Bigler (n 565) 159. Other examples for active market access include EMIR, art 77 and for passive market access BMR, art 30(1).

[575] EMIR, art 77(1).

[576] Emmenegger and Bigler (n 565) 159. However, they also emphasize that this is the exception rather than the rule. See also Dahmen and Kindermann (n 543) para 583.

[577] Explaining the passport using the example of CRD V: Dirk Schoenmaker, 'The UK Financial Sector and EU Integration after Brexit: The Issue of Passporting' in Nauro Campos and Fabrizio Coricelli (eds), *The Economics of UK-EU Relations* (Palgrave Macmillan 2017) 123f.

[578] Alienor Margerit, Marcel Magnus, and Benoit Mesnard, 'Third-country equivalence in EU banking legislation' IPOL Briefing PE 587.369 (12 July 2017) Box 2, 2 https://www.europarl.europa.eu/RegData/etudes/BRIE/2016/587369/IPOL_BRI(2016)587369_EN.pdf (accessed 12 November 2022).

full market access rights could be described as passporting extended to third countries. This comparison emphasizes the huge impact equivalence decisions may have. Ultimately, the internal market will no longer be limited to the EU's borders but will be extended to third countries in some areas.

V. Conclusion: Different look, but still similar

The categorization has shown that although equivalence regimes are all called the same, they are formulated differently and have different legal consequences. Some merely exempt third country products or service providers from certain obligations, while others offer complete market access. This seems to contradict the above finding that all equivalence provisions are based on a uniform concept.

1. Does the regulatory technique really matter?

The classification has revealed that the wording of the legal consequences of equivalence varies considerably, which creates the impression that they do not have much in common.

Category	Regulatory technique	Wording
1	Exemption from regulatory obligations	'are/may exempt from' 'shall not apply to' 'shall be deemed to have fulfilled'
2	Equal treatment	'shall be treated like' 'shall be considered to be equivalent to'
3	Partial market access	'may provide services in/to'; i.e. active market access
4	Full market access	'may be used in'; i.e. passive market access

The regulatory technique used has, however, hardly any impact on the legal consequences of equivalence. The same result can be achieved with different formulations. In relation to investment firms under MiFIR, the legislator described market access by stating that third country investment firms 'may provide investment services … to eligible counterparties and to professional clients … established throughout the Union'. Instead, the legislator could have achieved this outcome through a derogation (first category) or an equal treatment provision (second category). In the first case, the wording would have been that investment firms registered with ESMA are exempted from the authorization and further requirements when providing services to eligible counterparties and professional clients in the Union.[579] In the second case, the legislator would have prescribed that third country investment firms, once registered with

[579] The same works with the formulation 'shall be deemed to have fulfilled'.

ESMA, shall be treated like European investment firms for the purpose of providing services to eligible counterparties and professional clients.

This is not a purely hypothetical consideration. Equivalence provisions leading to market access can be found in all categories. Under Article 46(1) SAD, Member States may exempt third country auditors from registration and supervision following an equivalence decision, thereby granting them market access (first category). Reinsurance undertakings are granted market access through equal treatment of third country reinsurance contracts with European reinsurance contracts (second category).

But why did the legislator use different formulations? On the one hand, because equivalence mechanisms result in different degrees of liberalization. Some were supposed to exempt third country service providers from only a few prerequisites, while others resulted in a complete exemption from EU regulation. These levels of liberalization can be best expressed through different legal techniques. On the other hand, some regimes can only be formulated in a certain way because of the regulated object. For instance, the fact that the trading obligation can also be fulfilled on equivalent third country trading venues can only be expressed through an equal treatment provision (second category).

Consequently, different formulations are only due to varying degrees of liberalization or the specific product/service/object at issue. Sometimes the differences in wording are arbitrary and thus a sign of inconsistency in the legislation. In any case, they are not an indication of fundamental differences in content, which is why the wording should not be overstated.

2. From conflict avoidance instruments to passporting

In contrast to the general perception, equivalence is not just a tool for market access.[580] Most regimes serve as a corrective to the threats of legal and supervisory conflicts arising from an excessive extraterritorial application of the law by multiple jurisdictions. At the same time, they seek to retain regulatory and supervisory powers as far as possible with the EU. A prime example is the exemption from the trading and clearing obligation for derivatives under MiFIR.[581] The US, Switzerland, and the EU regulate derivatives traded (partially) outside their territory.[582] This inevitably leads to legal conflicts. All countries try to limit these conflicts by partially withdrawing their regulatory power in the form of deference without granting market access. Hence, these mechanisms can be described as 'conflict avoidance instruments'.

Other regimes are more focused on granting market access, such as the mechanisms relating to investment firms under MiFIR and relating to reinsurance undertakings under Solvency II. These regimes are not primarily about avoiding legal conflicts but

580 Emmenegger and Bigler (n 565) 158f.
581 MiFIR, art 33(3); another illustrative example is AIFMD, art 37(2).
582 See extensively Hans Kuhn, 'Kollisionsrechtliche Aspekte der Derivateregulierung' (2014) 86 SZW 362.

about expanding the range of services available to EU investors, increasing liquidity and opening up markets. In the case of provisions granting full market access, the legal consequences described above are almost the same as for passporting.

3. Same direction, same objective, same principle

As explained, the wording differences are only due to the regulatory techniques used but do not reflect a difference in substance. Nonetheless, equivalence provisions lead to a different degree of liberalization. Some can be classified as conflict avoidance instruments, which only exempt third country service providers from specific obligations, while others lead to full market access rights.

At first glance, these results do not have much in common. A closer look, however, reveals that they all share the same idea, which is to get rid of dispensable and costly double requirements and to create a legal system that does not rule out cross-border financial services. As soon as third countries have equivalent requirements that serve the same purpose and are as effective as those in the EU, there is no point in duplicating regulations. This can be true for just single requirements that are obsolete or the entire supervisory law.

Ultimately, although the legal consequences of equivalence regimes appear to be diverse at first sight, they are all based on the same philosophy, which again underlines the argument made above that equivalence provisions are part of a uniform concept. They are heading in the same direction, follow the same objective and are thus part of the same principle.

D) Tables on equivalence provisions: Article-by-Article overview

The following tables give an overview of all equivalence mechanisms, their prerequisites, and other special characteristics discussed in the course of the first two chapters, such as the process of equivalence or the category of legal consequences. Table 1 refers to equivalence in general, whereas Table 2 specifically describes the equivalence decision.

In both tables, the first column contains a number referring to a specific equivalence mechanism. The relevant provision to which reference is made can be identified with the help of the legend (see below). The following seven columns each refer to a *specific prerequisite* of equivalence. A green box indicates that the prerequisite is included in the mechanism, and a red box that it is not demanded. The next seven columns each refer to a *specific feature* of equivalence, which is further explained in the legend. Finally, the last four columns illustrate the competences for equivalence decisions or—if demanded—the second step of equivalence.

I. Legend 1

No	Legal act	Equivalence mechanism (table 1)	Equivalence decision (table 2)
1	Accounting Directive 2013/34/EU	Art 46(1)	Art 47
2	Transparency Directive 2004/109/EC	Art 23(1)	Art 23(4) subpara 1(ii) (General transparency requirements)
3	"	Art 23(1)	Art 23(4) subpara 3 (Accounting standards)*1
4	Statutory Audit Directive 2006/43/EC (SAD)	Art 45(5)(d)	Art 45(6)
5	"	Art 46(1)	Art 46(2)
6	"	Art 47(1)	Art 47(3)
7	Regulation (EC) 1060/2009 (CRA Regulation)	Art 5(1)	Art 5(6)
8	Regulation (EU) 909/2014 (CSDR)	Art 25(2) and (4)	Art 25(9)
9	Regulation (EU) 648/2012 (EMIR)	Art 1(6) and (4)	Art 1(6)
10	"	Art 2a(1) and (7)	Art 2a(2)
11	"	Art 13(3)	Art 13(2)
12	"	Art 25(1) and (2)	Art 25(6)
13	"	Art 77(1) and (2)	Art 75(1)
14	"	Art 76a(1)	Art 76a(2)
15	Regulation (EU) 2015/2365 (SFT Regulation)	Art 2(4) and (2)	Art 2(4)
16	"	Art 19(3) and (4)	Art 19(1)
17	"	Art 21(2)	Art 21(1)
18	Regulation (EU) 600/2014 (MiFIR)	Art 1(9) and (6)	Art 1(9)
19	"	Art 28(1)(d)	Art 28(4)
20	"	Art 33(3)	Art 33(2)
21	"	Art 38(1) and (2)	Art 38(3)
22	"	Art 46(1) and (2)	Art 47(1)
23	Directive 2014/65/EU (MiFID II)	Art 25(4)(a)(i) and (ii)	Art 25(4)(a) subparas 2-4
24	Regulation (EU) 596/2014 (MAR)	Art 6(5) and (1)	Art 6(5)
25	"	Art 6(6) and (3)	Art 6(6)
26	Regulation (EU) 236/2012 (SSR)	Arts 17(1) and 2(1)(k)	Art 17(2)
27	Benchmark Regulation (EU) 2016/1011 (BMR)	Art 30(1)	Art 30(2)
28	"	Art 30(1)	Art 30(3)
29	Prospectus Regulation (EU) 2017/1129	Art 29(1)	Art 29(3) subpara 2
30	Directive 2011/61/EU (AIFMD)	Art 21(3) subpara 2 and (6)	Art 21(6) subpara 3
31	"	Art 37(2)	Art 37(2)
32	Regulation (EU) 575/2013 (CRR II)	Art 107(3)	Art 107(4)
33	"	Art 114(7) subpara 1	Art 114(7) subpara 2
34	"	Art 115(4) subpara 1	Art 115(4) subpara 2
35	"	Art 116(5) subpara 1	Art 116(5) subpara 2
36	"	Art 142(1) no 4 and 153(2)	Art 142(2)
37	"	Art 391 subpara 1	Art 391 subpara 2
38	Directive 2009/138/EC (Solvency II)	Art 172(3)	Art 172(2)
39	"	Art 227(1) subpara 2	Art 227(4)
40	"	Art 260(1)	Art 260(3)

*1 Equivalence mechanisms concerning accounting standards can also be found in other legal acts, for example, the Prospectus Regulation. These mechanisms always refer to Commission Regulation (EC) No1569/2007. The equivalence regime of Art 23(4) subpara 3 Transparency Directive can therefore be seen as an example for the other mechanisms.

II. Legend 2

Prerequisites		
ED	=	Equivalence Decision
E	=	Equivalence of the supervisory law of the third country
RP	=	Reciprocity
HC	=	Home country authorisation and supervision (or in case of equivalence decision: subject to effective supervision and enforcement)
CA	=	Cooperation Agreement
SI	=	No systemic importance for financial stability and integrity of financial markets (complete prohibition or at least additional requirements that must be fulfilled)
IS	=	Compliance with specific international standards
M	=	Miscellaneous
Yes	=	
No	=	
Process of Equivalence		
P	=	Process of Equivalence
1-3	=	1 = one-step process
		2 = two-step process involving ESAs
		3 = two-step process involving NCAs
European Supervisory Authorities		
ESA	=	European Supervisory Authorities
1-3	=	1 = not involved in the process at all
		2 = somehow involved in the process (e.g. register, cooperation agreements or monitoring)
		3 = involved in the equivalence decision-making by the Commission
Addressee		
A	=	"Addressee" of the decision
1-2	=	1 = country
		2 = specific undertaking/product
Legal Consequences		
LC	=	Legal Consequences
1-2	=	1 = binding decision
		2 = discretion
Category of Legal Consequences		
CG	=	Category of Legal Consequences
1-5	=	1 = exemption from/modification of regulatory obligations
		2 = equal treatment
		3 = limited market access
		4 = full market access
		5 = special legal consequences
Withdrawal of Equivalence (Decision)		
W	=	Provision expressly regulating the withdrawal
1-3	=	1 = yes, concerning equivalence decision
	=	2 = yes, concerning registration/recognition/certification/equivalence decision at national level
	=	3 = no
Delegated Legislation		
DL	=	Delegated Legislation
1-2	=	1 = no power of delegated legislation
		2 = power of delegated legislation
Competence		
COM	=	Commission
ESAs	=	ESMA, EBA, or EIOPA not responsible but involved in **national***[1] decision-making
NCA	=	Competent authorities of the Member States not responsible but involved in the decision-making process
BE	=	Blocking effect of the COM's decision for authorities of the Member States if in principle both can decide Yes / Yes, but only partially / No

*[1] Where ESAs are involved in the Commission's equivalence decision, this involvement is indicated by a green 3 in the column dealing with ESAs.

III. Table 1: Equivalence

	ED	RP	HC	CA	SI	IS	M		P	ESA	A	LC	CG	W	DL		COM	ESA	NCA	BE
1									1	1	-	-	1	-	1		-	-	-	-
2									3	1	2	1	1	-	1		-	-		-
3									3	1	2	1	1	-	1		-	-		-
4									1	1	-	-	1	-	1		-	-	-	-
5									3	1	2	2	1	1	1					-
6									3	1	1	2	5	1	1					-
7									2	2	2	1	3	2	2					-
8									2	2	2	2	4	2	2					-
9									1	1	-	-	1	-	1		-	-	-	-
10									1	1	-	-	2	-	1		-	-	-	-
11									1	1	-	-	1	-	1		-	-	-	-
12									2	2	2	2	4	3	2					-
13									2	2	2	1	4	1	1					-
14									1	1	-	-	5	-	1		-	-	-	-
15									1	1	-	-	1	-	1		-	-	-	-
16									2	2	2	1	4	1	1					-
17									1	1	-	-	1	-	1		-	-	-	-
18									1	1	-	-	1	-	1		-	-	-	-
19									1	1	-	-	2	-	1		-	-	-	-
20									1	1	-	-	1	-	1		-	-	-	-
21									1	1	-	-	2	-	1		-	-	-	-
22									2	2	2	1	3	2	2					-
23									1	1	-	-	2	-	1		-	-	-	-
24									1	1	-	-	1	-	1		-	-	-	-
25									1	1	-	-	1	-	1		-	-	-	-
26									1	1	-	-	2	-	1		-	-	-	-
27									2	2	2	1	4	2	2					-
28									2	2	2	1	4	2	2					-
29									3	1	2	2	4	1	1					-
30									3	2	2	1	2	1	1					-
31*									1 3	1	2	1 2	1	1	2					-
32									1	1	-	-	2	-	1		-	-	-	-
33									1	1	-	-	2	-	1		-	-	-	-
34									1	1	-	-	2	-	1		-	-	-	-
35									1	1	-	-	2	-	1		-	-	-	-
36									1	1	-	-	2	-	1		-	-	-	-
37									1	1	-	-	2	-	1		-	-	-	-
38									1	1	-	-	2	-	1		-	-	-	-
39									3	2	2	2	2	1	1					-
40									3	2	2	1	2	1	1					-

* As this mechanism is a national process, much depends on the national law.

IV. Table 2: Equivalence decision

	E	RP	HC	CA	SI	IS	M			ESA	A	LC		W	DL		COM	ESA	MS	BE
1										1	1	2		1	2					-
2										3	1	1		1	2					
3										3	1	1		1	2					
4										1	1	2		1	2					
5										1	1	2		1	2					
6										1	1	2		1	2					
7										1	1	2		1	2					-
8										1	1	2		1	1					-
9	*1									1	2	1*2		1	1					-
10										1	2	2		1	1					-
11										2	1	2		3	1					-
12										2	1	2		3	1					-
13										1	1	2		1	1					-
14										1	1	2		1	1					-
15	*1									1	2	1*2		1	1					-
16										1	1	2		1	1					-
17										2	1	2		3	1					-
18	*1									1	2	1*2		1	1					-
19										1	1	2		1	1					-
20										2	1	2		3	1					-
21										1	1	2		1	1					-
22										2	1	2		3	2					
23										1	1	1*3		1	1					-
24	*1									1	2	1*2		1	1					-
25	*1									1	2	2		1	1					-
26										1	1	2		1	1					-
27										2	1	2		1	2					-
28										1	2	2		1	2					-
29										1	1	2		1	2					
30										1	1	1		1	2					-
31										1	2	1 2		1	2					-
32										1	1	2		1	1					-
33										1	1	2		1	1					-
34										1	1	2		1	1					-
35										1	1	2		1	1					-
36										1	1	2		1	1					-
37										1	1	2		1	1					-
38										3	1	2		3	2					-
39										3	1	2		3	2					
40										3	1	2		3	2					

*1 The term “equivalence” is not explicitly mentioned. Instead,a “comparative analysis” is often required.
*2 Binding decision only if the exemption is “necessary”.
*3 Binding decision only if at the request of the competent authority of a Member State.

3
A Liberal Access to Financial Markets in Switzerland: Equivalence and Appropriateness

Should foreign financial service providers or products be granted access to a domestic market and, if so, under what conditions? This is not a question specific to the EU, but one that each legal system has to deal with. Not surprisingly, the answers to this question vary. In this chapter, the approach of Switzerland will be analysed. Particular attention is paid to the question of whether and to what extent the Swiss legal system provides for mechanisms that are based on the idea of deference, i.e. the withdrawal of regulatory and supervisory powers in case the foreign law meets certain requirements.[1]

The Swiss approach to deference is of utmost importance to the EU. This follows from Switzerland's geographical location in the heart of Europe and the prominent role its financial industry plays.[2] The Swiss market is the second most important in terms of exports and imports of financial services to and from the EU's internal market. Furthermore, the study of the Swiss system is of significant importance because Switzerland offers a very liberal market access regime, which can be seen as a counterpart to the politicization in the EU and the restrictive market access in the US.

Switzerland's financial markets law has undergone a profound reform in recent years, which has led to the introduction of a cross-sectoral approach in many areas and closer alignment with the European system. The first section of this chapter gives a brief overview of this reform as well as the Swiss regulatory system in general (A)). Afterwards, a closer look is taken at the regulation of foreign financial service providers and products. Here, differences and similarities between the Swiss and EU approach with regard to foreign/third country firms and products will be evaluated (B)). Subsequently, general principles of the Swiss system will be deduced from the previous findings (C)). Finally, an attempt is made to identify reasons why Switzerland has taken this path (D)).

[1] Therefore, the analysis focuses on the question of whether the Swiss legal system contains legal instruments having the same or similar functions as equivalence in the EU, the so-called functional approach to comparative law. See Konrad Zweigert and Hein Kötz, *An Introduction to Comparative Law*, vol 1 (1st edn, North-Holland 1977) 27ff.

[2] See ch 3 D).

Equivalence and Substituted Compliance in Financial Markets Law. Jonas Schürger,
Oxford University Press. © Jonas Schürger 2023. DOI: 10.1093/oso/9780198876748.003.0003

A) Brief overview of Swiss financial regulation and its recent reform

Financial regulation in Switzerland has recently experienced a far-reaching transformation. The reform is referred to as a 'four-leaf clover-reform' (*Kleeblattreform*)[3] because it consists of four pillars. First, the Financial Market Supervision Act (FINMAG), which was already adopted before the financial crisis. Secondly, the Financial Market Infrastructure Act (FinfraG) from 2016 and more recently the Financial Services Act (FIDLEG) as well as the Financial Institutions Act (FINIG), both of which came into force on 1 January 2020.

FINMAG lays down the organization and supervisory instruments of the Swiss Financial Market Supervisory Authority (FINMA).[4] FINMA is the integrated supervisory authority responsible for the supervision of the financial market.[5] That means that FINMA is competent for those persons and entities who, under the financial market acts, require to be licensed, recognized, or registered as well as for collective capital investments.[6]

FinfraG deals with two different topics: first, the organization and operation of financial market infrastructures and, secondly, the conduct of financial market participants in securities and derivatives trading.[7] The term financial market infrastructure is defined rather broadly and encompasses not only CCPs, CSDs, trade repositories and payment systems but also trading venues.[8]

FIDLEG sets out requirements for the provision of services and the offering of financial instruments.[9] With regard to the provision of services, it demands sufficient knowledge of the client adviser, compliance with a code of conduct and adherence to organizational requirements.[10] One particularity of the Swiss system is that client advisers of Swiss financial service providers, who FINMA does not already supervise under Article 3 FINMAG, as well as client advisers of foreign financial service providers, must be entered into the newly created register of advisers (*Beraterregister*) in order to be able to carry out their activity in Switzerland.[11] With regard to the offering of financial instruments, FIDLEG, in principle, stipulates the duty to publish a prospectus and, if financial instruments are offered to retail clients, the production of a

[3] Peter V Kunz, 'Braucht es eine neue Architektur des Finanzmarktrechts für die Schweiz?' (2014) 87 Die Volkswirtschaft 18; Urs Zulauf, 'Koregulierung in den «Kleeblattentwürfen» zum Schweizer Finanzmarktrecht' in Felix Uhlmann (ed), *Private Normen und staatliches Recht* (Dike 2015) 61.

[4] FINMAG, art 1(2); see Peter Nobel, *Schweizerisches Finanzmarktrecht* (4th edn, Stämpfli 2019) § 5.

[5] See the list in FINMAG, art 1(1); Jean-Baptiste Zufferey and Franca Contratto, *FINMA: The Swiss Financial Market Supervisory Authority* (Helbing Lichtenhahn 2009); Urs Zulauf and David Wyss, *Finanzmarktenforcement* (3rd edn, Stämpfli 2022).

[6] FINMAG, art 3.

[7] FinfraG, art 1(1).

[8] See the list in FinfraG, art 1(2). This list is modelled after the CPSS-IOSCO Principles for Financial Market Infrastructures (PFMI) (April 2012); Lukas Fahrländer, 'Neuordnung der Finanzmarktregulierung in der Schweiz' (2019) 31 ZBB/JBB 225, 228.

[9] FIDLEG, art 1(2).

[10] FIDLEG, arts 6–27.

[11] FIDLEG, art 28; Nobel (n 4) § 10 para 95.

key information document.[12] Furthermore, FIDLEG also regulates the Ombudsman's office, a special kind of mediation to settle disputes between clients and financial firms.[13]

Finally, FINIG defines the prerequisites that apply to financial institutions. Financial institutions include portfolio managers, trustees, managers of collective assets, fund management companies and securities firms.[14] All these financial institutions generally require authorization.[15] The decisive criterion for the applicability of the authorization obligation is the physical presence of a financial service provider in Switzerland.[16]

The legislative acts are further specified in ordinances adopted by the Swiss Federal Council and in part by FINMA pursuant to Article 7(1)(a) FINMAG. Furthermore, FINMA frequently publishes circulars setting out its supervisory practice.[17] Although circulars play an important role in practice, they are not legally binding.[18]

One of the main goals of the reform was to introduce a cross-sectoral approach with general rules applying to all kinds of financial service providers and products.[19] This aim has only been partially achieved, as the reform does not cover banks and insurances.[20] Banks are dealt with under the Swiss Federal Act on Banks and Savings Banks (Banking Act), and insurers are regulated under the Insurance Supervision Law (VAG). Also, some financial products are still governed by special legislation, for example, in the *Pfandbriefgesetz* (PfG) or collective investment schemes in the Collective Investment Schemes Act (KAG).[21] The area of anti-money laundering was already designed in a cross-sectoral way before the reform since the Anti-Money Laundering Act (GwG) applies to all 'financial intermediaries', which is defined very broadly and also covers banks and insurances.[22]

The substantive regulatory requirements are very similar to that of the EU, as one of the aims of the legislator was to achieve regulatory equivalence to the EU.[23] This

[12] FIDLEG, arts 35 and 58; concerning crowdfunding see Fleur Baumgartner and Hans C von der Crone, 'Die Bewilligungs- und Prospektpflicht im schweizerischen Recht anhand des Crowdfundings' (2018) 90 SZW 726.

[13] See FIDLEG Title 5: 'Ombudsman's Offices'; Christoph B Bühler, 'Stärkung der Ombudsstelle' (2019) 91 SZW 559.

[14] FINIG, art 2(1).

[15] See especially FINIG, arts 5 and 7.

[16] Rashid Bahar and Bianca Nedwed, 'Grenzüberschreitendes Angebot von Finanzdienstleistungen und -produkten? Die Eidgenossenschaft schlägt zurück' (2019) 91 SZW 618, 624.

[17] See FINMAG, art 7(1)(b).

[18] Nobel (n 4) § 5 para 65; with regard to the legal nature also: Bundesgericht, judgment of 18 February 2016 [2016] BGer 2C_894/2014, para 4.6.1; Bundesgericht, judgment of 24 November 2015 [2015] BGer 2C_345/2015, para 5.3.

[19] Nobel (n 4) § 10 paras 29ff; Daniel Roth, 'Gesetzgebungsprojekte: FIDLEG, FINIG und FinfraG' (2014) 86 SZW 608, 608f.

[20] Rolf Sethe in Rolf Sethe and others (eds), *SK zum FinfraG* (Schulthess 2017) Einleitung para 7.

[21] Fahrländer (n 8) 226.

[22] See Anti-Money Laundering Act, art 2(2); Sethe (n 20) Einleitung para 7.

[23] Botschaft FinfraG, BBl 2014, 7483, 7509; regarding the alignment in general see Rolf Sethe, 'Rechtsangleichung im Schweizer Finanzmarktrecht' in Wolfhard Kohte and Nadinge Absenger (eds), *Festschrift für Armin Höland* (Nomos 2015) 345ff. The Supreme Court of Justice in Switzerland even supports an interpretation in conformity with European law if the Swiss legislator wanted to reproduce EU law. See Bundesgericht, judgment of 25 March 2003 [2003] BGE 129 III 335, para 30; Peter V Kunz, 'Amerikanisierung, Europäisierung sowie Internationalisierung im schweizerischen (Wirtschafts-)Recht' (2012) 23 recht 37, 49f.

already shows the influence the EU equivalence tool has. Even though Switzerland approximated its system to that of the EU, it kept certain special characteristics of its old system.[24] To give an example, Switzerland largely adhered to the principle of self-regulation because this approach has proved its worth in the legislator's eyes. Whether Switzerland has succeeded in creating equivalent frameworks in the respective areas remains to be seen. So far, the European Commission adopted some equivalence decisions, such as in the area of central counterparties,[25] but did not adopt decisions in other parts, for instance, for investment firms under MiFIR.[26] With regard to Swiss stock exchanges, the European Commission even refused to renew equivalence.[27]

B) Regulation of foreign service providers and products

Parallel to the EU, five general areas can be found in Swiss financial market regulation in which the idea of deference has been implemented to a greater or lesser extent. These are disclosure obligations (I.), gatekeepers and benchmarks (II.), financial intermediaries (III.), financial market infrastructures and market conduct (IV.), as well as exemptions for central banks and public bodies of foreign countries (V.).

I. Disclosure obligations under capital markets law

Disclosure obligations can be divided into three stages, depending on when they take effect. Either at market entry, i.e. on the primary market, on the secondary market or in the context of market exits.

1. First stage: Obligation to draw up a prospectus

The field of prospectus regulation is a prime example of the far-reaching changes brought about by the new reform. The duty to publish a prospectus was incomplete and dispersed across different legal acts before the reform.[28] With the introduction of FIDLEG and the corresponding ordinance (FIDLEV), there is now one harmonized duty to publish a prospectus for all public offers relating to the acquisition of securities and the admission of securities to trading on a trading venue.[29] In the case of a public offer, this duty applies only to offers made in Switzerland. The application of the prospectus duty in FIDLEG does not depend on the registered seat of the issuer

[24] See eg Botschaft FinfraG, BBl 2014, 7483, 7510.

[25] Commission Implementing Decision (EU) 2015/2042 of 13 November 2015.

[26] See for a detailed analysis Rolf Sethe, 'MiFIR/MiFID II: Drittstaatenzugang für die Schweiz und Äquivalenz von FINIG/FIDLEG' in Dieter Gericke (ed), *Private Equity VI* (Schulthess 2018) 156ff.

[27] Francesco Pennesi, 'The EU Equivalence Regime in Financial Services: An Effective Instrument to Preserve Financial Stability after Brexit?' (2020) ECMI Policy Brief No 27 5 http://www.eurocapitalmarkets.org/sites/default/files/the_eu_equivalence_regime_in_financial_services_ecmi_policy_brief.pdf (accessed 12 November 2022).

[28] See regarding the old regime Mirjam Eggen, 'Die schweizerische Prospektpflicht für Effekten—eine rechtsvergleichende Untersuchung der bestehenden Rechtslage' (2010) 82 SZW 203.

[29] FIDLEG, art 35(1); Till Spillmann and Richard Meyer, 'FIDLEG—Prospektregelung' in Thomas U Reutter and Thomas Werlen (eds), *Kapitalmarkttransaktionen X* (Schulthess 2016) paras 9ff.

but on the place where the product is offered.[30] Foreign issuers making a public offer in Switzerland are thus subject to the prospectus duty under FIDLEG. This reference point for the scope of application is the same as in the EU Prospectus Regulation.[31]

Just like the EU Prospectus Regulation, FIDLEG contains some exemptions from this duty.[32] Article 38 FIDLEG lays down exemptions for admission to trading. Among others, issuers offering securities already admitted to trading on a recognized foreign trading venue (lit c)) are exempted from the duty to publish a prospectus. A recognition requires that the regulation, supervision and transparency rules governing the foreign trading venue are appropriate.[33] This exemption facilitates dual listings and the admission to trading in the trading segments 'Sponsored Segments' of SIX Swiss Exchange AG.[34] The EU Prospectus Regulation does not provide for a similar exemption for cross-border dual listings.[35] This is unfortunate since investor protection and transparency are already ensured at the same level by the existing prospectus, which renders the obligation to draw up a new prospectus superfluous and overly burdensome.

Before a prospectus can be published, it must be submitted to a reviewing body in accordance with Article 51 FIDLEG, which checks the prospectus for completeness, coherence and clarity.[36] In relation to foreign prospectuses, the special regime of Article 54 FIDLEG applies, which contains two different procedures for the recognition. Under Article 54(1) FIDLEG, an individual prospectus drawn up in accordance with foreign law may be approved by the reviewing body. This recognition does not depend on the foreign prospectus meeting the requirements laid down in FIDLEG. The reviewing body may accept such a prospectus if it was produced in conformity with international standards and if the information duties of the respective country are equivalent to those of Switzerland.[37]

[30] Matthias Courvoisier, 'Prospektpflicht nach FIDLEG' (2020) 92 SZW 307, 310. Details concerning the determination of the place of the offer, especially in the case of internet offers, are controversial. See Till Spillmann and Andrea Giger, 'Ein modernes Prospektrecht für die Schweiz' (2019) 14 GesKR 182, 190.

[31] Prospectus Regulation, art 3(1) and (3); Rolf Sethe and Matthias Lehmann, 'Internationales Bank- und Finanzdienstleistungsrecht' in Christian Tietje (ed), *Internationales Wirtschaftsrecht* (3rd edn, De Gruyter 2021) § 15 paras 97 and 108.

[32] See extensively on the exemptions Patrick Schleiffer and Patrick Schärli, 'Ausnahmen von der Prospektpflicht unter dem künftigen Finanzdienstleistungsgesetz' (2018) 13 GesKR 1.

[33] See FIDLEV, art 48.

[34] Botschaft FIDLEG/FINIG, BBl 2015, 8901, 8973; Schleiffer and Schärli (n 32) 7. See eg the rules concerning dual listings in the Directive on the Listing of Foreign Companies as of 20 June 2019 of SIX Swiss Exchange, arts 12ff.

[35] In arts 1(5) and 14 of the Prospectus Regulation, dual listings within the EU are facilitated. However, the exemptions apply only to regulated markets as defined in MiFID II and do not cover third country trading venues. See Prospectus Regulation, art 2(j) and MiFID II, art 4(1) no 21; see Pim Horsten, '"Light" Disclosure Regime' in Danny Busch, Guido Ferrarini, and Jan P Franx (eds), *Prospectus Regulation and Prospectus Liability* (OUP 2020) paras 11.01ff. Nonetheless, article 14(2) subpara 4 of the Prospectus Regulation allows for relief at least insofar as third country issuers may, under certain conditions, file financial information in accordance with their equivalent national accounting standards.

[36] The reviewing body requires a licence by FINMA and must be domiciled in Switzerland. Foreign entities cannot act as reviewing bodies. See FIDLEG, arts 52 and 53 as well as FIDLEV, arts 71–77; on the reviewing process see Therese Grunder, 'Prüfung des Prospekts' (2019) 91 SZW 582.

[37] The recognition of a foreign prospectus has no effect on the duty to publish it under FIDLEG, art 64(1). See FIDLEV, art 70(1); Erläuternder Bericht Vernehmlassungsverfahren FIDLEV, FINIV, and AOV, 52.

Even more far-reaching than the procedure for individual recognition under Article 54(1) FIDLEG is the second procedure under Article 54(2) FIDLEG. Based on this procedure, the reviewing body has the competence to determine that all prospectuses approved in a certain country are considered to be approved in Switzerland.[38] The reviewing body is publishing a list of recognized countries.[39] Consequently, there will be no review of the individual prospectus in Switzerland.[40] This far-reaching exemption was drafted with the EU and US regimes in mind.[41] However, it is not clear from the wording whether the substantive requirements of Article 54(1) FIDLEG concerning the recognition of individual prospectuses, namely compliance with international standards and the existence of an equivalent regulation in the foreign country, also apply with regard to the general recognition of all prospectuses produced under the law of a foreign country in Article 54(2) FIDLEG. In view of the far-reaching consequences compared to paragraph 1 (*argumentum a fortiori*), the two states which the legislator had in mind as an example and which guarantee an equivalent level of protection for investors, and the fact that Swiss investors would otherwise be at risk, there are many reasons for transferring the requirements.[42] Automatic recognition is a significant relief for issuers from recognized countries. Issuers from these countries already know from the outset that their prospectus will be approved in Switzerland as soon as the approval in their home country has been completed, which increases legal certainty for them. Therefore, the general approval of Article 54(2) FIDLEG could be described as ex-ante approval. The individual approval under Article 54(1) FIDLEG, on the other hand, could be referred to as ex-post approval because the decision on approval in Switzerland is taken after the foreign authorities have approved the prospectus.

A recognition of prospectuses drafted under foreign legislation also exists in the EU Prospectus Regulation.[43] Yet the EU regime only contains a mechanism for the individual, ex-post approval of prospectuses—comparable to Article 54(1) FIDLEG—and not a general mechanism for all prospectuses from a specific country, as provided for in Article 54(2) FIDLEG. This makes the EU regime less liberal and exposes issuers to greater uncertainty as regards the chances of subsequent recognition of their prospectus.[44]

[38] FIDLEG, art 54(2); Alexander Vogel, Christoph Heiz, and Reto Luthiger (eds), *OFK FIDLEG/FINIG* (Orell Füssli 2020) FIDLEG, art 54 paras 6ff; Patrick Schleiffer and Patrick Schärli, 'Grenzüberschreitende Erbringung von Finanzdienstleistungen' (2020) 15 GesKR 24, 31f.

[39] FIDLEG, art 54(3).

[40] See FIDLEV, art 70(4) for the duties which continue to apply to these prospectuses, eg the duty to publish pursuant to lit c).

[41] See Botschaft FIDLEG/FINIG, BBl 2015, 8901, 8983.

[42] The Federal Department of Finance also seems to assume this when it requires a comparable level of transparency in the foreign state's legal system as a criterion for being included in the list under FIDLEG, art 54(3). See Erläuternder Bericht Vernehmlassungsverfahren FIDLEV, FINIV, und AOV, 52.

[43] Prospectus Regulation, art 29. The Swiss provision was modelled on the predecessor in Prospectus Directive, art 20(1). See Botschaft FIDLEG/FINIG, BBl 2015, 8901, 8983.

[44] Initially, the Swiss legislator also had doubts as to whether such a far-reaching ex-ante recognition would be appropriate. However, a double approval as required by the EU can rightly be described as unnecessary, which is why Switzerland's more liberal approach is to be welcomed. For a consenting view see Spillmann and Meyer (n 29) para 35; René Bösch, 'Das neue Schweizer Prospektrecht gemäss E-FIDLEG—eine Bestandesaufnahme und erste Würdigung' (2016) 135 ZSR 81, 96. Meanwhile, the Commission has also recognized this and is planning a far-reaching liberalization. See n 174 (ch 1).

A similar provision concerning recognition exists in FIDLEG regarding key information documents that have to be produced if the financial instrument is offered to retail clients.[45] Key information documents prepared in accordance with foreign law that is equivalent to the Swiss law on key information documents can be recognized.[46] This recognition does not affect the duty to publish the document.[47] Not surprisingly, given that the regulation of key information documents under FIDLEG is modelled on the EU PRIIP Regulation, the documents prepared in the EU are recognized as equivalent.[48] Contrary to Switzerland's liberal approach, EU law does not provide for a recognition mechanism in the PRIIP Regulation. This should be seen against the background that such key information documents are only required for offers to retail clients. When the interests of retail investors are at stake, the EU is generally very reluctant to recognize foreign regulation and supervision for reasons of investor protection.[49]

If neither an exemption applies nor a recognition of the prospectus drawn up in accordance with foreign law is possible, the question arises as to the required content of the prospectus. The provisions governing the content are included in Section 2 and are again liberal for foreign prospectuses. Even though English is not an official language in Switzerland, the prospectus can be drawn up in English.[50] With regard to the required semi-annual and annual accounts, all accounting standards recognized by the respective Swiss trading venue or the reviewing body are accepted.[51] This provision is a manifestation of Swiss self-regulation. SIX Swiss Exchange, for example, recognizes both US GAAP and IFRS.[52] In addition, the prospectus may also refer to foreign annual financial statements prepared in accordance with the accounting standards of the home country or to recognized foreign prospectuses.[53] The EU took a different path, as it does not rely on self-regulation in this area. The recognition of foreign accounting standards is thus not subject to the scrutiny of trading venues but to a separate equivalence mechanism.[54]

2. Second stage: Disclosure on the secondary market

a) *Periodic disclosure*

The most important periodic disclosure requirements exist in the area of financial reporting. Issuers whose securities are listed on a stock market must publish financial statements in accordance with Article 958e Law of Obligations (*Obligationenrecht*).

[45] FIDLEG, art 58(1).

[46] FIDLEG, art 59(2). Such foreign key information documents can even be used in Switzerland if the products were only designed for the Swiss market and are not offered abroad. See Vogel, Heiz, and Luthiger (n 38) FIDLEG, art 59 para 14.

[47] FIDLEG, art 66(1); see n 37 (ch 3).

[48] FIDLEV, Annex 10 no 1 and art 87; Bösch (n 44) 98.

[49] See ch 1C)II.6.a); see for an assessment of the level of investor protection achieved by the prospectus provisions of FIDLEG René Bösch, 'Das FIDLEG-Prospektrecht ante portas—Guter Anlegerschutz?' (2018) 90 SZW 451.

[50] FIDLEG, art 40(2); Vogel, Heiz, and Luthiger (n 38) FIDLEG, art 40 para 11.

[51] FIDLEV, art 51.

[52] Trading on SIX Swiss Exchange Module—Rules and Regulations as of December 2022 of SIX Swiss Exchange, s 3.2.2.

[53] FIDLEG, art 42 and FIDLEV, art 53(1)(b); Vogel, Heiz, and Luthiger (n 38) FIDLEG, art 42 para 4.

[54] Commission Regulation (EC) No 1569/2007, arts 2 and 3.

Additionally, they must publish annual and semi-annual reports pursuant to the respective Swiss stock exchange rules.[55] These statements must be drawn up in accordance with a financial reporting standard recognized by the Regulatory Board.[56] Regarding issuers incorporated in Switzerland, the accounting standards include Swiss GAAP FER, US GAAP and IFRS. Issuers incorporated outside of Switzerland may also use EU-IFRS or the Accounting standard of the People's Republic of China for business enterprises (Accounting Standards for Business Enterprises, 'ASBE').[57] In relation to banks—irrespective of a listing on a stock exchange—the special regime of Articles 6 et seq Banking Act applies.[58] With regard to Swiss branches of foreign banks, Article 8 Foreign Banks Ordinance-FINMA grants those branches the possibility to prepare their annual and interim accounts in accordance with the provisions applicable to the foreign bank if these provisions satisfy international accounting standards.

The disclosure of corporate governance issues is not required by law but is often demanded by stock exchanges as part of their self-regulation.[59] To mitigate legal conflicts, SIX Swiss Exchange applies its rules only to primary listings.[60] This gives the obligation an even smaller scope of application compared to the disclosure of corporate governance issues under the Accounting Directive in the EU.[61]

b) Event-driven disclosure

The disclosure of shareholdings, public takeover offers and inside information will be dealt with at a later stage because it is regulated under FinfraG and is therefore better suited in the part on market conduct.[62] The disclosure regime regarding directors' dealings does not contain specific rules with regard to foreign issuers.[63]

3. Third stage: Market exits

Disclosure obligations concerning market exits of financial institutions, especially delistings, do not exist in Switzerland.[64] However, Swiss trading venues adopted rules as part of their self-regulation. For example, SIX Exchange can make a delisting

[55] Listing Rules as of 15 July 2022 of SIX Swiss Exchange, arts 49 and 50 and Listing Rules as of 20 November 2020 of BX Swiss AG, art 15(1) and (2).

[56] Listing Rules as of 15 July 2022 of SIX Swiss Exchange, art 51 and Directive on Financial Reporting as of 6 December 2021 of SIX Swiss Exchange; Thomas C Jutzi, *Unternehmenspublizität* (Stämpfli 2017) paras 468ff; concerning the duty set out in the Code of Obligations see Verordnung über die anerkannten Standards zur Rechnungslegung (VASR) vom 21 November 2012.

[57] Directive on Financial Reporting as of 6 December 2021 of SIX Swiss Exchange, Annex 1.

[58] Jutzi (n 56) paras 497ff. The recognized accounting standards are specified in Accounting Standards-FINMA (RelV-FINMA), art 3(1).

[59] See eg Directive on Information relating to Corporate Governance as of 29 June 2022 of SIX Swiss Exchange. The BX Swiss only recommends the disclosure of corporate governance questions. See Jutzi (n 56) para 543. With regard to remuneration, FINMA published a circular: FINMA, 'Circ. 2010/01—Remuneration schemes' (21 October 2009); see Susan Emmenegger and Regula Kurzbein, 'Finanzmarktkrise und neue Corporate Governance von Banken' (2010) 5 GesKR 462.

[60] Directive on Information relating to Corporate Governance as of 29 June 2022 of SIX Swiss Exchange, art 3.

[61] See ch 1 C)II.1.b)aa).

[62] See ch 3 B)IV.1.b) to d).

[63] Jutzi (n 56) paras 709ff.

[64] Generally on delistings under Swiss law see Rudolf Tschäni, Hans-Jakob Diem, and Tino Gaberthüel, *Öffentliche Kaufangebote* (4th edn, Schulthess 2020) paras 847ff; Peter V Kunz, 'Kotierung sowie Dekotierung—oder: "Werden" und "Sterben" der Publikumsgesellschaften' (2006) 1 GesKR 117, 133ff.

conditional on timely notice by the issuer.[65] An equivalence regime in relation to these duties does not exist.

II. Gatekeepers and benchmarks

1. Credit rating agencies

Historically, rating agencies were hardly supervised for most of their existence.[66] This changed in the aftermath of the *Enron* scandal with the adoption of the Credit Rating Agency Reform Act of 2006 in the US.[67] As credit rating agencies were often accused of having been a major driver of the GFC, the US tightened its regulation.[68] The EU also responded with a strict regulation of these agencies, in particular with regard to foreign credit rating agencies.[69] In comparison, the reaction of Switzerland was more moderate. To date, there is no special legislation devoted to rating agencies. Instead, they are governed by the softer instrument of circulars issued by FINMA.

In 2008, FINMA published Circular 2008/26 on rating agencies, which was later replaced by Circular 2012/1 on credit rating agencies.[70] The Circular governs the recognition of credit rating agencies and applies when a rating is used for regulatory purposes by an institution supervised by FINMA. Using ratings for regulatory purposes is only feasible if the rating is issued by an agency recognized by FINMA. Contrary to the EU, FINMA does not supervise credit rating agencies on an ongoing basis.[71] This is one reason why the European Commission has not adopted an equivalence decision in relation to Switzerland.[72] Nevertheless, FINMA may review the recognition requirements at any time and withdraw the recognition if the requirements are no longer met.[73] The requirements for recognition by FINMA are laid out in paras 24ff of

[65] Listing Rules as of 15 July 2022 of SIX Swiss Exchange, art 58(1) no 1; more specifically see Directive on Delisting of Equity Securities, Derivatives and Exchange Traded Products as of 7 December 2018 of SIX Swiss Exchange.

[66] Kristina St Charles, 'Regulatory Imperialism: The Worldwide Export of European Regulatory Principles on Credit Rating Agencies' (2010) 19 Minn J Intl L 399, 402; John C Coffee Jr, 'Ratings Reform: The Good, the Bad, and the Ugly' (2011) 1 Harv Bus L Rev 231, 246.

[67] See John C Coffee Jr, 'Ratings Reform: The Good, the Bad, and the Ugly' (2011) 1 Harv Bus L Rev 231, 246ff.

[68] St Charles (n 66) 406ff.

[69] Rüdiger Veil, 'Rating Agencies' in Rüdiger Veil (ed), *European Capital Markets Law* (3rd edn, Hart Publishing 2022) § 27 paras 9ff; Harry McVea, 'Credit Rating Agencies, the Subprime Mortgage Debacle and Global Governance: The EU Strikes Back' (2010) 59 Intl & Comp LQ 701, 720ff.

[70] See FINMA, 'Circ. 2008/26—Rating Agencies' (20 November 2008) and FINMA, 'Circ. 2012/1—Credit Rating Agencies' (29 June 2011).

[71] FINMA, 'Circ. 2012/1—Credit Rating Agencies' (29 June 2011) paras 8 and 64; Matthias Lehmann, 'Internationales Finanzmarktrecht' in Jan von Hein (ed), *MüKo/BGB*, vol 13, pt 12 (8th edn, CH Beck 2021) para 446. See in the EU CRA Regulation, arts 21–25a; Christoph Kumpan and Ronny Grütze in Matthias Lehmann and Christoph Kumpan (eds), *European Financial Services Law* (Nomos 2019) CRA Regulation, arts 21–25a paras 5ff.

[72] The CRA Regulation demands in its art 5(6) subpara 2(a) that third country credit rating agencies are 'subject to effective supervision and enforcement on an ongoing basis'. This is not the case in Switzerland. See Nobel (n 4) § 7 para 643.

[73] FINMA, 'Circ. 2012/1—Credit Rating Agencies' (n 70) para 65.

the Circular and are closely modelled on the IOSCO Code of Conduct Fundamentals for Credit Rating Agencies.[74]

Since the major rating agencies are not domiciled in Switzerland,[75] the procedure governing foreign credit rating agencies gains in importance. In general, rating agencies are subject to the same requirements irrespective of their domicile, which means they must obtain FINMA recognition for their ratings to be used for regulatory purposes.[76] However, FINMA may simplify or waive proof of compliance with the recognition requirements if the foreign rating agency is already subject to ongoing supervision in its home country.[77] In the cases of Australia, the EU, Japan, and the US, FINMA has found that their supervision is 'sufficient'.[78] This mechanism is a manifestation of the principle of deference, as FINMA relaxes its rules with regard to foreign players that are already supervised. It is comparable to the EU's equivalence mechanism in that it demands a certain level of foreign regulation and supervision; more precisely, FINMA requires the foreign regulation and supervision to be 'sufficient'.[79] Nonetheless, the Swiss approach to deference is more liberal and far-reaching than that of the EU. It does not exclude systemically important agencies and also applies to ratings concerning entities established or financial instruments issued in Switzerland.[80] Remarkably, the depth of the Swiss third country regime (only two sentences) is far less than the EU's, which covers almost three pages.

More recently, Switzerland—following the FSB Principles for Reducing Reliance on CRA Ratings—attempted to reduce the reliance on credit ratings even more.[81] Already before this reform, only a few provisions of Swiss financial markets law required a rating, and these were mostly based on the Basel framework, such as in the area of capital adequacy and liquidity for banks.[82] As part of the action plan, FINMA amended its Ordinance on Collective Investment Schemes and removed all references to ratings.[83] This development shows that Switzerland prefers to reduce its dependency on ratings instead of strictly regulating them. FINMA encourages supervised institutions to 'maintain professional scepticism and limit their dependency on these credit ratings'. This approach also explains why FINMA does not carry out continuous monitoring. This would create the (false) impression that ratings can be relied upon blindly. The financial crisis has impressively taught us that this is not the case.

[74] ibid para 24; Jürgen Frick and Hanna Jost, 'Haftung von Ratingagenturen' in Thomas U Reutter and Thomas Werlen (eds), *Kapitalmarkt—Recht und Transaktionen XI* (Schulthess 2017) 146ff.

[75] There is just one recognized rating agency domiciled in Switzerland: fedafin AG based in St Gallen. For a full list of recognized rating agencies see FINMA, 'Recognised Credit Rating Agencies' (8 November 2022) https://www.finma.ch/en/~/media/finma/dokumente/finmapublic/bewilligungstraeger/ratingagenturen.pdf?sc_lang=en&hash=3EF6A5637E13BC76972B2B9670C3C0F3 (accessed 28 February 2023).

[76] FINMA, 'Circ. 2012/1—Credit Rating Agencies' (n 70) para 58.

[77] ibid paras 59f.

[78] ibid para 61.

[79] ibid para 60.

[80] In fact, this is the rule rather than the exception, as the duty of recognition only applies to institutions that are supervised by FINMA. See FINMA, 'Circ. 2012/1—Credit Rating Agencies' (n 70) para 1.

[81] FINMA, 'Action Plan for Reducing Reliance on CRA Ratings Switzerland' (10 January 2014) https://www.newsd.admin.ch/newsd/message/attachments/36274.pdf (accessed 12 November 2022).

[82] See, by way of an example, the analysis of a rating of a Swiss bank in Christian Schmid, 'Rating einer Kantonalbank' in Zafer Diab and Oliver Everling (eds), *Rating von Finanzinstituten* (2016 Springer) 155.

[83] See eg FINMA Collective Investment Schemes Ordinance (KKV-FINMA) as of 1 January 2009, arts 7, 8, and 33. The new ordinance of 27 August 2014 no longer includes these references.

2. External auditors

At the beginning of this century, auditing was an area subject only to self-regulation.[84] This changed with multiple scandals occurring in this field, including *Enron*, *Worldcom*, and *Tyco*. The US responded by enacting the Sarbanes-Oxley Act and establishing the Public Company Accounting Oversight Board. Shortly after the US, the EU initiated reforms and passed, inter alia, the Statutory Audit Directive. Because of this international pressure, Switzerland followed the example of other countries and reformed its substantive law concerning auditing as well as its supervisory law.[85] The Auditor Oversight Act (RAG), which is further specified in an ordinance (RAV) of the Federal Council, was adopted and the Federal Audit Oversight Authority (FAOA) was created.

a) Authorization and supervision of external auditors

Switzerland introduced a two-stage system in the RAG. External auditors must be licensed with the FAOA pursuant to Article 3(1) RAG if they want to conduct an audit as defined in Article 2(a) RAG. If the audit concerns a public interest entity, special registration with more stringent standards is required and the auditors are placed under public oversight.[86]

In the case of an audit in the sense of Article 2(a) RAG, the requirements are set out in Articles 4 to 6 RAG. Audit experts (*Revisionsexperten*), who have studied in a foreign country, can also meet the requirements for training and professional practice if their training is 'comparable' to that of Swiss experts.[87] Additionally, they must prove sufficient knowledge of the Swiss legal system. This recognition applies only if the foreign state concluded an international treaty with Switzerland in this area—which is the case for the EU—or if reciprocal treatment is ensured. The SAD in the EU contains a similar equivalence mechanism.[88]

In the case of an audit of a public interest entity, the situation is more complex. Here, the applicability of the RAG is not limited to the auditing of Swiss firms, but the RAG has an extraterritorial scope of application.[89] Pursuant to Article 8 RAG, foreign audit firms that audit foreign companies under foreign law that directly or indirectly use the Swiss capital market, for instance, by listing their shares on Swiss stock exchanges, must already be licensed and supervised by the FAOA. The extraterritorial reach of this provision is comparable to that of Article 45(1) SAD in the EU. To mitigate the extraterritorial effects of this rule, which led to practical problems and supervisory conflicts, the Swiss legislator introduced two exemptions to this obligation.[90] One of them provides that foreign audit firms must not adhere to the obligation if they are already licensed and supervised by their home country authority and if the Federal

[84] See for the historic development Peter V Kunz, *Wirtschaftsrecht* (Stämpfli 2019) 882f; Matthias Jeger, 'Internationale Regulierung von Auditdienstleistungen und Revisionsaufsicht' (2018) EF 874, 874f.

[85] Botschaft Änderung Obligationenrecht, BBl 2004, 3969, 3977ff.

[86] RAG, art 7(1).

[87] RAG, art 4(2)(d); see Urs Bertschinger in Rolf Watter and Urs Bertschinger (eds), *BSK-Revisionsrecht* (Helbing Lichtenhahn 2011) art 4 paras 20ff.

[88] See SAD, art 44(1) as well as arts 4 and 6–13.

[89] Urs Bertschinger, 'Das Finanzmarktaufsichtsrecht Mitte 2014 bis ins vierte Quartal 2015' (2015) 87 SZW 630, 644f.

[90] RAG, art 8(2) and (3); Bertschinger (n 89) 644f.

Council of Switzerland recognizes this authority.[91] The recognition is further specified in Article 10 RAV, which demands that the foreign oversight is equivalent. Important for this equivalence decision is, among other factors, whether other states or international organizations recognize the authority and whether the foreign legal system also contains a provision dealing with deference (element of reciprocity).[92] Countries whose authorities have been recognized include almost all EU Member States, the US, the UK, and many more.[93] Yet this exemption for foreign audit firms does not apply to the audit of Swiss firms under Swiss law. Hence, the audit of Swiss firms remains subject to Swiss supervisory law.[94] This mechanism is almost identical to the EU equivalence regime in Article 46(1) SAD, under which the European Commission has already adopted an equivalence decision in relation to Switzerland.[95]

In the event that recognition pursuant to Article 8(2) RAG has not been granted or—even if recognition has been granted—a Swiss company must be audited (exception under Article 9a(2) RAV), foreign audit companies need a special licence for such audits pursuant to Article 7(1) RAG. The requirements for the special registration are generally set out in Article 9(1) RAG. According to Article 9(2) RAG, the FAOA may grant the authorization based on a foreign authorization. This provision is designed to avoid unnecessary and burdensome administrative procedures where foreign authorities have already carried out detailed approval tests. To prevent circumvention of the requirements of Swiss law, the conditions of the RAG must still be respected.[96] This obligation was softened in 2015 when the Federal Council drafted Article 9a RAV, which contains special rules for the licensing of foreign-based audit firms. Now they must either fulfil the requirements of Article 9 RAG or equivalent requirements.[97] Additionally, the fulfilment of information and reporting obligations must be ensured, and the Swiss supervisory authority must have access to the audit firm.[98] By demanding the fulfilment of equivalent requirements, Switzerland's high level of supervision cannot be bypassed.

In 2017, the Federal Council amended Article 9a RAV and included paragraphs 3 and 4. Pursuant to paragraph 3, foreign audit entities, which are domiciled in a state whose authorities have been recognized as equivalent by Switzerland, cannot obtain a licence in Switzerland. As a licence is not needed for the audit of foreign firms in that scenario,[99] the new rule only applies to the audit of Swiss firms.[100] The purpose of

[91] See RAG, art 8(2).

[92] RAV, art 10(1).

[93] See the list in RAV, Annex 2. From the EU Member States, only Estonia and Cyprus are missing.

[94] See RAV, art 9a(2). This 'exception from the exception' was previously included in RAV, art 10(2) (as of 1 December 2010), which made sense, since it referred to the exception in RAV, art 10(1). The fact that the exception has been moved to RAV, art 9a(2) is very confusing, as the exception now comes before the rule. See on the old legal regime Felix R Ehrat and Daniel C Pfiffner in Rolf Watter and Urs Bertschinger (eds), *BSK-Revisionsrecht* (Helbing Lichtenhahn 2011) art 8 para 11.

[95] Commission Decision 2011/30/EU of 19 January 2011, art 1 no 9.

[96] RAG, art 9(2); Ehrat and Pfiffner (n 94) art 9 para 21.

[97] RAV, art 9a(1)(a).

[98] ibid.

[99] A licence is not required in this case because art 8(2) of the RAG and art 10(1) of the RAV restrict the extraterritorial scope of application provided for in art 8(1) of the RAG.

[100] This is because RAV, art 9a(2) restricts the recognition as provided for in RAG, art 8(2) and RAV, art 10(1).

this restriction remains unclear. Although it prevents supervisory conflicts, it creates a competitive disadvantage for equally regulated external auditors, a consequence that can hardly have been intended by the legislator.

b) Foreign audit standards

If an audit takes place under Swiss law, the question arises as to which audit standards must be applied.[101] Pursuant to Article 16a(2) RAG, the FAOA is responsible for determining the national and international standards which can be used in an audit. The FAOA addresses this question with regard to foreign standards in Article 3 of the FAOA Supervisory Ordinance (ASV-RAB). Paragraph 2 of this provision states that the FAOA may recognize other foreign standards if they are 'equivalent' to the standards of the International Auditing and Assurance Standards Board (IAASB). These standards of the IAASB are specified in para 4 of Circular 1/2008 of the FAOA.[102] In para 5 of this Circular, the FAOA recognizes that the US GAAP are equivalent to the standards of the IAASB. This recognition does, however, not apply to companies domiciled in Switzerland. Their annual and consolidated financial statements need to be additionally reviewed against the yardstick of the Swiss GAAP. This recognition of foreign accounting standards is also contained in a very similar form in the SAD, which allows the use of equivalent third country accounting standards in relation to foreign entities.[103]

c) Cooperation with foreign authorities and mutual support in cross-border audit procedures

As the exchange of information between different authorities and the mutual support in cross-border audit procedures is very important with regard to the audit of international firms, most legal systems also deal with these questions.[104] In Switzerland, Article 26 RAG allows the FAOA to request information and documentation from foreign authorities and to share information and documentation with them if the foreign authority fulfils certain requirements, such as that the information is only used for supervisory purposes or that the agency is bound by the rules of professional secrecy.[105] A similar provision applies to cross-border audit procedures, although the element of reciprocity plays a more important role here.[106] In both cases, the Federal Council may conclude international treaties with foreign authorities laying down further details.[107] In Europe, similar rules exist. Article 47 SAD allows the exchange of information if, inter alia, reciprocity is fulfilled. In addition, the EU framework demands

101 With regard to international audit standards see Frank Schneider, 'Internationales Standardsetting in der Wirtschaftsprüfung' (2015) 87 SZW 592.

102 FAOA, 'Circ. 1/2008—Recognition of auditing standards' (17 March 2008).

103 SAD, art 45(5)(c) and (6).

104 On the international background see extensively Ralph Malacrida and Till Spillmann in Rolf Watter and Urs Bertschinger (eds), *BSK-Revisionsrecht* (Helbing Lichtenhahn 2011) art 26 paras 1ff; highlighting the importance of international cooperation: Botschaft Änderung Obligationenrecht, BBl 2004, 3969, 4081.

105 Extensively on the requirement of professional secrecy: Malacrida and Spillmann (n 104) art 26 paras 33ff.

106 RAG, art 27; Malacrida and Spillmann (n 104) art 27 paras 34ff.

107 See RAG, arts 26(4) and 27(5).

that the foreign supervisory authority meets requirements that are 'adequate', which the European Commission has affirmed in the case of the FAOA.[108]

3. Benchmarks

Contrary to the EU, Switzerland has deliberately chosen not to adopt legislation governing benchmarks or their administrators.[109] Hence, (administrators of) benchmarks are neither supervised by FINMA nor do they have to comply with any special requirements. This applies to both Swiss as well as foreign benchmarks. Nevertheless, benchmark administrators may voluntarily comply with requirements set out in other countries' legislation. If they meet requirements as stringent as those of the EU Benchmark Regulation, individual benchmarks can be endorsed by regulated benchmark administrators of the EU. This happened in the case of benchmarks administered by SIX, a Swiss administrator.[110] Voluntary compliance through self-regulation, however, is not sufficient to qualify for a European Commission equivalence decision for two reasons. First, the administrator must be 'authorised and registered' and be 'subject to supervision' in its home country, which is not the case in Switzerland.[111] Secondly, the compliance must be of a 'binding' nature.[112]

From a global perspective, the lack of a special benchmark regime is not unusual. The US, for example, has not adopted specific legislation in this area.[113] Following the EU's example, on the other hand, Australia and Singapore have introduced benchmark regulations, which have already been recognized as equivalent by the European Commission.[114] The picture in this area is therefore mixed. From my point of view, Switzerland has refrained from regulation, as the EU endorsement regime suffices for the few Swiss benchmark providers operating at the international level. Regulation solely for reasons of greater legal certainty seemed too cumbersome in the eyes of the legislator.[115]

[108] SAD, art 47(1)(c) and (3); see Commission Decision 2010/64/EU of 5 February 2010, art 1 no 4.

[109] Federal Council, 'Derzeit kein Bedarf für Benchmark-Regulierung' Press Release (4 March 2016) https://www.admin.ch/gov/de/start/dokumentation/medienmitteilungen.msg-id-60870.html (accessed 12 November 2022); see also Beat Brändli, Basil Guggenheim and Matthias Jüttner, 'Financial Benchmarks: Bedeutung, Problematik und regulatorische Ansätze' (2016) 88 SZW 162.

[110] See SIX Swiss Exchange, 'Swiss Indices Endorsed Under the EU Benchmarks Regulation' Press Release (5 February 2020) https://www.six-group.com/en/newsroom/media-releases/2020/20200205-swiss-indices-endorsed.html (accessed 12 November 2022).

[111] See BMR, art 30(1)(b) and (2)(b).

[112] See BMR, art 30(2)(a); for a consenting view see Seraina Grünewald, 'Financial Benchmarks—Bedeutung und internationale Regulierungsbestrebungen' (2015) 87 SZW 586, 590, who therefore recommends the introduction of a Swiss regulation.

[113] Calling for a benchmark regulation see Gina-Gail S Fletcher, 'Benchmark Regulation' (2017) 102 Iowa L Rev 1929; see in more detail ch 4 B)II.3.

[114] See for Australia: ASIC Financial Benchmark (Administration) Rules 2018, F2018L00728; for Singapore: Securities and Futures (Financial Benchmarks) Regulations 2018, S 642/2018; regarding the equivalence decisions: Commission Implementing Decision (EU) 2019/1274 of 29 July 2019 in relation to Australia and Commission Implementing Decision (EU) 2019/1275 of 29 July 2019 in relation to Singapore.

[115] Critical of this view is Grünewald (n 112) 590f.

III. Financial intermediaries

One of the main objectives of the recent reform was the introduction of a cross-sectoral approach covering all financial intermediaries.[116] With regard to the duty to obtain authorization and questions of supervision, the Swiss legislator enacted FINIG to reach this goal (1.). Yet, the objective was not entirely achieved, as banks (2.) and insurance companies (3.) are still regulated separately, which is why the following analysis differentiates in this respect. In relation to the provision of financial services by financial intermediaries, the legislator introduced FIDLEG.

1. Financial intermediaries and FINIG, FIDLEG, and KAG

The regulation of financial intermediaries is divided into two legal acts: FINIG deals with the authorization, supervision and organization of financial institutions and FIDLEG with the conditions under which financial services may be provided. In addition, the KAG contains product-specific regulations concerning collective investment schemes.[117]

a) Financial institutions and FINIG

aa) Scope of application and cross-border services The scope of application of the new FINIG is defined in its Article 2. It covers portfolio managers, trustees, managers of collective assets, fund management companies, and securities firms. These institutions require authorization from FINMA under Article 5(1) FINIG, although certain authorizations also cover the activities of other institutions.[118] A banking authorization, for example, allows a bank to additionally operate as a securities firm under Article 6(1) FINIG. The territorial scope of FINIG is limited to financial institutions having a physical presence in Switzerland.[119] Accordingly, financial institutions domiciled abroad generally do not require FINMA approval, even if they provide services to Swiss investors on a cross-border basis. It is important to note in this context, however, that FIDLEG, which regulates the service itself, has a wider scope and also applies to purely cross-border financial services.[120]

The actual innovation of this authorization system—besides the unification and harmonization of different regimes—is that independent portfolio managers domiciled in Switzerland are now required to obtain authorization.[121] Previously, asset management by banks and securities firms was treated differently from that by independent asset managers because only the former were subject to comprehensive supervision.[122]

[116] See ch 3 A); Sethe (n 26) 156.

[117] Nobel (n 4) § 11 paras 9ff; Andreas Josuran and Vanessa Isler, 'Änderungen beim Vertrieb kollektiver Kapitalanlagen unter dem FIDLEG/FINIG' (2016) 11 GesKR 205, 205f.

[118] So-called *Bewilligungskaskade*; see the overview in Vogel, Heiz, and Luthiger (n 38) FINIG, art 6 para 7; Roth (n 19) 611f.

[119] Fahrländer (n 8) 233.

[120] See extensively ch 3 B)III.1.b).

[121] Sethe (n 26) 156f; see extensively Manuel Stutz, 'Die Aufsicht der unabhängigen Vermögensverwalter unter dem FINIG' (2017) 12 GesKR 293.

[122] Fahrländer (n 8) 234.

Different from the regulation of MiFID II,[123] independent client advisers are still not subject to the duty to obtain authorization under FINIG. However, they have the duty to register under FIDLEG and must have sufficient knowledge of the code of conduct.[124] The difference between portfolio managers and client advisers is that the former make independent investment decisions, whereas the latter only give recommendations, with the client making the final decision on an investment.[125] Because of this discrepancy in regulation between Switzerland and the EU, it is unclear whether the European Commission will adopt an equivalence decision under MiFIR in relation to Switzerland.[126]

Financial institutions domiciled in Switzerland and authorized by FINMA must be effectively managed from Switzerland pursuant to Article 10(1) FINIG. For securities firms domiciled and effectively managed from Switzerland but controlled by a foreign institution, the special rule of Article 43 FINIG applies. According to that rule, the provisions of the Banking Act on foreign-controlled banks apply by analogy. As a result, securities firms must comply with additional requirements, which the Swiss Federal Council can, however, waive in international treaties.[127]

bb) Branches of foreign financial institutions In case financial institutions domiciled abroad—so-called foreign financial institutions[128]—wish to establish a branch in Switzerland, they need to obtain authorization from FINMA in accordance with Article 52(1) FINIG. This regulatory approach is modelled on the Foreign Banks Ordinance-FINMA.[129] Although banking supervision has therefore not been integrated into FINIG, as originally intended by the reform, at least the cross-border provision of services by financial institutions and banks has been harmonized regarding the authorization requirement.

This authorization is granted if the conditions set out in Article 53 FINIG are met. This includes, among other things, that the foreign financial institution is subject to appropriate supervision in its home country, which also extends to the branch in question.[130] Furthermore, the foreign supervisory authority must not object to the establishment of the branch and must ensure administrative assistance to FINMA, two elements that are recurrent features of Swiss supervisory law with regard to the treatment of foreign branches.[131]

Such authorization is no longer sufficient if the foreign financial institution is effectively managed from Switzerland or executes its transactions exclusively or

[123] See MiFID II, art 5(1) and Annex I, s A, no 5 and art 4(1) no 4.

[124] FIDLEG, arts 28(1) and 6(1); see in detail the next section.

[125] Bundesgericht, judgment of 18 December 2014 [2014] BGer 4A_336/2014, paras 4.4.1 and 4.4; see extensively Nobel (n 4) § 10 paras 190ff.

[126] Rolf Sethe argues that this gap is compensated by the fact that the Swiss legislator subjects independent investment advisers in FIDLEG to criminal sanctions if they deliberately violate customer protection regulations. See Sethe (n 26) 160.

[127] Banking Act, art 3[bis](1); see concerning the exemption: Banking Act, art 3[quarter](1).

[128] See the definition in FINIV, art 76(1).

[129] Botschaft FIDLEG/FINIG, BBl 2015, 8901, 9035; Vogel, Heiz, and Luthiger (n 38) FINIG, art 53 para 1.

[130] The requirements are extremely high. See Vogel, Heiz, and Luthiger (n 38); FINIG, art 53 paras 2 and 7. The requirements are further specified in FINIV, arts 77ff.

[131] FINIG, art 59(1)(b); Foreign Banks Ordinance-FINMA, arts 4(1)(c) and 14(b).

predominantly in or from Switzerland.[132] In this scenario, the foreign financial institution must be organized under Swiss law and comply with all provisions governing domestic financial institutions.

The Swiss Federal Council has the competence to sign international treaties allowing financial institutions from the respective state to open branches without authorization from FINMA.[133] Such an agreement is subject to reciprocity and requires that the foreign regulation and supervision be equivalent to Switzerland's.

A priori excluded from the possibility to set up a branch are foreign fund management companies, as they must be organized as a Swiss company limited by shares with a registered and head office in Switzerland.[134]

cc) Representations of foreign financial institutions Similar rules as for the setting up of a branch apply to the establishment of a representation by a foreign financial institution. A representation is defined as the employment of persons in Switzerland who work for the foreign financial institution on a permanent and commercial basis in or from Switzerland.[135]

Again, an authorization by FINMA is necessary for the establishment of a representation.[136] The authorization is granted under conditions comparable to those applicable to branches, including an appropriate home country supervision as well as some degree of supervisory cooperation.[137] As with the regulation of branches, the Swiss Federal Council has the competence to sign international treaties allowing financial institutions from the respective state to open representations without authorization from FINMA if reciprocity, an equivalent regulation, and the supervision of the foreign financial institution is ensured. Foreign fund management companies are denied the possibility of setting up a representation, as they must be organized as a Swiss company limited by shares with a registered and head office in Switzerland.[138]

b) Provision of financial services and FIDLEG

aa) Scope of application As pointed out above, the scope of application of FIDLEG differs from that of FINIG.[139] The term financial service provider in FIDLEG also covers foreign institutions providing services to clients in Switzerland on a commercial basis.[140] Therefore, purely cross-border services are regulated under FIDLEG, but

[132] FINIV, art 76(2); Vogel, Heiz, and Luthiger (n 38); FINIG, art 52 para 7.

[133] FINIG, art 52(3).

[134] The exemptions in arts 52(2) and 58(2) of the FINIG therefore only have a clarifying function; see FINIG, art 33(1); Botschaft FIDLEG/FINIG, BBl 2015, 8901, 9037: only for purposes of legal certainty.

[135] The interpretation in FINIG is based on the definition in the Foreign Banks Ordinance-FINMA. Botschaft FIDLEG/FINIG, BBl 2015, 8901, 9037; Vogel, Heiz, and Luthiger (n 38) FINIG, art 58 para 6.

[136] FINIG, art 58.

[137] ibid art 59; Vogel, Heiz, and Luthiger (n 38) FINIG, art 59 paras 5ff.

[138] See FINIG, arts 58(2) and 33(1).

[139] Nobel (n 4) § 10 paras 105ff; for a critical view with regard to the different terminology used see Harald Bärtschi, 'Finanzmarktregulierung im Fluss: Zum neuen Finanzinstituts- und Finanzdienstleistungsgesetz' (2014) 86 SZW 459, 476.

[140] FIDLEG, art 3(d); Vogel, Heiz, and Luthiger (n 38) FIDLEG, art 2 para 6. On the scope of application see extensively Rolf Sethe, 'Einige kritische Anmerkungen zum geplanten Schweizer Finanzdienstleistungsgesetz' in Matthias Casper and others (eds), *Festschrift für Johannes Köndgen zum 70. Geburtstag* (RWS 2016) 604ff.

not under FINIG. However, excluded from the scope of application are services entered into at the express initiative of a client.[141] These cases of reverse solicitation are also excluded under EU law.[142]

As in MiFID II, the concept of a financial service is specified by a list of specific activities that qualify as such.[143] The services covered are similar to those of MiFID II. One major difference is that the term portfolio management applies to both individual and collective portfolio management, whereas the requirements in MiFID II only apply to individual portfolio management. The collective side is regulated in the UCITS, respectively, the AIFM-Directive.[144]

As a result of the broad scope of application, foreign financial service providers offering cross-border services to clients in Switzerland must have the required knowledge (Article 6 FIDLEG), must obey the code of conduct rules (Chapter 2) as well as the organizational measures (Chapter 3, Section 1) and must prevent any conflicts of interest (Chapter 3, Section 2). Because foreign service providers are not subject to ongoing prudential supervision in Switzerland, compliance with these obligations is not strictly monitored. To compensate for this limited supervision, violations of some of the rules will be prosecuted under criminal law (Article 89 FIDLEG).[145] This far-reaching extraterritorial regulation is one of the major changes brought about by the reform in this area,[146] aligning the system with the EU.

Remarkably, FIDLEG does not contain any deference mechanism in this area. It was the explicit aim of the legislator that foreign service providers should always comply with the code of conduct.[147] This absence of deference is also noteworthy because it makes the regime in some respects more restrictive than that of the EU, which contains an equivalence regime in MiFIR, at least for services to professional parties. However, given that the code of conduct of FIDLEG is modelled on MiFID II, little will change for EU service providers for whom compliance will therefore not be a major hurdle.[148]

bb) Register of advisers The reform of FIDLEG led to the introduction of a register of advisers. Client advisers of Swiss as well as foreign financial service providers, which are not already subject to FINMA supervision, have the duty to register if they address clients in Switzerland.[149] The registration applies only to the adviser—the natural person—and not the legal entity behind it and does not entail ongoing prudential supervision for either one of them. To be entered into the register, client advisers must

[141] FIDLEV, art 2(2).
[142] TFEU, arts 56 and 57; see eg AIFMD, recital 70; MiFIR, art 46(5) subpara 3; MiFID II, art 42.
[143] FIDLEG, art 3(c).
[144] Vogel, Heiz, and Luthiger (n 38) FIDLEG, art 3 para 81; see the exemption in MiFID II, art 2(1)(i).
[145] Admitting a weakened enforcement see Botschaft FIDLEG/FINIG, BBl 2015, 8901, 8916f; for a critical view see Sethe (n 26) 160.
[146] See extensively Bahar and Nedwed (n 16) 628ff.
[147] Botschaft FIDLEG/FINIG, BBl 2015, 8901, 8916f.
[148] ibid 8938: Service providers serving customers from both the EU and Switzerland should not have to comply with two different standards.
[149] FIDLEG, art 28(1); Vogel, Heiz, and Luthiger (n 38) FIDLEG, art 28 paras 1ff.

have sufficient knowledge of the code of conduct, the necessary expertise, professional indemnity insurance, and they must be affiliated to an ombudsman's office.

Exempted from the duty to register are client advisers of foreign financial service providers who are prudentially supervised in their home country and provide services exclusively for professional or institutional clients.[150] Like MiFID II/MiFIR, Swiss law allows for such segmentation of clients.[151] The exemption is not linked to a specific supervisory standard like appropriateness or equivalence in a foreign country.

At first sight, this exemption appears to be parallel to the equivalence mechanism under MiFIR, which also applies to services provided to professional clients and eligible counterparties. But the two have little in common.[152] MiFIR exempts third country investment firms—not client advisers—from the duty to authorize, EU supervision, and compliance with MiFID II, CRR II, and CRD V. On the contrary, Swiss supervisory law does not even contain a duty to obtain authorization for purely cross-border services in the first place, and there is no ongoing prudential supervision of foreign securities firms in relation to these services. Furthermore, the exemption from the duty to be registered does not exempt foreign service providers from compliance with the Swiss code of conduct. In addition, there are many other differences in detail, such as that the register in MiFIR is a public one managed by ESMA, whereas private entities run the register under FIDLEG.[153]

c) The reduced role of the KAG

Prior to the reform, the KAG, which regulates collective investment schemes and the persons responsible for them, contained provisions on the authorization and organization of such investment schemes, rules on the products, and the code of conduct. The former provisions were transferred to FINIG and the latter to FIDLEG. This leaves only product rules under the remit of the KAG.[154]

Part of these product rules is the duty for foreign collective investment schemes to obtain approval by FINMA (Article 120(1) KAG). Such approval is required for all foreign collective investment schemes offered in or from Switzerland to non-qualified investors. The conditions for approval are listed in Article 120(2) KAG. The investment scheme, fund management company and depositary must be subject to public supervision intended to protect investors. Moreover, the regulation concerning the organization, investor rights, and investment policy in that country must be equivalent. Also, the designation of the investment scheme must not provide grounds for confusion or deception, and the representative and paying agent must be appointed in Switzerland. Finally, cooperation between FINMA and the foreign supervisory

[150] FIDLEG, art 28(2) and FIDLEV, art 31.

[151] See also regarding the differences to MiFID II/MiFIR Sandro Abegglen and Thomas Hochstrasser, 'FIDLEG—was kommt gemäss Botschaft des Bundesrates auf die Finanzdienstleister zu?' (2016) 112 SJZ 369, 370ff; Guillaume Braidi, 'La classification des clients selon la loi sur les services financiers' (2018) 90 RSDA 486, 489ff.

[152] See the comparative analysis in Vogel, Heiz, and Luthiger (n 38) FIDLEG, art 28 paras 18f.

[153] On the register for client advisers see extensively Pascal Zysset, 'FIDLEG-Beraterregister als lex semiperfecta' (2020) 15 GesKR 271.

[154] Nobel (n 4) § 11 paras 9ff; Josuran and Isler (n 117) 205f.

authority must be ensured.[155] A simplified approval procedure may be applied for foreign investment schemes already approved by a foreign supervisory authority.[156]

According to Article 122 KAG, the Federal Council may conclude international treaties exempting foreign collective investment schemes from the duty to obtain authorization. Subsequently, the foreign collective investment scheme must only notify FINMA.[157] The Federal Council may enter into such international treaties if the foreign regulatory standards are equivalent and reciprocity is guaranteed. The consequence of such a treaty is that the foreign collective investment scheme must comply only with foreign regulation and is supervised only by its home country authority. One example of such an international treaty is the agreement between FINMA and BaFin.[158]

No FINMA approval is required for offers to qualified investors.[159] Moreover, it is no longer necessary to appoint a representative and a paying agent in Switzerland, contrary to the legal situation before the reform.[160]

d) *Two different approaches: Preventive ban with authorization option versus permission with reservation of prohibition*

The regulation outlined above differs from that of the EU in numerous smaller and larger details. Given that the regulatory structure is already completely different, it makes little sense to list these details here. Instead of a line-by-line comparison, the legal philosophies behind these regulations are evaluated. The EU follows an approach that could be described as a 'preventive ban with authorisation option'. At the outset, third country firms are not allowed to enter the EU market unless they get permission from national or European authorities. To obtain such authorization, they will often have to relocate to the EU by setting up a subsidiary or branch, or they must at least appoint a representative in the EU (i.e. forced territoriality). Once they are authorized, they still have to comply with EU regulations.

The Swiss approach to purely cross-border services is fundamentally different and could be characterized as a 'permission with reservation of prohibition' approach. Foreign firms are allowed to provide cross-border services without needing prior approval. They are not subject to ongoing prudential supervision by FINMA but are primarily supervised in their home country. Nevertheless, foreign firms must comply with Swiss supervisory law, such as the code of conduct, when providing cross-border services. If they violate these rules, they can be prosecuted by FINMA. Hence, the Swiss approach is liberal on market entry but becomes stricter afterwards.

[155] Extensively on the requirements see Stephanie Comtesse and Joël Fischer in René Bösch and others (eds), *BSK-KAG* (2nd edn, Helbing Lichtenhahn 2016) KAG, art 120 paras 16ff.

[156] KAG, art 120(3) and Collective Investment Schemes Ordinance (KKV), art 129, which makes this procedure subject to reciprocal treatment.

[157] Comtesse and Fischer (n 155) art 122 para 4.

[158] FINMA-Mitteilung 55 (2014) 3 https://www.finma.ch/de/~/media/finma/dokumente/dokumentencenter/4dokumentation/finma-mitteilungen-archiv/finma-mitteilung-55-2014.pdf?la=de (accessed 12 November 2022); Comtesse and Fischer (n 155) art 122 paras 7aff.

[159] *Argumentum e contrario* KAG, art 120(1); see Nobel (n 4) § 11 para 46.

[160] *Argumentum e contrario* resulting from KAG, art 120(4), which demands such an appointment only in the situation of an opting out. See Josuran and Isler (n 117) 210.

In the EU, equivalence decisions may exempt foreign financial service providers—at least in part—from the requirements described above. If the legal framework of the third country is deemed to be equivalent, the foreign company will be exempted either from individual duties of EU law (see Article 37(2) AIFMD) or from the entire regulation, including the authorization duty and ongoing supervision (see Article 46(1) MiFIR). Again, equivalence is designed as an ex-ante control: a preventive ban with the possibility of deference by way of an equivalence decision.

2. Banks and the Banking Act

Swiss regulation of cross-border banking services is extremely liberal compared to other legal systems in the world.[161] At the outset, the Swiss Banking Act applies to entities having their registered seat in Switzerland and performing banking services in Switzerland or abroad.[162] The scope of application is extended pursuant to Article 2(1) Banking Act to all branches of foreign banks established in Switzerland or representative offices of foreign banks in Switzerland.[163] *E contrario*, purely cross-border banking services provided by foreign banks, for instance via the internet, are not subject to the Banking Act, which is an extremely liberal approach.[164] The EU does not allow such licence-free cross-border services and only grants authorization if the legal person has its head office in a Member State (i.e. forced territoriality).[165] Such licence-free cross-border services are, however, subject to limitations under Swiss law. According to Article 1(2) Foreign Banks Ordinance-FINMA, a foreign bank must organize itself as a Swiss bank if it is factually managed from Switzerland or carries out a majority of its business in or from Switzerland. This forced territoriality prevents banks from establishing themselves in a foreign state merely to circumvent Swiss supervision, even though they primarily serve Swiss clients (so-called 'shell' banks).[166] The restriction is therefore marginal and is intended to prevent cases of abuse.

If a foreign bank does not wish to confine itself to providing purely cross-border services, it can set up a subsidiary, branch, or representative office in Switzerland.

[161] Even the Swiss Federal Banking Commission acknowledged this fact. See Eidgenössische Bankenkommission, 'Erläuterungen der Auslandbankenverordnung vom 21. Oktober 1996' (1997) 32 EBK Bulletinn 10 https://www.finma.ch/FinmaArchiv/ebk/f/publik/bulletin/pdf/bull32.pdf (accessed 12 November 2022).

[162] See regarding the requirements that must be met Rolf H Weber, 'Schweiz' in Peter Derleder, Kai-Oliver Knops, and Heinz Georg Bamberger (eds), *Deutsches und europäisches Bank- und Kapitalmarktrecht*, vol 2 (3rd edn, Springer 2017) § 113 para 9.

[163] This provision no longer includes agencies (*Agenturen*) previously covered by Foreign Banks Ordinance-FINMA, art 2(2). Nobel (n 4) § 7 para 272.

[164] Nobel (n 4) § 7 paras 269 and 459.

[165] See CRD V, art 13(2). As the authorization is granted only at the national level, this provision must be transposed. See eg KWG § 33(1) no 6 in Germany. Christoph Ohler, 'Europäisches Bankenaufsichtsrecht' in Peter Derleder, Kai-Oliver Knops, and Heinz Georg Bamberger (eds), *Deutsches und europäisches Bank- und Kapitalmarktrecht*, vol 2 (3rd edn, Springer 2017) § 90 para 38.

[166] Bundesgericht, judgment of 15 July 2004 [2004] BGE 130 II 351; Stefan Kramer, Urs P Roth, and Renate Schwob in Dieter Zobl and others (eds), *Bodmer/Kleiner/Lutz: Kommentar zum Bundesgesetz über die Banken und Sparkassen* (Schulthess 2015) art 2 para 2; concerning the phenomenon of shell banks see BCBS, 'Shell banks and booking offices' (January 2003) https://www.bis.org/publ/bcbs95.pdf (accessed 12 November 2022). The provision was introduced as a reaction to the collapse of the Bank of Credit and Commerce International, which was set up in such a way as to avoid effective regulation and supervision deliberately. See Eidgenössische Bankenkommission (n 161)n .

A legally independent subsidiary will generally be treated like a Swiss bank, which is why it needs a licence to operate as a bank.[167] Branches and representative offices are regulated separately, albeit in a similar manner, in the Foreign Banks Ordinance-FINMA. Pursuant to the ordinance, branches and representative offices require FINMA authorization. The Banking Act and Ordinance apply to them except provisions on capital adequacy and risk diversification.[168] However, FINMA may decide that branches and representative offices are fully subject to the Banking Act if the foreign bank's home country does not ensure equivalent mutual treatment of Swiss branches to the extent permitted by international law.[169] In any case, a licence can only be granted by FINMA if the foreign bank is subject to appropriate supervision, a certain degree of supervisory cooperation is ensured, and, in the case of representative offices, reciprocal treatment is granted.[170]

According to Article 2(3) Banking Act, the Swiss Federal Council may even exempt foreign banks from the duty to obtain FINMA authorization for the setting up of branches and representative offices. Such an exemption is subject to reciprocal treatment, equivalent regulation, and supervision abroad and is granted only through a treaty with the foreign country. The mechanism is very similar to those of Articles 52(3) and 58(3) FINIG. The concept of equivalence is interpreted broadly and is already fulfilled if the foreign legal system follows the recommendations of the Basel Committee.[171] The Swiss Federal Council has not yet concluded such a treaty, which would de facto introduce a single banking licence and thus make the Swiss system even more liberal.[172]

If a foreign bank sets up a subsidiary, branch, or representative office in Switzerland, these are regarded as being subject to a controlling foreign influence, which results in the application of additional requirements.[173] The Swiss Federal Council may waive these special licensing requirements in international treaties pursuant to Article 3^{quarter}(1) Banking Act.

Ultimately, the Banking Act is an extremely liberal law because, on the one hand, it does not regulate purely cross-border services, and, on the other hand, it does not overregulate branches and representative offices of foreign banks in Switzerland, but even allows for exemptions from regulation through treaties.

[167] Banking Act, art 3(1).

[168] Foreign Banks Ordinance-FINMA, arts 2(1) and 3(1). This licensing requirement applies separately to each branch or representative office of a foreign bank set up in Switzerland (Foreign Banks Ordinance-FINMA, arts 6(a) and 15(a)). The rules of the Banking Act and Banking Ordinance apply *mutatis mutandis* (*sinngemäß*), even though this is no longer expressly stated in the ordinance. See Kramer, Roth, and Schwob (n 166) art 2 paras 7ff.

[169] Foreign Banks Ordinance-FINMA, art 3(2); Kramer, Roth, and Schwob (n 166) art 2 para 8.

[170] The requirements in the Foreign Banks Ordinance-FINMA for branches (art 4(1)) and representative offices (art 14) differ in some respects. Cédric Chapuis in Rolf Watter and others (eds), *BSK-BankenG* (2nd edn, Helbing Lichtenhahn 2013) art 2 para 12.

[171] Kramer, Roth, and Schwob (n 166) art 2 para 55.

[172] Nobel (n 4) § 7 para 279.

[173] Banking Act, art 3bis(1). If they were already incorporated before they came under foreign influence, an additional licence is required. See Banking Act, art 3ter; Nobel (n 4) § 7 para 275.

3. Insurances and the VAG

The supervision of insurance companies and intermediaries is uniformly regulated in the Insurance Supervision Law (VAG). Its scope of application is set out in Article 2 VAG. First, it applies to Swiss direct and reinsurance companies, regardless of where they provide the insurance service. Secondly, it subjects insurance companies established outside of Switzerland to the regulation insofar as they offer insurance activities in or from Switzerland unless international agreements provide otherwise.[174] Consequently, purely cross-border services from foreign insurances are, contrary to the Banking Act, subject to the VAG.[175] However, Article 2(2)(a) VAG exempts foreign insurance companies providing reinsurance services exclusively from the regulation.[176] In this respect, Swiss law is more liberal than Solvency II of the EU, which grants an exception only if the respective third country regulation and supervision is equivalent.[177] Thirdly, insurance intermediaries are regulated by the VAG irrespective of where they are domiciled.[178] Finally, the VAG also applies to Swiss as well as foreign insurance groups and insurance conglomerates. In all cases, FINMA may waive supervision if the activities are only of minor commercial importance or cover only a small circle of insured parties.[179]

Insurance companies subject to the VAG must obtain approval from FINMA prior to providing insurance services.[180] Additional requirements are laid down in Article 15 VAG with regard to foreign insurance companies.[181] Among other things, they must be licensed in their home country and set up a branch in Switzerland. Thus, similar to Solvency II, the VAG requires the establishment of a branch office within its jurisdiction (i.e. forced territoriality), which constitutes a rather protectionist approach.[182]

Because insurance groups and conglomerates entail additional risks compared to individual insurance undertakings, they are generally subject to enhanced supervision.[183] This group or conglomerate supervision is carried out by FINMA pursuant to Article 65(1) VAG if the group or conglomerate is actually managed from Switzerland (lit a)). It will also be carried out by FINMA if the group/conglomerate is actually managed from abroad, but the foreign supervision is not equivalent to that of FINMA

[174] VAG, art 2(1)(b); Helmut Heiss and Ulrike Mönnich in Peter Ch Hsu and Eric Stupp (eds), *BSK-VAG* (Helbing Lichtenhahn 2013) VAG, art 2 paras 72ff.

[175] Nobel (n 4) § 12 para 61. For the definition of when an insurance activity is carried out in Switzerland see Supervisory Ordinance (AVO), art 1(1).

[176] Rolf H Weber and Rainer Baisch, *Versicherungsaufsichtsrecht* (2nd edn, Stämpfli 2017) § 4 para 43.

[177] See Solvency II, art 172.

[178] Weber and Baisch (n 176) § 4 para 38.

[179] VAG, art 2(3); Heiss and Mönnich (n 174) VAG, art 2 paras 143ff.

[180] VAG, art 3(1); with regard to the interplay between financial markets and insurance supervision see Monica Mächler-Erne, 'Finanzmarktrecht und Versicherungen: Stand und Perspektiven' (2005) 14 AJP/PJA 53.

[181] See extensively Weber and Baisch (n 176) § 5 paras 41ff; see also Supervisory Ordinance (AVO), arts 16ff.

[182] Solvency II, art 162(2)(b).

[183] Expertengruppe Finanzmartkaufsicht, 'Finanzmarktregulierung und -Aufsicht in der Schweiz' (Zufferey-Bericht) (November 2010) 51ff http://docplayer.org/108102443-Integrierte-finanzmarktaufsicht-gesetzgeberische-folgearbeiten-zum-schlussbericht-der-expertengruppe-finanzmarktaufsicht-bericht-zufferey.html (accessed 12 November 2022); see for definitions VAG, arts 64 and 72; on systemic risks in the insurance sector see Monica Mächler, 'Gelten die Überlegungen zu Systemrisiken im Bankensektor auch für den Versicherungssektor?' (2010) 82 SZW 493.

(lit b)). Group or conglomerate supervision is thus left to the foreign authority only if it supervises the group or conglomerate in an equivalent manner.[184] In the event of supervisory conflicts, the VAG urges FINMA to negotiate with the foreign supervisory authority and reach a cooperative solution.[185]

The distribution of competences is different in the EU, as the statutory seat of the group's parent company, rather than the effective management (i.e. the real seat), is the decisive criterion for the supervision of the group.[186] However, EU law also provides for the possibility to withdraw its supervisory competences in case equivalent foreign supervision exists.[187] This similarity is based on the international proposals of the IAIS, which advocated a broad recognition of foreign supervision and was followed by both the EU and Switzerland.

To put it in a nutshell, insurance law is not as liberal as banking law with regard to the cross-border provision of services in Switzerland. In this field, Swiss law is much closer to the EU's Solvency II Regulation.

IV. Financial market infrastructures and market conduct under FinfraG

FinfraG is divided into two major parts: the regulation of financial market infrastructures (Title II) and market conduct (Title III). Deviating from the order in the law, this analysis begins with the provisions on market conduct, as these set out the obligations applicable to trading, which must then be fulfilled at the second level by or through the use of market infrastructures. For example, if there is no reporting duty, the question of eligible market infrastructures—in this scenario trade repositories—does not arise.

1. Market conduct

The structure of the following analysis is guided by the structure of the chapters in the title on market conduct. First, derivatives trading is examined, which is regulated in the first chapter (a)).[188] Then cross-border aspects of the disclosure of shareholdings from the third chapter (b)) and public takeover offers from the fourth chapter (c)) are discussed. Finally, the prohibition of exploiting insider information and market manipulation as provided for in chapter five is assessed (d)).

a) Derivatives trading

Following the calls of the G20 and the introduction of strict regulation in the EU and the US, Switzerland also adopted a regulation regarding derivatives trading. This

[184] Weber and Baisch (n 176) § 4 para 41.

[185] VAG, arts 65(2) and 73(2).

[186] Solvency II, arts 260(1) and 247. However, art 247(3) of Solvency II allows for flexible solutions that also take into account the actual management and not only the formal group structure. See Irene Klauer and Olivier Hirsbrunner in Peter Ch Hsu and Eric Stupp (eds), *BSK-VAG* (Helbing Lichtenhahn 2013) art 65 para 8.

[187] See Solvency II, art 260(1) for the group supervision and Conglomerates Directive, art 18 for the supervision of conglomerates.

[188] The second chapter on position limits for commodity derivatives is not included in this analysis as it is not of particular relevance to cross-border issues discussed here.

regulation is modelled on EMIR, as Switzerland strives to be recognized as equivalent by the European Commission.[189] The chapter on derivatives trading is divided into a general section followed by multiple sections setting out specific obligations.

aa) General provisions The scope of the Swiss derivatives regulation is defined in the first section. Pursuant to Article 93(1) FinfraG, the regulation applies to financial and non-financial counterparties having their registered office in Switzerland. Consequently, activities of Swiss counterparties abroad—even if executed through foreign branches—are covered, whereas activities of foreign counterparties in Switzerland are not included.[190] Nonetheless, FINMA may subject Swiss branches of foreign market participants to the requirements of FinfraG if the third country does not provide for an equivalent regulation.[191] The foreign regulation is deemed equivalent if the legal requirements do not deviate 'to a significant extent' from those under FinfraG.[192]

The mere fact that generally only Swiss counterparties are subject to the regulation does not mean that conflicts of law cannot arise. Legal conflicts are particularly likely in cross-border derivatives transactions where one counterparty is domiciled in Switzerland and the other counterparty abroad.[193] In these cases, the transaction will often be regulated by the two legal systems whose counterparties are involved. To avoid such conflicts, Article 95 FinfraG provides that the duties regarding derivatives trading shall also be fulfilled if the requirements of a foreign regulatory regime are met. For this legal consequence to take effect, the foreign legal regime (lit a)) as well as the foreign market infrastructure which was used to fulfil the requirements of the foreign law (lit b)) must have been recognized as equivalent by FINMA. To prevent abuse, an objective connection with the respective legal system is demanded.[194]

The Federal Council has further specified the meaning of the concept of equivalence in an ordinance corresponding to FinfraG (FinfraV). Comparable to the EU's outcome-based approach, equivalence is understood to require that the foreign regulation achieves a 'comparable ... material impact'.[195] The Federal Council emphasizes in its reasoning that it is not individual requirements but the outcomes that count and

[189] Olivier Favre and Stefan Kramer in Rolf Sethe and others (eds), *SK zum FinfraG* (Schulthess 2017) Vor art 93 para 9; the Swiss legislator intensively analysed the regulation in EMIR: Botschaft FinfraG, BBl 2014, 7483, 7503ff; on further arguments why the legislator aligned with EU and US law see Hans Kuhn, 'Die Regulierung des Derivatehandels im künftigen Finanzmarktinfrastrukturgesetz' (2014) GesKR 161, 166f.

[190] Rashid Bahar, 'Derivative Trading under the Federal Act on Financial Markets Infrastructure' (2015) 87 SZW 479, 483; Daniel Haeberli, 'Finanzderivate in der Schweiz' in Jean-Claude Zerey (ed), *Finanzderivate* (4th edn, Nomos 2016) § 38 para 121.

[191] See FinfraG, art 93(5) and FinfraV, art 78, in which the Federal Council delegates the competence to FINMA; Favre and Kramer (n 189) art 93 paras 14f.

[192] FinfraV, art 78.

[193] According to a study by the Swiss National Bank, 81 per cent of all interest rate derivatives transactions in 2019 were concluded with foreign counterparties and were thus cross-border transactions. See Swiss National Bank, 'Turnover in foreign exchange and derivatives markets in Switzerland—BIS Triennial Survey' (April 2022) para 4.2 https://data.snb.ch/en/topics/texts/doc/ddum_2022 (accessed 28 February 2023).

[194] FinfraV, art 81(3); Dieter Gericke, Vanessa Isler, and Stefan Kramer, 'Derivatgeschäfte: Anwendung der FinfraG-Regulierung auf Schweizer Handels- und Industrieunternehmen' (2018) 90 SZW 232, 249; critical of this view is Favre and Kramer (n 189) art 95 para 32.

[195] FinfraV, art 81(1).

that the rejection of equivalence must be handled with restraint.[196] Hence, FINMA does not carry out a line-by-line assessment but rather a practical, principle- and outcome-based analysis. This practice differs fundamentally from that of ESMA.[197] An illustrative example is FINMA's one-page equivalence analysis of the EU derivatives regulation in EMIR.[198] Comparable technical advice from ESAs often exceeds 100 pages. Therefore, although similarly described in abstract terms, equivalence is carried out more liberally and pragmatically in Switzerland than in the EU.

In the EU, the regulation applicable to derivatives transactions depends on whether the derivative is traded OTC or on organized venues. In the former case, EMIR is applicable, and in the latter, MiFIR applies.[199] Such a differentiation is not alien to the Swiss derivatives regulation; however, the general section on derivatives trading relates to both kinds of derivatives.[200] To avoid legal conflicts, both EMIR and MiFIR contain equivalence mechanisms which provide that 'counterparties entering into a transaction subject to this Regulation shall be deemed to have fulfilled' certain obligations if they have met requirements of a foreign country which are equivalent to those of the EU.[201] Contrary to FinfraG, it is not sufficient to have an objective connection to the foreign country, but one counterparty must be established in that country. Apart from that, the regimes are similar.

bb) Clearing requirement Following international standards and in parallel to Article 4(1) EMIR, a clearing duty for OTC derivatives was implemented in FinfraG.[202] According to Article 97(1) FinfraG, OTC derivatives are considered derivatives transactions that have not been traded on a trading venue, i.e. a stock exchange or MTF pursuant to Article 26(a) FinfraG. Because this definition does not require the trading venue to be authorized or recognized, a derivative transaction conducted on a foreign trading venue does not qualify as an OTC derivative. It is therefore not subject to the clearing obligation.[203] This is different under EU law. In the EU, derivatives transactions conducted on third country trading venues are generally subject to the clearing obligation unless the third country trading venue is recognized as equivalent.[204] If a third country trading venue is not recognized as equivalent, derivative contracts

[196] Erläuterungsbericht FinfraV, 36f: 'Dabei soll nach Absatz 1 ein Vergleich der verschiedenen Rechtssysteme nicht auf Stufe Einzelregelung sondern ergebnisorientiert in einer Gesamtschau der zur Diskussion stehenden Pflicht erfolgen. Da die Gesetzesbestimmung in erster Linie dazu dient, Handelshindernisse als Folge nicht kompatibler Regelungen verschiedener Staaten zu verhindern, wird fehlende Gleichwertigkeit mit einer gewissen Zurückhaltung anzunehmen sein.'

[197] See regarding the practice of ESMA: ch 2 B)I.2.b)aa).

[198] FINMA, 'Guidance 01/2016—Financial Market Infrastructure Act: FINMA's Next Steps' (6 July 2016) 7 https://www.finma.ch/en/~/media/finma/dokumente/dokumentencenter/myfinma/4dokumentation/finma-aufsichtsmitteilungen/20160707-finma-aufsichtsmitteilung-01-2016.pdf?la=en (accessed 12 November 2022).

[199] See the definition in EMIR, art 2(7) and the subject matter in MiFIR, art 1(1)(c).

[200] Favre and Kramer (n 189) Vor art 93 para 30.

[201] See EMIR, art 13(3) and MiFIR, art 33(3).

[202] FinfraG, art 97(1). On the international development see FSB, 'Implementing OTC-Derivatives Market Reforms' (25 October 2010) https://www.fsb.org/wp-content/uploads/r_101025.pdf (accessed 12 November 2022).

[203] Bahar (n 190) 482.

[204] EMIR, arts 2(7) and 2a; see ch 1 C)II.4.b).

entered into on that trading venue are deemed to be OTC derivatives and are thus subject to the clearing obligation.

Generally, a clearing obligation does not exist for exchange-traded derivatives in Switzerland. However, the Federal Council can extend the clearing duty to derivatives transactions conducted via a trading venue or an organized trading facility (OTF). Such a decision would approximate the Swiss clearing obligation to that of the EU.[205]

The territorial scope of the clearing duty must be determined in accordance with the general rule of Article 93 FinfraG. Thereafter, the duty applies if the counterparties to the transaction are domiciled in Switzerland. Additionally, the clearing duty applies in cross-border transactions where only one party is domiciled in Switzerland and in which the foreign counterparty would be subject to the clearing duty if it had its registered office in Switzerland.[206] This test is called the 'as if' test and duplicates Article 4(1)(a)(iv) EMIR.[207] The Swiss Federal Council grants an exemption from this duty if the foreign counterparty has its registered office in a country whose legislation has been recognized as equivalent and where the specific transaction in question is not subject to the clearing duty under this foreign legislation.[208]

The extraterritorial scope of FinfraG does, nevertheless, not go as far as that of EMIR, which also applies to transactions between two counterparties domiciled in third countries 'that would be subject to the clearing obligation if they were established in the Union, provided that the contract has a direct, substantial and foreseeable effect within the Union or where such an obligation is necessary or appropriate to prevent the evasion of any provisions of this Regulation'.[209]

cc) **Reporting requirement** To enhance transparency, Switzerland—like the EU—has opted for a far-reaching reporting duty covering both exchange-traded derivatives as well as OTC derivatives.[210] Unlike the EU and following the example of the US, Switzerland has established a unilateral reporting regime in which only one party is obliged to report each transaction.[211] The applicability of the reporting duty is based on the general rule of Article 93 FinfraG.[212] Hence, it applies to participants domiciled in Switzerland and their foreign branches but not to foreign participants.

In transactions involving a Swiss and a foreign counterparty, Article 104(1)(c) FinfraG determines that the Swiss counterparty is responsible for the reporting if the foreign counterparty does not report the transaction. This allocation of responsibilities

[205] See MiFIR, art 29(1).
[206] FinfraG, art 102.
[207] See regarding the 'as if' test Bahar (n 190) 488.
[208] FinfraG, art 102 and FinfraV, art 90. The same result can be reached through a teleological interpretation. See Hans Kuhn, 'Kollisionsrechtliche Aspekte der Derivateregulierung' (2014) 86 SZW 362, 372.
[209] EMIR, art 4(1)(a)(v); Favre and Kramer (n 189) art 97 para 6; Bahar (n 190) 488.
[210] See FinfraG, art 104; Alexander Vogel, Christoph Heiz, and Reto Luthiger (eds), *OFK FinfraG/BEG* (Orell Füssli 2019) FinfraG, art 104 para 2. The counterpart in the EU is EMIR, art 9. See Paolo Lucantoni in Matthias Lehmann and Christoph Kumpan (eds), *European Financial Services Law* (Nomos 2019) EMIR, art 9(1) para 1.
[211] Bahar (n 190) 491.
[212] Vogel, Heiz, and Luthiger (n 210) FinfraG, art 104 para 4. The territorial scope of the Swiss clearing requirement is therefore also more limited than that of swap transactions under the Dodd-Frank Act. See ch 4 B)IV.

is intended to ensure that a report is made in any case.[213] According to the official justification, a foreign reporting is only recognized if submitted to an authorized or recognized trade repository.[214] The phrase 'recognised trade repository' is to be understood as a reference to the recognition pursuant to Article 80 FinfraG.[215]

dd) Risk mitigation Following the international trend,[216] Switzerland has also introduced duties with regard to risk mitigation techniques for OTC derivatives not cleared through authorized or recognized CCPs.[217] Although these duties only apply to Swiss counterparties pursuant to the general scope of application laid down in Article 93 FinfraG, the duties still have an extraterritorial dimension. Swiss counterparties, for instance, are dependent on the cooperation of foreign counterparties to fulfil certain requirements such as the exchange of collateral prescribed in Article 110 FinfraG.

Article 106 FinfraV attempts to mitigate frictions arising in a cross-border context. Pursuant to paragraph 1, the duty to exchange collateral does only apply in cases where the foreign counterparty would also be subject to this duty if it had its registered office in Switzerland. Paragraphs 2, 2bis and 2ter provide for more exemptions, inter alia, if the foreign counterparty has its registered office in a country whose legislation is recognized by FINMA as equivalent and if under the foreign legislation, the counterparty does not have to exchange collateral.

An interesting approach is provided for in paragraph 3, which does not focus on foreign legislation but allows the unilateral fulfilment of duties that usually require the other party's involvement if it 'corresponds to recognized international standards'. The emphasis on international standards is a common feature of Swiss financial markets law. This is a very liberal trait, as it does not place one's own legal system but rather the international trend at the centre of the analysis. If the foreign legal system is also deemed equivalent, the Swiss counterparty can directly fulfil the obligations under foreign law.

ee) Trading requirement Switzerland has also followed the call of the G20 to introduce a trading duty for derivatives (Article 112 FinfraG). The applicability of the duty, which was initially suspended, has meanwhile been activated by the Swiss Federal Council.[218] FINMA will further specify the types of derivatives subject to this duty. To date, FINMA has not addressed this issue.[219]

[213] Botschaft FinfraG, BBl 2014, 7483, 7573.

[214] ibid.

[215] See ch 3 B)IV.2.d); unclear in this respect are Markus Feller and Thomas Bischof in Rolf Sethe and others (eds), *SK zum FinfraG* (Schulthess 2017) art 104 para 19, who refer to equivalence under art 95 FinfraG instead of art 80 FinfraG. However, given that both equivalence mechanisms will often come to the same conclusions, the question is not of major relevance in practice.

[216] Olivier Favre and Jürg Frick in Rolf Sethe and others (eds), *SK zum FinfraG* (Schulthess 2017) art 107 paras 5f; see in the EU EMIR, art 11.

[217] Gericke, Isler, and Kramer (n 194) 243ff.

[218] See FinfraG, art 164(3); Verordnung über die abschliessende Inkraftsetzung des Finanzmarktinfrastr ukturgesetzes vom 5 Juli 2017.

[219] See Vogel, Heiz, and Luthiger (n 210) FinfraG, art 113 para 1; explaining the necessary steps: Marco Häusermann and Bertrand G Schott in Rolf Sethe and others (eds), *SK zum FinfraG* (Schulthess 2017) art 112 para 50.

The territorial scope of application of the trading requirement is determined by the general rule of Article 93(1) FinfraG, according to which the obligation covers only counterparties domiciled in Switzerland. Article 114 FinfraG extends this trading duty to cross-border transactions in case the foreign counterparty—if it had its registered office in Switzerland—would be subject to this duty. This rule prevents a drop in the level of protection where the foreign country does not provide for a trading duty. In this sense, Article 114 FinfraG mirrors Article 102, which deals with the clearing of cross-border transactions. Again, this extraterritorial scope does not go as far as that in the EU, which also regulates transactions between two third country counterparties if there is a 'direct, substantial and foreseeable effect' on the EU market.[220] To prevent legal conflicts, Article 111 FinfraV—similar to Article 90 FinfraV concerning trade repositories—exempts cross-border transactions with foreign counterparties having their registered office in a country whose legislation is recognized by FINMA as equivalent and which are not subject to the platform trading requirement under the legislation of that country.

To meet the preconditions of the trading duty, the derivatives trade must be executed either via a trading venue or an operator of an OTF authorized or recognized by FINMA. The recognition of foreign trading venues is regulated in Article 41 and will be discussed later.[221] As there is no provision regarding the recognition of OTFs, Article 110 FinfraV provides that Article 41 FinfraG shall be applied by analogy. However, different from the recognition of trading venues, an 'appropriate regulation and supervision' in the foreign country is not sufficient. Instead, Article 110 FinfraV demands a foreign regulation that is *equivalent* to that of Switzerland. By recognizing a foreign OTF, the trading requirement can also be fulfilled on this facility, although a foreign OTF does, in principle, neither require recognition nor approval.

b) Disclosure of shareholdings

The disclosure of major holdings is governed by Chapter 3 of FinfraG. Parallel to EU law, the disclosure of shareholdings is also structured in two phases, a notification duty of the acquirer (Article 120 FinfraG) and a subsequent duty of the company to inform (Article 124 FinfraG).[222] The notification duty under Article 120(1) FinfraG applies not only to investments in Swiss companies but also to investments in companies with their registered office abroad 'whose equity securities are mainly listed … in Switzerland'. The phrase 'mainly listed', pursuant to the definition in Article 115(1) FinfraV, means that the foreign company must fulfil at least the same duties for its listing and maintenance of its listing on a stock exchange in Switzerland compared to companies having their registered office in Switzerland. This will especially be the case in the event of a primary listing of the foreign company.[223] According to the SIX Swiss

[220] MiFIR, art 28(2); Häusermann and Schott (n 219) art 114 para 19; regarding the extraterritorial effects of the law of the US, the EU, and Switzerland see ibid art 112 paras 20, 36–38, and 54.

[221] See ch 3 B)IV.2.a).

[222] Jutzi (n 56) paras 609ff; Thomas Jutzi and Simon Schären in Rolf Sethe and others (eds), *SK zum FinfraG* (Schulthess 2017) art 124 para 2; critical with regard to the purpose pursued by the disclosure in this context: Christian Schmid, 'Fehlregulierung im schweizerischen Offenlegungsrecht?' (2018) 13 GesKR 194.

[223] Erläuterungsbericht Änderung Börsenverordnung, 2; Jutzi and Schären (n 222) art 124 para 95; Dieter Gericke, 'Von Marktrecht zu Marktsteuerung im Offenlegungs- und Übernahmerecht?' (2013) 8 GesKR 247, 248.

Exchange rules, a primary listing is only required if the company is not already listed on a trading venue recognized as equivalent by the Regulatory Board.[224] This limitation of the extraterritorial scope ensures that foreign companies are only partially subjected to these duties. This, in turn, makes an equivalence provision, as provided for under EU law,[225] less necessary as legal conflicts are much more unlikely. They will mainly arise in cases of two primary listings. As a result, EU and Swiss law achieve a similar result in two different ways: a far-reaching extraterritorial scope of application in combination with an equivalence mechanism on the side of the EU and an a priori limited extraterritorial scope of application on the side of Switzerland.

c) Public takeover offers

The regulation of public takeover offers was governed by the Swiss Stock Exchange Act (BEHG) before it was transferred to FinfraG in the course of the new reform.[226] The scope of the regulation is defined in Art 125(1) FinfraG.[227] It covers target companies with a registered office in Switzerland whose equity securities are at least partly traded on a stock exchange in Switzerland. Included are therefore also target companies whose shares are traded both in Switzerland and abroad, i.e. in cases of dual listings. In addition, the law applies to foreign target companies, i.e. those that are registered abroad but whose equity securities are at least in part mainly listed in Switzerland. Owing to the wide territorial scope, legal conflicts are very likely, which is why the legislator reacted by introducing a conflict avoidance rule in Article 125(2) FinfraG.[228] According to that rule, the Swiss Takeover Board may waive Swiss takeover law if Swiss and foreign law are simultaneously applicable, a legal conflict exists, and investors are protected in an equivalent manner under foreign law. By withdrawing its own law, a legal conflict is thus avoided.[229]

The EU does not have a similar mechanism in its Takeover Directive, even though the general concept of equivalence as a conflict avoidance instrument is well known to the EU, for instance, in Article 37(2) AIFMD.[230] The absence of such an instrument in the Takeover Directive is unfortunate.

[224] Directive on the Listing of Foreign Companies as of 20 June 2019 of SIX Swiss Exchange, art 4; Jutzi and Schären (n 222) art 124 para 96.

[225] Transparency Directive, art 23(1) and (4).

[226] See in detail on the new regime Jutzi (n 56) paras 632ff; on the old regime see Andrea Rüttimann, 'Offenlegung von Beteiligungen nach Art 20 BEHG und Art 31 BEHG sowie von Management-Transaktionen während des öffentlichen Übernahmeverfahrens' (2015) 10 GesKR 28.

[227] See extensively Beat M Barthold and Martina Isler in Rolf Sethe and others (eds), *SK zum FinfraG* (Schulthess 2017) art 125 paras 7ff.

[228] With particular reference to the dual listing scenario: Botschaft BEHG, BBl 2011, 6873, 6900; for a critical view of this broad extraterritorial scope of application already under the old regime of BEHG/BEHV see Gericke (n 223) 247f.

[229] Philippe Weber, Markus Kronauer, and Andrea Huber, 'Die Börsenzulassung in der Schweiz in ihrem rechtlichen und steuerlichen Umfeld' in Mathias Habersack, Peter O Mülbert, and Michael Schlitt (eds), *Unternehmensfinanzierung am Kapitalmarkt* (4th edn, Otto Schmidt 2019) § 44 para 212.

[230] See with regard to AIFMD, art 37(2): ch 1 C)II.3.d)bb)(2); concerning the concept of conflict avoidance instruments see ch 2 C)V.2.

d) *Insider dealing and market manipulation*

For a long time, the prohibition of insider dealing and market manipulation was not part of the supervisory law of Switzerland and was only based on circulars by FINMA that applied exclusively to the institutions it supervised.[231] This changed with the reform of the BEHG in 2013, whose rules on insider dealing and market manipulation were afterwards moved to FinfraG.[232] Consequently, the applicability of the rules is no longer limited to the institutions supervised by FINMA, and the rules cover 'all persons' who violate the prohibitions under Article 145 FinfraG.[233] The applicability is also not dependent on the place where the manipulation takes place as long as it impacts securities admitted to Swiss trading venues.[234] The Swiss law on insider dealing and market manipulation thus has a broad extraterritorial scope of application, similar to the MAR in the EU. With the exception of the special regime concerning central banks and public institutions,[235] there are no exemptions for foreign actors. Therefore, there is neither a general mechanism of deference in the MAR of the EU nor in the Swiss FinfraG.

2. Financial market infrastructures

All financial market infrastructures are regulated holistically under FinfraG in Switzerland. The title on market infrastructures (Title 2) is divided into a chapter applicable to all financial market infrastructures (Chapter 1: Common provisions) and chapters dealing with particular types of market infrastructures. This structure, known in Germany as *Klammertechnik*, greatly facilitates the comprehensibility of the law by avoiding unnecessary repetitions.[236]

The first section of chapter 1 sets out authorization conditions and duties applicable to all market infrastructures. Pursuant to Article 4(1) FinfraG, each financial market infrastructure requires authorization from FINMA.[237] This already is a big innovation for Swiss financial markets law, as prior to the reform, central counterparties, central securities depositories, and payment systems were supervised in specific cases only, and trade repositories were not supervised at all.[238] FinfraG generally applies solely to those infrastructures domiciled in Switzerland.[239] However, FinfraG is not limited

[231] FINMA, 'Circ. 2008/38—Market conduct rules' (20 November 2008); see Rolf Sethe and Lukas Fahrländer in Rolf Sethe and others (eds), *SK zum FinfraG* (Schulthess 2017) Vor art 142 paras 5–7 and 11–12.

[232] On the new regime see Jutzi (n 56) paras 667ff; Marc Hanslin, 'Marktmanipulation nach Art 143 FinfraG' (2016) 11 GesKR 45; concerning the old regime under the BEHG see Wolfgang Wohlers, 'Die neue Insiderstrafnorm' (2013) 8 GesKR 345.

[233] Jutzi and Schären (n 222) art 145 para 2. For a view that includes foreign institutions see Benedikt Maurenbrecher and Marc Hanslin in Rolf Watter and Rashid Bahar (eds), *BSK-FINMAG/FinfraG* (3rd edn, Helbing Lichtenhahn 2019) FinfraG, art 145 para 6.

[234] Sethe and Fahrländer (n 231) Vor art 142 para 99; Vogel, Heiz, and Luthiger (n 210) FinfraG, art 142 para 10.

[235] See ch 3 B)V.

[236] See eg the many provisions in EU law setting out obligations to register for different service providers and products. FinfraG manages this duty in just its art 4(1). See Sethe (n 20) Einleitung para 9.

[237] Although this obligation is restricted for payment systems in FinfraG, art 4(2). A good overview of the duties imposed on market infrastructures can be found in René Bösch and Stefan Kramer, 'Schweizer Finanzmarktrecht im Umbruch—Das Finanzmarktinfrastrukturgesetz als eine der neuen Säulen' (2014) 110 SJZ 249, 255f.

[238] Sethe (n 20) Einleitung para 73.

[239] Vogel, Heiz, and Luthiger (n 210) FinfraG, art 4 para 3; Sethe (n 20) Einleitung para 83.

to purely domestic situations. There are, for example, rules specifically applying to the cross-border activities of Swiss market infrastructures. To give an example, Article 17(a) FinfraG establishes the obligation to notify FINMA if a Swiss market infrastructure intends to establish, acquire, or close a foreign subsidiary, branch, or representative office.

In addition, there are several provisions dealing with the business of foreign market infrastructures in Switzerland, which will be examined in detail below. Sometimes foreign market infrastructures must be recognized; other times, they are even supervised by the Swiss National Bank if they are of systemic importance.[240]

The regulation of systemically important financial market infrastructures in the second section of Chapter 1 is also in line with the *Klammertechnik*. Since the legislator considered some infrastructures a priori as not systemically relevant, the regulation applies only to central counterparties, central securities depositories and payment systems.[241] For this reason, it is more advanced than the EU system, which does not holistically regulate the phenomenon of systemic relevance but deals with the issue separately for each infrastructure.[242] Another key difference between the two legal systems is that Swiss law imposes additional requirements on systemically important market infrastructures regardless of their location, whereas the system of the EU contains special regimes for systemically important infrastructures located in third countries only.

a) Trading venues and organized trading facilities

Chapter 2 FinfraG sets out specific rules applicable to trading venues (Section 1) and organized trading facilities (Section 2). The term trading venue covers both exchanges and multilateral trading facilities (MTFs) but not organized trading facilities (OTFs).[243] With regard to terminology, particular care is required, as the meaning of the terms MTF and OTF differs slightly between MiFIR/MiFID II and FinfraG.[244] OTFs, for instance, are always multilateral systems under MiFID II but can be bilateral systems under FinfraG. Such bilateral systems would be classified as systematic internalizers under EU law.

Even after the reform, Switzerland, contrary to the international trend, counts on self-regulation in the context of trading venues.[245] However, this self-regulation takes place under FINMA supervision and with some guard rails.[246]

[240] See eg National Bank Act, arts 41, 60, and 80, as well as art 19(2); Christoph Winzeler in Rolf Watter and Rashid Bahar (eds), *BSK-FINMAG/FinfraG* (3rd edn, Helbing Lichtenhahn 2019) FinfraG, art 4 para 6.

[241] The legislator justified this primarily with the lack of a counterparty risk as well as the substitutability of these infrastructures. See Botschaft FinfraG, BBl 2014, 7483, 7524; Hans Kuhn in Rolf Sethe and others (eds), *SK zum FinfraG* (Schulthess 2017) art 22 para 2.

[242] See eg EMIR, art 25(2)(e), which only covers systemically important CCPs.

[243] Critical in this respect because of terminological differences compared to EU law are Ansgar Schott and Markus Winkler in Rolf Sethe and others (eds), *SK zum FinfraG* (Schulthess 2017) art 26 paras 17ff.

[244] See extensively Simon Schären, Günther Dobrauz-Saldapenna, and Martin Liebi, 'Organisierte Handelssysteme im neuen FinfraG—Versuch einer regulatorischen Kategorisierung' (2016) 88 SZW 194, 194ff; see also Favre and Kramer (n 189) art 42 paras 5–17.

[245] See FinfraG, art 27; Schott and Winkler (n 243) art 27 paras 9ff.

[246] Daniel Daeniker and Stefan Waller in Rolf Watter and Rashid Bahar (eds), *BSK-FINMAG/FinfraG* (3rd edn, Helbing Lichtenhahn 2019) FinfraG, art 27 paras 14f.

aa) Authorization of foreign participants taking part in Swiss trading venues Article 34 FinfraG demands that trading venues, as part of their self-regulation, issue regulations on the admission, duties, and exclusion of participants. Foreign participants, also called remote members,[247] shall only be admitted to trading if FINMA authorizes them in accordance with Article 40 FinfraG.[248] Pursuant to this provision, FINMA must grant authorization to a foreign participant if the requirements of lit a) to d) and paragraph 2 are met. Hence, foreign participants have a right to be authorized by FINMA, but they do not have a right to be admitted by the trading venue.[249]

First, the foreign participant must be subject to appropriate regulation and supervision (lit a)). Before the reform, Article 53 Swiss Stock Exchange Ordinance (BEHV), which is no longer in force, only demanded appropriate supervision. The inclusion of an appropriate regulation adjusts the Swiss regulation to international standards, in particular to that of the EU, which always demands both.[250] Contrary to equivalence in the EU, the requirement of an *appropriate* and not equivalent regulation and supervision is used. This is not a coincidence because the Swiss legislator differentiates precisely between the terms appropriate and equivalent.[251] The notion of appropriateness is neither specified in ordinances nor the *Botschaft*. Unlike the term equivalence, the term appropriate does not have a fixed point of reference. Whether a regulatory and supervisory system is appropriate can be determined without a legal comparison to a particular, in this case, the Swiss legal system. Rather, comparisons must be made to different countries and their approaches as well as to international standards.[252] If foreign regulation and supervision fulfil international standards, it is generally to be regarded as appropriate, as the Swiss legislator attributes great importance to those standards, specifically within FinfraG.[253] As a result, the concept of appropriateness is less self-centred than equivalence in that it does not only refer to one's own system. Also, the required standard is less strict than that of equivalence. Ultimately, the concept of appropriateness is more liberal-minded.

Secondly, the foreign participant needs to observe a code of conduct and record-keeping as well as reporting duties, which are *equivalent* to the duties set out in Swiss regulations. In FINMA's opinion, a brief tabular comparison of the relevant provisions applicable in the country of domicile must be submitted for this purpose.[254] This description indicates a practical, principle- and outcome-based analysis similar to the

[247] Botschaft FinfraG, BBl 2014, 7483, 7537.

[248] See FinfraG, art 34(2)(c).

[249] Benjamin Leisinger in Rolf Sethe and others (eds), *SK zum FinfraG* (Schulthess 2017) art 40 paras 5ff.

[250] Botschaft FinfraG, BBl 2014, 7483, 7538; see eg MiFIR, art 28(4); Daniel Flühmann in Rolf Watter and Rashid Bahar (eds), *BSK-FINMAG/FinfraG* (3rd edn, Helbing Lichtenhahn 2019) FinfraG, art 40 para 13.

[251] See eg FinfraG, art 40(1)(b); for a consenting view see Vogel, Heiz, and Luthiger (n 210) FinfraG, art 40 para 2; Leisinger (n 249) art 40 para 11.

[252] There is a similar description in Simon Schären in Rolf Sethe and others (eds), *SK zum FinfraG* (Schulthess 2017) art 60 paras 20f.

[253] See Sethe (n 20) Einleitung para 71. The phrase 'international standards' is included 14 times in FinfraG alone.

[254] FINMA, 'Guidelines on Submitting Applications for Authorisation as a Foreign Participant (Remote Member)' (29 October 2018) 2 https://finma.ch/de/~/media/finma/dokumente/dokumentencenter/myfinma/1bewilligung/wl-remote-members.pdf?la=de (accessed 12 November 2022).

one under Article 95 FinfraG.[255] For reasons of systematic coherence, a parallel interpretation is also preferable, especially since there is no evidence of a divergent meaning.

Thirdly, it must be ensured that the activities are separated from the activities of any authorized Swiss entity. This obligation was introduced to prevent remote access from being used to circumvent the strict conditions for the authorization of a branch.[256]

Fourthly, the foreign supervisory authority in question must not have objected to the participant's activity in Switzerland and must render administrative assistance. The first part is a recurring element of Swiss deference provisions but is alien to EU law.[257] The second criterion is familiar to many EU equivalence mechanisms, which require a cooperation agreement to ensure effective administrative assistance.[258]

Finally, FINMA may refuse authorization if the state in which the foreign participant is established does not grant Swiss participants actual access to its markets or offer them the same competitive opportunities as those granted to domestic trading participants.[259] This prerequisite is the reciprocity principle provided for in many EU equivalence mechanisms. Contrary to EU law, Swiss law stipulates that no reciprocity is required if this is incompatible with international agreements, in particular the GATS. Switzerland regards the condition of reciprocal treatment as an exception to the MFN principle, which is why it initially included it in its list of Article II (MFN) Exemptions.[260] Under the Fifth Protocol to the GATS, Switzerland, like many other countries, including the EU, explicitly waived this exception.[261] Whether the requirement of reciprocity constitutes an exception to the MFN principle, however, is doubtful, as has been shown above.[262] In fact, the requirement is not an exception to MFN treatment and is in any case justified by the prudential carve-out. If one were to see it differently, the reciprocity requirement in the EU would also be a violation of the GATS.

bb) Recognition of foreign trading venues Article 41 FinfraG deals with the reverse scenario of foreign trading venues allowing Swiss participants supervised by FINMA direct access to their facilities. This provision has far-reaching extraterritorial effects, as one Swiss participant is sufficient to trigger the recognition obligation for foreign trading venues.[263] Recognition, however, is not followed by FINMA

[255] See ch 3 B)IV.1.a)aa).

[256] Leisinger (n 249) art 40 para 19.

[257] See eg FinfraG, arts 41(2)(b) no 1, 60(2)(b) no 1, and 80(2)(b) no 1; see also FINIG, arts 53(b) no 1 and 59(1)(b) and Foreign Banks Ordinance-FINMA, arts 4(1)(c) and 14(b).

[258] See eg EMIR, art 25(7); MiFIR, art 47(2); CRA Regulation, art 5(7).

[259] FinfraG, art 40(2).

[260] Switzerland, 'Final List of Article II (MFN) Exemptions' (GATS/EL/83) (15 April 1994) in the section on 'Banking and other financial services (excluding insurance)'.

[261] Botschaft WTO/GATS, BBl 3460, 3465; see Flühmann (n 250) FinfraG, art 40 para 31; extensively: Juliane Kokott, 'Liberalisierung der Finanzdienstleistungen im Rahmen der WTO—Auswirkungen auf Deutschland, Österreich und die Schweiz' (2000) 8 RIW 402.

[262] See ch 2 A)I.4.

[263] Verordnung über die Anerkennung ausländischer Handelsplätze für den Handel mit Beteiligungspapieren von Gesellschaften mit Sitz in der Schweiz vom 30 November 2018, art 1; critical

supervision. There is no such obligation at the EU level, but it is foreseen in some national regulations.[264]

The requirements for the recognition in Article 41 FinfraG are akin to those under Article 40 FinfraG. Again, appropriate regulation and supervision must be in place.[265] The foreign authority must not have any objections to the cross-border activity of the foreign trading venue and administrative assistance must be provided. In addition, FINMA may refuse to recognize foreign trading venues where no reciprocal treatment is guaranteed (paragraph 4).

Different from the authorization of foreign participants, the foreign authority must guarantee that they will inform FINMA if they detect violations of the law or other irregularities on the part of Swiss participants.[266] This obligation enables FINMA to exercise its supervision adequately, as FINMA will often be unable to detect violations on foreign trading venues without the foreign authority's notification. Such violations may damage the reputation of Switzerland as a financial centre.[267] Furthermore, the recognition of foreign trading venues, unlike the authorization of foreign participants, does not require equivalence.

The decisive difference in comparison to the authorization of foreign participants is that the recognition of foreign trading venues provides for a presumption of recognition in Article 41(3) FinfraG if FINMA finds that the state in which the trading venue is domiciled regulates and supervises its trading venues appropriately and the requirements with regard to supervisory cooperation—paragraph 2 lit b)—are met.[268] The presumption refers to all trading venues situated in the state and, contrary to the recognition in paragraph 2, does not work on an individual basis.[269] This presumption marks the liberal counterpart to the extensive extraterritorial application of the law.

cc) **Organized trading facilities** OTFs are not considered financial market infrastructures in the sense of Article 2(a) FinfraG. They, therefore, do not fall under the scope of the duty to obtain authorization pursuant to Article 4(1) FinfraG. Nevertheless, Article 43(1) sets out that anyone who operates an OTF 'requires authorization as a bank, securities dealer or DLT trading facility, or authorization or recognition as a trading venue', which is why at least an indirect duty to obtain authorization/recognition exists.[270]

already with regard to the old legal regime were Daniel Daeniker and Stefan Waller in Rolf Watter and Nedim P Vogt (eds), *BSK-BörsenG/FINMAG* (2nd edn, Helbing Lichtenhahn 2011) art 3 para 19.

264 Securities Trading Act (WpHG), § 102 in Germany and General Regulation of the Autorité des Marchés Financiers, art 513-3 (17 December 2016) in France; concerning the background of the German regulation in Jan von Hein in Eberhard Schwark and Daniel Zimmer (eds), *Kapitalmarktrechts-Kommentar* (5th edn, CH Beck 2020) WpHG, § 102 paras 1ff.

265 See extensively on this criterion Flühmann (n 250) FinfraG, art 41 paras 18ff.

266 FinfraG, art 41(2)(b) no 2.

267 Leisinger (n 249) art 41 para 21.

268 Vogel, Heiz, and Luthiger (n 210) FinfraG, art 41 para 8.

269 Flühmann (n 250) FinfraG, art 41 para 28.

270 Nobel (n 4) § 8 para 63.

This indirect duty applies only to OTFs operated from Switzerland.[271] Consequently, foreign OTFs do not need to be authorized or recognized.[272] Likewise, they are not subject to recognition proceedings under Article 41(1) FinfraG if they admit Swiss participants supervised by FINMA to trading. The same applies to foreign participants wishing to participate on Swiss OTFs. As Swiss OTFs are not considered trading venues, the duty of authorization in Article 40 FinfraG does not apply.[273] None of this, however, excludes voluntary recognition, which is necessary for the fulfilment of the trading obligation under Articles 112ff FinfraG. In cases of such recognition, Article 41 FinfraG is applied by analogy.[274]

Under MiFID II, the operation of an OTF inside the EU qualifies as an investment service subject to authorization.[275] Third country operators of OTFs, which are thus considered third country investment firms, must also obtain authorization if they grant EU clients access to their trading facility. Hence, the EU third country regimes dealing with third country investment firms apply: this includes the general regime of Articles 39ff MiFID II and, in relation to per se professional clients and eligible counterparties, the equivalence mechanism of Articles 46ff MiFIR. As a result, the EU regime is stricter than the Swiss approach, as granting access to EU clients is already sufficient to trigger regulation in the EU.[276]

b) Central counterparties

aa) Recognition of foreign CCPs The duty for CCPs to obtain authorization applies only to Swiss CCPs. A Swiss CCP is defined as a legal entity under Swiss law having its registered office and head office in Switzerland.[277] Additionally, it must be effectively managed from Switzerland.[278] *E contrario*, a foreign CCP is understood as a CCP having its registered and head office as well as its effective management outside of Switzerland.[279] Those foreign CCPs must obtain FINMA recognition pursuant to Article 60(1) FinfraG if they grant supervised Swiss participants direct access to their facilities (lit a)), provide services for Swiss financial market infrastructures (lit b)) or

[271] It is discussed whether the operation from Switzerland also requires a minimum presence of technical equipment in Switzerland or whether participants from Switzerland must be involved to trigger this indirect obligation. See Favre and Kramer (n 189) art 43 para 8.

[272] FINMA, 'Guidelines on Submitting Applications for Recognition of Foreign Trading Venues under Article 41 FMIA' (22 October 2020) 4 https://finma.ch/en/~/media/finma/dokumente/dokumentencenter/myfinma/1bewilligung/wl-boersen-ausl-d.pdf?la=en (accessed 12 November 2022); FINMA, 'Guidance 01/2016—Financial Market Infrastructure Act: FINMA's Next Steps' (6 July 2016) 9 https://www.finma.ch/en/~/media/finma/dokumente/dokumentencenter/myfinma/4dokumentation/finma-aufsichtsmitteilungen/20160707-finma-aufsichtsmitteilung-01-2016.pdf?la=en (accessed 12 November 2022).

[273] Consenting: Favre and Kramer (n 189) art 43 para 13.

[274] FinfraV, art 110; see ch 3 B)IV.1.a)ee).

[275] MiFID II, Annex I, s A, no (9) and art 5(1).

[276] Favre and Kramer (n 189) art 43 para 11.

[277] FinfraG, art 8(1); Winzeler (n 240) FinfraG, art 8 paras 2ff.

[278] FinfraV, art 7(1). The additional element is included because effective supervision is only feasible where the management is carried out from Switzerland. See Erläuterungsbericht FinfraV, 10.

[279] Schären (n 252) art 60 para 7. CCPs that have their registered office outside Switzerland but are actually managed from Switzerland are treated like Swiss CCPs and are not eligible for authorization. The same applies to CCPs having their registered office in Switzerland but which are managed from abroad. See Rashid

enter into interoperability agreements with Swiss CCPs (lit c)). Conversely, interoperability agreements are only approved by FINMA if the foreign CCP is recognized.[280]

Recognition by FINMA is subject to similar requirements as the recognition of foreign trading venues under Article 41 FinfraG. Again, the foreign regulation and supervision must be appropriate (lit a)), making recognition more liberal than the equivalence mechanism in Article 25 EMIR of the EU.[281] Recognition by FINMA also demands cooperation between supervisory authorities (lit b)) and reciprocity.[282] Unlike the recognition of trading venues, recognition of CCPs can only be granted on an individual basis.[283] Against the background that the legislator wanted to harmonize the regulation of market infrastructures, it can be assumed that the terminology is to be interpreted in the same way as in Article 41 FinfraG.[284]

In exceptional cases, FINMA may also exempt foreign CCPs from the obligation to obtain recognition if this does not adversely affect the protective purpose of FinfraG (Article 60(4) FinfraG). One use case of the exemption could be a CCP that only clears very small volumes.[285] This rule is the institutional counterpart to Article 97(5) FinfraG. According to this provision, FINMA may allow clearing by non-recognized foreign CCPs in exceptional cases where the recognition procedure is too burdensome compared to the trading volume.[286]

bb) Systemically important CCPs Since the GFC, the notion of systemic risk has gained in importance. Potential contagion effects resulting from the failure of individual institutions have been monitored much more closely ever since.[287] This development is reflected in the increased regulation of systemically important institutions, such as CCPs.[288]

In Switzerland, Article 22 FinfraG defines the conditions under which CCPs, central securities depositories and payment systems—irrespective of their domicile—are to be seen as systemically important, with paragraph 1 referring to the institution itself and paragraph 2 to the business process. First, these institutions are classified as systemically important if their non-availability can lead to serious losses, liquidity shortfalls, operational problems for financial intermediaries or other financial market infrastructures or can cause serious disruptions on financial markets. Secondly, systemic importance is given if a critical situation of one participant can spill over to other participants of the institution and lead to the same consequences. In both cases,

Bahar in Rolf Watter and Rashid Bahar (eds), *BSK-FINMAG/FinfraG* (3rd edn, Helbing Lichtenhahn 2019) FinfraG, art 60 para 3.

[280] FinfraG, art 57(2)(d).

[281] See EMIR, art 25(6)(a); see on the differences in meaning between appropriateness and equivalence ch 3 B)IV.2.a)aa).

[282] The caveat in paragraph 3 that reciprocity is only required in cases not involving world trade law is, as seen above, unjustified. See ch 3 B)IV.2.a)aa).

[283] Vogel, Heiz, and Luthiger (n 210) FinfraG, art 60 para 6.

[284] Botschaft FinfraG, BBl 2014, 7483, 7484; Flühmann (n 250) FinfraG, art 40 para 14.

[285] Botschaft FinfraG, BBl 2014, 7483, 7548.

[286] FinfraG, art 97(5); Patrick Hünerwadel in Rolf Watter and Rashid Bahar (eds), *BSK-FINMAG/FinfraG* (3rd edn, Helbing Lichtenhahn 2019) FinfraG, art 97 para 41.

[287] On the risks of CCPs see Beat Brändli, 'Die aufsichtsrechtliche Erfassung der Zentralen Gegenpartei im schweizerischen Kapitalmarkt' (2011) 83 SZW 2, 11f.

[288] With regard to FinfraG see Nobel (n 4) § 8 paras 36ff.

it must be assessed whether a hypothetical negative event can trigger further negative consequences. As this is a rather abstract task, the National Bank has established criteria to specify further factors which need to be considered.[289] These include the type of transactions cleared or settled, the transaction volumes and amounts, the currencies in which the transactions are cleared or settled, the participants, interdependencies, and substitutability.

The EU also recently adopted a special regime for systemically important CCPs in EMIR 2.2, in which the EU distinguishes between Tier 1 and Tier 2 CCPs, with the latter being defined as systemically important.[290] In contrast to Swiss law, this regime applies only to third country CCPs. Also, ESMA does not have to establish a hypothetical causality but can directly refer to various criteria set out in Article 25(2a) EMIR.[291] These criteria are almost identical to the criteria established by the Swiss National Bank, which is why the results are likely to be similar.

Following a classification as systemically important by the Swiss National Bank, market infrastructures must meet special requirements (Art 23 FinfraG), which are further specified in Section 2 of Chapter 4 of the National Bank Ordinance, and draw up a recovery plan in accordance with Article 24 FinfraG.[292] The supervision of systemically important infrastructures is exercised by the Swiss National Bank and is not limited to infrastructures domiciled in Switzerland but extends to infrastructures domiciled abroad if their activities have a substantial influence on the Swiss system.[293] To avoid regulatory and supervisory conflicts, foreign infrastructures may be exempted from compliance with the special requirements as well as the drawing up of a recovery plan pursuant to Article 23(4) FinfraG if they are subject to equivalent supervision and oversight (lit a)) and if the competent authorities cooperate with the Swiss National Bank, which is usually ensured by the conclusion of an MoU (lit b)).[294] Hence, the *appropriateness* of foreign regulation and supervision, as demanded for the recognition of foreign CCPs, is no longer sufficient. Instead, the foreign regulation and supervision must be *equivalent*. According to Swiss scholars, equivalence is fulfilled if the foreign legal order is based on the Principles for Financial Market Infrastructures (PFMI) of IOSCO.[295]

The equivalence mechanism of the EU in Article 25 EMIR is stricter in relation to systemically important CCPs from third countries. It is no longer sufficient for these Tier 2 CCPs to be regulated and supervised in an equivalent manner. They must additionally fulfil the requirements provided for in paragraph 2b. Inter alia, the third country CCP must obey many rules of EMIR unless it already complies with

[289] National Bank Ordinance, art 20; Vogel, Heiz, and Luthiger (n 210) FinfraG, art 22 paras 3ff; Martin Peyer in Rolf Watter and Rashid Bahar (eds), *BSK-FINMAG/FinfraG* (3rd edn, Helbing Lichtenhahn 2019) FinfraG, art 22 paras 29ff.

[290] Patrick Scholl, Marcel Hörauf, and Alexei Döhl, 'Derivateregulierung in EMIR—Umsetzung und Weiterentwicklung in der Praxis' (2019) 9 RdF 276, 282f.

[291] The criteria are further specified in Commission Delegated Regulation (EU) 2020/1303 of 14 July 2020; Sebastian Steuer, 'EMIR 2.2 und die Aufsicht über systemrelevante Drittstaaten-CCPs' (2021) 21 BKR 272, 274f.

[292] On the legal consequences see Peyer (n 289) FinfraG, art 22 paras 43f.

[293] National Bank Act, art 19(2).

[294] As regards the MoU and the extension to art 24 see Botschaft FinfraG, BBl 2014, 7483,7527.

[295] Kuhn (n 241) art 23 para 52.

comparable requirements in its home country.[296] If the Tier 2 CCP is of increased systemic importance, ESMA and the European Commission may even deny recognition altogether.[297]

All in all, Switzerland has created a special regime for all systemically important CCPs and not just for foreign CCPs like the EU. Switzerland only requires an equivalence assessment and thus sets lower obstacles for market access of systemically important CCPs than the EU, which imposes requirements that go beyond equivalence and, in some cases, even exclude recognition completely.

c) Central securities depositories

The term 'central securities depository' (CSD) and the comprehensive authorization requirement have been newly introduced to FinfraG following the example of the EU.[298] Although the definitions of CSDs in Swiss and EU law are similar, they are not identical.[299] The provision of settlement services as defined in Section A no 3 of the Annex of the EU CSDR, for example, is a constituent feature of a CSD under EU law, whereas in Switzerland the provision of settlement services is sufficient but not necessary to qualify as a CSD.

Different from the regulation of trading venues, CCPs and trade repositories, there is no recognition provision included in FinfraG with regard to foreign CSDs. Consequently, foreign CSDs may provide services to Swiss participants without being regulated or supervised in Switzerland.[300] In this respect, Swiss regulation is again more liberal than EU regulation, which requires an equivalence decision—at least for core services and the setting up of a branch—by the European Commission for this purpose.[301]

This—from Switzerland's point of view—unregulated provision of services has its limits with systemically important CSDs. Such systemically important CSDs are supervised by the Swiss National Bank and must fulfil additional requirements.[302] However, the Swiss National Bank may waive these obligations if the CSD is subject to equivalent supervision as well as oversight and supervisory cooperation is ensured.[303]

[296] So-called comparable compliance as laid down in EMIR, art 25a; Matthias Lehmann, 'CCP Supervision after Brexit' (2023) 18 CMLR 5, 24–25.

[297] EMIR, art 25(2c); referring to these CCPs as 'Tier 2 plus CCPs' see Lehmann (n 296) 22–24; Matthias Lehmann, 'Derivateclearing post-Brexit' (2021) 33 ZBB/JBB 177, 186.

[298] Botschaft FinfraG, BBl 2014, 7483, 7548; concerning the authorization requirement see FinfraG, art 4(1) and art 2(a)(4); Sarah Jungo, Oliver Zibung, and Daniel Roth in Rolf Sethe and others (eds), *SK zum FinfraG* (Schulthess 2017) art 4 para 6.

[299] See on similarities and differences Renato Costantini in Rolf Sethe and others (eds), *SK zum FinfraG* (Schulthess 2017) art 61 paras 43ff.

[300] This follows from the fact that the authorization requirement under art 4(1) FinfraG applies only to market infrastructures having its registered and head office in Switzerland pursuant to art 8(1) FinfraG. Therefore, foreign infrastructures may provide services to Swiss participants without a licence if there is no special recognition requirement along the lines of arts 41, 60, and 80 FinfraG. For CSDs such a recognition requirement does not exist. See Jungo, Zibung, and Roth (n 298) art 4 para 14 and art 8 para 8; misleading in this respect is Costantini (n 299) art 61 para 89.

[301] CSDR, art 25(2); see ch 1 C)II.4.c).

[302] See FinfraG, arts 22(1) and 23(1) as well as National Bank Act, art 19(2); see also Costantini (n 299) art 61 para 91.

[303] FinfraG, art 23(4); Patrick Schleiffer and Patrick Schärli in Rolf Watter and Rashid Bahar (eds), *BSK-FINMAG/FinfraG* (3rd edn, Helbing Lichtenhahn 2019) FinfraG, art 61 para 33.

Following an equivalence determination, even systemically important CSDs from other countries are exempted from Swiss regulation.[304]

d) Trade repositories

Where the reporting obligation pursuant to Article 104 FinfraG applies, it can only be fulfilled with a trade repository authorized in Switzerland or a recognized foreign trade repository. The recognition of foreign trade repositories is provided for in Article 80 FinfraG. The requirements are formulated almost identically to the recognition of foreign trading venues. In particular, the foreign trade repository must be subject to appropriate, but not equivalent, regulation and supervision. Likewise, Article 80 FinfraG contains two options for recognition: a recognition of individual trade repositories in paragraph 2 and a presumption of recognition valid for all trade repositories from a respective state in paragraph 3.[305] In light of the fact that the legislator wanted to harmonize the regulation of market infrastructures, it can be assumed that the terminology is to be interpreted in the same way as in Articles 41 and 60 FinfraG.[306] According to Article 22(1) FinfraG, trade repositories cannot be of systemic importance, which is why there is no special regime for them. The EU offers a similar recognition procedure in Articles 77(1) and 75(1) EMIR but requires an equivalent instead of an appropriate regulation of third country trade repositories.

e) Payment systems

A payment system is defined in Article 81 as an 'entity that clears and settles payment obligations based on uniform rules and procedures'. Payment systems are regarded as market infrastructures that generally require authorization by FINMA if they have their registered office in Switzerland.[307] However, Article 4(2) FinfraG restricts this duty for payment systems to situations in which an authorization is necessary for the proper functioning of the financial market or the protection of financial market participants and where the payment system is not operated by a bank, as an additional authorization is superfluous in that scenario.

As the chapter on payment systems does not address foreign payment systems, they do not fall under the scope of FinfraG, even if they provide services to Swiss clients.[308] In light of the fact that there are numerous and very different types of payment systems, recognition would also be very cumbersome. This absence of regulation could be perceived as a systemic threat to the Swiss financial market. However, if foreign payment systems are of systemic importance, they can also be supervised by the Swiss National Bank and are thus subject to FinfraG.[309] Excluded from this supervision are

[304] See extensively on the general mechanism concerning systemically important infrastructures in the context of CCPs: ch 3 B)IV.2.b)bb).

[305] The presumption is known from the recognition of foreign trading venues in art 41(3) FinfraG but alien to the recognition of foreign CCPs in accordance with art 60 FinfraG.

[306] Botschaft FinfraG, BBl 2014, 7483, 7484; Flühmann (n 250) FinfraG, art 40 para 14.

[307] See FinfraG, arts 4(1), 8(1), and 2(a) no 6; Daniel Flühmann, Peter Ch Hsu, and Tiffany Ender, 'Regulation of Electronic Payment Service Providers in Switzerland' (2017) 12 GesKR 5, 7.

[308] Flühmann, Ch Hsu, and Ender (n 307) 7.

[309] FinfraG, art 22(1); Martin Hess, André Kalbermatter, and Alexandra V Weiss in Rolf Sethe and others (eds), *SK zum FinfraG* (Schulthess 2017) art 81 para 41.

payment systems whose home country ensures equivalent supervision and oversight and whose authorities cooperate with the Swiss National Bank (Article 23(4) FinfraG).

The PSD II of the EU is not institution-based but service-based. The focus is on payment services and not on payment systems like in Switzerland.[310] The Directive requires that institutions offering payment services in the Union obtain authorization. It does not include an equivalence mechanism.[311]

V. Exemptions for central banks and public bodies of foreign countries

Like the EU, Switzerland exempts its National Bank and other public bodies from numerous obligations that normally apply to all other financial market players. In relation to derivatives trading, Article 94 FinfraG exempts the Swiss National Bank, other Swiss public bodies, and the Bank for International Settlement from the regulation.[312] The exemption under Swiss law is extended to foreign central banks, the ECB, the European Stability Mechanism, and others, except for the reporting duty.[313] However, exemptions from the reporting duty are also possible, provided reciprocity is granted.[314]

Comparable to the safe harbour rule under Article 6(5) MAR in the EU is Article 127(2) FinfraV. This provision exempts foreign central banks and public authorities, including EU Member States' central banks and the ECB, from the prohibition of exploiting inside information and market manipulation (Articles 142 and 143 FinfraG). The exemption applies if the transaction serves public tasks, reciprocity is guaranteed, and the transaction does not conflict with the legislative purpose.[315] Moreover, both legal systems exempt (foreign) central banks and public bodies from pre- and post-trade requirements. The counterpart to Article 1(9) MiFIR in this respect is Article 29 FinfraV.[316] Exceptions for foreign central banks and public bodies are granted if the transaction serves public tasks, reciprocity is ensured, and the transaction does not conflict with the legislative purpose.[317] Unlike EU law, which often requires a comparative analysis before an exemption is granted, the exemptions under Swiss law are not based on a qualitative assessment of the foreign legal system. The exemptions in Swiss law are thus not based on the idea of deference, as defined in this book.

[310] Hess, Kalbermatter, and Weiss (n 309) art 81 paras 53ff.

[311] Fahrländer (n 8) 231; see ch 1 C)II.3.b)cc).

[312] The parallel provision in the EU is EMIR, art 1(4).

[313] FinfraV, art 79(1); see EMIR, art 1(6) as the counterpart in EU law; Bahar (n 279) FinfraG, art 94 para 5; Bahar (n 190) 484f.

[314] FinfraV, art 79(2); Favre and Kramer (n 189) art 94 para 31.

[315] Sethe and Fahrländer (n 231) Vor art 142 paras 45f.

[316] Urs Kägi in Rolf Watter and Rashid Bahar (eds), *BSK-FINMAG/FinfraG* (3rd edn, Helbing Lichtenhah 2019) FinfraG, art 29 para 26.

[317] FinfraV, art 29(2) thus imposes the same requirements as FrinfraV, art 127(2).

C) The Swiss system of market access

From the above examination of the system of treatment of foreign service providers, distinctive characteristics of Swiss financial markets law in this area can now be derived. First, three features of financial markets law are identified that significantly influence market access for foreign market participants (I.). Secondly, common features of Swiss deference mechanisms are analysed (II.).

I. Characteristics of Swiss financial markets law

In terms of the regulation of market access for foreign service providers, three characteristics stand out. First, Switzerland does not apply its laws extraterritorially to the same extent as the EU or the US, making the Swiss system more liberal (1.). Secondly, self-regulation still plays an important role in Switzerland, and the risk of overregulation is countered more vigorously than in other jurisdictions (2.). Finally, Swiss regulation is principle-based and, therefore, significantly shorter, more comprehensible, and easier to apply (3.).

1. Less extraterritorial application of the law

Increasing globalization has led to a far-reaching integration of national financial markets. These markets are interconnected in so many ways that effects and risks no longer stop at national borders but spread across markets.[318] In the absence of a global regulator, states have expanded the scope of their regulation to areas outside their national territory. This phenomenon could be characterized as the denationalization or deterritorialization of regulation.[319]

A prime example of the expansive extraterritorial application of law in the wake of the GFC is the field of derivatives regulation.[320] Under section 2(i) of the US Commodity Exchange Act, the provisions relating to swaps apply to activities outside the US if they '(1) have a direct and significant connection with activities in, or effect on, commerce of the United States; or (2) contravene such rules or regulations as the Commission may prescribe or promulgate'.[321] The situation is similar in the EU, where EMIR's clearing obligation applies to transactions between two counterparties domiciled in third countries 'that would be subject to the clearing obligation if they were established in the Union, provided that the contract has a direct, substantial and

[318] Steven L Schwarcz, 'Systemic Risk' (2008) 97 George LJ 193, 243.

[319] Christoph B Bühler, 'Finanzmarktregulierung im Spannungsfeld von Recht und Politik' (2010) 106 SJZ 469, 476; Matthias Lehmann, 'Legal Fragmentation, Extraterritoriality and Uncertainty in Global Financial Regulation' (2017) 37 OJLS 406; more generally on extraterritoriality see Matthias Lehmann, 'New challenges of extraterritoriality: superposing laws' in Franco Ferrari and Diego P Fernández Arroyo (eds), *Private International Law* (Edward Elgar Publishing 2019) 258ff.

[320] John C Coffee Jr, 'Extraterritorial Financial Regulation: Why E.T. Can't Come Home' (2014) 99 Cornell L Rev 1259; Fabien Carruzzo in Rolf Sethe and others (eds), *SK zum FinfraG* (Schulthess 2017) Vor art 93 paras 284ff.

[321] 7 USC § 2(i).

foreseeable effect within the Union or where such an obligation is necessary or appropriate to prevent the evasion of any provisions of this Regulation'.[322]

As a general rule, Switzerland has resisted this trend and, at least in comparison to other jurisdictions such as the EU and especially the US, follows a rather strict territorial approach. The territorial scope of the Swiss clearing requirement, for instance, is limited to transactions where at least one party is domiciled in Switzerland.[323] In the case of cross-border transactions between a Swiss and a foreign counterparty, the foreign counterparty is further subjected to the clearing duty only if it meets the 'as if' test and is not exempted.[324]

This finding of a limited territorial scope is valid not only for the clearing obligation, but for the supervision of financial market infrastructures in Switzerland in general. The duty to obtain authorization in Article 4(1) FinfraG, in principle, applies only to infrastructures domiciled in Switzerland.[325] The concept that the obligation to obtain a licence is confined to situations where the foreign service provider establishes a physical presence in Switzerland can even be regarded as a general principle.[326] It can also be observed in the area of banking supervision. Purely cross-border banking services to Swiss clients are not subject to authorization and supervision. The same applies, in principle, to financial institutions under FINIG.

It can be concluded from this that Swiss financial markets law generally applies only if there is a physical presence in Switzerland. Contrary to the international trend, Switzerland, therefore, follows a more territorial approach that facilitates market entry for foreign firms.

2. More *laissez-faire* and self-regulation instead of state intervention

Countries with a market economy try to find the right balance between regulation on the one hand and free development of markets on the other. At least since the GFC, there has been an international trend towards more regulation and less market economy. As a rather small country, Switzerland has not been able to resist this development. Especially against the background of Switzerland's reliance on market access to the EU also via equivalence, Switzerland has often felt compelled to follow developments in the EU.

However, in contrast to other countries, efforts to avoid overregulation and excessive bureaucracy are still visible in Switzerland.[327] The goal of promoting Switzerland as a financial centre by avoiding regulation that disproportionately and unduly

[322] EMIR, art 4(1)(a)(v); Bahar (n 190) 488; Haeberli (n 190) § 38 para 121.

[323] FinfraG, arts 93 and 97; Favre and Kramer (n 189) Vor art 93 paras 83ff.

[324] See regarding the 'as if' test: Bahar (n 190) 488; concerning the exemption in case of equivalence see FinfraG, art 102 and FinfraV, art 90; Vogel, Heiz, and Luthiger (n 210); FinfraG, art 102 para 5.

[325] Vogel, Heiz, and Luthiger (n 210) FinfraG, art 4 para 3; Sethe (n 20) Einleitung para 83.

[326] Calling it a general rule see Bahar and Nedwed (n 16) 624. There are exceptions to almost every rule. In this case, for example, the insurance sector, the register of advisers under FIDLEG and the National Bank's supervision of systemically important infrastructures under art 22 FinfraG and art 19(2) National Bank Act can be mentioned. FIDLEG's register of advisers is criticized precisely against the background of the deviation from this general rule: ibid.

[327] See Peter Nobel, 'Was heisst "Überregulierung"?' (2014) 86 SZW 589, 593; Rolf H Weber, 'Theorie und Praxis der Finanzmarktregulierung' (2014) 86 SZW 577, 585f; see earlier explicitly Federal Department of Finance, 'Richtlinien für Finanzmarktregulierung' (September 2005) https://www.finews.ch/images/download/richtlinien.pdf (accessed 12 November 2022).

burdens market participants can be seen in many areas. It is an explicit goal of the legislator.[328] Before a legal act is adopted, the potential benefits are weighed against the burden the change will impose on market participants.[329]

One example of this assertion is the decision to refrain from regulating benchmarks.[330] Even though other countries have adopted such legislation (e.g. the EU, Australia, and Singapore), even though it might help Switzerland to get an equivalence decision from the EU and despite the scandals which occurred with regard to the manipulation of benchmarks, Switzerland repeatedly chose not to regulate benchmarks.[331] The situation is similar in relation to credit rating agencies. There is no law governing rating agencies, only a circular issued by FINMA, which is not legally binding.[332]

Another characteristic of Swiss financial markets law is the focus on self-regulation.[333] Switzerland allows fairly extensive self-regulation compared to other jurisdictions, although this trend has been weakened since the GFC. There are various modes of self-regulation, which can be distinguished primarily by the degree of state intervention.[334] Currently, a trend towards state-controlled self-regulation can be observed.[335] One example of this is the self-regulation of stock exchanges. Sometimes the state requires trading venues to issue regulations, for instance, in Article 28(1) FinfraG concerning the organization of orderly and transparent trading. Other times, the self-imposed regulation must be approved by supervisory authorities.[336] Whether rules stemming from self-regulation will be recognized as equivalent by the EU remains to be seen. Provided they are binding and effectively enforced, there is much to be said in favour of recognition.

3. Better regulation: Short and to the point

It is particularly striking that Swiss legislation is significantly shorter and more comprehensible than EU regulatory law. This applies both to supervisory law in general and deference in particular. Swiss law is based on the idea of principle-based and technology-neutral regulation.[337] Framework laws are adopted, which are further elaborated through ordinances and self-regulation.[338] This approach ensures that laws are formulated concisely and are not overloaded with too many details.[339]

[328] See Federal Council, 'Financial Market Policy for a Competitive Swiss Financial Centre' Report (November 2016) 19ff https://www.sif.admin.ch/dam/sif/en/dokumente/Publicationen/Bericht_Finanzmarktpolitik.pdf.download.pdf/Financial%20market%20policy%20for%20a%20competitive%20Swiss%20financial%20centre%20.pdf (accessed 12 November 2022).

[329] Concerning this analysis see n 328 (ch 3); see also Federal Department of Finance, 'Richtlinien für Finanzmarktregulierung' (n 327) 5.

[330] See extensively ch 3 B)II.3.

[331] Federal Council, 'Derzeit kein Bedarf für Benchmark-Regulierung' (n 109).

[332] FINMA, 'Circ. 2012/1—Credit Rating Agencies' (n 70); see ch 3 B)II.1.

[333] Sethe (n 20) Einleitung paras 66ff.

[334] See extensively on the different modes of self-regulation Pascal Zysset, *Selbstregulierung im Finanzmarktrecht* (Schulthess 2017) paras 363ff.

[335] Bühler (n 319) 475; regarding differences in terminology see Zysset (n 334) para 386.

[336] See eg FinfraG, art 27(4).

[337] Thomas C Jutzi, Ksenia Wess, and Damian Sieradzki, 'Die neue Finanzmarktarchitektur im europäischen Regulierungskontext' (2020) 29 AJP/PJA 587.

[338] Sethe (n 20) Einleitung para 70.

[339] Referring to the Swiss approach as better legislation see Sethe (n 20) Einleitung para 9.

The opposite is true for EU legislation. Although it is also based on framework regulations, which are to be specified at levels 2, 3, and 4 according to the *Lamfalussy* process, the EU never managed to streamline the legal acts by reducing the level of detail.[340] In the meantime, all levels are in such great detail that they are hardly comprehensible. This level of detail has also not achieved the desired effect of greater uniformity in Member States' laws. Rather, this approach has led to an inflexible, barely manageable legal order in which there continue to be numerous loopholes for Member States, and which consequently creates risks for the financial sector.[341]

Two examples in this context are the equivalence provisions governing CCPs and credit rating agencies. The regulation of third country CCPs in EMIR is set out over 20 pages in the *Official Journal* of the EU. This regulation will be accompanied by several Level 2 and Level 3 acts, which will take up many more pages. In contrast, the regulation on the recognition of foreign CCPs and systemically important CCPs does not even cover two pages in Switzerland.[342] The deference provision in FINMA's circular on credit rating agencies is only two sentences long, while the CRA Regulation in the EU covers almost three pages. These two examples underline the major differences that exist between the two legal orders in this respect.

II. Deference in Switzerland

At the outset, the system of deference in Switzerland is similar to that of the EU. This is not surprising, as most of the reforms were initiated at the international level, particularly by the G20. As will be shown in the following pages, Switzerland follows these international developments very closely for several reasons. First, it lacks the market power to set international standards, which is why Switzerland can only follow the standards if it wants to participate in the world market and try to influence them later.[343] Secondly, deference is a liberal way to grant market access to foreign service providers while at the same time reducing risks for investors and the financial system. Thirdly, attracting foreign service providers is an important segment of the Swiss economy, which is why it makes sense to introduce a coherent system of deference.[344] Fourthly, Switzerland often replicates EU law to achieve an equivalence status. An EU equivalence decision is often conditional on the third country offering EU service providers market access (reciprocity), a prerequisite that can be met by introducing deference provisions in Switzerland.[345] For all these reasons, it is not surprising that the starting points of the deference regimes are identical.

[340] Matthias Lehmann describes the situation since the GFC as a 'regulatory tsunami'. See Matthias Lehmann, 'Is EU Law Overly Complex?' in Jessica Schmidt, Carlos Esplugues, and Rafael A García (eds), *EU Law after the Financial Crisis* (Intersentia 2016) 65.

[341] ibid 66ff.

[342] See FinfraG, arts 22, 23, and 60.

[343] On the role of international standards for the financial market strategy of Switzerland see Rupert Schaefer, 'Internationale Standards in der schweizerischen Finanzmarktaufsicht' (2015) 87 SZW 607, 609f.

[344] Concerning the economic relevance see in detail ch 3 D)I.

[345] See CSDR, art 25(9); EMIR, art 25(6)(c); MiFIR, arts 28(1)(d), 38(3) subpara 2(b), and 47(1)(c).

However, the Swiss approach to deference also has distinctive features that clearly distinguish it from the one of the EU. The different approach already becomes apparent when comparing the motivation of the legislators to introduce deference provisions. For the European Commission,

> [e]quivalence is not a vehicle for liberalising international trade in financial services, but a key instrument to effectively manage cross-border activity of market players in a sound and secure prudential environment with third-country jurisdictions that adhere to, implement and enforce rigorously the same high standards of prudential rules as the EU.[346]

The Swiss government, in contrast, often explicitly intends to liberalize cross-border financial trading through deference.[347] These different strategic goals already explain many discrepancies between the Swiss and the EU approach to be presented in the following.

1. Finely graduated system: From non-regulation to appropriateness to equivalence

The Swiss legislator tries to balance two different goals. On the one hand, it pursues effective investor protection and the avoidance of systemic risks. At the same time, a close alignment with EU regulation is intended to establish a high level of regulatory convergence to be recognized as equivalent by the European Commission. On the other hand, the government strives to make Switzerland a strong financial centre that strengthens the domestic economy by attracting foreign players and capital. This attraction of foreign service providers and capital works best through an easily accessible capital market and a regulatory framework that is not overregulated. The legislator seeks to strike this balance through a finely graduated system that moves from non-regulation (level 1) to the requirement of an appropriate (level 2) to demanding an equivalent level of home country regulation and supervision (level 3).

The notion of non-regulation (level 1) is reflected in the rather strict territorial approach that can be observed in various areas of Swiss financial markets law. Mostly, there is no regulation for purely cross-border services. Only when there is a physical presence in Switzerland regulation applies and supervision takes place.[348] If the Swiss legislator is of the opinion that regulation and supervision is necessary, the first step is to require 'appropriate' regulation and supervision in the home country of the respective service provider (level 2). As has been outlined above, the concept of appropriateness does not refer to the Swiss legal system but takes into account international standards as well as the supervisory level in a multitude of states. It is less demanding and less self-centred than equivalence.[349] A similar term used in the context of credit

[346] Commission, 'EU Equivalence Decisions in Financial Services Policy: An Assessment' (Staff Working Document) SWD (2017) 102 final, 5.

[347] Vogel, Heiz, and Luthiger (n 38) FIDLEG, art 54 para 2.

[348] See the analysis in ch 3 C)I.1.; concerning the banking sector see Nobel (n 4) § 7 paras 269 and 459; Rashid Bahar and Eric Stupp in Rolf Watter and others (eds), *BSK-BankenG* (2nd edn, Helbing Lichtenhahn 2013) art 1 para 85; see ch 3 B)III.2.; with regard to financial institutions under FINIG see Fahrländer (n 8) 233.

[349] See ch 3 B)IV.2.a)aa).

rating agencies is that of 'sufficient' regulation and supervision.[350] The last step is to demand an equivalent foreign regulation and supervision (level 3). This third level is mainly found where the legislator considers market access relevant for systemic stability or particularly crucial for investor protection, or where a strong territorial link to Switzerland exists. It is also the level with the highest requirements when it comes to deference.[351]

Illustrative cases of these three levels can be found in the regulation of market infrastructures. Foreign CSDs may, for instance, provide services to Swiss participants without being regulated or supervised by FINMA (level 1).[352] The legislator deviates from this territorial approach in FinfraG if a foreign CSD is of systemic importance for Switzerland. In that scenario, the CSD is supervised by the Swiss National Bank and must fulfil additional criteria. An exemption can be provided if the foreign supervision and oversight is equivalent (level 3).

In contrast, foreign CCPs, which generally pose greater risks for the systemic stability of markets, must, in principle, obtain recognition from FINMA.[353] The recognition is conditional on the foreign CCP being subject to appropriate regulation and supervision (level 2). If the risks for systemic stability are even higher because the foreign CCP is of systemic relevance, CCPs are additionally supervised by the Swiss National Bank. Such supervision can be waived in case of an equivalent foreign supervision and oversight (level 3). Sometimes the legislator even draws precise differentiations within the third level. According to Article 78 FinfraV, the term equivalence is specified in that a foreign legal system is deemed to be equivalent if it does not deviate 'to a significant extent' from the legal requirements of FinfraV.[354] This standard seems to be less demanding than the usually employed equivalence standard, but higher than the standard of appropriateness.

These examples demonstrate that the Swiss legislator differentiates precisely in terms of the prerequisites required for market access for foreign players. The requested degree of regulatory convergence depends on the systemic relevance, the level of protection of Swiss investors deemed necessary and the extent of territorial linkage, i.e. whether market access takes place purely on a cross-border basis or with a physical presence.

2. More deference even if retail investors are affected

With regard to the fields in which equivalence provisions can be found, there are many parallels to the EU system. One important deviation, however, exists with respect to the use of deference when the interests of retail investors are involved. As described above, the EU is rather reluctant to implement equivalence in areas where the interests of retail investors are at stake.[355] Examples include the third country regime of MiFIR,

350 FINMA, 'Circ. 2012/1—Credit Rating Agencies' (n 70) para 60.

351 Only those regimes are stricter that do not include any deference mechanism for market access. One example of this is the market access for foreign insurance companies. See ch 3 B)III.3.

352 Jungo, Zibung, and Roth (n 298) art 4 para 14 and art 8 para 8; Schleiffer and Schärli (n 303) FinfraG, art 70 para 1; ch 3 B)IV.2.c).

353 FinfraG, art 60; ch 3 B)IV.2.b)aa).

354 Bahar (n 279) FinfraG, art 93 para 6.

355 See ch 1 C)II.6.a).

which is limited to per se professional clients and eligible counterparties, and the absence of equivalence provisions in deposit-taking and the PRIIP Regulation with regard to key information documents.

Switzerland's system is more liberal in this respect. FIDLEG contains an equivalence provision in Article 59(2) in relation to key information documents.[356] The Swiss system is also extremely liberal with regard to banking services. There is neither authorization nor supervision in the case of purely cross-border banking services without a physical presence. This liberal approach is mitigated in the area of investment services, where an exemption from the register of advisers exists exclusively for services to professional or institutional clients.[357] In view of the fact that the scope of FINIG is still limited to financial institutions with a physical presence in Switzerland and that (retail) investors can therefore use services even in the absence of permanent supervision of the institution by FINMA, the approach can nevertheless be described as liberal. Overall, the range of deference regimes in Switzerland is therefore similar to that in the EU. In relation to services for retail investors provided by foreign firms, the Swiss legislator is, however, less reluctant to implement equivalence.

3. Requirements

The Swiss system contains numerous deference provisions. The requirements of these provisions, although not completely identical, are largely similar. Four requirements are particularly noteworthy.

a) Equivalence and appropriateness decisions

Most provisions demand that the service provider or product is subject to equivalent or appropriate supervision and regulation in its home country. As in the EU, there needs to be a decision on this equivalence or appropriateness. There is no deference *ipso iure*. Different from the situation in the EU, where the decision at the European level always rests with the European Commission, the responsibilities in Switzerland are shared mainly between the Federal Council, the National Bank, and FINMA.[358] The Swiss Federal Council is responsible if the recognition is adopted by way of an international treaty. These provisions are akin to the former EU equivalence mechanisms, which were historically based on bilateral negotiations and not on unilateral decisions.[359] The Swiss National Bank is competent in cases of systemic important market infrastructures because these are—in the absence of an equivalence decision—supervised by the National Bank.[360] In most other cases, the decision-making authority lies with FINMA.

[356] Bösch (n 44) 98.

[357] See FIDLEG, art 28(2) and FIDLEV, art 31.

[358] In the exceptional case of FinfraG, art 125(2), the decision rests with the Swiss Takeover Board. With regard to the approval of foreign prospectuses, the reviewing body is responsible for the decision.

[359] The Swiss Federal Council is competent pursuant to Banking Act, art 2(3), KAG, art 122 and FINIG, arts 52(3) and 58(3).

[360] See FinfraG, art 23(4); eg ch 3 B)IV.2.b)bb).

b) International standards as benchmarks

Switzerland puts great emphasis on aligning its legal system with international standards.[361] This development reached a new peak with the recent reform.[362] The Swiss legislator explicitly wanted to align FinfraG with international standards, an intention that is expressed 16 times in the legal text of FinfraG.[363]

This focus on international standards is not limited to the internal perspective, i.e. the treatment of domestic market participants. Many deference regimes also refer to international standards as benchmarks. For example, the recognition of prospectuses drawn up under foreign law depends, among other things, on the foreign prospectus complying with IOSCO standards.[364] Even in the absence of an explicit reference, the legislator's objective of assigning an important role to international standards can be promoted by using international standards as a yardstick for determining whether a foreign regulation is 'appropriate'.[365] Such an interpretation underpins the international approach of Swiss financial markets law, emphasizes the difference to an *equivalent* regulation, which always refers to Switzerland's law, and allows flexible handling and adaptation of the law to future developments.

c) Reciprocity

Several Swiss deference provisions demand reciprocal treatment of Swiss service providers and products by foreign countries. This requirement is included in the deference mechanisms executed by the Federal Council through international treaties as well as in the provisions executed by FINMA through unilateral decisions.[366] It is not always formulated as a mandatory prerequisite but sometimes merely gives FINMA the right to refuse recognition if reciprocity is not guaranteed.[367] This design gives FINMA room for manoeuvre to react to situations where negotiation powers are unevenly distributed. However, it must not use the requirement to discriminate against other states, as this would not be permitted under GATS.[368]

Like in EU law, different degrees of reciprocity can be identified.[369] In the case of treaties, the other country must have actually recognized that the Swiss regulation is equivalent.[370] In cases where FINMA has the right to refuse recognition, it can do so either on the basis that 'actual access' to the foreign market has not yet been granted

[361] On international standards in the Swiss financial architecture see Schaefer (n 343); see also Stefan A Wandel, 'Global Financial Standards and Regulatory Reforms' (2015) 87 SZW 562.

[362] Peter Nobel, 'Was heisst "Internationale Standards"?' (2015) 87 SZW 556, 558.

[363] Botschaft FinfraG, BBl 2014, 7483, 7498; Nobel (n 362) 559.

[364] FIDLEG, art 54(1)(a); IOSCO, 'International Disclosure Standards for Cross-Border Offerings and Initial Listings by Foreign Issuers' (September 1998) https://www.iosco.org/library/pubdocs/pdf/IOSCOPD81.pdf (accessed 12 November 2022); Botschaft FIDLEG/FINIG, BBl 2015, 8901, 8983.

[365] For a consenting view see Schären (n 252) FinfraG, art 60 para 21; Bahar (n 279) FinfraG, art 60 para 11.

[366] See eg FINIG, arts 52(3) and 58(3) and FinfraV, art 79(2).

[367] See eg FinfraG, arts 40(2), 41(4), 60(3), and 80(4).

[368] Rolf Watter and Rashid Bahar (eds), *BSK-FINMAG/FinfraG* (3rd edn, Helbing Lichtenhahn 2019) FinfraG, art 40 para 30: 'wirtschaftspolitisches Entschliessungsermessen'. The general request of reciprocity is, contrary to many voices in the scientific community, compatible with world trade law. See ch 3 B)IV.2.a) aa).

[369] See ch 2 A)I.4.

[370] FINIG, arts 52(3) and 58(3) and Banking Act, art 2(3).

or that the foreign legal regime does not offer 'the same competitive opportunities as those granted to domestic' parties.[371]

d) Administrative cooperation

Given that deference is always based on trust in the home state's supervision, a rule ensuring administrative cooperation is also included in numerous regimes in Switzerland.[372] Although the goal of administrative cooperation is shared between the EU and Switzerland, the design of the rules differ. The EU's focus is on the conclusion of cooperation agreements. In contrast, Switzerland's approach builds on the (also unilateral) commitment of assistance by the foreign authority in particular cases. These commitments may take the form of MoUs, the exchange of letters or unilateral assurances.[373] The required commitments vary depending on the applicable regime. Among these are commitments that the foreign authorities have not objected to the cross-border activity of their service provider, that the authorities guarantee to inform FINMA if they detect any violations of the law and that the authorities provide FINMA with administrative assistance.[374] These commitments are not legally binding.

4. Legal consequences: Is deference an instrument to withdraw regulatory and supervisory powers in Switzerland?

The defining feature of deference is that the host state's law is not applied vis-à-vis foreign market participants to avoid legal conflicts and market fragmentation. This general idea is also the underlying principle of Swiss deference regimes. In some instances, the objective of eliminating legal conflicts is at the heart of the mechanisms. This applies, for example, to the exemption from obligations concerning derivatives trading.[375] In other cases, the objective of granting market access to foreign institutions is more at the centre, for example, with respect to the recognition of CCPs. The liberal objective of granting market access also promotes competition and increases the choice for investors, two goals that are equally pursued by the legislator.

However, a withdrawal of regulatory and supervisory powers does not always occur when the criteria of equivalence and appropriateness are used in Swiss regulation. If foreign banks establish a branch or representative office in Switzerland, these branches and representative offices require authorization from FINMA, which in turn presupposes that the foreign bank is subject to appropriate supervision in its home country. Even if the branch or representative office is authorized, it must still adhere to the Banking Act with the exception of capital adequacy and risk diversification rules.[376] Therefore, authorization and appropriate supervision do not lead to a withdrawal of regulatory and supervisory powers. Such a withdrawal occurs only following the

[371] See FinfraG, arts 40(2), 41(4), 60(3), and 80(4).

[372] See extensively on supervisory cooperation in Switzerland Urs Zulauf, 'Kooperation oder Obstruktion?—20 Jahre Amtshilfe im Finanzmarktrecht vom Börsengesetz zum FINFRAG' (2015) 10 GesKR 336.

[373] See Botschaft FinfraG, BBl 2014, 7483, 7539.

[374] See eg FinfraG, art 41(2)(b).

[375] See FinfraG, art 95(a); other examples include FinfraG, art 102 in connection with FinfraV, art 90; see also FinfraV, arts 106(2) and 111 as well as FinfraG, art 125(2).

[376] Article 2(1) of the Banking Act prescribes that the rules of the Banking Act apply *mutatis mutandis*; see Chapuis (n 170) art 2 paras 12ff.

conclusion of an international treaty by the Swiss Federal Council, which requires that foreign banking activities are supervised in an equivalent manner.[377] The situation is similar for the authorization of branches and representative offices of foreign financial institutions under FINIG. In these cases, there is also no withdrawal of supervisory law.[378]

Therefore, caution is required with regard to the criteria of appropriateness and equivalence. The Swiss legislator uses these prerequisites not only in the context of deference but also when regulating the market access for foreign institutions without a withdrawal of Swiss supervisory law.

D) Attempt to explain the differences between the EU and Switzerland: Why size matters

Despite similar approaches to deference, there are, as seen, considerable differences between the EU and Switzerland. There is no monocausal explanation for these discrepancies. Historical, cultural, and political factors play a role. From a cultural perspective, for example, the model of a responsible and enlightened citizen respectively investor is much more prevalent in Switzerland than in the EU.[379] Switzerland puts more trust in its investors and does not patronize them to the same degree as the EU. As mentioned above, Switzerland is also trying to pursue a more pragmatic and unbureaucratic approach, which is again based on the idea of a responsible citizen.[380] Nevertheless, one reason is predominant and common to all areas: the economic situation of Switzerland.

I. The economic situation: Facts, figures, and geography

The economic situation of Switzerland and its influence on financial regulation can best be described by looking at the role of the financial industry in Switzerland (1.) and the relevance of international business for this industry (2.). Moreover, Switzerland's geographical location in the middle of the Single European Market is crucial (3.). Based on these factors, Switzerland's strategic goals for financial market regulation, especially for the regulation of foreign service providers, can be identified (4.).

1. Role of the financial industry in Switzerland

The financial sector is a key sector for the Swiss economy. The financial sector accounted for 9 per cent of Switzerland's GDP in 2021.[381] In comparison, the financial

[377] Banking Act, art 2(3).

[378] See Bahar and Nedwed (n 16) 625ff.

[379] To the concept of an enlightened investor (*mündiger Anleger*) see Dieter Zobl and Stefan Kramer, *Schweizerisches Kapitalmarktrecht* (Schulthess 2004) 17.

[380] See ch 3 C)I.2.

[381] Federal Department of Finance, 'Swiss Financial Centre: Key Figures April 2022' (20 April 2022) p. 2, Figure 1 https://www.sif.admin.ch/dam/sif/en/dokumentation/kennzahlen/kennzahlen-sif-2022.pdf.download.pdf/sif-kennzahlen-2022-en.pdf (accessed 28 February 2023).

sector in Germany only contributed for 3.8 per cent of the GDP.[382] Looking at services exports, it is striking that the financial sector contributed 24 per cent of total services exports in 2019.[383] Also, 5.2 per cent of employees in Switzerland worked in the financial sector and 11.7 per cent of the total tax income was generated by it in 2021.[384]

In terms of the total number of freely tradable shares, SIX ranked third in Europe behind the LSE and Euronext and just ahead of Deutsche Börse.[385] These figures demonstrate that the financial sector is of major importance for the Swiss economy. Because of its crucial role, it is also high on the political agenda.

2. International business as the driving force

Much of the strength of the Swiss financial centre comes from international business. The export of financial services is of particular significance for Switzerland. In 2019, CHF 29.16 billion were generated from the export of financial and insurance services.[386] In the banking market in 2021, 94 out of 243 banks were foreign-controlled and foreign banks accounted for 10 per cent of the entire bank balance sheet.[387] In collective investment schemes, over 50 per cent of Swiss funds were domiciled in Luxembourg, and around 80 per cent were domiciled abroad.[388]

The abovementioned numbers show the enormous relevance of foreign business for the strength of the Swiss financial centre. With under ten million inhabitants, Switzerland's domestic market does not have enough inhabitants to be a globally significant hub. For this reason, foreign business plays a particularly important role for the Swiss legislator.

3. Relationship to the EU and UK

Switzerland's geographical position is characterized by a huge single market surrounding it with around 450 million inhabitants. This geographic situation is reflected in the enormous economic weight of the EU for Switzerland.[389] Out of Switzerland's total services trade volume in 2021, 49.22 per cent was generated with the EU and the UK.[390] Of the foreign direct investments in Switzerland in 2018, 77.68 per cent came from the EU and the UK.[391] Consequently, it is one of the key concerns of Switzerland to ensure market access to the EU and UK for its service providers.

[382] ibid p. 2, Figure 1.

[383] Federal Council, 'Leading worldwide, rooted in Switzerland' (4 December 2020) 5 https://www.sif.admin.ch/dam/sif/en/bilder/politik-finanzplatz-schweiz/politik-finanzplatz-schweiz-bericht.pdf.download.pdf/politik-finanzplatz-schweiz-bericht.pdf (accessed 12 November 2022).

[384] Federal Department of Finance (n 381) p. 3.

[385] Weber, Kronauer, and Huber (n 229) § 44 para 9.

[386] State Secretariat for Economic Affairs, 'Services Trade Cockpit 2020 Rev. 1' (January 2021) 4 https://www.seco.admin.ch/dam/seco/en/dokumente/Aussenwirtschaft/Wirtschaftsbeziehungen/Handel%20mit%20Dienstleistungen/services_trade_cockpit.pdf.download.pdf/Services%20Trade%20Cockpit%202020.pdf (accessed 12 November 2022).

[387] Federal Department of Finance (n 381) p. 5; for a legal determination see Nobel (n 4) § 2 para 139.

[388] Federal Department of Finance (n 381) p. 10.

[389] Describing the EU as the by far most important trading partner of Switzerland: Nobel (n 4) § 14 para 19.

[390] Directorate of European Affairs, 'Switzerland-EU in figures' (October 2022) 15 https://www.eda.admin.ch/content/dam/europa/de/documents/faq/schweiz-eu-in-zahlen_de.pdf (accessed 28 February 2023).

[391] ibid 21.

4. Summary: Strategic objectives

From the data found above, it can be deduced that two points are of critical importance for the strength of Switzerland as a financial centre and thus for the Swiss economy as a whole. On the one hand, it is crucial to attract financial players and capital to Switzerland. This can be achieved by providing a sound, secure, trustworthy, and predictable regulatory system. At the same time, the barriers to accessing the Swiss market must be minimized, as the limited number of customers does not offer great potential. This can be achieved, inter alia, by adjusting regulations to international standards. On the other hand, access for Swiss firms to the EU single market and to the markets of countries like the US and the UK must be ensured. In the absence of far-reaching trade deals encompassing financial services, market access can be obtained through regulatory alignment and accompanying equivalence decisions. These strategic goals are also explicitly spelt out in multiple policy papers.[392]

II. Coherence between the legal framework and strategic objectives

Against the background of the identified strategic goals, the current legal framework is easier to understand because the goals are clearly reflected in the regulation. To attract financial players and capital, Switzerland has modernized its regulatory system, placing great emphasis on aligning it with international standards.[393] As seen, Switzerland is also restrictive in applying its law extraterritorially to avoid legal and supervisory conflicts with other jurisdictions, which would ultimately hinder market access for foreign participants. Moreover, Switzerland pays particular attention to the avoidance of overregulation and principle-based regulation, which is comprehensible and predictable.[394] In addition, the wide-ranging introduction of deference and the use of a finely graduated system from non-regulation to appropriateness to equivalence facilitates market access.

But why can Switzerland pursue such a liberal approach to cross-border financial services without at the same time jeopardizing the protection of its investors and exposing itself to systemic risks? This phenomenon can also be explained against the backdrop of its geographical location. Switzerland is surrounded by the EU, which strictly regulates and supervises its service providers. Other large jurisdictions, such as the US, have also introduced stringent regulations, particularly since the GFC. Consequently, the risk of insufficiently regulated service providers or products entering the Swiss market is rather low. For this reason, Switzerland can be rather liberal when regulating foreign financial service providers and products. Moreover, foreign participants would not seek access to the Swiss market if the barriers to market entry were too high. Therefore, in contrast to the EU and the US, Switzerland cannot impose

[392] See eg Federal Department of Finance, 'Richtlinien für Finanzmarktregulierung' (n 327); Federal Council, 'Financial Market Policy for a Competitive Swiss Financial Centre' (n 328); Expertengruppe zur Weiterentwicklung der Finanzmarktstrategie, 'Schlussbericht' (Brunetti Bericht) (2014) https://www.newsd.admin.ch/newsd/message/attachments/37585.pdf (accessed 12 November 2022).

[393] See n 361 (ch 3).

[394] Jutzi, Wess, and Sieradzki (n 337) 587; Federal Department of Finance, 'Richtlinien für Finanzmarktregulierung' (n 327).

a strict preventive ban with a mere possibility of obtaining authorization, as it would otherwise deter foreign service providers and capital. Risks arising from foreign participants and products must be averted when arising on the Swiss market.

As seen, Switzerland also puts great emphasis on enabling market access of its service providers to other jurisdictions through equivalence.[395] By providing a liberal market access regime, Switzerland seeks to encourage other countries to do the same. The autonomous replication of EU law to achieve the status of equivalence is an explicit goal of the legislator and is reflected in almost all legal acts.[396] Since the UK has also adopted the EU equivalence mechanisms into its legal order with the Withdrawal Act, market access for Swiss firms to the UK can also be achieved via equivalence. Both Switzerland and the UK quickly reacted to Brexit by recognizing each other's stock exchanges[397] and working on a financial services agreement.[398] As a result, Switzerland's economic interests and geographical location provide a good explanation for its liberal regulatory framework.

[395] Expertengruppe Finanzmarktaufsicht, 'Finanzmarktregulierung und -Aufsicht in der Schweiz' (Zufferey-Bericht) (n 183) 25ff.

[396] Sethe (n 23) 345ff.

[397] See the decision of FINMA, 'Guidance 01/2021—Trading in Swiss shares: Recognition of various UK trading venues' (3 February 2021) https://www.finma.ch/en/~/media/finma/dokumente/dokumentencenter/myfinma/4dokumentation/finma-aufsichtsmitteilungen/20210203-finma-aufsichtsmitteilung-01-2021.pdf?la=en (accessed 12 November 2022).

[398] This agreement is supposed to be finalized by the end of summer 2023. See Federal Department of Finance, 'Last official visit as Federal Councillor' (22 December 2022) https://www.efd.admin.ch/efd/en/home/the-fdf/nsb-news_list.msg-id-92373.html (accessed 28 February 2023).

4
The Approach of Substituted Compliance in the United States

Owing to its size alone, the US capital market is one of the most influential in the world and historically the most developed 'market-based system'.[1] Therefore, the US is a standard-setter and an analysis of cross-border financial services cannot avoid examining the approach of the US to issues of globalization, extraterritoriality, fragmentation, and recognition of foreign regulation and supervision. Apart from that, an understanding of the US concept of deference is also crucial because it has and was influenced by the EU principle of equivalence. The developments and particularities of both approaches can hence only be understood from a comparative perspective.

The US has also developed a concept to withdraw regulatory and supervisory powers based on a qualitative assessment of a foreign legal system, i.e. a deference mechanism. This concept is commonly referred to as substituted compliance but is also discussed under the general heading of (mutual) recognition.[2] The following analysis attempts to assess this system of substituted compliance and identify similarities and differences with the EU and Swiss approaches.

At first, the historical development of substituted compliance is examined and put into context with the developments in the EU and Switzerland (A)). The second part looks at individual manifestations of substituted compliance and compares them with parallel regimes in Europe (B)). Finally, an overall picture is derived from this in-depth analysis (C)).

A) Historical development of substituted compliance

Like the concept of equivalence in the EU, the idea of substituted compliance in the US has changed and evolved over time. In both jurisdictions, the global financial crisis (GFC) has played a crucial role in shaping deference as it is today.[3] The following subdivision into three periods is based on the observations of Howell E Jackson.[4] The

[1] See in great detail the statistics provided for in SIFMA, '2022 Capital Markets Fact Book' (July 2022) https://www.sifma.org/wp-content/uploads/2022/07/CM-Fact-Book-2022-SIFMA.pdf (accessed 12 November 2022); on the differentiation between market-based and bank-based see Ross Levine, 'Bank-Based or Market-Based Financial Systems: Which Is Better?' (2002) 11 J Financ Intermediation 398.

[2] Howell E Jackson, 'Substituted Compliance' (2015) 1 JFR 169; Pierre-Hugues Verdier, 'Mutual Recognition in International Finance' (2011) 52 Harv Intl LJ 56; Cheryl C Nichols, 'Mutual Recognition Based on Substituted Compliance' (2008) 34 NC J Intl L & Com Reg 1; SEC, 'Unofficial Transcript of Roundtable Discussion on Mutual Recognition' (12 June 2007) https://www.sec.gov/news/openmeetings/2007/openmtg_trans061207.pdf (accessed 12 November 2022).

[3] Concerning the EU see ch 1 C)I.5.c).

[4] See Jackson (n 2).

Equivalence and Substituted Compliance in Financial Markets Law. Jonas Schürger, Oxford University Press. © Jonas Schürger 2023. DOI: 10.1093/oso/9780198876748.003.0004

focus will not be on the specifics of the respective systems but on a comparison of the underlying motives for deference in the US and the EU at different points in time, which are of paramount importance for understanding the systems.

I. Modified national treatment

The question of how foreign firms should be treated when they enter domestic markets gained in importance in the 1980s and 1990s with the rise of cross-border securities offerings, dual listings, and generally an increasing interconnectedness of national markets.[5] Until then, the predominant policy of the US was that of national treatment, according to which foreign firms are treated like domestic ones.[6] In order not completely to cut off foreign investments, firms and investors, it was necessary to modify this doctrine of national treatment, so-called modified national treatment. The Securities and Exchange Commission (SEC), for instance, made two caveats to the principle. First, it introduced a number of exceptions where foreign firms were exempt from US regulation, in particular, a registration with the SEC. Secondly, requirements for foreign firms that would likely lead to legal conflicts if they were registered with and supervised by the SEC were relaxed. In particular, corporate governance requirements were waived for foreign firms.[7]

The US was able to pursue the policy of modified national treatment mainly because of its dominance in the securities market. This dominance had the advantage that the SEC's standard was considered the 'gold standard' and was widely followed.[8] As a result, the US could effectively insist that other countries follow its standards to gain market access, which is why it rejected mutual recognition and demanded convergence at the beginning. This mindset is aptly reflected in Commissioner Roel C Campos' statement in Brussels in 2003, in response to EU calls for greater recognition: 'We are more inclined to a single set of rules for all participants in the US market, rather than mutual recognition.'[9]

This approach, however, came under growing pressure as the first decade of the twenty-first century progressed.[10] The potential threat of litigation with draconian sanctions in the US deterred foreign firms from registering with the SEC. Additionally, these firms became more mobile in a global financial market and learned how to

[5] Michael D Bordo, 'The Globalization of International Financial Markets: What Can History Teach Us?' in Leonardo Auernheimer (ed), *International Financial Markets: The Challenge of Globalization* (Chicago UP 2003) 29ff.

[6] This doctrine has its roots, inter alia, in the International Banking Act of 1978; concerning the doctrine of national treatment: Lily D Vo, 'Comment: Substituted Compliance: An Alternative to National Treatment for Cross-Border Transactions and International Financial Entities' (2015) 13 Geo JL & Pub Poly 85, 88ff.

[7] Jackson (n 2) 172f.

[8] Roberta S Karmel, 'The EU Challenge to the SEC' (2007) 31 Fordham Intl LJ 1692, 1711.

[9] Roel C Campos (Commissioner of SEC), 'Embracing International Business in the Post-Enron Era' Speech at Centre for European Policy Studies (11 June 2003) https://www.sec.gov/news/speech/spch061103rcc.htm (accessed 12 November 2022).

[10] Jackson (n 2) 174ff; Chris Brummer, *Minilateralism* (CUP 2014) 14ff.

circumvent SEC registration and supervision intentionally through the exemptions granted from national treatment.[11] Moreover, the absolute dominance of the US financial market declined compared to emerging markets in Asia and South America, as well as to the growing single market of the EU. This development was accompanied by a broad scientific discussion. The national treatment approach was increasingly criticized and various alternatives were proposed.[12] Among them were an increasing number of voices supporting the introduction of deference.[13]

Another crucial factor that led the US to change its strategy was the rise of equivalence in the EU. Roberta S Karmel argues that the EU equivalence regime was 'instrumental in moving [the SEC] from a policy of national treatment of foreign (non-U.S.) issuers to a policy of mutual recognition'.[14] After the EU had largely converged with US standards and its markets became stronger, it took the opportunity to stand up to the US and threatened to no longer accept US GAAP if it was not deemed equivalent to International Financial Reporting Standards (IFRS).[15] EU representatives also pushed for mutual recognition of equivalent regulatory standards in the US–EU Financial Markets Regulatory Dialogue.[16]

As a result of the shift in global power, the US was thus increasingly forced to move away from its strategy of modified national treatment. Especially the introduction and expansion of equivalence in EU law had a major impact on the turn to mutual recognition and deference.

II. First generation: 'in-bound' substituted compliance

A special feature of first-generation substituted compliance is that it was created on the drawing board before it was (at least partially) put into practice. Therefore, the following analysis starts with the abstract concept (1.) before a look is taken at the responses as well as the implementation of the concept in practice (2.).

[11] This increased mobility applies not only to issuers, but also to US investors, who could more easily invest in foreign assets. See Eric J Pan, 'Single Stock Futures and Cross-Border Access for U.S. Investors' (2008) 14 Stan JL Bus & Fin 221, 229ff.

[12] See eg the 'issuer choice approach' advocated in multiple articles: Roberta Romano, 'Empowering Investors: A Market Approach to Securities Regulation' (1998) 107 Yale LJ 2359; Stephen J Choi and Andrew T Guzman, 'Portable Reciprocity: Rethinking the International Reach of Securities Regulation' (1998) 71 S Cal L Rev 903; another suggestion was the 'issuer nationality approach': see Merritt B Fox, 'Securities Disclosure in a Globalizing Market' (1997) 95 Mich L Rev 2498. On this discussion and with another proposal see Kun Young Chang, 'Reforming U.S. Disclosure Rules in Global Securities Markets' (2003) 22 Ann Rev Bank & Fin L 237.

[13] See eg Edward F Greene, Daniel A Braverman, and Sebastian R Sperber, 'Hegemony of Deference: U.S. Disclosure Requirements in the International Capital Markets' (1995) 50 Bus Law 413, 436ff.

[14] Karmel (n 8).

[15] Extensively Karmel (n 8) 1700ff; consenting: Jackson (n 2) 178: 'realpolitik'.

[16] Frits Bolkestein (EU Commission), 'EU-US regulatory co-operation on financial markets: A matter of necessity' SPEECH/03/96 (24 February 2003); Alexander Schaub (DG Internal Market), 'Testimony before the Committee on Financial Services U.S. House of Representatives' (13 May 2004) https://www.iasplus.com/en/binary/resource/051304as.pdf (accessed 12 November 2022); generally on this dialogue see Kern Alexander and others, 'Transatlantic Financial Services Regulatory Dialogue' (2006) 7 EBOR 647.

1. Theoretical framework

The first generation of substituted compliance goes back to a proposal put forward by two SEC officials in an article in the *Harvard International Law Journal* in 2007. In this article, Ethiopis Tafara and Robert J Peterson proposed a new framework for dealing with foreign financial service providers accessing the US market.[17] The proposal was based on the observation that technology and globalization had changed the design of modern capital markets.[18] These markets were increasingly interconnected, which could be witnessed, among other things, by the global impact of some financial scandals.[19] These dangers of globalization materialized directly after the publication of the paper in the course of the GFC.

Remarkably, the main justification for the proposal was to strengthen investor protection, particularly that of retail investors.[20] Tafara and Peterson argued that it is difficult for US investors to invest overseas under the current system. While foreign investments were legally possible, in practice, they were hampered by significant transaction costs, as well as a lack of information.[21] Such overseas investments would, however, be reasonable for US investors because investments in foreign companies were in part very profitable and investors could better diversify their portfolios and thus reduce risks.[22] For this reason, it is hardly surprising that Tafara and Peterson chose cross-border access by foreign stock exchanges and foreign broker-dealers as examples for the application of substituted compliance. The underlying justification for the proposal was, therefore, the liberalization of market access to the US to strengthen the protection of US investors. Because market access was at the centre of the suggestion, Howell E Jackson characterized this system as 'in-bound' substituted compliance.[23]

The Tafara–Peterson draft was very close to the European Commission's conception of equivalence at that time. Access to US markets for EU exchanges and broker-dealers was a key concern for the EU. The European Commission had also brought forward the argument that such market access would be favourable to US investors.[24]

[17] Ethiopis Tafara and Robert J Peterson, 'A Blueprint for Cross-Border Access to U.S. Investors: A New International Framework' (2007) 48 Harv Intl LJ 31.

[18] ibid 33ff.

[19] ibid 37ff.

[20] ibid 32: 'The overarching objective of the framework is, first and foremost, to further the SEC's mandate of investor protection.' This justification constitutes a clear departure from the SEC's previous argumentation, which justified the strict regulation of foreign financial service providers precisely on the grounds of investor protection. See Jackson (n 2) 180; redrawing and complementing the arguments: Howell E Jackson, 'A System of Selective Substitute Compliance' (2007) 48 Harv Intl LJ 105, 109ff.

[21] Tafara and Peterson (n 17) 47f.

[22] ibid 41.

[23] Jackson (n 2) 199.

[24] See the speech delivered by Frits Bolkestein in 2003: 'I know that the issue of trading screens is of particular interest to you. The current situation is very unsatisfactory. Access to the US market via trading screens would be good for Europe but it would also be good for the US. US investors stand to benefit through reduced costs and wider access to the listed securities. I have raised the issue on numerous occasions with the SEC, including my last visit in February this year when I even put my head into the lion's den by visiting the New York Stock Exchange and debating the issue there.' Frits Bolkestein (EU Commission), 'Towards an Integrated European Capital Market, Some of the Major Issues Reconsidered' SPEECH/03/297 (13 June 2003) 5 https://ec.europa.eu/commission/presscorner/api/files/document/print/en/speech_03_297/SPEECH_03_297_EN.pdf (accessed 12 November 2022).

In addition, there are considerable similarities between the proposal and the design of equivalence in the EU. This concerns primarily the preconditions which must be fulfilled for deference to be granted. As has been extensively analysed above, equivalence in the EU means a functional equivalence of regulatory outcomes from a holistic perspective.[25] Similarly, the Tafara–Peterson proposal stated that market access or an exemption from regulatory requirements through substituted compliance is only granted after 'a set of regulatory preconditions' is fulfilled.[26] These included a so-called 'bilateral substituted compliance' which, inter alia, consisted of a comparability assessment of the foreign and US legal regime, in which the SEC was to examine whether the foreign country 'offers comparable regulatory oversight'.[27] The two legal systems did not need to be identical but 'sufficiently similar' so that the 'home jurisdiction regulation … achieve[s] the same objectives mandated by federal securities laws'.[28] Substituted compliance thus demanded that the foreign legal order achieves the regulatory objectives of US securities law to a sufficient degree. This is in line with the EU standard of equivalence.

Likewise, the other requirements that must be met for market access under substituted compliance are largely identical to those of EU equivalence provisions. Besides the comparability assessment, Tafara and Peterson suggested that reciprocity and co-operation agreements should be prerequisites for market access.[29] Both prerequisites are recurring elements of equivalence in the EU. Tafara and Peterson also advocated a 'Five-Year Comparability Review' in addition to the regular review of comparability.[30] The dual control of comparability is close to the European Commission's two-stage process of reviewing equivalence decisions, which consists of ongoing equivalence 'monitoring' on the one hand and ad hoc equivalence 'review' on the other hand.[31] Last but not least, the proposal emphasized the broad discretion to be granted to the SEC.[32] Similar discretionary powers also exist in EU law. However, the European Commission widens its room for manoeuvre to the extent that it includes political factors, an interpretation which is inadmissible under EU law[33] and that was not provided for in the proposal by Tafara and Peterson. On the contrary, the proposal advocated that the US remained 'nationality-neutral', a policy that would prohibit discrimination against foreign firms and investors, as well as discrimination between different foreigners.[34]

In light of the almost identical approaches and the role model function of European equivalence, the question arises as to why a different terminology has emerged in the

[25] See ch 2 B)I.1.a).

[26] Tafara and Peterson (n 17) 54; see also the characterization in Vo (n 6) 96.

[27] Tafara and Peterson (n 17) 55f.

[28] ibid 60.

[29] ibid 61ff; see also Nichols (n 2) 70ff. Highlighting the need for reciprocity see Edward F Greene, 'Beyond Borders: Time to Tear down the Barriers to Global Investing' (2007) 48 Harv Intl LJ 85, 88f.

[30] Tafara and Peterson (n 17) 63.

[31] See ch 2 B)III.

[32] Tafara and Peterson (n 17) 63f.

[33] See ch 2 A)I.1.c) and ch 2 B)II.2.

[34] Tafara and Peterson (n 17) 45ff and 51; Commission on the Regulation of U.S. Capital Markets in the 21st Century, 'Report and Recommendations' (March 2007) 40 https://www.uschamber.com/sites/default/files/legacy/reports/0703capmarkets_full.pdf (accessed 12 November 2022).

US. It is noteworthy in this context that neither the Tafara–Peterson proposal nor many of the subsequent discussions in the SEC mention the EU equivalence regime.[35] One reason could be that 'equivalence' was an emotive word for many in the SEC, and opposition to this concept had long been voiced.[36] By refraining from using the EU's terminology, resistance could therefore be reduced. Moreover, many expressed the intention to take a leadership role in spreading mutual recognition and deference worldwide.[37] It was important for this leadership role to develop a new terminology and not simply copy the European one. In this way, the SEC also had more leeway in shaping deference, as its approach was not directly compared to the concept of equivalence in the EU.

The underlying logic that substituted compliance shall liberalize international trade, facilitate market access and is particularly beneficial for retail investors was, as seen, in line with the understanding of the European Commission at that time. It is, however, contrary to the Commission's current conception of equivalence. The European Commission now stresses that '[e]quivalence is not a vehicle for liberalising international trade in financial services, but a key instrument to effectively manage cross-border activity of market players'.[38] The European Commission thus openly admits that it no longer sees equivalence primarily as an instrument for opening markets. The goal is not the liberalization of financial markets in the narrower sense by withdrawing regulatory and supervisory powers, but the less ambitious goal of avoiding frictions by eliminating legal and supervisory conflicts, while retaining one's own regulatory and supervisory powers to the greatest extent possible. This different approach is one reason why equivalence is often missing in the EU when interests of retail investors are at stake.[39] It also explains why market access is not always at the centre of EU equivalence regimes, but rather the avoidance of legal and supervisory conflicts in cross-border transactions.[40] The initiative of Tafara and Peterson was thus comparable to the European Commission's stance at the time, but it is clearly more liberal than the European Commission's current approach.[41] In terms of modern deference regimes, the substituted compliance proposal can rather be compared to the current Swiss approach, which still focuses on market access and does not leave out areas where retail investors are affected.[42]

[35] Tafara and Peterson (n 17); SEC (n 2).

[36] Roel C Campos (Commissioner of SEC), 'Convergence and Beyond' (U.S.–Europe Symposium: Program on International Financial Systems) (15 November 2003) 4ff https://www.sec.gov/news/speech/spch111503rcc.htm (accessed 12 November 2022); Campos (n 9); Annette L Nazareth (Director, Division of Market Regulation of SEC), 'Testimony Concerning Certain Pending Proposals by the European Commission' (22 May 2002) 2 https://www.sec.gov/news/testimony/052202tsaln.htm (accessed 12 November 2022).

[37] See eg SEC (n 2) 173.

[38] Commission, 'EU Equivalence Decisions in Financial Services Policy: An Assessment' (Staff Working Document) SWD (2017) 102 final, 5.

[39] See ch 1 C)II.6.a).

[40] See ch 2 C)V.2. This does not mean that the goal of conflict avoidance is not part of the Tafara–Peterson proposal. However, it plays a rather subordinate role. See Tafara and Peterson (n 17) 32, 53.

[41] This does not mean, however, that the Commission's view has prevailed in all cases. Equivalence mechanisms, such as the one in MiFIR in relation to third country investment firms, are clearly directed at market access. The current legal framework is therefore a mix of both approaches.

[42] See ch 3 C)II.

2. Response and practical implementation

The Tafara–Peterson proposal elicited a big and mostly positive response. A bipartisan, independent Commission set up by the US Chamber of Commerce recommended introducing substituted compliance.[43] The SEC initiated a roundtable to discuss issues of mutual recognition.[44] Moreover, multiple comments were published on the Tafara–Peterson suggestion in academia[45] and supportive speeches given by other SEC officials.[46] Because of this broad support, the proposal was also partly put into practice.

One of the first examples of substituted compliance was the SEC's decision to allow foreign issuers to prepare their financial statements in accordance with IFRS, thereby waiving the requirement to reconcile financial statements to US GAAP.[47] This decision was not a continuation of the idea of modified national treatment, as the SEC assessed the quality of foreign standards and made recognition conditional on a sufficient degree of convergence to the US standard.[48]

In March 2008, the SEC announced further steps to implement mutual recognition.[49] These steps included discussions with the regulators of Canada, Australia, and the EU to initiate mutual recognition frameworks based on substituted compliance.[50] An agreement was finally concluded with Australia, although exemptions did not follow due to the GFC.[51]

The implementation of substituted compliance as envisaged by Tafara and Peterson stagnated, however, and was never fully implemented.[52] Although some application

[43] Commission on the Regulation of U.S. Capital Markets in the 21st Century (n 34) 36ff.

[44] SEC (n 2).

[45] Supporting the proposal (at least in part) see Susan Wolburgh Jenah, 'Commentary on a Blueprint for Cross-Border Access to U.S. Investors' (2007) 48 Harv Intl LJ 69; Greene (n 29). Even more far-reaching is Eric J Pan's proposal to transfer the regime for intra-EU firms from MiFID I to the US. See Eric J Pan, 'A European Solution to the Regulation of Cross-Border Markets' (2007) 2 Brook J Corp Fin & Com L 133. For a critical view with regard to the proposal see George W Madison and Stewart P Greene, 'TIAA-CRED Response to a Blueprint for Cross-Border Access to U.S. Investors' (2007) 48 Harv Intl LJ 99.

[46] Christopher Cox (Chairman of SEC), 'Remarks to the New York Society of Security Analysts' (14 June 2007) https://www.sec.gov/news/speech/2007/spch061407cc.htm (accessed 12 November 2022); Erik R Sirri (Director, Division of Market Regulation of SEC), 'Trading Foreign Shares' (1 March 2007) https://www.sec.gov/news/speech/2007/spch030107ers.htm (accessed 12 November 2022).

[47] SEC, 'Acceptance from Foreign Private Issuers of Financial Statements Prepared in Accordance with International Financial Reporting Standards without Reconciliation to US GAAP' 72 Fed Reg 37962 (11 July 2007); extensively: Karmel (n 8) 1700ff.

[48] Jackson (n 2) 178.

[49] SEC, 'SEC Announces Next Steps for Implementation of Mutual Recognition Concept' Press Release 2008-49 (24 March 2008) https://www.sec.gov/news/press/2008/2008-49.htm (accessed 12 November 2022).

[50] SEC, 'Statement of the European Commission and the U.S. Securities and Exchange Commission on Mutual Recognition in Securities Markets' Press Release 2008-9 (1 February 2008) https://www.sec.gov/news/press/2008/2008-9.htm (accessed 12 November 2022); SEC, 'SEC Chairman Cox, Prime Minister Rudd Meet Amid U.S.-Australia Mutual Recognition Talks' Press Release 2008-52 (29 March 2008) https://www.sec.gov/news/press/2008/2008-52.htm (accessed 12 November 2022); SEC, 'Schedule Announced for Completion of U.S.–Canadian Mutual Recognition Process Agreement' Press Release 2008-98 (29 May 2008) https://www.sec.gov/news/press/2008/2008-98.htm (accessed 12 November 2022).

[51] US–Australia Mutual Recognition Arrangement (25 August 2008) para 61 https://download.asic.gov.au/media/1346672/SEC_framework_arrangement_aug_08.pdf (accessed 12 November 2022); Verdier (n 2) 82ff. On the agreement with Australia see Edward F Greene and Omer S Oztan, 'The Attack on National Regulation' (2009) 4 CMLJ 6, 18ff.

[52] Jackson (n 2) 184. This can already be seen from the reform of rule 15a-6 (17 CFR § 240.15a-6), which goes back to the early days of substituted compliance, but which is in the tradition of the old approach of modified national treatment. See ibid 181f.

areas can be identified, the suggestion has never spread across the entire legal framework and has only been implemented selectively. However, this failure is not due to the proposal's lack of persuasiveness. Rather, it is closely linked to personnel changes within the SEC[53] and the shift of the regulatory focus in the aftermath of the GFC, where liberalization of financial markets was no longer on the agenda.[54]

III. Second generation: 'out-bound' substituted compliance

After the GFC, the focus of regulators worldwide was rather on avoiding cross-border systemic risks, inter alia, by regulating the derivatives market and increasing the resilience of banks.[55] These reforms, especially in the area of derivatives, led to an increase in extraterritorial legislation and thus to a denationalization or deterritorialization of regulation in general.[56] This development resulted in a rise in legal fragmentation, as legal and regulatory conflicts occurred more frequently in cross-border transactions because they were often subject to multiple legal orders.[57]

Second generation substituted compliance mechanisms try to mitigate this legal fragmentation. They are no longer designed to facilitate market access (in-bound) but to exempt foreign activities and entities from being subjected to US law that would otherwise apply extraterritorially (out-bound).[58] Consequently, these rules do not primarily aim at liberalizing trade, but are instruments to enable and manage cross-border transactions in a globalized environment. This description is very close to the current European Commission's understanding outlined above, according to which equivalence is 'a key instrument to effectively manage cross-border activity of market players'.[59]

This change in the landscape has been accompanied by a change in the scope of substituted compliance. In contrast to the first generation, second generation substituted compliance mainly targets institutional investors, not retail investors.[60] The focus is also not on foreign stock exchanges and foreign broker-dealers, but substituted compliance is primarily to be found in the field of derivatives.[61] Both developments are also reflected in EU equivalence mechanisms, which have a limited scope of application in areas related to retail investors but often occur in the sphere of derivatives regulation. These differences do not imply that first and second generation substituted

[53] Verdier (n 2) 87 (n 153).

[54] Jackson (n 2) 199: 'one of the Global Financial Crisis's first regulatory casualties'; Alexey Artamonov, 'Cross-Border Application of OTC Derivatives Rules' (2015) 1 JFR 206, 209.

[55] Andreas Kerkemeyer, 'A Decade after Lehman: An Assessment of Key Regulatory Responses to the Global Financial Crisis' (2019) 16 ECFR 457. See the multiple contributions on different states in Eilís V Ferran and others (eds), *The Regulatory Aftermath of the Global Financial Crisis* (CUP 2012).

[56] Christoph B Bühler, 'Finanzmarktregulierung im Spannungsfeld von Recht und Politik' (2010) 106 SJZ 469, 476; Matthias Lehmann, 'Legal Fragmentation, Extraterritoriality and Uncertainty in Global Financial Regulation' (2017) 37 OJLS 406.

[57] Generally on fragmentation in international law see Matthias Herdegen, *The Dynamics of International Law in a Globalised World* (Vittorio Klostermann 2016) 31f.

[58] Jackson (n 2) 200.

[59] Commission (n 38) 5.

[60] Jackson (n 2) 200.

[61] ibid.

compliance are mutually exclusive. Rather, they coexist within one legal system. The differences do, however, highlight the diverging motivations and conceptions behind them, which are crucial for understanding substituted compliance.

IV. Evolution of deference in the US, the EU, and Switzerland

The previous analysis has shown that the treatment of foreign firms in the US has evolved from (modified) national treatment to in-bound substituted compliance and finally to out-bound substituted compliance. The initial US departure from the idea of national treatment was fostered by shifts in market power, the US–EU regulatory dialogue, the EU's call for mutual recognition, and the introduction and expansion of equivalence in the EU. In light of these dialogues and the resulting mutual influence, it is therefore not surprising that the initial concept of substituted compliance, as proposed by Tafara and Peterson, was almost identical to the EU approach of the time.

Following the GFC, both legal systems have at least to some extent moved away from the liberal spirit underlying early forms of deference. The US and the EU no longer consider substituted compliance, respectively equivalence primarily as a means of market liberalization. Rather, the focus is on overcoming problems that arose due to legal and supervisory conflicts in the deterritorialized law of the post-financial crisis era. Thus, the development of deference in the US and the EU has been largely parallel and both jurisdictions have constantly influenced each other.[62] However, the initiative to open markets for foreign service providers and products mostly came from the EU. To this day, the US has stuck to a rather strong territorial approach, which is relaxed only when external or internal pressure pushes the US to do so. Against this background, the development of deference can also be described as one of the US as a driven force.

Switzerland's liberal approach clearly stands out from this parallel development. Switzerland has maintained the liberal pre-GFC approach of the US and the EU. It applies its laws to a lesser degree extraterritorially and, with its appropriateness and equivalence rules, not only created instruments aimed at avoiding legal and supervisory conflicts, but primarily established a liberal framework for market access. This alternative conception is mainly due to the different market power and the different economic interests of Switzerland, which have been presented in detail above.

B) The current system of substituted compliance

The existence and scope of deference can be best examined by dividing the legal system into different areas. To ensure comparability, the following analysis is based on the same categorization used in the parts on the EU and Switzerland. The analysis starts with disclosure obligations under capital markets law (I.) and is followed by an

[62] This finding of a parallel development between the US and EU does not imply that there are no differences between the systems. These are presented in detail following the analysis of the individual manifestations of substituted compliance. See ch 4 B).

examination of gatekeepers and benchmarks (II.). The third part deals with financial intermediaries (III.). In the context of broker-dealers and investment advisers, a special focus is put on the general issue of whether US law can be applied extraterritorially in the aftermath of the Supreme Court's *Morrison* decision. Finally, special attention is devoted to financial market infrastructures, where substituted compliance, especially in the area of derivatives, plays a paramount role (IV.).

I. Disclosure obligations under capital markets law

The disclosure requirements can again be divided into three phases. The first phase of market access is mainly regulated by the Securities Act of 1933 (1933 Act). Disclosure obligations on the secondary market are contained in the Securities Exchange Act of 1934 (1934 Act), as well as in the Sarbanes–Oxley Act (SOX). The third level comprises market exits and the deregistration of issuers, which are also regulated under the 1934 Act.

1. First stage: Registration under the Securities Act of 1933

The 1933 Act is based on the idea of investor protection through disclosure.[63] At the heart of the 1933 Act is the prohibition to offer or sell any security to the public unless such offer is registered with the SEC.[64] Since the registration aims at providing sufficient information to potential investors and in view that a prospectus is an essential part of the registration statement that the issuer has to file, registration fulfils a similar function. It is thus comparable to the prospectus rules in the EU and Switzerland.

The duty to register applies to all offerings in the US, irrespective of the issuer's or underwriter's domicile.[65] The territorial scope of the duty is further specified in the safe-harbour regime of Regulation S. Pursuant to this, offers and sales are only subject to the registration duty if they occur within, but not outside, the US.[66] Whether an offer or sale occurs outside the US is a complex question that is addressed in rule 903.[67] The offer or sale must first be an offshore transaction, which is the case if the offer is made only to persons outside the US and either the buyer is, or the seller believes that the buyer is, outside the US, or the transaction is executed on a foreign trading floor.[68] Secondly, no directed selling efforts may be undertaken in the US, which encompasses any activity carried out for the purpose of conditioning US markets or that

[63] '[T]he 1933 Act is essentially only a "disclosure" statute'; see Thomas Lee Hazen, *Securities Regulation in a Nutshell* (11th edn, West Academic 2016) 51.

[64] 1933 Act, s 5(a) (15 USC § 77e(a)).

[65] Edward F Greene and others, *U.S. Regulation of the International Securities and Derivatives Markets*, vol 1 (12th edn, Wolters Kluwer 2017) 3–19; Louis Loss, Joel Seligman, and Troy A Paredes, *Fundamentals of Securities Regulation*, vol 1 (7th edn, Wolters Kluwer 2019) 359; see on the reach of the provision Choi and Guzman (n 12) 909ff.

[66] Regulation S, r 901 (17 CFR § 230.901); Greene and others (n 65) 8-3ff; Loss, Seligman, and Paredes (n 65) 372ff.

[67] Concerning Regulation S, r 903 (17 CFR § 230.901) see Roberta S Karmel and Mary S Head, 'Barriers to Foreign Issuer Entry into U.S. Markets' (1993) 24 Law & Poly Intl Bus 1207, 1222f; Richard M Kosnik, 'Comments on Barriers to Foreign Issuer Entry into U.S. Markets' (1993) 24 Law & Pol'y Intl Bus 1237, 1247f.

[68] Regulation S, rr 903(a)(1) and 902(h) (17 CFR § 230.903(a)(1) and 902(h)).

could reasonably be expected to have such an effect.[69] This includes, in particular, advertising published in media that is in 'general circulation' in the US.[70] Additional criteria apply depending on the type of security and the degree of US market interest in the offer or sale.[71]

The territorial scope of the US duty to register is comparable to the obligation to publish a prospectus under Swiss and EU law. Both jurisdictions also refer to the place of the offer and not to the domicile of the issuer.[72] In detail, however, the legal systems diverge with regard to the determination of the place where the offer occurs.[73]

a) Procedure and content of the registration

The registration process can be divided into three phases: the pre-filing, waiting, and post-effective period. At the end of the first period, the registration statement is turned in, the second period concludes with the effective date of the statement by the SEC, and the last period covers the time after that.[74] The SEC has released a number of forms specifying the content of the registration statement. With respect to foreign private issuers, most notably Forms F-1 and F-3 apply, which require fewer disclosures compared to the S-Forms applicable to US issuers.[75] These reliefs are not based on a qualitative analysis of the home country law of the foreign issuer. They are, therefore, not examples of substituted compliance but a form of modified national treatment.

The required content of the prospectus is set out in section 10(a) of the 1933 Act and is further specified in Regulation S-K regarding non-financial information and Regulation S-X regarding financial statements.[76] Foreign private issuers generally have the choice of whether they want to file their financial statements in accordance with US GAAP or other accounting standards. However, if they opt for the latter, they must reconcile these statements to US GAAP, which is time-consuming and costly.[77] In 2007, as one of the first substituted compliance regimes, the SEC waived this reconciliation requirement for financial statements prepared in accordance with IFRS due to the extensive convergence between IFRS and US GAAP.[78] Such a mechanism

[69] Regulation S, rr 903(a)(2) and 902(c) (17 CFR § 230.903(a)(1) and 902(c)).

[70] ibid r 902(c) second sentence (17 CFR § 230.902(c)).

[71] ibid r 903(a)(3) (17 CFR § 230.903(a)(3)); Raymer W McQuiston, 'Rule 144A, Regulation S and Amending Glass-Steagall Act' (1991) 17 Syracuse J Intl L & Com 171, 204ff.

[72] See ch 1 C)II.1.a) and ch 3 B)I.1.

[73] These differences become apparent, for example, when comparing the criteria used by the supervisory authorities to determine whether an offer via the internet falls under the registration, respectively the prospectus obligation. SEC, 'Use of Internet Web Sites to Offer Securities, Solicit Securities Transactions or Advertise Investment Services Offshore' Interpretation, IC-23071 (23 March 1998); Erläuternder Bericht Vernehmlassungsverfahren FIDLEV, FINIV und AOV, 21; ESMA has not yet specified when a security is offered to the public in the Union.

[74] Hazen (n 63) 69ff.

[75] Thomas Werlen and Stefan Sulzer, 'Aspekte der US-amerikanischen Securities Laws' in Mathias Habersack, Peter O Mülbert, and Michael Schlitt (eds), *Unternehmensfinanzierung am Kapitalmarkt* (4th edn, Otto Schmidt 2019) para 45.36; Greene and others (n 65) 3-21ff.

[76] See 15 USC § 77j(a) and 17 CFR Part 229; Loss, Seligman, and Paredes (n 65) 247ff and 325ff.

[77] 17 CFR § 210.4-01(a)(2). On the burdens that are associated with the obligation to carry out a reconciliation see Steven M Davidoff, 'Rhetoric and Reality: A Historical Perspective on the Regulation of Foreign Private Issuers' (2010) 79 U Cin L Rev 619, 635f; Chang (n 12) 242.

[78] SEC (n 47); Jackson (n 2) 176f.

of recognizing foreign accounting standards also exists both in the EU and in Switzerland.[79]

b) Private placement exemptions

The 1933 Act broadly distinguishes between two categories of exemptions: exempted securities in section 3 and exempted transactions in section 4.[80] A further distinction is made depending on whether the exemption suspends the duty to register for the issuer or any other person reselling the security.[81]

As part of the exempted transactions, section 4(a)(2) exempts 'transactions by an issuer not involving any public offering'.[82] Under what circumstances the offering qualifies as a private offering or placement is not specified in the 1933 Act but has been fleshed out by courts in their case law and by statements of the SEC.[83] The exemption applies regardless of whether the issuer is a US or foreign private issuer.

Given the limited scope of the exemption, resales of these securities by persons other than the issuer require SEC registration. For such resales, rule 144A contains a non-exclusive safe-harbour regime.[84] Registration is not required if a person other than the issuer resells the securities only to qualified institutional buyers, reasonable steps have been taken to ensure that the buyer was aware of the operation of the exemption, and the securities sold are not in a class of securities already registered under the 1934 Act.[85] Rule 144A was partly introduced to facilitate access to the US capital market for foreign companies.[86] Foreign issuers may use the private placement exemption under section 4(a)(2) of the 1933 Act to issue securities only to underwriters, who may then use the exemption under rule 144A to resell those securities only to qualified institutional buyers. This avoids the duty to register with the SEC for all transactions.[87]

Another exemption specifically tailored to foreign private issuers is rule 801.[88] According to this rule, rights offerings by foreign private issuers are exempt from the obligation to register if certain prerequisites are met, including that US holders hold no more than 10 per cent of the outstanding class of securities that is the subject of the rights offering. Other (private placement) exemptions that have no specific reference to foreign firms include rule 144, 'section $4(1^1/_2)$' transactions, and Regulation D.[89]

[79] Concerning the EU see Commission Regulation (EC) No 1569/2007, arts 2 and 3. In Switzerland, recognition is carried out by the trading venues as part of their self-regulation. See FIDLEV, art 51.

[80] 15 USC § 77c and § 77d.

[81] Generally on exemptions to the 1930 Act see Hazen (n 63) 80ff.

[82] 15 USC § 77d(a)(2); extensively see Loss, Seligman, and Paredes (n 65) 603ff.

[83] See eg *SEC v Ralston Purina Co* 346 US 119 (1953); see also egulation McQuiston (n 71) 178ff.

[84] 17 CFR § 230.144A; Luis F Moreno Trevino, 'Access to U.S. Capital Markets for Foreign Issuers: Rule 144A Private Placements' (1993) 16 Hous J Intl L 159; Karmel and Head (n 67) 1223ff; Loss, Seligman, and Paredes (n 65) 703ff.

[85] See r 144A(b) and (d) (17 CFR § 230.144A(b) and (d)); Thomas Lee Hazen, *Securities Regulation: Cases and Materials* (9th edn, West Academic 2016) 563f.

[86] Sara Hanks, 'Rule 144A: Another Cabbage in the Chop Suey' (1990) 24 Geo Wash J Intl L & Econ 305, 306f.

[87] Concerning this procedure and other ways to avoid registration see Andreas J Roquette, 'New Developments Relating to the Internationalization of the Capital Markets' (1994) 14 U Pa J Intl Bus L 565, 584.

[88] See 17 CFR § 230.801; Werlen and Sulzer (n 75) paras 45.113ff; Loss, Seligman, and Paredes (n 65) 370f.

[89] See 17 CFR § 144, and § 230.500; on these exemptions see egulation McQuiston (n 71) 181ff and 184ff; see extensively John C Coffee Jr, Hillary A Sale, and M Todd Henderson, *Securities Regulation* (2nd edn,

Overall, the US is at least somewhat responsive to the needs of foreign issuers through the private placement exemptions. However, there are neither substituted compliance rules—with the exception of IFRS recognition—nor far-reaching arrangements for recognition. The EU and even more so Switzerland have implemented considerably more liberal tools, for example, by recognizing prospectuses that have been drafted in accordance with equivalent or appropriate foreign law.[90]

2. Second stage: Disclosure on the secondary market

Disclosure obligations on the secondary market are mainly regulated in the 1934 Act. Since the field of disclosure is very broad, the following analysis will focus on those obligations containing specific rules in relation to foreign issuers. A general distinction can be made between disclosure obligations that arise in the course of the initial registration with the SEC under section 12 of the 1934 Act (a)), those that follow such registration at regular intervals (b)), and event-driven obligations such as the duty to disclose information on major holdings or insider information (c)).

a) Registration under the Securities Exchange Act of 1934

Section 12 of the 1934 Act requires registration of a class of securities in two instances. First, registration is needed if the security is traded on a national securities exchange (listed company).[91] Consequently, foreign issuers seeking a secondary listing on a US exchange must register with the SEC. There are no exceptions specifically tailored to foreign private issuers.

Secondly, registration is required if the security is traded over-the-counter (OTC) and the issuer has total assets exceeding US$10 million and a class of equity securities held by either 2,000 persons or 500 persons in the case of not accredited investors.[92] To not cut off US investors from foreign capital more than necessary and prevent foreign private issuers from being subjected to SEC regulation without their knowledge, the SEC introduced two exceptions to this rule.[93] According to rule 12g3-2(b), a foreign private issuer is exempt from the duty to register if it is not already required to file reports with the SEC under other provisions, the issuer is listed in a foreign jurisdiction in which its securities are primarily traded, and it has published certain information in English that may be relevant to US investors for their investment decisions.[94] Under rule 12g3-2(a), foreign private issuers are further exempt if fewer than 300 US

Foundation Press 2015) 370ff, 530ff, and 542ff; particularly on the s 4(1$^1/_2$) exemption see Carl W Schneider, 'Section 4(1-1/2)-Private Resales of Restricted or Control Securities' (1988) 49 Ohio State LJ 501.

[90] See Prospectus Regulation, art 29 and FIDLEG, art 54.

[91] 1934 Act, s 12(a) (15 USC § 78l(a)). This duty to register applies regardless of whether a public offer is placed. See Greene and others (n 65) 4-10.

[92] 1934 Act, s 12(g) (15 USC § 78l(g)).

[93] Greene, Braverman, Sperber (n 13) 424ff.

[94] 17 CFR § 240.12g3-2(b). The information required is based on the issuer's home country law, which is why this obligation is not a major hurdle. See Michael A Perino, 'American Corporate Reform Abroad: Sarbanes-Oxley and the Foreign Private Issuer' (2003) 4 EBOR 213, 218; Greene and others (n 65) 4-13ff.

investors hold the class of securities.[95] A general exemption based on the idea of substituted compliance does not exist.[96]

If registration is required in accordance with the above-mentioned provisions, the question arises as to the content of this registration. The SEC has published various forms that specify the content of the registration statement. In relation to foreign private issuers, as defined in rule 3b-4(c), Form 20-F applies.[97] Financial statements required under Item 17(a) of the form may be prepared either in accordance with US GAAP or with IFRS.[98] Owing to the SEC's decision from 2007 described above, which was based on the idea of substituted compliance, no reconciliation is required for IFRS financial statements.[99] If foreign private issuers use other generally accepted accounting principles, a reconciliation to US GAAP is still required.[100]

b) Periodic disclosure

Issuers registered with the SEC under the 1934 Act or subject to reporting requirements under section 15(d) 1934 Act must file annual and quarterly reports.[101] With respect to annual reports, foreign private issuers may use Form 20-F, which has been amended multiple times, most notably by section 404 SOX.[102] Financial statements required under Form 20-F can again be prepared in accordance with IFRS without the need for a reconciliation to US-GAAP.[103] However, there is no option to waive the duty to file Form 20-F as a whole if a comparable annual financial statement has already been published in the home country of the issuer.[104]

With regard to quarterly reports, special rules apply to foreign private issuers. They are generally exempt from filing these reports on Form 10-Q as long as they are required to furnish reports pursuant to Form 6-K, which is discussed in the next part.[105] Moreover, there are some specific periodic disclosure duties, such as the duty introduced by the Dodd-Frank Act to disclose all information regarding the use of conflict minerals and payments for extractive resources annually.[106]

c) Event-driven disclosure

There are a variety of events triggering disclosure obligations under US capital markets law. In many of these cases, foreign issuers are treated in the same way as US

[95] 17 CFR § 240.12g3-2(a).

[96] Such an approach based on greater deference was already advocated in 1995 but failed to gain acceptance: Greene, Braverman, and Sperber (n 13) 436ff.

[97] See in great detail on Form 20-F in Greene and others (n 65) 4-26ff; Loss, Seligman, and Paredes (n 65) 360ff.

[98] Form 20-F, item 17(c) first sentence.

[99] SEC (n 47).

[100] See Form 20-F, item 17(c) fourth sentence no (2). In addition, financial statements based on such other recognized accounting standards must include all other information required by US GAAP and Regulation S-X (17 CFR Part 210) that is not part of the financial statements and therefore not part of the reconciliation. See Form 20-F, item 18(b).

[101] See 1934 Act, s 13(a) and rr 13a-1 and 13a-13 (15 USC § 78m(a) and 17 CFR § 240.13a-1 and 13a-13). See Loss, Seligman, and Paredes (n 65) 793ff and 797ff.

[102] See 15 USC § 7262.

[103] See n 78 (ch 4).

[104] Such a far-reaching deference mechanism exists in the EU. See ch 1 C)II.1.b)aa).

[105] See r 13(b)(2) (17 CFR § 240.13a-13); Greene and others (n 65) 4-19f.

[106] See 1934 Act, s 13(p) and (q), as introduced by Dodd-Frank Act, ss 1502(b) and 1504 (15 USC § 78m(p) and (q)); Greene and others (n 65) 4-105ff.

issuers. One example of this is the disclosure obligation concerning major holdings. If a person acquires ownership of more than 5 per cent of a class of equity securities registered under section 12 of the 1934 Act, they must file a statement with the Commission in accordance with section 13(d) of the 1934 Act. This obligation applies regardless of the issuer's domicile, and there are no exemptions for foreign issuers.[107]

With regard to current reports, the situation is different. US issuers must file current reports on Form 8-K in a multitude of cases. These include signing, amending or terminating material definitive agreements not made in the ordinary course of business, bankruptcies or receiverships.[108] This duty does not apply to foreign private issuers required to make reports on Form 6-K.[109] Form 6-K must be filed each time the foreign issuer is required to disclose information under the rules of its home country or the stock exchange on which its securities are traded or when it is required to disclose information to its security holders.[110] This regime alleviates the situation for foreign issuers, as the reference to the home country rules achieves broad parallelism between the disclosure obligations in the US and the issuer's home country. The arrangement, therefore, takes into account the interests of foreign issuers. There is, however, no substituted compliance provision for event-driven disclosures.

3. Third stage: Market exits and deregistration

If an issuer wants to withdraw securities from listing on a US exchange or from registration under section 12(b) 1934 Act, it must file Form 25.[111] The form applies irrespective of the issuer's place of domicile. The filing of Form 25 is subject to several requirements, including compliance with the rules of the respective exchange and the issuance of a public notice.[112] The requirements apply equally to foreign and domestic issuers.

However, the filing of Form 25 does not affect the obligations following from the registration under section 12(g) 1934 Act and the reporting obligations under section 15(d) 1934 Act, which consequently continue to apply.[113] Deregistration from section 12(g) 1934 Act is subject to strict conditions, inter alia, that fewer than 300 persons hold the respective securities class.[114] In light of these strict requirements, many commentators feared that foreign issuers would be discouraged from registering in the first place, which would keep capital out of the US market and ultimately

[107] Greene and others (n 65) 6-8.

[108] See Form 8-K, ss 1–6 and 9; on quarterly and current reports see Loss, Seligman, and Paredes (n 65) 797ff.

[109] See r 13a-11(a) (17 CFR § 240.13a-11(a)).

[110] Form 6-K, 2; on this form see Greene and others (n 65) 4-20ff.

[111] See 1934 Act, s 12(d) second sentence and r 12d2-2(c)(1) (15 USC § 78l(d) and 17 CFR § 240.12d2-2(c)(1)); Greene and others (n 65) 4-168.

[112] See r 12d2-2(c)(2) (17 CFR § 240.12d2-2(c)(2)).

[113] See Preliminary Note No 1 to r 12d2-2 (17 CFR § 240.12d2-2).

[114] See 1934 Act, s 12(g)(4) and r 12g-4(a) (15 USC § 78l(g)(4) and 17 CFR § 240.12g-4(a)); Loss, Seligman, and Paredes (n 65) 816f.

harm US investors.[115] This concern was also recognized by the SEC, leading it to adopt special rules for foreign issuers.[116]

The most important easement of this reform for foreign private issuers was the adoption of rule 12h-6.[117] According to this rule, the decisive criterion for foreign issuers is no longer that their securities are held by fewer than 300 residents of the US, but that the average daily trading volume in their securities in the US has been no greater than 5 per cent of the average daily trading volume of that class of securities on a worldwide basis in a recent 12-month period.[118] Such deregistration also terminates and not just suspends the reporting obligations under section 15(d) 1934 Act.[119] These rules greatly facilitate the termination of registration for foreign issuers. They are designed in accordance with the concept of modified national treatment.[120] Since the special treatment of foreign issuers is not linked to qualitative criteria regarding the foreign legal system, this exemption is not based on the idea of substituted compliance.

II. Gatekeepers and benchmarks

1. Credit rating agencies

Rating agencies were barely regulated for a long time.[121] The US was one of the first jurisdictions to change this with the adoption of the Credit Rating Agency Reform Act of 2006, which added section 15E to the 1934 Act.[122] The backdrop to the reform were several financial scandals, especially one surrounding *Enron*, in which rating agencies assessed the company with an 'investment grade' rating until four days before its bankruptcy.[123] Following the GFC, further amendments were adopted, including the Dodd-Frank Act, which was intended to reduce reliance on ratings.[124]

115 Robert C Pozen, 'Can European Companies Escape U.S. Listings?' (2004) Harvard Law School Working Paper No. 464 https://ssrn.com/abstract=511942 (accessed 12 November 2022). For an economic analysis see András Marosi and Nadia Massoud, '"You Can Enter but You Cannot Leave . . . ": U.S. Securities Markets and Foreign Firms' (2008) 63 J Fin 2477.

116 SEC, 'Final Rule on Termination of a Foreign Private Issuer's Registration of a Class of Securities' 72 Fed Reg 16934 (5 April 2007) https://www.sec.gov/rules/final/2007/34-55540fr.pdf (accessed 12 November 2022). For the so-called 'deregistration rule' see Christopher Hung Nie Woo, 'United States Securities Regulation and Foreign Private Issuers: Lessons from the Sarbanes-Oxley Act' (2011) 48 Am Bus LJ 119, 149.

117 17 CFR § 240.12h-6; see Hung Nie Woo (n 116) 149f.

118 See r 12h-6(a)(4). In addition, some time limits have to be observed, in particular a one-year period during which there must have been a reporting obligation and no new registered offering has taken place in the US. The application must be made by filing Form 15F. See Greene and others (n 65) 4-169ff.

119 Greene and others (n 65) 4-169; concerning the suspension of the requirements see ibid 4-172f.

120 Jackson (n 2) 174.

121 See references in n 66 (ch 3).

122 See 15 USC § 78o-7; Elisabetta Conte and Federico Parmeggiani, 'The Regulation of Credit Rating Agency across USA and EU' (11 November 2008) 5ff http://ssrn.com/abstract=2214998 (accessed 12 November 2022).

123 Claire A Hill, 'Regulating the Rating Agencies' (2004) 82 Wash U L Q 43; John C Coffee Jr, *Gatekeepers: The Professions and Corporate Governance* (OUP 2006) 34f. On the legislative background see SEC, 'Report on the Role and Function of Credit Rating Agencies in the Operation of the Securities Markets' (January 2003) https://www.sec.gov/news/studies/credratingreport0103.pdf (accessed 12 November 2022).

124 See Dodd-Frank Act, s 939a (15 USC § 78o-7). As part of the implementation of this rule, the SEC deleted numerous references to ratings, for example, in Forms S-3 and F-3. See Mohammed Hemraj, *Credit Rating Agencies* (Springer 2015) 123ff.

To use a rating for regulatory purposes in the US, an agency can voluntarily apply for recognition as a 'nationally recognized statistical rating organization' (NRSRO). This mechanism entered into force in 1975.[125] This recognition applies regardless of the agency's domicile and therefore to both US and foreign agencies.[126] In contrast to the regulation of the EU and Switzerland, no substituted compliance provision exempts foreign rating agencies from the recognition procedure, let alone recognize foreign ratings.[127] This absence is likely attributable to the dominance of the US in the rating agency market and the resulting lack of pressure to open up the market in this area.

2. Statutory auditors

In the wake of several scandals at the beginning of this millennium, the US legislator reacted, inter alia, with the adoption of the Sarbanes–Oxley Act.[128] In its Title I, the Act lays the foundation for the establishment of the Public Company Accounting Oversight Board (PCAOB), which has the duty pursuant to section 101(c)(1) SOX to register public accounting firms that prepare audit reports for issuers in accordance with section 102 SOX.[129] The scope of application is not limited to US public accounting firms, but pursuant to section 106(a) SOX, it also encompasses foreign accounting firms preparing or furnishing an audit report with respect to any US issuer.[130] The clear wording refutes the presumption against extraterritoriality established by the Supreme Court in the *Morrison* case.[131] Therefore, these foreign accounting firms have to register with the PCAOB and are treated 'in the same manner and to the same extent as a public accounting firm that is organized and operates under the laws of the United States'. At the outset, the SOX, therefore, follows the principle of national treatment.

After the adoption of the SOX, great international resistance emerged. The EU called for an exemption from registration under section 106(c) SOX, which foresees such an exemption if it is 'determine[d] necessary or appropriate in the public interest or for the protection of investors'.[132] Since the exemption does not impose a qualitative

[125] On the historic dimension see Hill (n 123) 53ff; Chiara Picciau, 'The Evolution of the Liability of Credit Rating Agencies in the United States and in the European Union' (2018) 15 ECFR 339, 344ff. On the system in general see Coffee (n 123) 289ff.

[126] The list of NRSRO already includes foreign agencies, for instance, from Mexico and Japan; Ulrich G Schroeter, 'Grenzüberschreitende Verhaltenspflichten und Haftung von Rating-Agenturen' in Dirk A Zetzsche and Matthias Lehmann (eds), *Grenzüberschreitende Finanzdienstleistungen* (Mohr Siebeck 2018) § 11 paras 30f.

[127] In light of this restrictive and rather protectionist approach, the accusation of European regulatory imperialism raised by Kristina St Charles seems unjustified. See Kristina St Charles, 'Regulatory Imperialism: The Worldwide Export of European Regulatory Principles on Credit Rating Agencies' (2010) 19 Minn J Intl L 399.

[128] Extensively on the act see Byron F Egan, 'Major Themes of the Sarbanes-Oxley Act' (2008) 42 Tex J Bus L 339; see for a comparison between the Sarbanes–Oxley Act and the SAD in the EU Zeynep Sener, 'Effect of the Sarbanes-Oxley Act of 2002 on the EU Law Regarding Auditors and Auditors' Independence' (2010) 11 Bus L Intl 133, 136ff.

[129] See 15 USC § 7211(c)(1) and § 7212.

[130] See 15 USC § 7216(a); Hans C von der Crone and Katja Roth, 'Der Sarbanes-Oxley Act und seine extraterritoriale Bedeutung' (2003) 12 AJP/PJA 131, 132 and 137; see also Kathy H Y Hsu, Ronald G Cheek, and Harlan L Etheridge, 'The Impact of Sarbanes-Oxley Act on Non-U.S. Accounting Firms' (2005) 4 J of Intl Bus Research 1.

[131] See extensively ch 4 B)III.1.a).

[132] See 15 USC § 7216(c); Frits Bolkestein (EU Commission), 'Letter to Charles M Niemeier: Chairman of the PCAOB' (11 April 2003) 3 https://pcaob-assets.azureedge.net/pcaob-dev/docs/default-source/rulemaking/docket_001/042_european_union.pdf?sfvrsn=b04ad4b3_0 (accessed 12 November 2022).

requirement with regard to the foreign legal system, it is not a substituted compliance provision. To date, the PCAOB has not fully exempted any foreign jurisdiction from registration.[133] Instead, it has explicitly rejected a mutual recognition approach on the basis of deference.[134]

To avoid legal and supervisory conflicts and partly giving in to international pressure, the PCAOB, however, proclaimed a 'cooperative approach'.[135] This approach is primarily based on two pillars. On the one hand, foreign firms may withhold information from their application if providing the information would violate non-US law.[136] This provision represents a conflict avoidance instrument, which can also be found in the EU and Switzerland. Yet, it does not impose any qualitative requirements on the foreign law and thus does not constitute a substituted compliance provision.

On the other hand, rules 4011 and 4012 Bylaws and Rules of PCAOB allow foreign registered public accounting firms to request that the PCAOB relies on foreign inspections, i.e. on inspections by the home supervisory authority.[137] Such reliance and its extent depend primarily on the level of independence and rigour of the foreign system and whether it contains adequate standards.[138] The result is a 'sliding scale' where 'the more independent and robust a home country system [is], the higher the reliance on that system'.[139] The PCAOB further specified the standards for this sliding scale in a guidance in 2007, which also introduced the concept of 'full reliance', according to which the involvement of the PCAOB in foreign inspections is minimized when the standards of the foreign legal system are particularly rigorous.[140] This set-up partially follows the concept of substituted compliance. Although foreign audit firms must still comply with US law, which means, inter alia, that audits have to be conducted in

[133] On the contrary, the PCAOB has explicitly decided not to grant general exemptions from registration. See PCAOB, 'Registration System for Public Accounting Firms' Release No 2003-007 (6 May 2003) 13; confirming this decision: PCAOB, 'Request for Public Comment on Proposed Policy Statement: Guidance Regarding Implementation of PCAOB Rule 4012' Release No 2007-011 (5 December 2007) A1–3.

[134] PCAOB, 'Final Rules Relating to the Oversight of Non-U.S. Public Accounting Firms' Release No 2004-005 (9 June 2004) A2–6.

[135] See eg PCAOB, 'Briefing Paper: Oversight of Non-U.S. Public Accounting Firms' Release No 2003-020 (28 October 2003) 2; PCAOB, 'Proposed Rules Relating to the Oversight of Non-U.S. Public Accounting Firms' Release No 2003-024 (10 December 2003); summarizing the action by the PCAOB see Erin M Lyons, 'The Implications of the Sarbanes-Oxley Act for U.S. Foreign Relations' (2008) Thesis at the Ohio State University 62ff https://kb.osu.edu/bitstream/handle/1811/32187/Final_Erin_Lyons_Thesis.pdf (accessed 12 November 2022).

[136] See Bylaws and Rules of PCAOB, rr 2105 and 2207; Xiao Luo, 'Accessing Foreign Audit Work Papers and the Conflicting Non-U.S. Laws Defense' (2015) 18 NYU J Legis & Pub Pol'y 185, 192ff. On potential conflicts with Swiss supervisory law see Urs Bertschinger in Rolf Watter and Urs Bertschinger (eds), *BSK-Revisionsrecht* (Helbing Lichtenhahn 2011) art 1 para 121.

[137] The general provision for inspections is SOX, s 104(a) (15 USC § 7214(a)).

[138] Bylaws and Rules of PCAOB, r 4012(a)(1); see PCAOB, 'Proposed Rules Relating to the Oversight of Non-U.S. Public Accounting Firms' (n 135) 10ff and A2–2ff; PCAOB, 'Request for Public Comment on Proposed Policy Statement: Guidance Regarding Implementation of PCAOB Rule 4012' (n 133) A1–7ff.

[139] PCAOB, 'Briefing Paper: Oversight of Non-U.S. Public Accounting Firms' (n 135) 2.

[140] The exact criteria were the subject of a public consultation by the PCAOB, which allowed foreign authorities to submit comments on the PCAOB's proposal. These comments were then followed by a roundtable. See PCAOB, 'Request for Public Comment on Proposed Policy Statement: Guidance Regarding Implementation of PCAOB Rule 4012' (n 133); PCAOB, 'Roundtable on Proposed Policy Statement Regarding Rule 4012' (25 June 2008) https://pcaobus.org/news-events/events/event-details/pcaob-roundtable-on-proposed-policy-statement-regarding-rule-4012_286 (accessed 12 November 2022).

accordance with the US Generally Accepted Auditing Standards (GAAS) and thus no withdrawal of domestic law takes place,[141] the PCAOB withdraws its oversight competence on the basis of a qualitative evaluation of the foreign supervision. In this respect, the rules follow the idea of substituted compliance. Consequently, the PCAOB implemented a system of *mutual reliance* on foreign *supervision*, but not a system of *mutual recognition* of foreign *regulation*.[142]

A similar rule exists with regard to foreign investigations and adjudications.[143] Furthermore, the PCAOB adopted rules to facilitate inspections and investigations of US accounting firms by foreign authorities.[144] The bottom line is that the PCAOB has not fully followed the substituted compliance approach. However, it has created more and more regulatory and supervisory easements, some of which led to a retreat of regulatory enforcement. Compared to the EU and Switzerland, the US approach to deference is nevertheless far less developed and more restrictive in this area.

3. Benchmarks

Despite the many scandals surrounding benchmarks, the US has repeatedly decided against introducing ex-ante regulation of benchmarks.[145] Consequently, its legal system does not include substituted compliance provisions. Rather, authorities concentrate on ex-post prosecutions of violations, especially offences against the prohibition of market manipulation.[146]

As seen above, the US approach is in line with that of Switzerland but is opposed to the approach of the EU, which established extensive ex-ante regulation with the adoption of the Benchmark Regulation (BMR) in 2016.[147] Because the US feared that inclusion of their benchmarks in the EU would be made more difficult, they pushed for the introduction of liberal third country provisions.[148] US pressure was thus a major factor behind the current recognition and endorsement regime of the BMR.[149]

[141] PCAOB, 'Registration System for Public Accounting Firms' (n 133) 14.

[142] Bertschinger (n 136n) art 1 para 122.

[143] Bylaws and Rules of PCAOB, r 5113; see PCAOB, 'Proposed Rules Relating to the Oversight of Non-U.S. Public Accounting Firms' (n 135) A2–6f.

[144] Bylaws and Rules of PCAOB, rr 6001 and 6002; comparable provisions are RAG, art 26 in Switzerland and SAD, art 47 in the EU.

[145] Isabella Brosig, *Benchmark-Manipulation* (Nomos 2018) 279; see also Timothy Massad (Chairman of CFTC), 'Remarks before the Natural Gas Roundtable' (26 May 2015) https://www.cftc.gov/PressRoom/SpeechesTestimony/opamassad-23 (accessed 12 November 2022): 'The United States does not have a government-sponsored supervisory regime for benchmarks. That's simply not how our system works.' Critical of this is Gina-Gail S Fletcher, 'Benchmark Regulation' (2017) 102 Iowa L Rev 1929, 1962ff. For a mediating view see Andrew Verstein, 'Benchmark Manipulation' (2015) 56 BC L Rev 215, 250ff.

[146] See also with case examples Fletcher (n 145) 1936ff.

[147] See extensively ch 1 C)II.2.c) and ch 3 B)II.3.

[148] Huw Jones, 'U.S. Under Pressure to Match EU Rules on Market Benchmarks' *Reuters* (21 November 2014) https://www.reuters.com/article/us-usa-eu-regulations-idUSKCN0J51DN20141121 (accessed 12 November 2022); Philip Stafford, 'CFTC Warns EU Rules May Force Tighter US Derivative Regulation' *Financial Times* (20 November 2014) https://www.ft.com/content/d10bbd98-70ad-11e4-9129-00144feabdc0 (accessed 12 November 2022).

[149] Brosig (n 145) 361; Kristina L Gütte, *Regulierung finanzieller Referenzwerte* (Mohr Siebeck 2020) 372.

III. Financial intermediaries

1. Brokers, dealers, and investment advisers

US securities law distinguishes between brokers, dealers, and investment advisers.[150] Brokers and dealers, collectively called broker-dealers, are regulated under the 1934 Act. They are defined as persons engaging in the business either of 'effecting transactions in securities for the account others' (brokers) or of 'buying and selling securities ... for such person's own account through a broker or otherwise' (dealers).[151] Investment advisers are subject to the Investment Advisers Act 1940 (IAA). They are generally defined as 'any person who, for compensation, engages in the business of advising others ..., as to the value of securities or as to the advisability of investing in, purchasing, or selling securities'.[152] The activities of brokers, dealers and investment advisers are largely comparable to the activities and services of investment firms as set out in the Annex to MiFID II of the EU. It is therefore appropriate to compare their regulation with that of investment firms under MiFIR and MiFID II.[153]

Before the regulation of foreign broker-dealers (b)) and investment advisers (c)) is examined in more detail, the prior question of whether the duty to register with the SEC can be applied extraterritorially in the first place, i.e. to foreign firms, is addressed (a)). This question has been intensively discussed since the Supreme Court's landmark decision in *Morrison* but has not been adequately answered to date. The issue of extraterritoriality is closely linked to deference, as the degree of extraterritorial application of law determines the need for deference.

a) *The overarching problem of extraterritoriality*

aa) Impact of *Morrison* on registration of non-US broker-dealers and investment advisers Both broker-dealers and investment firms are generally required to register with the SEC before they are allowed to provide services to clients.[154] Traditionally, the SEC has interpreted these duties as applying to both US and non-US domiciled firms. To justify the extraterritorial application in the case of investment advisers, the SEC invoked the conduct and effects test.[155] With respect to broker-dealers, the SEC argued using an alleged presumption of extraterritoriality.[156]

[150] Criticizing this distinction see Christine Lazaro, 'The Future of Financial Advice: Eliminating the False Distinction Between Brokers and Investment Advisers' (2013) 87 St John's L Rev 381.

[151] See 1934 Act, s 3(a)(4) and (5) (15 USC § 78c(a)(4) and (5)).

[152] IAA, s 202(a)(11) (15 USC § 80b-2(a)(11)).

[153] See in MiFID II: Annex I, Section A, nos (1) and (2) for brokers, no (3) for dealers, and no (5) for investment advisers.

[154] See 1934 Act, s 15(a)(1) (15 USC § 78o(a)(1)) for brokers and dealers and IAA, s 203(a) (15 USC § 80b-3(a)) regarding investment advisers. There are further requirements on the state level for broker-dealers and investment advisers which are not addressed in this book. See Greene and others (n 65) 14-165f and 16-97ff.

[155] SEC (Division of Investment Management), 'Protecting Investors: A Half Century of Investment Company Regulation' (May 1992) 228ff https://www.sec.gov/divisions/investment/guidance/icreg50-92.pdf (accessed 12 November 2022).

[156] See SEC, 'Registration Requirements for Foreign Broker Dealers, Exchange Act' 54 Fed Reg 30013, 30016 (18 July 1989) https://www.sec.gov/rules/final/34-27017.pdf (accessed 12 November 2022). In this act, the SEC introduced an exemption for foreign broker-dealers in r 15a-6 (17 CFR § 240.15a-6).

Both lines of argumentation are highly questionable since the Supreme Court's *Morrison* ruling of 2010,[157] the facts of which are as follows. The National Australia Bank, a foreign bank whose shares are not traded on US exchanges, acquired HomeSide Lending, a company headquartered in Florida. This company allegedly manipulated its financial models, and the National Australia Bank officials allegedly knew about these manipulations. As a consequence of these manipulations, National Australia Bank had to write down the value of HomeSide's assets, which led to a fall in the price of its shares. As a result of this fall in the share price, shareholders suffered losses. Several *foreign* shareholders,[158] who had purchased shares of the *foreign* National Australia Bank before the write-down on *foreign* exchanges, brought an action before the Federal District Court for violation of sections 10(b) and 20(a) of the 1934 Act and SEC rule 10b-5.[159]

In its decision, the Supreme Court found that: 'Section 10(b) does not provide a cause of action to foreign plaintiffs suing foreign and American defendants for misconduct in connection with securities traded on foreign exchanges.'[160] Contrary to the first two instances, the Supreme Court did not consider the decisive issue to be one of jurisdiction. Rather, the question of whether a provision has an extraterritorial reach is one of merits.[161] The starting point for this determination is the presumption against extraterritoriality. According to the Supreme Court, '[w]hen a statute gives no clear indication of an extraterritorial application, it has none'.[162] The Court went on to reject the conduct and effects test that has long been used to determine extraterritoriality.[163] It criticized that this test neither leads to predictable results nor

Accordingly, the SEC had to assume that the general duty to register applies extraterritorially. Since the SEC does not provide any evidence for the alleged extraterritoriality, it must be inferred that it simply assumed extraterritoriality. See also Arthur B Laby, 'Regulation of Global Financial Firms After Morrison v. National Australia Bank' (2013) 87 St John's L Rev 561, 580 and 588f.

157 *Morrison v National Australia Bank* 561 US 247 (2010); see Elizabeth Cosenza, 'Paradise Lost: 10(b) after Morrison v National Australia Bank' (2010–2011) 11 Chic J Intl L 343; Edward F Greene and Arpan Patel, 'Consequences of Morrison v NAB, securities litigation and beyond' (2016) 11 CMLJ 145; Peter Mankowski, 'Extraterritoriale Reichweite des US-Wertpapierrechts?' (2010) 13 NZG 961; Linda J Silbermann, 'Morrison v. National Australia Bank: Implications for Global Securities Class Actions' (2010) 12 YPIL 123; Nathan Lee, 'The Extraterritorial Reach of United States Securities Actions After Morrison v. National Australian Bank' (2015) 13 Rich J Global L & Bus 623.

158 At the very beginning, a US investor named Morrison was also among the plaintiffs. However, when the case reached the Supreme Court, the plaintiffs were all Australians. Ironically, the case was still named after Morrison.

159 See 15 USC § 78j and § 78t, as well as 17 CFR § 240.10b-5. Because of all these foreign links, *Morrison* was also called 'foreign cubed' or 'f-cubed'. See Richard Painter, Douglas Dunham, and Ellen Quackenbos, 'When Courts and Congress Don't Say What They Mean' (2011) 20 Minn J Intl L 1, 5; Alex Reed, 'But I'm an American! A Text-Based Rationale for Dismissing F-Squared Securities Fraud Claims After Morrison v. National Australia Bank' (2012) 14 U Pa J Bus L 515.

160 *Morrison v National Australia Bank* (n 157).

161 ibid 253f.

162 ibid 280; see also American Law Institute, Restatement (Fourth) of the Foreign Relations Law of the US (2018), § 404.

163 *Morrison v National Australia Bank* (n 157) 261; reaffirming this ruling see *SEC v Gruss* 859 F Supp 2d 653, 661 (2012).

is it based on the intention of Congress. Consequently, a clear signal by Congress is needed to rebut the presumption and apply a rule extraterritorially.

On its face, the case has no regulatory implications, as it deals with private enforcement issues and whether foreign plaintiffs can sue foreign issuers in US courts.[164] On a closer look, however, fundamental regulatory questions arise.[165] When taking the presumption against extraterritorial application seriously, each regulatory obligation must be re-examined to determine whether Congress intended it to be applied extraterritorially, and thus whether it applies to foreign firms.[166]

With respect to broker-dealers, there would thus have to be a clear congressional intent indicating that 'any broker or dealer' in section 15(a) 1934 Act also includes foreign-based broker-dealers, thereby rebutting the presumption against extraterritoriality.[167] However, such a clear indication is difficult to find for several reasons.[168] First and foremost, the Supreme Court stated in *Morrison* that the 1934 Act has extraterritorial effects only in very limited cases. Consequently, 'any broker or dealer' generally only refers to US broker-dealers. Moreover, the Supreme Court rejected the argument that a general extraterritorial scope of the 1934 Act can be inferred from specific provisions like section 30(a) and (b) 1934 Act, which have an explicit extraterritorial scope.[169] Finally, no clear indication by Congress of a rebuttal of the presumption against extraterritoriality can be derived from section 929P Dodd-Frank Act.[170] According to this provision, district courts shall have jurisdiction in cases involving only foreign investors if the conduct occurs inside the US and in cases where the conduct occurs outside the US but has a foreseeable and substantial effect within the US.[171] On the one hand, section 929P Dodd-Frank Act refers only to jurisdictional issues and thus defines the circumstances in which US courts are competent. The Supreme Court, however, explicitly classified the issue as one of merits and not jurisdiction.[172] Hence, the Dodd-Frank Act does not tackle the right problem and

[164] This explains why most of the literature concerns these questions. See Katherine Florey, 'State Law, U.S. Power, Foreign Disputes: Understanding the Extraterritorial Effects of State Law in the Wake of Morrison v. National Australia Bank' (2012) 92 BU L Rev 535, 548f; Roger W Kirby, 'Access to United States Courts by Purchasers of Foreign Listed Securities in the Aftermath of Morrison v. National Australia Bank Ltd.' (2011) 7 Hastings Bus LJ 223, 225; Reed (n 159) 537f.

[165] Regulatory questions should be understood in this context as questions of ex-ante regulation. By contrast, questions involving ex-post regulation are those of enforcement.

[166] In *SEC v Benger*, the District Court applied the *Morrison* decision to the regulatory question of whether registration is required for foreign transactions by non-US brokers. It upheld the *Morrison* ruling and, as a result, denied a duty to register in the case at issue. See *US Securities & Exchange Commission v Benger* 934 F Supp 2d 1008 (ND Ill 2013).

[167] 15 USC § 78o.

[168] See extensively Laby (n 156) 590ff, who argues that the only way to justify an extraterritorial application in the case of broker-dealers might be to claim that rule 15a-6 (17 CFR § 240.15a-6) is an agency rule for which the SEC has discretion.

[169] See 15 USC § 78dd(a) and (b); *Morrison v National Australia Bank* (n 157) 248.

[170] 15 USC § 77v(c); see for an intensive discussion with further references to both sides: Raphael G Toman, 'The Extraterritorial Reach of the U.S. Securities Laws and Non-Conventional Securities' (2018) 14 NYU JL & Bus 657, 673ff.

[171] Dodd-Frank Act, s 929P(b)(1) (15 USC § 77v(c)).

[172] *Morrison v National Australia Bank* (n 157) 253f; George T Conway III, 'Extraterritoriality of the Federal Securities Laws After Dodd-Frank' (21 July 2010) http://www.wlrk.com/webdocs/wlrknew/WLRKMemos/WLRK/WLRK.17763.10.pdf (accessed 12 November 2022); Tamar Frankel and Arthur B Laby, *Regulation of Money Managers* (3rd edn, Wolters Kluwer 2020) 36-27ff.

cannot be used as a clear indication of extraterritoriality. On the other hand, the provision explicitly refers to 'Enforcement by the Commission' in its heading and later on to extraterritorial jurisdiction with respect to 'Antifraud Provisions of the Federal Securities Laws'. In light of this narrow scope, it could be argued that Dodd-Frank does not address issues of regulation and registration but is limited to ex-post enforcement of antifraud provisions.[173] In sum, it remains doubtful whether the SEC will be able to demonstrate that there is a clear congressional intent rebutting the presumption against extraterritoriality.

With regard to investment advisers, a clear indication of Congress would again be needed, which demonstrates that the registration requirement encompasses foreign investment advisers and thus applies extraterritorially.[174] Since the *Morrison* decision, it is no longer sufficient for the SEC to rely on the conduct and effects test.[175] The wording of section 203(a) IAA is unclear in this regard. A reference to the definition of 'interstate commerce', which also refers to foreign countries, is not enough as the Supreme Court held in *Morrison*.[176] An indication by Congress of the extraterritorial applicability of the registration requirement could, however, be inferred from the Dodd-Frank Act. Section 403 of the Act amends the exemption relating to foreign private advisers under section 203(b) IAA.[177] It could be concluded from the exemption that Congress generally wanted foreign advisers to register with the SEC. However, the Supreme Court in *Morrison* explicitly rejected a conclusion on the general extraterritoriality of a legal act from specific provisions.[178] Therefore, it is unlikely that the argument will be upheld in court.[179]

Ultimately, it is therefore highly doubtful whether the SEC can require foreign broker-dealers and investment advisers to register with it post-*Morrison*. These doubts, however, have not changed the SEC's practice of requiring such registration.[180] It remains to be seen whether courts will intervene and urge Congress to take a clearer stance to rebut the presumption against extraterritoriality.

bb) Interrelation between extraterritoriality and deference For a long time, US courts expanded the extraterritorial application of US law. This, in combination with the concept of punitive damages, not only attracted foreign litigation to the US but also caused headaches for numerous states that feared far-reaching legal conflicts crippling

[173] Laby (n 156) 585f; Arthur B Laby, 'The Extraterritorial Application of U.S. Financial Services Regulation' (2017) 89 SZW 174, 177.

[174] See 15 USC § 80b-3(a).

[175] *Morrison v National Australia Bank* (n 157) 261; Laby (n 156) 572ff.

[176] *Morrison v National Australia Bank* (n 157) 262f; Laby (n 156) 586.

[177] See 15 USC § 80b-3(b); on this exemption: Kenneth W Muller and Seth Chertok, 'A Detailed Analysis of How the US Dodd-Frank Act and Related Rules Will Impact Foreign Investment Advisers' (2011) 32 Bus L Rev 285.

[178] *Morrison v National Australia Bank* (n 157) 263f.

[179] Frankel and Laby (n 172) 36-24f; Laby (n 156) 586ff. Laby also raises the question of whether the IAA and the 1934 Act are of such fundamentally different nature that the application of the *Morrison* jurisprudence would not be justified, as the case *SEC v Gruss* indicates. However, the author convincingly rejects this idea. See ibid 588ff. *SEC v Gruss* (n 163).

[180] Frankel and Laby (n 172) 36-30.1ff.

the international economy.[181] These concerns grew as globalization progressed at an ever-increasing pace.

This development was stopped with the judgments in *Morrison*, *Kiobel*, and others.[182] The decision in *Morrison* should not be seen in isolation but as part of a series of judgments that together paved the way for a judicial retreat from extraterritoriality.[183] Through the rigorous application of the presumption against extraterritoriality, Congress was again directly confronted with these issues.

Interestingly, this development is in stark contrast to the general trend in capital markets law after the financial crisis. Following the GFC, there has been an increase in extraterritorial application of law in all major jurisdictions.[184] This trend is increasing the risk of legal and supervisory conflicts worldwide and thus the fragmentation of markets. To counter these dangers, states have promoted mechanisms of (mutual) recognition and deference. Remarkably, the presumption against extraterritoriality in the *Morrison* decision also pushes in this direction. Justice *Scalia* justified the decision, inter alia, with the risk of legal conflicts.[185] By transferring responsibility back to the political arena, policy-makers are forced carefully to assess the problems caused by an extraterritorial application of the law.[186]

Therefore, it can be concluded that the adoption of recognition and deference mechanisms in the form of substituted compliance by Congress and the rigorous application of the presumption against extraterritoriality by courts are two instruments that go hand in hand. Both reduce the risk of legal and supervisory conflicts and hence the fragmentation of markets. The more laws are restricted in their territorial reach, and the more recognition and deference mechanisms are adopted, the better economies flourish in the age of globalized and interconnected markets.

b) Broker-dealers

As seen above, the SEC requires domestic and foreign broker-dealers' registration and thus generally follows the principle of national treatment. Assuming the legality of this approach even post-*Morrison*, a more differentiated picture emerges, however, because the SEC recognizes various exemptions from the registration requirement for foreign broker-dealers.

[181] See eg Commission, 'United States Barriers to Trade and Investment: Report for 2007' (April 2008) 7 http://aei.pitt.edu/42336/1/2007_barriers.pdf (accessed 12 November 2022); Matthias Lehmann, 'Extraterritoriale Anwendung von US-Recht' (2010) RIW 841.

[182] See eg *Kiobel v Royal Dutch Petroleum Co* 569 US 108 (2013) and *RJR Nabisco Inc v European Community* 579 US ___ (2016); on *Morrison* and subsequent judgments in securities law see Louis Loss, Joel Seligman, and Troy A Paredes, *Fundamentals of Securities Regulation*, vol 2 (7th edn, Wolters Kluwer 2019) 2267ff.

[183] Austen L Parrish, 'Fading Extraterritoriality and Isolationism: Developments in the United States' (2017) 24 Ind J Global Legal Stud 207; Austen L Parrish, 'Kiobel, Unilateralism, and the Retreat from Extraterritoriality' (2013) 28 Md J Intl L 208; see also Edward T Swaine, 'Kiobel and Extraterritoriality: Here, (Not) There, (Not Even) Everywhere' (2016) 69 Okla L Rev 23.

[184] Describing and addressing this issue see Lehmann (n 56). For a view calling this development the 'return of unilateralism' see Hannah L Buxbaum, 'Transnational Legal Ordering and Regulatory Conflict' (2016) 1 UC Irvine J Intl Transnatl & Comp L 91, 108.

[185] *Morrison v National Australia Bank* (n 157) 269f; Lehmann (n 181) 845.

[186] See Lehmann (n 181) 849, who argues that due to a political pressure to compromise, fewer laws with an extraterritorial dimension will be passed.

The SEC adopted rule 15a-6, which exempts foreign broker-dealers from registration in four instances.[187] First, no registration is required when foreign broker-dealers act on behalf of persons not solicited by them.[188] This exemption is akin to the EU and Swiss concept of reverse solicitation, which is provided for, inter alia, in Article 46(5) subpara 3 MiFIR and Article 2(2) FIDLEV. Secondly, foreign broker-dealers may furnish research reports to major institutional investors in the US and execute transactions in the securities discussed in these research reports on behalf of these investors without a registration.[189] The exception is based on the low need for protection of those investors, who must at least manage assets in excess of US$100 million.[190] The assumption of a limited need for protection of certain investors resulting in a limited need for regulation is also a recurring element of the Swiss and EU systems, which differentiate between professional clients and non-professional clients.[191] The third and fourth exemptions are based on the involvement of regulated US firms, increasing the SEC's ability to exert influence and thereby reducing the need for regulatory intervention against foreign broker-dealers.[192]

Overall, the SEC pursues an approach of modified national treatment. It generally subjects foreign broker-dealers to registration but has introduced exemptions for them in rule 15a-6, which are often built on motives that are also visible in the system of Switzerland and the EU. In contrast to Switzerland and the EU, the SEC has not implemented deference regimes based on a qualitative assessment of the foreign legal system (substituted compliance),[193] although it extensively discussed this opportunity specifically with regard to broker-dealers in 2008.[194]

c) Investment advisers

The SEC always required foreign investment advisers to register with it and never recognized foreign registration and oversight.[195] Throughout the 1980s, it did so on an 'entity approach'.[196] This meant that, once registered, the SEC treated the investment adviser as a single entity and supervised all of its activities, even if the specific service in question occurred outside the US. As this practice created considerable problems for foreign advisers, the SEC changed its approach and allowed the establishment of an affiliate in the US, to which supervision was subsequently limited.[197] To prevent

[187] See extensively on these exemptions Greene and others (n 65) 15-23ff. On the practice of the SEC with regard to foreign broker-dealers see Loss, Seligman, and Paredes (n 182) 1281ff.

[188] See r 15a-6(a)(1) (17 CFR § 240.15a-6(a)(1)).

[189] See r 15a-6(a)(2) (17 CFR § 240.15a-6(a)(2)).

[190] See r 15a-6(b)(4) (17 CFR § 240.15a-6(b)(4)).

[191] See for Switzerland FIDLEG, art 28(2) and FIDLEV, art 31; ch 3 B)III.1.b)bb); in the EU, the differentiation can be found in the third country regime of investment firms when comparing MiFID II, art 39 to MiFIR, arts 46ff; Rolf Sethe, 'MiFIR/MiFID II: Drittstaatenzugang für die Schweiz und Äquivalenz von FINIG/FIDLEG' in Dieter Gericke (ed), *Private Equity VI* (Schulthess 2018) 146.

[192] See r 15a-6(a)(3) and (4) (17 CFR § 240.15a-6(3) and (4)).

[193] Greene and Oztan (n 51) 12.

[194] See SEC (n 2) 73ff.

[195] SEC (Division of Investment Management), 'Regulation of Investment Advisers by the U.S. Securities and Exchange Commission' (March 2013) 7f https://www.sec.gov/about/offices/oia/oia_investman/rplaze-042012.pdf (accessed 12 November 2022).

[196] Frankel and Laby (n 172) 36-11f.

[197] SEC, 'Protecting Investors: A Half Century of Investment Company Regulation' (n 155) 223f; see on this trend Greene and others (n 65) 16-3f and 16-13ff.

abuses of this restriction, the SEC imposed several conditions in the *Ellis* no-action letter designed to create a strong wall between the SEC-registered affiliate and other non-US advisers in the same entity.[198] As this approach was fraught with decisive disadvantages for foreign advisers, the SEC liberalized its approach again in 1992.[199] In a no-action letter to *Unibanco*, the SEC softened the conditions set by the no-action letter to *Ellis* based on criteria known from the conduct and effects test.[200] Despite these easements in the aftermath of registration, the SEC to date interprets the registration requirement very broadly in terms of its territorial scope.

The IAA also contains an exemption from the registration requirement for non-US advisers. The Dodd-Frank Act amended the provision and now reads that 'any investment adviser that is a foreign private adviser' does not need to register with the SEC.[201] The term 'foreign private adviser' is defined very narrowly in section 202(a)(30) IAA.[202] Only advisers that do not have a place of business in the US, have fewer than fifteen clients and investors, generally do not advise clients with more than US$25 million in assets, and do not hold themselves out to the public in the US are covered.

The SEC, therefore, continues to pursue a policy of national treatment by requiring the recognition of non-US investment advisers in the same way as that of US investment advisers. With the instrument of no-action letters and reliefs, the SEC staff tries to solve pressing issues.[203] They issued no-action letters, for example, when conflicts between the IAA and MiFID II arose.[204] Nevertheless, these selective reliefs cannot replace a comprehensive system of recognition in the form of substituted compliance, as it exists in the EU and Switzerland in the form of equivalence.

2. Banks

The regulation of foreign banks in the US is an area where the national treatment approach is very pronounced. The first federal regulation of foreign banks came into force with the International Banking Act of 1978.[205] Following several scandals, Congress tightened this regulation through the Foreign Bank Supervision Enhancement Act of 1991, which, inter alia, placed all foreign banks under the supervision of the Federal

[198] Richard Ellis Inc, SEC No-Action Letter (19 March 1981) https://www.sec.gov/divisions/investment/noaction/1981/richardellis031981.pdf (accessed 12 November 2022).

[199] SEC, 'Protecting Investors: A Half Century of Investment Company Regulation' (n 155) 228ff.

[200] Uniao de Bancos de Brasileiros SA (Unibanco), SEC No-Action Letter (28 July 1992) https://www.sec.gov/divisions/investment/noaction/1992/uniaodebancos072892.pdf (accessed 12 November 2022); see Frankel and Laby (n 172) 36-15f.

[201] IAA, s 203(b)(3) (15 USC § 80b-3(b)(3)); Christopher M Reimer, 'Private Trustees Beware: A Review of the Sweeping New SEC Registration Requirements under the Dodd-Frank Wall Street Reform and Consumer Protection Act' (2012) 12 J Bus & Sec L 337, 362f.

[202] See 15 USC § 80b-2(a)(30). The definition has been specified by the SEC in r 202(a)(30)-1 (17 CFR § 275.202(a)(30)-1).

[203] The letters are available at https://www.sec.gov/investment/investment-management-no-action-letters#investmentadviserregistration (accessed 12 November 2022).

[204] Proskauer Rose LLP, 'Analysis of the SEC's MiFID II No-Action Relief' (16 January 2018) https://www.proskauer.com/report/analysis-of-the-secs-mifid-ii-no-action-relief (accessed 12 November 2022).

[205] John L Carr Jr and John H More, 'Developments in the Regulation of Foreign Bank Operations in the United States' (1988) U Ill L Rev 255, 231f; Felix I Lessambo, *The U.S. Banking System* (Palgrave Macmillan 2020) 14f.

Reserve Board, making the Board the primary supervisor at the federal level.[206] These two acts are still the main basis for the regulation of foreign banks today, even though important adjustments have been made, for example, by the Dodd-Frank Act.[207] The regulatory framework regarding foreign banks is further specified in regulations, most notably Regulation K.[208]

When analysing the treatment of foreign banks, a distinction must be made between subsidiaries, branches, agencies, and representative offices.[209] A further differentiation can be made between federal and state entities.[210] Subsidiaries are separate legal entities, which is why they are treated like US banks.[211] They require a licence, but the range of services they are allowed to provide is the widest compared to the other types of establishments.

Foreign branches and agencies are often regulated together. The former can provide a comparable range of banking services as subsidiaries but are not considered separate entities. The latter are also not considered separate entities but are more restricted with regard to the banking services they may provide. Unlike branches, agencies are not allowed to accept conventional deposits from US citizens or residents.[212] Before a foreign bank may establish a branch or agency in the US, it must obtain a licence either from the competent authority of the state or, if it wishes to obtain a federal licence, from the Office of the Comptroller of the Currency.[213] Furthermore, it must obtain the approval of the Board of Governors of the Federal Reserve System.[214] This approval is subject, among other things, to the foreign bank being supervised and regulated comprehensively on a consolidated basis by the competent authorities in its home country, the consent of the home country supervisor to the proposed establishment, and sufficient financial and managerial resources of the foreign bank for the

[206] On the act in general and the scandals leading to it see L Todd Gibson, 'The Foreign Bank Supervision Enhancement Act of 1991' (1995) 27 Case W Res J Intl L 119; David W Fanikos, 'The Foreign Bank Supervision Enhancement Act of 1991' (1993) 16 Suffolk Transnatl L Rev 482, 492ff.

[207] The changes brought about include Dodd-Frank Act, s 165(b)(2) (12 USC § 5365(b)(2)), which amended Regulation YY (12 CFR Prt 252); Vo (n 6) 112ff.

[208] See egulation International Banking Organizations (12 CFR Prt 211) Regulation K; V Gerard Comizio, *International Banking Law* (West Academic 2016) 280ff.

[209] See extensively John C Dugan and others, 'Forms of Entry and Operation in the United States' in Randall D Guynn (ed), *Regulation of Foreign Banks & Affiliates in the United States* (9th edn, Thomson Reuters 2016) 28ff.

[210] See eg the regulation on the conversion of a foreign bank branch to a federal branch in the International Banking Act of 1978, s 4(f) (12 USC § 3102(f)). The following analysis is based on federal regulation. On state regulation of foreign banks see Kathleen A Scott, 'State Regulation of Foreign Banks' in Randall D Guynn (ed), *Regulation of Foreign Banks & Affiliates in the United States* (9th edn, Thomson Reuters 2016) 827ff.

[211] Matthias Lehmann, 'Internationales Finanzmarktrecht' in Jan von Hein (ed), *MüKo/BGB*, vol 13, pt 12 (8th edn, CH Beck 2021) para 197; John P Segala, 'A Summary of the International Banking Act of 1978' (1979) 65 Rich Econ Rev 16, 17.

[212] See the definition in the International Banking Act of 1978, s 1(b)(1) (12 USC § 3101(1)) and r 211.21(b) (12 CFR § 211.21(b)); see Segala (n 211). However, branches are also not allowed to accept retail deposits, i.e. deposits with an initial amount of less than US$250,000.

[213] Regarding the federal licence see the International Banking Act of 1978, s 4(a)(1) (12 USC § 3102(a)(1)).

[214] Foreign Bank Supervision Enhancement Act of 1991, s 2(a) (12 USC § 3105(d)(1)); Daniel B Gail, Joseph J Norton, and Michael K O'Neal, 'The Foreign Bank Supervision Act of 1991' (1992) 26 Intl Lawyer 993, 997.

international banking business.[215] Any branch or agency of a foreign bank operating in the US must fully comply with most US federal and state regulations.[216] The penalties for violations are rather strict, also apply to natural persons, and include criminal penalties.[217] If the parent foreign bank of the branch or agency has more than one billion consolidated bank assets worldwide, additional rules with regard to bank reserves apply to the branch or agency.[218] In addition, rules regarding deposit insurance and capital adequacy apply, including a study on the equivalency of foreign bank capital.[219]

Foreign representative offices are regulated separately from branches and agencies. The range of potential services they may offer is much smaller than that of subsidiaries, branches, and agencies. They are not allowed to grant loans or accept deposits but are restricted to maintaining and strengthening business contacts for their foreign bank.[220] If a foreign bank wants to establish a representative office in the US, it needs to obtain prior approval from the Federal Reserve Board.[221]

To sum up, the US treatment of foreign banks cannot be described as protectionist but was in fact liberal at the time of the enactment in the 1970s and 1990s. A primary goal of the US regulation of international banks has always been to create a level playing field between US and non-US banks and not discriminate against foreign banks.[222] Congress thought to achieve this goal through extensive national treatment of foreign banks.[223] Although ideas of recognition and deference were often discussed,[224] they never replaced the concept of national treatment.[225] This reluctance to embrace recognition and deference was certainly appropriate in the last century. However, given the global efforts and achievements with regard to harmonizing the regulation of banks, for example, through the Basel Accords, the approach of pure national treatment without elements of deference should be seen increasingly critically.

This criticism is all the more valid against the background that the US has recently made market access even more restrictive and thus more protectionist by introducing an intermediate holding company (IHC) requirement.[226] Pursuant to this rule,

[215] Foreign Bank Supervision Enhancement Act of 1991, s 2(a) (12 USC § 3105(d)(2) and (3)). See extensively on the requirements Gibson (n 206) 129ff; Ann E Misback, 'The Foreign Bank Supervision Enhancement Act of 1991' (1993) 79 Fed Res Bull 1, 5ff.

[216] International Banking Act of 1978, s 8(a)(1) (12 USC § 3106a(1)).

[217] Foreign Bank Supervision Enhancement Act of 1991, s 8 and Federal Deposit Insurance Corporation Improvement Act of 1991, s 213 (12 USC § 3110 and § 3111).

[218] International Banking Act of 1978, s 7(a) (12 USC § 3105(a)).

[219] Regarding deposit insurance see Gibson (n 206) 133. Concerning capital equivalency see Mark J Welshimer and Andrew R Gladin, 'U.S. Capital and Liquidity Regulation of Foreign Banking Organizations' in Randall D Guynn (ed), *Regulation of Foreign Banks & Affiliates in the United States* (9th edn, Thomson Reuters 2016) 558ff.

[220] Gail, Norton, and O'Neal (n 214) 1001.

[221] International Banking Act of 1978, s 10(a) (12 USC § 3107(1)(a)(1)); Gail, Norton, and O'Neal (n 214) 1001.

[222] Fanikos (n 206) with further references; Segala (n 211) 16ff.

[223] See with further references Carr and More (n 205) 231; see also Michael Malloy and William Lovett, *Banking and Financial Institutions Law in a Nutshell* (8th edn, West Academic 2019) 255, who speak of 'equalized regulatory discipline'.

[224] On early discussions see Segala (n 211). A rather new proposal can be found in Vo (n 6) 119ff.

[225] Daniel K Tarullo (Governor of US Board of Governors of Fed), 'Regulation of Foreign Bank Organizations' Speech (28 November 2012) 2 https://www.federalreserve.gov/newsevents/speech/files/tarullo20121128a.pdf (accessed 12 November 2022).

[226] Critical also is Katarzyna M Parchimowicz, 'Missed Targets and Misplaced Incentives? The Case of Parent Undertaking Requirement in the USA and in the EU' (2020) 21 J Bank Reg 212.

foreign banking organizations with average US non-branch assets of US$50 billion or more must establish a US intermediate holding company.[227] The EU has followed the US example and has introduced a comparable, so-called parent undertaking requirement.[228] This step has been understood as a retaliatory measure[229] and clearly shows that closures of national markets is answered with further shutdowns of markets and thus more protectionism—a development that once again highlights the need for more deference in this area.

3. Insurances

Unlike most financial services, insurance regulation in the US takes place largely at the state level, which makes a legal comparison with 'the US' difficult due to the different legal frameworks.[230] Foreign insurance companies are also not concentrated in one state but spread fairly evenly across the states.[231] One reason for this is that there is no nationwide licence, but, in principle, a separate licence is required for each state. Therefore, an insurer must be licensed in each state in which it intends to offer services.[232] Once a company is licensed as an insurer in one state, it is, however, much easier to obtain a licence in other states.[233]

In general, a distinction can be made between domestic, foreign, and alien insurers. Domestic insurers are those incorporated or organized under the laws of the state in question, whereas foreign insurers are incorporated or organized under the laws of

[227] Regulation YY, r 153(a) (12 CFR § 252.153(a)).

[228] See CRD V, art 21b, as introduced by Directive (EU) 2019/878 of 20 May 2019; Christoph Ohler, 'Die extraterritoriale Regulierung von internationalen Banken' (2018) 117 ZVglRWiss 478, 484f.

[229] Derek M Bush and Michael H Krimminger, 'EU Proposed Intermediate Holding Company Requirements for Non-EU Banks and Broker-Dealers' (17 December 2016) Harvard Law School Forum on Corporate Governance https://corpgov.law.harvard.edu/2016/12/17/eu-proposed-intermediate-holding-company-requirements-for-non-eu-banks-and-broker-dealers/ (accessed 12 November 2022); Heinrich Nemeczek and Sebastian Pitz, 'Intermediate EU Parent Undertaking Requirement for non-EU G-SIBs' (7 December 2016) OBLB https://www.law.ox.ac.uk/business-law-blog/blog/2016/12/intermediate-eu-parent-undertaking-requirement-non-eu-g-sibs (accessed 12 November 2022).

[230] John F Dobbyn and Christopher C French, *Insurance Law in a Nutshell* (5th edn, West Academic 2017) 509ff, with regard to licences see 514; critical is Willard Vasquez, *Modernizing U.S. Insurance Regulation and the Role of Global Reinsurance Markets* (Nova 2016) 68ff. See extensively on federal involvement Gary M Cohen, 'The Framework of Insurance Regulation' in Jeffrey E Thomas (ed), *New Appleman on Insurance Law Library Edition*, vol 2 (Lexis Nexis 2022) § 8.07. However, many state laws are based on model laws by the National Association of Insurance Commissioners. See eg regarding the reinsurance sector Kimberly M Welsh, 'Regulation of Reinsurance' in Jeffrey E Thomas (ed), *New Appleman on Insurance Law Library Edition*, vol 7 (Lexis Nexis 2022) § 8.01, [3].

[231] See NAIC, 'Insurance Department Resources Report, vol 1' (December 2022) 36 (Table 11) https://content.naic.org/sites/default/files/publication-sta-bb-volume-one.pdf (accessed 11 March 2023). For a list of alien insurers see NAIC, 'Quarterly Listing of Alien Insurers' (January 2023) https://content.naic.org/sites/default/files/QLS-AS-238.pdf (accessed 11 March 2023).

[232] A good overview is provided in Bradly J Condon, Joyce C Sadka, and Tapen Sinha, *Insurance Regulation in North America* (Kluwer Law International 2003) 155ff. See also Robert W Klein, 'The Insurance Industry and Its Regulation: An Overview' in Martin F Grace and Robert W Klein (eds), *The Future of Insurance Regulation in the United States* (Brookings Institution Press 2009) 13ff.

[233] Relaxations exist, for example, with regard to the obligation, to be discussed later, to deposit assets for US clients at an institution in the US. If a state is used as a 'port of entry', the obligation no longer has to be fulfilled in each state separately but can be fulfilled in one state. See Michigan Ins Code, s 431a. Richard G Liskov and John J Sarchio, 'U.S. Regulation of the Solvency and Insolvency of Alien Multi-National Insurers' in Jeffrey E Thomas (ed), *New Appleman on Insurance Law Library Edition*, vol 9 (Lexis Nexis 2022) § 103.01, [4][b].

any other state in the US.[234] Alien insurers are usually defined as insurance undertakings organized under a foreign legal system and are hence the relevant category here.[235] If alien insurers want to provide insurance services in the US, they can choose whether to establish a legally independent subsidiary or a branch.[236] The starting point of many states' regulations for both is that alien insurers have to comply with the same regulatory obligations as domestic insurers.[237] These states, therefore, follow the concept of national treatment. On top of that, some states impose additional requirements on alien insurers.[238] In many cases, they must deposit assets in a trust account with certain US institutions, which can then only be used for US policyholders and creditors.[239]

If an alien insurer does not want to set up a subsidiary or a branch, it can act as a non-admitted insurer. As the name suggests, these insurers are neither licensed nor admitted to provide insurance services in the respective state.[240] Even though they cannot offer insurance services directly, most states have enacted laws that allow them to offer insurance for very difficult or unusual risks through licensed brokers, so-called surplus line brokers.[241] However, the range of services that may be provided in this way is very narrow and the requirements are high.[242]

Consequently, alien insurers are often regulated quite strictly at the state level. They must, in any case, comply with the same obligations as domestic insurers and there are no recognition or deference mechanisms. Often, even more stringent requirements are imposed on alien insurers. The overall approach in the US is therefore similarly rigorous as that in the EU and Switzerland, although the latter at least provides deference in relation to reinsurers. To lower the market access barriers in this area, the US and the EU have concluded a bilateral agreement.[243] According to this agreement, both countries waive the obligation to require collateral for reinsurance contracts and no longer demand a local presence for reinsurers in relation to each other.

4. Investment companies and the custody of assets

In the US, funds are regulated under the Investment Company Act of 1940 (ICA). An investment company is defined in section 3(a)(1) ICA as an issuer engaged in the business of either primarily 'investing, reinvesting, or trading in securities' (lit (A)) or

[234] Irving Pfeffer, 'Non-Tariff Barriers to Alien Insurance in the United States' (1976) 43 J of Risk and Ins 275, 283. See e.g. NY Ins Law, s 107(a)(19) and (21); Indiana Code, s 27-1-2-3(e) and (f).

[235] James F Dowd, 'An Alien Insurer Seeking Entry into the United States: Factors to Consider' (1979) 11 NYU J Intl L & Pol 519. See ege.g. NY Ins Law, s 107(a)(5); Cal Ins Code, s 1580; Indiana Code, s 27-1-2-3(g).

[236] Liskov and Sarchio (n 233) § 103.01, [1][b].

[237] ibid § 103.01, [4][a]; see eg Indiana Code, s 27-1-17-2.

[238] See eg NY Ins Law, s 1106; Indiana Code, s 27-1-18.

[239] See eg NY Ins Law, ss 1312 and 1315 and Michigan Ins Code, s 431a.

[240] See eg Cal Ins Code, s 1760.1(n). For more detail see Julie Mix McPeak, 'Licensing of Insurers' in Jeffrey E Thomas (ed), *New Appleman on Insurance Law Library Edition*, vol 2 (Lexis Nexis 2022) § 9.09.

[241] Dowd (n 235) 534ff; e.g. see eg Indiana Code, s 27-1-15.8.

[242] In California, a surplus line broker may, for instance, only solicit a non-admitted insurer 'if that insurance cannot be procured from insurers admitted for the particular class or classes of insurance and that actually write the particular type of insurance in this state'. See Cal Ins Code, s 1763(a).

[243] Bilateral Agreement between the European Union and the United States of America on prudential measures regarding insurance and reinsurance https://home.treasury.gov/system/files/311/US_EU_Covered_Agreement_Signed_September_17_1.pdf (accessed 12 November 2022).

'of issuing face-amount certificates of the instalment type ...' (lit (B)) or 'of investing, reinvesting, owning, holding, or trading in securities, and owns or proposes to acquire investment securities having a value exceeding 40 per centum of the value of such issuer's total assets' (lit (C)).[244] There are some exceptions to this definition. Most importantly, issuers whose securities are not owned by more than 100 persons and issuers whose securities are exclusively owned by qualified purchasers do not qualify as investment companies and are consequently not subject to the ICA.[245]

Investment companies subject to the ICA are classified in face-amount certificate companies, unit investment trusts and management companies.[246] A further distinction is made between open-end and closed-end companies.[247] Unlike the EU regime, which has two different legal acts for different types of funds and their managers, the ICA applies irrespective of the type of investment company.

Investment companies organized or created under the laws of the US or any of its states are required to register with the Commission.[248] Foreign investment companies are prima facie excluded from registering with the SEC and are prohibited from using any means of inter-state commerce[249] to make a public offering.[250] The idea behind this exclusion was that foreign investment companies cannot be supervised as effectively as domestic companies.[251] This idea is also reflected in the EU regulatory framework, which only classifies companies as undertakings for collective investments in transferable securities if they are domiciled in an EU Member State. Third country undertakings can only be qualified as alternative investment funds and are thus regulated under the more stringent rules of the Alternative Investment Fund Managers Directive.

However, foreign investment companies are not completely denied access to the US market. The SEC may grant permission to foreign companies to register with the SEC under the second sentence of section 7(d) ICA. Such registration then allows foreign investment companies to address US investors. The SEC's permission is subject to two conditions. First, it must be legally and practically possible for the SEC to effectively enforce the obligations arising under the ICA against the foreign company. The wording of the provision already indicates that this is the exception rather than the rule.[252] Secondly, the permission needs to be in line with the public interest and

[244] See 15 USC § 80a-3(a)(1).

[245] ICA, s 3(c)(1) and (7) (15 USC § 80a-3(c)(1) and (7)). See Lehmann (n 211) para 397. With respect to foreign investment companies, the SEC has adopted specific exemptions, inter alia, in rules 3a-5 and following (17 CFR § 270.3a-5). See Greene and others (n 65) 15-17ff.

[246] See ICA, s 4(a) (15 USC § 80a-4(a)).

[247] ICA, s 5(a) (15 USC § 80a-5(a)); Hazen (n 63) 266ff.

[248] The registration is set out in ICA, s 8(a) (15 USC § 80a-8(a)); Teresa L Turner, 'Proposed Amendments to Section 7(d) of the Investment Company Act of 1940' (1993) 27 Geo Wash J Intl L & Econ 209, 212ff.

[249] When marketing via the internet, foreign funds must ensure that they do not target US investors and implement procedures to guard against sales or the provision of services to US persons. See SEC (n 73); Lisa A Mondschein, 'Solicitation and Marketing of Securities Offerings through the Internet' (1999) 65 Brook L Rev 185, 225ff.

[250] ICA, s 7(d) first sentence (15 USC § 80a-7(d)). *E contrario*, private offerings by foreign funds to US investors are permitted and not subject to registration. However, the exact limits for an offer to be considered private are unclear. See Frankel and Laby (n 172) 36-43ff. Also, private offerings by foreign funds are still extensively regulated. See Greene and others (n 65) 15-42ff.

[251] HR Rep No 2639, 76th Cong, 3d Sess, 13 (1940).

[252] It states that 'special circumstances or arrangements' must exist. This implies that the precondition is not fulfilled under ordinary circumstances.

the SEC's mandate to protect investors. The conditions are rigorous, which is underlined by the observation that only very few exceptions have been granted so far.[253] The exemption is therefore not a practical solution for market access by foreign investment firms.

In light of these difficulties, the SEC liberalized its approach towards foreign investment companies several times. It adopted rule 7d-1 with regard to Canadian companies.[254] Later on, it allowed so-called mirror fund solutions, which, however, never led to any significant relief for foreign investment companies.[255] The most far-reaching proposal of a mutual recognition approach was, although discussed in 1992, never implemented.[256] As a result, market access for foreign investment companies continues to be very restricted to this day.

A viable alternative for the SEC would be to exempt foreign investment companies from certain duties pursuant to section 6(c) ICA in cases where the foreign regime imposes a corresponding equivalent duty on its investment companies.[257] If the entire regulatory framework of a foreign country with respect to investment companies is equivalent, the SEC could even completely waive the applicability of and oversight under the ICA. Such a practice by the SEC would qualify as substituted compliance, since US regulatory law would be withdrawn on the basis of a qualitative assessment of a foreign legal order. It would bring US regulation closer to the EU and Swiss systems while at the same time taking up proposals long discussed within the SEC. Nonetheless, the SEC has so far largely refrained from issuing exemptions under section 6(c) ICA on a meaningful basis.[258]

To prevent the looting of assets, the ICA also prescribes special safeguards for the custody of investment companies' assets.[259] Pursuant to section 17(f) ICA, investment companies must place and maintain their investments in the custody of a bank, a company that is a member of a national securities exchange, or other registered companies subject to specific rules set out by the Commission.[260] With regard to foreign assets, the SEC has adopted special rules allowing the fund's board of directors to delegate specific responsibilities to a foreign bank regulated in its home country, so-called Qualified Foreign Banks.[261] This enables funds to place their foreign assets in the custody of an Eligible Foreign Custodian under strict conditions, including that the custodian is subject to standards of 'reasonable care' in its home jurisdiction.

[253] See Frankel and Laby (n 172) 36-31, who identified only one order that had been issued in a 30-year period. Some even consider the provision a de facto prohibition ('effectively prohibited'). See Greene and others (n 65) 15-17.

[254] 17 CFR § 270.7d-1; n Turner (n 248) 220ff.

[255] On mirror funds see SEC, 'Applications of Foreign Investment Companies Filed Pursuant to Section 7(4) of the Investment Company Act of 1940' IC-13691 (23 December 1998); on the development see Frankel and Laby (n 172) 36-35ff.

[256] SEC, 'Protecting Investors: A Half Century of Investment Company Regulation' (n 155) 185ff; critical of this is n Turner (n 248) 237ff.

[257] See 15 USC § 80a-6(a); Frankel and Laby (n 172) 36-31ff.

[258] Greene and others (n 65) 15-35ff.

[259] Hazen (n 63) 275.

[260] See 15 USC § 80a-17.

[261] See r 17f-5 (17 CFR § 270.17f-5); Greene and others (n 65) 58-82ff.

This rule is comparable, albeit not identical, to the EU equivalence rule concerning depositaries.[262]

IV. Trading venues and financial market infrastructures

The regulation of financial market infrastructures is a very broad field. In the cross-border context, problems arose in particular with regard to the regulation of trading venues and derivative transactions. In the first area, for example, the question of the territorial scope of the registration requirement must be addressed, i.e. under what conditions foreign trading venues must register with the SEC. This question has arisen in the past, especially with regard to the installation of foreign trading screens in the US.[263]

The regulation of derivatives has attracted much regulatory attention since the GFC. Following the recommendations of the G20, the US responded with the adoption of the Dodd-Frank Act, which changed the regulatory landscape of derivatives dramatically.[264] Because of the wide extraterritorial scope of the Act and the global nature of the derivatives market, regulation has become the area of US law where the concept of substituted compliance is most prevalent.

1. National securities exchanges and alternative trading systems

Exchanges are regulated under the 1934 Act and are defined in its section 3(a)(1).[265] Every exchange must register as a national securities exchange with the Commission if it uses means of inter-state commerce 'within or subject to the jurisdiction of the United States' unless the Commission exempts it due to the limited volume of transactions conducted on the exchange.[266] The conditions for registration as a national securities exchange are set out in more detail in section 6 1934 Act.[267]

Traditionally, the SEC has been strict in its interpretation of the registration requirement in the context of foreign exchanges.[268] Although it has never specified the territorial reach of the requirement in the form of concrete rules,[269] its administrative practice underlines its stringent approach. The SEC has, for example, always objected to the setting up of trading screens in the US unless full registration has been obtained.

262 The EU rule in question is AIFMD, art 21(6). It differs in that it only applies to non-EU funds, whereas the SEC rule also applies to US funds. However, the SEC rule is limited in that it applies solely to foreign assets of the fund.

263 See eg Howell E Jackson, Andreas M Fleckner, and Mark Gurevich, 'Foreign Trading Screens in the United States' (2006) 1 CMLJ 54.

264 For a comparative analysis of the US and EU derivatives framework see Levon Garslian, 'Towards a Universal Model Regulatory Framework for Derivatives' (2016) 37 U Pa J Intl L 941, 979ff.

265 15 USC § 78c(a)(1).

266 See the prohibition in 1934 Act, s 5 (15 USC § 78e).

267 15 USC § 78f; Loss, Seligman, and Paredes (n 65) 1169ff.

268 Pierre Schammo, 'Regulating Transatlantic Stock Exchanges' (2008) 57 Intl & Comp LQ 827, 837.

269 The SEC has published a fact sheet, but it is very vague about the scope of jurisdiction. It simply states that '[t]he non-U.S. exchange would only become subject to U.S. securities laws if that exchange is operating within the U.S.' without further defining the criteria of an operation in the US. See SEC, 'Fact Sheet on Potential Cross-Border Exchange Mergers' (16 June 2006) https://www.sec.gov/news/press/2006/2006-96.htm (accessed 12 November 2022).

This restrictive approach has received a great deal of criticism and was listed as a use case for substituted compliance in the Tafara–Peterson proposal.[270] The SEC would have also had the opportunity to grant exemptions based on its general exemptive authority under section 36 1934 Act.[271] Despite this criticism and the legal possibility of liberalization, the SEC has maintained its restrictive policy to date. Therefore, substituted compliance does not exist in relation to stock exchanges.

The situation is similar for electronic marketplaces or electronic communication networks (ECNs). These marketplaces have the choice to register either as a national securities exchange or as a broker-dealer under the additional requirements concerning alternative trading systems.[272] While the SEC made several proposals concerning the treatment of foreign electronic marketplaces when it adopted the regulation, none of these suggestions prevailed.[273]

2. Derivatives regulation by the SEC and CFTC

The competence to regulate derivatives is divided between the SEC and the Commodity Futures Trading Commission (CFTC). Historically, there have always been disputes between the authorities regarding the exact demarcation,[274] which has been amended several times.[275] In principle, the CFTC has exclusive jurisdiction over all commodity futures and options under the Commodity Exchange Act (CEA). The SEC has jurisdiction over options traded on national securities exchanges as well as on options on securities traded OTC. With regard to swaps, the Dodd-Frank Act assigned swaps that have a commodity as an underlying to the jurisdiction of the CFTC, security-based swaps to the jurisdiction of the SEC and mixed swaps to shared jurisdiction.[276]

In the following, the territorial scope of the Dodd-Frank Act is analysed using the example of the regulation of swap dealers and major swap participants (a)). Thereafter, the exchange trading (b)), the clearing (c)), and the reporting requirement (d)) are examined in relation to swaps.

[270] Tafara and Peterson (n 17) 64f; critical of this is Heiko Beck, 'Börsen- und kapitalmarktrechtliche Aspekte der grenzüberschreitenden Tätigkeit und Zusammenarbeit von Börsen' in Jens Ekkenga, Walther Hadding, and Horst Hammen (eds), *Festschrift für Siegfried Kümpel* (Erich Schmidt 2003) 46. A balanced discussion of all pros and cons can be found in Jackson, Fleckner, and Gurevich (n 263).

[271] Jan von Hein in Eberhard Schwark and Daniel Zimmer (eds), *Kapitalmarktrechts-Kommentar* (5th edn, CH Beck 2020) § 102 WpHG para 2; see also later ch 4 B)IV.2.b)bb).

[272] See Regulation ATS, rr 300ff (17 CFR §§ 242.300-304); Greene and others (n 65) 14-151ff; Gabriel Matus, 'Regulation of Alternative Trading Systems: Market Fragmentation and the New Market Structure' (2000) 44 NYLS L Rev 583.

[273] Roberta S Karmel, 'Regulatory Initiatives and the Internet: A New Era of Oversight for the Securities and Exchange Commission' (2001) 5 NYU J Legis & Pub Pol'y 33, 38; Christoph Kumpan, *Die Regulierung außerbörslicher Wertpapierhandelssysteme im deutschen, europäischen und US-amerikanischen Recht* (De Gruyter 2006) 161.

[274] *Chicago Mercantile Exchange v SEC* 883 F2d 537 (1989); Ronald H Filler and Jerry W Markham, *Regulation of Derivative Financial Instruments* (West Academic 2014) 47ff.

[275] See Jerry W Markham, 'Commodity Exchanges and Regulation' in H Kent Baker, Greg Filbeck, and Jeffrey H Harris (eds), *Commodities: Markets, Performance, and Strategies* (OUP 2018) 38f; extensively on the demarcation: Greene and others (n 65) 12-24ff.

[276] John C Coffee Jr, 'The Political Economy of Dodd-Frank' in Eilís V Ferran and others (eds), *The Regulatory Aftermath of the Global Financial Crisis* (CUP 2012) 349; Markham (n 275) 51.

a) Title VII of the Dodd-Frank Act and issues of extraterritoriality

One of the main objectives of the Dodd-Frank Act was to prevent the emergence of systemic risks and to ensure financial stability. To achieve this goal, Congress decided to include cross-border and purely foreign transactions in its regulation that could pose risks to the US market. The precise degree of this extraterritoriality has been specified by the CFTC for swaps and the SEC for security-based swaps. It is the subject of intense debates among scholars, the industry, and regulators worldwide.[277] As the question of extraterritorial application of legislation cannot be examined in the abstract but only on the basis of specific provisions, the regulation of (security-based) swap dealers and major (security-based) swap participants are used as examples in the following.

aa) CFTC cross-border guidance Section 722(d) of the Dodd-Frank Act amended the general territorial scope of the CEA.[278] It states that the rules of the CEA 'shall not apply to activities outside the United States unless those activities (1) have a direct and significant connection with activities in, or effect on, commerce of the United States; or (2) contravene such rules or regulations as the Commission may prescribe or promulgate as are necessary or appropriate to prevent the evasion of any provision of this chapter . . .'. The CFTC has specified this rule in an interpretive guidance from 2013.[279] The guidance sets out the circumstances under which the provisions of the CEA apply in cross-border situations, in particular, whether the parties to a swap must comply with the requirements of the CEA and register with the CFTC as swap dealers or major swap participants.[280] The CFTC interpreted the language in section 2(i) CEA as an express congressional intent that the Act applies extraterritorially in the situations described, thereby rebutting the presumption against extraterritoriality of *Morrison*.[281]

In the cross-border guidance, the CFTC identified a number of criteria that establish a sufficient nexus for applying the rules of the CEA. One crucial criterion is whether a party to the transaction is a 'U.S. person'.[282] A US person is defined very broadly as a person located in the US or a person domiciled outside the US whose swap activities have a 'direct and significant connection' to the US.[283] Under this broad

[277] Lucy McKinstry, 'Regulating a Global Market' (2013) 51 Colum J Transnatl L 776, 806ff. With regard to the CFTC approach see Jonathan Lindenfeld, 'The CFTC's Substituted Compliance Approach' (2015) 14 J Intl Bus & L 125, 138.

[278] CEA, s 2(i) (7 USC § 2(i)). For great detail on the extraterritorial approach of the CFTC see Edward F Greene and Ilona Potiha, 'Issues in the Extraterritorial Application of Dodd-Frank's Derivatives and Clearing Rules, the Impact on Global Markets and the Inevitability of Cross-Border and US Domestic Coordination' (2013) 8 CMLJ 338, 346ff.

[279] CFTC, 'Interpretive Guidance and Policy Statement Regarding Compliance With Certain Swap Regulations' 78 Fed Reg 45292 (26 July 2013) 45297 https://www.cftc.gov/sites/default/files/idc/groups/public/@lrfederalregister/documents/file/2013-17958a.pdf (accessed 12 November 2022). This guidance expresses only the general policy of the CFTC and is not binding. See John C Coffee Jr, 'Extraterritorial Financial Regulation: Why E.T. Can't Come Home' (2014) 99 Cornell L Rev 1259, 1277ff.

[280] The duty to register for swap dealers and major swap participants is set out in CEA, s 4s (7 USC § 6s), as introduced by Dodd-Frank Act, s 731. On the parties covered see Levon Garslian, 'Towards a Universal Model Regulatory Framework for Derivatives' (2016) 37 U Pa J Int'l L 941, 991ff.

[281] CFTC (n 279) 45299; see for a detailed analysis on the relationship between the extraterritoriality of the Dodd-Frank Act and the *Morrison* ruling: McKinstry (n 277) 806ff.

[282] CFTC (n 279) 45301ff; Sean J Griffith, 'Substituted Compliance and Systemic Risk: How to Make a Global Market in Derivatives Regulation' (2014) 98 Minn LR 1291, 1332f.

[283] CFTC (n 279) 45301f.

definition, a foreign branch of a US person is, for instance, considered a US person and the CEA, therefore, applies to its transactions.[284] With respect to the applicable regulation, the CFTC distinguishes between entity-level and transaction-level requirements and develops further subgroups within the two categories.[285] This approach creates a very nuanced and complex landscape in terms of the extraterritorial applicability of individual rules to specific transactions and parties. The extensive extraterritoriality of the CFTC cross-border guidance persists with regard to the registration requirement of swap dealers and major swap participants. Non-US persons are also subject to the duty to register if their transactions with US persons exceed a de minimis threshold further specified in the CFTC rules.[286] Some commentators disagree with the extensive extraterritoriality created by the CFTC guidance.[287] The US District Court, however, confirmed that the extraterritorial interpretation in the CFTC's cross-border guidance is consistent with Title VII of the Dodd-Frank Act.[288]

To mitigate the effects of this extensive extraterritoriality, the CFTC introduced a system of substituted compliance in its cross-border guidance.[289] According to this system, certain US requirements can be substituted by compliance with comparable rules of the home country's law of one of the parties. This approach of restricting extraterritoriality rather than granting market access through substituted compliance has been referred to above as second generation 'out-bound' substituted compliance.[290] Substituted compliance is available only to swap dealers and major swap participants organized and domiciled outside the US.[291] Because of the above-mentioned distinction between entity-level and transaction-level requirements, the possibility of substituted compliance must be determined separately for each category of requirements.[292] This renders the determination of the applicable law to foreign swap dealers extremely difficult and makes the substituted compliance approach even more fragmented than its European counterpart.[293] This is reflected in the fact that there is not one substituted compliance determination, but many different ones, such as a 'Capital Comparability Determination'.[294] Moreover, there are further substituted compliance determinations that are not in the hands of the CFTC, such as the exemption for foreign exchange

[284] ibid 45317. For more detail see Lindenfeld (n 277) 134f.

[285] ibid 45331ff and 45335ff. On the differentiation see Lindenfeld (n 277) 131f.

[286] CFTC (n 279) 45317ff; see for the definition of swap dealers and the de minimis exception: 17 CFR § 1.3; these de minimis thresholds are specified for cross-border situations in 17 CFR § 23.23; Christian Johnson, 'Regulatory Arbitrage, Extraterritorial Jurisdiction, and Dodd-Frank' (2014) 14 Nev LJ 542, 591.

[287] Scott D O'Malia (Commissioner of CFTC), 'Regulatory Harmonization, Not Imperialism: A Workable Cross-Border Framework' Keynote Address at the Global Forum for Derivatives Market (26 September 2013) http://www.cftc.gov/PressRoom/SpeechesTestimony/opaomalia-29 (accessed 12 November 2022); see with more references Lindenfeld (n 277) 138.

[288] *Securities Industry & Financial Markets Association v US Commodity Futures Trading Commission* 67 F Supp 3d 373 (2014).

[289] CFTC (n 279) 45340ff; Lindenfeld (n 277) 137ff.

[290] See ch 4 A)III.

[291] CFTC (n 279) 45347; see 17 CFR § 23.101(a)(5) and (b)(4)).

[292] A substituted compliance determination in relation to transaction-level requirements is rather unusual. See also Griffith (n 282) 1333f; see extensively Johnson (n 286) 592ff.

[293] This complexity is reflected in the attempt to present the applicable rules in tabular form by Fabien Carruzzo in Rolf Sethe and others (eds), *SK zum FinfraG* (Schulthess 2017) Vor art 93 paras 301ff; critical of this view is Johnson (n 286) 617f.

[294] See 17 CFR § 23.106.

swaps and forwards following a comparability determination by the Secretary of the Treasury.[295]

Overall, the picture is very confusing. The CFTC has chosen to attach great importance to the extraterritoriality inherent in Dodd-Frank and has therefore interpreted the territorial scope extremely broadly. In an attempt to counter the resulting risk of a far-reaching fragmentation of the derivatives market and thus the emergence of legal and supervisory conflicts, the CFTC implemented a system of substituted compliance. The CFTC's effort to create nuanced and appropriate rules, however, resulted in such complex regulations that the success of this system can be doubted.[296] The approach of the CFTC is even more fragmented than the one of the EU.

bb) SEC cross-border release The SEC has also clarified the cross-border reach of the rules of the Dodd-Frank Act to security-based swaps. Unlike the CFTC, the SEC has done so in the form of binding rules rather than a mere interpretive guidance.[297] The result of this clarification, however, is no less controversial.

Pursuant to section 15F(a)(1) and (2) 1934 Act, it is unlawful for 'any person' to act as a security-based swap dealer or major security-based swap participant unless registered with the Commission.[298] The two terms are defined in section 3 of the 1934 Act.[299] According to the Supreme Court's decision in *Morrison*, the term 'any person' is to be understood as referring only to US persons unless there is a clear congressional intent that overrides the presumption against extraterritoriality. Some commentators argued that there is no such congressional intent and that the registration requirement should therefore be interpreted strictly territorially.[300] In addition to the *Morrison* jurisprudence, they referred to section 30(c) 1934 Act to justify the limitation of the SEC's jurisdiction.

Contrary to these comments, the SEC has not adopted a strict territorial approach but extends the application of the registration requirement to different cross-border situations.[301] Non-US persons are, for instance, required to register as security-based swap dealers if they exceed a de minimis threshold. A territorial distinction is drawn by the SEC in connection with the calculation of the de minimis threshold. Which positions are aggregated for the calculation depends on whether the person is a US or non-US person.[302] In the case of US persons, the SEC follows an entity approach and includes all swap transactions for the de minimis threshold, regardless of whether the transaction took place abroad or even through a foreign branch.[303] In the case of

[295] CEA, ss 1a and 1b (7 USC §§ 1a and 1b).

[296] Very critical also is Johnson (n 286) 617f.

[297] The SEC has explained its motives in great detail and also put them up for discussion in a public proceeding. See SEC, 'Cross-Border Security-Based Swap Activities' Release No 34-69490 (21 August 2013) https://www.sec.gov/rules/proposed/2013/34-69490.pdf (accessed 12 November 2022).

[298] See 15 USC § 78o-10(a)(1) and (2), as introduced by Dodd-Frank Act, s 764(a).

[299] Concerning security-based swap dealers see 1934 Act, s 3(a)(71) (15 USC § 78c(a)(71) and 17 CFR § 240.3a71-1); concerning major security-based swap participants see 1934 Act, s 3(a)(67) (15 USC § 78c(a)(67) and 17 CFR § 240.3a67-1).

[300] SEC (n 297) 45ff and 67ff; see for a discussion: McKinstry (n 277) 806ff.

[301] However, the SEC claims to follow a territorial approach when stating: 'We differ from commenters, however, in our understanding of what a territorial approach means in the context of a global security-based swap market.' See SEC (n 297) 48.

[302] The term 'U.S. person' is defined in 17 CFR § 240.3a71-3(a)(4).

[303] SEC (n 297) 51f; see 17 CFR § 240.3a71-3(b)(1)(i).

non-US persons, generally, all swap transactions conducted either with US persons or within the US count towards the de minimis threshold.[304] If the non-US person exceeds the threshold and must therefore register with the SEC, the rules of the 1934 Act subsequently apply to all transactions, including those that take place abroad and are concluded with foreign counterparties.[305]

The claim of the SEC to follow a 'territorial approach' is therefore rather questionable, although its approach is admittedly less extraterritorial than that of the CFTC.[306] The SEC justifies this broad understanding of territoriality primarily with the telos of the Dodd-Frank Act, which aims at preventing the emergence of systemic risk and ensuring systemic stability in the US. It argues that these objectives can only be achieved in a global market, such as the market for security-based swaps, if conduct occurring outside the US is also subjected to US regulation under certain circumstances.[307] Whether this broad extraterritorial interpretation is still based on a clear congressional intent or whether the SEC has not rather introduced a presumption of extraterritoriality through the back door remains a question to be discussed.

Since this broad extraterritoriality leads to legal and supervisory conflicts, the SEC, just like the CFTC, introduced provisions based on the concept of substituted compliance.[308] Accordingly, registered non-US swap dealers may also satisfy certain requirements of US law by complying with their home state law.[309] A substituted compliance determination by the SEC presupposes that the foreign rules are comparable to the US rules at issue in terms of their scope and objective and that they are effectively complied with and enforced.[310] Additionally, a supervisory and enforcement MoU or similar arrangement with the foreign regulator must be in place.[311] In July 2021, the SEC issued for the first time such a substituted compliance decision with respect to French security-based swap dealers and major security-based swap participants.[312] All in all, the approach of the CFTC and the SEC to cross-border transactions is, therefore, similar.[313]

b) *National securities exchanges, swap execution facilities, and designated contract markets*

One important lesson from the GFC was that too many derivatives were traded OTC, resulting in a lack of transparency. For this reason, states agreed to implement a far-reaching platform trading obligation at the G20 summit in Pittsburgh.[314] This trading

[304] SEC (n 297) 53; see 17 CFR § 240.3a71-3(b)(1)(iii); Griffith (n 282) 1336.
[305] SEC (n 297) 54.
[306] The CFTC defines a 'U.S. person' in an even broader manner than the SEC. See Griffith (n 282) 1336.
[307] SEC (n 297) 49.
[308] 17 CFR § 240.3a71-6.
[309] This substituted compliance is limited to the prerequisites listed in 17 CFR § 240.3a71-6(d) and applies only to non-US persons.
[310] 17 CFR § 240.3a71-6(a)(i).
[311] 17 CFR § 240.3a71-6(a)(ii).
[312] SEC, 'SEC Issues Substituted Compliance Determination for France' Press Release 2021-138 (26 July 2021) https://www.sec.gov/news/press-release/2021-138 (accessed 12 November 2022).
[313] Griffith (n 282) 1335: '[t]he architecture of the SEC's Cross-Border Release in fact largely copies that of the CFTC.'
[314] G20 Pittsburgh Summit, 'G20 Leaders' Statement' (24–25 September 2009) para 13 third bullet point http://www.g20.utoronto.ca/2009/2009communique0925.html (accessed 12 November 2022).

obligation is referred to as the 'exchange trading requirement' in the US and was introduced by the Dodd-Frank Act.

aa) Jurisdiction of the CFTC For swaps under the jurisdiction of the CFTC, the obligation is set out in section 2(h)(8)(A) CEA.[315] The scope of the duty is based on that of the clearing obligation described below,[316] which means that the two duties are synchronized. Likewise, the exemptions granted in relation to the clearing obligation also apply to the trading obligation. The CFTC does not allow substituted compliance in relation to transaction-level requirements, i.e. in this case with regard to the exchange trading requirement.[317]

Swap transactions can generally only be executed on a board of trade designated as a contract market or on swap execution facilities.[318] Both designated contract markets and swap execution facilities must be registered with the CFTC to be permitted to operate as a facility for the trading or processing of swaps.[319] Only if they are registered will a transaction conducted on them meet the exchange trading requirement. However, the CFTC may exempt foreign swap execution facilities from registration if 'the facility is subject to comparable, comprehensive supervision and regulation on a consolidated basis by ... the appropriate governmental authorities in the home country of the facility'.[320] As the applicability of US law is withdrawn based on a qualitative assessment of the foreign legal system, the exception is based on the idea of substituted compliance.

bb) Jurisdiction of the SEC Security-based swaps under the jurisdiction of the SEC are also subject to the mandatory trade execution requirement if such swaps fall under the remit of the clearing requirement.[321] This is the case for cross-border transactions where one of the parties is a US person.[322] This trade execution requirement can be fulfilled either by trading on an exchange or a security-based swap execution facility registered with the SEC or exempt from registration.

Pursuant to section 3D(a)(1) 1934 Act, all persons operating a swap execution facility must be registered with the SEC.[323] This registration requirement covers all

[315] See 7 USC § 2(h)(8)(A), as amended by Dodd-Frank Act, s 723(a); Ligia C Arias-Barrera, *Regulation and Supervision of the OTC Derivatives Market* (Routledge 2018) 220ff.

[316] See under ch 4 B)IV.2.c).

[317] CFTC, 'Cross-Border Application of Certain Swaps Provisions of the Commodity Exchange Act' 77 Fed Reg 41214, 41230 (12 July 2012) https://www.cftc.gov/sites/default/files/idc/groups/public/@lrfederalregister/documents/file/2012-16496a.pdf (accessed 12 November 2022).

[318] An exception exists only if the swap transaction is not made available on an eligible platform. See CEA (7 USC § 2(h)(8)(B)).

[319] CEA, s 5h(a)(1) (7 USC § 7b-3(a)(1)).

[320] CEA, s 5h(g) (7 USC § 7b-3(g)).

[321] 1934 Act, s 3C(h)(1) (15 USC § 78c-3), as amended by Dodd-Frank Act, s 763(a); Garslian (n 280) 1000.

[322] In parallel with the clearing requirement, a proposed rule by the SEC that would have included transactions by two non-US persons under certain circumstances was later dropped. See proposed r 3Ch-1(a)(2); SEC, 'Application of Certain Title VII Requirements to Security-Based Swap Transactions Connected with a Non-U.S. Person's Dealing Activity That Are Arranged, Negotiated, or Executed By Personnel Located in a U.S. Branch or Office or in a U.S. Branch or Office of an Agent' Release No 34-74834 (29 April 2015) 114ff. Accordingly, the Commission's possibility to grant substituted compliance in those cases has also been repealed. This substituted compliance mechanism was foreseen in r 3Ch-2(b). See SEC (n 297) 336ff.

[323] See 15 USC § 78c-4, as introduced by Dodd-Frank Act, s 763(c).

execution facilities as defined in section 3(a)(77) 1934 Act. Whether it also applies to facilities domiciled in foreign states depends on whether these facilities take affirmative actions to induce execution or trading on its markets by US persons or non-US persons located in the US.[324] This is the case, for example, when foreign swap facilities provide US persons direct access to their market by setting up electronic screens.[325]

If the trade execution requirement applies, the swap transaction cannot only be fulfilled on a registered swap execution facility but also a facility exempt from registration by the Commission. There is an express exemption with respect to swap execution facilities that are already subject to comparable supervision and regulation by the CFTC.[326] In relation to foreign facilities subject to comparable supervision and regulation under their home country jurisdiction, an explicit exemption does not exist. However, the Commission stated that it is willing to grant such exemptions under the general rule of section 36 1934 Act to reduce the risk of regulatory and supervisory conflicts.[327] Not only would such an exemption require comparability of the foreign legal system, in particular comparability with the core principles applicable to US swap execution facilities, but the Commission may request additional conditions, such as the conclusion of MoUs or a certification by the foreign facility that it will provide the Commission with prompt access to its books and records.[328]

c) Derivative clearing organizations and clearing agencies

Another key lesson from the GFC was that OTC derivatives should be cleared through central counterparties in order to reduce counterparty risk.[329] Accordingly, the Dodd-Frank Act introduced such a clearing requirement in the US for both swaps under the jurisdiction of the CFTC and the jurisdiction of the SEC.

aa) Jurisdiction of the CFTC The clearing requirement for swaps is set out in section 2(h)(1)(A) CEA.[330] Whether a particular transaction is subject to the clearing obligation is a complex question that depends on the type of swap, the applicability of an exemption and the compliance schedule and dates.[331] The clearing requirement is a transaction-level requirement for which a substituted compliance determination is possible only in very limited circumstances.[332] As a general rule, any swap transaction in which a counterparty is a US person is subject to the clearing obligation without the possibility of substituted compliance. This constitutes a considerably more restrictive

324 SEC (n 297) 226.
325 ibid 227.
326 1934 Act, s 3D(e) (15 USC § 78c-4(e)).
327 SEC (n 297) 230.
328 ibid 231.
329 G20 Pittsburgh Summit (n 314).
330 See 7 USC § 2(h)(1)(A), as amended by Dodd-Frank Act, s 723(a); see also 17 CFR § 50.2.
331 See CEA, s 2(h)(7) (7 USC § 2(h)(7)) and also 17 CFR § 50.4, § 50.5, §§ 50.25f, and §§ 50.50ff.
332 CFTC, 'Cross-Border Application of Certain Swaps Provisions of the Commodity Exchange Act' (n 317); Griffith (n 282) 1334.

approach than that of the EU and Switzerland, both of which provide for exemptions via equivalence also for the clearing requirement.[333]

When the clearing requirement takes effect, all persons executing such transactions must submit the swap for clearing to a registered or an exempt derivatives clearing organization.[334] Foreign clearing organizations have two opportunities to be eligible for the clearing requirement. They can either register with the CFTC, subject to 'alternative application procedures'.[335] To be approved, they must first demonstrate to the Commission that they are subject to regulation in their home state that ensures compliance with the core principles of the CEA to which domestic registered derivatives clearing organizations are subject.[336] If they meet this requirement, they must no longer comply with the core principles. In addition, they must be in good regulatory standing in their home country, which is the case if there has not been a finding by the home country regulator of material non-observance of the Principles for Financial Market Infrastructures or other relevant home country legal requirements.[337] This prerequisite shows that the US puts an emphasis on the observance of international standards. Moreover, they must not pose a substantial risk to the US financial system.[338] Finally, an MoU or similar arrangement between the Commission and the home country regulator must be in place, which, inter alia, ensures effective information sharing.[339] As a result of the registration, the applicability of part of the US regulation is withdrawn in exchange for compliance with equivalent foreign rules. This represents a mechanism of substituted compliance that is limited in that although some regulatory requirements are removed (i.e. the core principles), supervisory oversight is not.

The second alternative of market access as a so-called 'exempt derivatives clearing organization', in contrast, constitutes a comprehensive substituted compliance mechanism that leads to a complete exemption from the CEA and CFTC supervision.[340] Pursuant to section 5b(h) CEA, the Commission may exempt derivatives clearing organizations from registration if the Commission finds that it is already subject to 'comparable comprehensive supervision and regulation' in its home country.[341] Additional

333 See in the EU EMIR, art 13 and MiFIR, art 33; see in Switzerland FinfraG, art 102 and FinfraV, art 90.

334 For the registration of a derivatives clearing organization see CEA, s 5b (7 USC § 7a-1).

335 17 CFR § 39.3(3) and § 39.51. See extensively on this procedure Evariest Callens, *Regulation of Central Counterparties (CCPs) in Light of Systemic Risk* (Intersentia 2022) 526–33.

336 17 CFR § 39.3(3) fourth sentence and § 39.51(a)(i). The core principles applicable to domestic derivatives clearing organizations are laid out in CEA, s 5b(c)(2) (7 USC § 7a-1(c)(2)) and specified in 17 CFR §§ 39.10–39.27.

337 17 CFR § 39.51(a)(ii); the definition of the term 'good regulatory standard' can be found in 17 CFR § 39.2.

338 17 CFR § 39.3(3) first sentence and § 39.51(a)(iii). The foreign derivatives clearing organization poses such a risk if it holds 20 per cent or more of the required initial margin of US clearing members for swaps across all derivatives clearing organizations and 20 per cent or more of the initial margin requirements for swaps at that derivatives clearing organization are attributable to US clearing members. See the definition in 17 CFR § 39.2.

339 17 CFR § 39.51(a)(iv).

340 Callens (n 335) 533–40; Paolo Saguato, Guido Ferrarini, and Eric Pan, 'Financial Market Infrastructures: The International Approach and the Current Challenges' in Jens-Hinrich Binder and Paolo Saguato (eds) *Financial Market Infrastructures* (OUP 2022) para 4.23.

341 See 7 USC § 7a-1(h) and 17 CFR § 39.6(a)(1). The definition of an exempt derivatives clearing organization is set out in 17 CFR § 39.2.

prerequisites for the exemption, which are similar to the requirements of the alternative application procedure described above, are laid down in § 39.6(a).[342] Accordingly, the clearing organization must be in good regulatory standard and an MoU or similar arrangement must be concluded between the competent authorities. The clearing organization must also be subject on an ongoing basis to rules which are consistent with the Principles for Financial Market Infrastructures.

The result of this set-up is a clear split. With regard to transaction-level requirements, there are hardly any deference regimes, which stands in contrast to the legal situation in the EU and Switzerland. In relation to entity-level requirements, the CFTC allows for substituted compliance. These substituted compliance mechanisms are akin to the entity-level equivalence provisions of the EU and Switzerland.

bb) Jurisdiction of the SEC The Dodd-Frank Act also introduced a mandatory clearing requirement for security-based swaps.[343] Following a determination by the SEC, certain classes or groups of security-based swaps must be cleared by a clearing agency registered with or exempt from registration with the SEC. The clearing requirement applies in cross-border transactions if at least one of the counterparties is a US person. Initially, the SEC proposed applying the clearing requirement also to transactions between two non-US persons as long as the transaction was conducted within the US.[344] After massive criticism, the SEC, however, refrained from imposing such a far-reaching requirement.[345] Like the CFTC, the SEC has hardly introduced any exemptions from transaction-level requirements based on substituted compliance. Therefore, an exemption from the clearing requirement via substituted compliance is not possible.[346]

In case the clearing requirement applies to a specific transaction, the parties must have the clearing carried out by a clearing agency.[347] Clearing agencies using means of inter-state commerce must generally register with the SEC prior to providing any clearing services.[348] The SEC interpreted this registration duty as covering all clearing agencies, regardless of their place of business, incorporation or organization, if they perform clearing functions within the US, which is the case if they provide clearing services to a US party.[349] The Commission may, however, exempt clearing agencies from the duty to register if the clearing agency is subject to comparable and comprehensive regulation and supervision in its home country.[350] Such an exemption based on the concept of substituted compliance requires a comparability determination by the Commission. The Commission will only grant such an exemption if the extent of

342 17 CFR § 39.6(a).

343 See Dodd-Frank Act, s 763(a), which added section 3C to the 1934 Act (15 USC § 78c-3); on the clearing requirement and potential exemptions see Garslian (n 280) 998ff.

344 Proposed r 3Ca-3(a)(2); see extensively SEC (n 297) 281ff.

345 SEC, 'Application of Certain Title VII Requirements to Security-Based Swap Transactions Connected with a Non-U.S. Person's Dealing Activity That Are Arranged, Negotiated, or Executed By Personnel Located in a U.S. Branch or Office or in a U.S. Branch or Office of an Agent' (n 322) 114ff, particularly at 126.

346 Griffith (n 282) 1336.

347 For the definition of a clearing agency see 1934 Act, s 3(a)(23)(A) (15 USC § 78c(a)(23)(A)).

348 1934 Act, s 17A(b) (15 USC § 78q-1(b)); 17 CFR § 240.17Ab2-1.

349 SEC (n 297) 184ff.

350 1934 Act, s 17A(k) (15 USC § 78q-1(k)).

the clearing house's activities in the US is rather small, and therefore registration is not necessary.[351] Even if no exemption is granted and the clearing agency must therefore register with the SEC, the Commission may consider applying other criteria to foreign-based clearing agencies, thereby granting some relief.[352]

Against the background that there is no substituted compliance for transaction-level requirements, the SEC has recognized that it may not be appropriate to require clearing through a registered or exempt clearing agency for every swap transaction, especially if there are duplicative or conflicting clearing requirements. In such cases, the SEC has therefore extended substituted compliance at the entity-level by allowing parties to clear swaps through clearing agencies that are neither registered nor exempt. The Commission can adopt such exemptions in individual cases based on the general substituted compliance rule 0-13, which is based on section 36 of the 1934 Act.[353] This substituted compliance regime is limited to foreign clearing agencies that do not have staff and do not provide services in the US. It is subject to a comparability determination by the SEC, in which it analyses the similarity of the foreign regulatory framework based on the regulatory scope and objectives, as well as effective compliance and enforcement by the foreign authorities.[354] This extended entity-level exemption is very close to the transaction-level exemptions of the EU and Switzerland.

d) Swap data repositories

Besides the clearing and trading requirement, the reporting requirement is the third cornerstone of the new regulatory framework for swaps under the Dodd-Frank Act. The obligation to report data on swap transactions to data repositories sheds some light on the derivatives market. The resulting transparency puts market participants and supervisors in a position to identify risks more easily and react appropriately.

aa) Jurisdiction of the CFTC Pursuant to section 2(a)(13)(G) CEA, each swap, whether cleared or uncleared, must be reported to a registered swap data repository.[355] The same applies to swaps that were not accepted for clearing by any derivatives clearing organization.[356] These duties are established for swap dealers and major swap participants in section 4s(f)(1) CEA.[357] In relation to registered swap dealers and major swap participants who are non-US persons, exemptions in accordance with the idea of substituted compliance are available.[358]

Such a report is only accepted if made to an entity registered with the CFTC as a swap data repository. Any person who uses means of inter-state commerce and performs the functions of a swap data repository must be registered with the CFTC.[359]

351 SEC (n 297) 188.
352 1934 Act, s 17A(i) (15 USC § 78q-1(i)); SEC (n 297) 188f.
353 See 15 USC § 78mm and 17 CFR § 240.0-13.
354 SEC (n 297) 334.
355 7 USC § 2(a)(13)(G), as added by Dodd-Frank Act, s 727; Garslian (n 280) 1000f.
356 See CEA, s 4r (7 USC § 6r), as added by Dodd-Frank Act, s 729.
357 7 USC § 6s(f)(1), as added by Dodd-Frank Act, s 731.
358 Whether an exemption is available depends on whether the requirement is a Category A or a Category B transaction-requirement and whether the counterparty to the transaction is a US or non-US person. See CFTC (n 279) 45350ff; regarding entity-level requirements see ibid 45338.
359 CEA, s 21 (7 USC § 24a), as introduced by Dodd-Frank Act, s 728.

This also applies to data repositories located in foreign jurisdictions.[360] An exception for foreign data repositories based on the concept of substituted compliance is not foreseen in the regulation.

bb) Jurisdiction of the SEC The reporting requirement under the 1934 Act is set out in two provisions. Pursuant to section 13A(a)(1)1934 Act, all security-based swaps not accepted for clearing must be reported.[361] Additionally, section 13(m)(1)(G) 1934 Act prescribes that each security-based swap, whether cleared or uncleared, must be reported to a registered swap data repository.[362] The Commission specified these duties in Regulation SBSR, in particular in rule 901.[363] The cross-border application of the reporting requirement is specified in rule 908.[364] Under rule 908(a), a swap is subject to the duty, among other situations, where a party of the transaction is a US person or the swap is cleared or executed by an entity in the US. Originally, the Commission planned a rule with a much wider extraterritorial scope but refrained from doing so after facing considerable criticism. The personal scope of the duty is further limited by rule 908(b).

In case one of the parties is a non-US person or a foreign branch of a US person, the reporting requirement can also be fulfilled in accordance with the rules of a foreign country.[365] For this exception to apply, a substituted compliance determination by the Commission is demanded, in which the Commission finds that the foreign legal framework is comparable to that of the US.[366] This substituted compliance determination, in turn, requires the conclusion of an MoU or similar arrangement with the foreign supervisory authority.[367]

If the swap transaction is not exempted from the reporting requirement, it must be reported to a registered security-based data repository.[368] Each data repository domiciled in the US must be registered with the SEC in accordance with section 13(n)(1) 1934 Act.[369] Data repositories that are not residing or incorporated in the US, so-called non-resident security-based swap data repositories, are only required to register if they perform functions within the US.[370] The SEC derived this from the reference to means of inter-state commerce in section 13(n)(1) 1934 Act.[371] In case an MoU or

[360] This follows from r 49.7 (17 CFR § 49.7), which requires foreign data repositories to guarantee that they are legally allowed to provide the Commission with access to their books and records and to consent to onsite inspections and examinations.

[361] 15 USC § 78m-1(a)(1), as introduced by Dodd-Frank Act, s 766(a).

[362] 15 USC § 78m(m)(1)(G), as introduced by Dodd-Frank Act, s 763(i).

[363] Regulation on Reporting and Dissemination of Security-Based Swap Information—Regulation SBSR (17 CFR §§ 242.900–242.909); see John Welling, 'In Defense of the Dealers' (2016) 85 Fordham L Rev 909, 920f.

[364] See 17 CFR § 242.908.

[365] See r 908(c)(1) (17 CFR § 242.908(c)(1)).

[366] See r 908(c)(2)(i) (17 CFR § 242.908(c)(2)(i)). Parties may file an application for such a determination (see under (ii)). When adopting a substituted compliance determination, the Commission must take into account certain specified factors (see under (iii)).

[367] See r 908(c)(2)(iv) (17 CFR § 242.908(c)(2)(iv)).

[368] Security-based swap data repositories are defined in 1934 Act, s 3(a)(75) (15 USC § 78c(a)(75)), as added by Dodd-Frank Act, s 761(a).

[369] 15 USC § 78m(n)(1); concerning the registration procedure see r 13n-1 (17 CFR § 240.13n-1).

[370] See the definition in r 13n-1(a)(1) (17 CFR § 240.13n-1(a)(1)). If these non-resident data repositories must be registered, the special requirements of r 13n-1(f) apply.

[371] SEC (n 297) 196.

similar arrangement with the competent foreign supervisory authorities exists, which addresses issues of confidentiality of data and access to data by the Commission, a non-US person performing functions of a security-based data repository within the US shall be exempted from the duty to register.[372] When determining whether to enter into such an agreement, the SEC may take into account various factors, such as reciprocal assistance, whether the conclusion of an MoU is in the public interest or whether the foreign data repository ensures that data is kept confidential and shared with the SEC.[373] As this exemption theoretically applies to all foreign data repositories regardless of the comparability of the level of regulation in their home country, the exemption is not founded on the idea of substituted compliance.

3. Administrative practice and substituted compliance

The above analysis has shown that numerous rules based on the concept of substituted compliance exist in the area of derivatives regulation. In fact, substituted compliance is most prevalent in this part of US capital markets law, making the administrative interpretation and implementation of the concept particularly important here. In the intra-US context, the practice of the CFTC can be compared with that of the SEC, and the practice in the US more generally with that of the European Commission and the Financial Market Supervisory Authority (FINMA).

Both the SEC and the CFTC intended to align their policies on cross-border transactions to the greatest extent possible from the outset.[374] As the above analysis shows, their approaches are indeed similar, albeit not identical, which is not surprising as a full harmonization of the practices of two independently acting authorities with different legal bases is not realistic. The most notable difference is of a formal nature, namely that the CFTC released an interpretive guidance, while the SEC proposed binding rules.[375]

On the substantive level, both agencies have a shared understanding of what substituted compliance roughly means.[376] Both view the concept as one in which foreign entities can substitute compliance with US law for compliance with the law of their home country if the rules are comparable to their respective US counterparts.[377] There is also agreement that the comparability determination does not require that the other state's rules are identical.[378] This understanding goes hand in hand with the claim of both agencies to follow an outcome-based approach, where the focus of the analysis is on regulatory outcomes rather than the exact wording or regulatory technique used

372 See r 13n-12(b) (17 CFR § 240.13n-12(b)).

373 SEC (n 297) 198.

374 CFTC (n 279) 45296. This goal was also formulated by the SEC, which at the same time acknowledged that complete harmonization will not be possible. SEC (n 297) 344f. The desire for a uniform approach is also reflected in the fact that the CFTC and the SEC initially adopted common rules in this area. See SEC, 'Further Definition of "Swap Dealer," "Security-Based Swap Dealer," "Major Swap Participant," "Major Security-Based Swap Participant" and "Eligible Contract Participant"' 77 Fed Reg 30596 (23 May 2012) https://cftc.gov/sites/default/files/idc/groups/public/@lrfederalregister/documents/file/2012-10562a.pdf (accessed 12 November 2022).

375 Artamonov (n 54) 211.

376 On the policies of the CFTC and the SEC see Griffith (n 282) 1329ff.

377 SEC (n 297) 25; CFTC (n 279) 45340.

378 SEC (n 297) 311; CFTC (n 279) 45342; Artamonov (n 54) 212f.

by the foreign legislator.[379] In addition, both agencies request that MoUs or similar agreements be entered into with the foreign regulator and advocate periodic reviews of comparability determinations.[380]

Despite all these similarities, two major differences persist. With respect to the comparability determination, one difference between the SEC and the CFTC is that the SEC proclaims a holistic approach. In contrast, the CFTC conducts comparability determinations on a requirement-by-requirement basis.[381] This makes the SEC approach more principle-based and less focused on specific rules.[382] At the same time, it exposes the CFTC's method to the risk of being overly fragmented and not sufficiently taking into account the overall regulatory level of the foreign state.[383] On closer inspection, however, this difference weighs less heavily, as the SEC and the CFTC both conduct comparisons on the basis of categories and neither holistically for the entire regulation nor on the basis of individual requirements. Only the number of categories used by the CFTC—13—is greater than the four categories developed by the SEC.[384] The second divergence lies in the applicability of substituted compliance for certain transaction-level requirements. In this regard, the SEC has created a much more comprehensive system of substituted compliance.[385]

In stark contrast to this far-reaching system of substituted compliance created by the SEC, however, is its practice. The SEC has been very reluctant to adopt substituted compliance determinations until recently.[386] The practice of the CFTC is quite different. It began to issue substituted compliance determinations already at an early stage, which is why its practice is more liberal than that of the SEC.[387] In practice, therefore, the CFTC has so far proved to be more liberal than the SEC, even if this is not reflected in the abstract rules.[388]

The CFTC's and SEC's described policies on substituted compliance are broadly in line with those of the European Commission and FINMA.[389] All agencies advocate an outcome-based approach and do not require the foreign regulatory framework to be identical. Like the SEC, the European Commission and FINMA take a holistic

379 SEC (n 297) 26; CFTC (n 279) 45342f.

380 The CFTC wants to re-evaluate substituted compliance determinations every four years. See CFTC (n 279) 45345. The SEC also provides for the possibility of withdrawal, for example, in r 240.3a71-3(d)(2)(iii) (17 CFR § 240.3a71-3(d)(2)(iii)). Concerning the need for an MoU see CFTC (n 279) 45344; the SEC demands such an MoU, for instance, in r 240.3a71-3(d)(1)(iii)(A) (17 CFR § 240.3a71-3(d)(1)(iii)(A)).

381 SEC (n 297) 26; CFTC (n 279) 45343.

382 Griffith (n 282) 1337f; Lindenfeld (n 277) 145f.

383 Johnson (n 286) 617f.

384 Artamonov (n 54) 212f; Coffee (n 279) 1284: 'This means that the SEC's approach is less holistic than it first appears.'

385 These differences are presented very concisely in the form of a table in Artamonov (n 54) 216.

386 The SEC has only started to adopt substituted compliance determinations in 2020. See https://www.sec.gov/page/exchange-act-substituted-compliance-and-listed-jurisdiction-applications-security-based-swap (accessed 12 November 2022). See also n 312 (ch 4).

387 The CFTC has already issued a number of decisions in 2013 in relation to the EU, Switzerland, Japan, Hong Kong, Australia, and Canada. See https://www.cftc.gov/LawRegulation/DoddFrankAct/CDSCP/index.htm (accessed 12 November 2022). On the relationship between the CFTC and the EU see extensively Stuart Weinstein, 'Transatlantic Extraterritoriality and the Regulation of Derivatives' (15 November 2018) SWIFT Institute Working Paper No 2013-003, 13ff https://ssrn.com/abstract=3285814 (accessed 12 November 2022).

388 Toman (n 170) 701f.

389 Consenting on the similarity of the US and EU systems see Lindenfeld (n 277) 145.

perspective when assessing foreign legal systems. However, when looking at individual decisions, differences emerge. A politicization of deference decisions, as practised by the European Commission in its equivalence decisions, does not take place in the US. While the CFTC and the SEC are similarly—or even more—restrictive in adopting deference decisions than the EU, this restraint is based on a great fear of regulatory arbitrage and distrust in the ability of foreign regulations to ward off systemic risks. Both policies stand in contrast to Switzerland's liberal and pragmatic approach, which is not as risk-averse as that of the EU and the US.

V. Exemptions for central banks and public bodies of foreign countries

Like the legal orders of the EU and Switzerland, the US legal system also exempts central banks and other public bodies from certain regulatory obligations. 'International financial institutions', for instance, are exempt from the CEA's clearing requirement.[390] These exemptions do not involve a qualitative analysis of the foreign legal system, which is why they are not based on the concept of substituted compliance. For this reason, they are more akin to Swiss than to EU law.[391]

C) An Atlantic divide: The US deliberately lagging behind

The analysis of the US system has revealed that there are significant differences between deference in the US and its counterparts in the EU and Switzerland. These include primarily the extent to which deference has been embedded in the legal systems of the US, the EU, and Switzerland (I.). In terms of prerequisites, the concepts are quite similar (II.1.), whereas the legal consequences of deference on both sides of the Atlantic are again fairly different (II.2.).

Whether the more territorial and restrained approach to deference of the US or the more open approach in Europe will prevail in the future remains to be seen. This book predicts that the US is lagging behind. As international pressure grows due to increasing globalization and the continuing rise of emerging markets, the US will change course and liberalize as well as reinforce the concept of substituted compliance, thereby aligning it with the EU and Swiss approach (III.).

I. Modified national treatment trumps substituted compliance

From a historical perspective, the US approach to the issue of market access for foreign firms and investors has always been that of (modified) national treatment. This has changed only slightly with the first generation of legislation based on the idea of substituted compliance. The exemption from the duty to reconcile IFRS to US GAAP

390 See 17 CFR § 50.76.

391 For more detail on the EU system see ch 1 C)II.5.; on the Swiss exemptions see ch 3 B)V.

is one of the few cases that persist. The second generation of substituted compliance, which followed the GFC, is also far from being implemented in most areas of the financial market. In fact, it is most prevalent in derivatives regulation, where multiple mechanisms are in place. But even in the field of derivatives regulation, substituted compliance is often restricted to entity-level requirements—at least under the framework of the CFTC—and does not cover transaction-level requirements.[392] This again reduces the scope of application of deference in US capital markets law. This very limited scope of substituted compliance in the US regulatory system leads to a much lower importance of the concept compared to that of equivalence in the EU and Switzerland. Although equivalence in the EU and Switzerland cannot be found in all areas of financial markets law, it is embedded in numerous areas and does not represent a singular phenomenon like in the US.

II. Less developed, less comprehensive, and less far-reaching deference

1. Prerequisites

Equivalence mechanisms in the EU often consist of several pages of regulations and set out the requirements in great detail.[393] Swiss equivalence provisions, however, are rather brief and less obsessed with detail.[394] Yet, in Switzerland, the essential requirements for equivalence are also defined by the legislator. This type of legislation is typical for civil law countries and differs considerably from the American common law approach.

In the US, very few substituted compliance requirements are directly spelt out by Congress in legal acts, and much is therefore left to the Federal Agencies. For instance, in the area of derivatives, the SEC and the CFTC have a wide room for manoeuvre.[395] The SEC and the CFTC use this leeway in part to specify the requirements for substituted compliance through rules. However, also these rules are much less detailed in comparison to EU equivalence mechanisms. Whether reciprocal treatment is required in order for an agency to make a comparability determination or whether the foreign legal system must adhere to international standards is often not explicitly laid down in the regulation but left to administrative practice. This gives the authorities more flexibility in individual cases but leads to greater legal uncertainty for the states and financial institutions involved, especially if there is only minimal or inconsistent administrative practice. Therefore, it is fair to say that equivalence provisions in the EU are more comprehensive and, given the rather limited administrative practice in the US in this area, also more developed.

[392] See eg ch 4 B)IV.2.c)aa). For a view that is very critical of this see Johnson (n 286) 616f.

[393] See eg the equivalence mechanism in EMIR, arts 25ff and MiFIR, arts 46ff.

[394] See ch 3 C)I.3.

[395] This is already visible in the agencies' documents consisting of hundreds of pages in which they explain their approaches. See eg the 83-page CFTC, 'Cross-border Guidance' (n 279) and the 600+ page SEC (n 297) remarks. The wide room for manoeuvre is also reflected in the extensive administrative legislation, which is not limited to laying down minor details, but rather contains the key policy decisions.

2. Legal consequences

The analysis of the legal consequences of equivalence in the EU has shown that the regimes are, in part, very diverse. They range from a mere exemption from specific requirements to granting partial market access to unlimited market access where third country firms are not being subjected to any host state regulation or supervision.[396]

This spectrum can also be found in US substituted compliance rules. This can be seen, for example, with respect to the recognition of foreign clearing organizations. These clearing organizations can either register with the Commission subject to an alternative application procedure. As part of this procedure, they can be exempted from compliance with the US core principles if they are already subject to comparable requirements in their home state.[397] This substituted compliance mechanism consequently exempts foreign clearing organizations only from certain regulatory requirements. Alternatively, foreign clearing organizations can be completely exempted from registration if they are already subject to comparable comprehensive supervision and regulation in their home country.[398] This substituted compliance regime leads to a complete exemption from the CEA and CFTC supervision.

However, the majority of US substituted compliance provisions are more territorial and less far-reaching compared to the EU and Switzerland.[399] This fact is already reflected in the categorization as 'second-generation' substituted compliance. The provisions in this category, as seen, are not primarily designed as a tool of market access but rather as a conflict avoidance instrument.[400] These limited legal consequences and the absence of deference in many key areas make access to the US markets quite restrictive.

III. Are the US stuck in the old world?

In the last century, the US financial market was by far the most evolved and biggest in the world. Consequently, the US did not feel any need to defer to other legal systems, as its market was powerful enough to attract foreign firms, capital, and investors, even if the process of market access was cumbersome. This market position allowed the US to follow the approach of national treatment with few exceptions. On the international level, the US always feared regulatory arbitrage in case of deference and therefore strived for complete harmonization.[401]

[396] See ch 2 C).

[397] 17 CFR § 39.3(3) fourth sentence and § 39.51(a)(i). The core principles applicable to domestic derivatives clearing organizations are laid out in CEA, s 5b(c)(2) (7 USC § 7a-1(c)(2)) and specified in 17 CFR §§ 39.10–39.27.

[398] See 7 USC § 7a-1(h) and 17 CFR § 39.6(a)(1). The definition of an exempt derivatives clearing organization is set out in 17 CFR § 39.2.

[399] Francesco Pennesi, 'Equivalence in the Area of Financial Services' (2021) 58 CMLR 39, 40 and 62ff; Francesco Pennesi, *Equivalence in Financial Services* (Palgrave Macmillan 2022) 45.

[400] Jackson (n 2) 174, 199f.

[401] See Campos (n 9): 'We are more inclined to a single set of rules for all participants in the US market, rather than mutual recognition.'

This policy changed only when international pressure on the US grew. The US facilitated market access through the concept of modified national treatment by exempting foreign firms from certain requirements. These easements were, however, limited in their effect, as a waiver of US regulation for all foreign countries irrespective of the level of their regulation was only possible to a limited extent if the US did not want to endanger its investors and market stability. A system that would have allowed for more far-reaching deference was proposed in the form of first-generation substituted compliance regimes. This proposal was a very liberal piece that could have changed the policy of the US. This change of policy was, however, only short-lived and its implementation was suddenly stopped by the GFC. The GFC marks a turning point in this development, as liberalization of markets was no longer on the agenda worldwide and international pressure to change course, therefore, decreased for the US. Instead of strengthening deference, the US reacted with a growing extraterritorial regulation to fight systemic risks. Again, the US preferred harmonization over deference because they feared regulatory arbitrage. Although the SEC and CFTC implemented second-generation substituted compliance regimes, these regimes only reduce legal fragmentation and are not designed as a liberal alternative to national treatment. They rather mitigate frictions that arise because of the still predominant approach of national treatment and do not represent a real change in policy as envisaged in 2007.[402]

The analysis of the current system of market access for foreign financial service providers has shown that the US continues to operate predominantly with the old instrument of (modified) national treatment from the 1980/90s. Even if it uses substituted compliance, the concept is too piecemeal, too restricted, and too protectionist. It mainly aims at reducing regulatory conflicts and seldomly grants market access rights for foreign firms. The US has missed the departure to an approach that fits better into modern, globalized times. The increasing market power of emerging countries in South America and Asia and the continuing rise of China and the EU will push the US to change its course if it does not want to suffer competitive disadvantages. The US will have to liberalize market access to continue to attract investors by expanding deference. Like with the initial emergence of substituted compliance, where the US was also pushed particularly by the EU equivalence approach, history will repeat itself, and the US will get another push to more deference. Recent evidence for this hypothesis can already be seen from a more liberal practice of the SEC with regard to substituted compliance and CFTC officials pushing for liberalizations.[403]

The disadvantage of lagging behind the time is that it will be increasingly hard for the US to shape the worldwide system of deference.[404] The US is no longer at the

[402] On this historic development see Greene and others (n 65) 3-7ff.

[403] See on the SEC's increasing activities in this area https://www.sec.gov/page/exchange-act-substituted-compliance-and-listed-jurisdiction-applications-security-based-swap (accessed 12 November 2022); see n 312 (ch 4); on the CFTC reform proposals see J Christopher Giancarlo (Chairman of CFTC), 'Cross-Border Swaps Regulation Version 2.0' White Paper (1 October 2018) https://www.cftc.gov/sites/default/files/2018-10/Whitepaper_CBSR100118_0.pdf (accessed 12 November 2022).

[404] The risk of lagging behind the time was already recognized in 2007 at the roundtable on mutual recognition, where scholars pushed for a quick implementation in order to 'be a leader in the area of mutual recognition'. See SEC (n 2) 173.

forefront, which reduces its influence. However, the US has another chance to get into the driver's seat. The EU is currently preoccupied with Brexit and the future role of the UK's financial market for the EU. This fight has led to an increasing politicization of equivalence which hampers the concept and renders it inappropriate for an era of globalized markets. The US could use this opportunity to regain control over future developments by expanding and strengthening its concept of substituted compliance.

5
The Future of Deference in the World and Equivalence in the EU

The first four chapters of this book have provided an in-depth analysis of the current system of deference by examining the EU and Swiss concept of equivalence as well as the approach of substituted compliance in the US. The last chapter leaves the current legal framework and focuses on the future of deference in general and the EU concept of equivalence in particular. Two questions will be addressed: first, what role should deference play in an increasingly globalized financial system (A)); and, secondly, how can the EU strengthen and further enhance equivalence *de lege ferenda* (B))?

A) Deference as a cornerstone of a new global financial market architecture

The globalization of financial markets is not at all a new development. In fact, financial markets were already much more globalized at the end of the nineteenth century than is sometimes assumed.[1] However, this globalization was shattered by the First World War, the financial crisis of 1929, and the Second World War. It was not until the 1960s that the liberalization of financial markets began, and globalization took off again.[2] This development was caused by rapid technological innovation on the one hand and by a number of state policy decisions on the other.[3]

This liberalization led to increasingly interconnected and interdependent markets and the emergence of systemic risks that were initially overlooked and finally culminated in the global financial crisis (GFC) of 2007/2008. Unlike after the world financial crisis of 1929, states did not react by isolating their national markets. Given the degree of technological advancement, globalization could have hardly been stopped anyhow, let alone did it make economic sense to do so. Instead, the major market economies focused on the avoidance of systemic risks by increasing the extraterritorial application of their supervisory law.[4] States realized that foreign financial firms and products

[1] On the rise and fall of the economy at that time, including capital markets see Martin Wolf, *Why Globalization Works* (Yale UP 2005) 106ff.

[2] On the historical dimensions see Michael D Bordo, 'The Globalization of International Financial Markets: What Can History Teach Us?' in Leonardo Auernheimer (ed), *International Financial Markets: The Challenge of Globalization* (Chicago UP 2003) 29ff.

[3] On the influence of technology see Walter B Wriston, 'Technology and Sovereignty' (1988) 67 Foreign Aff 63, 71; on the influence of policy decisions by states see Eric Helleiner, 'Explaining the Globalization of Financial Markets: Bringing States Back In' (1995) 2 Rev Intl Polit Econ 315.

[4] Stefano Pagliari, 'A Wall around Europe? The European Regulatory Response to the Global Financial Crisis and the Turn in Transatlantic Relations' (2012) 35 J Eur Integr 391; John C Coffee Jr, 'Extraterritorial Financial Regulation: Why E.T. Can't Come Home' (2014) 99 Cornell L Rev 1259.

Equivalence and Substituted Compliance in Financial Markets Law. Jonas Schürger,
Oxford University Press. © Jonas Schürger 2023. DOI: 10.1093/oso/9780198876748.003.0005

could pose similar risks to the domestic market as local ones. As a result, they concluded that systemically relevant foreign firms and products had to be subjected to their regulation and supervision. This development can be observed in almost all prominent jurisdictions, most notably in the EU and the US.[5] This far-reaching extraterritoriality has, however, created new challenges that have not been adequately addressed to date.[6] These include an increase in legal and supervisory conflicts leading to greater fragmentation, which makes it unattractive for financial service providers to enter new markets.[7] This fragmentation causes considerable welfare losses.[8]

This is exacerbated by several worrying political developments in recent years. The idea of open markets is coming under increasing pressure worldwide and protectionism is on the rise. This is exemplified by the election of populist governments in major Western countries during the last decade, trade conflicts between China and the US, and the tightening of its foreign trade policy by the EU. One outcome of this development and particularly significant for financial markets was the UK's withdrawal from the EU.

The unlawful Russian invasion of the Ukraine on 24 February 2022 and the terrible war that has raged since then is another low point. It shows in a brutal but exemplary way the prevailing imperialist thinking of some states that reject the concept of a rules-based world order. This turning point reinforces the call for a depoliticization of deference made in this book. Since the Russian attack, the West has come closer together. This can be seen, for example, in the United Nations General Assembly Resolution ES-11/1 condemning Russia's war of aggression, which was supported by 141 countries.[9] Deference in financial law primarily addresses market access between these Western states. In this context, the term 'West' is not understood geographically but historically and ideologically. It includes all democratic states that follow the principles of a democratic and rule-based international order and more specifically in financial terms of an open market economy. In these times it is precisely the Western nations that must cooperate more closely. As far as the integration of financial markets through deference is concerned, greater openness and liberality and fewer political conflicts are needed. In view of the West moving closer together, the call for more deference and less politicization is more realistic than ever.

Numerous alternatives to the current framework have been developed to tackle these issues, some of which are briefly presented and discussed in the following section (I.). The next section then argues that an expansion of deference is the only

[5] ibid.

[6] Far-reaching extraterritoriality in the sense used here refers in particular to what Chris Brummer calls a 'direct' extraterritoriality. See Chris Brummer, 'Territoriality as a Regulatory Technique: Notes from the Financial Crisis' (2010) 79 U Cin L Rev 499, 506f. See eg the strong warnings of the FSB and IOSCO in FSB, 'FSB Report on Market Fragmentation' (4 June 2019) https://www.fsb.org/wp-content/uploads/P040619-2.pdf (accessed 12 November 2022); IOSCO, 'Market Fragmentation & Cross-border Regulation' Report (June 2019) https://www.iosco.org/library/pubdocs/pdf/IOSCOPD629.pdf (accessed 12 November 2022).

[7] ibid.

[8] International Federation of Accountants, 'Regulatory Divergence: Costs, Risks, Impacts' (11 April 2018) https://www.ifac.org/system/files/publications/files/IFAC-OECD-Regulatory-Divergence.pdf (accessed 12 November 2022).

[9] UN General Assembly, 'Aggression against Ukraine' A/RES/ES-11/1, Resolution adopted by the General Assembly on 2 March 2022.

realistic option to reduce market fragmentation, while at the same time preventing the emergence of systemic risks (II.). The third section concludes (III.).

I. Globalization of financial markets and regulatory responses: A variety of proposals, their merits, and drawbacks

In the aftermath of the GFC, a range of concepts was developed regarding the new design of a global financial market architecture that sought to ensure, on the one hand, that globalization is not reversed and, on the other hand, that the emergence of systemic risks is avoided. This debate and the advantages and disadvantages of the proposals can only be presented very roughly in the following.[10] The suggestions can be broadly classified according to the level at which regulation and supervision should take place.

1. A global regulator and harmonization of supervisory law

Some scholars promote the idea of a financial architecture in which the main competences lie at the global level.[11] In its most extreme form, an institution at the global level would have the authority to adopt supervisory law in the form of hard law as well as to supervise financial institutions worldwide directly. This set-up would have the advantage of entirely preventing regulatory arbitrage.[12] Also, the fragmentation of national markets would be reduced, as there would generally be only one world market governed by the same rules and supervised by the same authority.[13] This approach would massively reduce compliance costs for financial firms providing services on a cross-border basis and, as a result, increase overall welfare.[14] In addition, expertise that is now scattered across dozens of regulatory agencies could be pooled at the global level. One argument that is always put forward in this context is that companies are becoming more and more international, and thus supervision should also be organized globally. In short, global firms need a global regulator.[15]

This approach is, however, fraught with considerable disadvantages.[16] Complete elimination of competition between legal orders will, on the one hand, prevent

[10] For an interesting discussion of the different approaches using the example of derivatives regulation see Andrew Godwin, Ian Ramsay, and Edwin Sayes, 'Assessing Financial Regulatory Coordination and Integration with Reference to OTC Derivatives Regulation' (2017) 12 CMLJ 38, 49ff; for a similar discussion see Francesco Pennesi, *Equivalence in Financial Services* (Palgrave Macmillan 2022) 39ff.

[11] Kern Alexander, Rahul Dhumale, and John Eatwell, *Global Governance of Financial Systems* (OUP 2005) 161ff; Emilios Avgouleas, *Governance of Global Financial Markets* (CUP 2012) 429ff; see also Tajinder Singh and Chris Brummer, 'Does Today's World Need a Global Financial Regulator?' (2014) 33 Intl Fin L Rev 18, 18f.

[12] Rhys Bollen, 'The Slow Journey towards a Global Regulator' (2008) 5 Macquarie J Bus L 255, 268; Chris Brummer, *Soft Law and the Global Financial System* (2nd edn, CUP 2015) 328f.

[13] Pointing to a more consistent implementation of rules see Vanessa Blackmore and Esther Jeapes, 'The Global Financial Crisis: One Global Regulator or Multiple Regulators?' (2009) 4 CMLJ S112, S113.

[14] With further references: John M Fontecchio, 'The General Agreements on Trade in Services: Is it the Answer to Creating a Harmonized Global Securities System' (1994) 20 NC J Intl L & Com Reg 115, 117.

[15] Ross P Buckley, 'How the International Financial System, to Its Detriment, Differs from National Systems, and What We Can Do about It' (2004) 34 Hong Kong LJ 321, 331f.

[16] Edward F Greene, 'Beyond Borders Part II' (May 2007) 4ff http://www.sechistorical.org (accessed 12 November 2022); Annelise Riles, 'Managing Regulatory Arbitrage: A Conflict of Laws Approach' (2014) 47 Cornell Intl LJ 63, 77ff.

any improvements of regulation as the idea of trial and error is abolished.[17] On the other hand, weaknesses in the regulatory set-up will have even more dramatic consequences, as all markets and jurisdictions will be affected simultaneously.[18] Moreover, a regulator at the global level will necessarily be far away from the supervised entities and the developments in the local markets. While this may promote impartiality, it carries the danger that local particularities and associated risks will be overlooked.

What is more, a financial architecture of this extreme shape is unrealistic and impracticable.[19] States will fight fiercely for their sovereignty and will not allow a global institution to dictate the rules; much less will they delegate the exercise of oversight powers to a global body.[20] A global institution of this kind would also lack democratic legitimacy and accountability as long as there are no elections and no judicial control at this level.[21] There would also be many unanswered questions regarding the composition of such an institution. Who should be part of it and, if all states were represented, would it even work?

These shortcomings and challenges show that a truly global regulator and harmonized hard law at the global level are neither desirable nor likely to be implemented in the near future.[22] This does not mean, however, that some elements of this approach are not viable. In practice, especially after the GFC, many harmonizing initiatives have emerged from global institutions such as the Financial Stability Board (FSB) or the International Organization of Securities Commissions (IOSCO). These international standards in the form of soft law have helped considerably to make deference feasible in the first place. In fact, the development of international standards and deference are not mutually exclusive, as will be shown later. They are not alternatives but two complementary components of a functioning financial market architecture.

2. Host state regulation

Since the first proposal is not practicable and has not been able to gain acceptance to date, states predominantly follow the principle of host state regulation and supervision. According to this principle, states regulate and supervise not only their domestic financial service providers but also those seeking access to their territory or markets and thus become the guest of the respective state. The decisive question is at what level of linkage the respective host country applies its laws; the answer to this question

[17] Roberta Romano, 'For Diversity in the International Regulation of Financial Institutions' (2014) 31 Yale J Reg 1; Roberta Romano, 'The Need for Competition in International Securities Regulation' (2001) 2 Theoretical Inq L 387. An economic analysis of regulatory competition is provided for in Larry E Ribstein and Bruce H Kobayashi, 'An Economic Analysis of Uniform State Laws' (1996) 25 J Legal Stud 131.

[18] Sean J Griffith, 'Substituted Compliance and Systemic Risk: How to Make a Global Market in Derivatives Regulation' (2014) 98 Minn LR 1291, 1293f and 1349; extensively see Charles K Whitehead, 'Destructive Coordination' (2011) 96 Cornell L Rev 323.

[19] See Brummer (n 12) 329, who states: 'Despite the potential attractions of a global regulator, the likelihood of the sort of supranational authority described above is small to nonexistent.'

[20] Singh and Brummer (n 11) 19. In that article, Chris Brummer stresses that such a process would also be extremely time-consuming.

[21] On these issues and with further references see Brummer (n 12) 193ff; Claire R Kelly, 'Financial Crises and Civil Society' (2011) 11 Chic J Intl L 505, 534ff. With regard to international standards see Stefan A Wandel, *International Regulatory Cooperation* (Schulthess 2014) 139ff.

[22] For further arguments see the convincing discussion in Blackmore and Jeapes (n 13) S115ff.

determines the degree of extraterritoriality.[23] As we have seen, states have considerably expanded the territorial reach of their law in the aftermath of the GFC.[24]

A further distinction can be made within this approach depending on the type of regulation to which foreign firms are subjected. The most common one is a form of modified national treatment, in which foreign companies are treated, with certain exceptions, in the same way as domestic ones.[25] Another differentiation can be made based on whether an establishment in the form of a subsidiary or branch office is required, i.e. forced territoriality.[26]

The approach of host state regulation has the advantage that blind spots in regulation and supervision are largely avoided. It also prevents some forms of regulatory arbitrage and creates a level playing field by subjecting all market participants to the same regulation regardless of their country of origin.[27] Also, the emergence of systemic risks can be adequately countered, as states can already regulate financial firms and products when there is minimal contact with their markets. However, this quest for an extensive influence of one's own regulation and supervision has led to a high degree of extraterritoriality, especially in the field of derivatives, where states apply their laws even to transactions between two foreign parties in certain situations.[28]

The downside of extraterritoriality is that legal and supervisory conflicts are growing as certain firms and transactions are regulated simultaneously by more and more states.[29] This trend will increase as the importance of emerging markets grows, which will eventually also apply their laws to cross-border transactions. This development also raises opportunity costs for companies that are subjected to more and more legal orders and are under the supervision of numerous different authorities. All this leads to fragmented markets and overall welfare losses.[30] Therefore, a pure system of

[23] From the perspective of public international law, the limits are very broad. The existence of a 'genuine link' is generally sufficient. See landmark decisions in *S.S. Lotus* (*France v Turkey*) (Judgment) [1927] PCIJ Series A No 10; *Nottebohm Case* (*Liechtenstein v Guatemala*) (second phase) (Judgment) [1955] ICJ Rep 4; *Barcelona Traction, Light and Power Co Case* (*Belgium v Spain*) (Judgment) [1970] ICJ Rep 6; see also American Law Institute, Restatement (Fourth) of the Foreign Relations Law of the US § 402 (2018); Cedric Ryngaert, *Jurisdiction in International Law* (2nd edn, OUP 2015) 43 and 84ff.

[24] Pagliari (n 4).

[25] The US especially follows this approach of modified national treatment to a large extent. See Edward F Greene and Ilona Potiha, 'Issues in the Extraterritorial Application of Dodd–Frank's Derivatives and Clearing Rules, the Impact on Global Markets and the inevitability of Cross-border and US Domestic Coordination' (2013) 8 CMLJ 338, 344; Lily D Vo, 'Comment: Substituted Compliance: An Alternative to National Treatment for Cross-Border Transactions and International Financial Entities' (2015) 13 Geo JL & Pub Pol'y 85, 88ff; see ch 4 A)I.

[26] Examples of forced territoriality can be found especially in the insurance sector. See art 162(2)(b) of the Solvency II in the EU and art 15(1)(b) of the VAG in Switzerland. In the US, this forced territoriality comes in the form of an obligation to deposit assets exclusively for US investors and creditors with an institution in the US. See eg NY Ins Law, ss 1312 and 1315 and Michigan Ins Code, s 431a. A counter-example in the field of investment services can be found in MiFID II, art 39(1), which leaves it up to the Member States to decide whether they will require third country firms to establish a branch for the provision of investment services.

[27] Greene and Potiha (n 25) 344.

[28] See extensively with further references on the US approach ch 4 B)IV.2.a); see also for a comparative analysis Stuart Weinstein, 'Transatlantic Extraterritoriality and the Regulation of Derivatives' (15 November 2018) SWIFT Institute Working Paper No 2013-003 https://ssrn.com/abstract=3285814 (accessed 12 November 2022).

[29] See Hannah L Buxbaum, 'Transnational Legal Ordering and Regulatory Conflict' (2016) 1 UC Irvine J Intl Transnatl & Comp L 91, 93ff; see also the strong warnings of the FSB and IOSCO in FSB (n 6); IOSCO (n 6).

[30] International Federation of Accountants (n 8).

host country regulation and supervision no longer offers an adequate framework in times of globalized markets. It must at least be combined with approaches that tackle the issue of market fragmentation.

3. Home state regulation or country-of-origin principle

Instead of regulating and supervising foreign firms and products upon market entry, a state can rely on the service provider's home state or country-of-origin supervision.[31] Broadly speaking, there are two forms: one where this reliance is unconditional and another in which the host state requires the home state's legal system to meet certain conditions in return for withdrawing regulatory and supervisory powers.

a) Unconditional withdrawal of regulation and supervision

A complete withdrawal of regulatory and supervisory powers by the host state has the advantage of a clear distribution of supervisory competences, as these are exercised only by the authority in whose jurisdiction the company is domiciled. This set-up eliminates market fragmentation to a large extent and minimizes opportunity costs for financial firms. In contrast to a global supervisor, the authorities are also close to the institutions they supervise and have a good understanding of local specificities. The approach preserves competition between legal orders, which would be lost with a global system.

However, an unlimited recognition of foreign supervisory systems would have negative consequences. States will try to exploit the system by attracting foreign firms into their markets through lowering regulatory standards. Such behaviour will trigger a race to the bottom and foster regulatory arbitrage.[32] For this reason, such a system without restrictions cannot be found in any country. One notable exception is the concept of passports in the EU.[33] However, there is no risk of a race to the bottom in the EU because there is a single rulebook for large parts of capital markets law, compliance is monitored not only by national but also European authorities, and there is even judicial review before the Court of Justice of the European Union on a supranational level.

b) Conditional withdrawal of regulation and supervision

A race to the bottom, as is feared in the case of unconditional recognition, can be prevented by solely recognizing foreign legal systems that meet a certain quality standard that the host country must assess. This is the underlying idea of deference. The standard required depends on the applicable deference mechanism. Some refer only to the adherence to international standards, while others demand an appropriate, equivalent, or comparable foreign legal system. The advantages and disadvantages

[31] On the principle in the context of the EU see Karsten E Sørensen, 'The Country-of-Origin Principle and Balancing Jurisdiction between Home Member States and Host Member States' (2019) 30 EBLR 37; Matthias Lehmann, 'Internationales Finanzmarktrecht' in Jan von Hein (ed), *MüKo/BGB*, vol 13, pt 12 (8th edn, CH Beck 2021) paras 123ff.

[32] Sørensen (n 31) 46. On regulatory arbitrage see Victor Fleischer, 'Regulatory Arbitrage' (2010) 89 Tex L Rev 227.

[33] Regarding the concept of passporting see Wulf-Henning Roth, 'Mutual Recognition' in Panos Koutrakos and Jukka Snell (eds), *The Law of the EU's Internal Market* (Edward Elgar Publishing 2017) 446ff; Niamh Moloney, *EU Securities and Financial Markets Regulation* (3rd edn, OUP 2014) 108ff, 217ff, 290ff, and 396ff; see ch 1 B)I.1.

associated with deference mechanisms depend on the specific design of the applicable regime, which is why they are presented in detail in the next part.

II. Deference: Equivalence and substituted compliance as the best compromise

It will be argued in the following that deference should be a cornerstone of any well-functioning financial architecture. In the near future, only deference can realistically prevent fragmentation and, at the same time, ensure a well-functioning and stable financial order. To achieve this, it is crucial that deference mechanisms, whose design, as seen, varies considerably around the world, have specific characteristics. These characteristics will be outlined below (1.), followed by a discussion of the advantages associated with such designed mechanisms (2.).

1. Details matter: How deference should be designed

a) Equivalent or comparable does not mean identical

The system of deference is based on the assumption that there is no uniform global regulation and that different regulatory approaches can achieve similar outcomes.[34] This assumption is taken *ad absurdum* when a comparison of legal systems is carried out through a line-by-line analysis, examining whether the foreign legal system has completely replicated the domestic regulation.

Such an approach not only leads to a situation in which hardly any deference decisions will be issued but also causes further disadvantages. A call for complete uniformity of regulation would destroy the essential advantage of a financial architecture in which different jurisdictions compete with each other to find the right solution and learn from their own and other countries' mistakes (trial and error).[35] Also, weaknesses of a regulatory system are likely to have far more drastic consequences in the case of financial crises if all states have the same regulation and thus the same weaknesses. Moreover, the desire for absolute equality of regulation always goes hand in hand with one side giving up its current regulatory approach. This will lead to a situation in which not the best system, but the system of the most powerful market will prevail. As a result, many states will feel like 'rule-takers' whose sovereignty is under attack.[36] This, in turn, will make the worldwide breakthrough of the idea of deference more difficult or even impossible and thus destroy the system.

This risk of demanding a complete adoption of one's own law is particularly evident in some analyses conducted by EU authorities, in which the foreign legal system

[34] Greene (n 16) 5. This starting point is undisputed in all legal systems examined: Commission, 'Equivalence in the area of financial services' (Communication) COM (2019) 349 final, 7f; SEC, 'Cross-Border Release', 311 and 315; Erläuterungsbericht FinfraV, 36f.

[35] Romano, 'The Need for Competition in International Securities Regulation' (n 17).

[36] A case in point is the discussion in the wake of Brexit, in which the UK often saw itself forced into the role of a 'rule-taker'. See Caroline Binham, 'Fear EU Deal Puts City of London at Risk of "Rule-taking"' *Financial Times* (23 January 2020) https://www.ft.com/content/d56ee33a-3d3d-11ea-b232-000f4477fbca (accessed 12 November 2022).

is closely examined line-by-line.[37] At times it would be beneficial for the EU to look at the more risk-sensitive and pragmatic approach of the Swiss Financial Market Supervisory Authority (FINMA) in this regard.[38] A step in the right direction is the EU's recent focus on issues like risk-sensitivity and proportionality.[39] If an equivalence decision in a certain area entails lower risks, the analysis should be shorter and more pragmatic.[40]

One manifestation of such a risk-sensitive approach is Switzerland's finely graduated system, in particular the regimes based on the appropriateness of a foreign legal order, which in this regard could serve as a blueprint for other states.[41] In cases involving the regulation of non-systemically relevant service providers, products, or infrastructures, it may be sufficient to require 'appropriate' rather than 'equivalent' foreign regulation and supervision because exposure to systemic risks in these cases is low.[42] The criterion of appropriateness not only results in a greater latitude for recognition but has the effect that the analysis not only takes into account domestic law but instead focuses on international standards and other foreign legal orders. This broadens the perspective of the comparability assessment, which otherwise carries the risk of being too introspective.

b) Depoliticization is key

The central challenge of the concept of equivalence in the EU is its increasing politicization. As explained in detail in Chapter 2, the compatibility of this politicization with EU law and world trade law is highly doubtful.[43] Apart from this legal aspect, it is also detrimental to the goal of creating a functioning global financial system for two reasons.

First, the idea of regulatory competition only works if there are mechanisms to ensure that the 'best' and not the legal system of the strongest state prevails.[44] The 'best'

[37] See eg the analysis of capital requirements by EIOPA. EIOPA, 'Advice to the European Commission: Equivalence assessment of the Bermudan supervisory system in relation to articles 172, 227 and 260 of the Solvency II Directive' EIOPA-BoS-11-029 (2011), 41ff. Overall, equivalence decisions in the EU are, nonetheless, still based on an outcome-based approach that demands comparability rather than identity, as the analysis of EU practice has shown. See ch 2 B)I.2.

[38] One example of this is Switzerland's quick and pragmatic reaction to Brexit. Switzerland and the UK immediately entered into negotiations on a mutual recognition agreement. See Federal Department of Finance, 'Switzerland and United Kingdom Deepen Relationship in Financial Sector' (27 January 2021) https://www.efd.admin.ch/efd/en/home/the-fdf/nsb-news_list.msg-id-82134.html (accessed 12 November 2022).

[39] Commission (n 34) 5ff; Commission, 'EU Equivalence decisions in financial services policy: An assessment' (Staff Working Document) SWD (2017) 102 final, 8 and 11; see also the reforms MiFIR and EMIR, which pay particular attention to the issues of risk-sensitivity and proportionality; see ch 2 B)I.1.a)dd).

[40] In favour of such a risk-sensitive approach: IOSCO, 'Good Practices on Processes for Deference' Report (June 2020) 16ff (Good Practice 3) https://www.iosco.org/library/pubdocs/pdf/IOSCOPD659.pdf (accessed 12 November 2022).

[41] See ch 3 B)IV.2.a)aa) and ch 3 C)II.1.

[42] An example of this is the Swiss system in relation to foreign CCPs. See FinfraG, arts 60(2)(a) and 23(4)(a); see ch 3 C)II.1.

[43] Jeremy Bacharach, 'L'équivalence: entre question technique et instrument de realpolitik' Centre de droit bancaire et financier (19 August 2019) https://www.cdbf.ch/1081/ (accessed 12 November 2022); Pierre-Henri Conac, 'The International Organisation of Securities Commissions (IOSCO), Europe, Brexit, and Rethinking Cross-border Regulation' (2020) 17 ECFR 72, 76ff; see ch 2 B)II.2.

[44] Fearing such a '"War of the Clubs" Scenario' see Chris Brummer, 'Post-American Securities Regulation' (2010) 98 Cal L Rev 327, 374f.

legal order in this context is understood as the one that in the most efficient way provides the greatest protection for investors, safeguards the functioning of markets, and prevents the emergence of systemic risks. However, if states use their economic power to pursue political goals unrelated to financial market regulation, this competition no longer functions properly. One example of such misguided competition due to a politicization is the non-renewal of the recognition of Swiss stock exchanges by the EU.[45]

Second, an increasing politicization leads to a downward spiral. When market access is denied solely for political reasons unrelated to regulatory aspects, other countries will feel like 'rule-takers' and will be offended in their national pride.[46] This causes them to close their markets to service providers from other countries as an act of defiance. Other countries may follow and thus unleash a downward spiral.

To prevent such harmful politicization, various measures can be taken. The responsibility for comparability determinations can, for example, be shifted to technical authorities, thereby withdrawing it from the political arena. A proposal along these lines, which aims at strengthening the competences of European supervisory authorities (ESAs) in the EU, is presented below.[47] Furthermore, states can strengthen and expand the availability of legal remedies at both the national level and at that of the World Trade Organization (WTO). Increased judicial control will limit the possibilities of political abuse. Another remedy could be to provide more detailed justifications of deference decisions, enabling other states to understand the technical reasons underlying the decisions better and allowing states to react to these accordingly, for example, by adapting their law.[48] To avoid the inclusion of political considerations in the first place, it is also essential to define and implement a methodology for such decisions, as has been suggested in Chapter 2 above.[49]

c) International standards as the baseline for deference

Requiring conformity with international standards as a prerequisite for deference and thus using them as a baseline for comparability assessments has many benefits. The prospect of market access for their financial service providers incentivises countries to comply with these standards. This will foster the harmonization of international standards and promote convergence of financial regulation.[50] Conversely, recognition of foreign regulation is often only feasible if both regulations are based on a shared regulatory goal. This common ground is usually an internationally agreed standard, which forms the foundation for sufficient comparability. Therefore, the extent to which international standards are implemented depends on deference on the one hand, and the success of deference depends on harmonized international standards on the other. There is thus a mutual interdependency.

[45] Peter Nobel, *Schweizerisches Finanzmarktrecht* (4th edn, Stämpfli 2019) § 2 para 70; see ch 2 B)II.2.a).
[46] On such 'retaliatory measures' see Francesco Pennesi, 'Equivalence in the Area of Financial Services' (2021) 58 CMLR 39, 57; describing this phenomenon as the 'political economy problem': Brummer (n 6) 509ff.
[47] See ch 5 B)II.1.
[48] This is also suggested by IOSCO, 'Good Practices on Processes for Deference' Report (June 2020) (n 40) 18f (Good Practice 7).
[49] See ch 2 B)I.2.c).
[50] Roberta S Karmel, 'IOSCO's Response to the Financial Crisis' (2012) 37 J Corp L 849, 900f; Caroline Bradley, 'Private International Law-Making for the Financial Markets' (2005) 29 Fordham Intl LJ 127.

Furthermore, competitive disadvantages for domestic service providers, who need to comply with those standards anyway because most of the supervisory law in the EU, the US, and Switzerland are based on them, are eliminated. In cases where strict international standards already exist, it may even be appropriate to grant equivalence on the basis of compliance with those standards.[51]

All in all, it is therefore advisable to extend the requirement of conformity with international standards to all deference mechanisms where such standards exist. A positive example in this regard is again Switzerland. Its equivalence and appropriateness provisions are largely based on international standards, and compliance with these is sometimes considered sufficient for recognition.[52]

d) Reciprocity as an essential element

Another essential component of deference is reciprocity. The prerequisite of reciprocity is not without controversy. British and US authorities, in particular, were critical of the concept during the European Market Infrastructure Regulation (EMIR) negotiations.[53] However, the opposition from the US is contradictory because the US substituted compliance regimes themselves sometimes demand reciprocity.[54] Switzerland is also reluctant to apply reciprocity vis-à-vis WTO member states.[55]

These concerns are based primarily on two aspects. The first is an alleged incompatibility with WTO law.[56] However, as explained above, such incompatibility does not exist.[57] Secondly, some fear that market access barriers are too high if reciprocity is required.[58] This point can be mitigated as many reciprocity provisions only demand the opportunity for foreign market participants to gain access to the foreign market. This abstract reciprocity is the most common form in the EU and does not render market access overly burdensome.[59]

Instead, there are many strong arguments supporting the call for reciprocity.[60] One claim is that reciprocity promotes the creation of a level playing field. Without

[51] See on this approach, which is partly pursued under Swiss financial markets law: ch 3 C)II.3.b); Rashid Bahar in Rolf Watter and Rashid Bahar (eds), *BSK-FINMAG/FinfraG* (3rd edn, Helbing Lichtenhahn 2019) FinfraG, art 60 para 11.

[52] ibid.

[53] House of Lords, 'MiFID II: Getting it Right for the City and EU Financial Services Industry' European Union Committee—Second Report (2012) paras 53ff https://publications.parliament.uk/pa/ld201213/ldselect/ldeucom/28/2802.htm (accessed 12 November 2022); see Lucia Quaglia, 'The Politics of 'Third Country Equivalence' in Post-Crisis Financial Services Regulation in the European Union' (2015) 38 West Eur Pol 167, 178f.

[54] See eg CFTC, 'Comparability Determination for the European Union' 82 Fed Reg 48394, 48412 (18 October 2017) https://www.cftc.gov/sites/default/files/idc/groups/public/@lrfederalregister/documents/file/2017-22616a.pdf (accessed 12 November 2022).

[55] See eg second sentence of FinfraG, arts 40(2), 41(4), 60(3), and 80(4).

[56] See eg in Switzerland Benjamin Leisinger in Rolf Sethe and others (eds), *SK zum FinfraG* (Schulthess 2017) art 40 para 26; in the UK see House of Lords (n 53) para 56.

[57] See ch 2 A)I.4.

[58] See opinion of Emilios Avgouleas in House of Lords (n 53) para 57; more generally see Susan Emmenegger and Andrea Bigler, 'Fortress Europe: Die Äquivalenzverfahren der EU im Bereich der Finanzdienstleistungen' (2019) 91 SZW 155.

[59] See ch 2 A)I.4.

[60] See Edward F Greene, 'Beyond Borders: Time to Tear Down the Barriers to Global Investing' (2007) 48 Harv Intl LJ 85, 88f; on self-interest and reciprocity see Matthias Herdegen, *The Dynamics of International Law in a Globalised World* (Vittorio Klostermann 2016) 33ff.

reciprocity, financial service providers from the recognizing state would face competitive disadvantages. They would not be able to compete with service providers on foreign markets but would instead have more competition on their domestic markets.[61] Another reason to demand reciprocity is that foreign supervisors will be much more diligent in their supervision if they are also dependent on other supervisors because risks are distributed more symmetrically when financial firms from both sides enter the foreign market. Hence, an externalization of risks can be avoided.[62] Finally, reciprocity is a decisive leverage factor. The offer to open up a national market usually constitutes a considerable incentive for other countries to do the same. As a result, the general fragmentation of markets can be reduced. For these reasons, it is advisable to demand reciprocal treatment when opening domestic markets via deference. To avoid setting the barriers to market entry too high, abstract reciprocity, as set out in many EU provisions, should be sufficient.

e) Withdrawal as a corollary to deference

Once a comparability finding has been adopted and deference granted, the future development of the two jurisdictions in question must be monitored. A frequently expressed risk of deference is that one state tries to gain unfair competitive advantages over the other state by lowering the standard of regulation and supervision.[63] This can lead to countermeasures by the other state, which in turn reduces its regulatory and supervisory standards. The result is a race to the bottom, with dramatic consequences for investor protection and financial stability.[64]

The fear of this scenario, however, is largely unfounded. The instrument of withdrawal can provide a sufficient safeguard against such developments. Since no state is obliged to grant foreign service providers and products market access via deference, states can revoke market access rights if the preconditions are no longer met. This gives states an alternative course of action: they do not have to lower their regulatory standards but can revoke market access for foreign firms by withdrawing the comparability determination. This opportunity of revoking market access rights thus prevents a race to the bottom.

On the contrary, deference can even initiate a race to the top.[65] Following a deference decision, states are free to raise the level of their regulation. If they do so, other states must follow to ensure that their regulation and supervision are still regarded as equivalent or comparable and that they continue to have market access. Examples

[61] Matthias Lehmann and Dirk A Zetzsche, 'How Does It Feel to Be a Third Country? The Consequences of Brexit for Financial Market Law' in Oonagh E Fitzgerald and Eva Lein (eds), *Complexity's Embrace* (Queen's UP 2018) 114.

[62] Dirk A Zetzsche, 'Competitiveness of Financial Centers in Light of Financial and Tax Law Equivalence Requirements' in Ross P Buckley, Emilios Avgouleas, and Douglas W Arner (eds), *Reconceptualising Global Finance and Its Regulation* (CUP 2016) 398.

[63] Tzung-bor Wei, 'The Equivalence Approach to Securities Regulation' (2007) 27 NW J Intl L & Bus 255, 293f; Vo (n 25) 103.

[64] Pennesi (n 46) 49f.

[65] Referring to a 'race to optimality' under a recognition regime see Greene (n 16) 6; see also on a race towards the top in an intra-US context John C Coffee Jr, 'Racing towards the Top: The Impact of Cross-Listing and Stock Market Competition on International Corporate Governance' (2002) 102 Colum L Rev 1757, 1811ff.

of such a race to the top can be observed in the context of Switzerland's autonomous replication of EU standards and following the Multijurisdictional Disclosure System (MJDS) between Canada and the US.[66] At the same time, this mechanism also protects the sovereignty of states, which are free to choose between adjusting their regulation to preserve market access rights and maintaining their regulation and thus give up their rights to market access. If there is a threat of overregulation in one state, market access becomes less attractive for foreign service providers, and other states will not follow the regulatory changes. In this respect, the system of deference also disciplines states. To continue to attract foreign capital, states must always consider when amending their regulation whether they can convince other states to follow them.

To sum up, the possibility of withdrawing deference is essential to prevent a race to the bottom. A withdrawal regime also promotes competition between different regulatory systems and fosters a moderate race to the top. How exactly such provisions should be designed to avoid the disadvantages that can accompany them[67] is the subject of the last section of this chapter.[68]

f) Multilateralization of deference

A more long-term and far-reaching reform goal would be the multilateralization of deference mechanisms. Matthias Lehmann and I have developed such a proposal, which allows me to remain brief at this point and refer to it for further details.[69]

In a nutshell, multilateralization of deference means transferring the comparability analysis to an international organization. In a first step, this organization should determine whether a particular national system has implemented the international standards in a particular area. In a second step, the national legal systems are then to be compared with each other. The analysis ends with a non-binding recommendation for a specific state to recognize the system of another state as comparable or not. On the basis of the findings of the comparative analysis, nation states can then continue to decide autonomously whether to issue a deference decision in the form of equivalence, appropriateness, comparability, or substituted compliance decision. It is within their sovereign right to deviate from the recommendations made by the international organization in charge of the comparability assessment.

2. Supposed downsides and benefits of deference

The greatest strength of deference is that it combines the best of both worlds. It builds on the advantages of a global approach without suffering from its disadvantages. At the same time, deference promotes the implementation of global standards. It also avoids the downsides associated with host country regulation without creating systemic risk

[66] Susan Wolburgh Jenah, 'Commentary on a Blueprint for Cross-Border Access to U.S. Investors' (2007) 48 Harv Intl LJ 69, 78.

[67] See ch 2 B)III. On the withdrawal decision see Eddy Wymeersch, 'Third-Country Equivalence and Access to the EU Financial Markets Including in Case of Brexit' (2018) 4 JFR 209, 227f.

[68] See ch 5 B)III.3.b).

[69] Matthias Lehmann and Jonas Schürger, 'Multilateralizing Deference: A Proposal for Reforming Global Financial Law' (2021) EBI Working Paper Series No 107 https://ssrn.com/abstract=3981699 (accessed 12 November 2022).

or enabling regulatory arbitrage. Deference can therefore be described as the best compromise.[70]

a) Supposed downsides

One of the main arguments against deference is that it could lead to regulatory arbitrage and a race to the bottom.[71] Once a state's regulation and supervision are recognized, and its service providers and products subsequently gain market access, that state may be tempted to lower its regulatory standards to gain competitive advantages over the other state. This problem is resolved, however, by the possibility of the recognizing state to withdraw market access in this case. As seen above, the option to withdraw deference prevents a race to the bottom and may even foster a race to the top.[72]

Another concern is that if supervision is left to home country authorities, they will not have much interest in looking for risks to other markets but will focus on threats to their own domestic markets. For example, if UK central counterparties (CCPs) provide clearing services to EU counterparties via equivalence, UK authorities may focus on risks to UK counterparties rather than counterparties in the EU. This risk can be mitigated if deference requires reciprocal treatment. Reciprocity has the effect that both supervisory authorities are mutually dependent on each other and thus also have an incentive to monitor strictly the risks posed by domestic firms to other markets. Reciprocity, therefore, avoids an externalization of risks.

Finally, states may be afraid of competitive disadvantages if they allow foreign financial firms to enter their markets without requiring them to comply with domestic regulatory requirements.[73] However, this concern is unjustified as these firms must comply with an equivalent regulation in their home country. If another state succeeds in creating a regulatory regime with significantly lower costs for its financial service providers while providing an equivalent level of regulation, this constitutes a prime example of better regulation. In this case, the host country should adjust its regulation. This process of adaptation would be an expression of a functioning competition between regulatory systems.[74]

b) Advantages over global regulation

Apart from the perception that establishing a worldwide uniform supervisory law and a global supervisory authority are unrealistic, such a purely global approach would also have various disadvantages, as has been shown. Many of these deficiencies would be mitigated or completely avoided by strengthening and expanding deference. First, a beneficial competition of different national approaches is preserved and thus the

[70] On this classification as a middle way see Dirk A Zetzsche and Robin Veidt, 'The AIFMD's Third-Country Rules and the Equivalence Concept' in Dirk A Zetzsche (ed), *The Alternative Investment Fund Managers Directive* (3rd edn, Wolters Kluwer 2020) 831f.

[71] Vo (n 25) 101ff.

[72] Extensively see Zetzsche and Veidt (n 70) 832f.

[73] Wei (n 63) 293f; Vo (n 25) 103.

[74] For an explanation of the difference between fruitful regulatory competition and regulatory arbitrage see Ethiopis Tafara and Robert J Peterson, 'A Blueprint for Cross-Border Access to U.S. Investors: A New International Framework' (2007) 48 Harv Intl LJ 31, 52f; Griffith (n 18) 3126ff. On regulatory competition in resolution regimes see Wolf-Georg Ringe, *Regulatory Competition in Global Financial Markets* (Annals of Corporate Governance 2016) 175.

concept of trial and error.[75] At the same time, states have an incentive to strengthen their regulation to gain access to foreign markets through the recognition of their legal system as adequate, equivalent, or comparable.[76] Ultimately, regulatory competition will lead to an overall enhancement of regulatory regimes.

Secondly, the concept of subsidiarity, according to which regulation and supervision should be as close as possible to local authorities which are more familiar with the particularities of their markets, is better reflected than with a global authority.[77] Thirdly, the concept of deference better protects national sovereignty because it leaves it up to each state whether or not to open its market, which at the same time enhances democratic legitimacy and accountability. Finally, deference allows states to react more flexibly to changing circumstances because no agreement must first be reached between the various actors at the global level.[78]

Nonetheless, deference and elements of a global regulatory architecture are not antagonists. On the one hand, deference is only feasible when global standards exist. If the general objectives of regulation are not coordinated, comparability is not achieved, and recognition is impossible. A far-reaching and robust system of deference, on the other hand, strengthens the implementation of international standards. States have a strong incentive to transpose these into their legal system to gain access to the markets of other states whose legal systems are based on these standards. In this way, deference and international standards are mutually dependent and mutually reinforcing.

c) Advantages over host state regulation

As has previously been pointed out, the current financial system is suffering especially from increasing fragmentation, which is caused by the extensive extraterritorial application of the law by major jurisdictions under the principle of host state regulation. This fragmentation can be reduced primarily by strengthening and expanding deference. If states withdraw regulatory and supervisory powers, legal and supervisory conflicts and thus the fragmentation of markets will be reduced. This will lead to more open markets and will intensify competition between service providers and financial products that have to compete globally. This development is also beneficial for investors.[79]

If financial firms have to adhere to one set of regulations only, this will drastically reduce compliance costs. This is particularly true in cases where host states demand the establishment of a subsidiary or branch office on its territory. If compliance costs for service providers decrease, it will be easier for investors to invest in foreign assets, which in turn reduces their transaction costs.[80] All in all, deference, therefore, enhances the efficiency of cross-border investments.[81]

[75] Pierre-Hugues Verdier, 'Mutual Recognition in International Finance' (2011) 52 Harv Intl LJ 56, 65. On the advantages of regulatory competition see Griffith (n 18) 1328.

[76] Tafara and Peterson (n 74) 56f; Brummer (n 6) 522.

[77] Verdier (n 75) 65.

[78] ibid; Greene (n 16) 6.

[79] Tafara and Peterson (n 74) 56.

[80] ibid.

[81] Vo (n 25) 97; Lucy McKinstry, 'Regulating a Global Market' (2013) 51 Colum J Transnatl L 776, 828f.

In addition to saving opportunity costs on the part of the supervised entities, the supervisory authorities themselves also save time and costs.[82] Increasing extraterritorial supervision is extremely costly and wastes supervisory resources for transactions that are already subject to supervision by other authorities. If the supervisory authorities concerned cooperate closely in such cross-border transactions, regulatory gaps can also be closed to a greater extent.[83]

III. Conclusion: Deference as a central pillar of any global financial market architecture

The analysis has shown that none of the three principal ways of regulating market access is without weaknesses. However, the concept of deference is, to a large extent, capable of mitigating the disadvantages and maximizing the benefits of each of the three approaches. That is why deference should be expanded and strengthened.

This is not to say that all eggs should be put in one basket. On the contrary, the current 'multi-layered approach' of global soft law and national implementation has proven its worth. The combination of harmonized standards at the international level, their strict implementation and additional regulation by home country regulators and, where this is not the case, additional robust regulation in cross-border transactions by host country authorities constitutes a financial architecture that largely prevents systemic risks and at the same time does not render the worldwide provision of services impossible. However, once home country authorities ensure effective supervision based on international standards, deference is necessary in order to not unduly diminish the benefits of globalization. Therefore, deference is not the one solution but an important cornerstone of a financial architecture that needs to be strengthened and further developed.[84]

This development of deference has slowed down globally because the implementation of deference, although recommended by the G20, is ultimately a voluntary decision by the states. While this voluntary nature should be maintained to safeguard national sovereignty, sufficient incentives must be set to make implementation profitable for states. These incentives are created when states adhere to the characteristics recommended above. These include that comparable and not identical foreign regulatory systems are required, depoliticization is promoted, compliance with international standards is demanded, and reciprocal treatment is ensured. Finally, states should provide for the possibility of withdrawing comparability determinations. Deference will only become globally accepted and successful if these characteristics are observed.

[82] Vo (n 25) 97; Steven Clark (OECD), 'A Policy Framework for Investment: Tax Policy' (2005) 1 https://www.oecd.org/investment/investmentfordevelopment/35488855.pdf (accessed 12 November 2022).

[83] Vo (n 25) 97.

[84] Once the system of deference is working smoothly, one could think about introducing a system of 'portable reciprocity' in which financial firms can choose the regulatory regime to which they are subjected from different legal systems that are recognized as being comparable or equivalent. See the proposal by Stephen J Choi and Andrew T Guzman, 'Portable Reciprocity: Rethinking the International Reach of Securities Regulation' (1998) 71 S Cal L Rev 903, 914ff. However, this presupposes a system of deference that is already established and well-functioning on a global scale.

B) Equivalence in the EU *de lege ferenda*

The last section derives proposals for enhancing equivalence in the EU *de lege ferenda* from the deficiencies identified in the first two parts and the insights gained from the legal comparison with the systems of Switzerland and the US. First, an alternative to the current obligation-based approach is presented (I.). Subsequently, reform proposals in relation to the equivalence decision are discussed (II.). The final section examines proposals aimed at further harmonization and increasing the juridification of equivalence (III.).

I. Overcoming the obligation-based approach

1. Weaknesses of the current obligation-based approach

The current approach of the EU with regard to equivalence can be described as obligation-based. This means that most equivalence provisions refer to a specific obligation under EU law from which they exempt third country service providers or products. As a result, there is often more than one equivalence provision dealing with a particular service provider or product.[85] This obligation-based approach led to the adoption of 40 different equivalence mechanisms to date, albeit equivalence is still missing in important areas.[86] There are, for instance, three provisions governing insurances, multiple provisions dealing directly or indirectly with accounting principles and six mechanisms concerning the calculation of exposures to third country institutions. A good example of the obligation-based approach concerns trade repositories. The Securities Financing Transactions (SFT) Regulation entails a reporting obligation for securities financing transactions.[87] A similar rule exists in EMIR concerning derivative contracts.[88] Both reporting obligations can only be fulfilled by a trade repository that is either registered or, following an equivalence decision, recognized by the European Securities and Markets Authority (ESMA). Yet, there is not one equivalence mechanism but two separate regimes.[89] Taking into account that the SFT Regulation even partly refers to the requirements set out in EMIR regarding the regulation of trade repositories and that the wording of the equivalence provisions is almost identical, it is clear that one mechanism is redundant. The same holds true for Article 21 SFT Regulation, which replicates Article 13(2) and (3) EMIR. Another example is the

[85] For a comprehensive overview see the tables provided for in ch 2 D).

[86] Lehmann and Zetzsche (n 61) 111f. For a sector specific analysis see Eilís V Ferran, 'The UK as a Third Country Actor in EU Financial Services Regulation' (2017) 3 JFR 40, 45ff; Wymeersch (n 67) 234ff.

[87] SFT Regulation, art 4(1).

[88] EMIR, art 9(1).

[89] See SFT Regulation, art 19 and EMIR, art 77; regarding the effects of EMIR, art 77; Paola Lucantoni in Matthias Lehmann and Christoph Kumpan (eds), *European Financial Services Law* (Nomos 2019) EMIR, art 77 para 3.

interplay between Article 13 EMIR and Article 33 Markets in Financial Instruments Regulation (MiFIR), which both exempt derivatives from the clearing obligation: one time for OTC derivatives and the other time for derivatives traded on regulated markets.[90]

Such an approach leads to unnecessary duplication of equivalence provisions. It turns equivalence into a complex and confusing construct in an area that is hardly understandable anyway.[91] This complexity even increases in regimes where two equivalence decisions are required in order for the legal consequences to take effect.[92] Legal acts already consisting of hundreds of pages are also unduly prolonged by this obligation-based approach, which wastes huge amounts of paper. For example, the regulation of third country CCPs in EMIR alone is set out over 20 pages in the *Official Journal* of the EU.[93] Moreover, supervisory resources, which are urgently needed, are not efficiently used. ESAs have to provide legal advice on many different equivalence regimes and monitor and review each of them following an equivalence decision, even though the content of the various assessments often overlap. Another and from a substantive law perspective probably the most significant shortcoming of an obligation-based approach is the occurrence of inconsistencies. Provisions that have been drafted twice or even three times entail the risk of unintended deviations, especially if they do not originate from the same author—for example, different Directorates-General within the European Commission—or are the result of political compromises. Also, if these equivalence mechanisms are reformed at different points in time, inconsistencies between them will inevitably occur, even if they concern an (almost) identical object. This leads to an unequal treatment of similar situations without objective justifications, which is problematic from a constitutional point of view.[94] It also creates legal uncertainty. In addition, many equivalence provisions are drafted in a very technical and detailed manner.[95] By introducing a sectoral approach, equivalence provisions need to be much more general as they will in that case cover multiple different obligations. This will reduce the technicality, level of detail, and complexity of equivalence, making it more transparent. Switzerland serves as a good example of such better law-making.[96]

[90] See regarding the systematic context of art 33 of MiFIR: Matthias Lehmann in Matthias Lehmann and Christoph Kumpan (eds), *European Financial Services Law* (Nomos 2019) MiFIR, art 33 paras 2f.

[91] See on the difficulties and shortcomings of modern EU law Matthias Lehmann, 'EU Law-Making 2.0: The Prospect of a European Business Code' (2020) 28 Eur Rev Priv L 73, 85ff; Matthias Lehmann, 'Lässt sich die Rechtsetzungsmethode der EU reformieren? Der Versuch eines Europäischen Wirtschaftsgesetzbuchs' Speech—Zentrum für Europäisches Wirtschaftsrecht No 225 (20 January 2020) 3ff.

[92] See eg MiFIR, art 38(1).

[93] Another illustrative example is AIFMD, art 37, which consists of 23 paragraphs and extends over seven pages in the *Official Journal* of the EU.

[94] On the legislator's duty of equal treatment see Case C-127/07 *Arcelor Atlantique and Lorraine and Others* ECLI:EU:C:2008:728; Case T-13/99 *Pfizer Animal Health v Council* ECLI:EU:T:2002:209; Hans D Jarass in Hans D Jarass (ed), *Charta der Grundrechte der EU* (4th edn, CH Beck 2021) art 20 paras 19f; Denis Martin in Manuel Kellerbauer, Marcus Klamert, and Jonathan Tomkin (eds), *Commentary on the EU Treaties and the Charter of Fundamental Rights* (OUP 2019) CFR, art 20.

[95] See eg EMIR, arts 25ff.

[96] See ch 3 C)I.3.

2. Introduction of a sectoral approach

One way to overcome these disadvantages is a consolidation of equivalence provisions.[97] The ideal situation would be to have only one mechanism applying to all kinds of service providers and products. However, the question arises whether this would be a realistic goal. This presupposes that the numerous equivalence regimes dealing with different service providers and products and having different legal effects are sufficiently similar to be merged into a single provision. This is not the case. To give an example, equivalence provisions exempting central banks and other public institutions from specific duties are not comparable to the far-reaching provisions concerning market access rights.[98] The latter demand more stringent requirements, such as reciprocity, effective supervision of the service provider in question by its home country authority, and the conclusion of cooperation agreements. None of this is—or reasonably should be—required for equivalence provisions exempting central banks and other public institutions from regulation. Moreover, if there is just one equivalence assessment covering all different service providers and products, the assessment will become even more complicated, and supervisory resources will not be saved as envisaged. Such cost advantages will only materialize if the subjects of the evaluation overlap to a large extent. This does not only apply to the initial decision on equivalence but also to the subsequent reviewing process. Monitoring an equivalence regime ranging from the market access for reinsurers to the exemption from the duty of large undertakings or public-interest entities to perform country-by-country reports is costly and inefficient. Finally, if there is just one equivalence provision, clashes between the different ESAs can be expected, as it would be unclear how to separate the insurance from the banking and securities sector.[99] Consequently, the reduction to just one mechanism is neither a realistic goal nor would it be a preferred solution, as it does not save resources and is connected to undesirable side-effects.

A less radical approach would be to consolidate equivalence provisions without reducing them to a single mechanism. Here, the challenge is to identify along which lines such a consolidation should take place. On the one hand, the fewer regimes, the better in terms of consistency and economical use of resources. On the other hand, it is important to consider the particular characteristics of certain service providers or products adequately. Consequently, it is appropriate to preserve separate mechanisms for different service providers or products and not to treat, for example, insurances in the same way as banks. However, to enable consolidation in the first place, it is necessary to abandon the obligation-based approach, which has been identified as the main reason for the large number of equivalence provisions. Instead of including a special

[97] The legislator itself expresses the aim of creating a uniform and consistent system. See MiFIR, recital 41: 'It is appropriate to introduce a common regulatory framework at Union level. The regime should harmonise the existing fragmented framework, ensure certainty and uniform treatment of third-country firms accessing the Union.' So far, however, the legislator has not been successful in achieving this goal.

[98] Examples of the first group include EMIR, art 1(6), SFT Regulation, art 2(4), and MiFIR, art 1(9). The latter category includes equivalence provisions dealing with third country investment firms, credit rating agencies, and CCPs.

[99] For a critical discussion of the tripartite approach see Wolf-Georg Ringe, Luis Morais, and David Ramos, 'A Holistic Approach to the Institutional Architecture of Financial Supervision and Regulation in the EU' in Veerle Colaert, Danny Busch, and Thomas Incalza (eds), *European Financial Regulation: Levelling the Cross-Sectoral Playing Field* (Hart Publishing 2019) 405ff.

regime for each obligation, it would be better to draft one mechanism for each service provider or product. Consequently, there would be just one mechanism for trade repositories, trading venues, insurances, or credit institutions. This method could be described as a sectoral approach.

A sectoral approach has the advantage of being able to react to the peculiarities of certain service providers or products while at the same time drastically reducing the number of equivalence provisions. It could be argued against a sectoral approach that it is not feasible in view of the many particularities of some equivalence regimes, even in relation to the same service provider or product, i.e. within the same sector. Indeed, there are several mechanisms with 'special requirements' which are not found in other regimes of the same sector.[100] However, most of these requirements are superfluous and can be eliminated or reserved for Level 2 legislation.[101] Therefore, these 'special requirements' do not interfere with a sectoral approach.

3. Trading venues as an illustrative example of the sectoral approach

To make the proposal of a sectoral approach more concrete, it is illustrated in the following example. A redundant duplication of equivalence exists concerning trading venues. As a reaction to the GFC, the G20 recommended, among other things, that 'standardized OTC derivative contracts should be traded on exchanges or electronic trading platforms, where appropriate'. The EU implemented this proposal in Article 28 MiFIR.[102] To avoid the necessity of duplicative trading that occurs when different countries foresee a trading obligation with extraterritorial effects in their legal system, the EU also accepts when trading takes place on an equivalent third country trading venue.[103] The criteria necessary to determine equivalence are laid down in more detail in lit a) to d) of Article 28(4) sub-para 3 MiFIR. An almost identical wording can be found in Article 25(4)(a) sub-para 4(i) to (iv) Markets in Financial Instruments Directive II (MiFID II), as well as in Article 17(2) sub-para 3(a) to (d) SSR. In the first case, execution-only services are exempted from the completion of a suitability and appropriateness assessment. In the latter case, the provision provides for an exemption of market making activities from the requirements and restrictions of the SSR.

Why would it be appropriate to consolidate these provisions? Basically, all the general reasons described above—saving paper, clearer and more comprehensible legislation, more efficient use of supervisory resources, and eliminating inconsistencies between equivalence provisions—apply. The existence of inconsistencies is particularly problematic and will be illustrated in the following. All these equivalence decisions are designed as discretionary acts. Accordingly, in the Short Selling Regulation (SSR) and MiFID II, a third country legal and supervisory framework *may*

[100] 'Special requirements' refer to those preconditions which are not common to many mechanisms. See ch 2 A)II. and the overview tables in ch 2 D) with a list of all equivalence provisions containing such special requirements.

[101] See ch 5 B)III.2.b).

[102] G20 Pittsburgh Summit, 'G20 Leaders' Statement' (24–25 September 2009) para 9 http://www.g20.utoronto.ca/2009/2009communique0925.html (accessed 12 November 2022); Matthias Lehmann in Matthias Lehmann and Christoph Kumpan (eds), *European Financial Services Law* (Nomos 2019) MiFIR, art 28 paras 2f.

[103] Matthias Lehmann in Matthias Lehmann and Christoph Kumpan (eds), *European Financial Services Law* (Nomos 2019) MiFIR, art 28 para 25.

be considered equivalent if four requirements are fulfilled.[104] In contrast, Article 28(3) sub-para 3 MiFIR states that a third country's legal and supervisory framework *is* considered to have equivalent effect if the same four conditions are met. This raises the question of why, although all three are discretionary decisions, the substantiated requirements for equivalence are formulated as a discretionary element in two provisions and as a binding element in the other. There seems to be no rational explanation for this difference in wording. Another discrepancy is that Article 28 MiFIR refers to 'trading venues in that third country', whereas MiFID II and the SSR, although having the same definition for trading venues,[105] use the term 'markets'. This divergence in terminology does not seem to be rooted in a difference in content either. Finally, it is unclear whether there is an objective reason why equivalence under Article 28 MiFIR demands reciprocity, whereas it is not required in MiFID II and the SSR, even though it makes sense to include it in those acts as well.

II. Reform of the equivalence decision

In addition to the shortcomings associated with an obligation-based approach, current equivalence mechanisms are inextricably linked with further disadvantages, which have already been identified in Chapter 2. The critical point of the process is the equivalence decision, which is why three suggestions are presented below on how the decision-making can be amended *de lege ferenda*.

1. Turning equivalence into what it really is: An implementing technical decision

The assessment of equivalence by the European Commission is not based on a uniform methodology and is strongly affected by political considerations. Consequently, the process is opaque, and the results are hardly predictable and appear arbitrary. This has negative consequences for the ability to seek legal protection and for the confidence in the administration in general. These disadvantages derive from the fact that the Commission is responsible for an administrative decision, i.e. the equivalence decision, although it is primarily a political institution. The Commission was initially designed as a technocratic authority (High Authority) but has gained more and more legislative powers and has become more political.[106] As a

[104] MiFID II also contains the specification that 'at least' the listed requirements must be met. It is unclear whether this allows the Commission to demand further requirements and, if so, what such requirements should be. The Commission apparently assumes that the four conditions are exhaustive. See Commission Implementing Decision (EU) 2017/2320 of 13 December 2017, recital 29. It also remains unexplained why this phrase ('at least') is only included in MiFID II, but not in SSR, art 17(2) subpara 2, which otherwise has completely identical wording.

[105] A 'trading venue' is defined in MiFID II, art 4(1) no 24. MiFIR refers to this definition in its art 2(1) no 16 and the SSR refers to the old definition under MiFID I in its art 2(1)(l), which is to be understood as a reference to the current version of MiFID II (see MiFID II, art 94(2) and Annex IV). See Klaus U Schmolke in Matthias Lehmann and Christoph Kumpan (eds), *European Financial Services Law* (Nomos 2019) SSR, art 17 para 2.

[106] For an interesting analysis see Christoph Möllers, *Die Drei Gewalten* (Velbrück 2008) 183ff; Philipp Dann, 'The Political Institutions' in Armin von Bogdandy and Jürgen Bast (eds), *Principles of European Constitutional Law* (2nd rev edn, Hart Publishing 2009) 257ff.

result, it is involved at many stages and tends to mix up legislative and administrative functions.[107]

a) ESAs as competent authorities: Conflicts with Meroni*?*

These drawbacks can be overcome by shifting away power from the European Commission. A radical approach would be to put ESAs in charge of the decision. Since ESAs are agencies with high technical expertise and experience in regulatory dialogues with third countries, the decision-making would be depoliticized and therefore more objective.[108] The restriction to technical considerations is explicitly provided for in the regulations governing ESAs.[109] The assumption is furthermore supported on the one hand by experience, namely with the technical advice issued by ESMA, and on the other hand by the explicit self-limitation of ESAs.[110]

It is questionable, however, whether such a reform would be in conformity with the Treaties, more specifically the *Meroni* case law of the European Court of Justice (ECJ).[111] According to this case law, discretionary powers implying a wider margin of appreciation may generally not be delegated to institutions not entrusted with competences under the Treaties. Consequently, equivalence decisions as discretionary acts must not be transferred to ESAs.

However, in a more recent case, the ECJ upheld the validity of Article 28 SSR, which authorizes ESMA to adopt acts of general application.[112] Hence, the mere fact that equivalence decisions are of a general nature does not infringe the Treaties. In the same case, Advocate General Jääskinen goes even further by drawing a clear distinction between delegated powers under Article 290 and Article 291 TFEU and concluding that decisions under the latter may be delegated to ESAs.[113] According to this interpretation, equivalence decisions, as implementing decisions based on Article 291(2) TFEU, could be carried out by ESAs. Such a clear demarcation between acts under Articles 290 and 291 TFEU irrespective of the degree of discretion associated with the act in the individual case is, however, not appropriate, as the ECJ has based its case

[107] See ch 2 B)II.2.a).

[108] Moloney (n 33) 907f and 992ff; Thomas Schmitz-Lippert, 'International Co-operation between Financial Supervisory Authorities' (2010) 7 ECFR 266; Niamh Moloney, 'International Financial Governance, the EU, and Brexit' (2016) 17 EBOR 451, 465ff.

[109] See eg ESMA Regulation, art 15(1) second sentence: 'Implementing technical standards shall be technical, shall not imply strategic decisions or policy choices and their content shall be to determine the conditions of application of those acts.'

[110] See concerning this practice ch 2 B)I.2.b)aa); see concerning the limitation 'focusing on "technical criteria" and "not taking into account any considerations of a political nature"'. CESR, 'Technical Advice to the European Commission on the Equivalence between the Japanese Regulatory and Supervisory Framework and the EU Regulatory Regime for Credit Rating Agencies' CESR/10-333 (9 June 2010) para 8; see also ESMA, 'Final report: Technical advice on third country regulatory equivalence under EMIR—US' ESMA/2013/1157 (1 September 2013) 6.

[111] Case C-9/56 *Meroni v High Authority* ECLI:EU:C:1958:7; Moloney (n 33) 909f; see on the general discussion Edoardo Chiti, 'European Agencies' Rulemaking: Powers, Procedures and Assessment' (2013) 19 Eur LJ 93; Madalina Busuioc, 'Rule-Making by the European Financial Supervisory Authorities: Walking a Tight Rope' (2013) 19 Eur LJ 111.

[112] Case C-270/12 *United Kingdom v European Parliament and Council* ECLI:EU:C:2014:8, paras 65f.

[113] Opinion of Advocate General Jääskinen delivered on 12 September 2013 in Case C-270/12 *United Kingdom v Parliament and Council* ECLI:EU:C:2013:562, paras 60ff and particularly paras 86 and 87. The ECJ did not address this issue in its judgment. See also Simone Gabbi, 'The Principle of Institutional (Un) Balance after Lisbon' (2014) 5 Eur J Risk Reg 259.

law primarily on the institutional balance of the EU, which does not necessarily go hand in hand with the qualification as a delegated or implementing act.[114] Given the broad discretion and the enormous consequences resulting from equivalence, the legitimacy of ESAs remains at least doubtful. In light of the relatively weak democratic legitimacy of ESAs, it, therefore, seems wise to divide competences between ESAs and the Commission to achieve a better institutional balance.[115] Therefore, a complete transfer of responsibility for equivalence decisions to ESAs is legally and democratically doubtful and should be avoided.

b) Equivalence decisions as implementing technical decisions

A less radical approach is to classify equivalence decisions as implementing *technical* standards, respectively decisions in the sense of Article 15 ESAs Regulations. Such standards derive from implementing acts under Article 291 TFEU.[116] Strictly speaking, an equivalence determination is a technical comparison of two legal systems and the outcomes they produce. It is not a policy choice as indicated by the Commission because the political goals have been conclusively expressed at Level 1 and in the regulatory technical standards at Level 2. Therefore, it is better to qualify equivalence decisions as what they truly are: implementing *technical* decisions. Such a classification would also unbundle policy and technical decisions, which are of a completely different nature, as expressed in the second sentence of Article 15(1) ESAs Regulations.

If they were qualified as implementing technical standards under Article 15, the procedure for equivalence decisions would then consist of the following steps.[117] At the start, ESAs conduct open public consultations and perform a cost-benefit analysis before submitting a draft to the Commission. The Commission immediately forwards this draft for information to the Parliament and the Council.[118] Usually, the Commission has three months to endorse, amend, or reject the draft. If the Commission amends or rejects the draft, it will have to justify its decision to the competent ESA, which then has the opportunity to amend and resubmit its draft. This strictly regulated process has many advantages compared to the current approach. First and foremost, powers are shifted to ESAs, which will depoliticize the decisions. Unlike the current procedure, ESAs would be in charge of initiating equivalence assessments. By conducting open public consultations, third country stakeholders can already put forward their interests at the beginning of the procedure. Moreover, the

[114] Case C-9/56 *Meroni v High Authority* (n 111).

[115] On questions of accountability and governance see Elizabeth Howell, 'EU Agencification and the Rise of ESMA' (2019) 78 Cambridge LJ 324.

[116] ESAs Regulation, art 15(1) subpara 1; Niamh Moloney, *The Age of ESMA* (Hart Publishing 2018) 121; Paul Craig, 'Comitology, Rulemaking, and the Lisbon Settlement' in Carl F Bergström and Dominique Ritleng (eds), *Rulemaking by the European Commission* (OUP 2016) 198f.

[117] On the process see Moloney (n 116) 121; for detail on ESMA's modes of action see also Rüdiger Veil, 'Kapitalmarktgesetzgebung im Zeitalter der ESMA' in Klaus J Hopt and Dimitris Tzouganatos (eds), *Das Europäische Wirtschaftsrecht vor neuen Herausforderungen* (Mohr Siebeck 2014) 100ff; Christoph Ohler, 'Finanzmarktregulierung und -aufsicht' in Matthias Ruffert (ed), *Europäisches Sektorales Wirtschaftsrecht* (2nd edn, Nomos 2020) § 10 paras 114ff.

[118] It is important to note that the Parliament and Council do not have a veto power in this procedure but are merely informed. See Moloney (n 116) 121.

Commission can no longer reject assessments of ESAs without a justification.[119] This obligation to state reasons will bring light into the evaluation of the Commission and allow for effective judicial review. Also, if the justification does not persuade the competent ESA, it may resubmit the draft and thus get another chance. Yet, the ultimate decision still rests with the Commission, which is preferable from a democratic standpoint and for maintaining the institutional balance.[120] Furthermore, the right to timely treatment under Article 41(1) CFR is strengthened because the procedure explicitly stipulates time limits, for instance, regarding the Commission's endorsement.

Another major advantage of the classification as an implementing technical standard is that the examination procedure under Article 5 Comitology Regulation no longer applies. Binding technical standards do not involve 'strategic decisions or policy choices' (Article 15 ESAs Regulations), which renders the implementing decision one that does not require the control of Member States. This need for Member State control is, however, a prerequisite for the Comitology Regulation to apply.[121] Hence, the references to the Comitology Regulation in the equivalence provisions at Level 1 can be removed. In turn, this eliminates the danger already described above[122] of Member States unduly interfering in the technical decision through political considerations or national interests. To sum up, transforming equivalence decisions into implementing technical decisions will further enhance juridification, increase transparency, and amplify the technical nature of the decision.

2. From country-oriented to subject-specific analyses

Another possibility to objectify the evaluation is to shift the focus from a country-oriented to a subject-specific analysis.[123] So far, most of the equivalence analyses have been country-oriented, which means that the legal framework of a particular country is compared to that of the EU.[124] This method entails the risk of including prejudiced assumptions about certain countries in the assessment. Moreover, this approach contains the long-term risk of inconsistencies between different equivalence decisions. If the decisions are influenced by policy considerations or prejudices, a coherent and consistent system will not evolve.

Instead of comparing legal systems of specific countries, it would be better to focus on comparing abstract rules and their consequences, irrespective of the country in question. An example of a more subject-specific analysis was the Commission's comparison of the International Financial Reporting Standards (IFRS) with the Generally Accepted Accounting Principles (GAAP).[125] Here, the focus was not on the third country in question but rather on the accounting system itself. A more subject-oriented

[119] Moloney (n 33) 923; see also Eddy Wymeersch, 'The Reforms of the European Financial Supervisory System: An Overview' (2010) 7 ECFR 240.

[120] For the call for more parliamentary oversight and legitimation of ESMA see Niamh Moloney, 'Reflections on the EU Third Country Regime for Capital Markets in the Shadow of Brexit' (2020) 17 ECFR 35, 68ff.

[121] The Comitology Regulation applies only pursuant to its art 1, where a basic act 'requires that the adoption of implementing acts by the Commission be subject to the control of Member States'.

[122] See ch 2 A)I.1.a) and ch 2 B)III.

[123] For such a differentiation see Wymeersch (n 67) 220.

[124] See ch 2 B)I.2.

[125] Wymeersch (n 67) 220.

approach would consist of two steps. The first step is to identify the problem which the EU legislator deemed to be in need of regulation. Afterwards, different possibilities and solutions must be developed on how this specific problem could be addressed. These solutions can then be reflected by abstract rules (A, B, C, and D). Subsequently, it must be evaluated whether rules A, B, C, or D solve the respective issue in an equivalent manner by looking at both the abstract rule, as well as the consequences that these rules produce on markets. In a second step, it must be examined whether the legal framework of the respective country to be assessed contains a rule A, B, C, or D or a comparable rule. If this is the case, the solution found with regard to the abstract rule can be transferred to the specific country.

Such a subject-specific analysis must not, however, exclude the possibility of taking peculiarities of the third country legal system in question into consideration during the second step. Issues like the enforcement of rules or effective supervision can only be adequately addressed with regard to a particular country. Ultimately, equivalence decisions are always taken in relation to a specific third country. Nevertheless, the preliminary assessment of such decisions can be based on a subject-specific analysis. All in all, a subject-specific approach would lead to more objective, less biased, and transparent results. It would therefore promote the building of a consistent and coherent system of equivalence decisions in the long run.

3. Tiering and comparable compliance: Current developments in MiFIR and EMIR

In the face of Brexit, the EU has amended two key third country regimes, namely in MiFIR regarding investment firms and in EMIR regarding CCPs.[126] Both reforms concern the element of systemic importance in equivalence but differ considerably in detail. These reforms are introduced (a)) and critically evaluated (b)) in the following pages. The reforms also triggered reactions in academia, including a proposal by Niamh Moloney, which will be discussed later. Finally, a new proposal based on the changes in MiFIR is presented (c)).

a) Reforms of MiFIR and EMIR

Although the amendments in MiFIR and EMIR deal with systemic importance in the context of equivalence, on closer examination they do not have much in common. Following the reform of MiFIR, the Commission must consider in its equivalence decision whether the activities performed by investment firms from the third country in question 'are likely to be of systemic importance for the Union'.[127] If this is the case, the Commission may only adopt an equivalence decision 'after a detailed and granular assessment', specifically taking into account 'the supervisory convergence between the third country concerned and the Union'. Additionally, the Commission can attach 'specific operational conditions to equivalence decisions'.[128] Hence, the criterion of

[126] See ch 2 A)I.6. On Brexit and derivatives clearing see Karel Lannoo, 'Derivatives Clearing and Brexit' (2017) ECMI Policy Brief No 25 https://www.ceps.eu/wp-content/uploads/2017/11/ECMI_PB25_KL_BrexitClearing.pdf (accessed 12 November 2022). On the reform see Moloney (n 120).

[127] MiFIR, art 47(1) subpara 2.

[128] ibid; see Jan Ceyssens and Andreas Tarde, 'Äquivalenz im Finanzdienstleistungsrecht der Europäischen Union' (2019) 31 EuZW 805, 809f.

systemic importance is applied only at the first level—the equivalence decision—and not at the second level—the registration with ESMA. Moreover, the element of systemic importance relates not to single investment firms in the third country but the entirety of them.

Unlike in MiFIR, the amendments in EMIR do not concern the equivalence decision but take effect at the second level, the recognition by ESMA. The question of systemic importance is thus not part of the equivalence assessment. Rather, a special regime was introduced for the recognition of individual CCPs that have been determined as systemically important by ESMA (Tier 2 CCPs).[129] ESMA cannot recognize Tier 2 CCPs under the 'ordinary' equivalence procedure.[130] Instead, Tier 2 CCPs can be either completely excluded from the provision of services (paragraph 2c) or recognized pursuant to paragraph 2b under the additional obligation to obey the requirements as set out in Article 16 and Titles IV and V of EMIR.[131] Thus, recognition by ESMA no longer exempts such Tier 2 CCPs from compliance with large parts of the regulation under EMIR. This new approach can be described as an 'on-shored system'.[132] A Tier 2 CCP recognized under this procedure may nevertheless request to be exempted from adhering to the requirements under Article 16 and Titles IV and V of EMIR. This exemption requires that the Tier 2 CCP complies with comparable requirements in its home country (so-called comparable compliance).[133]

b) EMIR as an aberration: A critical analysis

The introduction of the criterion of systemic importance into equivalence provisions is in principle to be welcomed, as systemic stability is one of the main objectives, especially of post-GFC EU legislation.[134] However, the question remains as to how this introduction is best implemented.[135] The approach in EMIR can be described as an aberration. The extraterritorial application of EU law in the case of Tier 2 CCPs constitutes a break with the guiding idea of equivalence, which can be characterized as deference for trust. EU supervisory law is not applied extraterritorially after an equivalence decision has been adopted because the laws of a third country have been found to be equivalent and efficiently enforced. If systemic risks for EU markets increase as a result of an equivalence decision, the third country legal framework is not equivalent and should not be recognized as such. Therefore, contrary to EMIR, the criterion of systemic importance should be part of the equivalence decision and not the recognition process.

[129] Henning Berger and Nikolai Badenhoop, 'Financial Services and Brexit: Navigating Towards Future Market Access' (2018) 19 EBOR 679, 687f.

[130] EMIR, art 25(2)(e).

[131] Matthias Lehmann, 'Derivateclearing post-Brexit' (2021) 33 ZBB/JBB 177, 184ff.

[132] Moloney (n 120) 59.

[133] EMIR, arts 25(2b)(a) and 25a; Danny Busch, 'A Stronger Role for the European Supervisory Authorities in the EU27' in Danny Busch, Emilios Avgouleas, and Guido Ferrarini (eds), *Capital Markets Union in Europe* (OUP 2018) paras 3.81ff; see specifying the criteria for the assessment Commission Delegated Regulation (EU) 2020/1304 of 14 July 2020, arts 2–4.

[134] See ch 2 A)I.6.; Philipp Hartmann and Olivier de Bandt, 'Systemic Risk in Banking after the Great Financial Crisis' in Allen N Berger, Philip Molyneux, and John OS Wilson (eds), *The Oxford Handbook of Banking* (3rd edn, OUP 2019) 847ff.

[135] For further points of criticism see Pennesi (n 10) 198–99.

Moreover, the reform in EMIR creates inconsistencies between the equivalence decision and the decision on comparable compliance. Some stakeholders have argued that the decisions are 'one in the same'.[136] Indeed, both decisions are very similar, which has led ESMA to explain the differences in its technical advice.[137] ESMA highlights that its decision is 'entity-based', while the equivalence decision is 'jurisdiction-based'. ESMA also claims that the decision on comparable compliance is stricter than the equivalence decision and based on a requirement-by-requirement assessment. Also, internal rules and procedures of individual CCPs can be taken into account in the entity-based decision on comparable compliance. These differentiations, however, are neither convincing nor do they demonstrate the necessity of such a decision. ESMA's answer rather reveals that they only argued that way because they miss a 'viable alternative'.[138] Both decisions assess the equivalence of the third country legal system and compliance with these rules. If individual CCPs do not comply with the requirements under their jurisdiction and their home country authorities do not intervene, effective supervision and enforcement are not ensured, and ESMA is not allowed to register a CCP pursuant to the general rules, irrespective of the systemic importance of the CCP in question.[139] This constellation, therefore, does not justify a second decision by ESMA. Moreover, the alleged strictness of the decision on comparable compliance because of risks associated with market access for systemic relevant CCPs can also be taken into account at the level of the equivalence decision. Hence, the two decisions are basically taken on the same subject by two different authorities (ESMA and the Commission), which will create conflicts between them. ESMA attempts to mitigate the risk of such collisions in its delegated regulation,[140] but it cannot completely eradicate them. Furthermore, there is no apparent reason why equivalence to Article 16 and Title V EMIR is required for Tier 2 CCPs in the decision concerning comparable compliance but not for Tier 1 CCPs in the equivalence decision. It would make more sense to include these criteria directly into the equivalence decision.

Another challenge for the concept of mutual trust between supervisory authorities is the emerging idea of extraterritorial enforcement of supervisory measures on foreign soil. Article 25h EMIR, for instance, allows on-site inspections of ESMA on any business premises, land, or property of Tier 2 CCPs, even in foreign countries.[141] A similar rule is provided for in Article 47(2)(c) MiFIR. If EU supervisors even personally control foreign entities on foreign soil, it is hard to imagine that mutual trust can be established in an environment of omnipresent distrust. Equivalence, however, does not work without mutual trust.[142] Thus, a trend towards more "direct

[136] ESMA, 'Final Report: Technical advice on Comparable Compliance under article 25a of EMIR' ESMA70-151-2649 (11 November 2019) 13.

[137] ibid 10f.

[138] ibid 13; critical also Sebastian Steuer, 'EMIR 2.2 und die Aufsicht über systemrelevante Drittstaaten-CCPs' (2021) 21 BKR 272, 278f.

[139] See EMIR, art 25(2)(b), which applies to all CCPs regardless of their systemic relevance.

[140] See Commission Delegated Regulation (EU) 2020/1304, of 14 July 2020, recital 4 and art 3(2).

[141] See Matthias Lehmann, 'La coopération avec les États tiers en matière bancaire et financière: La confiance n'exclut pas le contrôle' (2020) RB 35, 41; Matthias Lehmann, 'CCP supervision after Brexit' (2023) 18 CMLR 5, 25–26; see also MiFIR, art 47(2)(c).

[142] This fact is even underlined by the Commission itself, which states: 'Cooperation contributes to building mutual understanding and trust among jurisdictions, which is a pre-requisite for managing cross-border risks'; see Commission (n 34) 1 and 10.

'on-shoring'" for high-impact jurisdictions, as advocated by some scholars,[143] is dangerous because it is at odds with the concept of equivalence itself.

Ultimately, the impression could arise that the new reform is not about avoiding the emergence of systemic risk but rather about pushing Tier 2 CCPs to relocate to the EU.[144] Such a location policy is not per se harmful, but it should at least be implemented consistently. From a systematic point of view, the market access for Tier 2 CCPs granted under the new rules has little to do with equivalence and should thus not be part of the mechanism.

The Commission's current proposal to deepen the Capital Markets Union, which is being discussed in the context of the EU Listing Act, moves even further away from the concept of equivalence. The draft contains the proposal to insert a new subparagraph 3 in Article 25(6) EMIR. According to this, the Commission has the power to adopt an equivalence decision even if the regulation and supervision in a third country is not equivalent, as long as such a decision is 'in the interests of the Union'. Such proposals reduce the principle of equivalence to absurdity.

c) MiFIR as a role model for future equivalence mechanisms?

With the amendments in MiFIR, the legislator managed to implement similar objectives to those in EMIR in a way that fits much better into the system of equivalence.[145] Integrating the question of systemic relevance into the equivalence decision is more suitable since third country service providers should only be granted market access through equivalence if the third country legal framework guarantees systemic stability in an equivalent way. The idea that equivalence assessments must be more detailed and granular in cases involving high-impact countries is also plausible, in light of the enormous consequences associated with market access for service providers from those countries.[146] A tiering of third countries depending on the impact that market access of their service providers has on EU markets is therefore reasonable. This is, however, not a political decision, but it is an empirical question that depends, inter alia, on the market size of the third country in question.[147]

As a result, the introduction of gradual tiering from low-impact to high-impact countries is also recommended for other equivalence mechanisms. That way, the granularity of the equivalence assessment always correlates with the impact the granting of market access has on EU markets. The tendency to politicize such questions

[143] Moloney (n 120) 68.

[144] The ECB has pursued this policy for quite some time. See ECB, 'Eurosystem Oversight Policy Framework' (July 2011) 9 https://www.ecb.europa.eu/pub/pdf/other/eurosystemoversightpolicyframework2011en.pdf (accessed 12 November 2022). The UK successfully challenged this practice before the GC. See Case T-496/11 *United Kingdom v ECB* ECLI:EU:T:2015:133, para 110. Now it seems that this policy is being pursued by other means, namely equivalence. On the drawbacks of a relocation see Paolo Saguato, Guido Ferrarini, and Eric Pan, 'Financial Market Infrastructures: The International Approach and the Current Challenges' in Jens-Hinrich Binder and Paolo Saguato (eds), *Financial Market Infrastructures* (OUP 2022) paras 4.48–4.51; Evariest Callens, *Regulation of Central Counterparties (CCPs) in Light of Systemic Risk* (Intersentia 2022) 514–18.

[145] The only exception is the rule in MiFIR, art 47(2)(c) regarding onsite inspections, which was criticized above because it is at odds with one of the underlying prerequisites of deference, namely the existence of mutual trust. See ch 5 B)II.3.b).

[146] Commission (n 39) 11; Conac (n 43) 87.

[147] Dissenting: Moloney (n 120) 68.

and expand the extraterritorial application of the law is, nonetheless, a worrying development that cannot serve as a model for other equivalence provisions.

III. Strengthening equivalence: Enhancement of consistency and further juridification

In addition to reforming the equivalence decision, the concept of equivalence as a whole could be further strengthened if the various mechanisms were made more consistent and legal certainty was enhanced. Three points, in particular, are worth discussing: an extension of the scope of application (1.); a harmonization of the process, prerequisites as well as legal consequences (2.); and a further juridification by establishing a right to an equivalence decision, as well as defining rules governing the withdrawal of equivalence (3.).

1. Extension of the scope of application?

The system of equivalence is often criticized for being piecemeal.[148] A simple way out would be to call for an extension of equivalence to all areas which are not yet covered. This primarily concerns payment services, the management of UCITS, market access for banks and direct insurers, and investment services to retail investors.

However, as outlined above, the legislator has (at least in part) legitimate reasons justifying this fragmented picture.[149] The first reason relates to areas strongly influenced by the concept of investor protection, specifically retail investors. The second idea is to safeguard the functioning of the financial system by providing markets with enough liquidity while at the same time restricting market access to the minimum. The third and final theme concerns the intention to avoid dependencies on foreign supervision and the corresponding aim of attracting financial market players to Europe to remain competitive.

Nevertheless, there are two dangers. First, the system might become incomprehensible and too complex to work.[150] One way to reduce complexity has been proposed in this book with the introduction of a sectoral approach leading to a consolidation of equivalence mechanisms. Secondly, despite legitimate reasons to restrict market access through equivalence, the concept is the most suitable approach in a globalized world to regulate financial markets.[151] Equivalence promotes regulatory harmonization, improves market access opportunities for EU service providers, and reduces market fragmentation, while at the same time guaranteeing a high level of investor protection and a stable financial system. Deference is advocated by the G20 and is

[148] Niamh Moloney, 'Brexit, the EU and Its Investment Banker: Rethinking "Equivalence" for the EU Capital Market' (2017) LSE Working Paper Series 5/2017, 46 http://eprints.lse.ac.uk/73429/1/WPS2017-05_Moloney.pdf (accessed 12 November 2022); Niccolò Lorenzotti, 'Third-country Equivalence and Its Suitability in the Context of Brexit' (2019) 22 Fin Reg Intl 1, 9; for an extensive overview of the areas (not) covered by equivalence see ch 1 C)II.

[149] See ch 1 C)II.6; justification by the Commission can be found in Commission (n 34) 4ff.

[150] See Ferran (n 86) 55ff; see also referring to the question of market access in general Hans Kuhn, 'Handel mit Dienstleistungen' in Herbert Kronke, Werner Melis, and Hans Kuhn (eds), *Handbuch Internationales Wirtschaftsrecht* (2nd edn, Otto Schmidt 2017) pt C para 299: 'heillos zersplitterter Rechtsrahmen'.

[151] See extensively ch 5 A).

widely spread in the world.[152] All in all, it is reasonable to promote equivalence rather than to restrict it. However, the right balance remains a genuine political question.

2. Harmonization of equivalence by eliminating inconsistencies

Throughout the previous chapters, inconsistencies between different equivalence mechanisms have often been identified as one of the main shortcomings of the concept.[153] Some of the discrepancies can be eliminated by a more systematic interpretation, as advocated in this book. Others can only be resolved by the legislator. Some parts of equivalence, where the legislator could advance harmonization, will be examined in the following remarks.

a) Process

Equivalence mechanisms can be divided into three categories, namely one-step processes and two-step processes involving either ESAs or national competent authorities (NCAs).[154] Because each category has its advantages and disadvantages, there is a need to analyse the allocation of equivalence mechanisms to one of the categories and identify the most appropriate category for the potential adoption of new equivalence provisions.

One-step processes have the advantage for third countries that the process is fairly short, as only one decision is required. Because of this reduction to a single decision, and thus the lack of involvement of ESAs and NCAs at the second level, the mechanisms usually have few preconditions. These characteristics seem particularly suitable for equivalence mechanisms that do not entail far-reaching legal consequences and should therefore be easy and quick in their implementation. Conversely, they are not appropriate for mechanisms leading to extensive market access rights. Hence, it makes sense to draft equivalence in the form of a one-step process only if the regime operates with few requirements and does not have far-reaching legal consequences.

Two-step processes involving NCAs preserve the sovereignty of Member States but are connected with various disadvantages. They serve as a gateway for political interferences, are more complex and cumbersome and interfere with the goal of a single market. Thus, they should not play a major role in the medium and long term. In areas where no EU authority is yet competent, such as for the approval of prospectuses, the involvement of the national level is still necessary, but these areas will diminish as harmonization progresses. With fewer non-harmonized areas, the number of mechanisms consisting of two-step processes involving ESAs will increase. This type of process is best suited for complex and significant equivalence mechanisms, such as granting market access to CCPs, credit rating agencies, or investment firms.

[152] See Mark Carney (Chairman of the FSB), 'Financial Reform: Progress and Challenges' Letter to G20 Finance Ministers and Central Bank Governors (17 February 2014) 1 http://www.financialstabilityboard.org/publications/r_140222.pdf (accessed 12 November 2022), who recommends that the G20 states defer 'to each other's market regulatory regimes where they achieve equivalent outcomes'; G20 St Petersburg Summit, 'G20 Leaders' Declaration' (6 September 2013) para 71 http://www.g20.utoronto.ca/2013/2013-0906-declaration.html (accessed 12 November 2022).

[153] Wymeersch (n 67) 221f.

[154] See extensively ch 1 C)III.

To sum up, it is not appropriate to confine equivalence mechanisms to a particular process. The most suitable process depends on the equivalence provision at hand. As a rule of thumb, one-step processes are adequate for less complex and less extensive regimes, while two-step processes are the best option for cumbersome and far-reaching mechanisms. It is generally better to resort to two-step processes involving only the European and not the national level.

b) Prerequisites

Equivalence usually consists of six key requirements and is thus not as diverse as one might think at first sight.[155] All these requirements are based on legitimate considerations, and their introduction is to be supported in principle. As a rule, modern equivalence mechanisms require more of these six prerequisites than older ones.[156] If equivalence provisions miss out on certain preconditions, there is often a legitimate reason for this. What makes equivalence inconsistent is the existence of tailor-made requirements beyond the above-mentioned key requirements. Therefore, it would be best to exclude them from equivalence, and there are multiple possibilities to accomplish this.

First, some of the requirements are superfluous and could thus be removed. One example is the Credit Rating Agencies (CRA) Regulation requirement that the third country's regulatory regime must keep authorities or other public bodies from interfering in the content of the credit rating or the methodology.[157] Such influences must certainly be prevented for ratings used for regulatory purposes, as politically influenced ratings fail to achieve their objective.[158] However, a legal system that allows interventions in the independence of rating agencies is not equivalent to the EU framework. That is why the consideration could be included in the general equivalence assessment under lit b) and does not need to be stipulated separately. The same applies to the liability of third country depositaries to the alternative investment fund (AIF) as required under the Alternative Investment Fund Managers Directive (AIFMD).[159] Again, this consideration can be included in the equivalence decision, as the requirement is an integral part of the European legislation.[160] Such inclusion has the side benefit of clearing up requirements in equivalence mechanisms that are in danger of becoming incomprehensible.

Secondly, some requirements could be phrased in a more general way so that they could apply to different equivalence provisions. One case of application is the obligation of equivalent professional secrecy.[161] There is no need for a tailor-made approach

[155] These requirements are the equivalence decision, home country authorization, and supervision of service providers, the existence of cooperation agreements, reciprocity, conformity with international standards, and the criterion of systemic importance. See ch 2 A)I.

[156] Compare, for instance, the requirements of the new mechanisms in MiFIR, art 46(1) and EMIR, art 25(1) with older ones such as Transparency Directive, art 23(1) or Solvency II, art 172(3).

[157] CRA Regulation, art 5(6) subpara 2(c).

[158] See CRA Regulation, arts 1 and 6; Rüdiger Veil, 'Rating Agencies' in Rüdiger Veil (ed), *European Capital Markets Law* (3rd edn, Hart Publishing 2022) § 27 paras 31ff.

[159] AIFMD, art 21(6) subpara 1(e).

[160] AIFMD, art 21(12) and (13); see also Ulf Klebeck and Catia Meyer, 'Drittstaatenregulierung der AIFM-Richtlinie' (2012) 2 RdF 95.

[161] See eg MiFIR, art 33(2)(b); SFT Regulation, arts 19(1) subpara 1(c) and 21(1)(b); EMIR, arts 13(2)(b), 75(1) subpara 1(c), and 76a(2)(c).

here. Instead, it could be required that the legal system of the third country provides for an equivalent method of professional secrecy when such information is at stake. A more general formulation is also possible in the area of disclosure requirements to European authorities, as demanded in some provisions.[162]

Thirdly, some very technical requirements could be removed from the basic act and included in the delegated act at Level 2 of the *Lamfalussy* process. This would avoid an overload of the already complex provisions at the level of the basic act, and a better picture of what equivalence provisions genuinely want to achieve would be conveyed.[163] An illustrative example of this is the duty of third country investment firms to have arrangements and procedures in place which enable them to inform ESMA about their services extensively.[164] The basic act even specifies the timeframe within which investment firms must have the information on orders and transactions at the disposal of ESMA.[165] Such technical details overload equivalence provisions. These three suggestions show that there are multiple possibilities to consolidate equivalence rules, thereby making them more transparent, comprehensible, and less contradictory.

c) Legal consequences

The legal consequences of equivalence provisions are formulated very differently, although they all head in the same direction, follow the same objective, and are part of a uniform concept.[166] Some of these differences can be explained by the different degrees of liberalization or the specific characteristics of the regulated subject or object. However, in many cases, divergent formulations are a sign of inconsistency between different pieces of legislation and are not based on objective reasons. These discrepancies need to be reduced.

Equivalence provisions in category 1[167] mainly use three different formulations to establish an exemption from regulatory obligations: 'are/may exempt from'; 'shall not apply to'; and 'shall be deemed to have fulfilled'. The first two are interchangeable, which is why the legislator should opt for one formulation and use it exclusively.[168] The third expression best reflects that the third country service provider/product already fulfils equivalent obligations in its home country and is therefore not unregulated. Consequently, this wording should always be used where such equivalent obligations exist.[169]

162 SFT Regulation, arts 19(1) subpara 1(d) and 21(1)(d); EMIR, arts 77(2) subpara 1(b), 75(2), and 76a(2)(d).

163 Critical towards those hardly comprehensible mechanisms are Aleksandra Visekruna, 'The Access to the EU Financial Market for the Companies from Non-Member States' (2018) 2 ECLIC 656, 664; Ferran (n 86) 56; Karel Lannoo, 'EU Financial Market Access after Brexit' (2016) 51 Intereconomics 255, 258: 'highly complex puzzle'.

164 MiFIR, art 46(2)(d) and (6a) subpara 1.

165 MiFIR, art 46(6a) subpara 3 and (6b) subpara 1.

166 See ch 2 C)V.3.; on legal consequences of equivalence see Emmenegger and Bigler (n 58) 158ff.

167 For the categorization see ch 2 C).

168 This uniform terminology is already used with regard to the derogations for public bodies and central banks of third countries, where the legislator always phrases: 'shall not apply to'. See EMIR, art 1(4); MiFIR, art 1(6); MAR, art 6(1) and (3); SFT Regulation, art 2(2).

169 This includes all equivalence provisions in this category, except for the derogations for public bodies and central banks of third countries. Such a formulation is already used in art 13(3) of EMIR, art 21(2) of the SFT Regulation, and art 33(3) of MiFIR. A redrafting is recommended for art 23(1) of the Transparency Directive, art 46(1) of the Accounting Directive, and art 37(2) of the AIFMD.

The regulatory technique used for category 2—equal treatment—is mainly due to the nature of the regulated subject. It concerns, in particular, trading venues that cannot actively enter a market and where the legal consequences cannot be formulated in the form of an exception. In such cases, the regulatory technique of equal treatment should be maintained.

Regulation is particularly inconsistent in cases where equivalence leads to market access rights. Market access is formulated partly as an exception to the duty to register (category 1; e.g. statutory auditors), partly by way of equal treatment with EU contracts (category 2; e.g. reinsurance contracts) and mostly through explicit permission to provide services (categories 3 and 4; e.g. investment firms and CCPs). These different regulatory techniques and expressions are confusing, not based on objective reasons and should therefore be harmonized. This raises the question, however, of whether the legal consequence of market access should be formulated as an exception (category 1) or rather as an explicit permission (categories 3 and 4). One advantage of drafting market access by way of an exception is that it would be clear from which rules third country financial service providers are exempted. This is not always the case for equivalence provisions in categories 3 and 4 because the scope of the exemption is determined by the extent of the equivalence decision, which sometimes cannot be accurately defined.[170] This concern about wording equivalence by way of explicit permission can be mitigated by a more precise specification of the scope of the equivalence decision at Level 2, as already foreseen in many mechanisms. A more detailed definition of the scope of equivalence decisions will indirectly clarify the extent of their legal consequences. In addition, a list of all duties from which third country actors are to be exempted would make equivalence regimes even longer and more incomprehensible. This could be avoided by expressing market access by way of an explicit permission. Such wording is also easier to understand because it explicitly prescribes the desired consequence, i.e. market access. Hence, it would be best to formulate market access by way of an explicit permission (categories 3 and 4).

3. Further juridification: Strengthening the legal position of financial service providers

One of the key concerns of this book has been to enhance the juridification of equivalence by developing an orderly framework for the concept that meets the requirements demanded by fundamental principles such as the principle of legal certainty, effective legal protection, and separation of powers. As a result of this aim, a common methodology on how equivalence is to be assessed has been developed, and the nature of equivalence as a technical and not a political question as well as specific limits to the decision-making resulting from constitutional as well as administrative principles have been identified.[171] Moreover, the possibilities of legal protection have been

[170] See eg the confusion over the scope of the exemption for investment firms under MiFIR. This is accurately described in Rolf Sethe, 'Das Drittstaatenregime von MiFIR und MiFID II' (2014) 86 SZW 615, 626; Thierry R Ammann, *Der europäische Marktzugang für Schweizer Banken* (Dike 2020) paras 293f; for a dissenting view see Mirjam Eggen and Rupert Schaefer, 'Regulierung grenzüberschreitender Tätigkeiten im Finanzmarktrecht' (2013) 8 GesKR 368, 378, who only recognize an exemption from the code of conduct rules.

[171] See ch 2 B)I. and II.

evaluated.[172] In this chapter, further proposals have been made, such as the introduction of a sectoral approach to reduce the bewildering variety of equivalence mechanisms, as well as reforms regarding the equivalence decision and the elimination of inconsistencies between the different regimes. All of this helps further to crystallize the principle behind equivalence and enhance juridification. This last section strives to complete this process of juridification by proposing further reforms. It is advocated to codify a right to an equivalence decision, including detailed requirements governing this right (a)). Furthermore, it is recommended to specify the right to withdraw equivalence decisions (b)).

a) Right to a decision

As outlined above, there is, in principle, already a right to a decision, even if it is usually not explicitly stipulated.[173] For third country firms, such a right arises directly from the applicable equivalence provision. For the third country itself, such a right derives from world trade law.[174] This right is, nonetheless, somewhat limited in its effects because of the discretion granted to the Commission and the practical difficulties to prove equivalence. In many cases, the right to a decision only exists in the form of a right to request a decision free of any errors of assessment or even only in the form of a right to a lawful consideration of a request.

The first question to be answered is whether a codification of a right to a decision is at all advisable. Since the right to a decision exists anyway, the legislator would not limit its scope for action. A codification will also demonstrate the EU's willingness to open its markets in a globalized world if other countries adopt the same high supervisory standards. What is more, the legislator would have the opportunity to specify further the conditions applying to the right to a decision. Hence, the codification of a right to a decision is advisable.

This finding raises the question of how such a right should be designed. Three aspects can be highlighted. First, the legislator should require a prior request from the third country in question before a decision on equivalence is taken. This request should be accompanied by a duty to provide extensive information on the third country's legal framework and economic data on its financial markets. Such an obligation does not yet exist, although ESAs already demand information in their consultations.[175] EMIR 2.2 even provides for such a duty in the context of the comparable compliance decision in relation to Tier 2 CCPs.[176] This approach is the most efficient way to gain first-hand knowledge and allows the best understanding of the third country legal framework. It also saves ESAs time and resources.

Secondly, the drafting of such an obligation is the perfect time for the legislator to define time limits for the decision-making of the administration. This prevents time

[172] See ch 2 B)IV.

[173] See in more detail ch 2 B)II.5, also with references to dissenting voices in the literature.

[174] This is at least the view expressed here. Whether the ECJ recognizes such a right that follows directly from world trade law, however, seems very doubtful. See with more references ch 2 B)II.5.

[175] See ch 2 B)I.2.b).

[176] See EMIR, art 25a(1); Berger and Badenhoop (n 129) 688.

delays for political reasons.[177] In addition, time limits increase legal certainty and allow third country service providers to plan better in advance.

Finally, the legislator should establish criteria in which order third countries can expect an equivalence assessment in response to their application. This would, in turn, enhance legal certainty. Also, the definition of clear criteria by the legislator, instead of an unregulated order chosen by the administration, is preferable from the standpoint of the principle of democracy. But what should the relevant criteria be? The European Insurance and Occupational Pensions Supervisors (CEIOPS) has already listed some points in its advice to the Commission.[178] It would be harmful to the effectiveness of equivalence to politicize the matter. Rather, 'hard' economic factors should be at the centre. To what degree does granting market access to service providers from a third country lead to a wider range of financial services for EU investors compared to other third countries? By how much does a specific equivalence decision increase liquidity in EU markets and thus lead to more efficiency and more stable EU markets? What are the risks for investors and financial markets if foreign service providers gain access to EU markets? In addition, it could be considered whether the third country legal system is remarkably similar to the one of the EU, and therefore, equivalence is easier to establish. These states could then be examined with priority. All these factors should be reflected in the criteria defined by the legislator with regard to the right to a decision.

b) Restriction of the right to withdrawal

The right to withdrawal is often identified as one of the main shortcomings of equivalence from the perspective of third country firms.[179] The right has two opposing facets. On the one hand, the permanent risk of a sudden loss of market access rights weakens equivalence. The possibility of a withdrawal is like the sword of Damocles hanging over service providers. This is particularly problematic in an area such as financial law, which is to a high degree dependent on trust and stable conditions.[180] This potential risk harms the concept of equivalence and is not just a disadvantage for third country service providers. If service providers do not trust in market access through equivalence, the EU will be supplied with fewer financial services. This is detrimental to the EU as less supply is available to EU investors, markets become more fragmented, and less liquidity reaches the EU, leading to inefficient markets.[181] Because of the principle

[177] Examples for such political delays include the EU–US deal on equivalence concerning the recognition of CCPs and the equivalence mechanism regarding non-EU AIFM marketing AIF in the EU. See IRSG, 'The EU's Third Country Regimes and Alternatives to Passporting' (23 January 2017) 102 https://www.irsg.co.uk/assets/IRSG-Full-report-The-EUs-third-country-regimes-and-alternatives-to-passporting.pdf (accessed 12 November 2022); see also ch 2 B)II.2.a).

[178] CEIOPS, 'Advice to the European Commission: Equivalence assessments to be undertaken in relation to Articles 172, 227 and 260 of the Solvency II Directive' CEIOPS-DOC-92-10 (31 August 2010) 3.

[179] Scott Morrison, 'Third-country Equivalence: A Brexit Scenario for UK Financial Services' (2018) 29 ICCLR 1, 6; Saima Hanif, 'Equivalence: Panacea or Pandora's Box?' (2016) 31 BJ Intl Ban & Fin L 567, 568.

[180] See on the concept of trust Peter O Mülbert and Alexander Sajnovits, 'The Element of Trust in Financial Markets Law' (2017) 18 German LJ 1.

[181] With regard to Brexit see IMF, 'Financial Services Sector Assessment Program, Financial System Stability Assessment' IMF Country Report (1 June 2016) https://www.imf.org/~/media/Websites/IMF/imported-full-text-pdf/external/pubs/ft/scr/2016/_cr16167.ashx (accessed 12 November 2022); Sir Hector Sants and others (Oliver Wyman), 'The Impact of the UK's Exit from the EU on the UK-based Financial

of reciprocity, as provided for in many equivalence mechanisms,[182] restricted market access for third country service providers also means it is more difficult for EU service providers to access third country markets. On the other hand, the EU has a legitimate interest to protect investors and its markets if legal frameworks of third countries are no longer equivalent to that of the EU, if their supervision is no longer as effective or if the EU wants to introduce stricter supervisory measures and the third country does not intend to follow.[183] The general possibility of withdrawing equivalence is also essential to prevent regulatory arbitrage and a race to the bottom, as already explained above.[184]

The crucial problem is to find the right balance between these poles. The EU has introduced detailed rules on this matter in more recent equivalence mechanisms, albeit only in relation to the withdrawal of the registration or recognition at the second stage and not with regard to the withdrawal of equivalence decisions.[185] One model for a withdrawal arrangement could be the recently concluded EU–Japan Economic Partnership Agreement. In its Annex 8-A on Regulatory Cooperation on Financial Regulation, it stipulates in No 12 that

> [e]ach Party may rescind at any time its decision to rely on the regulatory and supervisory framework of the other Party and revert to the application and enforcement of its own rules, if rules and supervision of the other Party are no longer equivalent in outcome, if the other Party fails to enforce its rules effectively or if there is insufficient cooperation of the other Party in the supervision of financial institutions. The Parties shall consult with each other in an appropriate manner prior to reverting to the application and enforcement of their own rules.[186]

Two aspects are of particular importance here: first, the determination of reasons for a withdrawal and, secondly, the procedural rules to be observed in a withdrawal. Regarding the reasons for withdrawal, the provision lists three grounds that can be summarized with non-equivalent rules and supervision, a lack of enforcement, and insufficient supervisory cooperation. It should be emphasized that a withdrawal for political reasons is neither part of the reasons listed in the EU–Japan Economic Partnership Agreement, nor would it be legal to include it in equivalence provisions.[187]

Equally important for service providers from third countries as the grounds for withdrawal is the procedural side. According to the provision in the EU–Japan Economic Partnership Agreement, the parties shall consult each other prior to a withdrawal. This obligation has the function of warning the other party and allowing it to comment on the grounds for the impending withdrawal and react accordingly

Services Sector' (2016) https://www.oliverwyman.com/content/dam/oliver-wyman/global/en/2016/oct/OW%20report_Brexit%20impact%20on%20Uk-based%20FS.pdf (accessed 12 November 2022).

182 See ch 2 A)I.4.
183 Wymeersch (n 67) 227f.
184 See in more detail ch 5 A)II.1.e).
185 See eg MiFIR, art 49 and EMIR, art 25p.
186 Council Decision (EU) 2018/1907 of 20 December 2018.
187 See extensively ch 2 B)II.2.b) and III.

to prevent it.[188] Often, a withdrawal, which should only be an *ultima ratio*, may be avoided through intensive dialogue. This duty to consult each other in due time is also provided for in other provisions of the EU–Japan Economic Partnership Agreement, namely in the case of planned regulatory initiatives to allow the other party to comment and possibly adapt its legal system.[189]

What is missing in the agreement, but should be included in equivalence provisions, are transitional arrangements following a withdrawal.[190] Even though the period is relatively short, the US–Australia Mutual Recognition Arrangement, which contained a transitional period of 61 days, may serve as an example.[191] It is of paramount importance to provide for appropriate transitional periods. A loss of market access rights might force service providers to relocate, which takes time.[192] Thus, it would be appropriate to include a transitional period of 6–12 months following the withdrawal of an equivalence decision, during which service providers keep their market access rights. Only in cases where the systemic stability is under an imminent threat or where investors are exposed to significant risks should this transitional period not apply. Besides a transitional period, there should also be a legacy clause.[193] This clause would ensure that contracts concluded under the equivalence framework prior to the revocation can still be fulfilled. Comparable regulations were also enacted at the national level in response to Brexit.[194] The Commission can already issue such a rule under the current legal framework as part of the withdrawal decision. However, a statutory obligation to do so would increase legal certainty and thus be conducive to the overall goal of this book: greater juridification.

[188] In this direction see IOSCO, 'Good Practices on Processes for Deference' Report(June 2020) 19ff (Good Practices 8–10) https://www.iosco.org/library/pubdocs/pdf/IOSCOPD659.pdf (accessed 12 November 2022).

[189] See eg EU–Japan Economic Partnership Agreement, no 7 and no 9.

[190] Similarly, the proposal by IOSCO, 'Good Practices on Processes for Deference' Report (June 2020) (n 40) 22 (Good Practice 11).

[191] US–Australia Mutual Recognition Arrangement (25 August 2008) para 61 https://download.asic.gov.au/media/1346672/SEC_framework_arrangement_aug_08.pdf (accessed 12 November 2022).

[192] See Lehmann and Zetzsche (n 61) 105. See in relation to banks ECB, 'Relocating to the euro area' (2017) www.bankingsupervision.europa.eu/banking/relocating/html/index.en.html (accessed 12 November 2022).

[193] Pennesi (n 46) 56f.

[194] See eg in Germany Banking Act (KWG), § 53b(12); Payment Services Supervision Act (ZAG), § 39(8); Securities Trading Act (WpHG), § 102(4). However, the German regulations impose excessive requirements on the possibility of continuing existing contracts, which is why they cannot serve as a model. On the German response: Matthias Lehmann and Jonas Schürger, 'Brexit-Steuerbegleitgesetz und Brexit-Übergangsgesetz: Sicherheit trotz Unsicherheit?' (2019) 19 BKR 365, 367ff; on the problem in general see Matthias Hanten, 'Contract Continuity under Brexit' (2019) 9 RISF/JFS 28.

Summary

Chapter 1 Access to Financial Markets in the EU

Deference describes the withdrawal of regulatory and supervisory powers over foreign service providers and products by a state when this state deems the foreign regulation and supervision to be comparable to its domestic one. In the EU, the concept of deference exists in the form of equivalence, which is now embedded in most areas of financial market regulation. Nonetheless, there are still some areas that are not covered by equivalence, including market access for banks and direct insurers, as well as numerous sectors where the interests of retail investors are particularly affected.[1]

The procedure within which equivalence is granted in the 40 mechanisms can be divided into three categories.[2] In some equivalence provisions, the Commission's equivalence decision is sufficient to bring about legal consequences. In other EU legal acts, the third country firm is required to register in some way with one of the European Supervisory Authorities (ESAs) after the equivalence decision has been adopted. The third type consists of two different discretionary acts: an equivalence decision by the Commission at the first level and a decision by a national authority at the second level.

Chapter 2 Equivalence in the EU

A) Equivalence as a uniform concept

All equivalence mechanisms of the EU are based on a uniform concept. The defining element of each provision is the decision on equivalence by the European Commission. Moreover, most regimes consist of the same key requirements.[3] It follows from this that the term 'equivalence' has the same meaning in all mechanisms, that the administrative and constitutional limits governing the entire process are the same, and that the same limitations apply to withdrawal decisions. Likewise, the possibilities for and the level of judicial review are similar.

[1] See ch 1 C)II.
[2] See ch 1 C)III.
[3] See ch 2 A)I.

B) Equivalence decision as the crucial point

I. Pivotal question: What is meant by equivalence, and how can it be determined?
The decision on equivalence by the European Commission is the defining and core element of equivalence. An equivalence decision does not presuppose an identical but a foreign legal system that is 'equal in value'. The regulatory aims of the EU legislator must be fulfilled by the third country legal system on an equal footing. Consequently, the outcomes on financial markets and market participants in relation to the goals of investor protection, the functioning of financial markets as well as financial stability are at the centre of the assessment. In this regard, specific EU provisions do not need a counterpart, but the third country legal system as a whole must achieve the same regulatory outcome. Hence, equivalence means a functional equivalence of regulatory outcomes from a holistic perspective (so-called outcome-based approach).[4]

More problematic than the abstract meaning is the process of determining equivalence in practice.[5] The ESAs apply a similar methodology, which can be compared to the well-known functional method from comparative law by *Zweigert/Kötz*.[6] One challenge, however, is that no methodology exists regarding the weighing of differences, which is the last and decisive step. Ultimately, the principle of efficiency in the form of a *Kaldor-Hicks improvement*[7] is the most appropriate method. Using this criterion, at least as an aid for the argumentation, will objectify the balancing process and make it fairer, more predictable, and more transparent.

II. Administrative decision-making leeway
Currently, the EU Commission misuses its discretionary powers in a political way by including aspects in the decision-making process that are not related to financial market regulation. Using equivalence as a bargaining chip for goals unrelated to financial regulation is not only unwise from a political point of view but is even unlawful.[8] A political decision is not envisaged in the legal texts of the equivalence provisions and violates the European Treaties. Moreover, the involvement of policy arguments in the equivalence decision violates the Most-Favoured-Nation Treatment set out in the GATS. Policy arguments cannot be justified on the basis of the prudential carve-out and are thus not in line with world trade law.

The fact that equivalence decisions consist of a purely technical comparison of two legal systems does not mean that the Commission has no discretionary powers. The Commission should retain a large margin of discretion when weighing up the differences and similarities, as this process contains prognostic elements and particularly complex economic questions. Here, the level of judicial scrutiny is limited, which does not mean, however, that the CJEU may completely give up judicial control.[9]

[4] See ch 2 B)I.1.
[5] See ch 2 B)I.2.
[6] Konrad Zweigert and Hein Kötz, *An Introduction to Comparative Law*, vol 1 (1st edn, North-Holland 1977) 23–41.
[7] Nicholas Kaldor, 'Welfare Propositions of Economics and Interpersonal Comparisons of Utility' (1939) 49 Economic J 549; John R Hicks, 'The Foundations of Welfare Economics' (1939) 49 Econ J 696.
[8] See ch 2 B)II.2.b).
[9] See ch 2 B)II.3.

Furthermore, third countries and their service providers have a right to an equivalence decision deriving from WTO law, respectively EU law.[10] This right is typically limited to a right to a lawful consideration of the request to be recognized as equivalent. In exceptional circumstances that are partly fulfilled vis-à-vis the UK post-Brexit, this right may, however, evolve into a right to a decision free of any errors of assessment or even into a right to be granted equivalence.

III. Withdrawal of equivalence decisions

Some equivalence mechanisms contain a provision regarding the revocation of equivalence. But even in the absence of such a provision, the Commission can withdraw equivalence. For such withdrawals, the same legal limits apply as to the initial equivalence decision, which means inter alia that political considerations must not be part of the decision-making process. Apart from the threat of political decisions, the revocation of equivalence poses four other challenges for third country financial service providers. First, it remains unclear on what grounds equivalence decisions can be withdrawn. Secondly, it is potentially dangerous for service providers that the withdrawal process may be influenced by the Member States. Thirdly, the withdrawal of equivalence may take place at little or even no notice. Fourthly, the process of withdrawal is rather opaque, making it difficult to anticipate such decisions, which in turn increases legal uncertainty.[11]

IV. Judicial review of equivalence decisions

Whether and in what form legal protection is available depends on many factors, including the procedure according to which equivalence is granted and the claimant in question (third country or their service providers). Contrary to the view of some commentators, legal protection is generally available for service providers from third countries before the CJEU.[12]

As the EU is a member of the WTO, the rules of the GATS apply to equivalence. It follows from the GATS that third countries not only have a right to a decision deriving from world trade law but also have a corresponding right to bring actions before the Dispute Settlement Body of the WTO.[13]

C) Legal consequences

The legal consequences of equivalence provisions are not homogeneous but can be divided into four categories depending on the regulatory technique applied. Equivalence can waive certain regulatory obligations (category 1), provide equal treatment with EU firms or products (category 2), or grant partial (category 3), or full market access (category 4) to third country firms or products.[14] The regulatory technique used to

[10] See ch 2 B)II.5.
[11] See ch 2 B)III.
[12] See ch 2 B)IV.1.
[13] See ch 2 B)IV.2.
[14] See ch 2 C)I–IV.

describe the legal consequences does not affect the substance and is in part an expression of inconsistent legislation. What varies is the degree of liberalization that follows from equivalence.

Ultimately, legal consequences of equivalence regimes, although they appear to be diverse at first sight, are all based on the same philosophy, which again underlines the argument made above that equivalence provisions are part of a uniform concept. They are heading in the same direction, follow the same objective, and are thus part of the same principle.[15]

Chapter 3 A Liberal Access to Financial Markets in Switzerland

Deference is anchored in Swiss law to a similar extent as is equivalence in EU law, albeit Switzerland is more liberal in the area of retail investors and has implemented deference rules here as well.[16] Like in the EU, deference in Switzerland exists primarily in the form of equivalence. However, Switzerland has also implemented the more liberal concept of appropriateness. As a rule of thumb, Switzerland imposes fewer requirements, and the third country regimes are more concise. Besides, Switzerland attaches particular importance to international standards in its deference mechanisms. Furthermore, Switzerland follows a more pragmatic approach in the adoption of deference decisions, generally relies more on self-regulation than state intervention, and applies its laws to a lesser extent extraterritorially.[17]

Switzerland's liberal approach aims at attracting foreign capital, investors, and financial service providers while at the same time opening foreign markets to domestic firms. The policy of open markets is no coincidence but is rooted in Switzerland's geographical and economic position, in particular the predominant role of the Swiss financial industry.

Chapter 4 The Approach of Substituted Compliance in the United States

The legal situation in the US regarding deference is very different from that in the EU and Switzerland. Here, the approach of national treatment and later that of modified national treatment has traditionally prevailed over deference.[18] After the first generation of substituted compliance did not gain widespread acceptance, in recent years, the second generation of substituted compliance appeared on the regulatory landscape.[19] This second generation does not aim at granting market access but seeks

[15] See ch 2 C)V.3.
[16] See extensively on the scope of application of deference in Switzerland ch 3 B).
[17] On the Swiss system of market access and its peculiarities see ch 3 C).
[18] See ch 4 A)I.
[19] See ch 4 A)II. and III.

to reduce regulatory and supervisory conflicts by exempting foreign participants and transactions from certain requirements. These substituted compliance provisions are mainly limited to the derivatives sector, and neither the legislator nor the supervisory authorities have so far implemented substituted compliance extensively in other areas of financial regulation.[20] The concept of substituted compliance is therefore not as widespread as deference in the EU and Switzerland. At the same time, it is less far-reaching than its European and Swiss counterparts because it rarely leads to a complete exemption from licensing requirements and supervision, but only specific obligations are waived.[21]

Overall, the territorial and restrictive approach of the US lags behind on an international scale. The US will have to liberalize market access by extending and strengthening deference to retain its influence and dominant role. Similar to the initial emergence of substituted compliance, where the US was pushed particularly by the EU equivalence approach, history will repeat itself, and the US will get another push to more deference.[22]

Chapter 5 The Future of Deference in the World and Equivalence in the EU

Deference is the only instrument capable of reducing market fragmentation and meeting the needs of a globalized world.[23] Further expansion, strengthening, and improvement of deference is therefore essential for the current international financial system to function.

In the further development, some important points should be observed that will also aid the global breakthrough of deference: states should not demand foreign legal systems to be identical but allow them some room for experimentation; deference decisions should be depoliticized; more reference should be made to international standards to shift the focus away from the domestic legal system as the perceived best solution; and finally, the requirement of reciprocal treatment should be included in any deference mechanism to incentivize other states to defer as well.[24]

When developing EU equivalence *de lege ferenda*, some additional points should be taken into account. To reduce the complexity of the current regulation and create a consistent and coherent system of equivalence, the obligation-based approach must be replaced by a sectoral approach with only one equivalence regime for each sector.[25] In addition, equivalence decisions should be transformed into implementing technical decisions, thereby giving ESAs more competences.[26] At the same time, the focus

[20] See the extensive overview in ch 4 B).
[21] See ch 4 C)I. and II.
[22] See ch 4 C)III.
[23] See ch 5 A)I.
[24] See ch 5 A)II.
[25] See ch 5 B)I.
[26] See ch 5 B)II.1.

of equivalence determinations should be more subject-specific rather than country-specific.[27] Finally, it is advisable to eliminate inconsistencies in the procedure, prerequisites, and legal consequences of equivalence, to standardize and define a right to an equivalence decision, and to restrict the right to withdraw equivalence in the sense of determining grounds for a withdrawal, as well as to specify procedural rules and introduce rules regarding transitional arrangements.[28]

[27] See ch 5 B)II.2.
[28] See ch 5 B)III.

Bibliography

Abegglen S and Hochstrasser T, 'FIDLEG—was kommt gemäss Botschaft des Bundesrates auf die Finanzdienstleister zu?' (2016) 112 SJZ 369

Akehurst M, 'Jurisdiction in International Law' (1972–1973) 46 Brit Y B Intl L 145

Albors-Llorens A, 'Judicial Protection before the Court of Justice of the European Union' in Barnard C and Peers S (eds), *European Union Law* (3rd edn, OUP 2020)

Alexander K, Dhumale R, and Eatwell J, *Global Governance of Financial Systems* (OUP 2005)

Alexander K, Ferran EV, Jackson HE, and Moloney N, 'Transatlantic Financial Services Regulatory Dialogue' (2006) 7 EBOR 647

Alexander K, 'The GATS and Financial Services' in Alexander K and Andenas M (eds), *The World Trade Organization and Trade in Services* (Martinus Nijhoff 2008)

Alexander K, 'The UK's Third-Country Status Following Brexit' in Alexander K, Barnard C, Ferran EV, Lang A, and Moloney N (eds), *Brexit and Financial Services: Law and Policy* (Hart Publishing 2018)

Ammann TR, *Der europäische Marktzugang für Schweizer Banken* (Dike 2020)

Amtenbrink F and Heine K, 'Regulating Credit Rating Agencies in the European Union: Lessons from Behavioural Finance' (2013) 2013 DQ 2

Andenas M and Zleptnig S, 'Proportionality and Balancing in WTO Law: A Comparative Perspective' in Alexander K and Andenas M (eds), *The World Trade Organization and Trade in Services* (Martinus Nijhoff 2008)

Andersen PK, *EU Trading Venues* (Djøf Forlag 2018)

Arias-Barrera LC, *Regulation and Supervision of the OTC Derivatives Market* (Routledge 2018)

Armour J, Awrey D, Davies P, Enriques L, Gordons JN, Mayer C, and Payne J, *Principles of Financial Regulation* (OUP 2016)

Armour J, 'Brexit and Financial Services: Bargaining in the Shadow of Equivalence' in Armour J and Eidenmüller H (eds), *Negotiating Brexit* (CH Beck 2017)

Armstrong KA, 'Mutual Recognition' in Barnard C and Scott J (eds), *The Law of the Single European Market* (Hart Publishing 2002)

Arner DW, Barberis J, and Buckley RP, 'The Evolution of FinTech: A New Post-Crisis Paradigm' (2016) 47 Geo J Intl L 1271

Arner DW, Avgouleas E, Busch D, and Schwarcz SL (eds), *Systemic Risk in the Financial Sector: Ten Years after the Great Crash* (CIGI 2019)

Artamonov A, 'Cross-Border Application of OTC Derivatives Rules' (2015) 1 JFR 206

Assmann H-D, Schneider UH, and Mülbert PO (eds), *Wertpapierhandelsrecht* (8th edn, Otto Schmidt 2023)

Avgouleas E, *Governance of Global Financial Markets* (CUP 2012)

Axelrod R, *The Evolution of Cooperation* (Basic Books 1984)

Ayling DE, *The Internationalisation of Stockmarkets* (Gower 1986)

Bacharach J, 'L'équivalence: entre question technique et instrument de realpolitik' Centre de droit bancaire et financier (19 August 2019) https://www.cdbf.ch/1081/ (accessed 12 November 2022)

Bahar R, 'Derivative Trading under the Federal Act on Financial Markets Infrastructure' (2015) 87 SZW 479

Bahar R and Nedwed B, 'Grenzüberschreitendes Angebot von Finanzdienstleistungen und -produkten? Die Eidgenossenschaft schlägt zurück' (2019) 91 SZW 618

Bar von C and Mankowski P, *Internationales Privatrecht*, vol 1 (2nd edn, CH Beck 2003)

Barfield CE, 'Free Trade, Sovereignty, Democracy, The Future of the WTO' (2001) 2 Chic J Intl L 403

Bartels L, 'The Chapeau of the General Exceptions in the WTO GATT and GATS Agreements: A Reconstruction' (2015) 109 AJIL 95

Bärtschi H, 'Finanzmarktregulierung im Fluss: Zum neuen Finanzinstituts- und Finanzdienstleistungsgesetz' (2014) 86 SZW 459

Bast J, 'New Categories of Acts After the Lisbon Reform: Dynamics of Parliamentarization in EU Law' (2012) 49 CMLR 885

Baumgartner F and von der Crone HC, 'Die Bewilligungs- und Prospektpflicht im schweizerischen Recht anhand des Crowdfundings' (2018) 90 SZW 726

Beck H, 'Börsen- und kapitalmarktrechtliche Aspekte der grenzüberschreitenden Tätigkeit und Zusammenarbeit von Börsen' in Ekkenga J, Hadding W, and Hammen H (eds), *Festschrift für Siegfried Kümpel* (Erich Schmidt 2003)

Bennett A and Vines D, 'The EU–UK Trade and Cooperation Agreement' (2022) 38 Oxf Rev Econ Policy 68

Berger H and Badenhoop N, 'Financial Services and Brexit: Navigating Towards Future Market Access' (2018) 19 EBOR 679

Bergström M, 'Judicial Protection for Private Parties in European Commission Rulemaking' in Bergström CF and Ritleng D (eds), *Rulemaking by the European Commission* (OUP 2016)

Berrisch GM, 'Beihilferecht: Direktklagen gegen beihilferechtliche Entscheidung der Kommission nach Art 263 IV AEUV' (2014) 25 EuZW 228

Bertschinger U, 'Das Finanzmarktaufsichtsrecht Mitte 2014 bis ins vierte Quartal 2015' (2015) 87 SZW 630

Binham C, 'Fear EU Deal Puts City of London at Risk of "rule-taking"' *Financial Times* (23 January 2020) https://www.ft.com/content/d56ee33a-3d3d-11ea-b232-000f4477fbca (accessed 12 November 2022)

Blackmore V and Jeapes E, 'The Global Financial Crisis: One Global Regulator or Multiple Regulators?' (2009) 4 CMLJ S112

Bleckmann A, 'Die actus-contrarius-Doktrin' (1988) 28 JuS 174

Blomeyer W and Schachtschneider KA, *Die Europäische Union als Rechtsgemeinschaft* (Duncker & Humblot 1995)

Bollen R, 'The Slow Journey towards a Global Regulator' (2008) 5 Macquarie J Bus L 255

Bordo MD, 'The Globalization of International Financial Markets: What Can History Teach Us?' in Auernheimer L (ed), *International Financial Markets: The Challenge of Globalization* (Chicago University Press 2003)

Borselli A, 'Insurance Group Supervision in the European Union' in Marano P and Siri M (eds), *Insurance Regulation in the European Union* (Palgrave Macmillan 2017)

Bösch R and Kramer S, 'Schweizer Finanzmarktrecht im Umbruch—Das Finanzmarktinfrastrukturgesetz als eine der neuen Säulen' (2014) 110 SJZ 249

Bösch R, Rayroux F, Winzeler C, and Stupp E (eds), *BSK-KAG* (2nd edn, Helbing Lichtenhahn 2016)

Bösch R, 'Das neue Schweizer Prospektrecht gemäss E-FIDLEG—eine Bestandesaufnahme und erste Würdigung' (2016) 135 ZSR 81

Bösch R, 'Das FIDLEG-Prospektrecht ante portas—Guter Anlegerschutz?' (2018) 90 SZW 451

Bradley C, 'Private International Law-Making for the Financial Markets' (2005) 29 Fordham Intl LJ 127

Braidi G, 'La classification des clients selon la loi sur les services financiers' (2018) 90 RSDA 486

Brambring M, *Zentrales Clearing von OTC-Derivaten unter EMIR* (Mohr Siebeck 2017)
Brändli B, 'Die aufsichtsrechtliche Erfassung der Zentralen Gegenpartei im schweizerischen Kapitalmarkt' (2011) 83 SZW 2
Brändli B, Guggenheim B, and Jüttner M, 'Financial Benchmarks: Bedeutung, Problematik und regulatorische Ansätze' (2016) 88 SZW 162
Brosig I, *Benchmark-Manipulation* (Nomos 2018)
Brummer C, 'Territoriality as a Regulatory Technique: Notes from the Financial Crisis' (2010) 79 U Cin L Rev 499
Brummer C, 'Post-American Securities Regulation' (2010) 98 Cal L Rev 327
Brummer C, *Soft Law and the Global Financial System* (2nd edn, CUP 2015)
Brummer C, *Minilateralism* (CUP 2014)
Brunsden J, 'Brussels Signals Tough Stance on UK Bank Bonuses after Brexit' *Financial Times* (19 December 2017) https://www.ft.com/content/98c9a2b4-e4a0-11e7-97e2-916d4fbac0da (accessed 12 November 2022)
Brunsden J, Stafford P, and Keohane D, 'EU Regulators Seek Solution to Post-Brexit Derivatives Rule Clash' *Financial Times* (16 November 2020) https://www.ft.com/content/ad60293f-cdb4-4566-8644-b970ecf98ad4 (accessed 12 November 2022)
Buckley RP, 'How the International Financial System, to Its Detriment, Differs from National Systems, and What We Can Do about It' (2004) 34 Hong Kong LJ 321
Buckley RP and Arner DW, 'Redesigning the Architecture of the Global Financial System' (2010) 11 Melb J Intl L 1
Buckley RP, Avgouleas E, and Arner DW (eds), *Reconceptualising Global Finance and Its Regulation* (CUP 2016)
Bühler CB, 'Finanzmarktregulierung im Spannungsfeld von Recht und Politik' (2010) 106 SJZ 469
Bühler CB, 'Stärkung der Ombudsstelle' (2019) 91 SZW 559
Bungenberg M 'Europäisches Verwaltungsrecht und WTO-Recht' in Terhechte JP (ed), *Verwaltungsrecht der Europäischen Union* (Nomos 2011)
Bureau D and Muir Watt H (eds), *Droit international privé*, vol 1 (4th edn, Thémis 2017)
Burling J, 'The Potential Effect of Brexit on Insurance Regulation in the UK' in Marano P and Siri M (eds), *Insurance Regulation in the European Union* (Palgrave Macmillan 2017)
Busch D and Louisse M, 'MiFID II/MiFIR's Regime for Third-country Firms' in Busch D and Ferrarini G (eds), *Regulation of the EU Financial Markets: MiFID II and MiFIR* (OUP 2017)
Busch D, 'A Stronger Role for the European Supervisory Authorities in the EU27' in Busch D, Ferrarini G, and Franx JP (eds), *Prospectus Regulation and Prospectus Liability* (OUP 2020)
Bush DM and Krimminger MH, 'EU Proposed Intermediate Holding Company Requirements for Non-EU Banks and Broker-Dealers' (17 December 2016) Harvard Law School Forum on Corporate Governance https://corpgov.law.harvard.edu/2016/12/17/eu-proposed-intermediate-holding-company-requirements-for-non-eu-banks-and-broker-dealers/ (accessed 12 November 2022)
Busuioc M, 'Rule-Making by the European Financial Supervisory Authorities: Walking a Tight Rope' (2013) 19 Eur LJ 111
Buxbaum HL, 'Transnational Legal Ordering and Regulatory Conflict' (2016) 1 UC Irvine J Intl Transnatl & Comp L 91
Callens E, *Regulation of Central Counterparties (CCPs) in Light of Systemic Risk* (Intersentia 2022)
Callens E, 'Third Country CCP Supervision as a Catalyst for More Centralized EU CCP Supervision?' (2023) EBI Working Paper Series No 134 https://ssrn.com/abstract=4349597 (accessed 5 March 2023)
Calliess C and Ruffert M (eds), *EUV/AEUV* (6th edn, CH Beck 2022)
Cane P and Kritzer HM (eds), *The Oxford Handbook of Empirical Legal Research* (OUP 2010)

Carr JL Jr and More JH, 'Developments in the Regulation of Foreign Bank Operations in the United States' (1988) U Ill L Rev 255

Ceyssens J and Tarde A, 'Äquivalenz im Finanzdienstleistungsrecht der Europäischen Union' (2019) 31 EuZW 805

Chang KY, 'Reforming U.S. Disclosure Rules in Global Securities Markets' (2003) 22 Ann Rev Bank & Fin L 237

Chipman JS, 'Compensation Principle' in Vernengo M, Caldentey EP, and Rosser BJ Jr (eds), *The New Palgrave Dictionary of Economics* (3rd edn, Macmillan 2018)

Chiti E, 'An Important Part of the EU's Institutional Machinery: Features, Problems and Perspectives of European Agencies' (2009) 46 CMLR 1395

Chiti E, 'European Agencies' Rulemaking: Powers, Procedures and Assessment' (2013) 19 Eur LJ 93

Choi SJ and Guzman AT, 'Portable Reciprocity: Rethinking the International Reach of Securities Regulation' (1998) 71 S Cal L Rev 903

Christiansen T and Dobbels M, 'Non-Legislative Rule Making after the Lisbon Treaty: Implementing the New System of Comitology and Delegated Acts' (2013) 19 Eur LJ 42

Clarkson D, Jaecklin S, and Kaczmarski K (Oliver Wyman), 'Domiciles of Alternative Investment Funds' (2014) https://www.oliverwyman.com/content/dam/oliver-wyman/global/en/2014/dec/Oliver_Wyman_Domiciles_of_Alternative_Investment_Funds.pdf (accessed 12 November 2022)

Classen CD, 'Der EuGH und die Herausbildung eines europäischen Verwaltungsrechts' in Schenke RP and Suerbaum J (eds), *Verwaltungsgerichtsbarkeit in der Europäischen Union* (Nomos 2016)

Coester-Waltjen D, 'Das Anerkennungsprinzip im Dornröschenschlaf?' in Mansel H-P, Hausmann R, Kohler C, Kronke H, and Pfeiffer T (eds), *Festschrift für Erik Jayme*, vol 1 (Sellier 2004)

Coffee JC Jr, 'Racing towards the Top: The Impact of Cross-Listing and Stock Market Competition on International Corporate Governance' (2002) 102 Colum L Rev 1757

Coffee JC Jr, *Gatekeepers: The Professions and Corporate Governance* (OUP 2006)

Coffee JC Jr, 'Ratings Reform: The Good, the Bad, and the Ugly' (2011) 1 Harv Bus L Rev 231

Coffee JC Jr, 'The Political Economy of Dodd-Frank' in Ferran EV, Moloney N, Hill JG, and Coffee JC Jr (eds), *The Regulatory Aftermath of the Global Financial Crisis* (CUP 2012)

Coffee JC Jr, 'Extraterritorial Financial Regulation: Why E.T. Can't Come Home' (2014) 99 Cornell L Rev 1259

Coffee JC Jr, Sale HA, and Henderson MT, *Securities Regulation* (2nd edn, Foundation Press 2015)

Cohen GM, 'The Framework of Insurance Regulation' in Thomas JE (ed), *New Appleman on Insurance Law Library Edition*, vol 2 (Lexis Nexis 2022)

Colaert V and Busch D, 'Summary and Conclusions' in Colaert V, Busch D, and Incalza T (eds), *European Financial Regulation: Levelling the Cross-Sectoral Playing Field* (Hart Publishing 2019)

Collin PH, Janssen S, and Kornmüller A (eds), *PONS: Fachwörterbuch Recht* (Ernst Klett 1990)

Comizio VG, *International Banking Law* (West Academic 2016)

Conac P-H, 'The International Organisation of Securities Commissions (IOSCO), Europe, Brexit, and Rethinking Cross-border Regulation' (2020) 17 ECFR 72

Condon BJ, Sadka JC, and Sinha T, *Insurance Regulation in North America* (Kluwer Law International 2003)

Conte E and Parmeggiani F, 'The Regulation of Credit Rating Agency across USA and EU' (11 November 2008) http://ssrn.com/abstract=2214998 (accessed 12 November 2022)

Contratto F, 'Sanktionen: Neue Gretchenfrage im Ringen um den Marktzugang in die EU?' (2018) 90 SZW 653
Conway III GT, 'Extraterritoriality of the Federal Securities Laws After Dodd-Frank' (21 July 2010) http://www.wlrk.com/webdocs/wlrknew/WLRKMemos/WLRK/WLRK.17763.10.pdf (accessed 12 November 2022)
Cosenza E, 'Paradise Lost: 10(b) after Morrison v National Australia Bank' (2010–2011) 11 Chic J Intl L 343
Courvoisier M, 'Prospektpflicht nach FIDLEG' (2020) 92 SZW 307
Craig PP, 'Delegated Acts, Implementing Acts and the New Comitology Regulation' (2011) 36 Eur L Rev 671
Craig PP, 'Comitology, Rulemaking, and the Lisbon Settlement' in Bergström CF and Ritleng D (eds), *Rulemaking by the European Commission* (OUP 2016)
Craig PP, *EU Administrative Law* (3rd edn, OUP 2018)
Crawford J, *Brownlie's Principles of Public International Law* (9th edn, OUP 2019)
Curtis R, 'Solvency as a Focal Point of Prudential Regulation' in Liedtke PM and Monkiewicz J (eds), *The Future of Insurance Regulation and Supervision* (Palgrave Macmillan 2011)
Dahmen L and Kindermann J, 'Zwischen Passport und Niederlassungszwang' in Teuber H and Schröer H (eds), *MiFID II/MiFIR: Umsetzung in der Bankpraxis* (Finanz Colloquium 2015)
Dale R, *The Regulation of International Banking* (Woodhead-Faulkner 1984)
Dann P, 'The Political Institutions' in Bogdandy von A and Bast J (eds), *Principles of European Constitutional Law* (2nd rev edn, Hart Publishing 2009)
Danwitz von T, 'Eigentumsschutz in Europa und im Wirtschaftsvölkerrecht' in Danwitz von T, Depenheuer O, and Engel C (eds), *Bericht zur Lage des Eigentums* (Springer 2002)
Danwitz von T, *Europäisches Verwaltungsrecht* (Springer 2008)
Danwitz von T in Dauses MA and Ludwigs M, *Handbuch des EU-Wirtschaftsrechts* (CH Beck as of February 2021)
Dasgupta S, 'Environmental Regulation and Development: A Cross-country Empirical Analysis' (2001) 29 Oxf Dev Stud 173
Davidoff SM, 'Rhetoric and Reality: A Historical Perspective on the Regulation of Foreign Private Issuers' (2010) 79 U Cin L Rev 619
De Arriba-Sellier N, 'The Brexit Reform of European Financial Supervision: Lost in Transition?' (2019) 30 EBLR 695
De Búrca G, 'The Principle of Proportionality and its Application in EC Law' (1993) 13 YBEL 105
De Manuel Aramendía MJ, 'Third Country Rules for Alternative Investments: Passport flexibility comes at a price' ECMI Commentary No 27/16 (December 2010) https://www.ceps.eu/wp-content/uploads/2010/12/ECMI%20Commentary%20No%2027.pdf (accessed 12 November 2022)
Deipenbrock G, 'Direct Supervisory Powers of the European Securities and Markets Authority (ESMA) in the Realm of Credit Rating Agencies' (2018) 29 EBLR 169
Delimatsis P and Hoekman B, 'National Tax Regulation, Voluntary International Standards, and the GATS: Argentina–Financial Services' (2018) 17 World Trade Rev 265
Dervisopoulos J, 'Nichtigkeitsklage' in Rengeling H-W, Middeke A, and Gellermann M (eds), *Handbuch des Rechtsschutzes in der Europäischen Union* (3rd edn, CH Beck 2014)
Dervisopoulos J, 'Untätigkeitsklage' in Rengeling H-W, Middeke A, and Gellermann M (eds), *Handbuch des Rechtsschutzes in der Europäischen Union* (3rd edn, CH Beck 2014)
Dietl C-E and Lorenz E (eds), *Dictionary of Legal, Commercial and Political Terms*, pt 1 (6th edn, CH Beck 2000)
Djankov S, Glaeser E, La Porta R, Lopez-de-Silanes F, and Shleifer A, 'The New Comparative Economics' (2003) 31 J Comp Econ 595

Dobbyn JF and French CC, *Insurance Law in a Nutshell* (5th edn, West Academic 2017)
Dornseifer F, Jesch TA, Klebeck U, and Tollmann C (eds), *AIFM-Richtlinie* (CH Beck 2013)
Dougan M, 'The Treaty of Lisbon 2007: Winning Minds, not Hearts' (2008) 45 CMLR 617
Dowd JF, 'An Alien Insurer Seeking Entry into the United States: Factors to Consider' (1979) 11 NYU J Intl L & Pol 519
Dowell-Jones M and Kinley D, 'Minding the Gap: Global Finance and Human Rights' (2011) 25 Ethics & Intl Aff 183
Dreher M, *Treatises on Solvency II* (Springer 2015)
Dugan JC, Plotkin MW, Noreika KA, and Nonaka M, 'Forms of Entry and Operation in the United States' in Guynn RD (ed), *Regulation of Foreign Banks & Affiliates in the United States* (9th edn, Thomson Reuters 2016)
Dür A, 'Fortress Europe or open door Europe? The external impact of the EU's single market in financial services' (2011) 18 J Eur Public Policy 619
Egan BG, 'Major Themes of the Sarbanes-Oxley Act' (2008) 42 Tex J Bus L 339
Eggen M and Schaefer R, 'Regulierung grenzüberschreitender Tätigkeiten im Finanzmarktrecht' (2013) 8 GesKR 368
Eggen M, 'Die schweizerische Prospektpflicht für Effekten—eine rechtsvergleichende Untersuchung der bestehenden Rechtslage' (2010) 82 SZW 203
Eichhorn J and Klebeck U, 'Drittstaatenregulierung der MiFID II und MiFIR' (2014) 4 RdF 189
Eidenmüller H, *Effizienz als Rechtsprinzip* (4th edn, Mohr Siebeck 2015)
Eliantonio M and Stratieva N, 'From Plaumann, through UPA and Jego-Quere, to the Lisbon Treaty: The Locus Standi of Private Applicants under Article 230(4) EC through a Political Lens' (2010) 2010 RRDE 43
Emmenegger S and Kurzbein R, 'Finanzmarktkrise und neue Corporate Governance von Banken' (2010) 5 GesKR 462
Emmenegger S and Bigler A, 'Fortress Europe: Die Äquivalenzverfahren der EU im Bereich der Finanzdienstleistungen' (2019) 91 SZW 155
Fahrländer L, 'Neuordnung der Finanzmarktregulierung in der Schweiz' (2019) 31 ZBB/JBB 225
Fanikos DW, 'The Foreign Bank Supervision Enhancement Act of 1991' (1993) 16 Suffolk Transnatl L Rev 482
Farrell S and Cankett M, 'EU Benchmark Regulation: Our Translation, Your Transition and the Timeframe' (2018) 10 J of Sec Oper & Cust 279
Faust F, 'Economic Analysis of Law' in Reimann M and Zimmermann R (eds), *The Oxford Handbook of Comparative Law* (2nd edn, OUP 2019)
Fehling M, 'Europäisches Verwaltungsverfahren und Verwaltungsprozessrecht' in Terhechte JP (ed), *Verwaltungsrecht der Europäischen Union* (Nomos 2011)
Feldkamp J, 'Alle ein bisschen LIBOR? Die neue Referenzwertordnung und ihre Folgen' (2016) 6 RdF 180
Ferran EV, *Building an EU Securities Market* (CUP 2004)
Ferran EV, 'After the Crisis: The Regulation of Hedge Funds and Private Equity in the EU' (2011) 12 EBOR 379
Ferran EV, 'Financial Supervision' in Mügge D (ed), *Europe and the Governance of Global Finance* (OUP 2014)
Ferran EV, 'The UK as a Third Country Actor in EU Financial Services Regulation' (2017) 3 JFR 40
Ferran EV, 'Regulatory Parity in Post-Brexit UK–EU Financial Regulation' in Alexander K, Barnard C, Ferran EV, Lang A, and Moloney N (eds), *Brexit and Financial Services: Law and Policy* (Hart Publishing 2018)

Filler RH and Markham JW, *Regulation of Derivative Financial Instruments* (West Academic 2014)

Fischer R and Schulte-Mattler H (eds), *KWG, CRR-VO* (6th edn, CH Beck 2023)

Fisher J and Bewsey J, *The Law of Investor Protection* (Sweet & Maxwell 1997)

Fleischer V, 'Regulatory Arbitrage' (2010) 89 Tex L Rev 227

Fletcher G-GS, 'Benchmark Regulation' (2017) 102 Iowa L Rev 1929

Florey K, 'State Law, U.S. Power, Foreign Disputes: Understanding the Extraterritorial Effects of State Law in the Wake of Morrison v. National Australia Bank' (2012) 92 BU L Rev 535

Flühmann D, Hsu PCh, and Ender T, 'Regulation of Electronic Payment Service Providers in Switzerland' (2017) 12 GesKR 5

Fontecchio JM, 'The General Agreements on Trade in Services: Is it the Answer to Creating a Harmonized Global Securities System' (1994) 20 NC J Intl L & Com Reg 115

Fox MB, 'Securities Disclosure in a Globalizing Market' (1997) 95 Mich L Rev 2498

Frankel T and Laby AB, *Regulation of Money Managers* (3rd edn, Wolters Kluwer 2020)

Frenz W, *Handbuch Europarecht*, vol 4 (Springer 2009)

Frick J and Jost H, 'Haftung von Ratingagenturen' in Reutter TU and Werlen T (eds), *Kapitalmarkt—Recht und Transaktionen XI* (Schulthess 2017)

Fritzsche A, 'Discretion, Scope of Judicial Review and Institutional Balance in European Law' (2010) 47 CMLR 361

Fuerea A, 'The ECJ Case-Law on the Annulment Action: Grounds, Effects and Illegality Plea' (2017) 24 Lex ET Scientia Intl J 61

Funken K, *Das Anerkennungsprinzip im internationalen Privatrecht* (Mohr Siebeck 2009)

Gabbi S, 'The Principle of Institutional (Un)Balance after Lisbon' (2014) 5 Eur J Risk Reg 259

Gail DB, Norton JJ, and O'Neal MK, 'The Foreign Bank Supervision Act of 1991' (1992) 26 Intl Lawyer 993

Garner BA (ed), *Black's Law Dictionary* (11th edn, West 2021)

Garslian L, 'Towards a Universal Model Regulatory Framework for Derivatives' (2016) 37 U Pa J Intl L 941

Gary SN, 'Best Interests in the Long Term: Fiduciary Duties and ESG Integration' (2019) 90 U Colo L Rev 731

Geiger H, 'Transnational supervisory recognition' in Burling J and Lazarus K (eds), *Research Handbook on International Insurance Law and Regulation* (Edward Elgar Publishing 2011)

Geiger R, Khan D-E, and Kotzur M (eds), *European Union Treaties* (CH Beck 2015)

Gericke D, 'Von Marktrecht zu Marktsteuerung im Offenlegungs- und Übernahmerecht?' (2013) 8 GesKR 247

Gericke D, Isler V, and Kramer S, 'Derivatgeschäfte: Anwendung der FinfraG-Regulierung auf Schweizer Handels- und Industrieunternehmen' (2018) 90 SZW 232

Gibson LT, 'The Foreign Bank Supervision Enhancement Act of 1991' (1995) 27 Case W Res J Intl L 119

Girard O, 'Les méthodes de suppression des frontières au plan mondial dans le domaine bancaire et financier' (2007–2008) 3 EUREDIA 349

Gkoutzinis A, 'International Trade in Banking Services and the Role of the WTO' (2005) 39 Intl Lawyer 877

Glander H and Ağırman Y, 'Auswirkungen des Brexit auf die deutsche Fondsindustrie und den Marktzugang von UK-Finanzdienstleistern' (2019) 9 RdF 4

Glander H and Lühmann D, 'Auswirkungen der europäischen ESG-Regulierung auf Asset Manager' (2020) 10 RdF 12

Glaser A, *Die Entwicklung des Europäischen Verwaltungsrechts aus der Perspektive der Handlungsformenlehre* (Mohr Siebeck 2013)

Gleeson S, 'The Prospectus Regime and Brexit' in Busch D, Ferrarini G, and Franx JP (eds), *Prospectus Regulation and Prospectus Liability* (OUP 2020)
Golland A, 'Datenschutzrechtliche Anforderungen an internationale Datentransfers' (2020) 73 NJW 2593
Godwin A, Ramsay I, and Sayes E, 'Assessing Financial Regulatory Coordination and Integration with Reference to OTC Derivatives Regulation' (2017) 12 CMLJ 38
Goodhart C, *The Basel Committee on Banking Supervision* (CUP 2011)
Görlitz N and Kubicki P, 'Rechtsakte „mit schwierigem Charakter"' (2011) 22 EuZW 248
Gornig G and Trüe C, 'Die Rechtsprechung des EuGH und des EuG zum europäischen allgemeinen Verwaltungsrecht' (2000) 55 JZ 446
Gortsos C, *Fundamentals of Public International Financial Law* (Nomos 2012)
Grabitz E, Hilf M, and Nettesheim M (eds), *Das Recht der Europäischen Union* (76th edn, CH Beck 2022)
Greenbaum SI, Thakor AV, and Boot AWA, *Contemporary Financial Intermediation* (4th edn, Elsevier 2021)
Greene EF, Braverman DA, and Sperber SR, 'Hegemony of Deference: U.S. Disclosure Requirements in the International Capital Markets' (1995) 50 Bus Law 413
Greene EF, 'Beyond Borders: Time to Tear down the Barriers to Global Investing' (2007) 48 Harv Intl LJ 85
Greene EF, 'Beyond Borders Part II' (May 2007) http://www.sechistorical.org (accessed 12 November 2022)
Greene EF and Oztan OS, 'The Attack on National Regulation' (2009) 4 CMLJ 6
Greene EF and Potiha I, 'Issues in the Extraterritorial Application of Dodd-Frank's Derivatives and Clearing Rules, the Impact on Global Markets and the Inevitability of Cross-border and US Domestic Coordination' (2013) 8 CMLJ 338
Greene EF, Silverman LN, Braverman DA, Sperber SR, Grabar N, and Fleisher AE, *U.S. Regulation of the International Securities and Derivatives Markets*, vol 1 (12th edn, Wolters Kluwer 2017)
Gregory J, *Central Counterparties* (Wiley 2014)
Griffith SJ, 'Substituted Compliance and Systemic Risk: How to Make a Global Market in Derivatives Regulation' (2014) 98 Minn LR 1291
Grunder T, 'Prüfung des Prospekts' (2019) 91 SZW 582
Grünewald S, 'Financial Benchmarks—Bedeutung und internationale Regulierungsbestrebungen' (2015) 87 SZW 586
Guohua Y, 'The Causes of the Crisis Confronting the WTO Appellate Body' (2019) 9 J WTO & China 102
Gütte KL, *Regulierung finanzieller Referenzwerte* (Mohr Siebeck 2020)
Haeberli D, 'Finanzderivate in der Schweiz' in Zerey J-D (ed), *Finanzderivate* (4th edn, Nomos 2016)
Haentjens M and de Gioia-Carabellese P, *European Banking and Financial Law* (2nd edn, Routledge 2020)
Hahn M, 'The Day After: Access to the Single Market in Times of Brexit, Equivalence and Extraterritoriality' (2018) 21 ZEuS 409
Hallstein W, *Der unvollendete Bundesstaat* (Econ 1969)
Hallstein W, *Die Europäische Gemeinschaft* (Econ 1973)
Hanif S, 'Equivalence: Panacea or Pandora's Box?' (2016) 31 BJ Intl Ban & Fin L 567
Hanks S, 'Rule 144A: Another Cabbage in the Chop Suey' (1990) 24 Geo Wash J Intl L & Econ 305
Hanslin M, 'Marktmanipulation nach Art 143 FinfraG' (2016) 11 GesKR 45

Hanten M and Sacarcelik O, 'Pandora's Box: EU Market Access for UK-Based Banks and Investment Firms After Brexit' (2018) 15 ECL 126
Hanten M, 'Contract Continuity under Brexit' (2019) 9 RISF/JFS 28
Harbo T-I, 'The Function of the Proportionality Principle in EU Law' (2010) 16 Eur LJ 158
Hartmann P and de Bandt O, 'Systemic Risk in Banking after the Great Financial Crisis' in Berger AN, Molyneux P, and Wilson JOS (eds), *The Oxford Handbook of Banking* (3rd edn, OUP 2019)
Hatzopoulos V, 'Forms of Mutual Recognition in the Field of Services' in Lianos I and Odudu O (eds), *Regulating Trade in Services in the EU and the WTO* (CUP 2012)
Häusermann DM, 'Eine annahmenbasierte Rechtssetzungsmethode für das Handelsrecht' (2015) 6 RW 49
Hazen TL, *Securities Regulation in a Nutshell* (11th edn, West Academic 2016)
Hazen TL, *Securities Regulation: Cases and Materials* (9th edn, West Academic 2016)
Hein von J (ed), *MüKo/BGB*, vol 12, pt 1 (8th edn, CH Beck 2021)
Hein von J (ed), *MüKo/BGB*, vol 13, pt 12 (8th edn, CH Beck 2020)
Helleiner E, 'Explaining the Globalization of Financial Markets: Bringing States Back In' (1995) 2 Rev Intl Polit Econ 315
Helleiner E and Pagliari S, 'The End of an Era in International Financial Regulation? A Post-Crisis Research Agenda' (2011) 65 Intl Organization 169
Hemraj M, *Credit Rating Agencies* (Springer 2015)
Herbst J and Kent R, 'Q: Is Equivalence a Backdoor Route for UK Firms to Maintain Access to EU Markets' (2017) 36 Intl Fin L Rev 14
Herdegen M, 'Grundrechte der Europäischen Union' in Isensee J and Kirchhof P (eds), *Handbuch des Staatsrechts*, vol 10 (3rd edn, CF Müller 2012)
Herdegen M, *Principles of International Economic Law* (2nd edn, OUP 2016)
Herdegen M, *The Dynamics of International Law in a Globalised World* (Vittorio Klostermann 2016)
Herdegen M, *Europarecht* (24th edn, CH Beck 2023)
Hicks JR, 'The Foundations of Welfare Economics' (1939) 49 Econ J 696
Hill CA, 'Regulating the Rating Agencies' (2004) 82 Wash U L Q 43
Hill JG, 'Regulatory Cooperation in Securities Market Regulation: Perspectives from Australia' (2020) 17 ECFR 11
Hirte H and Möllers TMJ (eds), *Kölner Kommentar zum WpHG* (2nd edn, Carl Heymanns 2014)
Hobbes T, *Leviathan* (Liberal Arts Press 1958)
Hofmann HCH, Rowe GC, and Türk AH, *Administrative Law and Policy of the European Union* (OUP 2011)
Hong M, 'Subjektive Rechte und Schutznormtheorie im europäischen Verwaltungsrechtsraum' (2012) 67 JZ 381
Hooghiemstra SN, 'Depositary Regulation' in Zetzsche DA (ed), *The Alternative Investment Fund Managers Directive* (3rd edn, Wolters Kluwer 2020)
Hoops C, 'Die Drittstaatenregelung von MiFIR/MiFID und ihre Umsetzung im geplanten Fina nzmarktnovellierungsgesetz' (2016) 28 ZBB/JBB 47
Höpfner C, *Die systemkonforme Auslegung* (Mohr Siebeck 2008)
Hopt KJ, *Der Kapitalanlegerschutz im Recht der Banken* (CH Beck 1975)
Horsten P, '"Light" Disclosure Regime' in Busch D, Ferrarini G, and Franx JP (eds), *Prospectus Regulation and Prospectus Liability* (OUP 2020)
Houben A and Teunissen M, 'The Systemicness of Insurance Companies' in Liedtke PM and Monkiewicz J (eds), *The Future of Insurance Regulation and Supervision* (Palgrave Macmillan 2011)
Howell E, 'EU Agencification and the Rise of ESMA' (2019) 78 Cambridge LJ 324

Howell E, 'Post-"Brexit" Financial Governance' (2020) 83 MLR 128
Howse R, 'The World Trade Organization 20 Years On: Global Governance by Judiciary' (2016) 27 EJIL 9
Hsu KHY, Cheek RG, and Etheridge HL, 'The Impact of Sarbanes-Oxley Act on Non-U.S. Accounting Firms' (2005) 4 J of Intl Bus Research 1
Hsu PC and Stupp E (eds), *BSK-VAG* (Helbing Lichtenhahn 2013)
Hug S, *Die Substitution im internationalen Privatrecht. Anhand von Beispielen aus dem internationalen Familienrecht* (Florentz 1983)
Hung Nie Woo C, 'United States Securities Regulation and Foreign Private Issuers: Lessons from the Sarbanes-Oxley Act' (2011) 48 Am Bus LJ 119
Hüpkes E, 'Globale Finanzstabilität—Wer setzt die Standards?' (2015) 87 SZW 570
Iglesias-Rodriguez P, 'Supervisory Cooperation in the Single Market for Financial Services: United in Diversity' (2018) 41 Fordham Intl LJ 589
Imm T, *Der finanz- und kapitalmarktrechtliche Gleichwertigkeitsmechanismus* (Mohr Siebeck 2020)
IRSG, 'The EU's Third Country Regimes and Alternatives to Passporting' (23 January 2017) https://www.irsg.co.uk/assets/IRSG-Full-report-The-EUs-third-country-regimes-and-alternatives-to-passporting.pdf (accessed 12 November 2022)
Itzcovich G, 'The Interpretation of Community Law by the European Court of Justice' (2009) 10 German LJ 537
Jackson HE, Fleckner AM, and Gurevich M, 'Foreign Trading Screens in the United States' (2006) 1 CMLJ 54
Jackson HE, 'A System of Selective Substitute Compliance' (2007) 48 Harv Intl LJ 105
Jackson HE, 'Substituted Compliance' (2015) 1 JFR 169
Janssens C, *The Principle of Mutual Recognition in EU Law* (OUP 2013)
Jarass HD (ed), *Charta der Grundrechte der EU* (4th edn, CH Beck 2021)
Jayme E and Bucher A, 'Première Commission/First Commission Résolution' (2008) 28 IPrax 297
Jeger M, 'Internationale Regulierung von Auditdienstleistungen und Revisionsaufsicht' (2018) EF 874
Jenah SW, 'Commentary on a Blueprint for Cross-Border Access to U.S. Investors' (2007) 48 Harv Intl LJ 69
Jingxia S and Fangyan B, 'A Practical Response to the WTO Appellate Body Crisis: Utilizing Arbitration to Resolve Trade Disputes' (2019) 9 J WTO & China 35
Johnson C, 'Regulatory Arbitrage, Extraterritorial Jurisdiction, and Dodd-Frank' (2014) 14 Nev LJ 542
Jones H, 'U.S. under Pressure to Match EU Rules on Market Benchmarks' *Reuters* (21 November 2014) https://www.reuters.com/article/us-usa-eu-regulations-idUSKCN0J51DN20141121 (accessed 12 November 2022)
Jordan C, *International Capital Markets: Law and Institutions* (OUP 2014)
Josuran A and Isler V, 'Änderungen beim Vertrieb kollektiver Kapitalanlagen unter dem FIDLEG/FINIG' (2016) 11 GesKR 205
Jutzi TC and Feuz C, 'MiFID II, AIFMD und UCITSD: Auswirkungen des EU-Vermögensverwaltungsrechts auf das grenzüberschreitende Geschäft Schweizer Finanzintermediäre' (2016) Jusletter Next 1
Jutzi TC, *Unternehmenspublizität* (Stämpfli 2017)
Jutzi TC, Wess K, and Sieradzki D, 'Die neue Finanzmarktarchitektur im europäischen Regulierungskontext' (2020) 29 AJP/PJA 587

Kading BL and Madeiros L, 'Insurance Regulation: Mutual Recognition, Equivalence and International Standards' in Liedtke PM and Monkiewicz J (eds), *The Future of Insurance Regulation and Supervision* (Palgrave Macmillan 2011)
Kaldor N, 'Welfare Propositions of Economics and Interpersonal Comparisons of Utility' (1939) 49 Econ J 549
Kalss S, 'Kapitalmarktrecht' in Riesenhuber K (ed), *Europäische Methodenlehre* (4th edn, De Gruyter 2021)
Kanska K, 'Towards Administrative Human Rights in the EU: Impact of the Charter of Fundamental Rights' (2004) 10 Eur LJ 296
Karmel RS and Head MS, 'Barriers to Foreign Issuer Entry into U.S. Markets' (1993) 24 Law & Pol'y Intl Bus 1207
Karmel RS, 'Regulatory Initiatives and the Internet: A New Era of Oversight for the Securities and Exchange Commission' (2001) 5 NYU J Legis & Pub Pol'y 33
Karmel RS, 'The EU Challenge to the SEC' (2007) 31 Fordham Intl LJ 1692
Karmel RS, 'IOSCO's Response to the Financial Crisis' (2012) 37 J Corp L 849
Kellerbauer M, Klamert M, and Tomkin J (eds), *Commentary on the EU Treaties and the Charter of Fundamental Rights* (OUP 2019)
Kelly CR, 'Financial Crises and Civil Society' (2011) 11 Chic J Intl L 505
Kerkemeyer A, 'A Decade after Lehman: An Assessment of Key Regulatory Responses to the Global Financial Crisis' (2019) 16 ECFR 457
Khan M and Stafford P, 'EU-based Traders Caught in Swiss "Equivalence" Spat' *Financial Times* (30 June 2019) https://www.ft.com/content/41091f2c-9ad0-11e9-9c06-a4640c9feebb (accessed 12 November 2022)
Kirby RW, 'Access to United States Courts by Purchasers of Foreign Listed Securities in the Aftermath of Morrison v. National Australia Bank Ltd.' (2011) 7 Hastings Bus LJ 223
Kischel U, *Comparative Law* (OUP 2019)
Kissinger H, *World Order* (Penguin 2014)
Klebeck U and Meyer C, 'Drittstaatenregulierung der AIFM-Richtlinie' (2012) 2 RdF 95
Klein RW, 'The Insurance Industry and Its Regulation: An Overview' in Grace MF and Klein RW (eds), *The Future of Insurance Regulation in the United States* (Brookings Institution Press 2009)
Klöhn L, 'Lafonta/AFM: Die neue cause célèbre des europäischen Insiderrechts?' (2014) 35 ZIP 945
Klöhn L (ed), *Marktmissbrauchsverordnung* (CH Beck 2018)
Kluttig B, 'Die Klagebefugnis Privater gegen EU-Rechtsakte in der Rechtsprechung des Europäischen Gerichtshofes: Und die Hoffnung stirbt zuletzt ... ' (2004) 30 Beiträge zum Transnationalen Wirtschaftsrecht 5
Koch O, *Der Grundsatz der Verhältnismäßigkeit in der Rechtsprechung des Gerichtshofs der Europäischen Gemeinschaften* (Duncker & Humblot 2003)
Kokott J, 'Liberalisierung der Finanzdienstleistungen im Rahmen der WTO—Auswirkungen auf Deutschland, Österreich und die Schweiz' (2000) 8 RIW 402
Kokott J, 'Soft Law Standards under Public International Law' in Nobel P (ed), *International Standards and the Law* (Bern 2005)
Köpfer VE-M, *Anwendung und Auswirkungen des europäischen Kapitalmarktrechts auf Akteure aus Drittstaaten* (2015) https://www.e-helvetica.nb.admin.ch/api/download/urn%3Anbn%3Ach%3Abel-523480%3Adis4410.pdf/dis4410.pdf (accessed 12 November 2022)
Kosnik RM, 'Comments on Barriers to Foreign Issuer Entry into U.S. Markets' (1993) 24 Law & Pol'y Intl Bus 1237
Kronke H, Melis W, and Kuhn H (eds), *Handbuch Internationales Wirtschaftsrecht* (2nd edn, Otto Schmidt 2017)

Kuhn H, 'Die Regulierung des Derivatehandels im künftigen Finanzmarktinfrastrukturgesetz' (2014) GesKR 161
Kuhn H, 'Kollisionsrechtliche Aspekte der Derivateregulierung' (2014) 86 SZW 362
Kuhn H, 'From the Board: The US Attack on the WTO Appellate Body' (2018) 45 Legal Issues of Econ Integ 1
Kumpan C, *Die Regulierung außerbörslicher Wertpapierhandelssysteme im deutschen, europäischen und US-amerikanischen Recht* (De Gruyter 2006)
Kunz PV, 'Kotierung sowie Dekotierung—oder: "Werden" und "Sterben" der Publikumsgesellschaften' (2006) 1 GesKR 117
Kunz PV, 'Amerikanisierung, Europäisierung sowie Internationalisierung im schweizerischen (Wirtschafts-)Recht' (2012) 23 recht 37
Kunz PV, 'Braucht es eine neue Architektur des Finanzmarktrechts für die Schweiz?' (2014) 87 Die Volkswirtschaft 18
Kunz PV, *Wirtschaftsrecht* (Stämpfli 2019)
La Porta R, Lopez-de-Silanes F, and Shleifer A, 'What Works in Securities Laws?' (2006) 61 J Fin 1
Laby AB, 'Regulation of Global Financial Firms After Morrison v. National Australia Bank' (2013) 87 St John's L Rev 561
Laby AB, 'The Extraterritorial Application of U.S. Financial Services Regulation' (2017) 89 SZW 174
Lagarde P, *La reconnaissance des actes publics dans les règlements européens de droit international privé* (Pedone 2013)
Lang A, 'The "Default Option"? The WTO and Cross-Border Financial Services Trade after Brexit' in Alexander K, Barnard C, Ferran EV, Lang A, and Moloney N (eds), *Brexit and Financial Services: Law and Policy* (Hart Publishing 2018)
Lange M, 'Sustainable Finance: Nachhaltigkeit durch Regulierung?' (2020) 20 BKR 216 (pt 1)
Lange M, 'Sustainable Finance: Nachhaltigkeit durch Regulierung?' (2020) 20 BKR 261 (pt 2)
Lannoo K, 'EU Financial Market Access After Brexit' (2016) 51 Intereconomics 255
Lannoo K, 'Derivatives Clearing and Brexit' (2017) ECMI Policy Brief No 25 https://www.ceps.eu/wp-content/uploads/2017/11/ECMI_PB25_KL_BrexitClearing.pdf (accessed 12 November 2022)
Lauterpacht H, 'Recognition of States in International Law' (1944) 53 Yale LJ 385
Lawless RM, Robbennolt JK, and Ulen TS (eds), *Empirical Methods in Law* (2nd edn, Wolters Kluwer 2016)
Lazaro C, 'The Future of Financial Advice: Eliminating the False Distinction Between Brokers and Investment Advisers' (2013) 87 St John's L Rev 381
Lee N, 'The Extraterritorial Reach of United States Securities Actions After Morrison v. National Australian Bank' (2015) 13 Rich J Global L & Bus 623
Legrand A and Wiener C, *Le droit public* (La Documentation française 2017)
Lehmann M, 'Extraterritoriale Anwendung von US-Recht' (2010) RIW 841
Lehmann M, *Grundriss des Bank- und Kapitalmarktrechts* (CF Müller 2016)
Lehmann M, 'Is EU Law Overly Complex?' in Schmidt J, Esplugues C, and García RA (eds), EU Law after the Financial Crisis (Intersentia 2016)
Lehmann M, 'Legal Fragmentation, Extraterritoriality and Uncertainty in Global Financial Regulation' (2017) 37 OJLS 406
Lehmann M and Zetzsche DA, 'How Does It Feel to Be a Third Country? The Consequences of Brexit for Financial Market Law' in Fitzgerald OE and Lein E (eds), *Complexity's Embrace* (Queen's UP 2018)
Lehmann M and Kumpan C (eds), *European Financial Services Law* (Nomos 2019)

Lehmann M and Schürger J, 'Brexit-Steuerbegleitgesetz und Brexit-Übergangsgesetz—Sicherheit trotz Unsicherheit?' (2019) 19 BKR 365

Lehmann M, 'New Challenges of Extraterritoriality: Superposing Laws' in Ferrari F and Fernández Arroyo DP (eds), *Private International Law* (Edward Elgar Publishing 2019)

Lehmann M, 'Lässt sich die Rechtsetzungsmethode der EU reformieren? Der Versuch eines Europäischen Wirtschaftsgesetzbuchs' Speech—Zentrum für Europäisches Wirtschaftsrecht No 225 (20 January 2020)

Lehmann M, 'EU Law-Making 2.0: The Prospect of a European Business Code' (2020) 28 Eur Rev Priv L 73

Lehmann M, 'Global Rules for a Global Market Place? The Regulation and Supervision of FinTech Providers' (2020) 38 BU Intl LJ 118

Lehmann M, 'La coopération avec les États tiers en matière bancaire et financière—La confiance n'exclut pas le contrôle' (2020) RB 35

Lehmann M, 'Jurisdiction, Locus Standi and the Circulation of Judgments in the Banking Union' in Zilioli C and Wojcik K-P (eds), *Judicial Review in the European Banking Union* (Edward Elgar Publishing 2021)

Lehmann M, 'Derivateclearing Post-Brexit' (2021) 33 ZBB/JBB 177

Lehmann M, 'CCP Supervision after Brexit' (2023) 18 CMLR 5

Lehmann M and Schürger J, 'Multilateralizing Deference: A Proposal for Reforming Global Financial Law' (2021) EBI Working Paper Series No 107 https://ssrn.com/abstract=3981699 (accessed 12 November 2022)

Leible S and Domröse R, 'Die primärrechtskonforme Auslegung' in Riesenhuber K (ed), *Europäische Methodenlehre* (4th edn, De Gruyter 2021)

Lenaerts K and Gutierrez-Fons JA, 'To Say What the Law of the EU Is: Methods of Interpretation and the European Court of Justice' (2014) 20 Colum J Eur L 3

Lenaerts K, Maselis I, and Gutman K, *EU Procedural Law* (OUP 2014)

Leroux EH, 'Trade in Financial Services under the World Trade Organization' (2002) 36 JWT 413

Lessambo FI, *The U.S. Banking System* (Palgrave Macmillan 2020)

Leuz C, 'IAS versus U.S. GAAP: Information-Asymmetry Based Evidence from Germany's New Market' (2003) 41 J Acct Res 445

Levine R, 'Bank-Based or Market-Based Financial Systems: Which Is Better?' (2002) 11 J Financ Intermediation 398

Lewald H, 'Règles générales des conflits de lois' (1939) 69 Rec des Cours 5

Lezzi L, *Regulierung und Aufsicht über kollektive Kapitalanlagen für alternative Anlagen* (Schulthess 2012)

Lieverse K, 'The Obligation to Publish a Prospectus and Exemptions' in Busch D, Ferrarini G, and Franx JP (eds), *Prospectus Regulation and Prospectus Liability* (OUP 2020)

Lindenfeld J, 'The CFTC's Substituted Compliance Approach' (2015) 14 J Intl Bus & L 125

Liskov RG and Sarchio JJ, 'U.S. Regulation of the Solvency and Insolvency of Alien Multi-National Insurers' in Thomas JE (ed), *New Appleman on Insurance Law Library Edition*, vol 9 (Lexis Nexis 2022)

Loff D, 'Die Nutzung des vereinfachten Marktzugangs für Schweizer Banken' (2014) 9 GesKR 376

Loff D and Lembke J, 'Zugang von Drittstaaten-Finanzmarktakteuren in die EU' (2016) 6 RdF 101

Lorenzotti N, 'Third-country Equivalence and Its Suitability in the Context of Brexit' (2019) 22 Fin Reg Intl 1

Loss L, Seligman J, and Paredes TA, *Fundamentals of Securities Regulation*, vols 1 and 2 (7th edn, Wolters Kluwer 2019)

Luo X, 'Accessing Foreign Audit Work Papers and the Conflicting Non-U.S. Laws Defense' (2015) 18 NYU J Legis & Pub Pol'y 185

Lüttringhaus JD, 'Substitution' in Basedow J, Rühl G, Ferrari F, and de Miguel Asensio P (eds), *Encyclopedia of Private International Law*, vol 2 (Edward Elgar Publishing 2017)

Lyons EM, 'The Implications of the Sarbanes-Oxley Act for U.S. Foreign Relations' (2008) Thesis at the Ohio State University https://kb.osu.edu/bitstream/handle/1811/32187/Final_Erin_Lyons_Thesis.pdf (accessed 12 November 2022)

Mächler-Erne M, 'Finanzmarktrecht und Versicherungen: Stand und Perspektiven' (2005) 14 AJP/PJA 53

Mächler M, 'Gelten die Überlegungen zu Systemrisiken im Bankensektor auch für den Versicherungssektor?' (2010) 82 SZW 493

Madir J, 'Introduction: What is FinTech?' in Madir J (ed), *FinTech: Law and Regulation* (Edward Elgar Publishing 2019)

Madison GW and Greene SP, 'TIAA-CRED Response to a Blueprint for Cross-Border Access to U.S. Investors' (2007) 48 Harv Intl LJ 99

Maduro MP, 'Interpreting European Law: Judicial Adjudication in a Context of Constitutional Pluralism' (2008) 1 Eur J Legal Stud 137

Malloy M and Lovett W, *Banking and Financial Institutions Law in a Nutshell* (8th edn, West Academic 2014)

Mankowski P, 'Extraterritoriale Reichweite des US-Wertpapierrechts?' (2010) 13 NZG 961

Marcacci A, 'IOSCO: The World Standard Setter for Globalized Financial Markets' (2012) 12 Rich J Global L & Bus 23

Marchetti J, 'The GATS Prudential Carve-Out' in Delimatsis P and Herger N (eds), *Financial Regulation at the Crossroads* (Kluwer Law International 2011)

Marjosola H, 'Regulate Thy Neighbour' (2016) EUI Working Papers 2016/01 http://hdl.handle.net/1814/39022 (accessed 12 November 2022)

Markham JW, 'Commodity Exchanges and Regulation' in Baker HK, Filbeck G, and Harris JH (eds), *Commodities: Markets, Performance, and Strategies* (OUP 2018)

Marosi A and Massoud N, '"You Can Enter but You Cannot Leave ...": U.S. Securities Markets and Foreign Firms' (2008) 63 J Fin 2477

Matsushita M, Schoenbaum TJ, Mavroidis PC, and Hahn M, *The World Trade Organization* (3rd edn, OUP 2015)

Mattoo A, 'MFN and the GATS' in Cottier T and Mavroidis PC (eds), *Regulatory Barriers and the Principle of Non Discrimination* (University of Michigan Press 2000)

Matus G, 'Regulation of Alternative Trading Systems: Market Fragmentation and the New Market Structure' (2000) 44 NYLS L Rev 583

Mayer P, 'Les méthodes de la reconnaissance en droit international privé' in *Le droit international privé: esprit et méthodes, Mélanges en l'honneur de Paul Lagarde* (Dalloz 2005)

McKinstry L, 'Regulating a Global Market' (2013) 51 Colum J Transnatl L 776

McNulty L, 'Here Is the UK-EU Brexit Deal for Finance' *Financial Times* (1 April 2021) https://www.fnlondon.com/articles/here-is-the-uk-eu-brexit-deal-for-finance-20210401 (accessed 12 November 2022)

McPeak JM, 'Licensing of Insurers' in Thomas JE (ed), *New Appleman on Insurance Law Library Edition*, vol 2 (Lexis Nexis 2022)

McQuiston RW, 'Rule 144A, Regulation S and Amending Glass-Steagall Act' (1991) 17 Syracuse J Intl L & Com 171

McVea H, 'Credit Rating Agencies, the Subprime Mortgage Debacle and Global Governance: The EU Strikes Back' (2010) 59 Intl & Comp LQ 701

Ménard C and du Marais B, 'Can We Rank Legal Systems According to Their Economic Efficiency?' (2008) 26 Wash U J L & Pol'y 55

Mendes J, 'Delegated and Implementing Rule Making: Proceduralisation and Constitutional Design' (2013) 19 Eur LJ 22
Mendes J, 'Bounded Discretion in EU Law: A Limited Judicial Paradigm in a Changing EU' (2017) 80 MLR 443
Meng W, *Extraterritoriale Jurisdiktion im öffentlichen Wirtschaftsrecht* (Springer 1994)
Merkt H, *Unternehmenspublizität* (Mohr Siebeck 2001)
Meyer J and Hölscheidt S (eds), *Charta der Grundrechte der Europäischen Union* (5th edn, Nomos 2019)
Michaels R, 'Functional Method' in Reimann M and Zimmermann R (eds), *The Oxford Handbook of Comparative Law* (2nd edn, OUP 2019)
Misback AE, 'The Foreign Bank Supervision Enhancement Act of 1991' (1993) 79 Fed Res Bull 1
Mitchell AD, Hawkins JK, and Mishra N, 'Dear Prudence: Allowances under International Trade and Investment Law for Prudential Regulation in the Financial Services Sector' (2016) 19 JIEL 787
Möllers C, *Die Drei Gewalten* (Velbrück 2008)
Möllers TM, 'Efficiency as a Standard in Capital Market Law' (2009) 20 EBLR 243
Moloney N, 'The Legacy Effects of the Financial Crisis on Regulatory Design in the EU' in Ferran EV, Moloney N, Hill JG, and Coffee JC Jr (eds), *The Regulatory Aftermath of the Global Financial Crisis* (CUP 2012)
Moloney N, *EU Securities and Financial Markets Regulation* (3rd edn, OUP 2014)
Moloney N, 'International Financial Governance, the EU, and Brexit' (2016) 17 EBOR 451
Moloney N, 'Brexit, the EU and Its Investment Banker: Rethinking "Equivalence" for the EU Capital Market' (2017) LSE Working Paper Series 5/2017 http://eprints.lse.ac.uk/73429/1/WPS2017-05_Moloney.pdf (accessed 12 November 2022)
Moloney N, 'The European Union in International Financial Governance' (2017) 3 RSF 138
Moloney N, *The Age of ESMA* (Hart Publishing 2018)
Moloney N, 'Capital Markets Union, Third Countries, and Equivalence' in Busch D, Avgouleas E, and Ferrarini G (eds), *Capital Markets Union in Europe* (OUP 2018)
Moloney N, 'Reflections on the EU Third Country Regime for Capital Markets in the Shadow of Brexit' (2020) 17 ECFR 35
Mondschein LA, 'Solicitation and Marketing of Securities Offerings through the Internet' (1999) 65 Brook L Rev 185
Mooney A, 'Will London Be Berned Like the Swiss?' *Financial Times* (6 July 2019) https://www.ft.com/content/fe903f9b-926d-36c8-b950-f2f56e014cff?ftcamp=engage%2Femail%2Fnewsletters%2Fsmart_brief%2Fsmartbriefnewsletterscontraf (accessed 12 November 2022)
Moreno Trevino LF, 'Access to U.S. Capital Markets for Foreign Issuers: Rule 144A Private Placements' (1993) 16 Hous J Intl L 159
Morrison S, 'Third-country Equivalence: A Brexit Scenario for UK Financial Services' (2018) 29 ICCLR 1
Mülbert PO and Sajnovits A, 'The Element of Trust in Financial Markets Law' (2017) 18 German LJ 1
Muller KW and Chertok S, 'A Detailed Analysis of How the US Dodd-Frank Act and Related Rules Will Impact Foreign Investment Advisers' (2011) 32 Bus L Rev 285
Müller W, *Duden: Sinn- und sachverwandte Wörter und Wendungen*, vol 8 (Duden 1972)
Nästegård E, 'Equivalence Decisions in the EU and UK Financial Services Sectors Post-Brexit' (2022) 33 EBLR 463
Nemeczek H and Pitz S, 'Cross-Border Business of UK Credit Institutions and Investment Firms with German Clients in light of Brexit, MiFIR and MiFID II' (2018) 29 EBLR 425
Nemeczek H and Pitz S, 'Intermediate EU Parent Undertaking Requirement for non-EU G-SIBs' (7 December 2016) OBLB https://www.law.ox.ac.uk/business-law-blog/blog/2016/12/intermediate-eu-parent-undertaking-requirement-non-eu-g-sibs (accessed 12 November 2022)

Nettesheim M, 'Subjektive Rechte im Unionsrecht' (2007) 132 AöR 333
Ng L, 'Market Abuse Update' (2016) OBLB https://www.law.ox.ac.uk/business-law-blog/blog/2016/06/market-abuse-update (accessed 12 November 2022)
Nichols CC, 'Mutual Recognition Based on Substituted Compliance' (2008) 34 NC J Intl L & Com Reg 1
Nicolaïdis K, 'Non-Discriminatory Mutual Recognition' in Cottier T and Mavroidis PC (eds), *Regulatory Barriers and the Principle of Non Discrimination* (University of Michigan Press 2000)
Nobel P, 'Was heisst "Überregulierung"?' (2014) 86 SZW 589
Nobel P, 'Was heisst "Internationale Standards"?' (2015) 87 SZW 556
Nobel P, *Schweizerisches Finanzmarktrecht* (4th edn, Stämpfli 2019)
O'Brien M, 'Case C-452/04, Fidium Finanz AG v. Bundesanstalt für Finanzdienstleistungsaufsicht, judgment of the Court of Justice (Grand Chamber) of 3 October 2006, [2006] ECR I-9521' (2007) 44 CMLR 1483
Ohler C, 'Europäisches Bankenaufsichtsrecht' in Derleder P, Knops K-O, and Bamberger HG (eds), *Deutsches und europäisches Bank- und Kapitalmarktrecht*, vol 2 (3rd edn, Springer 2017)
Ohler C, 'Die extraterritoriale Regulierung von internationalen Banken' (2018) 117 ZVglRWiss 478
Ohler C, 'Finanzmarktregulierung und -aufsicht' in Ruffert M (ed), *Europäisches Sektorales Wirtschaftsrecht* (2nd edn, Nomos 2020)
Ortino M, 'The Role and Functioning of Mutual Recognition in the European Market of Financial Services' (2007) 56 Intl & Comp LQ 309
Pagliari S, 'A Wall around Europe? The European Regulatory Response to the Global Financial Crisis and the Turn in Transatlantic Relations' (2012) 35 J Eur Integr 391
Painter R, Dunham D, and Quackenbos E, 'When Courts and Congress Don't Say What They Mean' (2011) 20 Minn J Intl L 1
Pan EJ, 'A European Solution to the Regulation of Cross-Border Markets' (2007) 2 Brook J Corp Fin & Com L 133
Pan EJ, 'Single Stock Futures and Cross-Border Access for U.S. Investors' (2008) 14 Stan JL Bus & Fin 221
Pan EJ, 'Challenge of International Cooperation and Institutional Design in Financial Supervision: Beyond Transgovernmental Networks' (2010) 11 Chic J Intl L 243
Papaconstantinou GA, 'The GATS and Financial Regulation: Time to Clear-House?' (2020) 19 World Trade Rev 379
Paranque B, Perez R, and Sun W (eds), *Finance Reconsidered: New Perspectives for a Responsible and Sustainable Finance* (Bingley Emerald 2016)
Parchimowicz KM, 'Missed Targets and Misplaced Incentives? The Case of Parent Undertaking Requirement in the USA and in the EU' (2020) 21 J Bank Reg 212
Parisi F and Ghei N, 'The Role of Reciprocity in International Law' (2003) 36 Cornell Intl LJ 93
Parrish AL, 'Kiobel, Unilateralism, and the Retreat from Extraterritoriality' (2013) 28 Md J Intl L 208
Parrish AL, 'Fading Extraterritoriality and Isolationism: Developments in the United States' (2017) 24 Ind J Global Legal Stud 207
Payne J, 'The Role of Gatekeepers' in Moloney N, Ferran EV, and Payne J (eds), *The Oxford Handbook of Financial Regulation* (OUP 2015)
Payne J and Howell E, 'The Creation of a European Capital Market' in Koutrakos P and Snell J (eds), *The Law of the EU's Internal Market* (Edward Elgar Publishing 2017)
Pechstein M, *EU-Prozessrecht* (4th edn, Mohr Siebeck 2011)
Pechstein M, Nowak C, and Häde U (eds), *Frankfurter Kommentar*, vols 1 and 4 (Mohr Siebeck 2017)

Peers S, Hervey T, Kenner J, and Ward A (eds), *The EU Charter of Fundamental Rights* (Hart Publishing 2014)
Pennesi F, 'The EU Equivalence Regime in Financial Services: An Effective Instrument to Preserve Financial Stability after Brexit?' (2020) ECMI Policy Brief No 27 http://www.eurocapitalmarkets.org/sites/default/files/the_eu_equivalence_regime_in_financial_services_ecmi_policy_brief.pdf (accessed 12 November 2022)
Pennesi F, 'Equivalence in the Area of Financial Services' (2021) 58 CMLR 39
Pennesi F, *Equivalence in Financial Services* (Palgrave Macmillan 2022)
Perino MA, 'American Corporate Reform Abroad: Sarbanes-Oxley and the Foreign Private Issuer' (2003) 4 EBOR 213
Pfeffer I, 'Non-Tariff Barriers to Alien Insurance in the United States' (1976) 43 J of Risk and Ins 275
Philipponnat T, 'The Landscape for Post-Brexit European Financial Services' in Armour J and Eidenmüller H (eds), *Negotiating Brexit* (CH Beck 2017)
Picciau C, 'The Evolution of the Liability of Credit Rating Agencies in the United States and in the European Union' (2018) 15 ECFR 339
Poelzig D and Bärnreuther M, 'Die finanzmarktrechtlichen Konsequenzen des Brexit' in Kramme M, Baldus C, and Schmidt-Kessel M (eds), *Brexit: Privat- und wirtschaftsrechtliche Folgen* (2nd edn, Nomos 2020)
Poelzig D, 'Drittstaaten und Gleichwertigkeit' in Klöhn L and Mock S (eds), *Festschrift 25 Jahre WpHG* (De Gruyter 2020)
Polinsky AM and Shavell S (eds), *Handbook of Law and Economics*, vols 1 and 2 (Elsevier 2007)
Polinsky AM, *An Introduction to Law and Economics* (5th edn, Wolters Kluwer 2019)
Posner RA, *Economic Analysis of Law* (9th edn, Wolters Kluwer 2014)
Pozen RC, 'Can European Companies Escape U.S. Listings?' (2004) Harvard Law School Working Paper No 464 https://ssrn.com/abstract=511942 (accessed 12 November 2022)
Prieß H-J and Berrisch GM, 'Die Geltung und Durchsetzung des WTO-Rechts im Gemeinschaftsrecht' in Prieß H-J and Berrisch GM (eds), *WTO-Handbuch* (CH Beck 2003)
Proskauer Rose LLP, 'Analysis of the SEC's MiFID II No-Action Relief' (16 January 2018) https://www.proskauer.com/report/analysis-of-the-secs-mifid-ii-no-action-relief (accessed 12 November 2022)
Prüm A, 'Brexit: Options for Banks from the UK to Access the EU Market' (2017) 28 EuZW 988
Quaglia L, 'The Politics of 'Third Country Equivalence' in Post-Crisis Financial Services Regulation in the European Union' (2015) 38 West Eur Pol 167
Raffan M, 'International Standards' in Herbst J and Lovegrove S (eds), *Brexit and Financial Regulation* (OUP 2020)
Reed A, 'But I'm an American! A Text-Based Rationale for Dismissing F-Squared Securities Fraud Claims After Morrison v. National Australia Bank' (2012) 14 U Pa J Bus L 515
Reimer CM, 'Private Trustees Beware: A Review of the Sweeping New SEC Registration Requirements under the Dodd-Frank Wall Street Reform and Consumer Protection Act' (2012) 12 J Bus & Sec L 337
Ribstein LE and Kobayashi BH, 'An Economic Analysis of Uniform State Laws' (1996) 25 J Legal Stud 131
Riesenhuber K, 'Die Auslegung' in Riesenhuber K (ed), *Europäische Methodenlehre* (4th edn, De Gruyter 2021)
Riles A, 'Managing Regulatory Arbitrage: A Conflict of Laws Approach' (2014) 47 Cornell Intl LJ 63
Ringe W-G, '"Alternativen: Keine"? Gesetzesfolgenabschätzung in der Finanzmarktregulierung' in Casper M, Klöhn L, Roth W-H, and Schmies C (eds), *Festschrift für Johannes Köndgen zum 70. Geburtstag* (RWS 2016)

Ringe W-G, *Regulatory Competition in Global Financial Markets* (Annals of Corporate Governance 2016)

Ringe W-G, Morais L, and Ramos D, 'A Holistic Approach to the Institutional Architecture of Financial Supervision and Regulation in the EU' in Colaert V, Busch D, and Incalza T (eds), *European Financial Regulation: Levelling the Cross-Sectoral Playing Field* (Hart Publishing 2019)

Roer-Eide H and Eliantonio M, 'The Meaning of Regulatory Act Explained: Are There Any Significant Improvements for the Standing of Non-Privileged Applicants in Annulment Actions' (2013) 14 German LJ 1851

Romano R, 'Empowering Investors: A Market Approach to Securities Regulation' (1998) 107 Yale LJ 2359

Romano R, 'The Need for Competition in International Securities Regulation' (2001) 2 Theoretical Inq L 387

Romano R, 'For Diversity in the International Regulation of Financial Institutions' (2014) 31 Yale J on Reg 1

Roquette AJ, 'New Developments Relating to the Internationalization of the Capital Markets' (1994) 14 U Pa J Intl Bus L 565

Roth D, 'Gesetzgebungsprojekte: FIDLEG, FINIG und FinfraG' (2014) 86 SZW 608

Roth W-H, 'Mutual Recognition' in Koutrakos P and Snell J (eds), *The Law of the EU's Internal Market* (Edward Elgar Publishing 2017)

Rüttimann A, 'Offenlegung von Beteiligungen nach Art 20 BEHG und Art 31 BEHG sowie von Management-Transaktionen während des öffentlichen Übernahmeverfahrens' (2015) 10 GesKR 28

Ryngaert C, *Jurisdiction in International Law* (2nd edn, OUP 2015)

Saguato P and Ferrarini G, 'Clearing House and Systemic Risk' in Arner DW, Avgouleas E, Busch D, and Schwarcz SL (eds), *Systemic Risk in the Financial Sector: Ten Years after the Great Crash* (CIGI 2019)

Saguato P, Ferrarini G, and Pan E, 'Financial Market Infrastructures: The International Approach and the Current Challenges' in Binder J-H and Saguato P (eds) *Financial Market Infrastructures* (OUP 2022)

Sajnovits A, 'Die Auswirkungen des Brexit auf die Verwendung des LIBOR und anderer UK-Benchmarks' (2018) 27 WM 1247

Samuel G, *An Introduction to Comparative Law Theory and Method* (Hart Publishing 2014)

Sandberger C, 'Die EU-Prospektrichtlinie: "Europäischer Pass für Emittenten"' (2004) 12 EWS 298

Sants H, Austen M, Naylor L, Hunt P, and Kelly D (Oliver Wyman), 'The Impact of the UK's Exit from the EU on the UK-based Financial Services Sector' (2016) https://www.oliverwyman.com/content/dam/oliver-wyman/global/en/2016/oct/OW%20report_Brexit%20impact%20on%20Uk-based%20FS.pdf (accessed 12 November 2022)

Sasse T, 'Die Grundrechtsberechtigung juristischer Personen durch die unternehmerische Freiheit gemäß Art 16 der Europäischen Grundrechtecharta' (2012) 47 EuR 628

Sauter W, 'Proportionality in EU Law: A Balancing Act' (2012–2013) 15 Cambridge YB Eur Legal Stud 439

Savigny von FC, *System des heutigen Römischen Rechts*, vol 1 (Veit 1840)

Schaefer R, 'Internationale Standards in der schweizerischen Finanzmarktaufsicht' (2015) 87 SZW 607

Schäfer H-B and Ott C, *Lehrbuch der ökonomischen Analyse des Zivilrechts* (6th edn, Springer 2020)

Schammo P, 'Regulating Transatlantic Stock Exchanges' (2008) 57 Intl & Comp LQ 827

Schammo P, *EU Prospectus Law* (CUP 2011)

Schären S, Dobrauz-Saldapenna G, and Liebi M, 'Organisierte Handelssysteme im neuen FinfraG—Versuch einer regulatorischen Kategorisierung' (2016) 88 SZW 194
Scheiwe K, 'Was ist ein funktionales Äquivalent in der Rechtsvergleichung?' (2000) 83 KritV 30
Schiltknecht R, 'Internationale Standards in den Vorlagen zur neuen Finanzmarktarchitektur' (2015) 87 SZW 598
Schleiffer P and Schärli P, 'Ausnahmen von der Prospektpflicht unter dem künftigen Finanzdienstleistungsgesetz' (2018) 13 GesKR 1
Schleiffer P and Schärli P, 'Grenzüberschreitende Erbringung von Finanzdienstleistungen' (2020) 15 GesKR 24
Schmid C, 'Rating einer Kantonalbank' in Diab Z and Everling O (eds), *Rating von Finanzinstituten* (2016 Springer)
Schmid C, 'Fehlregulierung im schweizerischen Offenlegungsrecht?' (2018) 13 GesKR 194
Schmid O, 'Rebuilding the Fallen House of Cards: A New Approach to Regulating Credit Rating Agencies' (2012) 2012 Colum Bus L Rev 994
Schmidt-Aßmann E, 'Der Europäische Verwaltungsverbund und die Rolle des Verwaltungsrechts' in Schmidt-Aßmann E and Schöndorf-Haubold B (eds), *Der Europäische Verwaltungsverbund* (Mohr Siebeck 2005)
Schmies C, 'Germany' in van Setten L and Busch D (eds), *Alternative Investment Funds in Europe* (OUP 2014)
Schmitz BM, *Die Entwicklung des Anlegerschutzes beim regulären Delisting in Deutschland* (Peter Lang 2019)
Schmitz-Lippert T, 'International Co-Operation between Financial Supervisory Authorities' (2010) 7 ECFR 266
Schneider CW, 'Section 4(1-1/2)-Private Resales of Restricted or Control Securities' (1988) 49 Ohio State LJ 501
Schneider F, 'Internationales Standardsetting in der Wirtschaftsprüfung' (2015) 87 SZW 592
Schoenmaker D, 'The UK Financial Sector and EU Integration after Brexit: The Issue of Passporting' in Campos N and Coricelli F (eds), *The Economics of UK-EU Relations* (Palgrave Macmillan 2017)
Schoenmaker D and Schramade W, *Principles of Sustainable Finance* (OUP 2018)
Scholl P, Hörauf M, and Döhl A, 'Derivateregulierung in EMIR—Umsetzung und Weiterentwicklung in der Praxis' (2019) 9 RdF 276
Schreiber V, *Internationale Standards—Neues Recht für die Weltmärkte* (Haupt 2005)
Schroeter UG, 'Grenzüberschreitende Verhaltenspflichten und Haftung von Rating-Agenturen' in Zetzsche DA and Lehmann M (eds), *Grenzüberschreitende Finanzdienstleistungen* (Mohr Siebeck 2018)
Schuster G, 'A Tightened European Framework for Banks Following Brexit' (2019) 31 ZBB/JBB 297
Schuster G and Nemeczek H, 'IFR, IFD und WpIG—Neuer Rechtsrahmen für Wertpapierfirmen (Teil 1)' (2021) 33 ZBB/JBB 35
Schütze R (ed), *European Constitutional Law* (3rd edn, OUP 2021)
Schwarcz SL, 'Systemic Risk' (2008) 97 George LJ 193
Schwark E and Zimmer D (eds), *Kapitalmarktrechts-Kommentar* (5th edn, CH Beck 2020)
Schwarze J, 'Rechtsstaatliche Grundsätze für das Verwaltungshandeln in der Rechtsprechung des Gerichtshofs' in Colneric N, Edward D, Puissochet JP, and Colomer DR (eds), *Une Communauté de droit: Festschrift für Gil Carlos Rodriguez Iglesias* (BWV 2003)
Schwarze J, Becker U, Hatje A, and Schoo J (eds), *EU-Kommentar* (4th edn, Nomos 2019)
Schwennicke A, 'Die künftige Beaufsichtigung der Wertpapierfirmen in Deutschland' (2021) 21 BKR 150
Scott HS, *International Finance: Law and Regulation* (Sweet & Maxwell 2004)

Scott HS, 'International Finance' in Guzman AT and Sykes AO (eds), *Research Handbook in International Economic Law* (Edward Elgar Publishing 2007)
Scott HS, *The Global Financial Crisis* (New York Foundation Press 2009)
Scott J, 'The New EU "Extraterritoriality"' (2014) 51 CMLR 1343
Scott KA, 'State Regulation of Foreign Banks' in Guynn RD (ed), *Regulation of Foreign Banks & Affiliates in the United States* (9th edn, Thomson Reuters 2016)
Segala JP, 'A Summary of the International Banking Act of 1978' (1979) 65 Rich Econ Rev 16
Sener Z, 'Effect of the Sarbanes-Oxley Act of 2002 on the EU Law regarding Auditors and Auditors' Independence' (2010) 11 Bus L Intl 133
Sergakis K, *The Law of Capital Markets in the EU: Disclosure and Enforcement* (Palgrave Macmillan 2018)
Sethe R, 'Das Drittstaatenregime von MiFIR und MiFID II' (2014) 86 SZW 615
Sethe R and Lehmann M, 'Internationales Bank- und Finanzdienstleistungsrecht' in Tietje C (ed), *Internationales Wirtschaftsrecht* (3rd edn, De Gruyter 2021)
Sethe R, 'Rechtsangleichung im Schweizer Finanzmarktrecht' in Kohte W and Absenger N (eds), *Festschrift für Armin Höland* (Nomos 2015)
Sethe R, 'Einige kritische Anmerkungen zum geplanten Schweizer Finanzdienstleistungsgesetz' in Casper M, Klöhn L, Roth W-H, and Schmies C (eds), *Festschrift für Johannes Köndgen zum 70. Geburtstag* (RWS 2016)
Sethe R, Favre O, Hess M, Kramer S, and Schott A (eds), *SK zum FinfraG* (Schulthess 2017)
Sethe R, 'MiFIR/MiFID II: Drittstaatenzugang für die Schweiz und Äquivalenz von FINIG/FIDLEG' in Gericke D (ed), *Private Equity VI* (Schulthess 2018)
Shaw MN, *International Law* (9th edn, CUP 2021)
Siems MM, 'Numerical Comparative Law: Do We Need Statistical Evidence in Law in Order to Reduce Complexity' (2005) 13 Cardozo J Intl & Comp L 521
Siems MM, 'What Does Not Work in Comparing Securities Laws: A Critique on La Porta et al.'s Methodology' (2005) 16 ICCLR 300
Siems MM, 'Statistische Rechtsvergleichung' (2008) 72 RabelsZ 354
Silbermann LJ, 'Morrison v. National Australia Bank: Implications for Global Securities Class Actions' (2010) 12 YPIL 123
Simitis S, Hornung G, and Spiecker I (eds), *Datenschutzrecht: DSVGVO mit BDSG* (Nomos 2019)
Sims S, Brandt P, and Norman G, 'AIFMD Passport: Europe Must Try Harder' (2016) 17 J Invest Compliance 10
Singh T and Brummer C, 'Does Today's World Need a Global Financial Regulator?' (2014) 33 Intl Fin L Rev 18
Sørensen KE, 'The Country-of-Origin Principle and Balancing Jurisdiction between Home Member States and Host Member States' (2019) 30 EBLR 37
Spillmann T and Meyer R, 'FIDLEG—Prospektregelung' in Reutter TU and Werlen T (eds), *Kapitalmarkttransaktionen X* (Schulthess 2016)
Spillmann T and Giger A, 'Ein modernes Prospektrecht für die Schweiz' (2019) 14 GesKR 182
Spindler G and Tancredi S, 'Die Richtlinie über Alternative Investmentfonds (AIFM-Richtlinie)—Teil I' (2011) 67 WM 1393
Spindler G and Tancredi S, 'Die Richtlinie über Alternative Investmentfonds (AIFM-Richtlinie)—Teil II' (2011) 67 WM 1441
Srivastava A and Moffatt N, 'EU Equivalence Regime' in Herbst J and Lovegrove S (eds), *Brexit and Financial Regulation* (OUP 2020)
St. Charles K, 'Regulatory Imperialism: The Worldwide Export of European Regulatory Principles on Credit Rating Agencies' (2010) 19 Minn J Intl L 399

Stafford P, 'CFTC Warns EU Rules May Force Tighter US Derivative Regulation' *Financial Times* (20 November 2014) https://www.ft.com/content/d10bbd98-70ad-11e4-9129-00144feabdc0 (accessed 12 November 2022)
Stegeman R and Berket A, 'Derivatives' in Busch D and Ferrarini G (eds), *Regulation of the EU Financial Markets: MiFID II and MiFIR* (OUP 2017)
Steuer S, 'EMIR 2.2 und die Aufsicht über systemrelevante Drittstaaten-CCPs' (2021) 21 BKR 272
Stoffel WA, 'Place of Performance-Jurisdiction and Plaintiff's Interests in Contemporary Societies' (2002) 4 Eur JL Reform 185
Stutz M, 'Die Aufsicht der unabhängigen Vermögensverwalter unter dem FINIG' (2017) 12 GesKR 293
Swaine ET, 'Kiobel and Extraterritoriality: Here, (Not) There, (Not Even) Everywhere' (2016) 69 Okla L Rev 23
Tafara E and Peterson RJ, 'A Blueprint for Cross-Border Access to U.S. Investors: A New International Framework' (2007) 48 Harv Intl LJ 31
Talmon S, *Recognition in International Law* (Martinus Nijhoff 2000)
Tanzer G, 'Substituted Compliance: An Australian Regulator's Perspective' (2007) 48 Harv Intl LJ Online 21
Tarrant A, Holmes P, and Kelemen RD, 'Equivalence, Mutual Recognition in Financial Services and the UK Negotiating Position' (January 2019) University of Sussex Briefing Paper No 27 https://blogs.sussex.ac.uk/uktpo/files/2019/01/BP27print.pdf (accessed 12 November 2022)
Terhechte JP, 'Europäisches Verwaltungsrecht und europäisches Verfassungsrecht' in Terhechte JP (ed), *Verwaltungsrecht der Europäischen Union* (Nomos 2011)
Thiele A, *Europäisches Prozessrecht* (2nd edn, CH Beck 2014)
Tietje C and Lehmann M, 'The Role and Prospects of International Law in Financial Regulation and Supervision' (2010) 13 JIEL 663
Toman RG, 'The Extraterritorial Reach of the U.S. Securities Laws and Non-Conventional Securities' (2018) 14 NYU JL & Bus 657
Toni M and Hungerbühler L, 'Neue Handelspflicht für Aktien in der EU' (2017) 12 GesKR 205
Towfigh EV and Petersen N (eds), *Ökonomische Methoden im Recht* (2nd edn, Mohr Siebeck 2017)
Tschäni R, Diem H-J, and Gaberthüel T, *Öffentliche Kaufangebote* (4th edn, Schulthess 2020)
Türk AH, *The Concept of Legislation in European Community Law* (Wolters Kluwer 2006)
Türk AH, *Judicial Review in EU Law* (Edward Elgar Publishing 2009)
Turner TL, 'Proposed Amendments to Section 7(d) of the Investment Company Act of 1940' (1993) 27 Geo Wash J Intl L & Econ 209
Usher JA, 'The Evolution of the Free Movement of Capital' (2008) 31 Fordham Intl LJ 1533
Vahldiek W, 'GATS und Bankenaufsichtsrecht' (2003) 3 BKR 971
Valiante D, 'CMU and the Deepening of Financial Integration' in Busch D, Avgouleas E, and Ferrarini G (eds), *Capital Markets Union in Europe* (OUP 2018)
Van Cleynenbreugel P, 'Accountability Challenges for EU Agencies in the Context of Third Country Equivalence Assessments' in Hofmann HCH, Vos E, and Chamon M (eds), *The External Dimension of EU Agencies and Bodies* (Edward Elgar Publishing 2019)
Van den Bossche P, 'The Making of the "World Trade Court"' in Yerxa R and Wilson B (eds), *Key Issues in WTO Dispute Settlement: The first ten years* (CUP 2005)
Van Venrooy GJ, *Internationalprivatrechtliche Substitution* (Hartung-Gorre 1999)
Vasquez W, *Modernizing U.S. Insurance Regulation and the Role of Global Reinsurance Markets* (Nova 2016)
Veil R, 'The Reform of the Transparency Regime in European Capital Markets Laws' (2013) 10 ECFR 18

Veil R, 'Europäische Kapitalmarktunion' (2014) 43 ZGR 544
Veil R, 'Kapitalmarktgesetzgebung im Zeitalter der ESMA' in Hopt KJ and Tzouganatos D (eds), *Das Europäische Wirtschaftsrecht vor neuen Herausforderungen* (Mohr Siebeck 2014)
Veil R (ed), *European Capital Markets Law* (3rd edn, Hart Publishing 2022)
Verdier P-H, 'Mutual Recognition in International Finance' (2011) 52 Harv Intl LJ 56
Verstein A, 'Benchmark Manipulation' (2015) 56 BC L Rev 215
Visekruna A, 'The Access to the EU Financial Market for the Companies from Non-Member States' (2018) 2 ECLIC 656
Vo LD, 'Comment: Substituted Compliance: An Alternative to National Treatment for Cross-Border Transactions and International Financial Entities' (2015) 13 Geo JL & Pub Pol'y 85
Vogel A, Heiz C, and Luthiger R (eds), *OFK FinfraG/BEG* (Orell Füssli 2019)
Vogel A, Heiz C, and Luthiger R (eds), *OFK FIDLEG/FINIG* (Orell Füssli 2020)
Von der Crone HC and Roth K, 'Der Sarbanes-Oxley Act und seine extraterritoriale Bedeutung' (2003) 12 AJP/PJA 131
Von der Groeben H, Schwarze J, and Hatje A (eds), *Europäisches Unionsrecht*, vols 1–4 (7th edn, Nomos 2015)
Wagner G, 'Prävention und Verhaltenssteuerung durch Privatrecht—Anmaßung oder legitime Aufgabe' (2006) 206 AcP 352
Wakefield J, *The Right to Good Administration* (Wolters Kluwer 2007)
Waline J, *Droit administratif* (28th edn, Dalloz 2020)
Wandel SA, *International Regulatory Cooperation* (Schulthess 2014)
Wandel SA, 'Global Financial Standards and Regulatory Reforms' (2015) 87 SZW 562
Wang W, 'The Prudential Carve-Out' in Alexander K and Andenas M (eds), *The World Trade Organization and Trade in Services* (Martinus Nijhoff 2008)
Warren III MG, 'Regulatory Harmony in the European Communities: The Common Market Prospectus' (1990) 16 Brook J Intl L 19
Watter R and Bertschinger U (eds), *BSK-Revisionsrecht* (Helbing Lichtenhahn 2011)
Watter R and Vogt NP (eds), *BSK-BörsenG/FINMAG* (2nd edn, Helbing Lichtenhahn 2011)
Watter R, Vogt NP, Bauer B, and Winzeler C (eds), *BSK-BankenG* (2nd edn, Helbing Lichtenhahn 2013)
Watter R and Bahar R (eds), *BSK FINMAG/FinfraG* (3rd edn, Helbing Lichtenhahn 2019)
Weber P, Kronauer M, and Huber A, 'Die Börsenzulassung in der Schweiz in ihrem rechtlichen und steuerlichen Umfeld' in Habersack M, Mülbert PO, and Schlitt M (eds), *Unternehmensfinanzierung am Kapitalmarkt* (4th edn, Otto Schmidt 2019)
Weber RH and Sethe R, 'Äquivalenz als Regelungskriterium im Finanzmarktrecht' (2014) 110 SJZ 569
Weber RH and Baisch R, *Versicherungsaufsichtsrecht* (2nd edn, Stämpfli 2017)
Weber RH and Koch R, 'Relevance of WTO Law for Financial Services Lessons from "Argentina—Financial Services"' (2017) 89 SZW 163
Weber RH, 'Schweiz' in Derleder P, Knops K-O, and Bamberger HG (eds), *Deutsches und europäisches Bank- und Kapitalmarktrecht*, vol 2 (3rd edn, Springer 2017)
Weber RH, 'Theorie und Praxis der Finanzmarktregulierung' (2014) 86 SZW 577
Wei T-b, 'The Equivalence Approach to Securities Regulation' (2007) 27 NW J Intl L & Bus 255
Weinstein S, 'Transatlantic Extraterritoriality and the Regulation of Derivatives' (15 November 2018) SWIFT Institute Working Paper No 2013-003 https://ssrn.com/abstract=3285814 (accessed 12 November 2022)
Weiß W, *WTO Law and Domestic Regulation* (CH Beck 2020)
Welling J, 'In Defense of the Dealers' (2016) 85 Fordham L Rev 909
Welsh KM, 'Regulation of Reinsurance' in Thomas JE (ed), *New Appleman on Insurance Law Library Edition*, vol 7 (Lexis Nexis 2022)

Welshimer MJ and Gladin AR, 'U.S. Capital and Liquidity Regulation of Foreign Banking Organizations' in Guynn RD (ed), *Regulation of Foreign Banks & Affiliates in the United States* (9th edn, Thomson Reuters 2016)

Werlen T and Sulzer S, 'Aspekte der US-amerikanischen Securities Laws' in Habersack M, Mülbert PO, and Schlitt M (eds), *Unternehmensfinanzierung am Kapitalmarkt* (4th edn, Otto Schmidt 2019)

Widmer B, *Verwaltungsermessen im Recht der Europäischen Union* (CH Beck 2014)

Wittenberg T, 'Regulatory Evolution of the EU Credit Rating Agency Framework' (2015) 16 EBOR 669

World Trade Organization, *A Handbook on the WTO Dispute Settlement System* (2nd edn, CUP 2017)

Wohlers W, 'Die neue Insiderstrafnorm' (2013) 8 GesKR 345

Wolf M, *Why Globalization Works* (Yale University Press 2005)

Wolfrum R, Stoll P-T, and Feinäugle C (eds), *WTO—Trade in Services* (Martinus Nijhoff 2008)

Wouters J, Hoffmeister F, De Baere G, and Ramopoulos T (eds), *The Law of EU External Relations* (3rd edn, OUP 2021)

Wriston WB, 'Technology and Sovereignty' (1988) 67 Foreign Aff 63

Wymeersch E, 'The Future of Financial Regulation and Supervision in Europe' 42 CMLR (2005) 987

Wymeersch E, 'The Reforms of the European Financial Supervisory System: An Overview' (2010) 7 ECFR 240

Wymeersch E, 'Third-Country Equivalence and Access to the EU Financial Markets Including in Case of Brexit' (2018) 4 JFR 209

Yokoi-Arai M, 'GATS' Prudential Carve Out in Financial Services and Its Relation with Prudential Regulation' (2008) 57 Intl & Comp LQ 613

Young P (Norton Rose Fulbright), 'Market Access after Brexit: Prospectus Equivalence' (May 2017) https://www.nortonrosefulbright.com/de-de/wissen/publications/79f084b3/market-access-after-brexit-prospectus-equivalence (accessed 12 November 2022)

Zaring D, 'International Institutional Performance in Crisis' (2010) 10 Chic J Intl L 475

Zepeda R, 'To EU, or Not to EU: That Is the AIFMD Question' (2014) 29 JIBLR 82

Zetzsche DA, 'Drittstaaten im Europäischen Bank- und Finanzdienstleistungsrecht' in Bachmann G and Breig B (eds), *Finanzmarktregulierung zwischen Innovation und Kontinuität in Deutschland, Europa und Russland* (Mohr Siebeck 2014)

Zetzsche DA, 'Competitiveness of Financial Centers in Light of Financial and Tax Law Equivalence Requirements' in Buckley RP, Avgouleas E, and Arner DW (eds), *Reconceptualising Global Finance and Its Regulation* (CUP 2016)

Zetzsche DA and Lehmann M, 'Das Vereinigte Königreich als Drittstaat?—Die Auswirkungen des Brexit auf das Finanzmarktrecht' (2017) 62 AG 651

Zetzsche DA and Veidt R, 'The AIFMD's Third-Country Rules and the Equivalence Concept' in Zetzsche DA (ed), *The Alternative Investment Fund Managers Directive* (3rd edn, Wolters Kluwer 2020)

Zetzsche DA, Arner DW, and Buckley RP, 'Decentralized Finance' (2020) 6 JFR 172

Zobl D and Kramer S, *Schweizerisches Kapitalmarktrecht* (Schulthess 2004)

Zobl D, Schwob R, Weber RH, Winzeler C, Kaufmann C, and Kramer S (eds), *Bodmer/Kleiner/Lutz: Kommentar zum Bundesgesetz über die Banken und Sparkassen* (Schulthess 2015)

Zufferey J-B and Contratto F, *FINMA: The Swiss Financial Market Supervisory Authority* (Helbing Lichtenhahn 2009)

Zulauf U and Wyss D, *Finanzmarktenforcement* (3rd edn, Stämpfli 2022)

Zulauf U, 'Kooperation oder Obstruktion?—20 Jahre Amtshilfe im Finanzmarktrecht vom Börsengesetz zum FINFRAG' (2015) 10 GesKR 336

Zulauf U, 'Koregulierung in den «Kleeblattentwürfen» zum Schweizer Finanzmarktrecht' in Uhlmann F (ed), *Private Normen und staatliches Recht* (Dike 2015)
Zúñiga Schroder H, *Harmonization, Equivalence and Mutual Recognition of Standards in WTO Law* (Wolters Kluwer 2011)
Zweigert K and Kötz H, *An Introduction to Comparative Law*, vol 1 (1st edn, North-Holland 1977)
Zysset P, *Selbstregulierung im Finanzmarktrecht* (Schulthess 2017)
Zysset P, 'FIDLEG-Beraterregister als lex semiperfecta' (2020) 15 GesKR 271

Index

For the benefit of digital users, indexed terms that span two pages (e.g., 52–53) may, on occasion, appear on only one of those pages.